P9-DUZ-169

SEVENTH EDITION

# Criminology

## A Canadian Perspective

## Rick Linden

*University of Manitoba*

NELSON / EDUCATION

# NELSON / EDUCATION

Criminology: A Canadian Perspective,
**Seventh Edition**

by Rick Linden

**Vice President, Editorial**
**Higher Education:**
Anne Williams

**Executive Acquisitions Editor:**
Lenore Taylor-Atkins

**Marketing Manager:**
Terry Fedorkiw

**Developmental Editor:**
Suzanne Simpson Millar

**Photo Researcher:**
Kathy Mo

**Permissions Coordinator:**
Kathy Mo

**Content Production Manager:**
Christine Gilbert

**Production Service:**
Integra

**Copy Editor:**
Jessie Coffey

**Proofreader:**
Integra

**Indexer:**
Integra

**Manufacturing Manager—Higher**
**Education**
Joanne McNeil

**Design Director:**
Ken Phipps

**Managing Designer:**
Franca Amore

**Interior Design:**
Jennifer Stimson

**Cover Design:**
Martyn Schmoll

**Cover Image:**
Connie Coleman/Getty Images

**Compositor:**
Integra

**Printer:**
Edwards Brothers

**COPYRIGHT © 2012, 2009**
by Nelson Education Ltd.

Printed and bound in the United
States of America
1  2  3  4   14  13  12  11

For more information contact
Nelson Education Ltd.,
1120 Birchmount Road, Toronto,
Ontario, M1K 5G4. Or you can visit
our Internet site at
http://www.nelson.com

Statistics Canada information is used
with the permission of Statistics
Canada. Users are forbidden to copy
this material and/or redisseminate
the data, in an original or modified
form, for commercial purposes,
without the expressed permissions
of Statistics Canada. Information on
the availability of the wide range of
data from Statistics Canada can be
obtained from Statistics Canada's
Regional Offices, its World Wide Web
site at <http://www.statcan.gc.ca>,
and its toll-free access number
1-800-263-1136.

**ALL RIGHTS RESERVED.** No part of
this work covered by the copyright
herein may be reproduced,
transcribed, or used in any form or
by any means—graphic, electronic,
or mechanical, including
photocopying, recording, taping,
Web distribution, or information
storage and retrieval systems—
without the written permission of
the publisher.

For permission to use material
from this text or product, submit
all requests online at
www.cengage.com/permissions.
Further questions about
permissions can be emailed to
permissionrequest@cengage.com

Every effort has been made to
trace ownership of all copyrighted
material and to secure permission
from copyright holders. In the
event of any question arising as
to the use of any material, we will
be pleased to make the necessary
corrections in future printings.

**Library and Archives Canada**
**Cataloguing in Publication Data**

Criminology: a Canadian
perspective / [edited by] Rick
Linden. — 7th ed.

Includes bibliographical references
and index.
ISBN 978-0-17-650337-6

    1. Criminology—Canada—
Textbooks.  I. Linden, Rick

HV6807.c76 2011   364.971
C2011-906936-9

ISBN-13: 978-0-17-650337-6
ISBN-10: 0-17-650337-4

To Christopher, who gave so much and asked so little
and
Dan Koenig, a wonderful colleague and friend

# Brief Contents

# Contents

## PART 2: EXPLANATIONS OF CRIME   255

## PART 3: PATTERNS OF CRIMINAL BEHAVIOUR    491

# Preface

Since it was first published in 1987, *Criminology: A Canadian Perspective* has been used to introduce this field to more than 50 000 students across the country. At that time, most criminology courses in Canada were taught using American texts. It was our intention to provide a text that was written *by* Canadians, *for* Canadians. Over the past three decades, the discipline of criminology has grown from a few widely scattered faculty members to a large community of academics, researchers, practitioners, and students. The seventh edition of *Criminology: A Canadian Perspective* continues to reflect their work. That said, criminology remains a small and underfunded discipline in Canada. As a result, much of the new theoretical and empirical work in the field continues to come from the United States and Europe. This seventh edition represents our continued effort to provide you with the best Canadian scholarship in combination with the most relevant research from other countries.

## Advantages of a Multi-authored Text

The many different theories proposed to explain criminality are continually being revived and revised. Often the popularity of a particular theory owes as much to ideological commitment and academic fashion as it does to the explanatory power of the theory. As a result of this unresolved diversity, the pages of many texts are littered with the bodies of straw men, set up only to be sacrificed to the author's favourite approach. The authors of this text are among Canada's leading criminologists. The advantage of having such a multi-authored text is that the diverse perspectives of criminology can be fairly represented. In this book, each chapter is written by someone who has used the perspective in his or her own research and who understands its strengths and weaknesses.

## Organization of the Text

This book is intended as a text for a one-term course in introductory criminology. While the book deals extensively with theories about the causes of crime (which have largely been developed elsewhere), its purpose is to provide students with information about crime in Canada.

The chapters of this text have been organized into three parts. **Part I: Crime and Society** provides some of the basic information about crime: the sources of criminal law, the legal elements of crime, the sources of information about crime, the social correlates of criminal behaviour, a discussion of women and crime, and a look at victimization and at the role of victims in the justice system. This part provides the student with the background necessary to assess the theories of crime causation presented in Part II. In **Part II: Explanations of Crime**, all the major theories are covered, including biological, psychological, and sociological explanations. In **Part III: Patterns of Criminal Behaviour**, two of the most serious and frequent types of crime—organized crime and white-collar crime—are discussed. The way we have arranged the chapters is just one way of presenting the material, but instructors are encouraged to assign these chapters in whatever order best suits their course needs.

## Features of the Text

Each chapter begins with a brief *Introduction* and a list of *Learning Objectives* and concludes with a *Summary, Questions for Critical Thinking, Net Work* (Internet activities), a list of *Key Terms*, and a *Bibliography*. This text also features margin notes, *Web Links* in the margin to interesting related websites, and a *Running Glossary*, which defines the key terms next to the paragraph in which they first appear. A full *Glossary* is at the end of the text.

## ANCILLARIES

The **Nelson Education Teaching Advantage (NETA)** program delivers research-based instructor resources that promote student engagement and higher-order thinking to enable the success of Canadian students and educators.

Instructors today face many challenges. Resources are limited, time is scarce, and a new kind of student has emerged: one who is juggling school with work, has gaps in his or her basic knowledge, and is immersed in technology in a way that has led to a completely new style of learning. In response, Nelson Education has gathered a group of dedicated instructors to advise us on the creation of richer and more flexible ancillaries that respond to the needs of today's teaching environments. In consultation with this editorial advisory board, Nelson Education has completely rethought the structure, approaches, and formats of our key textbook ancillaries. We've also increased our investment in editorial support for our ancillary authors. The result is the Nelson Education Teaching Advantage, featuring *NETA Assessment*.

*NETA Assessment* relates to testing materials. Under *NETA Assessment*, Nelson's authors create multiple-choice questions that reflect research-based best practices for constructing effective questions and testing not just recall but also higher-order thinking. Our guidelines were developed by David DiBattista, a 3M National Teaching Fellow whose recent research as a professor of psychology at Brock University has focused on multiple-choice testing. All Test Bank authors receive training at workshops conducted by Prof. DiBattista, as do the copyeditors assigned to each Test Bank. A copy of *Multiple Choice Tests: Getting Beyond Remembering,* Prof. DiBattista's guide to writing effective tests, is included with every Nelson Test Bank/Computerized Test Bank package.

For *Criminology: A Canadian Perspective,* a Computerized Test Bank was created under the *NETA Assessment* program to ensure that high-quality multiple choice questions are available to instructors. A printable version of the Test Bank is also available. In addition, a full set of PowerPoint® slides is available to facilitate testing and augment teaching. A companion website is also available, at **www.lindencriminology7e.nelson.com**, to facilitate learning. This site includes additional information such as quizzes and links to criminology associations.

## New to the Seventh Edition

This edition of *Criminology: A Canadian Perspective* provides us with the opportunity to update crime statistics, to add new research material, and to make some major revisions that have been suggested by reviewers. In this edition, these major revisions include three new chapters:

- Chapter 7: "Victimology, Victim Services, and Victim Rights in Canada," written by Irvin Waller, introduces the very important issue of the consequences of victimization and the way in which victims are treated in the justice system.

- Chapter 15: "Deterrence, Routine Activity, and Rational Choice Theories," written by Rick Linden and Dan Koenig, examines several related theories based on the notion that people choose to commit crimes. Many of these theorists are concerned with crime reduction, so this chapter also discusses the best ways of lowering Canada's crime rates.

- Chapter 16, "Organized Crime," written by Stephen Schneider, replaces an earlier chapter covering organized crime.

Many revisions and updates to the remaining chapters are also included in this edition. Chapter 1, "Crime, Criminals, and Criminology," continues to introduce new areas of criminology with the discussion of the new criminological field of terrorism studies. A new box dealing with a brutal and tragic murder on a Greyhound bus has been added to Chapter 9, "Psychological Perspectives on Criminality," to illustrate the insanity defense. Chapter 11, "Conflict Theories," has an interesting new box on honour killings while Chapter 14, "Social Control Theory," discusses a fascinating experiment involving marshmallows that illustrates the importance of self-control in criminal behaviour. Finally, Chapter 17, "Corporate and White-Collar Crime," includes new discussions of the Ponzi schemes orchestrated by Bernie Madoff and by Earl Jones as well as a discussion of how illegal behaviour helped to produce the 2008 financial crisis. Chapter 17 also has new material on medical misconduct and a new box showing how the actions of people working with the justice system can lead to wrongful convictions.

## ACKNOWLEDGEMENTS

It has become traditional for authors to thank families for not making demands, and spouses, or close friends, both for moral support and for those unspecified but essential services that writing seems to require. Since my wife and children had already reached their tolerance limit with my work schedule, I decided that I couldn't just disappear into my office and reappear two years later with a book. Thus it is to them that I owed my wise decision to get help from the friends and colleagues who co-authored the text. For the time I did spend writing, I thank for their support Olive, Brad, Chris, Robin, Shawn, Tyler, and Amanda. By the fourth edition, all my children were old enough that they no longer cared about my working hours. However, their place at my work table was taken by pets, and I thank Nicholas, Morris, Annie, and

Edward for ensuring that each page in this manuscript has been stepped on or slept on by an orange cat. Callie also added some black cat hair to my computer keyboard.

As usual, working with the people at Nelson Education has been a delightful experience. For significant improvements in this seventh edition, I thank Lenore Taylor-Atkins and Suzanne Simpson Millar, and Jessie Coffey for her editorial skills. Joanne Minaker, Grant MacEwan University, has done a wonderful job with the ancillary material.

Special thanks to the reviewers who have given us good advice over the various editions. Reviewing textbooks is an onerous process and the help of many colleagues is very much appreciated. Among the reviewers of this and previous editions have been: Bill Avison, Jane Barker, Marilyn Belle-McQuillan, Thomas Bernard, Augustine Brannigan, David Brownfield, Tullio Caputo, Elaine DeCunha-Bath, Sange de Silva, Robert Drislaine, Karlene Faith, Thomas Gabor, Colin Goff, Jim Hackler, Stephanie Hayman, Sheilagh Hodgins, Carl Keane, Gail Kellough, John Martin, Robynne Neugebauer, Gary Parkinson, Michael Petrunik, Karen Richter, Vincent F. Sacco, Les Samuelson, Bernard Schissel, Alfredo Schulte-Bockholt, Phillip C. Stenning, Lee Stuesser, Diane Symbaluk, David Ryan, Heather A. Kitchin, Norman Okihiro, Austin T. Turk, and James Williams.

I would also like to thank each of the authors who contributed to the book. I appreciate your enthusiastic responses to revision suggestions and your efforts to meet deadlines. I continue to enjoy and to learn from your work.

Individual authors wished to make the following acknowledgements:

J. Evans and A. Himelfarb (Chapter 4)—"The authors wish to thank the Canadian Centre for Justice Statistics for providing much of the data presented in this chapter."

T.F. Hartnagel (Chapter 5)—"I wish to thank Kerri Calvert of the Sociology Information Centre, University of Alberta, for her help in locating references and generally keeping me informed of recent material. I also wish to acknowledge the research assistance of Marianne Nielson, Hannah Scott, Cora Voyageur, and Xavier Cattarinich, who helped me with the various editions of this text."

*Rick Linden*
*University of Manitoba*

# Crime and Society

Part 1 of this book provides some basic information about crime: the origins of our criminal law, the legal elements of crime, the sources of information about crime, and the social correlates of criminal behaviour.

Chapter 1 introduces you to the discipline of criminology, which is the scientific study of crime and criminals. This chapter explores the role played by rules and shows how these rules are sometimes formalized in laws. The chapter also looks at several different ways of defining crime and points out that because crime is socially defined, the definition of crime can change over time. The chapter concludes with discussions of "green" criminology and terrorism studies which are two of the newest sub-fields of criminology to show you how the discipline continues to evolve.

In Chapter 2, we learn how our system of law has developed as we have evolved from simple hunting and gathering societies to modern industrial ones. With the increased complexity and growth of modern societies comes the need for a formal legal system to maintain order. We also learn why some social harms are defined as illegal while others are not.

The legal elements of a crime are *actus reus* (the physical element) and *mens rea* (the mental element). These are discussed in Chapter 3, along with the defences available to an accused, a history of criminal procedure, and an outline of the social factors affecting the definition of specific types of crime.

We cannot study crime systematically unless we can measure it. Chapter 4 details some of the ways we count crime, such as official government statistics, victimization surveys, and self-report surveys. None of these methods is completely adequate; you will learn the strengths and weaknesses of each.

Before we can explain a phenomenon such as crime, we must know something about the way it is distributed demographically. In Chapter 5, a number of correlates of crime are discussed, including age, sex, race, and social class. In recent years, there has been an increased recognition of the importance of looking at the issue of women and crime. Because of this, Chapter 6 considers this correlate in more depth. The explanations of crime discussed in Part 2 of the book should be judged according to how well they account for these regularities.

Finally, Chapter 7 discusses the difficulties faced by victims of crime. About one in four Canadian adults are victimized by crime each year and the cost to these victims is estimated at $80 billion a year. While there are several important international protocols to guide the ways in which countries treat victims, Canadian governments have failed to provide adequate victim services. Instead of investing to support victims and to prevent future victimization, governments have chosen to invest billions of dollars in the traditional institutions of police, courts, and prisons.

# Crime, Criminals, and Criminology

**Rick Linden**

UNIVERSITY OF MANITOBA

Canadians have an endless fascination with crime. Our newspapers and television news broadcasts are saturated with stories about crime and criminals. Movies, television shows, and video games are filled with depictions of violence and other criminal behaviour. While crime is a matter of public concern and a favourite form of entertainment, it is also the subject of serious academic study. This chapter will introduce you to the discipline of criminology, which is the scientific study of crime and criminals.

## Learning Objectives

After reading this chapter, you should be able to

- Define the term *criminology*.
- Understand the different subject areas studied by criminologists.
- Explain the role played by rules in our daily lives and understand how these rules can become formalized in law.
- Understand the different ways of defining crime: a strict legal definition, an expanded legal definition that goes beyond just considering the criminal law, a definition based on the protection of people's human rights, and a definition that places acts of deviance and crime on a continuum ranging from minor acts of deviance to serious offences that almost everyone agrees are wrong.
- Explain how crime is socially defined and how people's ideas about crime change over time.
- Understand the two main theoretical perspectives (conflict and consensus) on how some acts get defined as criminal and others do not.
- Understand the new sub-fields of green criminology and terrorism studies.

## A Violent Crime: The Sand Brothers

Robert and Danny Sand grew up in an Alberta family with their father, Dennis, and their mother, Elaine. Robert was born in 1978 and Danny was born in 1980. Dennis Sand, who had served time in jail in his youth for a variety of crimes including armed robbery, gave up crime when he was 20 and later supported his family by doing a variety of jobs. He lives in a small Alberta community where Elaine runs a business and both are respected community members (Staples, 2002). As youngsters, Robert and Danny were constantly in trouble, along with several of their closest friends who made up a group composed of the only mixed-race boys in their town. The boys had difficulty in school and they were frequently suspended. In junior high they got into more serious trouble and at age 15 Danny was sent to a youth centre for beating up another student. The boys began to steal cars and to use drugs. Newspaper reporter David Staples described the situation of the brothers and their friends:

> Their contact with adults was minimal. No teachers, because the teens had all dropped out. No parents, because most didn't live at home. They relied on each other to figure out the world, believing their friends were closer and wiser than any adult. They're all there to protect each other, and they can't see past that, says [one of the mothers]. The teens suffered from the moral blindness of those who have achieved nothing in life and have nothing to lose. But they weren't entirely lacking in vision. They had an inkling of the difference between right and wrong. They certainly understood when someone did wrong to them, or to one of their closest friends. They just didn't see it as a problem to rob or injure someone outside of their group. It was us vs. them, with them being teachers, the RCMP, car owners, property owners, anyone with something they wanted to grab. (Staples, 2002, D2)

In 1998, after several armed robberies, Robert received a seven-year jail sentence. He became a model inmate, though counsellors said he could never explain why he had behaved the way he did. Danny also ended up in jail for a number of crimes, including attacking a police officer. After his release, Danny got involved in another incident that foretold the crime that would result in his death. An Edmonton police officer used his cruiser car to block an alley where Danny Sand was suspiciously parked in a stolen truck. Instead of giving up, Danny sped toward the cruiser and seemed to swerve toward the police officer. After this incident, he joined Robert in Drumheller Penitentiary, where he continued to get into trouble and where he got a stomach tattoo that read "Fearless, Painless, Senseless." After his release Danny told people that he would never go back to jail.

In October of 2001, Robert was released to a halfway house. He could find only menial work and began to fear that he had cancer. He reunited with Laurie Bell, a former girlfriend who was a heavy drug user. He left the halfway house, which violated his parole. On December 18, Robert and Laurie—along with Danny, who was also violating his parole—headed for the Maritimes where they had vague plans for making a new life. They never made it past Manitoba.

In the midst of a crime spree that included robbing a bank, breaking into homes, and stealing several vehicles, the three made it to the town of Russell, Manitoba. Shortly after midnight on December 21, 2001, Danny drove onto the main highway without first stopping at a stop sign. When RCMP constables Brian Auger and Dennis Strongquill tried to stop the vehicle, Robert fired several shotgun blasts at the police. When the police drove away, Danny chased the police SUV into town. He rammed the SUV after it stopped at the Russell

RCMP Detachment. Robert jumped out of the truck and fired at Constable Strongquill, who was trapped in the damaged police vehicle. Four of the shots hit Constable Strongquill and he died almost immediately.

The RCMP tracked the trio to a motel near Wolseley, Saskatchewan. A police sniper fatally wounded Danny Sand; Robert Sand and Laurie Bell were captured and charged with first-degree murder. While in prison awaiting trial, Robert kept a diary in which he reflected on the shooting:

> I was in one of my moods so I asked to see the pictures again of my case. There are pics of trucks burnt, crashed shot up etc. Homes broken into, property of ours and others and of course pics of the dead cop, shot up cop cars and Dan. Now I've seen them before and without emotion, I've no more tears to shed. But I was looking at this man, on a table. And I started to think, he's just a man, and shouldn't be dead. He had a family and friends, and now he's a body on a table. I realized it's not the man I hated, but the uniform he wore. His flag, colours of war. But seeing him without his uniform I felt bad for the loss of his life. But then I flipped to the pics of Dan, and my thoughts changed. Cause now I felt that the other man is right where he should be. And losses on both sides are to be expected, only Dan took my place. And when I looked upon the cop car I felt pride, and remembered the battle, I remembered how these enemy soldiers fled in fear and cowardess. I saw how much damage I'd caused to their unit and smiled, from the knowledge that the enemy isn't as strong as they want us to believe. But they should beware that the moment they fly their flag, wear their uniform. That they're at war and people die in war, everyone has their enemies. (McIntyre, 2003, 195)

Robert Sand, who physically attacked his own lawyer in court at the end of his trial, is serving a life sentence after being convicted of first-degree murder; Laurie Bell was convicted of manslaughter.

One of the challenges of the discipline of criminology is to make sense of cases such as this one. Why did the Sand brothers live such wild and undisciplined lives? Why did they aggressively pursue Constable Strongquill and his partner? Why did Robert see the world as a war zone? Is there anything we can do to prevent tragedies like this in the future?

Criminologists have considered a wide range of theories to explain crime, and you will learn about many of these theories in this text. Some focus on biology—could Robert and Danny have inherited traits from their parents that made their criminality more likely? Others look at an individual's psychological make-up—were the Sand brothers psychopaths or could other mental conditions have caused their behaviour? Other theories are sociological—what role did their family and friends play in their violence? Could the schools have done a better job motivating the brothers to study and to become involved in legitimate outlets for their energy? What role did racism and the brothers' poor economic prospects play in their lives?

These questions are very complex and we may never be able to adequately explain individual cases such as this one. However, even if we could explain the factors that led Robert Sands to kill Constable Strongquill, would the same explanation apply to another homicide case that was being dealt with while Robert Sands was facing the court on murder charges? This case involves Diego Zepeda-Cordera, a Toronto barber, who was a member of the Missionary Church of Christ (Galloway, 2003). His 19-year-old son, Walter, began to behave in a way that troubled Zepeda-Cordera. Walter began going out to bars, smoking, and he wouldn't help out around the house. His parents found a satanic magazine in his room. His father became extremely concerned when Walter began to speak in gibberish at a religious meeting. Believing his son was possessed by the devil, Mr. Zepeda-Cordero and a friend tied Walter to two metal chairs in their apartment building. Their minister and many church members came to the home to pray over Walter to exorcise the devil they believed was inside him. Walter remained tied to the chairs, often with duct tape over his mouth, for seven days before he died of dehydration. Although the judge in the case believed that the men genuinely thought Walter was possessed and sought to help him, he sentenced them to four years in jail after they pleaded guilty to manslaughter.

As these two examples suggest, there are many different patterns of homicide that have little in common other than the death of a victim. Some involve intoxicated people who stab friends during drinking parties; others involve a settling of accounts among organized criminals; some abusive men kill their wives and children; some corporate executives kill their customers by selling defective products in order to enhance their profits, or kill their employees by providing unsafe working conditions; and some predators kill children after having sex with them. In your criminology course, you will learn about these and many other patterns of criminal behaviour.

# A White-Collar Crime: The Downfall of Conrad Black

White-collar crime further illustrates the diversity of the behaviour studied by criminologists. For much of the spring of 2007 the Canadian media covered the trial of Conrad Black and several co-accused who were charged in the United States with a variety of offences relating to the fraudulent acquisition of funds that should have gone to shareholders of Hollinger International; the funds instead were taken by the accused, who were managers of the company.

Black's background was very different from that of the Sand brothers. His father was a wealthy businessman and Conrad had a very comfortable childhood. As a boy he attended Toronto's Upper Canada College, an elite private school, but was unhappy with its regimentation and discipline. While at the college, he broke into school offices to steal and alter school records. On one occasion, he and several accomplices stole several final exam papers. Perhaps anticipating his later business career, Black had previously taken copies of the academic records of all the students in the school, so he knew which students would be prepared to pay the most for the exam papers. His motivation was not entirely commercial:

I was going to reduce the school's whole academic system ... to utter chaos while achieving a spectacular mark for myself having done virtually no work. ...By the last week of the school year, I had almost completely undermined the system. ...I had more power than our jailers. I penetrated the Masters' Common Room and reassigned the faculty to supervisory tasks by typing up and substituting my own assignment sheet, assuring among other things that our examinations were presided over by the least vigilant people available, the music and printing teachers, as I recall. (Black, 1993, 15)

The scheme unravelled when one of Black's customers confessed to cheating and Black was expelled from the school.

After graduating from Laval University's law school, Black began a career in the newspaper business. Along with two partners, he bought a small, money-losing Quebec paper, the *Sherbrooke Record*. Black and his partners quickly discovered a formula that would eventually make them very rich. They fired 40 percent of the employees (a step that Black was reported to have described as "drowning the kittens" [Plotz, 2001, n.p.]), modernized the production process, and began to make a profit. They cut costs relentlessly. When one employee brought Black's partner David Radler a petition signed by newspaper staff complaining about some of the cost-cutting measures taken by the new management, Radler deducted two cents from the man's pay for wasting the piece of paper (Black, 1993). At the same time Black reports beginning a pattern of behaviour that later led to serious legal problems:

[At the same time as they were cutting even the most minor expenses at the newspaper] we operated ... what amounted to a modest slush fund for our preferred causes and tenuously business-connected expenses. (Black, 1993, 72)

Throughout his business career Black attempted, on several occasions, to transfer money from the corporations he ran—but which were owned by public shareholders—to his personal accounts.

Black began buying other small papers and eventually acquired a very important British paper, the *Telegraph*, as well as the *Jerusalem Post*, Canada's *National Post*, and the *Chicago Sun-Times*. At one point through his corporation Hollinger International, he ran hundreds of daily papers—including 60 percent of the papers published in Canada—and controlled the world's third-largest newspaper chain (McNish and Stewart, 2004). Black moved to London, England and, in 2001, he gave up his Canadian citizenship so he could accept admission to the British House of Lords and the title of Lord Black of Crossharbour. Shortly after taking his seat in the House of Lords in 2001, Black's financial empire began to unravel when he was challenged by investors at Hollinger's annual shareholders meeting. Some investors wanted to know why their investment in Hollinger was not profitable while Black and other senior executives were getting very wealthy. He was ultimately forced to step down from his position as chief executive officer of Hollinger and an investigation committee established by the board of directors accused Black and other executives of running a "corporate kleptocracy" that conspired to steal $400 million from

Hollinger that should have been paid out to shareholders. The report concluded that "Black and Radler were motivated by a 'ravenous appetite for cash' ... and Hollinger International, under their reign, 'lost any sense of corporate purpose, competitive drive or internal ethical concerns' as the two executives looked for ways to 'suck cash' out of the company" (McNish and Stewart, 2004, 288). In 2005 this action was followed by criminal fraud charges filed in the United States against Black and three other executives.

During much of the period when his actions were under investigation, Black demonstrated the imperious attitude that had characterized his career. In response to criticisms of his extravagance, like his use of company jets, he responded:

> There has not been an occasion for many months when I got on our plane without wondering whether it was really affordable. But I'm not prepared to reenact the French Revolutionary renunciation of the rights of nobility. We have to find a balance between an unfair taxation on the company and a reasonable treatment of the founder-builder-managers. We are proprietors, after all, beleaguered though we may be. (McNish and Stewart, 2004, 92)

Black and several colleagues were charged with conspiring to take funds from Hollinger International for their own personal gain. This is illegal because the corporation was owned by shareholders, not by the men who ran the company. How did they take the money? Over a period of years, Black sold off Hollinger's newspapers. When he sold the papers, the buyers also paid for agreements that Hollinger would not start competing papers in those markets. However, rather than paying these non-compete fees to Hollinger and its shareholders, they went directly to Black and his colleagues. They were alleged to have diverted over $83 million by these transactions. In some of the cases, the non-compete agreements were not even requested by the purchasers but were put in the agreement at the request of Black and his colleagues. The money to pay these fees was simply diverted from the purchase price, so the funds that went to Black were essentially taken from Hollinger's shareholders. In one transaction, in which Black himself purchased a newspaper from Hollinger, Black was even paid a fee to agree to not compete with himself. In other transactions Black and his colleagues received personal non-compete fees and additional fees were also paid to a company that they owned (McNish and Stewart, 2004). In effect, they were being paid twice for the same thing at the expense of Hollinger shareholders who actually owned the papers being sold.

Black was also charged with misusing corporate money for personal expenses. One of the key examples of this presented by the prosecution at his trial was his use of more than $40 000 of Hollinger money to pay for a lavish birthday party for his wife. Because of an incident when he and his chauffeur were videotaped violating a court order by removing a number of boxes of documents from his Toronto office, he also faced charges of obstruction of justice. Key to the case against Black was testimony from his partner, David Radler, who had pled guilty and received a relatively lenient 29-month sentence in exchange for his testimony against Black.

Black's defence was relatively straightforward. His lawyers claimed that the non-compete payments were approved by Hollinger's board of directors and were therefore legal. They also claimed that his use of Hollinger funds for parties, trips, and other expenses was legal because the expenses were business-related. For example, his wife's birthday party was held after a board meeting and involved making contacts with other business people. Also, Black paid a portion of the expenses from his own funds to cover the personal component of the event. Finally, they claimed that David Radler was lying in order to get lenient treatment. In fact, Radler had consistently lied about his involvement prior to his guilty plea and he did receive lenient treatment, so his testimony was vulnerable to those charges by the defence.

In July 2007 Black was convicted on four charges and acquitted on nine others. He was convicted of obstruction of justice because of the documents he removed from his office. The other convictions related to non-competition agreements that were not requested by the buyers of several Hollinger newspapers and to the sale in which Black was paid handsomely for agreeing not to compete with himself. He was sentenced to six-and-a-half years in prison and ordered to make restitution of $6.1 million (U.S.). In 2010, after serving two years of his sentence in a Florida prison, the U.S. Supreme Court set aside his fraud convictions, sent the case back to lower courts for reconsideration, and Black was released from prison on bail. An Illinois appeal court upheld both his convictions for fraud and for obstruction of justice. In June 2011 Black's sentence was reduced to 42 months and he was ordered back to prison to serve the remainder of his term.

A Timeline of Conrad Black's Case
http://www.cbc.ca/news/canada/story/2010/06/25/f-conrad-black-timeline.html

# What Is Criminology?

The term **criminology** is used in a number of different ways. Detectives in mystery novels, forensic scientists, and crime analysts on television shows are sometimes referred to as criminologists. The term is also sometimes applied to physicists and chemists who specialize in studying the trajectories of bullets or the ink used in counterfeit money. Most commonly the term is applied to academics who study crime and the criminal justice system. In this text, we will follow the definition of the discipline given by two well-known American criminologists, Edwin Sutherland and Donald Cressey: "Criminology is the body of knowledge regarding crime as a social phenomenon. It includes within its scope the processes of making laws, of breaking laws, and of reacting to the breaking of laws. … The objective of criminology is the development of a body of general and verified principles and of other types of knowledge regarding this process of law, crime, and treatment" (1960, 3). This definition implies that criminologists take a scientific approach to the study of crime.

**criminology**

The body of knowledge regarding crime as a social phenomenon. It includes the processes of making laws, breaking laws, and reacting to the breaking of laws. Its objective is the development of a body of general and verified principles and of other types of knowledge regarding this process of law, crime, and treatment.

## Why Should We Study Crime?

There are three reasons why it is important for us to know more about crime. First, social scientists believe that it is intrinsically worthwhile to learn more about all aspects of our social lives, including criminal behaviour and society's response to this behaviour. Learning about crime can tell us a great deal about our society. For example, the United States has a much higher rate of violent crime, particularly firearms crime, than Canada. The United States also has a much harsher justice system than Canada (see Chapter 15). These differences highlight important value differences between the two countries. Second, just as an understanding of a disease helps medical scientists develop cures, before we can reduce crime we need to understand it. For example, Richard Tremblay tracked the behaviour of children in Montreal as they grew up. One of his findings was that boys whose violent behaviour had not followed the normal pattern of declining by age 16 were more likely than other boys to be the sons of young mothers with low levels of education. The Quebec government has used this research to develop support programs for mothers who fit these risk profiles to see if this support will help to reduce the criminality of their children (Blumstein, 2003). Finally, crime directly or indirectly affects all of us. Many of us have been victims of crime and all of us pay for the costs of crime and the crime control system. Also, many Canadians are employed in the justice system or in security-related businesses.

# FOCUS BOX 1.1

## CRIME AND THE MEDIA

Most Canadians learn about serious crime through the media rather than from first-hand experience. Stories on television and radio programs and in newspapers, magazines, and books shape our views about crime and criminals. Writers of television shows and movies use violence to attract viewers and to sell tickets. Newspaper editors and television reporters select the crime news we hear and construct the way in which this news is presented to us in order to attract an audience.

Unfortunately, the picture of crime we receive from the media is often inaccurate. For example, while most crime is property crime the majority of media stories deal with violent crime. Typical of research in this area was a review of all the crime-related stories reported over two months in an Ottawa newspaper (Gabor, 1994). Over half the stories focused on violent crimes, particularly murders. However, violent crimes made up only seven percent of reported crimes in Ottawa, and the city averaged just six murders per year. While violent crimes were over-reported, property crimes rarely received much attention and white-collar and political crimes were almost never discussed.

The portrayal of crime in the fictional media is even more distorted. Consider the partial list of the 221 violent acts depicted in *South Park: Bigger, Longer & Uncut*, the R-rated movie based on the animated series *South Park*, and ask whether the list reflects the reality of the lives of today's young people:

> 130 weapons fire (with multiple killings), 18 electric shocks, 10 blows to the body, 8 blood spatterings, 3 burnings, 3 hanging-body scenes, 1 breaking of body in half, 1 assault with chain saw, 1 attempted electrocution, and 1 dog attack. (Media Index, 1999)

The popularity of programs such as the various incarnations of *CSI* (the original program, set in Las Vegas, has spun off both *CSI: Miami* and *CSI: New York*) has affected people's perceptions of the justice system. Some prosecutors have spoken about the *CSI* effect, which they feel has caused crime victims and juror members to expect more definitive forensic evidence than is available outside the fictional laboratories of a television show (Dowler et al., 2006).

Why do the media misrepresent crime? The primary goal of the media is to make profits by selling advertising. Stories that attract viewers

*(continued)*

or readers will boost ratings and circulation even if these stories do not represent the reality of crime. The informal news media rule "If it bleeds, it leads" reflects the fact that the public is fascinated by sensationalized, bloody stories such as mass murders or attacks against helpless senior citizens. Commenting on his experience with the media, the executive director of the Nova Scotia Bar Society said, "If there's no blood and gore, or there's no sex, it's not newsworthy. And if it falls into the category of being newsworthy, then they have to show the dead body. They've got to show the corpse" (McCormick, 1995, 182). Some parts of the media also have an ideological agenda and they favour 'tough on crime' policies which are more likely to be supported by a public that fears being victimized by violent crime.

The media's misrepresentation of crime has several consequences. First, Canadians greatly over-estimate the amount of violent crime and have a fear of crime that is higher than the actual risk of victimization. Second, the media provide a distorted stereotype of offenders. Violent crimes are most often committed by relatives, friends, and acquaintances—not by the anonymous stranger so many of us fear. Our fear of crime and our image of the criminal have an impact on government policy toward crime. Actual crime trends are irrelevant—if the public feels crime is out of control, it demands that government do something about it. Although crime rates are declining, a combination of increasing media coverage of crime and pressure from a variety of interest groups has led the federal government to tighten several laws, including those dealing with immigration, young offenders, and firearms.

The media may also contribute to crime. There is some evidence that children who are exposed to a great deal of television violence are more likely to be violent themselves. This linkage is complex and people disagree about the degree to which television influences behaviour rather than simply reflecting an interest in violence; however, there is some anecdotal evidence that the media do play a role in individual cases.

For example, Virginia teenager Josh Cooke was a fan of the movie *The Matrix*. He had a large poster from the film in his room and had a trench coat like the one worn by the protagonist, Keanu Reeves' character Neo. He also bought a shotgun similar to one used by Reeves in his movie fight against the "agents." In 2003, Cooke used the shotgun to kill his father and mother; he then turned himself in to the police. His defence was that he was attempting to escape the matrix. Several other killers across the United States have also claimed to be affected by *The Matrix*. Two of these accused have been found not guilty by reason of insanity (Jackman, 2003). Lee Boyd Malvo, the young man accused of being one of the Washington snipers who killed 10 people in 2002, has written,

> Wake up! Free your mind, you are a slave to matrix "control." …The outside force has arrived. Free yourself of the matrix "control". Free first your mind. Trust me!! The body will follow. Remove fear, doubt, distrust, watch the change then. (Jackman, 2003, 3)

While it is obvious that most people who see movies such as *The Matrix* do not commit murders, many researchers believe that media exposure can influence people who are already vulnerable or predisposed to commit violence.

Some have blamed the media for failing to cover the story of large numbers of missing women in Canada until Robert Pickton was charged with 26 murders. While a missing child from a middle-class home will generate an avalanche of publicity, the stories of dozens of missing lower-class women—many of whom were sex-trade workers—were not seen as important. Robert Pickton's trial generated international coverage but the media focused on the gruesome crimes and did not consider larger social issues such as legal policies that endanger sex trade workers, the structural reasons why so many of the victims were Aboriginal, and the role of the state in producing socially impoverished neighbourhoods such as Vancouver's Downtown Eastside where Pickton found most of his victims (Hugill, 2010).

**Criminal Code of Canada**
http://laws.justice.gc.ca/en/c-46/

## The Discipline of Criminology

The discipline of criminology includes six major areas: the definition of crime and criminals, the origins and role of law, the social distribution of crime, the causation of crime, patterns of criminal behaviour, and societal reactions to crime.

**The Definition of Crime and Criminals**  Not all social harms are criminal nor are all criminal acts harmful. Thus it is necessary to specify what kinds of acts are defined as crimes. There is also some question concerning who should be defined as a criminal for the purposes of criminological research. For example, should we include someone who has been charged with a criminal offence but has not been convicted? What about the person who has committed a criminal offence but not been charged? And how about the person who has been convicted of violations of laws governing a safe workplace after an employee was killed on the job, when these laws are not part of the Criminal Code?

**The Origins and Role of the Law**  It is important to understand the social origins of our laws as well as the role that law plays in society. Why are some acts defined as criminal, while others are dealt with under other types of legislation or are not sanctioned at all?

**The Social Distribution of Crime**  In order to understand crime we must know such things as the characteristics of people who commit crimes; trends in the occurrence of crime over time; and differences between cities, provinces, and countries in the rates and types of crime. These and other dimensions of the social distribution of crime help criminologists to understand the causes of crime.

**The Causation of Crime**  One of the most important questions for criminologists is why some people commit crimes, while others live more law-abiding lives. In this text you will learn about a wide variety of explanations of criminal behaviour.

**Patterns of Criminal Behaviour**  Criminal acts are defined by law in particular categories such as homicide, theft, and sexual assault. Criminologists have conducted a great deal of research analyzing the patterns of these offences. Among the questions asked by criminologists are these: Who are the offenders? Who are the victims? Under what social circumstances are offences most likely to take place? What are the consequences for the victims of crime? How can particular types of crime be prevented?

**Societal Reactions to Crime**  Historically, societies have responded to crime in many different ways and the issue of how best to deal with offenders is an important one. In our society we normally process law violators through a criminal justice system that includes the police, the courts, and the corrections system. Criminologists have studied each of these institutions very extensively.

This text does not cover the criminal justice system because at most colleges and universities it is covered in a separate course. However, a brief overview of the system will help you to understand how people charged with criminal offences are dealt with in Canada. As you will learn in Chapter 3

("Criminal Law") under the Constitution Act of 1867, the federal Parliament has exclusive jurisdiction over criminal law and procedure; therefore, the provinces and territories cannot pass or amend the criminal law. However, the provinces are responsible for the administration of justice. Because of this division of powers, the Canadian criminal justice system is quite complex. For example, there are many different levels of responsibility for policing. The federal police force—the Royal Canadian Mounted Police—enforces some federal laws, such as the Controlled Drugs and Substances Act, for which it is responsible in all provinces and territories. It also acts as a provincial police force in all jurisdictions except Ontario, Quebec, and parts of Newfoundland and Labrador, which have their own provincial police forces. The provinces pay the RCMP for these services under a provincial policing contract. The RCMP further acts as a municipal police force in some communities. While most of these are small communities, they also do urban policing under contract in larger communities, most notably in the Lower Mainland of British Columbia. Thus, while the city of Vancouver has its own municipal force like most of Canada's larger municipalities, the adjoining cities of Burnaby and Richmond are policed by the RCMP. In 2010 there were almost 70 000 police officers in Canada (Statistics Canada, 2010).

The courts also come under both federal and provincial jurisdiction. The provinces are responsible for appointing some judges and for administering the "lower" courts that deal with most criminal cases, including those involving young offenders. Higher-level courts that try serious criminal cases are the responsibility of the federal government, as are the provincial appeal courts. Appeal courts do not try cases, but hear appeals of cases decided by other courts. At the top of the hierarchy of courts is the Supreme Court of Canada, which hears appeals of decisions made by provincial courts of appeal.

Offenders who receive sentences of less than two years are dealt with by the provincial government. This includes offenders who receive community dispositions, such as probation or restitution. Those who are imprisoned go to institutions that are run by the provinces. A sentence of two years or more must be served in a federal institution that is run by the Correctional Service of Canada. This service also supervises offenders who are released into the community prior to the expiration of their sentences. The release decision is made by a separate body, the National Parole Board.

# Rules and Laws

## The Regulation of Behaviour

All groups have rules that guide their members' behaviour. Society cannot function without them—if we are to live and to work with others, rules are necessary. We must also have a reasonable expectation that other people will obey the rules. Think of the chaos that would result if each driver decided which side of the road she would drive on each day, or which stop sign he would decide to obey. Most of the time most of us conform to the norms our group prescribes. Of course, not all members of the group obey all the time. All of you have broken many rules, perhaps some of them important ones. In this text, we shall consider the topic of crime—behaviour that breaks the rules. How do rules get established? Why do people break them? How do groups respond to this violation?

We learn most rules so well that we follow them without thinking about them. Following accepted ways of walking and talking is almost automatic because these **norms** have been internalized. Often we cannot even specify all the rules that govern a particular behaviour—we just follow them. For example, when you try to learn a foreign language you suddenly become aware of all sorts of rules, such as those governing verb tenses, that you aren't consciously aware of when you are using your first language. Other rules are not followed in this routine fashion. Many of us may wish to drive above the speed limit, park illegally, or use marijuana but refrain from doing so because of our fear of penalties while some people may break these rules whenever they get a chance.

**norms**

Established rules of behaviour or standards of conduct.

Think of some of the informal rules (or folkways) that govern your conduct. When you were younger, your parents probably tried to persuade you to eliminate some of your favourite habits such as eating with your fingers, dipping food in your milk, and banging your toys on the furniture. These are very basic rules—others can be more complex. For example, how do you address the Queen or the lieutenant-governor if you meet them? Whose name do you mention first when you introduce your 22-year-old spouse to your 60-year-old employer? What are we to make of these rules that seem, on their face, to be trivial or silly? Rules help us to select from the vast numbers of potential behaviours of which we are capable. Do we bow, kiss, or shake hands as a greeting? Which of two persons holds a door for the other? Who gets served first and last at dinner? How do we handle important milestones such as marriage and death? While the way each society solves these little problems may vary widely, each society has provided solutions.

Not only do these solutions avert potential chaos, but following the rules enhances our sense of belonging. The penalties for not following these rules are normally informal ones—the disapproval of family, friends, or colleagues, or perhaps a reprimand from an organization to which the violator belongs. However, we normally don't think of the penalties but continue to obey these rules because we have been taught to obey them and because they are part of belonging to the group.

In our society, not all actions are governed only by these informal means of social control. Why do some informal rules become more formal regulations or laws? Consider the early days of the automobile. Driving was not regulated and the only rules of the road were those that applied to horse-drawn carriages. When automobiles were open and speeds slow, drivers gave right of way to other drivers who had higher social status, just as was done when walking down the street. However, as speeds became higher and as drivers ranged farther from their homes, this became impractical and the state had to establish more formal regulations. In this and in many other cases, we might say that the law exists when order can no longer be maintained through informal rules. The law also deals with behaviour that is too serious to be left to informal mechanisms.

## What Is a Crime?

As you will read in Chapter 2, the concept of crime has been developed relatively recently. That does not mean that people didn't do harmful things to one another in earlier times, but this harmful behaviour was handled quite differently than it is now. Prior to the 18th century, in most societies offences were handled privately by the wronged individual and his or her family. The early courts in Europe and North America dealt with religious and civil law rather than with criminal law.

**The Legal Definition of Crime**  The most common definition of crime is a *legalistic* one that defines a crime as an act that violates the criminal law and is punishable with jail terms, fines, and other sanctions. This **legal definition of crime** is satisfactory for most purposes and will fit most of the crimes discussed in this text. However, some criminologists—in particular, Edwin Sutherland, Herman and Julia Schwendinger, and John Hagan—have argued for a sociological definition of crime that encompasses a broader range of harmful behaviour than this strict legal definition provides.

**legal definition of crime**
Crime is an act that violates the criminal law and is punishable with jail terms, fines, and other sanctions.

**Is White-Collar Crime Really Crime?**  Edwin Sutherland was one of the most important figures in the development of criminology. In his famous presidential address to the American Sociological Association in 1939, Sutherland (1940) argued that focusing only on violations of the criminal law presented a misleading picture of crime. Limiting criminological research to offences such as burglary, assault, and theft that were dealt with in the criminal courts led to the conclusion that crime was primarily a lower-class phenomenon. However, Sutherland pointed out that many **white-collar crimes** were committed by middle- and upper-class people in the course of their business activities. Criminologists neglected these crimes because they were not dealt with by the criminal courts:

**white-collar crime**
Crime that is committed by middle- and upper-class people in the course of their legitimate business activities.

> The crimes of the lower class are handled by policemen, prosecutors, and judges, with penal sanctions in the form of fines, imprisonment, and death. The crimes of the upper class either result in no official action at all, or result in suits for damages in civil courts, or are handled by inspectors, and by administrative boards or commissions, with penal sanctions in the form of warnings, orders to cease and desist, occasionally the loss of a license, and only in extreme cases by fines or prison sentences. (Sutherland, 1940, 8)

Sutherland argued that even though they may not be dealt with in criminal court, the great harm caused by white-collar criminals made it imperative that criminologists study them. Thus he was suggesting that the legal definition of crime be expanded to encompass the violation of other types of laws.

## Human Rights Violations as Crime

Another attempt to expand the definition of crime was made by Herman and Julia Schwendinger (1970), who advocated a definition of crime based on **human rights** rather than on legal statutes. If an action violated the basic rights of humans to obtain the necessities of life and to be treated with respect and dignity, criminologists should consider it a crime. Thus government policies that create poverty and homelessness should be studied as crimes along with other practices that cause social harm, including imperialism, sexism, and racism. Advocates of this approach feel that the criminal law has been established by those in power so that acts committed by powerful people are not criminalized. Therefore, they feel the law is biased against the poor. The

**human rights**
The minimum conditions required for a person to live a dignified life. Among the rights set out by the Universal Declaration of Human Rights are the right to life, liberty, and security of the person; the right to be free of torture and other forms of cruel and degrading punishment; the right to equality before the law; and the right to the basic necessities of life.

Schwendingers' proposal explicitly places criminology on the side of the poor and powerless.

Proponents of green criminology, discussed later in this chapter, take a similar view. Many corporations engage in practices that do enormous harm to the environment and to individuals, but do not violate laws or environmental regulations. For example, multinational companies have built factories in China where environmental regulations are very lax (Shuqin, 2010). While legal, many of these factories contribute massive amounts of pollution. Green criminologists argue that practices such as these should be studied, despite their legality, because of the harm they cause (Gibbs et al., 2010).

## A Continuum of Crime and Deviance

Universal Declaration of
Human Rights
http://www.un.org/en/documents/
udhr/index.shtml

While few criminologists today would limit their work to the strict legal definition of crime, most would not make the definition as broad as the human rights approach would suggest. John Hagan (1985) has proposed an approach to defining crime that reflects the way most criminologists view their discipline. Hagan says that a definition of crime must encompass not only violations of the criminal law, but also "a range of behaviors that for all practical purposes are treated as crimes (e.g., Sutherland's white-collar crimes), as well as those behaviors that across time and place vary in their location in and outside the boundaries of criminal law. In other words, we need a definition that considers behaviors that are both actually and potentially liable to criminal law" (1985, 49). Hagan proposed that deviance and crime be considered as a continuum ranging from the least serious to most serious acts. Seriousness can be assessed on three dimensions:

- *The degree of consensus that an act is wrong.* Most people feel that mass murder is wrong, but there is much less agreement over the issue of using marijuana.

- *The severity of the society's response to the act.* Murder is punishable by death in some societies and by life imprisonment in others. On the other hand, possession of small amounts of marijuana may be ignored by the police, and many U.S. states have decriminalized this behaviour.

- *The assessment of the degree of harm of the act.* Drug use, illegal gambling, and prostitution are often considered to be "victimless" crimes that harm only the offender, while serious crimes of violence are considered to be very harmful.

Although these three dimensions are normally closely related, this is not always the case. For example, the operators of the Westray mine, whose unsafe practices resulted in the death of 26 miners in Nova Scotia, caused a great deal of harm (see Box 17.1). However, even though most Canadians would probably agree that this negligence was wrong, none of the people responsible for the mine were penalized for their actions. This approach recognizes that "the separation of crime from other kinds of deviance is a social and political phenomenon" (Hagan, 1985, 49) and allows criminologists to consider a broad range of behaviours, including some types of deviance that may not be against the law. Hagan's approach is illustrated in Figure 1.1, which shows four major categories of crime and deviance: consensus crimes, conflict crimes, social deviations, and social

**FIGURE 1.1  Hagan's Varieties of Deviance**

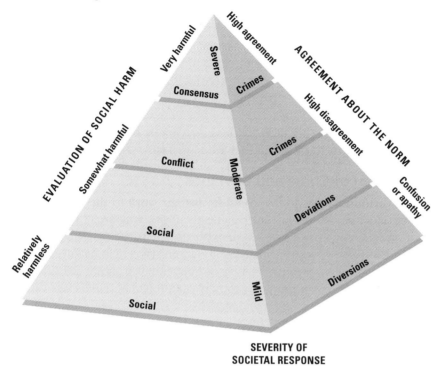

Source: John Hagan. (1991). *The Disreputable Pleasures: Crime and Deviance in Canada,* 3rd ed. Toronto: McGraw-Hill Ryerson. p. 13. Reprinted with permission.

diversions. Although this text will not specifically consider social deviations and social diversions, the distinction between consensus and conflict crimes is an important one that will be discussed in several chapters.

## Crime Is Socially Defined

Can you think of any type of behaviour that everybody condemns? Most people might consider killing another person to be an act that is always evil, but this is not the case. Soldiers are considered heroes for killing the enemy during times of war. Society allows police officers to kill under some circumstances, and all of us have the right to kill a person who is threatening us with lethal force. Even those who commit what most of us would call murder are not always classified as murderers by the courts. For example, a man may kill his neighbour and be found not guilty by reason of insanity (now formally called "not criminally responsible on account of mental disorder"). If the same man were sane but intoxicated at the time of the offence, he might be found guilty only of manslaughter. Even for an act as serious as killing another person, we must understand the social context of the act before we can determine whether it is deviant and how it should be classified.

Just as murder is socially defined, so are other types of crime and other forms of deviance. An act is deviant only from the point of view of a set of rules and regulations, and these vary widely from society to society and from group to group. There are some broad similarities in acts that are defined as deviant. For example, most societies, most of the time, frown upon members killing one  another or plotting the violent overthrow of the government. However, there are also great differences between societies and within societies over time. Some societies consider as unlawful many acts that are tolerated or even encouraged in Canada while others permit practices that we restrict. For example, in Saudi Arabia women are not permitted to drive cars or wear short skirts, in Singapore it is unlawful to possess chewing gum (it creates messy streets and transit vehicles), and on some French beaches it is unlawful to wear clothes. All these practices are quite acceptable here. On the other hand, Canada and most western countries have laws against helping a terminally ill person to commit suicide (see Box 3.1), while in Holland doctor-assisted suicide is common.

Thus there is nothing inherent in any act that makes it unlawful. We can define deviance as behaviour that violates the rules, whatever those rules may be. However, this definition leaves us with problems. Whose rules are to be followed? Consider the case of the Muslim father living in Winnipeg who went to court because he wanted his 14-year-old daughter to marry her 27-year-old fiancé. Such a marriage is not permitted by Manitoba law, which sets the minimum age for marriage at 16 (*Winnipeg Free Press*, 1993). Therefore, behaviour that is normative from the father's perspective is considered deviant from the province's perspective. What about a person who belongs to an outlaw motorcycle gang? Behaviour that conforms to the standards of the group will often violate the rules of the broader society. The same is true of those who use terrorism to fight what they feel is an unjust political system. If the revolution is successful, they will be heroes. Many political leaders, including Menachem Begin of Israel, Fidel Castro of Cuba, and China's Mao Zedong, began their political careers by using violence to achieve power. However, if the revolution fails, the leaders will be killed or imprisoned. This important question of "Who sets the rules?" will be discussed more fully later in this chapter.

## The Relativity of Crime

Another implication of the fact that crime is socially defined is that the rules can change. A situation in the United States a few years ago highlighted just how relative the law can be. Because of pressure from the federal government, many states raised their legal drinking age from 18 to 21. At least one state did this in stages, with the drinking age rising one year each January 1. In a television interview, one university student whose 18th birthday was in late November described what he was facing for the next three years. Each year, he would be able to legally drink alcohol from his November birthday until midnight on December 31. Since the drinking age changed with the new year, he had to return to soft drinks until the following November when he turned 19. This would go on every year until he was 21, which meant that he could legally drink for less than six months out of the 36 months between his 18th and 21st birthdays.

A more important example is the fact that several decades ago, the sexual acts of gays and lesbians were prohibited by the Criminal Code and subject to maximum penalties ranging from five to fourteen years, depending on the specific act (Rodgers, 1962). When former prime minister Pierre Trudeau was the Minister of Justice, he declared that the "state has no place in the bedrooms of the nation" and removed these sections from the Criminal Code. Since that time there have been dramatic changes. Gays and lesbians now have the right to get married and much of the controversy over gay rights has disappeared.

These examples show that criminal and non-criminal are not two distinct categories. There is an overlap between the two, and the line between them can be very ambiguous. We often speak as if the world were divided between criminals and non-criminals. However, we have all broken the law at times—does this mean we are "criminals"? In fact, phrases like "everybody does it" are used to justify crimes that are committed by "respectable" people, including stealing from employers, not reporting tips and other income on tax forms, and copying computer software (Gabor, 1994). How do people draw the line between respectable citizens who occasionally do bad things and those they consider "criminals"? What are the implications of thinking of crime as being a matter of degree?

## Who Makes the Rules? Conflict Versus Consensus Theories of Law

Of course the law is not completely subjective or arbitrary. Many criminal laws reflect serious social harms that are illegal in most societies and that most people condemn. However, as you have just read, the exact form of the laws and the specific behaviour prohibited vary greatly in different places and at different times. Why do some acts become subject to criminal sanctions while others do not?

One of the most important questions in the study of criminology is "Who sets the rules?" Who decided that selling marijuana is illegal while selling cigarettes is a respectable business? Who determined that an impaired driver who causes the death of a pedestrian can be severely sanctioned, while an employer whose violation of workplace safety rules causes death may receive only a small fine? We have seen that rules can take many different forms, so the issue of how rules come to have a specific content is an important one. There have been two distinct approaches to this question—the consensus and conflict perspectives.

### The Consensus Approach

**Consensus theorists** believe that law represents the consensus of the people. That is, the law is simply a codification of the **values** shared by most members of a society. For example, several Muslim countries have institutionalized sharia law, which is explicitly based on the Koran, and so the law reflects those societies' religious values. Similarly, many of the early European settlers in the United States were Puritans who left England for the colony of Massachusetts so that they would be free to practise their religious beliefs. Not surprisingly, the legal code of the new colony reflected these beliefs. Much of their legal code of 1648 was taken directly from the Bible, and many crimes were punishable by death. These capital crimes included "idolatry, witchcraft, blasphemy,

**consensus theory**
Laws represent the agreement of most of the people in society that certain acts should be prohibited by the criminal law.

**value**
A collective idea about what is right or wrong, good or bad, and desirable or undesirable in a particular culture.

bestiality, sodomy, adultery, rape, man stealing, treason, ... cursing or smiting of a parent, stubbornness or rebelliousness on the part of a son against his parents, and homicide committed with malice prepense, by guile or poisoning" (Haskins, 1969, 37). Of course, religious values are not the only ones enshrined in law, but they do illustrate how values become codified in law.

Support for the consensus view is also found in the fact that there is a broad agreement regarding many laws, particularly those that deal with street crimes such as robbery, burglary, and murder. Several studies have asked people to rate the seriousness of a broad range of criminal offences. These studies have demonstrated that there is considerable agreement among people from Canada and the United States concerning the rankings of these offences (Normandeau, 1966; Akman et al., 1967).

## The Conflict Approach

**class conflict theory**

Laws are passed by members of the ruling class in order to maintain their privileged position by keeping the common people under control.

Conflict theorists do not share the view that our laws reflect a consensus of members of society. This is particularly apparent in the work of **class conflict theorists,** who take the view that laws are passed by members of the ruling class to maintain their privileged position by keeping the common people under control. Activities that threaten those with power are defined as illegal, and the legal mechanism of the state is used to enforce the laws. One example from Canada's early history shows how the law can be used to further the aims of the politically powerful at the expense of the common people. After the Riel Rebellion in 1885, Hayter Reed, the assistant commissioner of Indian Affairs, used the Indian Act to control the Aboriginal population. He deposed many of the chiefs he felt were disloyal and undermined the authority of other Aboriginal leaders by instructing his staff to deal directly with individuals and families rather than with the bands. He also confined Indians to their reserves by ordering the implementation of a pass system that had no justification in law:

> Officials of the [North West Mounted Police] were never comfortable with the absence of any legal foundation for the pass system. The lack of a legal basis in this case undermined the validity of all NWMP operations: they were trying to demonstrate to the Indians that the police enforced a rational system of laws that operated to the benefit of all. ... In 1893 a circular letter was issued directing all police officers to refrain from ordering Indians without passes back to their reserves.
>
> Hayter Reed would have none of these weak-kneed, legalistic concerns. He urged the police to continue enforcing the pass system on the grounds that the "moral responsibilities of the Indian Department transcended treaty obligations." Reed's views triumphed. By at least 1896 the police had reversed their position. In that year Commissioner Herchmer issued a circular letter instructing police who encountered any Indian without a pass to "use all possible pressure to persuade him to return to his reserve." (Carter, 1990, 153–54)

Reed was able to use the legal system to restrict the movement of Aboriginal people who were believed to represent a threat to those holding power—the government and the white settlers who were moving onto the Prairies.

While the pass system has been abolished, the effects of another discriminatory legal intervention targeted at powerless people persist today. Canada has very harsh penalties for the possession and sale of illicit drugs. Though rarely imposed, the maximum penalty for trafficking drugs such as heroin is life imprisonment, and in 2011 the Conservative government is planning to legislate mandatory prison terms for growing six plants of marijuana or more if there is evidence that the marijuana is being trafficked.

Why are these drugs punished so severely while other harmful substances such as alcohol and tobacco are legally available? The answer dates back to the early 1900s. Between 1908 and 1929 Parliament passed a series of harsh anti-drug laws, most of which are still on the books. Cook (1969) attributed the severity of these laws to several factors, including racial hostility against Asian immigrants. Not only were the Chinese viewed as inferior, but they had low social status and little power to resist legislation that was clearly targeted at them. While addiction was common among Caucasians who were using opium-based prescription and over-the-counter drugs, the focus of legislators was on those Chinese immigrants who smoked opium rather than on the doctors and pharmaceutical companies. Drug laws still disproportionately affect socially disadvantaged Canadians, many of whom are members of racial minority groups.

Consensus and conflict theories each provide explanations of the formation and persistence of some laws. However, as Hagan's definition of crime suggests, neither provides a complete explanation. While the majority of the populace does benefit from many laws, others benefit the powerful at the expense of the rest of us. Some laws fit in neither category. For example, there is no consensus in our society about the propriety of abortion, gambling, or prostitution, but laws regulating these behaviours do not reflect any particular class interest. Thus, some feel that the most accurate way of describing the process of law formation is group conflict theory. This perspective recognizes that all laws are the result of a political process, and that this process typically involves a conflict or a debate between different interest groups. You will learn more about these theories later in this text.

# Criminology Is an Evolving Discipline: The New Fields of Green Criminology and Terrorism Studies

Like other academic disciplines, criminology is constantly changing. To show how the criminological perspective can help us understand contemporary issues, this chapter will conclude with a discussion of two of criminology's newest branches: green criminology and terrorism studies. Other new areas of study for criminologists include genocide (Woolford, 2011) and the political aspects of modern surveillance systems (Haggerty and Ericson, 2005). Each of these new areas challenges the discipline by presenting new ways of defining and understanding crime as criminologists engage with significant changes in the world.

## Green Criminology

Some criminologists have begun to develop a "green criminology" because they feel criminologists should contribute to the debate about the causes and consequences of environmental destruction and should use their expertise to help deal with this problem.

Green criminologists believe that criminology should not just study actions that violate the criminal law but also actions that are socially harmful. Some environmental harms are illegal. One of Canada's most serious environmental disasters was a case of water pollution in Walkerton, Ontario, that caused more than 2000 people to fall seriously ill and led to seven deaths. The operators of the water treatment plant who failed to test the water and who falsified test results were successfully prosecuted, though politicians such as former Ontario premier Mike Harris, whose government's policies contributed in a major way to the tragedy (O'Connor, 2002) were not prosecuted. However, many actions that are much more serious in the long term, such as the emission of huge quantities of greenhouse gases in the production of oil from Alberta's tar sands (Smandych and Kueneman, 2010) and clear-cutting tropical rainforests, are not against the law. Green criminologists argue that the damage to the Earth caused by destructive environmental practices can be far more serious than the illegal acts that have traditionally been the subject matter of criminological study (Lynch and Stretesky, 2007). The impact of global warming could cause mass starvation, migration from countries where drought has led to the collapse of agriculture, and conflict between countries over water resources and food supplies (South, 2010).

Green criminology has its roots in the environmental and animal rights movements, though more green criminologists have focused on environmental issues than on animal rights. The environmental focus of green criminology covers the study of environmental damage, including air and water pollution and harm to natural ecosystems such as oceans and forests. Those interested in animal rights study "individual acts of cruelty to animals and the institutional, socially-acceptable human domination of animals in agribusiness, in slaughterhouses and abattoirs, in so-called scientific experimentation and, in less obviously direct ways, in sports, colleges and schools, zoos, aquaria and circuses" (Beirne and South, 2007, xiv) (see Box 1.2). These theorists have introduced the concept of "speciesism," which refers to discrimination against non-human animals. Thus green criminology encompasses a broad range of behaviours ranging from acts that are clearly harmful, such as dumping toxic waste in the ocean, to acts that many people consider to be acceptable, such as eating meat or wearing leather shoes.

The range of work done by green criminologists has been outlined this way:

- It has documented the existence of law-breaking with respect to pollution, disposal of toxic waste, and misuse of environmental resources.

- It has raised questions relating to the destruction of specific environments and resources in ways that are "legal" but ecologically very harmful to plants, animals, and humans.

- It has challenged corporate definitions of good environmental practice and emphasized the claims of non-human nature to ecological justice.

# FOCUS BOX 1.2

## ANIMAL CRUELTY LAWS IN CANADA

In several chapters of this book you will learn that laws do not just happen; they are the result of a complex social process. Whether or not particular laws are passed depends on the influence of individuals and groups whose interests would be affected by the law. Green criminologists are very critical of the fact that the voices of environmentalists are often not heard by politicians who are also being lobbied by corporate interests who can profit from environmental damage. Current attempts to improve Canada's animal cruelty legislation show how different groups try to ensure that legislation does not interfere with their interests.

Canada has made only minor changes in its animal cruelty legislation since 1892 and there is widespread agreement that stronger laws are needed to prevent animal abuse. Many critics of the current legislation cite an Edmonton case in which two men tied a dog to a tree and beat it to death with a baseball bat. The men were not convicted of animal cruelty because the evidence showed that the dog had died when it was first hit with the bat so it did not suffer cruelty. It is also very difficult to get convictions for people who neglect their animals because the Crown must prove that the neglect is "willful." Thus a farmer whose animals have starved to death will be acquitted unless it can be proved that he acted willfully. As a result, very few people in Canada have been convicted of animal abuse.

New animal cruelty laws have been before Parliament since 1999. However, the proposed legislation has been opposed by hunters, trappers, farmers, and medical researchers who experiment on animals and who fear that the laws would affect their livelihoods. In 2008 Parliament was faced with two competing bills. The first, (S-203) involved minimal changes beyond making the penalties tougher for existing offences. The second (C-229) would have added significant protection for animals. It would have removed the 'willful neglect' provision and would have made it more difficult to kill stray animals. The second bill was supported by many groups, including the Canadian Veterinary Medical Association and virtually all of Canada's humane societies and animal support organizations. On the other side were groups such as the Canadian Sportfishing Industry Association, which claimed that the proposed legislation would jeopardize the $10 billion-a-year sportsfishing industry by making it "possible for a Grandfather to face a federal criminal prosecution for taking his grandchildren fishing" (Canadian Sportfishing Industry Association, 2007). Other opponents claimed that the bill would give animals the same legal standing as humans and would encourage animal rights "terrorists" to keep attacking medical researchers (Senate Committee on Legal and Constitutional Affairs, 2006). Proponents of Bill C-229 argued that the bill excluded harming animals for lawful reasons such as hunting and medical experimentation, but this interpretation was challenged by opponents. The Conservative government was able to pass S-203 in 2008 but the bill that would do much more to protect animals (C-229) has not been passed.

- It has emphasized the dynamic links between distribution of environmental "risk" and distinct communities, particularly how poor and minority populations experience disproportionate exposure to environmental harm.

- It has investigated the specific place of animals in relation to issues of "rights" and human–non-human relationships on a shared planet.

- It has criticized the inadequacies of environmental regulation in both philosophical and practical terms.

- It has exposed corporate attempts to stifle environmental critique and dissent through the use of public relations propaganda and strategic lawsuits against public participation.
- It has reconsidered the nature of victimization in relation to environmental changes and events, including social and governmental responses to this victimization.
- It has explored the ways in which law enforcement officials—particularly the police but also environmental protection authorities—have intervened with regard to regulation of fisheries, prosecution of polluters, and conservation of specific environs and species.*

The work of green criminologists is grounded in the philosophy of ecological citizenship. This means that notions of morality and rights should be extended to "non-human nature" (White, 2007, 35) and that societies should adopt a notion of ecological citizenship that obliges them to recognize that the environment must be protected for future generations. This will require a global perspective because the effects of environmental crimes go far beyond the borders of any single country.

## Terrorism Studies

A global perspective is also important in the growing field of terrorism studies. Criminologists became more interested in terrorism after the al-Qaeda attacks on the United States on September 11, 2001. Criminologists have looked at several dimensions of terrorism, including the recruitment and training of terrorists, the organization of terrorist organizations, links between terrorism and other types of criminality, and the social control of terrorism. In this chapter we will consider two of the most interesting aspects of terrorism studies: the social definition of terrorism and the degree to which Western nations have violated the rule of law in their "war on terror".

**terrorism**

The illegitimate use of force to achieve a political objective by targeting innocent people.

**The Social Definition of Terrorism**  Terrorism is difficult to define and there is no universal agreement on its definition. However, a simple definition that captures much of our sense of what terrorism involves is: "Terrorism constitutes the illegitimate use of force to achieve a political objective by targeting innocent people" (Laqueur, 1987: 72).

One reason why finding an agreed upon definition is difficult is because terrorism is a socially constructed term. Turk has clearly stated the issue:

> Contrary to the impression fostered by official incidence counts and media reports, terrorism is not a given in the real world but is instead an interpretation of events and their presumed causes. And these interpretations are not unbiased attempts to depict truth but rather conscious efforts to manipulate perceptions to promote certain interests

---

*Rob White. (2007). "Green Criminology and the Pursuit of Social and Ecological Justice." In Piers Beirne and Nigel South (eds.), *Issues in Green Criminology: Confronting Harms Against Environments, Humanity and Other Animals* (pp. 33–34). Portland: Willan Publishing.

at the expense of others. When people and events come to be regularly described in public as terrorists and terrorism, some governmental or other entity is succeeding in a war of words in which the opponent is promoting alternative designations such as 'martyr' and 'liberation struggle'. (2004: 272)

Thus the 9/11 al-Qaeda attack on the United States is generally defined as terrorism by Western countries but is seen by some living in other countries as martyrdom for a just cause. The subsequent U.S. invasion of Iraq was not considered terrorism by political authorities in western countries because the Americans resisted this labelling even though thousands of innocent people were killed during the Iraq war. Actions such as the intensive firebombing of German and Japanese cities by the Allies during World War II were not defined as terrorism because those who won the war were able to impose their definitions of these actions.

Another definitional complication is that while we normally consider terrorism to refer to acts committed against a government, the term can also be applied to actions committed by a government against its own people. Dictators such as Joseph Stalin, who ruled the Soviet Union from 1924 to 1953, and Mao Zedong, who controlled China from 1949 to 1976, each killed millions of their own people in order to maintain their political control.

# FOCUS BOX 1.3

## TERRORISM IN CANADA

Most Canadians are probably unaware that Canada has had problems with terrorism. Kellett (2004) tracked over 400 terrorist incidents in Canada between 1960 and 1992. The majority of these incidents involved Canadians attacking domestic targets, and most of these were committed by two groups: the FLQ and the Sons of Freedom Doukhobors. The FLQ (Front de Liberation du Quebec) were committed to the separation of Quebec from Canada. They financed their political activities through crimes such as credit card fraud and robbery. During the 1960s they were responsible for nearly 100 bombings, including an attack on the Montreal Stock Exchange which injured 27 people. They also kidnapped and murdered Quebec cabinet minister Pierre Laporte in 1970.

The Sons of Freedom Doukhobors were a very different group. They were a pacifist religious group who rejected government involvement in their lives and who refused to send their children to school, to pay taxes, or to register births and deaths. As a result, the British Columbia government removed many of their children from their homes and forced them into residential schools. The group's protests against the government and against other Doukhobors culminated in over 100 bombings and arson attacks on public facilities such as schools and power lines between 1960 and 1962.

The worst incident of Canadian-based terrorism was the 1985 bombing of Air India flight 182. A bomb placed in a Boeing 747 in Vancouver exploded over the Atlantic Ocean, killing all 329 people on board. At almost the same time a bomb placed on another Air India flight from Vancouver exploded at Japan's Narita airport killing two baggage handlers. The bombings were blamed on Canadian militant groups supporting a Sikh homeland in India. One man, Inderjit Singh Reyat, pleaded guilty to a charge of manslaughter and building the

*(continued)*

bombs; he received a 15-year jail sentence. The men accused of placing the bombs, Ajaib Singh Baghri and Ripudaman Singh Malik, were later acquitted. In 2010, Reyat was convicted of perjury in the Baghri and Malik trial and sentenced to an additional nine years in prison.

Terrorist activities have continued over the past decade. In 2006, 18 men were arrested in the Toronto area on charges of planning terrorist attacks in Canada. While not a well-trained or well-organized group, they had plans to detonate several truck bombs and to storm the Parliament building and behead Prime Minister Harper. They held training camps north of Toronto (which featured the uniquely Canadian touch of visits to Tim Hortons along with lessons in using firearms and discussions of jihad) and tried to order several tonnes of ammonium nitrate to use in their truck bombs. They were arrested before they got a chance to put any of their plans into action. Eleven of the men have been convicted of a variety of charges and their leader received a sentence of life imprisonment.

Most recently, a group of Ottawa men bombed a Royal Bank branch in 2010 to protest globalization and a Quebec group bombed a Canadian Forces recruiting centre in Trois Rivières to protest Canada's role in the war in Afghanistan.

Source: From MURRAY/LINDEN/KENDALL. *Sociology in Our Times*, 5E. © 2011 Nelson Education Ltd. Reproduced by permission. www.cengage.com/permissions

**Terrorism and Rule of Law**  Ericson (2007) has observed that Western societies have placed a high priority on preventing terrorism at all costs: "Normal legal principles, standards, and procedures must be suspended because of a state of emergency, extreme uncertainty, or threat to security with catastrophic potential. The legal order must be suspended to save the social order" (2007: 26). To fight terrorism the state has assumed greater powers. Enhanced methods of surveillance and control have been put in place and normal restraints, such as the need for due process and the rights of accused persons, have been ignored in the search for security. For example, the American government has held hundreds of Muslim prisoners in Guantanamo Bay, which is U.S.-controlled territory in Cuba, so that normal American due process rights do not apply. These prisoners are not classified by the Americans as prisoners of war but as 'unlawful enemy combatants', so the rights provided to such prisoners by the Geneva Convention also do not apply.

The mandates of Canadian security agencies have broadened since 9/11 (Murphy, 2007). Billions of dollars were added to the budgets of security agencies, including the RCMP, the Canadian Security and Intelligence Service (CSIS), and the Canadian Border Services Agency. New anti-terrorism legislation has expanded the powers of the police and other security agencies. In addition to these new powers, the emphasis on prevention requires that the police use extraordinary tactics, including "the use of paid community informants, extensive community surveillance, broad intelligence-gathering, targeted ethnic and religious profiling, and a preventative security-policing tactic called 'threat disruption'" (Murphy, 2007: 456).

Many governments have violated the rights of some of their citizens in the war on terror. The most notorious Canadian case (discussed in more detail in Chapter 12) involved Maher Arar, a Syrian born Canadian citizen. Arar was returning from a holiday in Tunisia in 2002 when he was apprehended in New

York by U.S. officials. Because of suspected ties to al-Qaeda Arar was immediately sent to Syria (a practice known as rendition) where he was tortured in a Syrian prison, likely to provide information to American intelligence agencies. He was allowed to return to Canada after a year in Syrian custody.

The Canadian government held an inquiry into the Arar case. The inquiry concluded that the RCMP had violated its own policies by providing American authorities with information about Arar that was inaccurate and unfairly negative (Commission of Inquiry into the Actions of Canadian Officials in Relation to Maher Arar, 2006). The RCMP and CSIS did not work co-operatively with the Foreign Affairs Department to help secure Arar's return to Canada, and Canadian officials leaked inaccurate classified information about Arar to the media following his return to Canada. The RCMP had also concealed information from senior government officials about their handling of the case.

Following the inquiry, the Canadian government formally apologized to Arar and paid him $10.5 million in compensation. U.S. Senator Patrick Leahy's comment on the Arar case provides an eloquent expression of the impact of anti-terrorism programs on the rule of law in many countries: "Maher Arar's case stands as a sad example of how we have been too willing to sacrifice our core principles to overarching government power in the name of security when doing so only undermines the principles we stand for—and makes us less safe" (*Ottawa Citizen*, 2007).

## Summary

- The term *criminology* is used in a number of ways. In this text it will refer to the body of knowledge regarding crime as a social phenomenon. It includes within its scope the processes of making laws, breaking laws, and reacting to the breaking of laws. The objective of criminology is the development of a body of general and verified principles and of other types of knowledge regarding this process of law, crime, and treatment.

- The discipline of criminology includes six major areas: the definition of crime and criminals, the origins and role of law, the social distribution of crime, the causation of crime, patterns of criminal behaviour, and societal reactions to crime.

- Our behaviour is strongly influenced by norms, many of which we have internalized. Much of the time we don't even consciously think about the rules that govern our behaviour. Most of the time, rules are enforced through informal means such as the disapproval of our family and friends; however, in some cases the rules are formalized into laws.

- The strict legal definition of crime is an act that violates the criminal law and is punishable with jail terms, fines, and other sanctions. Sociologists have expanded this definition in a number of different ways. In his discussion of white-collar crime, Sutherland said that criminologists should also include violations of other types of laws in addition to criminal law. The Schwendingers proposed that crime be defined as a violation of human rights. Hagan felt that criminologists should consider deviance and crime as a continuum ranging from the minor acts of deviance to serious crimes.

■ Crime is socially defined. No behaviour is inherently good or evil and we must understand the social context of an act before we can determine whether it is deviant and how it should be classified. Also, the form of laws and the specific behaviour that is prohibited vary greatly in different places and at different times.

■ Consensus theorists believe that laws represent the will of most of the people in a particular society. On the other hand, conflict theorists feel that law reflects power relationships in society, as those with power use the law to help maintain their position. Some laws fit each of these perspectives.

■ Like other disciplines, criminology continually moves into new research areas. Two of the newest sub-fields in criminology are green criminology and terrorism studies.

## QUESTIONS FOR CRITICAL THINKING

1. Look at Figure 1.1, which shows different types of crime and deviance. Can you think of examples of behaviours that fit into each of the four categories (consensus crimes, conflict crimes, social deviations, and social diversions)? How can particular behaviours move from one category to another? Can you think of examples of behaviours that have moved from one category to another?

2. Look at the way your local newspaper handles crime stories. What picture does the newspaper provide of crime in your community? If you have a tabloid paper (such as the *Toronto Sun*, the *Winnipeg Sun*, or the *Vancouver Province*) in your community, does it handle crime stories in a different manner from other newspapers?

3. Think of a law people are currently lobbying to change. What changes are being advocated? Why do some people want to change the law? If anyone is resisting the legal change, why are they offering this resistance? What do you think will be the outcome of this attempt at legal change?

4. Discuss some of the advantages and disadvantages of the Schwendingers' suggestion that crime be broadly defined as a violation of human rights.

5. Many college and university students have used drugs, and some who work as restaurant servers do not declare all of their income on their tax forms. Should these students be called criminals? Why do you feel they should or should not be called criminals?

## NET WORK

A group led by criminologist Delbert Elliott has established a website dedicated to the prevention of violence. The group has assessed over 600 violence prevention programs and has selected a small number that have a demonstrated ability to reduce violence. Go to the website for Blueprints for Violence Prevention at

**www.colorado.edu/cspv/blueprints/model/overview.html**. Look at three of the model programs that have been selected by the project. For each of these programs, can you determine what aspect of the child's social environment the program planners are trying to change? What does the success of the three programs you have selected tell you about the causes of crime?

## KEY TERMS

class conflict theory; pg. 20
consensus theory; pg. 19
criminology; pg. 9
human rights; pg. 15

legal definition of crime; pg. 15
norms; pg. 14
value; pg. 19
white-collar crime; pg. 15

## BIBLIOGRAPHY

Akman, D.D., A. Normandeau, and S. Turner. (1967). "The Measurement of Delinquency in Canada." *Journal of Criminal Law, Criminology and Police Science* 58: 330–37.

Beirne, Piers, and Nigel South. (2007). *Issues in Green Criminology: Confronting Harms Against Environments, Humanity and Other Animals*. Portland: Willan Publishing.

Black, Conrad. (1993). *A Life in Progress*. Toronto: Key Porter Books.

Blumstein, Alfred. (2003). "The Kid Whiz: Richard Tremblay." *Time* May 26: 54.

Canadian Sportfishing Industry Association. (2007). "Federal Animal Cruelty Legisltion." Available at http://www.csia.ca/media/FEDERAL_ANIMAL_CRUELTY_LEGISLATION.pdf; accessed August 18, 2007.

Carter, Sarah. (1990). *Lost Harvests*. Montreal: McGill-Queen's University Press.

Chunn, Dorothy, Susan Boyd, and Robert Menzies. (2002). "'We All Live in Bhopal': Criminology Discovers Environmental Crime." In Susan Boyd, Dorothy Chunn, and Robert Menzies (eds.), *Toxic Criminology: Environment, Law and the State in Canada* (pp. 7–24). Halifax: Fernwood.

Commission of Inquiry into the Actions of Canadian Officials in Relation to Maher Arar. (2006). *Report of the Events Relating to Maher Arar: Analysis and Recommendations*. Ottawa: Public Works and Government Services Canada.

Cook, Shirley. (1969). "Canadian Narcotics Legislation, 1908–1923: A Conflict Model Interpretation." *Canadian Review of Sociology and Anthropology* 6: 36–46.

Croall, Hazel. (2007). "Food Crime." In Piers Beirne and Nigel South (eds.), *Issues in Green Criminology: Confronting Harms Against Environments, Humanity and Other Animals* (pp. 206–29). Portland: Willan Publishing.

Dowler, Ken, Thomas Fleming, and Stephen Muzzatti. (2006). "Constructing Crime: Media, Crime and Popular Culture." *Canadian Journal of Criminology and Criminal Justice* 48: 837–50.

Ericson, Richard. (2007). *Crime in an Insecure World*. Cambridge: Polity Press.

Gabor, Thomas. (1994). *Everybody Does It: Crime by the Public*. Toronto: University of Toronto Press.

Galloway, Gloria. (2003). "Parents Sentenced for Exorcism Gone Wrong." *Globeandmail.com*. Available at http://www.theglobeandmail.com/servlet/story/RTGAM.20030522.ue; accessed May 28, 2007.

Gibbs, Carole, Meredith Gore, Edmund McGarrell, and Louie Rivers III. (2010). "Introducing Conservation Criminology: Towards Interdisciplinary Scholarship on Environmental Crimes and Risks." *British Journal of Criminology* 50: 124–44.

Hagan, John. (1985). *Modern Criminology: Crime, Criminal Behaviour, and Its Control.* New York: McGraw-Hill.

Haggerty, Kevin, and Richard Ericson. (2005). *The New Politics of Surveillance and Visibility.* Toronto: University of Toronto Press.

Haskins, George Lee. (1969). "A Rule to Walk By." In Richard Quinney (ed.), *Crime and Justice in Society* (pp. 33–54). Boston: Little, Brown and Company.

Hugill, David. 2010. Missing Women, Missing News: Covering Crisis in Vancouver's Downtown Eastside. Halifax/Winnipeg: Fernwood Publishing

Jackman, Tom. (2003). "Murder Defendants Claim Connection with Hit Movie." *HoustonChronicle.com.* Available at http://www.chron.com/cs/CDA/printstory.hts/nation/1923147; accessed May 28, 2007.

Kellett, Anthony. (2004). "Terrorism in Canada: 1960–1992." In Jeffrey Ian Ross (ed.), *Violence in Canada: Sociopolitical Perspectives*, 2nd edn (pp. 284–312). New Brunswick, NJ: Transaction Press.

Laqueur, Walter. (1987). *The Age of Terrorism.* Boston: Little, Brown.

Lynch, Michael J., and Paul Stretesky. "Green Criminology in the United States." In Piers Beirne and Nigel South (eds.), *Issues in Green Criminology: Confronting Harms Against Environments, Humanity and Other Animals* (pp. 248–69). Portland: Willan Publishing.

McCormick, Chris. (1995). *Constructing Danger: The Misrepresentation of Crime in the News.* Halifax: Fernwood Publishing.

McIntyre, Mike. (2003). *Nowhere to Run: The Killing of Constable Dennis Strongquill.* Winnipeg: Great Plains Publications.

McNish, Jacquie, and Sinclair Stewart. (2004). *Wrong Way: The Fall of Conrad Black.* Toronto: Viking Canada.

Media Index. (1999). "South Park Gets Nasty at Record-Setting Pace." *Austin American-Statesman* July 16: E1.

Murphy, Christopher. (2007). "'Securitizing' Canadian Policing: A New Paradigm for the Post 9/11 Security State?" *The Canadian Journal of Sociology* 32: 449–75.

Murray, Jane Lothian, Rick Linden, and Diana Kendall. (2011). *Sociology in Our Times* (5th edn). Toronto: Nelson.

Normandeau, Andre. (1966). "The Measurement of Delinquency in Montreal." *Journal of Criminal Law, Criminology, and Police Science* 57: 172–77.

O'Connor, The Honourable Dennis R. (2002). *Report of the Walkerton Inquiry: Part One: Summary.* Toronto: Queen's Printer for Ontario.

Ottawa Citizen. (2007). "Arar on Time's '100 Most Influential' List, But He's Still Not Welcome in U.S." *Ottawa Citizen*, May 4. Available at http://www.canada.com/nationalpost/news/story.html?id=54c8383c-6315-43c4-ac9c-ddbf2fff7167&k=97087; accessed May 18, 2011.

Plotz, David. (2001). "Conrad Black." *Slate* August 31. Available at http://www.slate.com/id/114605.

Rodgers, R.S. (1962). *Sex and Law in Canada: Text, Cases and Comment.* Ottawa: Policy Press.

Schwendinger, Herman, and Julia Schwendinger. (1970). "Defenders of Order or Guardians of Human Rights." *Issues in Criminology* 5: 123–57.

Senate Committee on Legal and Constitutional Affairs. (2006). "Evidence." December 4.

Shuqin, Yang. (2010). "The Polluting Behaviour of the Multinational Corporations in China." In Rob White (ed.), *Global Environmental Harm: Criminological Perspectives* (pp. 150–58). Cullompton, Devon: Willan Publishing.

Smandych, Russell, and Rodney Kueneman. (2010). "The Canadian-Alberta Tar Sands: A Case Study of State-Corporate Environmental Crime." In Rob White (ed.), *Global Environmental Harm: Criminological Perspectives* (pp. 87–109). Cullompton, Devon: Willan Publishing.

South, Nigel. (2010). "The Ecocidal Tendencies of Late Modernity." In Rob White (ed.), *Global Environmental Harm: Criminological Perspectives* (pp. 228–47). Cullompton, Devon: Willan Publishing.

Staples, David. (2002). "Fearless, Painless, Senseless: The Sand Brothers." *Edmonton Journal*, March 31: D1.

Statistics Canada. (2010). "Police Personnel and Expenditures 2010." Ottawa: Statistics Canada. Available at http://www.statcan.gc.ca/pub/85-225-x/2010000/part-partie1-eng.htm.

Sutherland, Edwin. (1940). "White-Collar Criminality." *American Sociological Review* 5: 1–12.

Sutherland, Edwin, and Donald Cressey. (1960). *Principles of Criminology* (6th ed.). Philadelphia: J. B. Lippincott.

Turk, Austin. (2004). "Sociology of Terrorism." *Annual Review of Sociology* 30: 271–86.

White, Rob. (2007). "Green Criminology and the Pursuit of Social and Ecological Justice." In Piers Beirne and Nigel South (eds.), *Issues in Green Criminology: Confronting Harms Against Environments, Humanity and Other Animals* (pp. 32–54). Portland: Willan Publishing.

*Winnipeg Free Press*. (1993). "Law, Religion Clash over Child Marriage." September 24.

Woolford, Andrew. (2010). "Criminological Nightmares: A Canadian Criminology of Genocide." In Aaron Doyle and Dawn Moore (eds.), *Critical Criminology in Canada: New Voices, New Directions* (pp. 136–61). Vancouver: UBC Press.

# 2

# The Origins and Role of Law in Society

**Rodney Kueneman**

**UNIVERSITY OF MANITOBA**

People in all human societies have disputes, and every human group has developed mechanisms for restoring social order. Today, the law plays a prominent role in the restoration process; however, not all communities have relied on formally enacted laws enforced by the power of a state. In small-scale societies of the past, victims or their relatives were responsible for settling disputes, and the major goal of dispute settlement processes was to restore harmonious relationships between the conflicting parties. In this chapter, you will learn how our system of formal laws has developed.

## Learning Objectives

After reading this chapter, you should be able to

- Trace the changes from community-based dispute resolution processes in small-scale societies to state-controlled processes in more complex societies.

- Explain why knowledge of social context is important in understanding the existence and operation of different dispute settlement systems.

- Understand the emergence and consolidation of social and economic power in human societies and how the consolidation has made it difficult to control the actions of those who have power.

- Explain why the rule of law has become a primary force in modern societies and understand the limitations of law as a means of controlling behaviour.

- Understand the importance of restorative dispute settlement processes in small-scale societies and explain why they are once again becoming popular.

Throughout most of human existence we lived in small hunting and gathering communities. Cooperation, mutual aid, and kinship within these communities were the essential means of preserving harmony and restoring order. The absence of a centralized power structure meant that these communities had to rely on different mechanisms to keep the peace. One of the tasks of this chapter is to show how different dispute settlement mechanisms can be understood only within their social context. As patterns of societal organization changed, different forms of dispute settlement emerged. The general role of dispute settlement processes in all societies is the restoration of order; however, the nature of these different social orders, and the groups who have received the most advantage within them, have changed significantly. As we shall see, dispute settlement processes are intimately involved in the structuring of social relationships.

This textbook is about crime. It is important to realize that crime does not exist in all societies. In a technical sense, a crime is a violation of a law, and not all societies have had formulated laws. While each society has had to develop a moral order complete with stated expectations for acceptable behaviour, not all societies have developed laws to restrain their members. The formulation of law requires the existence of a central body, such as a **state**, that develops law and enforces compliance with it. This is not only a matter of semantics. For much of human history, social order was maintained by other means. It is equally important to note that criminal law, as we know it, has not been part of the social fabric for most of human history. Harms between individuals were resolved by various forms of redress in societies without a state. Even in societies with a state apparatus, many disputes are regulated by civil law. Under civil law, the state adjudicates between the parties to the dispute in an effort to repair the damage. Criminal law comes into existence at the point when the state declares itself to be the injured party for certain types of infractions. In its narrowest sense, criminology is concerned with this limited subset of laws and social infractions. But in order to understand the broad question of social order, it is important to see criminal law within an historical and social context that considers the full spectrum of dispute settlement practices.

Finally, it is important to reflect on the human condition. In place of the instincts that order so much of the lives of other animals, human beings fashion their collective stability by way of culture. While humans share common emotional, intellectual, and motivational attributes, they have produced an amazing variety of solutions to the problems they have faced. Equipped with a powerful imagination, members of our species have introduced both inspiring and terrifying innovations to their communities. This human imagination has contributed to the development of human culture. But it is also a principal source of instability that has threatened to erode, weaken, and destroy the social fabric it has created. Humans have the ability to create disputes and to upset social arrangements. Law and other forms of dispute settlement are at the heart of our efforts to limit and to recover from the harm that is inflicted. Although there are many differences between societies, each social order must be recognized as a response to the need to construct a moral, or at least a legal, order.

**state**
As defined by Max Weber (1864–1920), the state is an institution that claims the exclusive right to the legitimate exercise of force in a given territory through the use of police to enforce laws or the army to maintain civil stability. While there have been stateless societies, most complex societies have state systems of formal government and administrative bureaucracies.

# Patterns of Human Social Organization

Cultures have been classified in many different ways. Lenski (1966) emphasized the **mode of production** used by societies. He developed the following classification: hunting and gathering, pastoral, horticultural, agricultural, and industrial societies.

It will not be possible here to provide a detailed description and analysis of the vast array of human cultures. Instead, our inquiry will examine two patterns of social organization: hunting and gathering societies and industrial societies.

**mode of production**
The dominant form of social and technical organization of economic production in a society. Historically, a variety of modes of production can be distinguished based on both technology and the structure of social relationships.

The rest of this chapter will outline the basic characteristics of the dominant social forms and will show how the dispute settlement processes used in these different settings were a part of the social fabric. It will become clear that any discussion of custom, law, and dispute settlements must be placed within its social context in order to understand how each human society settles the troubles that spring up within it.

## Small-Scale Society

In this section, the general characteristics of small-scale societies will be described as a prelude to a discussion of their typical practices for settling disputes. Although such attributes are not present in all small-scale societies, they do appear in virtually all hunting and gathering societies and hence are useful as "ideal types" for the purposes of analysis.

Without underestimating the often harsh realities of the small-scale society, there is no question that such communities were characterized by a strong **collective solidarity**. Whether living in the High Arctic, on the plains, or in the tropical rainforests, hunters and gatherers were well aware that they were part of a natural ecosystem that had forces they could not control. They understood their individual vulnerability and realized that their collective life was an exercise in mutual survival. The cooperative, mutual-aid character of these societies was not accidental. The near certainty of death for those who lacked the assistance of the group strengthened the group's solidarity.

## The Need for Self-Restraint

Hunting and gathering groups were small communities of approximately 50 members who were closely related kin. In these small, face-to-face communities, social networks were dense and characterized by a high degree of social visibility. The mutual-aid character of such social relationships meant there was an expectation that the relationship would continue throughout their lifetime. The absence of a complex division of labour made it necessary for each individual in the group to fulfill a number of roles. This **diffuseness of roles** placed a premium on cooperation because each member was intimately involved with others. Continuous interaction with other group members provided each person with feedback concerning the acceptability of certain types of behaviour. It also created a climate for the development of common norms and the cultivation of a consensus.

In such close and intimate quarters, members were reluctant to offend one another because of their mutual interdependence. Each member learned to cultivate personal restraint and impulse control in order to prevent the breakdown of a working order. Colson (1974) shows how these social circumstances fostered the development of forbearance, the avoidance of disputes, the sharing of resources, and the tolerance of human foibles. She relates how the Tonga of Zambia attempted to sidestep controversial issues and how they were reluctant to allow others to drag them into disputes. Their social structure, as well as their fear of attack by sorcerers, worked against the outbreak of violence or other forms of retaliation and contributed to the development of self-restraint.

**ideal type**
An ideal type is a theoretical construct which is abstracted from experience and brings together observed characteristics of real social relationships. Observed empirical instances are combined to create a social form that has a conceptual coherence which is never entirely observed in any actual community but can be used as a standard against which to compare any real community.

**collective solidarity**
A state of social bonding or interdependency that rests on similarity of beliefs and values, shared activities, and ties of kinship and cooperation among members of a community.

**diffuseness of roles**
A characteristic of relatively simple societies in which people encounter one another in a variety of overlapping roles—there is little occupational specialization and no clear separation of private and public spheres of life. People are continuously reminded of their extensive bonds with others.

Colson notes that these people did not lack "occasion for quarrels and hostility but they learn that they must control their hostility, their greed, and their envy if they are to survive" (1974, 61). Such communities could effectively punish any individual who consistently went his or her own way. The self-restraint that members exercised stemmed not only from the close, intimate, and friendly ties that are a product of common life, but also out of the fear of reprisal and the desire to keep hostilities from surfacing and disturbing the business of living. Rupert Ross (1989), a Crown attorney in northern Ontario, relates how the principle of emotional restraint still operates in some remote Ojibway communities (see Box 2.1). The practice of "burying" old disputes and declining to revisit the emotions that they evoke was an exercise in individual restraint that kept these disruptions of the past from damaging current social relations.

## Mutual Benefit

Living in a subsistence economy where little or no surplus could be generated made it necessary for the group to share the fruits of a day's hunting or foraging. Typically, everyone received an equal and adequate share, regardless of the extent and nature of each one's contribution. In such a distribution system, there may have been collective scarcity if food was not found, but there was never poverty in the sense that some ate while others went hungry. Though a member was not expected to love everyone else, each one was expected to care for all members of the community. This ensured they, too, would be taken

# FOCUS BOX 2.1

## THE PRINCIPLE OF EMOTIONAL RESTRAINT IN THE OJIBWAY COMMUNITY

Grief, anger, and sorrow [should] be quickly buried. They should not be expressed, for that only serves to burden the person who hears. They should not be explored or indulged privately, for doing so results in a lessened capacity to contribute the fullest energy, attention and skills which the hunter-gatherer society needed to maintain survival. Expressions of anger or criticism would serve only to create friction, a dangerous luxury to a people who required the maximum cooperation of all. Even the *thinking* of critical thoughts about others was to be avoided. Quite simply, the past was the past, and its negative parts were to be buried and forgotten as quickly as possible. . . .

While such overt observances of these rules are declining, it remains a central tenet of life in many communities that it is wrong to speak of your hurts and angers and criticisms, wrong to indulge your private emotions. Instead, you bury and you carry on, resisting the backwards glance. I recall one teenage rape victim who refused to testify when her assailant finally came to trial more than a year after the event; her reason was simply that he should have paid his penalty by now and be getting on with his life. For her, it was simply too late to put him through it. The past was the past.

Asking a Native accused to explain what it was that aggravated him to such a degree that he attacked his victim is the subject of a special constraint, already referred to, which forbids the criticism of others.

Source: Rupert Ross. (1989). "Leaving Our White Eyes Behind: The Sentencing of Native Accused." 3 *Canadian Native Law Reporter* 1 at 4.

care of in the non-productive times of their life such as childhood, old age, and sickness. This mutual benefit model helped to keep greed and the desire for personal advantage in check.

## A Community of Belief

The structure of small-scale societies fostered both moderation and compassion, which acted as powerful curbs to selfishness. A shared system of customs and patterns of behaviour in domestic, economic, and political life grew out of the personal and interpersonal accommodations that were required of such intimate social actors. There is no question that this type of society was coercive; there was virtually no freedom of belief. One's location in the kinship system established basic duties, obligations, rights, and privileges. Failure to meet obligations jeopardized one's relationship with many members of this primary group and, especially, the face-to-face interaction with one's immediate kin. The notion of collective responsibility, which was prevalent in such communities, made kin groups accountable for the behaviour of their members. The positive dimension of community membership was that throughout the life cycle, the customary ways provided meaning for members. Their common purpose helped foster commitment to community beliefs and practices.

## The Absence of Surplus, Stratification, and the State

Hunters and gatherers lived cooperatively. The inability to produce or to keep large amounts of food on hand meant food gathering was a regular activity that included all able-bodied members. The division and distribution of food to all community members underscored the understanding that everyone had a right to this collective activity; food was a group possession. The need to move regularly limited the amount of personal belongings a person could accumulate, and since each member had access to the same raw materials, there was little difference in the individuals' possessions. The possibility of generating any significant **surplus** under these conditions was limited. Small-scale society, then, acted as a brake on the human tendency to secure an advantageous individual position. By identifying one's "self" with the interests of the entire group, the individual self so familiar to our society was superseded by a social or collective self-concept.

The absence of surplus suppressed the emergence of economic stratification and any form of state-like structure or political institution. Small-scale societies had no distinct source of social power or authority independent of the collective will. The only form of power available to special individuals in such societies was influence. Influence was based on status derived from hunting skill, sex, wisdom, or generosity, and not on differential access to, or accumulation of, material resources. Social status was a group property, not a personal attribute. The members of the group could give it and take it away. Hoebel (1973, 82) comments on the position of the Inuit headman:

> The headman possesses no fixed authority; neither does he enter into formal office. He is not elected, nor is he chosen by any formal process. When other men accept his judgement and opinions, he is headman. When they ignore him, he is not.

**surplus**

The excess of production over the human and material resources used up in the process of production. In simple societies, there was often little if any surplus since the production from hunting and gathering was entirely used up in subsistence. With the development of animal herding and settled agriculture, production exceeded immediate subsistence needs, and social inequality and class division became possible when particular individuals or groups were able to take control of this surplus.

Thus, if an esteemed individual became arrogant or tried to force others to comply in ways that were deemed inappropriate, the special status was removable. All aspects of group life worked in a systematic fashion to control and limit the will of the individual in the best interests of the group.

## Dispute Settlement in Small-Scale Society

The major goal of dispute settlement in small-scale societies was to restore harmonious relations between parties involved in a conflict. It was essential that problems be settled as quickly as possible in mutually agreeable ways so as not to impede group life. The absence of an independent political institution meant that disputants typically had to resolve their differences without the assistance of an adjudicator (Gulliver, 1979). Community pressure was applied to the parties in a dispute to meet and to bring an end to the discord. Each party had to give and to receive information from the other in order to learn of the other party's needs and expectations. In a series of such educational exchanges, an attempt was made to move toward a mutually agreeable outcome and the restoration of harmonious interaction.

This type of approach to discord led to a general airing of all the issues that created friction between the parties. This ensured that an effort was made to keep the conflict from escalating and to lead the discordant parties to a mutually satisfying conclusion to their problem. Potential troublemakers had to recognize that at some point they would have to confront those whom they had directly harmed, rather than being processed by some impersonal system of justice acting on behalf of a victim who was a stranger. Inside this general framework, there was some variation in the types of disputes and the form of the settlement practices.

## Types of Disputes and Their Settlement

Newman (1983) provides rich detail concerning the types of disputes that arose in hunting and gathering societies. Many disputes among hunting and gathering peoples concerned women. Because women were valuable producers, adultery, failure to honour marriage agreements, and the taking of a woman by an enemy caused serious disruptions. While women were not necessarily considered the property of their fathers or husbands, there was an interest in controlling them as valuable resources to the kin system. Other causes of conflict involved such acts as improper food distribution, asymmetrical gift exchange, laziness, stinginess, theft, and murder. Theft was an infrequent offence among nomadic foragers because of the relative absence of property. Murders were relatively infrequent and almost always resulted from disputes concerning women. Because of the emergence of the notion of property among sedentary food collectors, however, there was a greater incidence of theft and disputes over the use of land in those societies.

The primary method of redress in small-scale society itself was self- or kin-based redress. Other methods, used less frequently, were advisor or mediator systems.

**Self- or Kin-Based Redress** The range of responses available in self- or kin-based redress included public criticism, shaming rituals, temporary ostracism, expulsion from the group, blood feuds, and reprisal killings. Some sedentary food gatherers also developed a scale of fines for certain types of infractions. Less harsh methods were often employed initially, and only when they failed were more punitive responses called forth. In some instances, a disputant may simply have chosen to leave the group and join another on a temporary or permanent basis.

The injured party had to initiate the dispute process because there was no centralized authority. This does not mean that the victim was free to do to an offender whatever the victim chose. The society had customary expectations about the appropriateness of different reprisals. Too harsh a response could evoke group disapproval and sanctions. If the reprisal was considered to be more serious than the original offence, the initial offence would be expunged and the original offender would become the injured party. An individual could lose the support of his or her family by retaliating too vigorously. It is important to emphasize here that self-redress is a regulated social process. The image of small-scale societies as violent and constantly feuding is inaccurate. While it is true that disputes did escalate into blood feuds and cycles of revenge killings, even these proceeded in an orderly fashion. Furthermore, small-scale society had a body of custom that was coupled with the fear of reprisal; this acted as a brake on such escalation by defining an appropriate level of redress for various offences.

Clearly defined notions of right and wrong behaviour existed in spite of the absence of third-party authority figures. Formalized civil or criminal law was not necessary for these small, kin-based communities to restore order. If an individual violated a custom, he or she suffered the consequences. His or her kin did not provide protection from legitimate retaliation. If the punishment was too harsh or unfairly exacted, a retaliation was initiated and conflict continued until both sides were satisfied with the resolution of the situation. An exchange of gifts often signalled the end to hostilities.

**Advisor Systems** The advisor system was really only an extension of the self-redress method of dispute settlement because it was once again ultimately the victim or kin who would enforce any retaliation. Disputants approached advisors, who tended to be men who were distinguished warriors, hunters, or speakers. They were mature, although not always the oldest men of the community, and they were regarded as public repositories of wisdom about customs and rituals.

The dispute settlement process was activated when one or both parties sought out one of these high-status figures. They were not required to turn to this third party, but it was expected that they would do so. Each party presented its case and, after considering the facts, the advisor recommended what should be done. He interpreted the case with respect to custom and it was his role to ensure that the social group's conception of appropriate behaviour was protected. He was a moral authority, but he could not enforce compliance. He could, however, attempt to influence disputants with shaming rituals and his ability to make compelling arguments. Among some groups, the advisor could take a more active role by indicating which side his own kin group would back in the event of a reprisal. Here, too, the advisor could not direct his kin group, but only report its position with reference to the dispute. The advisor was, essentially, a communication link between parties and attempted to coordinate a settlement without violence. An advisor gained status by being able to settle disputes without the outbreak of revenge activity. A demonstrated ability to resolve disputes peacefully strengthened his moral authority. If the advisor overstepped his bounds and tried to make his authority too exacting, the community would stop using him in his capacity of advisor. Thus the advisor system was still firmly controlled by the community.

Most hunting and gathering societies relied on self-redress; a smaller proportion developed an advisor system. In general, the dispute settlement processes used by small-scale societies were designed to restore social integration and harmony. These societies tried to contain problems involving members of the community and sought to resolve them through compromise and reconciliation. Each member was tied to other members for a variety of social purposes. The discord created by disputants interfered with these other positive and necessary ties. These people simply could not afford to have long-standing anger and discord. As Ross (1989) points out, traditional Inuit and Ojibway dispute settlement mechanisms provide a poignant contrast to the assumptions of the Canadian criminal justice system (see Box 2.2).

On the whole, small-scale society had considerable success in avoiding the outbreak of serious trouble. Each member of the community was able to exercise some measure of control over others, so power remained diffuse. As a community, members were able to deal with discord in such a way that victim and offender could once again enter into harmonious interaction after a mutually agreeable settlement of a dispute had been made.

# The Transformation from Small-Scale Society to the State

Within the last 6000 to 8000 years, most hunting and gathering societies have been transformed into pastoral, horticultural, agricultural, and industrial societies—as a result either of their own development or the invasion of an outside culture. The transformation of some small-scale societies to state societies will be outlined in this section, along with a discussion of the way in which this transformation affects the dispute settlement process.

## The Slow Emergence of Social Power

Hunting and gathering communities were long able to resist any aspirations to autonomy and power by their members. While positions of influence did exist for those who made special contributions to the group, this status was not consolidated by greater access to material resources. Influential members still had to be responsive to the opinions, expectations, and judgments of the rest of their community in order to retain their special status.

At some point, the mutuality of **tribalism** was ruptured. The emergence of the concept of private property slowly and progressively created social power for families and individuals. Privately owned land and livestock

**tribalism**
Where social bonds are based primarily on people's real or assumed common descent from an ancestor or group of ancestors, and this shared identification distinguishes the group from outsiders. In such societies, all social relationships tend to be direct and quasi-familial.

# FOCUS BOX 2.2

## TRADITIONAL INUIT AND OJIBWAY DISPUTE SETTLEMENT

The practice in one Inuit village was to call the entire village together and to put the actual event forward as a *hypothetical* event which might happen some time in the future. All people—including the miscreant and his victim—were required to put forward their views as to how things might be handled peacefully and properly were the situation ever to arise. There was no blaming, no pointing of fingers, and no requirement of explanation; nor was there ever any discussion, much less imposition, of either punitive or restitutionary response. At an Ojibway Reserve in my district similar dynamics governed. While the miscreant and his victim were summoned before an Elders Panel, there was never any discussion of what had happened and why, of how each party felt about the other or of what might be done by way of compensation. Nor was there any imposition of punishment. Each party was instead provided with a counselling Elder who worked privately to "cleanse his spirit." When both counselling Elders so signified by touching the peace pipe, it would be lit and passed to all. It was a signal that both had been "restored to themselves and to the community." If they privately arranged recompense of some sort, that was their affair. As far as the community was concerned, the matter was over. While I have not learned what the private counselling did consist of, I have been told that it did not involve retrieval and re-examination of the past in either its factual or emotional facets. It concentrated upon the future, and its spiritual component was central.

As a footnote, such ethics also cast the behavior of native victims in a very different light. Refusal or reluctance to testify or, when testifying, to give anything but the barest and most emotionless recital of events, may of course have been prompted by fear of the accused, by fear of the court, by love for and forgiveness of the accused or by any other such "sensible" reason (including the possibility, of extreme rarity in my experience, that they are uncomfortable because they are lying). Another reason, culturally foreign to us, could be that giving testimony face to face with the accused is simply considered wrong. It was not part of the traditional processes described above, where in fact every effort seems to have been made to *avoid* such direct confrontation. I recall one Indian woman who repeated her entire story of abuse to me in vivid detail before going into court and then asked me to do whatever I could to have the court send her very dangerous assailant to jail for as long as possible. Ten minutes later she took the witness stand and absolutely refused to say anything of an accusatory nature. When such witnesses regularly ask why they have to repeat their stories in court when they have already told "us" (meaning the police and the Crown), I have come to suspect that it is more than fear or embarrassment at work. I suspect instead that it is perceived as ethically wrong to say hostile, critical, implicitly angry things about someone *in their presence*, precisely what our adversarial trial rules have required. . . . In fact, we have taken this legal challenge into our daily lives, exhorting each person to open up with the other, to be honest and up front, to get things off our chests, etc., all of which are, to traditional native eyes, offensive in the extreme. When they refuse to follow the exhortations of our rules, we judge them as deficient in rule-obedience or, worse still, rule-less. In our ignorance we have failed to admit the possibility that there might be rules other than ours to which they regularly display allegiance, an allegiance all the more striking because it is exercised in defiance of our insistent pressures to the contrary.

Source: Rupert Ross. (1989). "Leaving Our White Eyes Behind: The Sentencing of Native Accused." 3 *Canadian Native Law Reporter* 1 at 5–6.

meant the more fortunate members of the community were able to generate a surplus (Newman, 1983). This surplus enabled them to rely less on the community for their survival. Under such circumstances, some of the ancient patriarchs began to define women as property, to secure not only control of their labour, but also their reproductive capacities "in order to ensure that there would be determinate heirs to function as the designatable future owners of individually held accumulations of private property" (Clark and Lewis, 1977, 113).

## The Evolution of Inequality

The power constellation of small-scale society was "horizontal" or "flat" and under the control of the community as a whole. It was the community that moved against the interests of individuals or factions when their actions were viewed as a serious threat to the group. New forms of power necessitated important changes. The emergence of surplus, stratification, and the basis for factional power gave rise to the "pyramidal" power constellation of modern societies and the development of the state in rudimentary form. The changing role of mediators, elders' councils, restricted councils, and then chieftainships, shows the slow yet progressive development and consolidation of a social form of power independent of the community as a whole.

In small-scale societies, each individual was expected to discharge his or her obligations directly to other community members. Slowly, the social elites were able to redirect this exchange to enhance their position in the changing social order. The goods that had been readily available to all members in a simple economy of sharing became distributed in patterns that reflected the stratified nature of pastoral, horticultural, agricultural, and industrial orders. These new modes of production made it increasingly possible for powerful groups and individuals to extract surplus value from those who turned to them in order to make a living. The ability to have other people help generate their personal wealth greatly accelerated the formation of structured inequality. Less powerful segments in society found it increasingly difficult to resist those social forces that were compromising their interests.

Ultimately, the state emerged in agricultural society, and it championed and represented the interests of the powerful. The growing size and complexity of social systems gave rise to the need for large bureaucracies and a class of officials whose personal interests would become fused with those of the state. Human history was firmly established on a course that would generate hitherto unseen levels of surplus, poverty, and social inequality. The interests of whole groups of individuals were devalued and subordinated to the interests of powerful factions and the state. The equality of condition in small-scale societies had been replaced by a class system rife with disparities.

The dispute settlement practices that emerged with these different social forms and the types of offences committed in such societies reflected the basic changes in social structure that have been outlined in this section. Attention will now be focused on the dispute process and the changes that took place that created law as it exists today.

# Transformation in the Forms of Dispute Settlement

As societies changed so did the types of disputes that arose in them. For example, with the emergence of private property, theft became possible. The concepts of rent and the violation of contracts became grounds for disagreement. The emergence of contracts and wills contributed to the need for more codified conventions and a body of civil law. Finally, the emergence of surplus meant disputes could be settled by the payment of various types of fines to compensate the party who had been wronged. For example, under Anglo-Saxon law, if a woman was raped a compensatory fee was paid to either her husband or her father, depending on who exercised the rights of ownership over her at the time of the offence. The fee was not paid directly to the woman herself because she was not considered to be the person who had been wronged by the act (Clark and Lewis, 1977).

Increased productive capacity resulted in disputes concerning property, accompanied by increasingly complex legal codifications to deal with them. The creation of chiefdoms, and eventually states, was accompanied by the emergence of offences such as treason, slander, and libel, and, in general, the possibility for criminal law as defined as offences against the Crown. Failure to pay taxes or to work on public projects became offences and sources of litigation. In this section, some of the basic features of elders' councils, chieftainships, and paramount chieftainships will be examined. These are the dominant structural elements in dispute settlement that distinguish societies lying between small-scale societies and state systems.

## Elders' Councils

Elders' councils performed legal, political, economic, and administrative functions. Disputants were required to submit their dispute to these councils, whose verdicts were binding. There were often several levels of councils, including local and regional councils with different powers; for example, one level would hear appeals. The membership in these councils was representative of the influential segments of the society and may have included all married males or the oldest male in each family. Each family was represented, therefore membership was basically democratic. Participation was not contingent upon wealth, although there was a clear sex bias. Eventually, most men in the community would have occasion to sit on the elders' councils.

Council procedures were marked by a high degree of formality. This is uncharacteristic of the forms of dispute settlement discussed so far. Formal language, recourse to precedents, and rules of conduct all marked the seriousness of the occasion. The conclusions of these councils carried considerable weight because they were made by a representative group of elders who had the duty of determining a dispute in the best interests of the community. Community pressure dictated the obligation to accept the judgment of the council. If an individual was recalcitrant, the council could enlist local men to threaten the offender and deprive him or her of property, or direct the kinsmen of the victim to retaliate. This was the only type of self-redress that was available in these systems.

## Chieftainships

A chief was the highest political authority in the community and was recognized as having the ultimate power in settling disputes. The chief's decisions were binding, although others may have been required to enforce them. Chieftainships tended to be based on heredity or supernatural knowledge, and were primarily made up of rich men from influential families. They also were expected to display oratorical skills, wisdom, and knowledge of customary ways. Chiefs usually served on a permanent basis and held office through their productive years, either voluntarily relinquishing it when they judged themselves incapable of continuing or being overthrown by rebellions when they fell from popularity. Chiefs often had the right to select their successor, although this was contingent upon community approval.

Chieftainships made possible a formalization and institutionalization of the legal system. The chief was able to intervene in a dispute without being requested to do so and heard appeals if more informal attempts to settle a dispute failed. Chiefs had the power to order executions, beatings, public reprimands, and economic sanctions such as fines and destruction or confiscation of property. No form of self-redress was allowed unless the approval of the chief had been secured. The chief had considerable power, although he often consulted community members prior to making a decision.

## Paramount Chieftainships

The **paramount chieftainship** took a significant step away from the participatory and democratic features of other models. Paramount chieftainships were much like kingdoms. They were based on hereditary aristocracies and drew together a large number of communities or villages that retained some level of local autonomy. Paramount chieftainships were complex, hierarchical structures. The chief was surrounded with retainers and nobles who performed judicial and administrative tasks. Many such chieftainships had a "civil service" recruited from the ranks of royalty to handle daily affairs. This apparatus allowed a more formal and structured legal system to develop. In this way, the paramount chief was able to extend control over a large geographical region and a sizeable population.

The paramount chief held court in a capital city and district or circuit courts settled most disputes. The more serious cases came under the jurisdiction of the paramount chief who might consult with an advisory council made up of royalty, but who had the final authority to make binding decisions from a full range of options. From the structure of paramount chieftainship, it was a small step to the creation of the state.

**paramount chieftainship**

A political system similar to a kingdom that brings together a number of partly autonomous villages or communities under the hierarchical rule of a grand chief.

The transformation of the hunting and gathering social form and the attendant dispute-settling processes are dramatic when considered in this comparative framework. But the changes occurred so gradually that the historical actors barely noticed them. Once the checks on the accumulation of wealth and power that bound small-scale society together were undercut, there seemed to be a likely chain of events that led to the emergence of a state system. Some of the reasons for this steady and cumulative development have been discussed in general terms. In the next section of this chapter, the modern state system will be examined in greater detail.

## Modern State Systems

The emergence of the state in the past 3000 or 4000 years has created a rich and complex social tapestry. We will outline the essential changes in social-power constellations that transformed land-based **feudalism** into the modern capitalist state which would ultimately result in the emergence of modern commercial, industrial society. The case of England provides the basis for the analysis of the emergence of law in Western democratic states. This focus is clearly appropriate when seeking to understand the legal system in Canada and the United States of America. The analysis of law in state systems in other historical circumstances is beyond the scope of this chapter.

### From Tribalism to Feudalism

The primary basis for social order prior to feudalism was tribal kinship. In this social order military leaders were emerging in a class system where conquered individuals were tied to them with reciprocal obligations (Jeffery, 1969; Kennedy, 1976). In essence, feudalism was a social system based on the tenure of land, which was the dominant form of capital in an agrarian mode of production. The use of land was granted to the vassal in return for military service, compulsory labour, tribute or, in later years, for rent. This relationship, while based on subjection, had a quasi-familial tone and the lord had a duty to protect and feed his serfs in hard times. The lord controlled the use of the land and a serf could lose the right to use it only for neglect of the land or failure to meet obligations.

No central power existed in the early period of feudalism. In tribal times, blood feuds were the primary dispute settlement mechanism. As feudalism developed and the notion of collective responsibility was replaced with that of individual responsibility, money settlements and fines were used to settle serious disputes. Compliance with these was through local custom since no centralized source of power had emerged to enforce them. Once Anglo-Saxon lords were able to consolidate some power in England, they began to develop a body of law to deal with disputes. Under this system, trial by ordeal (using such methods as walking on hot coals or reaching into boiling water to pick up a pebble) was the means to establish guilt or innocence for those disputants who could not find some other way to settle a dispute. The pattern is clear; kin-based dispute settlement practices were being continuously undermined and replaced by feudal lords and their laws.

**feudalism**

A system of economic and social organization found historically in several areas of the world. In western Europe, feudalism was at its height between about 1000 and 1500. The economic foundation of the system was the feudal manor that included a central farm owned by a landlord and small land holdings for a class of bonded farm labourers (serfs). The serfs were required to work the central manorial farm and to provide the lord with produce and money payments in return for their right to use the land. The system gradually declined as cities and towns grew and power became centralized in nation-states under monarchies.

## The Emergence of the Centralized State

With the success of the Norman Invasion in 1066, William the Conqueror declared himself the "supreme landlord" of all England, so that all individuals who held land held his land. Over the succeeding centuries, the English kings slowly expanded and consolidated their power over the feudal landscape. As a result, compensation was paid to kings, lords, and bishops, rather than to kinship groups. The Norman kings saw themselves as the injured party when a crime was committed because the harm was against their peace. Since some crimes were now against the Crown, criminal law became a reality. The Crown replaced the victim as the injured party, and compensation to the victim's family was replaced by punitive fines that were payable to the Crown.

A central authority had emerged in England to replace the authority of feudal lords and the king's system of royal courts and royal writs created a **common law** which became available to all individuals who sought the jurisdiction of the Crown rather than that of their families or local lord. As Jeffery (1969) has stated, "The family was no longer involved in law and justice. The State was the offended unit, and the State was the proper prosecutor in every case of crime." The law and the courts played a pivotal role in this undertaking to consolidate centralized political and economic power. The growth of trade and the rise of the merchant class also contributed to the decline of the feudal system and to the rise of towns and cities at the expense of the rural manors. Cities began to arise during the reign of King John (1199–1216) and, although they were situated on land controlled by feudal lords, they fell under the jurisdiction of the Crown. A new system of social relationships developed that was based on commerce instead of on feudal obligations.

## The Coalition of Merchants and Monarchs

William the Conqueror created a state apparatus when he made all nobles take an oath to establish him as their feudal overlord. With this came the power to create laws to govern the kingdom, royal officials to protect the king's interests, and royal courts to dispense the king's justice. This state apparatus was superimposed on feudalism. While feudalism was dominant, the king used the state apparatus to defend the common interests of feudal lords. However, the breakdown of feudal obligations and the feudal tax system also meant a loss of revenue for the Crown, which needed to find new ways to finance war and the state. This was accomplished by going outside the feudal system to negotiate loans with merchants, using land as collateral. The king wanted his power consolidated and needed political support and financial assistance, while the merchants wanted a unified and safe trading area (Chambliss, 1969; Hall, 1969a). The state was to become the vehicle that the Crown and its merchant allies would use to overcome resistance to the development of the new social order. In return for their support, Henry VIII conceded that Parliament would have control over tax revenues and the legislative function. Thus the state, which was staffed by the **bourgeois class**, would become the mechanism for change by statute. Laws would be passed by Parliament.

The merchants benefited from this new arrangement because they were able to gain greater access to land. The feudal lords' losses in war brought the

"Historical Origins of Government's Monopoly on Criminal Justice" National Center for Policy Analysis (USA)
www.ncpa.org/studies/s181/s181c.html

**common law**

The common law tradition found in English Canada derives from feudal England, where it had become the practice for the king to resolve disputes in accordance with local custom. Customs that were recognized throughout the country were called common custom, and decisions made by the king and by subsequent courts set up to settle disputes became known as common law.

**bourgeois class**

The term *bourgeois class*, or *bourgeoisie*, was used by Marx to refer to the capitalist or ruling class in modern societies.

merchants the land that the lords had put up as collateral for loans. When Henry VIII expropriated church land, more than one-sixth of the land in England was removed from its connection to feudalism. Henry sold this land to friends and allies, for whom he created peerages with seats in the House of Lords. This action more than doubled his revenue, placed a large block of land outside feudal control, and made it available for the money market. As the feudal system declined, many lords were tied into feudal land arrangements of rent, which were driving them into financial ruin. Eventually, their lands also were freed of feudal ties and became part of the commodity market to be bought and sold as private property in the interest of profit. In 1540, Henry VIII also gave his support to the Statute of Wills, which made most land in England transmittable by will. The role of the Crown had changed from that of shared owner of land under feudalism to that of land regulator via the state, which was becoming a separate and sovereign entity.

The labour of serfs, who had been tied to the land under feudalism, was freed from the land, as were the lords. In addition, much of the land that had been controlled by the church was also made available as commons for serfs to graze their animals. However, the new owners enclosed a great deal of this land for wool production and thoroughly disrupted the lives of the commoners. The right of commoners to hunt, fish, and gather wood on their lord's manor was extinguished under the new property relations. The Black Act of 1723 increased the number of offences for which the courts could impose the death penalty. These harsh measures were seen as necessary to compel the common people to abandon these feudal practices (Thompson, 1976). The new land regulations displaced the rural workforce, which then became the new urban workforce in the factories made possible by technological innovation.

These fundamental changes contributed to the increased importance of commerce and money. The close and personal ties of fealty and its reciprocal duties and obligations were being eclipsed by the abstract, anonymous trans-actions of money in commercial enterprise. The growth of banking institutions, the use of paper currency, and other instruments of credit created new occasions for theft by trusted third parties. The famous Carrier's Case of 1473 made it clear that the law of theft would need to be refined in order to prevent intermediaries from keeping goods put in their possession for transport (Hall, 1952). International trade, which was spurred by Britain's colonial empire, also necessitated an expansion and refinement of the concept of theft. Hall (1969b) recounts how the law governing embezzlement was enacted to make theft of paper money and commercial bonds a crime. If a business was run by members of a household, behaviour was regulated by custom and by family ties. However, when businesses grew they needed to hire employees from the larger communities who had no other ties to the owners. Transactions between anonymous parties would henceforth be regulated by law because of the absence of cus-tomary ties between them.

Law and lawyers would figure prominently in the regulation of the new social relationships. To chart the consolidation of state power within the con-text of law, it is essential to study the activities of various interest groups with respect to commerce and contract law. The consolidation of a new form of social life based on contract was achieved within the context of commerce and the rise of the bourgeois class.

## Commerce, Contracts, and the Primary Role of Law

The growth of commerce, spurred by the Industrial Revolution and the expansion of trade, required greater uniformity and enforceability of trading arrangements. Towns, cities, and even nation-states realized that a system of law, and a court system to apply it, would be essential if trade was to stabilize and grow. The volume of trade, its growing impersonality, the practice of joint ventures, and the long distances involved in international trade created the need for a mechanism to secure the interests of traders. Legal contracts, which had existed since Roman times, became the dominant mechanism that would tie social relationships together in the new social order. Tönnies (1887) argued that modern society came to exist as a superior power to enforce the terms set out in the contracts of the merchants and capitalists. Lawyers grew in number and importance as new contract forms were developed to meet the increasingly complex trade arrangements of the time. Contracts, which had been private agreements, now became widely used to bind together individuals in the new social order.

During the mid-1500s, the king sought to consolidate power, and he found that great inroads could be made into common law by throwing his support behind merchant law in support of the merchant class. In return for taxes and loans, the Crown placed the power of the state behind the laws of commerce and enforced these laws. The merchant class supported the legislative and judicial power of the Crown in exchange for the development of legal mechanisms that would strengthen their class position, increase their fortunes, and consolidate their power. The law and lawyers had been guaranteed a primary role in the new industrial, capitalist mode of production. The bourgeois had helped to strengthen the power of the monarch in order to be protected by his state apparatus. The king's support of merchant law as the law of the land helped to stabilize the necessary social and legal conditions for commerce.

The power of the nation-state was solidified around the interests of commerce, and the role of custom and kinship was eroded. The basis for the new social order was predicated on law, in the realm of both commercial and criminal activity. While the primary interest of this chapter is criminal law, it is important to track the rise of the institution of law in the modern state—and this was primarily within the context of merchant interests.

The merchant class had supported the aspirations of the Crown because its members needed a stable and modified system in order to conduct their affairs. However, once the land had been redistributed and feudal village life had been disrupted, the bourgeois became interested in forming a new alliance so as to curb the Crown's ability to restrict trade. Tigar and Levy (1977) have documented the new alliance with common-law lawyers.

## The Consolidation of Bourgeois Ascendance

Contracts under merchant law were enforced in merchant courts, as well as in chancery and admiralty courts. Common-law lawyers realized that the portion of law that they administered was shrinking with the decline of the landed nobility. Some of them were eager to have merchant law enforced in their courts. The bourgeois supported this change because it would make them less dependent on the king and his special courts. Common-law lawyers made a concerted effort to make their courts more receptive to bourgeois legal principles. By 1600, an alliance between the common-law lawyers and the bourgeois succeeded in introducing the bourgeois theory of contract into common-law courts. A conflict between the Crown and the merchant class ensued because the Crown wanted to control merchant activity through the monarch's court, and the bourgeois wanted to evade the Crown's attempts at controlling trade by having matters handled through the common-law courts.

The merchant class gained a stronghold on the Parliament as the landed aristocracy's power waned. Parliament used its control over tax revenues to limit the king's control of trade. This conflict was resolved in the English Civil War of 1642–1648 by a reduction in the power of the monarchy and the establishment of the bourgeois-controlled Parliament as the sole source of political control.

Peasants and workers were not represented in this early Parliament, and, as a result, the modern state developed under the influence of the bourgeois. The rise of the labour movement would come later, but according to Miliband (1969) the power of organized labour has never matched that of organized business. Whatever advances have been made in democratizing the state apparatus, it remains a political and legal structure to protect the interests of property. In the arena of modern political life, various interest groups bring pressure on the state to protect their interests under the rule of law.

## State, Law, and Interest Groups

As the structures of feudalism declined, the state became the dominant institution regulating social order and settling disputes. State decisions were backed up by military and police organizations. The state stood as the superior force behind the contractual arrangements of business and property in order to ensure that the terms of these agreements were observed.

The law has become the dominant means of regulating human affairs: legislation and administrative directives are the legal apparatus that create the bases of modern nation-states: property, commerce, real estate, labour, and contractual agreements are all regulated by law; municipalities and corporations are governed by law; the protection of the environment is regulated by law; and disputes over person and property are handled through family, civil, and criminal law. In short, the law is the principal means whereby human activity is prohibited, permitted, or required, and the state and the law are intimately meshed in the creation of the modern social order.

As shown in earlier sections, the merchant class was quite successful in promoting and protecting its interests as it helped shape the nature of the state and the law. But business interest groups are not the only ones that approach the state to promote their interests. A variety of cultural, ethnic, minority, class, economic, and political interest groups lobby the state in order to promote their own interests. The modern state has become a vehicle sought after by a variety of groups, each seeking certain guarantees and protections. The heterogeneous nature of modern societies and the antagonistic relationships between various groups ensure that the state cannot promote the interests of all groups. Choices need to be made. Given the nature of electoral politics, the state is under some pressure to promote the values and interests of the majority as well as those of powerful minorities in order to maintain legitimacy and popularity. In the remainder of this chapter, several examples will be reviewed to show the range of interest groups seeking to influence the content and role of law in modern society. Given the sheer volume of law and the complexity of modern society, this review can be only illustrative of the role of law in modern society.

# Regulation by Law

Some criminologists argue that the law reflects the values of the majority of the population, while others analyze various laws to show that powerful minority interests have shaped the content of the law. There is no reason to conclude that only one of these positions is correct. It is clear that some laws reflect the values of the majority, and it is also clear that other laws clearly do not reflect the values of the majority but instead reflect the values of powerful minorities. The significant impact of powerful interests on the content of law is a topic that is subject to much debate. This section will provide examples that represent both points of view.

## Consensus and the Law

There is general consensus regarding laws that seek to protect individuals from common assault in public places, from breaking and entering, and from theft of property from their residence. There is also considerable agreement about what constitutes serious crime. Rossi and Waite (1974) replicated the earlier work of Sellin and Wolfgang (1964) on the ranking of seriousness of crimes and concluded "[t]he norms defining how serious various criminal acts are considered to be, are quite widely distributed among blacks and whites, males and females, high and low socio-economic levels, and among levels of educational attainment" (237). This basic consensus about what constitutes crime against person and property should not be understated.

**Interest Groups and the Law**   However, most of the research on law over the past 40 years shows the operation of interest groups. Chambliss (1969) demonstrated how various interest groups have been able to influence the content and the use of vagrancy law to suit their interests. Feudal lords used it to press the idle into work during times of labour shortages. In the 17th century, the law was used to deal with the "roadmen" who were disrupting early commercial trade and stealing goods in transport. After the emancipation of the slaves in the United States, plantation owners and industrialists encouraged the arrest of freed African Americans under vagrancy legislation so that they could then be leased to work without pay for those who had previously used slave labour.

Hagan and Leon (1977) and Platt (1969) showed the operation of "moral entrepreneurs" who were part of a child-saving movement and the responsiveness of the state in creating a separate juvenile court for young offenders.

West and Snider (1985) have also documented the operation of interest groups in this movement, but they expand the argument by suggesting that their motives were to both save children and deal with an excess labour supply.

Research on drug legislation also showed the state responding to various forms of pressure. Becker (1963) concluded that drug legislation in the United States was the result of the efforts of a civil servant, Harry Anslinger, who was primarily a moral entrepreneur. Dickson (1968) further argued that this bureaucrat was able to use his access to government services not only to foster particular moral objectives, but possibly also to save his organization and help it expand. The research of Shirley Small (1978) into Canadian narcotics legislation suggested that strong racist sentiments against Asians were a motivating force in the push for drug laws. Comack (1985) demonstrated that these anti-Asian sentiments were best understood as being grounded in labour disputes that were being handled in racial terms instead of in class terms.

Graham's (1976) analysis of amphetamine legislation also demonstrated the operation of special interests. In spite of strong support from the American public and the president, attempts to change the Federal Drug Administration's (FDA) control of amphetamine production failed because of pressure from the powerful drug companies. A legislative remedy would have gone a long way in promoting the common good with regard to this significant problem, but the power of a sizeable lobby stifled the attempted changes. This fact was hidden from public view.

Analyses of the history of rape legislation (Brownmiller, 1975; Clark and Lewis, 1977; Kinnon, 1981) showed that such laws were enacted to protect the transmission of property in the male line of descent. Fathers used rape laws to avoid transferring property to men of whom they disapproved but who had taken their daughters by bride capture. They also sought compensation for the reduction of bride price that they suffered because their daughters had lost virginal status. Husbands wanted to secure control over their wives' reproductive capacity to ensure that they transferred their property to their own sons. Therefore, women and children became the property of the man of the household and the act of rape became an offence against the husband. Over time, and as the result of concerted feminist activity, the act of sexual assault has been reconceptualized as a crime against the woman who has been victimized; in some jurisdictions, including Canada, the husband can now be prosecuted for the rape of his wife (Chapter 5). This, of course, means that women have succeeded in having themselves redefined as persons and not merely as the property of their fathers or husbands.

Research conducted on anti-combines legislation in Canada also provided the kind of evidence that demonstrated the operation of class-based interest groups in the framing of the law. Smandych (1985) outlined a confrontation that was brewing in the 1880s between labour and capital. The Knights of Labour movement specifically focused on the monopolistic nature of industrial capitalism and demanded the elimination of combines. A royal commission was established, and it submitted its report in the same year that the first anti-combines legislation was enacted. But as Goff and Reasons (1978) pointed out, the wording of the statute was weakened in comparison with proposals in preliminary drafts. So the statute appeared to constrain capital interests when, in fact, it hardly did so.

More changes to this statute in the 1970s further liberalized the circumstances under which mergers were permissible. Thus, not only was the state unwilling to champion the interests of organized labour in the legislation but as Goff and Reasons (1978) and Snider (1980) have shown, the act has been applied only to small firms in Canada. In spite of the evidence of higher prices under conditions of oligopoly and in spite of protests by organized labour, the Canadian government has been unwilling to regulate the larger corporations in order to make Canada competitive in the international market. The government appears to fear the loss of investor confidence and the flight of capital.

**The Canadian Centre for Occupational Health and Safety**
www.ccohs.ca

The history of occupational health and safety legislation is also very instructive. Friedman and Ladinsky (1980) traced the changes in the law governing industrial accidents and relate that, initially, employers were held responsible for injuries to workers under tort law, even if such injury resulted from the negligence of another employee. But this doctrine of *respondeat superior* was slowly replaced by the fellow-servant rule, which did not allow an employee to sue the employer in the case of injury unless harm was caused by the employer's personal misconduct. This move effectively prevented thousands of lawsuits in the United States, but the large number of accidents generated a continuing series of cases. Pressure was exerted by workers and their unions and, in some jurisdictions, legislation was introduced to exclude the application of the fellow-servant rule. Workers' compensation schemes were proposed but employers showed little interest in them until judges began awarding damages to employees. The compensation legislation that was finally enacted was based on a compromise. Employers and employees would both contribute to the cost of the program, which would guarantee the injured employee compensation based on statutory schedules. However, the employer would be protected from the bulk of civil liability litigation because employee claims would be handled by an administrative agency instead of by the courts.

While this compensation program has been more or less acceptable to workers and owners, Walters (1983) showed how the Ontario government had undertaken changes in occupational health and safety legislation in an effort to reduce the cost of running its health-care system. It has been estimated that $1.4 billion was added to the health-care system's bill every year because of industrial accidents. Here is an interesting case of the state enacting legislation not to promote or protect the interests of any specific interest group but rather to reduce its own deficit. It is interesting to note that Snider (1994) found that the greatest gains in the regulation of dangerous corporate behaviour have been in the realm of occupational health and safety.

These examples demonstrate that the process of law creation is heavily influenced by various interest groups and the pressure that they bring to bear on the state. It seems quite clear that the state often does find itself in situations in which it can make decisions based on the wishes and interests of the majority. At other times, it finds itself hard pressed to regulate effectively some of the special interest groups.

## The Failure to Regulate: The Eclipse of the State?

There is growing concern among some analysts that **transnational corporations** operating in countries all over the globe have amassed so much economic power

**transnational corporation**

A corporation that has sales and production in many different nations. As a result of their multinational reach, these corporations are often thought to be beyond the political control of any individual nation-states.

that they are getting beyond the control of nation-states. These corporations are expanding at two to three times the rates of growth of national economies, and the scale of such organizations gives them considerable power to resist the efforts of nation-states to regulate them. These corporations can, and do, bring considerable pressure to bear on national governments. If a government is too restrictive in its regulatory policies, a transnational corporation can relocate operations to another country with laws more to its liking. It is clear that corporations are responsible for environmentally damaging practices that are harmful to individuals, societies, and nature itself and these harms are not being effectively controlled by the state and the rule of law. The following examples help make the point.

**Victims of Avoidable Harms** Reasons et al. (1981) analyzed numerous instances in which Canadian workers were needlessly exposed to risks in the workplace that resulted in injury and death. Many of these dangers were known to employers and were avoidable, which led Reasons et al. to suggest that these casualties were "victims without crimes," and that such injuries should be conceptualized as "assaults" on the worker. Stone (1975) recounted cases of corporate actions involving injury that would have resulted in criminal trials and possibly death sentences had they been committed by individuals. Dowie (1977) reported that the design problems of the Ford Pinto that resulted in passenger injury and death were known by the auto manufacturer, that these problems could have been addressed by cost-effective measures, and that the corporation chose not to make the improvements. Internal Ford memos revealed that the costs of design changes had been compared to the costs of potential litigation for death, dismemberment, and injury, and that the company decided to put Pinto passengers at risk. It is hard to conceive of the death and injury created by the Pinto as accidental when such injury and death were anticipated and could have been avoided. It could be argued that these deaths were homicides and that such harmful behaviour ought to come under the control of the Criminal Code. Ford was, in fact, charged with homicide for one of the Pinto accidents but was acquitted by an Indiana jury. This kind of reckless corporate behaviour persists and it is clear that the modern consumer-citizen is not being protected under the rule of law from dangerous corporate misbehaviour.

The courts could move in the direction of holding corporations and their managers accountable for harms such as the one that took place in Cook County, Illinois. On July 1, 1985, three former executives of a silver-recycling plant were convicted of murder and each received a sentence of 25 years in prison and a fine of $10 000 for the death of an employee. The company had exposed workers to cyanide gas by intentionally concealing warnings of hazards from immigrant workers. These murder convictions are believed to be the first in the United States of corporate officials in a job-related death. But to date, governments have not pursued a vigorous policy of bringing such corporate harms under the appropriate sections of the Criminal Code. This case turned out to be a rarity and not a harbinger of greater corporate accountability.

Finally, Brodeur (1985) provided a detailed analysis of problems associated with the asbestos industry in the United States and Canada. It has come to light that the industry had been aware of the health hazards related to the inhalation

The Asbestos Institute Online
www.asbestos-institute.ca

of asbestos particles since the 1930s, but that it withheld this information from workers and did not take steps to improve the safety of the workplace. *Facts on File* has kept track of the significant developments related to the claims against asbestos companies. The key developments will be tracked here in some detail because they demonstrate the legal complexities involved as the various stakeholders attempt to use the law to protect their interests against those of other interested parties. It is estimated by a U.S. Federal Appeals Court "that the number of current and future claimants [is] expected to reach several million" (*Facts on File*, 1997). Further, "analysts estimated total asbestos liability to be as high as $50 billion" (*Facts on File*, 2000). Asbestos firms have been flooded with lawsuits in which courts have been finding them responsible for the resultant illnesses and deaths and have awarded victims sizable punitive damages. "$53.5 million dollar judgment [was awarded] in favor of the estate of Stephen Brown, a former mechanic who died of mesothelioma in December 2000. The verdict handed down in a State Court in New York City, was the largest ever awarded to a single asbestos plaintiff" (*Facts on File*, 2002). In 1982, the Johns-Manville Corporation, with assets of more than $2 billion, filed for bankruptcy in the United States in an effort to escape paying the damages assessed for its harmful business practices. By 2000, 25 companies had filed for bankruptcy protection due to asbestos litigation. The U.S. government was put under considerable corporate pressure to grant this request. However, it was also faced with pressure to hold corporate citizens accountable to the same laws that ordinary citizens are bound to obey. It is increasingly clear that the government's response to this situation is to make use of *civil* rather than *criminal* courts. Reasons et al. (1981) made a compelling case in arguing that many "accidents" in the workplace are not unforeseen and therefore are not accidents. They argued that they should properly be conceptualized as "assaults on the workers" and handled by way of the Criminal Code rather than by occupational health and safety legislation, offering the following example: "It has been revealed that asbestos companies continued to expose workers to that substance in spite of the fact that they had had evidence concerning its fatal effects for some thirty years. Such conscious, premeditated, and rational behaviour undoubtedly led to thousands of deaths and disabilities. Nonetheless, asbestos companies are only liable to civil lawsuits" (6).

The court system initially declined to allow victims to bring forward class action suits; however, in 1991 the judicial panel on multidistrict litigation allowed more than 26 000 personal injury cases involving asbestos to be consolidated "in order to reduce delays and rising costs in asbestos litigation, which many lawyers said had reached a crisis level, with plaintiffs dying or depleting their resources before a verdict was handed down" (*Facts on File*, 1991). Since then, other courts have also consolidated asbestos cases because they are the largest number of civil cases in U.S. federal courts. This decision has made it easier for victims to gain access to damage awards. (Similar class action, or "mass tort," cases have also been used or contemplated in actions against tobacco companies as well as the manufacturers of the Dalkon Shield, Agent Orange, and silicone breast implants.) In an effort to limit their liability in future claims, large asbestos companies proposed a settlement under which "220 companies and their insurers would resolve outside of court as many as 100,000 new asbestos-injury claims for $1 billion over the next decade" (*Facts on File*, 1993). This settlement was an attempt by the companies to set a limit on monetary damages that they would be liable to pay to claimants after the number of claims and the size of settlements being awarded threatened to bankrupt many of them. An appeals court struck down the settlement package in May 1996. The appeals court ruled "that the agreement, which would bar individuals from pursuing future claims against the manufacturers, could compromise the rights of people who were currently unaware that they had been exposed to asbestos" (*Facts on File*, 1997). This decision was upheld by the Supreme Court on June 25, 1997.

So the outcome of this episode of corporate deviance is far from settled. The state finds itself in the middle between the rights of individuals to damages and the needs of the corporations to limit damages so that they can remain in business. The state clearly has an interest in keeping corporations in business because they are the major employers in an industrial economy. Many jurisdictions are considering legislation that could limit the amount of damages for which corporations could be sued. It remains to be seen whether the United States is prepared to hold major corporations responsible under the law for their reckless and harmful behaviour. The asbestos companies are encountering financial fallout in any event. For example, in December 7, 2001, Halliburton, a multinational corporation with operations in over 120 countries, "saw its stock tumble 42% after a Baltimore, MD jury that day had ordered the company to pay $30 million in damages in an asbestos exposure lawsuit" (*Facts on File*, 2001). Halliburton also owned the Energy Services Group, which provided technical products and services for *oil* and *gas* exploration and production, and had a subsidiary, KBR, which undertook major construction of *refineries*, *oil fields*, *pipelines*, and *chemical plants*. KBR was the corporate entity involved in the asbestos litigation. In 2004, the U.S. Bankruptcy Court approved a deal between Halliburton and Equitas, a reinsurance firm, that would pay Halliburton $575 million (25 percent of the $2.3 billion that Halliburton sought) to finance an asbestos trust fund (*Facts on File*, 2004). In 2005, Halliburton "finalized a $5.1 billion settlement that ended its past and future liability to asbestos lawsuits" with regard to claims by more than 400 000 people (*Facts on File*, 2005). On April 5, 2007, Halliburton announced that it had broken ties with KBR, which had been its contracting, engineering, and construction unit for 44 years.

The mining, sale, and use of asbestos in the industrialized world has become a risky venture for corporations and the state has developed restrictive policies and funded asbestos removal programs in Canada and the United States. Quebec now has a zero tolerance policy for the use of asbestos as it deals with the health crisis it has created. In 2009, the Quebec Worker's Compensation Board showed that 60 percent of occupational deaths were caused by asbestos. These constraints should have spelled the end of asbestos mining in Quebec, but it has not. A consortium of international investors is planning to buy the Jeffrey Mine and convert it from an open pit into an underground mine. The proposal involves expanding production more than tenfold—to 180 000 tonnes in 2012 and eventually to 225 000 tonnes. The provincial government is considering guaranteeing a $58 million loan to the mine in Asbestos, Quebec. This expanded mining operation would preserve the 340 current jobs and could create 400 direct jobs and 1000 indirect jobs in the region. The benefit of these jobs must be measured against the consequences of endorsing a product the World Health Organization says kills 90 000 annually.

In an open letter (http://hesa.etui-rehs.org/uk/newsevents/files/Letter_Premier_ Charest.pdf) to Quebec Premier Jean Charest in 2010, more than 100 prominent scientists in 28 countries challenged the premier to put and end to the double standard which bans the use of asbestos at home while approving its export to other countries. The pressure has intensified with the publication of an article in the prestigious British medical journal *The Lancet*. The article, titled "Canada accused of hypocrisy over asbestos exports" (2010, Dec 11, 376 (9757), 1973–74), comes at a time when there are protests in London, Quebec, and various Asian cities by groups advocating a ban on asbestos. Anti-asbestos activists came from Japan, South Korea, and India in December 2010 to meet with provincial officials to urge them to get out of the asbestos industry. Activists made it clear that those using asbestos in their countries do not understand the dangers associated with exposure to even a miniscule amount of chrysotile asbestos and so the export of this substance is causing tragic and avoidable health consequences. Under these circumstances, it is hard to understand why the Canadian government still allows asbestos to be exported from a health perspective. However, when the matter is looked at from the point of view of corporate business practice, it is quite understandable.

Transnational corporations exist to make profits for investors, but the pursuit of profit has often been maximized by reckless and dangerous behaviour. The growing evidence of the serious harm to employees, customers, and the environment that has resulted suggests that a very powerful set of human actors is currently operating beyond the control of law. For example, Marchak (1991) described some of the serious harms that stem from the creation of **free trade zones** within Third World countries. Free trade zones are created by countries within their borders to attract corporations to set up businesses. The corporations that work within these zones have often been able to negotiate very favourable terms, including freedom from taxation, exemptions from labour and environmental legislation, and very favourable labour regulations that allow them to hire workers very cheaply. One of the more harmful practices discussed by Marchak is the use of noncitizen, female workers from neighbouring states in microchip production and in the garment industry. For example, "Singapore has imported Malaysian, Thai, Filipina, and Indonesian women as guest workers. These women have no citizen rights and no civil rights, and are deported if their eyesight or productivity fails to please, or if markets slow down" (Marchak, 1991, 147). When they are sent back home, they receive no compensation or benefits and typically face severe financial difficulties.

At present, many such harms cannot be brought to the courts for remedy because the state has not defined them as disputes or crimes. It may be asked whether the modern state has truly established the rule of law when serious sources of harm escape regulation and control. In some important ways, the legal power of the state has been superseded by the economic power of the modern corporation. The law cannot restore order in areas of social life where the state does not establish its jurisdiction. The absence of protection from the raw economic power of corporations places individuals, and perhaps even humanity, in harm's way.

**free trade zone**

A specially designated geographical area within a nation that is exempt from the regulations and taxation normally imposed on business. These zones are intended to facilitate cross-border production and trade. Examples of these zones are found along the United States–Mexico border, where they are referred to as *maquilladora*.

Snider (1999, 2000) carefully illustrated many of the acts of corporate impropriety in Canada and documented the steps taken by the Canadian government to "make corporate crime disappear." She recounted how, in 1986, the House of Commons passed legislation that abolished the Combines Investigation Act and replaced it with the Competition Act. Among other things, this change removed criminal sanctions from the merger and monopoly sections and removed the public interest criterion that had previously been used when evaluating proposed mergers. Snider showed how these changes further eroded the weak record of Canadian government scrutiny and intervention in corporate mergers that have harmed other groups in Canadian society. She noted that "the significance of the disappearance of corporate crime speaks volumes about the potential of state law to harness capital. The corporate counter-revolution illustrates how profoundly dependent the promulgation and enforcement of nation-state law is on the balance of powers operating within a society" (Snider, 1999, 204). She noted that when unions or social movements are strong, such as in Europe or Scandinavia, corporate "downsizing and decriminalization will be resisted longer and more effectively" (204). When they are weak, as in Canada and the United States, corporate wrongdoing is increasingly decriminalized and subject to decreasing scrutiny. Further, she stressed that progressive social movements have a vital role to play in developing and applying pressure on the state to use law as a mechanism for controlling harmful corporate behaviour.

The unwillingness or inability of the state to regulate forms of behaviour that have serious deleterious consequences has resulted in growing cynicism about the legitimacy of an ineffective "social contract" and "rule of law." It is important to reflect on some of the serious concerns raised about the harm caused by the state's failure to protect us from corporate crime (see also Chapter 17).

## A Coming Crisis in State Legitimacy?

An essential function of the law is to foster a willingness to comply with legal prescriptions of good conduct. The rule of law depends in large measure on the willingness of the majority of citizens to comply with legal prescriptions and prohibitions. In situations of widespread, sustained levels of disobedience, the social control apparatus may be unable to cope or even be overwhelmed. Thus it is essential that the state system be seen as providing peace, security, good government, and protection from harm. Any state that fails to live up to its end of the social contract sooner or later faces a crisis of nonconfidence. In numerous quarters, dissatisfaction is growing with the evident failure of the nation-state system to regulate serious forms of harmful behaviour that have not been criminalized or limited by legal sanctions. If this situation is allowed to persist, it is reasonable to expect an increase in cynicism, which may lead to a crisis in the legitimacy of the "rule of law." Four of the most glaring examples of uncontrolled harm are the following:

1. The un(der)regulated business practices of major corporations result in the daily introduction of massive amounts of toxins into the air, water,

soil, and food chain, which is having serious and evident consequences for human health. The rapidly growing incidence of cancers, birth defects, sterility, and other man-made misery are clear signs that the state has not been fully effective in providing basic security from harm. Its limited effectiveness in regulating corporate behaviour is of growing concern. The responsibility to curb the harm caused by irresponsible corporations properly falls within the jurisdiction of the state since corporations are created by charters of incorporation that are approved by the state. The history of incorporation clearly documents how the American state forfeited the tight control of corporations that had been imposed when they were first brought into being (Grossman and Adams, 1993). This ineffectiveness may make people critical not only of the corporations but also of the state itself.

2. The systematic assaults on entire ecosystems, in the pursuit of profit, have resulted in loss of diversity, loss of habitat, species extinctions, and deformities of plant and animal life forms. The cumulative consequences are so serious that they threaten the very integrity of the world's ecosystem and have been referred to as an "ecocide" (Broswimmer, 2002). The fact that such destructive behaviour is not criminalized undermines the legitimacy of the nation-state system. Citizens expect the state to protect them and future generations from human-created sources of harm.

3. Extreme levels of economic inequality continue to grow. When "the world's 587 billionaires are now worth more than the combined income of the bottom half of humanity [3.2 billion]" (Cavanagh and Mander, 2004, 48), there have been growing calls for some form of state intervention into the distribution of wealth. The state has the legal means to limit class disparities through the use of legal sanctions and taxation programs that would effect a redistribution of wealth in order to provide basic security, health, and social justice for a greater number of people. Such progressive legislation had been used in the past and there are increasing calls for its reintroduction. While it is true that this private wealth is private property, it is important to remember that the notion of private property is a human invention regulated by the nation-state. The inaction of nation-states in setting limits on the egregious disparities in access to wealth denies a major portion of humanity from a decent standard of living. This invites contempt for an unfeeling state apparatus and a questioning of the legitimacy of the status quo and those institutions that make it possible.

4. The annual world military expenditure is some $1464 billion. Lester Brown (2006, 255–260) argues that an annual expenditure of $77 billion is needed to meet basic social goals at the global level and that $110 billion is needed for earth restoration goals. This $187 billion would require the redirection of 13 percent of the world's military budget. When the governments of the world invest in the death industry rather than the life-enhancing forms of human endeavour, can they really count on the continuing compliance of ordinary citizens to a rule of law that fails to protect the bulk of humanity from the excesses of the powerful few?

A pessimistic view of this situation suggests the possibility that at some time in the not-too-distant future, the growing concern about escalating ecological deterioration and the increasing misery caused by mounting social injustice may cross a threshold that will precipitate a massive challenge to the rule of law and spell the end of the social ordering principles of modernity.

## The Dilemma and Challenge for the Modern State

In this chapter, the changing forms of social order have been traced from early small-scale societies to the complex arrangements of the modern era. Small communities based on self-restraint and mutual dependence were transformed into large industrial states in which social life is controlled by political and economic power. Societies that based their order on customary beliefs have been eclipsed by those that are organized according to differential access to surplus and the resultant stratification. These changing patterns of organization did not always happen as a result of historical developments within a single society. Important external forces often played an essential role in shaping the form and content of law. This is well illustrated by the case of Canada's legal inheritances in Box 2.4.

The nature of dispute settlement has undergone a dramatic transformation from the small-scale society in which every member had direct access to the process of redress, to the present era in which not everyone can afford the costs of seeking a remedy through the courts. Furthermore, some serious harms are not currently subsumed under the law and, without a crime, there are few alternatives available for victims to seek redress. The concentration of social power has seen the state come to play a central role in the dispute settlement process. Since **Tudor** times, the administration and control of the legal process have been the prerogative of the state. While the interests of all members formed the basis of customary practice in small-scale communities, the interests of the merchant class have been given a special place in law in Western industrial societies. The promotion and protection of the interests of this wealthy and increasingly powerful minority has increasingly put ordinary citizens at risk. The modern state has not extended protection to all interest groups under the law since the heterogeneous nature of contemporary society and inherent conflicts of interest of various groups make this impossible. Nevertheless, there is growing pressure on the state to regulate the business practices of transnational corporations when they cause serious harm to human beings and the natural environment.

However, some argue convincingly that nation-states lack the ability, or the will, to regulate such powerful organizations, which have come to dominate the social landscape in the past 50 years. The very health of the economy in liberal democracies depends on the decisions made by those who privately own the "means of production." So the state needs to provide a "favourable climate for investment" in order to have those businesses operate in their country. And yet those very same companies are often involved in activities that are harmful to the ecosystems, employees, consumers, and the general health of the economy—activities for which they should be disciplined. It is because the liberal state has conjoined interests with the propertied class that it finds it difficult to regulate their harmful behaviour, even when there is strong

"The Harvard Negotiation Project
www.pon.harvard.edu/hnp/index
.shtml

**Tudor**

Refers to the period of English history from 1485 to 1603, when the nation's monarchs were descended from Owen Tudor and Catherine (1401–1437), widow of Henry V.

public pressure from citizens to do so. It remains very much an open question whether the state and its legal system are up to the task of bringing these behemoths back under the rule of law. It is unrealistic to expect continuing compliance of the majority of humanity with the rule of law if it does not afford them some measure of security and social justice.

## Full Circle: Restorative Justice and a Return to Original Forms of Dispute Settlement?

Restorative Justice Online
www.restorativejustice.org/

While controlling modern corporations will require new and innovative legal methods, developments on other fronts bring this discussion of the evolution of law back to where we began. Many critics of the current justice system have advocated returning to a fundamentally different way of approaching criminal justice, to a system that is intended to restore social relationships rather than simply to punish. Advocates of restorative justice seek to return the focus of the justice system to repairing the harm that has been done to the victim and the community. A key element of restorative justice is the involvement of the victim and other members of the community as active participants in the process. The focus of the restorative justice approach is to reconcile offenders with those they have harmed and to help communities *reintegrate* victims and offenders. The source of peace and order lies in a strong, active, and caring community, and proponents of restorative justice feel that a more humane and satisfying justice system can help to rebuild communities that may have been weakened by crime and other social ills.

## FOCUS BOX 2.3

### CANADA'S LEGAL INHERITANCES

*Canada's Legal Inheritances* is a collection of scholarly research reports that trace some of the key "threads in the tapestry that is Canada's current law. The weave is created from a complex of colonial, federal, provincial and local jurisdictions, ancient and recent, patterned from a multiplicity of statutes, judgments, behavioural rules and by-laws, some written and many oral, each coloured by religious values, private interests, moral maxims, public needs, and raw power."

While many people live out their lives close to the place of their birth and are guided by the culture of that place, many others move great distances, take their birth-culture with them and yet must learn the cultural expectations of their new residence. This phenomenon is part of the experience of many people in "an immigrant constructed country like Canada."

Canadian law is the product of several legal inheritances that include "indigenous laws and imported laws" reaching back to the 1620s when "the French were settling the northern St. Lawrence River valley and the English annually visiting Newfoundland, importing their respective legal inheritances; but, at least for that century, they applied their laws almost exclusively

*(continued)*

to themselves, as the Hudson's Bay Company would later in Rupert's Land. Aboriginal peoples, whether Algonquin or Huron, were repeatedly described . . . by the Jesuits as having and applying their own legal inheritances to themselves. . . . The French had their indigenous laws, now transplanted, and the First Nations had theirs with neither importing the other into their indigenous laws. Likewise for Newfoundland, so long as the fishing fleet English remained seasonal visitors, the Beothuk legal inheritance did not connect with English admiralty law, any more than it did with the laws of other regular fishing fleets from Spain and Portugal. . . .

"By the end of the eighteenth century, approximately nine generations of imported European laws, in Lower Canada (Quebec), the Maritimes, Newfoundland and Rupert's Land had begun a more deliberate extension westward. The French led as coureurs de bois, soon followed by the English and Scots for the fledgling Hudson's Bay Company after 1670 and its later Montreal-based competitors. Then came an even larger group, the Loyalist immigrants fleeing the thirteen southerly secessionist New England colonies after 1774, mainly into Upper Canada (Ontario). . . . The Loyalists imported after 1774 an English common law shaped by their New England experiences. By then, there was little European sensitivity left for recognition of Canada's first indigenous Aboriginal law, a century and a half after the first European settlements. By mid-century, French and English laws had become the indigenous laws in their respective territories, awaiting the next wave of immigrants, largely from the newly formed United States. Nevertheless, Canada's three legal inheritances were in place: Aboriginal, French and English."

Significant changes came in 1763 when the "Treaty of Paris (3 September 1763) vested France's Lower Canada (Quebec), and lands east of the Mississippi River, in Great Britain's empire. Then Britain's Royal Proclamation of 1763 (7 October) played a double role in Canada's

legal inheritances. It imposed the complete replacement of French civil law with the English common law in Lower Canada: '. . . as near as may be agreeable to the Laws of England.' The Proclamation had grown alongside events beginning with Quebec's capture in 1759 and become an instrument to neutralise Britain's expanded array of Aboriginal peoples. It did so by recognising their use of reserved lands, without mention of any rights, and only according to the English law based on royal prerogative, not on parliamentary or judge-made law, and not on any formal recognition of Aboriginal law. Defeating Old France had not translated into winning New France, and Britain soon had to restore French civil laws and procedures to Lower Canada (1774), albeit retaining the English criminal law." The British then set out to pacify "Aboriginal peoples without acknowledging their laws."

"Lord Durham's Report (1839), in the wake of Quebec's *patriote rebellion*, effectively imposed an English transplanted stability on the two territorial legal inheritances, which was institutionalised in the confederation created by the British North America Act (1867). Shortly thereafter the need to people the vast continent, at the expense of the Aboriginal birth and residence cultures, became too great to be limited to more English and French immigrants. The gates opened to Icelanders and Mennonites on the prairies, Irish in Newfoundland, Chinese in British Columbia." Each immigrant group brought its own "birth-culture laws and most kept them as their new residence-culture laws" to the extent possible. And so Canadian law emerged and continues to re-emerge from a multitude of local and imported legal inheritances that have continued to refashion the codes of conduct in the many locales of Canadian life.

Source: DeLloyd J. Guth and W. Wesley Pue (eds.). (2001). *Canada's Legal Inheritances*. Canadian Legal History Project, Faculty of Law, The University of Manitoba, Winnipeg.

Canada and New Zealand have led the way in the field of restorative justice. This is due at least in part to the influence of Aboriginal people in these two countries. Rupert Ross (1996) discusses some of the steps being undertaken in Aboriginal communities to place a renewed emphasis on healing as the community response to individual wrongdoing. Many community leaders view the restorative justice approach as a way to restore harmonious relationships and to foster the development of healthy communities.

The restorative approach is not just limited to Aboriginal communities. The Young Offenders Act and its successor, the Youth Criminal Justice Act, mandated youth courts to look for alternative measures to traditional punishment, and options such as restitution, alternative dispute resolution, victim–offender reconciliation, community group conferences, and sentencing panels are being used much more frequently for both juvenile and adult offenders. Braithwaite and Mugford (1994) have discussed some of the ways in which the traditional practices of shame, reintegration, and healing might be introduced into modern urban settings. As outlined earlier, there are important differences in the make-up of small-scale and modern communities. When an offence occurs within the intimacy of small-scale communities it typically involves a victim and an offender who have an established bond. The trouble between them has weakened or shattered the bond, and the dispute settlement process seeks to restore the bond to the satisfaction of both parties and to reintegrate the offender into the community as a member in good standing. In modern communities, no such bond exists between many victims and offenders who are, more often than not, strangers to each other until the offense creates a connection between them. The goal of the restorative approach within this context is not to re-establish a nonexistent earlier bond; rather it is to intervene in such a way that the parties to the conflict can transform the negative ties they have to each other into positive ties. In this sense, conflict can actually create the opportunity for the establishment of positive bonds between former strangers whereas the normal adversarial court practice would solidify their interconnection into a permanent negative tie between them. In other respects, the similarities are worth noting. Not only are the offender and the victim touched by the offence, so too are their immediate circles of family and friends. To the extent that the restorative justice approach can mobilize these "communities of care" (Johnstone, 2002, 51) in support of the healing process and involve them in the development of a solution that they also endorse, a larger community can be created where none existed previously. The restorative approach helps to empower the victims of crime in any community and increases their participation in the dispute resolution process rather than requiring them to surrender their voice to lawyers. While it is too soon to know the degree to which these practices will replace more punitive methods of justice, it is clear that these traditional ideas are being actively reconsidered.

W W W

"Aboriginal Corrections Publications" Public Safety Canada

www.publicsafety.gc.ca/res/cor/apc/apc-eng.aspx

# FOCUS BOX 2.4

## RESTORATIVE JUSTICE: PRESENT PROSPECTS AND FUTURE DIRECTIONS

There is a genuine difference of opinion about whether the restorative justice process can work in communities that do not have strong social ties prior to the commission of an offence. Elmar Weitekamp (2002, 325) sees it as follows:

> Looking at the newest developments of restorative justice within the context of existing justice systems, one finds that they resemble in fact very old and ancient forms of restorative justice as used in acephelous societies and other forms of humankind: family group conferences, family conferences, peace circles, community circles, or circle hearings as used by indigenous people such as the Aboriginals, Maori, Inuit, the Native Indians of North America and African peoples. The new concepts and models treat crime as an offence against human relationships, recognize that crime is wrong and when it happens can further alienate the community, the family of the victim and the offender and lead to damage, disrespect, disempowerment and feelings of insecurity. The chance of the restorative justice approach is to recognize the injustice, so that in some form, equity will be restored, thus leading the participants of this process to feel safer, more respected and more empowered. It is somewhat ironic that, at the beginning of the new millennium, we have to go back to methods and forms of conflict resolution which were practised some millennia ago by our ancestors.

Source: Elmar G. M. Weitekamp. (2002). "Restorative Justice: Present Prospects and Future Directions." In Elmar G.M. Weitekamp and Hans-Jürgen Kerner (eds.), Restorative Justice: Theoretical Foundations. Oregon: William Publishing.

In this view, we need to recover the restorative practice and apply it to our efforts to repair the damage done and restore peace between parties to a dispute. There is no call for a change in the overall make-up of social relationships or other social practices of modern society. This view may be overly optimistic about the ability of the restorative justice principle alone to restore peace between the offender, victims, and their respective communities of care. Barbara Gray and Pat Lauderdale (2007, 218) do not think that solely relying on restorative principles will be sufficient:

> Restorative justice is dependent on the foundational traditional preventative structures and practices that work together to create justice and prevent injustice. Focusing on the restorative aspects of justice without incorporating the preventative mechanisms creates injustice, for it breaks the Circle of Justice and leaves individuals and the community without the necessary cultural foundational structures to heal and prevent crime.

Source: Barbara Gra and Pat Lauderdale. (2007). "The Great Circle of Justice: North American Indigenous Justice and Contemporary Restoration Programs." Contemporary Justice Review 10:2 (June): 215–25. Reprinted with permission of the publisher (Taylor & Francis Group, http://www.informaworld.com).

Their point is that the restorative principles are but a part of a much larger social fabric that has other ways to contribute to the achievement of a Circle of Justice within the community. "The preventative mechanisms are found within the traditional teachings—for example, in ceremonies, songs, dances, stories, kinship relations, and healing and warrior societies" (218). Teachings within traditional societies promote the development of the "good mind" in each member by implanting "the concepts of love, unity, peace, equity, coexistence, cooperation, power, respect, generosity, and reciprocity" (218). By using these concepts, each member of the community is encouraged to live in accordance with these teachings and to retain "balance by respecting and protecting each other and the rest of the natural order" (217). "The foundational narratives of many American Indian nations contain teachings about how humans are to live with each other and the rest of the natural world. They also provide the blueprints for societal structures: the

*(continued)*

political and spiritual form of governance, kinship relations, and specific duties and responsibilities in maintaining justice within the community. One has a duty to self and to the community to prevent injustice.... The duties and responsibilities of each person in the society are given and reaffirmed every time the people come together for ceremonies and social activities" (219). "The Great Law of Peace [of the Haudenosaunee], then, is a system of checks and balances that depends not only on people not wanting to commit a transgression, but on people understanding and having the will to prevent others from breaching the peace" (220). From this perspective, the attempt to use the restorative aspect without also providing the work necessary to build the larger set of preventative peace-keeping practices is unlikely to be adequate to the task.

It is enticing to imagine that the use of a limited set of restorative justice principles could help to repair the damage created by anonymity, excessive individualism, a heightened form of self-interest, the erosion of cohesive communities, the competitiveness and materialism of modern society, and the great inequalities of power and wealth. This is the attraction: we can repair the damage between people who are estranged from each other without repairing the social fabric which made them indifferent strangers to each other in the first place. While this is a small contribution to building community cohesion, it should not be underrated. There is genuine value in creating justice, the foundation for apology and forgiveness, as well as the creation of peace and good will in the social circles that were disrupted by the harm done.

## Summary

- For most of human history, we lived in small groups. Because individuals lacked the resources to live independently, such societies were coercive in their enforcement of codes of conduct.

- In small-scale societies, disputes were primarily settled by the parties to the dispute or by their kinship groups. The individual was expected to show a considerable degree of self-restraint because the survival of the group depended upon the cooperation of all its members.

- While people in small-scale societies were relatively equal to one another, changes in methods of production led to new social formations in which some families and individuals gained greater access to material surplus. This resulted in the growth of social power, the stratification of society, and the emergence of rulers. This process eventually gave rise to the development of the state.

- The rise of the central authority of the state undermined local kinship-based methods of resolving disputes. The harm was seen to be done to the ruler, who displaced the real victim of harm.

- As the merchant class grew, social life became increasingly regulated by contracts that were regulated and enforced by a strong central state. The interests of the capitalist class became central to the modern state, and the rule of law became the dominant means of regulating all aspects of human affairs.

- In democratic political structures, some laws reflect a broadly based consensus that certain behaviours need to be discouraged; however, other laws are passed because of the influence of groups with the power to have their interests reflected in legislation.

- The ineffectiveness of the nation-state system to provide peace, security, good government, and protection from harm to large portions of humanity threatens to undermine the very legitimacy of the rule of law. A loss of legitimacy will be very corrosive of the willingness to conform, which is the foundation of the modern legal order.

- In recent years, we have seen a return to restorative justice practices that are similar to those used in small-scale societies.

## QUESTIONS FOR CRITICAL THINKING

1. Proponents of restorative justice are advocating that we move away from legalistic, punishment-oriented ways of dealing with social conflict. Do you think this will work in our contemporary society? Can you think of examples of restorative justice programs in your own community?

2. This chapter has discussed the role played by special interest groups in the passage and enforcement of particular laws. What are some of the laws that reflect the interests of some groups at the expense of others? What are some examples of laws that reflect the consensus of most members of society?

3. Assume you live in a small city. A local chemical company has been found to be improperly disposing of hazardous wastes by burying them underground. The wastes have leached into local wells and contaminated the water supply. Some say the company should be prosecuted and its operations shut down; however, the company is the largest employer in the community. Describe several ways in which the community might approach this problem. What sort of outcome is most likely?

4. One of the problems with dispute resolution systems based on intervention by the victims or their kinship groups is that such a system can lead to feuds or vendettas among groups that do not agree with the manner in which a conflict was resolved. How did small-scale societies avoid prolonging these disputes?

## NET WORK

You have learned in this chapter that one of the major trends in criminal justice is the return to methods of restorative justice. To earn more about methods of restorative justice, go to the Correctional Service of Canada website at **http://www.cscscc.gc.ca/text/pblct/satisfy/index_e.shtml**. This will give you access to a report written by the Church Council on Justice and Corrections. Using this report, answer the following questions:

1. What do the authors mean by "satisfying justice"? How can you use this concept to understand the dissatisfaction most Canadians seem to have with our current criminal justice system?

2. Describe four different types of restorative justice programs, and give an example of each.

## KEY TERMS

bourgeois class; pg. 45

collective solidarity; pg. 34

common law; pg. 45

diffuseness of roles; pg. 34

feudalism; pg. 44

free trade zone; pg. 55

ideal type; pg. 34

mode of production; pg. 33

paramount chieftainship; pg. 43

state; pg. 33

surplus; pg. 36

transnational corporation; pg. 51

tribalism; pg. 39

Tudor; pg. 58

## BIBLIOGRAPHY

Becker, Howard. (1963). "Moral Entrepreneurs." In Becker (ed.), *The Outsiders*. New York: Free Press.

Braithwaite, John, and S. Mugford. (1994). "Conditions of Successful Reintegration Ceremonies." *British Journal of Criminology* 34 (2):139–71.

Brodeur, Paul. (1985). "The Asbestos Industry on Trial." In *The New Yorker*, June 10, June 17, June 24, July 1.

Broswimmer, Franz. (2002). *Ecocide: A Short History of the Mass Extinction of Species*. London: Pluto Press.

Brown, Lester R. (2009). *Plan B 4.0: Mobilizing to Save Civilization*. New York: W.W. Norton and Company.

Brownmiller, Susan. (1975). *Against Our Will: Men, Women and Rape*. New York: Simon and Schuster.

Cavanagh, John, and Jerry Mander (eds.). (2004*). Alternatives to Economic Globalization: A Better World Is Possible* (2nd ed.). San Francisco: Berrett-Koehler Publishers.

Chambliss, William. (1969). "The Law of Vagrancy." In Chambliss (ed.), *Crime and the Legal Process* (pp. 51–63). New York: McGraw-Hill.

Clark, Lorenne, and Debra Lewis. (1977). *Rape: The Price of Coercive Sexuality*. Toronto: The Women's Press.

Colson, Elizabeth. (1974). *Tradition and Contract: The Problem of Order*. Chicago: Aldine Publishing.

Comack, Elizabeth. (1985). "The Origins of Canadian Drug Legislation: Labelling versus Class Analysis." In Thomas Fleming (ed.), *The New Criminologies in Canada: State, Crime and Control* (pp. 65–86). Toronto: Oxford University Press.

Dickson, Donald. (1968). "Bureaucracy and Morality: An Organizational Perspective on a Moral Crusade." *Social Problems* 16(2) (Fall):143–56.

Dowie, Mark. (1977). "Pinto Madness." *Mother Jones* 2(8) (September/October).

*Facts on File*. (1991). 51 (August 8):2646.

———. (1993). 53 (March 25):2718.

———. (1997). 57 (June 26):2951.

———. (2000). 60 (December 31):1017.

———. (2001). 61 (December 31):1031.

———. (2002). 62 (December 31):1012.

———. (2004). 64 (June 3):403.

———. (2005). 65 (January 20):36.

Friedman, Lawrence, and Jack Ladinsky. (1980). "Social Change and the Law of Industrial Accidents." In William Evan (ed.), *The Sociology of Law* (pp. 395–414). New York: Free Press.

Goff, Colin, and Charles Reasons. (1978). *Corporate Crime in Canada*. Scarborough: Prentice Hall.

Graham, James. (1976). "Amphetamine Politics on Capital Hill." In William Chambliss (ed.), *Whose Law, What Order?* (pp. 107–22). New York: Wiley.

Gray, Barbara, and Pat Lauderdale. (2007). "The Great Circle of Justice: North American Indigenous Justice and Contemporary Restoration Programs." *Contemporary Justice Review* 10(2) (June):215–25.

Grossman, Richard L., and Frank T. Adams. (1993). *Taking Care of Business: Citizenship and the Charter of Incorporation*. Available at http://www.ratical.org/corporations/TCoB.html

Gulliver, P. H. (1979). *Disputes and Negotiations: A Cross-Cultural Perspective*. New York: Academic Press.

Guth, DeLloyd J., and W. Wesley Pue (eds.). (2001). *Canada's Legal Inheritances*. Canadian Legal History Project, Faculty of Law, The University of Manitoba, Winnipeg.

Hagan, John, and Jeffrey Leon. (1977). "Rediscovering Delinquency: Social History, Political Ideology and the Sociology of Law." *American Sociological Review* 42 (August):587–98.

Hall, Jerome. (1952). *Theft, Law, and Society* (2nd ed.). Indianapolis: Bobbs-Merrill.

———. (1969a). "Theft, Law and Society: The Carrier's Case." In William Chambliss (ed.), *Crime and the Legal Process* (pp. 32–51). New York: McGraw-Hill.

———. (1969b). "Crime and the Commercial Revolution." In Donald Cressey and David Ward (eds.), *Delinquency, Crime and Social Process* (pp. 100–10). New York: Harper and Row.

Hoebel, E. Adamson. (1973). *The Law of Primitive Man*. New York: Atheneum Press.

Jeffery, Clarence Ray. (1969). "The Development of Crime in Early English Society." In William Chambliss (ed.), *Crime and the Legal Process* (pp. 12–32). New York: McGraw-Hill.

Johnstone, Gerry. (2002). *Restorative Justice: Ideas, Values, Debates*. Oregon: Willan Publishing.

Kennedy, Mark. (1976). "Beyond Incrimination: Some Neglected Facets of the Theory of Punishment." In William Chambliss (ed.), *Whose Law, What Order?* (pp. 34–65). New York: Wiley.

Kinnon, Dianne. (1981). *Report on Sexual Assault in Canada*. Report to the Canadian Advisory Council on the Status of Women.

Kirby T. (2010). "Canada Accused of Hypocrisy over Asbestos Exports." *Lancet* 376 (9757) (December 11):1973–74.

Lenski, Gerhard. (1966). *Power and Privilege: A Theory of Social Stratification*. New York: McGraw-Hill.

Marchak, Patricia. (1991). *The Integrated Circus: The New Right and the Restructuring of Global Markets.* Montreal: McGill-Queen's University Press.

Miliband, Ralph. (1969). *The State in Capitalist Society.* London: Quarter Books.

Newman, Katherine. (1983). *Law and Economic Organization: A Comparative Study of Pre-industrial Societies.* London: Cambridge University Press.

Platt, Anthony. (1969). *The Child Savers: The Invention of Delinquency.* Chicago: University of Chicago Press.

Reasons, Charles, Lois Ross, and Craig Paterson. (1981). *Assault on the Worker.* Toronto: Butterworths.

Ross, Rupert. (1989). "Leaving Our White Eyes Behind: The Sentencing of Native Accused." 3 *Canadian Native Law Reporter* 1 at 4.

———. (1996). Return to the Teachings: Exploring Aboriginal Justice. Toronto: Penguin.

Rossi, Peter, and Emily Waite. (1974). "The Seriousness of Crimes: Normative Structure and Individual Differences." *American Sociological Review* 39 (April):224–37.

Sellin, Thorsten, and Marvin Wolfgang. (1964). *The Measurement of Delinquency.* New York: Wiley.

Small, Shirley. (1978). "Canadian Narcotics Legislation, 1908–1923: A Conflict Model Interpretation." In W. Greenaway and S. Brickey (eds.), *Law and Social Control in Canada* (pp. 28–42). Scarborough: Prentice Hall.

Smandych, Russell. (1985). "Marxism and the Creation of Law: Re-examining the Origins of Canadian Anti-Combines Legislation 1890–1910." In Thomas Fleming (ed.), *The New Criminologies in Canada: State, Crime and Control* (pp. 87–99). Toronto: Oxford University Press.

Snider, Laureen. (1980). "Corporate Crime in Canada." In Robert Silverman and James Teevan (eds.), *Crime in Canadian Society* (2nd ed.) (pp. 348–68). Toronto: Butterworths.

———. (1994). "The Regulatory Dance: Understanding Processes in Corporate Crime." In Ronald Hinch (ed.), *Readings in Critical Criminology* (pp. 276–305). Scarborough: Prentice Hall.

———. (1999). "Relocating Law: Making Corporate Crime Disappear." In Elizabeth Comack (ed.), *Locating Law: Race, Class/Gender Connections* (pp. 183–207). Halifax: Fernwood Publishing.

———. (2000). "The Sociology of Corporate Crime: An Obituary." *Theoretical Criminology* 4(2):169–206.

Stone, Christopher. (1975). Where the Law Ends: Social Control of Corporate Behavior. New York: Harper and Row.

Thompson, Edward P. (1976). *Whigs and Hunters: The Origin of the Black Act.* New York: Pantheon Books.

Tigar, Michael, and Madeleine Levy. (1977). *Law and the Rise of Capitalism.* New York: Monthly Review Press.

UNICEF. (2005). *Progress for Children.* A Report Card on Immunization: Number 3, September.

Walters, Vivienne. (1983). "Occupational Health and Safety Legislation in Ontario: An Analysis of Its Origins and Content." *Canadian Review of Sociology and Anthropology* 20(4) (November):138–69.

Weitekamp, Elmar G.M. (2002). "Restorative Justice: Present Prospects and Future Directions." In Elmar G.M. Weitekamp and Hans-Jürgen Kerner (eds.), *Restorative Justice: Theoretical Foundations.* Oregon: William Publishing.

West, Gordon, and Laureen Snider. (1985). "A Critical Perspective on Law in the Canadian State: Delinquency and Corporate Crime." In Thomas Fleming (ed.), *The New Criminologies in Canada: State, Crime and Control.* Toronto: Oxford University Press.

# 3

# Criminal Law

**Simon N. Verdun-Jones**

SIMON FRASER UNIVERSITY

Criminology is concerned with crimes and the individuals who commit them. It is necessary for criminologists to acquire a basic understanding of the criminal law because it is this body of legal rules and principles that designates which types of behaviour should be prohibited and punished and whether those persons who are accused of committing crimes should be convicted and officially labelled as criminals.

## Learning Objectives

After reading this chapter, you should be able to

- Define a crime.
- Identify the sources of Canadian criminal law.
- Distinguish between regulatory offences and "true crimes."
- Analyze criminal offences in terms of the *actus reus* (physical) and *mens rea* (mental) elements.
- Understand the differences between subjective and objective *mens rea* requirements.
- Describe the different ways in which a person may become a party to a criminal offence.
- Identify the basic components of the inchoate crimes of counselling, attempt, and conspiracy.
- Describe the major defences that may be raised in response to a criminal charge: not criminally responsible on account of mental disorder, mistake of fact, mistake of law, intoxication, necessity, duress, provocation, and self-defence.

## What Is a Crime?

**crime**
Conduct that is prohibited by law and that is subject to a penal sanction (such as imprisonment or a fine).

For a lawyer, the definition of a **crime** is remarkably simple: namely, the coupling of a *prohibition* against certain conduct with a *penal sanction* (such as imprisonment or a fine). In Canada, all crimes are the products of a legislative process and are contained in statutes such as the *Criminal Code*. Some crimes may reflect an almost universal social consensus that certain conduct is wrong and should be punished (for example, murder and sexual assault). Other crimes may not be based on such a general consensus and a significant proportion of Canadians may not consider them to be inherently wrong and deserving of punishment (for example, assisting a terminally ill patient to commit suicide when he or she is in great pain). While legislators need to wrestle with the ongoing task of trying to bring the criminal law into line with emerging community notions of crime and justice, the police and the judiciary are required to enforce the existing criminal law, regardless of their own private views as to whether particular conduct should or should not be defined as a crime (see Box 3.1). Therefore, while it is important to be aware of the intensely political nature of the process that results in the enactment of legislation dealing with crime and punishment, such considerations fall outside the scope of a chapter dealing with the contents of the existing criminal law.

# FOCUS BOX 3.1

## CONFLICT OF VALUES: THE CASE OF EUTHANASIA

If a person is suffering from a terminal illness, is in great pain, and wishes to end his or her life, should a physician be able to grant that wish by, for example, administering a lethal injection? In Canada, the *Criminal Code* (section 14) clearly prohibits anyone, including a physician, from killing another human being—even if that person has given an unequivocal consent to the taking of his or her life. As a consequence, in Canada a so-called mercy killing constitutes murder under the *Criminal Code*. However, in both the Netherlands and Belgium legislation has been passed that permits physicians to perform euthanasia on their patients in certain, strictly defined circumstances. Does the existing criminal law in Canada reflect current values? What should the Parliament of Canada do if Canadians are profoundly divided on this issue?

In October 1993, Robert Latimer, a Saskatchewan farmer, killed his severely disabled daughter, Tracy. Although the 12-year-old Tracy was not capable of giving consent, the homicide was portrayed by many as a "mercy killing." Ultimately, Latimer was convicted of second-degree murder. Under the *Criminal Code* [section 745(c)], the minimum sentence that may be imposed for second-degree murder is life imprisonment with no possibility of parole for a period of 10 years. Some Canadians argued that this sentence should not apply to a father who had killed his daughter in order to spare her further pain and suffering. In fact, polls consistently indicated that most Canadians believed

that the sentence was excessively harsh. On the other hand, other Canadians asserted that if the courts were to impose a more lenient sentence on Latimer because his motive was that of compassion they would be implicitly diminishing the value of the lives of persons with disabilities. After all, Tracy was not consulted as to her fate: her father made the decision for himself that her life was not worth living. In 2001, the Supreme Court of Canada ruled that the mandatory sentence in the *Criminal Code* did not contravene the *Canadian Charter of Rights and Freedoms* and that Latimer was not entitled to receive a so-called constitutional exemption that would relieve him of the penalty of life imprisonment. However, the Court did point out that the government of Canada has the power to exercise the "Royal Prerogative of Mercy" [*Criminal Code*, section 748(1)] and grant Latimer an early release. Was Latimer's sentence too harsh? The prerogative of mercy was not exercised in Latimer's case. He was released on day parole in 2008 and granted full parole in 2010 (having served the 10-year non-eligibility period for consideration of parole).

For further reading, see *R. v. Latimer*, [2001] 1 S.C.R. 3, available online at http://www.canlii.org/en/ca/scc/doc/2001/2001scc1/2001scc1.html. See also H. Heavin. (2001). "Human Rights Issues in *R. v. Latimer* and their Significance for Disabled Canadians." *Saskatchewan Law Review* 64 (2): 613–30; and K. Mukhida. (2007). "Loving Your Child to Death: Considerations of the Care of Chronically Ill Children and Euthanasia in Emil Sher's Mourning Dove." *Paediatrics & Child Health* 12 (10): 859–65.

# What Is Criminal Law?

**criminal law**

A body of jurisprudence that includes the definition of various crimes, the specification of various penalties, a set of general principles concerning criminal responsibility, and a series of defences to a criminal charge.

The body of jurisprudence known as **criminal law** includes not only the definitions of the various crimes and the specification of the respective penalties but also a set of general principles concerning criminal responsibility and a series of defences to a criminal charge. The main focus of this chapter will be on the general principles underlying Canadian criminal law and the major defences that have been developed both by the Parliament of Canada and by judges in the course of deciding specific cases that have come before them.

# The Sources of Criminal Law

A basic question about criminal law is "Where does it come from?" There are two primary sources of Canadian criminal law: (i) legislation and (ii) judicial decisions that either interpret such legislation or state the "common law."

## Federal Legislation and Criminal Law

Since Canada is a federal state, legislation may be enacted both by the Parliament of Canada and by the legislatures of the various provinces and territories. However, under the terms of the Canadian Constitution, there is a distribution of specific legislative powers between the federal and provincial or territorial levels of government. Under the terms of the *Constitution Act, 1867*, the federal Parliament has the exclusive jurisdiction to enact "criminal law and the procedures relating to criminal matters." One might think that it is relatively simple to define the term *criminal law* for the purpose of interpreting the scope of the federal criminal law power under the *Constitution Act, 1867*. However, this task is not quite as straightforward as it may appear at first glance. It was noted above that, for most purposes, a crime can be defined in terms of two basic elements: (i) a *prohibition* against certain conduct and (ii) a *penalty* for violating that prohibition. However, when the courts are required to decide whether Parliament has enacted legislation that legitimately falls within the scope of its criminal law power, a third element must be added to the definition of a crime. More specifically, the Supreme Court of Canada has ruled that the prohibition and penalty must be directed against a "public evil" or some form of behaviour that is having an injurious effect on the Canadian public. If any of these three elements is missing, the legislation concerned may not be considered to fall within the legitimate scope of the federal criminal law power; indeed, it may be ruled invalid insofar as it intrudes into areas of legislative authority that have been specifically allocated to the provincial and territorial legislatures. Consider the problem of environmental pollution. In the case of *Hydro-Québec* (1997), the Supreme Court of Canada held that the Parliament of Canada could use its criminal law power to enact legislation that imposes penalties on those individuals who engage in serious acts of pollution. The particular legislation in question in this case was the *Canadian Environmental Protection Act*, R.S.C. 1985, c. 16. In the words of Justice La

Forest, "Pollution is an 'evil' that Parliament can legitimately seek to suppress." Therefore, the *Canadian Environmental Protection Act* was considered to constitute "criminal law" because the Parliament of Canada was unequivocally concerned with the need to safeguard public health from the devastating consequences of toxic pollution. If the Supreme Court had ruled that this statute was not a genuine exercise of the Parliament of Canada's criminal law power, then the Court would have ruled that the Act was invalid. Similarly, in *R. v. Malmo-Levine; R. v. Caine* (2003), the Supreme Court of Canada ruled that Parliament had the authority, by virtue of its criminal law power, to prohibit the simple possession of marijuana. Even though simple possession may be viewed as a "victimless crime," the criminal law power may nevertheless be used to protect the users of marijuana from self-inflicted harm. The "evil or injurious or undesirable effect" that Parliament sought to address is "the harm attributed to the non-medical use of marijuana." The Supreme Court, therefore, upheld the constitutional validity of the relevant provisions of the *Narcotic Control Act*, R.S.C. 1985, c. N-1.*

What important pieces of legislation has the Canadian Parliament enacted in the field of criminal law? Undoubtedly, the most significant federal statute dealing with both the *substantive criminal law* and the *procedural* law relating to criminal matters is the *Criminal Code*, R.S.C. 1985, c. C-46 (first enacted in 1892). "Substantive criminal law" refers to legislation that defines the nature of various criminal offences (such as murder, manslaughter, and theft) and specifies the various legal elements that must be present before a conviction can be entered against an accused person. The term also refers to the legislation that defines the nature and scope of such defences as provocation, duress, and self-defence.

The term **criminal procedure** refers to legislation that specifies the procedures to be followed in the prosecution of a criminal case and defines the nature and scope of the powers of criminal justice officials. For example, the procedural provisions of the *Criminal Code* classify offences into three categories: (i) *indictable offences*, (ii) offences punishable on *summary conviction*, and (iii) *"mixed" or "hybrid" offences* that may be tried either as indictable or as summary conviction offences. These provisions then specify the manner in which these different categories of offences may be tried within the system of criminal courts. For example, they spell out whether these offences may be tried by a judge sitting alone or by a judge and jury, and indicate whether they may be tried before a judge of the Superior Court or a judge of the Provincial (or Territorial) Court. Indictable offences carry the most serious penalties upon conviction of the accused. The procedural provisions of the *Criminal Code* are also concerned with defining the nature and scope of the powers of such officials as police officers. For example, these provisions stipulate the nature and scope of the powers of the police in relation to the arrest and detention of suspects. Likewise, the *Criminal Code* articulates the powers of judges in relation to the important task of sentencing convicted offenders.

**criminal procedure**
A body of legislation that specifies the procedures to be followed in the prosecution of a criminal case and defines the nature and scope of the powers of criminal justice officials.

---

*This Act was repealed in 1996. Possession of marijuana is now prohibited by section 4 of the *Controlled Drugs and Substances Act*, S.C. 1996, c. 19 (which came into force on May 14, 1997).

In addition to the *Criminal Code*, a number of other federal statutes unquestionably create "criminal law." These include the *Controlled Drugs and Substances Act*, S.C. 1996, c. 19, and the *Youth Criminal Justice Act*, S.C. 2002, c. 1.

## Federal and Provincial or Territorial Regulatory Legislation: Quasi-Criminal Law

Under the *Constitution Act, 1867*, the provincial and territorial legislatures have been granted exclusive jurisdiction to enact legislation in relation to such issues as health, education, highways, liquor control, and hunting and fishing. This legislation may be enforced through the imposition of "a fine, penalty or imprisonment." At first blush, it may seem that the use of punishments of these types would persuade the courts to treat such legislation as criminal law—an area of legislative authority that is reserved exclusively for the Parliament of Canada. However, such regulatory legislation does not constitute "real" criminal law for the purpose of the distribution of powers under the Constitution because such legislation lacks the necessary element of "public evil" that was discussed earlier. Indeed, regulatory legislation is concerned with the orderly regulation of activities that are inherently legitimate (such as driving a vehicle or operating a business). Criminal law is directed toward the control of behaviour that is considered to be inherently wrong (namely, **"true crimes"** such as theft, assault, sexual assault, and wilful damage to property). **Regulatory offences**, therefore, are quite distinct from the "true crimes" that arise under the *Criminal Code* or the *Controlled Drugs and Substances Act*, and they are, therefore, classified as quasi-criminal law ("quasi" means seeming, not real, or halfway).

Regulatory offences are generally far less serious in nature than "true crimes." Indeed, the maximum penalties that may be imposed for violation of regulatory offences are generally no more than a fine or a maximum term of imprisonment of six months or both. Under the *Criminal Code* or the *Controlled Drugs and Substances Act*, however, the penalties may range as high as a life term of imprisonment.

Regulatory offences are also to be found in a broad range of federal statutes that regulate activities that fall within the jurisdiction of the Parliament of Canada: for example, the *Competition Act*, R.S.C. 1985, C. c-34; the *Fisheries Act*, R.S.C. 1985, c. F-14; the *Food and Drugs Act*, R.S.C. 1985, F-27; the *Freezing Assets of Corrupt Foreign Officials Act*, S.C. 2011, c. 10; the *Species at Risk Act*, S.C. 2002, c. 29; and the *Tobacco Act*, S.C. 1996, c. 13. Taken together with the quasi-criminal offences created under provincial and territorial legislation, these federal regulatory offences contribute to a vast pool of quasi-criminal law that has become increasingly complex as modern society has developed. Even the average lawyer is acquainted with only a fraction of the hundreds of thousands of regulatory offences that currently exist under both federal and provincial or territorial legislation. However, ignorance of the law is no excuse for those who commit regulatory offences.

## Judge-Made Criminal Law

The second major source of criminal law in Canada is the large body of judicial decisions that either interpret criminal legislation or expound the

**"true crime"**

A "true crime" occurs when an individual engages in conduct that is not only prohibited but also constitutes a serious breach of community values; as such, it is perceived by Canadians as being inherently wrong and deserving of punishment. Only the Parliament of Canada, using its criminal law power under the *Constitution Act, 1867*, may enact a "true crime."

**regulatory offences**

Regulatory offences arise under legislation (either federal, provincial, or territorial) that regulates inherently legitimate activities connected with trade, commerce, and industry or with everyday living (driving, fishing, etc.). These offences are not considered to be serious in nature and usually carry only a relatively minor penalty upon conviction.

"**common law**"—a term that refers to that body of judge-made law that evolved in areas that were not covered by legislation. Parliament cannot possibly provide for every possibility or provide comprehensive definitions of every term used in the legislation that it enacts; therefore, there is always great scope for judicial interpretation of the *Criminal Code*. For example, in section 380 of the *Code*, Parliament has created the offence of fraud. According to section 380, fraud may be committed by "deceit, falsehood, or other fraudulent means." However, the term "other fraudulent means" was left undefined and it was left to the Supreme Court of Canada to provide a working definition in the case of *R. v. Olan, Hudson and Hartnett* (1978), namely, "all other means which can properly be stigmatized as dishonest."

As far as the common law is concerned it is important to recognize that, historically, much of the English criminal law, upon which the *Criminal Code* of 1892 was loosely based, was developed by judges who were required to deal with new situations and challenges that were not dealt with by the legislation of the day. In Canada, one common law offence still exists—contempt of court. However, with the exception of contempt of court, the *Criminal Code* (section 9) has, since 1954, made it clear that judges cannot create any new common law crimes. On the other hand, the judges have developed a number of common law defences that were not dealt with by legislation. For example, Canadian courts have developed a defence of necessity even though it is not mentioned in the *Criminal Code*; hence, necessity is known as a common law defence. Section 8(3) of the *Criminal Code* preserves any common law "justification," "excuse," or "defence" to a criminal charge "except in so far as they are altered by or are inconsistent with this act or any other act of the Parliament of Canada." This provision is particularly significant because it means that common law defences, such as necessity, may still be developed by Canadian judges.

**common law**

The body of judge-made law that has evolved in areas not covered by legislation.

# Impact of the *Canadian Charter of Rights and Freedoms* on Criminal Law

The enactment of the *Canadian Charter of Rights and Freedoms* as part of the *Constitution Act, 1982*, heralded a dramatic new era in the relationship between judges and the elected members of the Parliament of Canada and the legislative assemblies of the various provinces and territories. As an entrenched bill of rights, the *Charter* empowers judges to declare any piece of legislation to be invalid—and of no force or effect—if the latter infringes on an individual's *Charter* rights (such as the presumption of innocence [section 11(d)] or the right not to be deprived of the right to life, liberty, and security of the person except in accordance with the principles of fundamental justice [section 7]). Canadian judges have demonstrated a willingness to use this extraordinary power when they believe it is absolutely necessary to do so. For example, in *R. v. Morgentaler, Smolig and Scott* (1988), the Supreme Court of Canada declared the controversial abortion provisions of the *Criminal Code* (section 287) to be invalid because they unjustifiably infringed the right of Canadian women to "security of the person" (protected by section 7 of the *Charter*). However, the courts are bound

*Charter*

The *Canadian Charter of Rights and Freedoms,* enacted by the *Canada Act 1982 (UK)* c. 11 (see glossary for extended definition).

to take into account the provisions of section 1 of the *Charter*, which permit Parliament or the provincial or territorial legislatures to impose "such reasonable limits [on *Charter* rights] as can be demonstrably justified in a free and democratic society." This provision requires Canadian courts to engage in an elaborate balancing act in which they must decide whether the infringement of an individual's *Charter* rights can be justified in the name of some "higher good." For example, in *R. v. Sharpe* (2001), the Supreme Court of Canada ruled that certain aspects of the child pornography provisions of the *Criminal Code* (section 163.1) infringed the accused person's right to "freedom of thought, belief, opinion and expression"—a right that is guaranteed by section 2(b) of the *Charter*. However, the Court also ruled that the child pornography provisions constituted a "reasonable limitation" on the accused's section 2(b) right and were, therefore, justified under section 1 of the *Charter*.

## The Basic Elements of a Crime: *Actus Reus* and *Mens Rea*

The study of criminal law invariably begins with the statement that every criminal offence can be analyzed in terms of two major elements: namely, *actus reus* and *mens rea*. These terms are derived from the Latin maxim, *actus non facit reum nisi mens sit rea* (which, translated literally, means that an act does not render a person guilty unless his or her mind is also guilty). Based on this principle, it can be stated that an accused person may not be convicted of a criminal offence unless the prosecution can prove the following beyond a reasonable doubt:

(a) that a particular event or state of affairs was "caused" by the accused person's conduct (*actus reus*); and

(b) that this conduct was simultaneously accompanied by a certain state of mind (*mens rea*).

In essence, the concept of *mens rea* refers to the mental elements of an offence while the term *actus reus* refers to all the other elements that must be proved by the Crown. However, there is an important gloss that must be placed on this seemingly simple formulation: namely, that the *actus reus* of a criminal offence includes an element of voluntariness. As Justice McLachlin said, in delivering the judgment of the majority of the justices of the Supreme Court of Canada in the case of *Théroux* (1993),

> The term *mens rea*, properly understood, does not encompass all of the mental elements of crime. The *actus reus* has its own mental element; the act must be the voluntary act of the accused for the *actus reus* to exist.

### The *Actus Reus* Elements of a Crime

**actus reus**

All the elements contained in the definition of a criminal offence—other than the mental elements (*mens rea*).

In general, it is possible to divide the ***actus reus*** into three separate components:

1. conduct (a voluntary act or omission constituting the central feature of the crime),
2. the surrounding or "material" circumstances, and
3. the consequences of the voluntary conduct.

For example, in order to prove that an accused person is guilty of the offence of assault causing bodily harm (section 267 of the *Criminal Code*), the Crown must establish that the accused applied force to the body of the victim (conduct); that the force was applied without the consent of the victim (circumstances); and that the application of force caused bodily harm (consequences). Bodily harm is defined in section 2 of the *Criminal Code* as meaning "any hurt or injury to a person that interferes with the health or comfort of the person and is more than merely transient or trifling in nature." For example, a swollen face and bleeding nose have been considered to constitute "bodily harm" and Canadian courts have also ruled that the term even includes psychological harm.

There are some significant exceptions to the division of the *actus reus* into three elements. For example, perjury (section 131 of the *Criminal Code*) is an offence that does not require proof of any consequences. Provided the accused person knowingly makes a false statement with intent to mislead a court, he or she will be guilty of perjury even though not a single person actually believed the false statement. However, consequences do constitute a crucial element of the *actus reus* of most criminal offences. Consider, by way of illustration, the offences of dangerous operation of a motor vehicle causing death or dangerous operation of a motor vehicle causing bodily harm (section 249 of the *Criminal Code*); these carry maximum penalties of 14 and 10 years, respectively. In contrast, the "simple" offence of dangerous operation of a motor vehicle (where the Crown does not have to prove the consequences of death or bodily harm) carries a maximum penalty of only five years. Occasionally, the *actus reus* of an offence does not contain the requirement that the accused engage in conduct of any kind; instead, the Crown must prove that the accused was found in a particular "condition" or "state." For example, it is an offence [section 351(1) of the *Criminal Code*] to be in possession of housebreaking instruments without a lawful excuse for having them. It is not necessary for the prosecution to establish that the accused person actually used the housebreaking instruments; it is enough that the accused person was found in possession of the instruments concerned. The rationale for this type of offence is that it is often necessary to use the criminal law in a preventative manner; it is undoubtedly preferable to stop the break-in before it occurs and it is only "guilty" possession that is the target of section 351(1) of the *Criminal Code*.

An important question that must be addressed is whether a mere failure to act (an omission) can qualify as the conduct element of the *actus reus* of an offence. The answer is that a failure to act can constitute a crime only if the accused was under a pre-existing legal duty to act. A good illustration is the duty owed by a parent to a small child to provide the latter with the "necessaries of life"—for example, by feeding the child and providing him or her with necessary medical care (section 215 of the *Criminal Code*). Under Canadian criminal law, there is no duty to rescue a stranger who is in serious danger. However, there is a duty to rescue when the person in danger is a child or spouse of the accused person or is in some other relationship that imposes a duty to act (for example, a prisoner is owed such a duty by the officer in charge of the jail in which the prisoner is being held). It has been argued that the criminal law is seriously deficient insofar as it does not require every adult citizen to take active steps to rescue a person who is in danger provided, of course, that the rescue may be undertaken without an unreasonable degree of danger to the rescuer. However, it may be very difficult to enforce such a duty in practice. For example, suppose a radio message is broadcast that informs listeners that volunteers are needed to help rescue children in a collapsed school building. Should everyone who hears that message be legally required to forsake what they are doing and rush to the scene of the disaster?

A final point that needs to be made about the *actus reus* component of an offence concerns the requirement that the accused's conduct be voluntary. If a driver is repeatedly stung by a swarm of bees and crashes his or her vehicle, the accident would be considered the consequence of a series of reflex actions that were beyond the driver's control; clearly, they did not flow from the free exercise of his or her will. Similarly, if an accused person's consciousness is impaired to such an extent that he or she is unable to control his or her actions, it may be concluded that there was no *actus reus* of any criminal offence because the accused acted involuntarily; when this situation occurs, the accused may raise the defence of automatism. In fact, automatism is a rare—and somewhat exotic—defence and may be successfully raised only in a very limited number of situations. For example, if an individual is hit on the head and immediately thereafter enters a state of impaired consciousness and assaults another person, he or she may claim the benefit of the defence of automatism—provided it is established that the assault constituted an involuntary action. In practice, automatism is a difficult defence to claim successfully because, in the *Stone* case (1999), the Supreme Court of Canada ruled that the burden of proving the defence is placed on the accused person who raises it (normally, the Crown is required to prove every element of the *actus reus* and *mens rea* components of an offence). Stone had been charged with the murder of his wife, following a series of provocative statements that she had directed at him. The accused had stabbed his wife 47 times but claimed that, at the time, he was in a state of dissociation following the shock of the "psychological blow" that had been inflicted on him by his spouse's hurtful words; more specifically, he stated that a "whoosh" sensation had swept over him and that he was unaware of what he was doing. Ultimately, the jury concluded that the claim of automatism had not been proved by Stone. However, Stone was convicted of manslaughter rather than murder because the jury concluded that there had been provocation (within the meaning of section 232 of the *Criminal Code*). Stone's conviction of manslaughter was later affirmed by the Supreme Court of Canada, where Justice Bastarache stated that the plausibility of a claim of automatism in such cases is significantly reduced if the victim is alleged to be the "trigger" of the violence directed at him or her. A successful defence of automatism presupposes that accused persons are plunged into such a state of impaired consciousness that they are barely aware of what is happening around them. In Stone's case, the accused responded directly to what he perceived to be insults and the jury evidently believed that his actions were those of a man who knew where he was and what he was doing.

## The *Mens Rea* Elements of a Crime

Basically, *mens rea* refers to all the mental elements (other than voluntariness) that the Crown must prove (beyond a reasonable doubt) in order to obtain a

**mens rea**

The mental elements (other than voluntariness) contained in the definition of a criminal offence.

conviction of a criminal offence. *Mens rea* is rather like a chameleon insofar as it changes its nature from one offence to another. Obviously, the *mens rea* for murder is very different from that required for theft. Furthermore, *mens rea* is not one mental state but rather a combination of mental states; indeed, it is necessary to analyze the *mens rea* required in relation to each of the three elements of the *actus reus* of any particular crime—that is, conduct, circumstances, and consequences.

The requirement that the prosecution prove *mens rea* reflects basic values that Canadians hold in relation to civil liberties. In essence, the *mens rea* requirement ensures that only those defendants who are morally blameworthy are convicted of "true crimes" under the *Criminal Code*. As Justice McLachlin said in the Supreme Court of Canada's decision in *Théroux* (1993),

> *Mens rea* . . . refers to the guilty mind, the wrongful intention, of the accused. Its function in the criminal law is to prevent the conviction of the morally innocent—those who do not understand or intend the consequences of their acts.

## Subjective and Objective *Mens Rea*

There are two very distinct types of *mens rea* requirements in Canadian criminal law: (1) subjective and (2) objective.

**Subjective *mens rea*** is based on the notion that accused persons may not be convicted of a criminal offence unless (a) they *deliberately intended* to bring about the consequences prohibited by the law, (b) *subjectively realized* that their conduct might bring about such prohibited consequences but recklessly continued with that conduct in spite of their knowledge of the risks involved, or (c) were *wilfully blind* in that they deliberately closed their minds to the obvious criminality of their actions. As Justice McLachlin explained in the Supreme Court of Canada's decision in *Creighton* (1993),

> The requisite intention or knowledge may be inferred from the act and its circumstances. Even in the latter case, however, it is concerned with "what was actually going on in the mind of this particular accused at the time in question."

Subjective *mens rea*, therefore, constitutes a requirement that the accused *deliberately chose to do something wrong*.

**Objective *mens rea*** is predicated on the principle that accused persons should be convicted of certain offences, not because they intended to bring about the prohibited consequences or acted recklessly, but rather because *reasonable* people, in the same situation, would have appreciated that their conduct created a risk of causing harm and would have taken action to avoid doing so. Here the fault of the accused does not lie in deliberately choosing to do something wrong; instead, the culpability lies in the fact that the accused person had the capacity to live up to the standard of care expected of a reasonable person and failed to do so. As the Supreme Court of Canada stated in *Beatty* (2008): "objective *mens rea* is based on the premise that a reasonable person in the accused's position would have been aware of the risks arising from the conduct.  The fault lies in the absence of the requisite mental state of care."

**subjective *mens rea***
The *mens rea* elements of a criminal offence are considered to be subjective if they are based on a determination of "what actually went on in the accused person's mind." The forms of subjective *mens rea* are intention and knowledge; recklessness; and wilful blindness.

**objective *mens rea***
The *mens rea* elements of a criminal offence are considered to be objective if they are based on a determination of whether a reasonable person, in the same circumstances and with the same knowledge as the accused, would have appreciated the risk involved in the accused's conduct and would have taken steps to avoid the commission of the *actus reus* elements of the crime in question.

Who is the "reasonable person"? The answer to this question is simply that it is up to the judge or jury (if there is one) to decide what is reasonable in all the circumstances of the case and, no doubt, they call upon their own reservoir of life experience to determine what they think is reasonable. Nevertheless, this means that it is always difficult to predict whether a judge or jury will determine that a specific defendant in a criminal trial acted reasonably.

In the *Creighton* case (1993), Justice McLachlin emphasized that the "moral fault of the offence must be proportionate to its gravity and penalty"; in other words, the most serious crimes, carrying the most severe penalties, should generally be based on a subjective *mens rea* requirement. Significantly, in the case of *Martineau* (1990), the Supreme Court of Canada ruled that the crime of murder is so serious and carries such a high degree of stigma that criminal responsibility for this offence must be based on subjective *mens rea*; indeed, the Court stated that the *Charter* requires that the Crown prove either that the accused deliberately intended to kill or, at the very least, subjectively foresaw that his or her conduct was likely to cause death. However, in *Creighton* (1993), the Supreme Court held that responsibility for manslaughter could be based on an objective *mens rea* requirement because the degree of stigma and the penalties attached to it were considerably less severe than is the case for murder. In Creighton's case, the accused had injected a quantity of cocaine into the arm of the victim. In order to convict Creighton of manslaughter, the Crown first had to prove that he had intentionally committed an unlawful act that had resulted in death. The unlawful act was the offence of trafficking in narcotics (trafficking includes the act of administering a drug) and there was no doubt that the victim died as a direct consequence of the injection. The *mens rea* for so-called unlawful act manslaughter is objective in nature. Therefore, the second task confronting the Crown was to prove that any reasonable person would have foreseen the risk of non-trivial bodily harm as a consequence of committing the unlawful act. The Supreme Court of Canada had no doubt that Creighton was correctly convicted of manslaughter because any reasonable person who administered a dangerous drug intravenously would foresee the risk of some degree of bodily harm.

There are three forms of subjective *mens rea* that the Crown may be required to prove in a criminal prosecution: (1) intention and knowledge, (2) recklessness, and (3) wilful blindness.

Section 155(1) of the *Criminal Code* provides a typical example of the subjective *mens rea* requirement of intention and knowledge; indeed, it provides that an individual commits incest if, knowing that another person is "by blood relationship his or her parent, child, brother, sister, grandparent or grandchild," he or she intentionally has sexual intercourse with that person. Usually, the *Criminal Code* will require the Crown to prove a specific mental element in addition to intention and knowledge. Take, for example, the offence of first-degree murder. Section 231(2) of the *Code* states that this offence is committed when murder is both "planned and deliberate." In order to convict an accused person of murder, the Crown must establish that this person either intended to kill or intended to inflict bodily harm that he or she knew was likely to cause death and was reckless (did not care) whether death ensued or not [section 229(a)]. However, if the offender is to be convicted of first- as opposed to second-degree murder, then normally the Crown must also prove that the killing was planned and deliberate in the sense that the accused did not act impulsively and was following some pre-existing plan to kill someone. Intoxicated defendants who are found to have the necessary *mens rea* for murder will often be acquitted of first-degree murder because they acted on impulse or without thinking about what they were going to do ahead of time; these accused persons will instead be convicted of second-degree murder.

Recklessness is a form of subjective *mens rea* where the accused knows that his or her conduct could cause certain prohibited consequences but deliberately proceeds with that conduct because he or she does not care one way or the other. Take the case of arson. Section 434 of the *Criminal Code* states that a person who "intentionally or recklessly causes damage by fire or explosion to property that is not wholly owned by that person" is guilty of an indictable offence and may be sentenced to a maximum of 14 years in prison. If Nero throws a lighted cigarette onto a haystack, realizing that there is a good chance the haystack will catch fire, he will be convicted of arson even if he can demonstrate that he did not start the fire deliberately and that, in fact, he hoped very sincerely that there would not be any blaze as a consequence of his actions. Nero is guilty of arson because his recklessness constitutes one of the forms of *mens rea* that is necessary for conviction under the terms of section 434.

Wilful blindness is the final form of subjective *mens rea*. It exists where accused persons have every reason to make some kind of inquiry as to whether there are circumstances that would render their conduct criminal but deliberately choose to shut their eyes to the obvious because they wish to avoid being convicted of an offence. As the Supreme Court of Canada stated in *Briscoe* (2010): "wilful blindness imputes knowledge to an accused whose suspicion is aroused to the point where he or she sees the need for further inquiries, but deliberately chooses not to make those inquiries." The most common example of wilful blindness occurs in relation to the crime of being in possession of stolen property [section 354(1) of the *Criminal Code*]. Suppose that an accused person pays for goods at a relatively small fraction of their known value but deliberately refrains from asking whether they are stolen because he or she wants to deny actual knowledge when subsequently confronted by the police. Such a person would be considered to have been wilfully blind as to the criminality of his or her actions and would be treated as though there had been actual knowledge that the goods were stolen.

Objective *mens rea* has been applied to a significant number of offences under the *Criminal Code*. For example, the following offences have all been characterized by the courts as requiring proof only of objective, rather than subjective, *mens rea*: manslaughter, dangerous operation of a motor vehicle, assault causing bodily harm, and criminal negligence causing death or bodily harm. However, it is important to bear in mind that the courts have consistently stated that accused persons may not be convicted of "true crimes" under the *Criminal Code* merely because they were "careless" in the sense that their conduct fell below the standard of care expected of a reasonable person acting prudently in the same circumstances as the accused. As Justice McLachlin said in the *Creighton* case (1993), "The law does not lightly brand a person as criminal." Therefore, for crimes that are based on objective *mens rea*, the

Crown must prove that there was a *marked departure* from the standard of care expected of the reasonable person acting prudently. Furthermore, the Supreme Court of Canada has repeatedly stated that the courts should apply a "modified objective test" in such cases. This means that a judge or jury (if there is one) must ask what the accused person in the case before them actually knew about the circumstances surrounding their actions. The judge or jury must then decide whether the accused's behaviour constituted a marked departure from the standard of care expected of a reasonable person who faces the identical circumstances as the accused and who is armed with exactly the same knowledge of those circumstances. Suppose, for example, an accused person suffers an epileptic fit while driving a vehicle and he or she crosses over the centre of the road and causes a fatal collision with a car that is travelling in the opposite direction. On the face of it, straying over the centre line and causing a collision constitutes a marked departure from the standard of care expected of a reasonable person. However, if the accused did not know that he or she was likely to suffer from an epileptic fit, there would be no conviction on a charge of dangerous operation of a motor vehicle causing death [section 249(4) of the *Criminal Code*]. A reasonable driver, with no knowledge of the likelihood that he or she might suffer an epileptic fit, would have behaved in the same way as the accused. However, the situation would be very different if the accused person knew that he or she was suffering from epilepsy or subject to sudden fainting spells and, without first obtaining medical clearance, continued to drive a motor vehicle. Clearly, a reasonable person armed with this knowledge would never attempt to take a vehicle on the road; therefore, the accused's conduct would almost certainly be considered a marked departure from the standard of care expected of the reasonable person.

Although it may appear somewhat harsh to convict individuals of serious crimes on the basis of objective *mens rea*, it is clear that the courts have watered down the objective test of liability by requiring that the judge or jury take into account the subjective knowledge accused people have of the relevant circumstances surrounding their actions. Furthermore, if an accused person lacks the normal capacity of the reasonable person to appreciate that his or her conduct might create a risk of harm, that person may not be convicted of a crime, even if it is based on proof of objective *mens rea*. For example, suppose a 20-year-old man has a mental age of 10 and he hits a neighbour with a metal bar. Tragically, the neighbour dies from his injuries. In the case of an ordinary person who does not suffer from a severe disability, it would be relatively easy for the Crown to prove a charge of manslaughter. The *mens rea* requirements are objective in nature. The accused must be proved to have intentionally applied force to the victim and the Crown must then proceed to establish that a reasonable person would have foreseen the risk of non-trivial bodily harm. Any reasonable person would foresee the risk of fairly serious bodily harm if an attack is carried out with a metal bar; therefore, most accused persons would be routinely convicted of manslaughter in such circumstances. However, if the accused is so developmentally disabled that he or she cannot foresee that their actions may cause non-trivial bodily harm, then that individual may not be convicted of manslaughter. The essence of culpability in objective *mens rea* is the notion that the accused had the capacity to foresee—and avoid—the risk of physical harm but did not do so. If the accused lacks this basic capacity, to convict him or her of manslaughter would amount to punishing someone who lacks any blameworthiness. In *Creighton* (1993), the Supreme Court of Canada ruled that such an outcome would infringe the fundamental principles of justice that are enshrined in the *Charter* (section 7).

## *Mens Rea* and Regulatory Offences

Earlier in this chapter, a distinction was drawn between regulatory offences ("quasi-criminal law") and "true crimes." Where "true crimes" are concerned, the Crown usually has to prove the required *mens rea* of the offence beyond a reasonable doubt. However, most regulatory offences are considered to be offences of strict liability. This means that the Crown only has to prove the *actus reus* elements of the offence; the onus is then on the accused to prove, on the balance of probabilities, that he or she was not negligent (or that he or she "acted with due diligence"). The rationale for strict liability is that it would be extremely difficult to conduct effective prosecutions of regulatory offences if the Crown were required to prove that accused persons were negligent. Usually, it is the accused person who has the best knowledge of the steps that he or she has taken to comply with the regulations that apply to his or her field of manufacturing or business activities, and so on; therefore, it is not unfair to require the accused to present this evidence and prove that he or she acted with the due diligence expected of a reasonable person in the same circumstances. Furthermore, the penalties for regulatory offences are comparatively lenient, since they rarely include imprisonment as a realistic sentencing alternative. In any event, strict liability is infinitely preferable to a regime of absolute liability, in which the accused is not permitted to claim a lack of *mens rea* as a defence. Prior to the decision of the Supreme Court of Canada in the case of *Sault Ste. Marie (City of)* in 1978, the majority of regulatory offences imposed absolute liability and accused persons were prevented from asserting that their actions were not blameworthy. However, since the *Sault Ste. Marie* case, by far the greatest proportion of regulatory offences have been considered to impose a regime of strict liability, leaving the accused with the opportunity to prove that he or she has done all that reasonably could be expected to be done in order to comply with the relevant regulations that apply to his or her business, occupation, industry, and so on.

In the *Wholesale Travel Group Inc.* case (1991), the accused had been charged with the regulatory offence of false or misleading advertising, under the federal *Competition Act*, R.S.C. 1970, c. C–23. The Act clearly imposed strict liability insofar as it permitted the accused to raise a defence of having acted "with due diligence." Essentially, the defence would be available where the accused proved that the "act or omission giving rise to the offence" was the "result of error" and that he or she "took reasonable precautions and exercised due diligence to prevent the occurrence of such error." It was contended before the Supreme Court of Canada that, because strict liability requires accused persons to prove their innocence, it infringed the presumption of innocence enshrined in section 11(d) of the *Charter*, and was, therefore, invalid. However, the Supreme Court of Canada ultimately held that strict liability was not invalid under the provisions of the Charter. The *Wholesale Travel Group Inc.*

case is, therefore, a decision of great importance since it has affirmed the legitimacy of the basic principles of liability that are at the heart of the vast network of regulatory legislation that governs the everyday lives of all Canadians.

## Becoming a Party to a Criminal Offence

Individuals can be convicted of criminal offences even if they are not the persons who actually commit them. For example, section 21(1) of the *Criminal Code* provides that anyone is a party to a criminal offence who (i) actually commits it, (ii) aids another person to commit it, or (iii) abets (encourages) any person to commit it. In a homicide case the person who actually commits the offence would be the individual who, for example, actually stabs a victim to death. However, the person who intentionally provides assistance and/or encouragement is liable to be convicted of murder on the same basis as the actual killer. Section 21(1), therefore, provides the courts and, in particular, prosecutors, with a significant degree of flexibility. Take, for example, the notorious case of *Pickton* (2010). William Pickton was involved in one of the most horrific series of murders in any country in modern times. In this case, although the evidence appeared to indicate that Pickton committed the murders himself, the defence suggested that others may have been involved in the killings. The Supreme Court of Canada held that section 21(1) places the person who aids and or abets a murder on exactly the same footing as a person who actually commits it. Therefore, it does not matter whether members of the jury believed that Pickton actually committed the murders himself or whether he aided and/or abetted others to do so: in either case, he should be convicted of murder. Section 22 of the *Criminal Code* provides a similar degree of flexibility to the courts insofar as it provides that a person who counsels ("procures," "solicits," or "incites") another to commit a crime becomes a **party to that crime** even if "the offence was committed in a way different from that which was counselled" (section 22 of the *Criminal Code*).

An individual may also become a party to a criminal offence that has been committed by other people when he or she had previously formed a common intention with them to commit a crime. Section 21(2) of the *Criminal Code* deals with the situation in which two or more persons have agreed to commit a crime and to assist one another in carrying out this "common purpose." Each of these individuals is considered a party to any offence committed by the other person(s) who entered the original agreement provided (i) that this other offence was committed in order to carry out the "common purpose" and (ii) that these individuals either knew or ought to have known that the commission of this other offence "would be a probable consequence of carrying out the common purpose." Suppose that Arthur, Benedict, and Cassio agree to commit a robbery and to help one another in carrying out this "common intention." Cassio—without consulting his colleagues in crime—kills one of the robbery victims. In these circumstances, Arthur and Benedict would be convicted of manslaughter if they either knew or ought to have known that inflicting nontrivial bodily harm on the intended victim(s) would be a probable consequence

**party to a crime**
The *Criminal Code* specifies that one is a party to—and liable to conviction of—a criminal offence if one actually commits it, aids and/or abets it, becomes a party to it by virtue of having formed a common intention with others to commit a crime, or counsels the commission of an offence that is actually committed by another person.

of implementing their common intention to commit robbery. Since robbery necessarily involves an element of violence or threatened violence, any reasonable person would foresee the probability that someone may be seriously hurt; therefore, Arthur and Benedict would almost certainly be found guilty of manslaughter. The use of the phrase "or ought to have known" indicates that the *mens rea* elements are objective in nature and this means that the scope of potential liability under section 21(2) is remarkably broad. The only exception to this form of objective liability arises where the offence of murder is concerned. Since the Supreme Court of Canada has ruled [in *Martineau* (1990)] that an accused person may be convicted of murder only where there was an actual intention to kill or subjective foresight of the likelihood of death, Arthur and Benedict would be convicted of murder only if they subjectively realized that death was a probable consequence of carrying out their common intention to commit robbery.

One question that immediately springs to mind when discussing section 21(2) is whether an individual who agreed with others to commit a crime and to provide the necessary assistance to achieve his goal should be entitled to change his or her mind and withdraw from the common intention. The answer is that an individual may withdraw from the common intention, but may do so effectively only when he or she gives unequivocal notice to the other party or parties of his or her wish to abandon the criminal enterprise. Once effective notice has been given, the individual is no longer liable for any subsequent crimes committed by the other party or parties in pursuit of the common intention.

# The Use of Criminal Law as a Preventative Tool: Inchoate Offences

Any system of criminal law will permit the police to intervene and arrest those who, in some way, demonstrate that they are about to embark upon the commission of a serious crime. If members of a gang of professional kidnappers agree to abduct a particular victim and to hold him or her to ransom, the police do not have to wait until the abduction is actually carried out before they intervene. Even though the kidnapping may exist only in the intentions of the members of the gang, it is undoubtedly legitimate for the state to punish them for having participated in a conspiracy to commit kidnapping. Conspiracy is an **inchoate crime** (literally, a crime "in embryo"); once their agreement to commit a crime has been reached, the accused may be convicted of the crime of conspiracy even though the offence that they originally planned to commit is never brought to fruition. Other inchoate crimes are criminal attempt and counselling an offence that is not committed.

Inchoate crimes raise serious questions about the civil liberties of those who are charged with having committed them. In general, it is accepted that the criminal law should not punish people simply for entertaining evil thoughts. However, society does have the right to prevent individuals from translating their evil thoughts into criminal acts. The problem lies in defining the point at which the state is justified in laying a charge against someone who has not yet committed

**inchoate crime**

A criminal offence that is committed when the accused person seeks to bring about the commission of a particular crime but is not successful in doing so. The three inchoate offences in the *Criminal Code* are attempt, conspiracy, and counselling.

the crime that he or she has in mind. Basically, accused persons must take some form of action that manifests their intention to commit a crime; in counselling, the accused must encourage another person to commit a crime; in attempt, the accused must take a substantial step toward completion of a crime; and, in conspiracy, the accused must enter into an agreement to commit a crime.

## Counselling an Offence That Is Not Committed

**counselling**

Procuring, soliciting, or inciting another person to commit a crime.

According to section 22 of the *Criminal Code*, it is a crime to **counsel** another person to commit an offence that is not ultimately brought to fruition. Since the main focus of the offence is on the accused person's intentions, it does not matter that no one is actually influenced by the accused person's efforts to procure, solicit, or incite someone to commit a crime. Furthermore, once their counselling action is completed, accused persons cannot escape criminal conviction merely because they change their minds and renounce their criminal intent. Box 3.2 illustrates how technological change can affect the interpretation and application of the criminal law.

# Criminology and the Media   Box 3.2

## COUNSELLING CRIME OVER THE INTERNET

Canadian courts are constantly faced with the need to adapt the criminal law to deal with the many opportunities that rapidly developing communication technologies create for novel methods of committing crimes. *R. v. Hamilton* (2005) furnishes a noteworthy example of a case in which the Supreme Court of Canada very cautiously adapted the existing principles of criminal law to deal with a situation in which it was alleged that the Internet was used to communicate information that was likely to incite other individuals to commit criminal offences.

Hamilton had used the Internet to sell computer files and documents to a number of individuals. These files contained detailed instructions for bomb making, burglary, and a program that generated credit card numbers that might be used for fraudulent purposes. Hamilton was charged with counselling the commission of four offences that were not in fact committed; namely, making explosive substances with intent, doing anything with intent to cause an explosion, break and enter with intent, and fraud. At his trial, Hamilton readily admitted that he had read a computer-generated list of the files concerned but denied that he had actually read the

contents of those files. Although he had generated some credit card numbers, he had never used them and there had been no complaints from the bank concerning their misuse.

At his trial, the Judge acquitted Hamilton of all the charges against him because, in her view, Hamilton never intended that the persons to whom he sent the computer files should actually commit the offences described in them. The Crown took the case to the Supreme Court of Canada, which articulated the *mens rea* that must be proved before an accused person may be convicted of counselling an offence. According to Justice Fish,

the *mens rea* consists in nothing less than an accompanying *intent* or *conscious disregard* of the substantial and unjustified risk inherent in the counselling: that is, it must be shown that the accused either intended that the offence counselled be committed, or knowingly counselled the commission of the offence while aware of the unjustified risk the offence counselled was in fact likely to be committed as a result of the accused's conduct. [at para. 29] (Emphasis in original)

*(continued)*

Prior to the *Hamilton* case, the courts had always applied the principle that, in order to obtain a conviction for counselling, the Crown must prove that the accused person actually intended that the offence be committed. However, the Supreme Court ruled in *Hamilton* that an accused person may also be convicted if he or she was *extremely reckless* as to the likelihood that the offence would be committed. Nevertheless, even with this expanded definition of the necessary *mens rea*, the Supreme Court affirmed Hamilton's acquittal on all the counselling charges except the charge of counselling fraud. The Supreme Court ordered a new trial on the charge of counselling fraud because it took the view that the trial judge should have found that Hamilton had the necessary *mens rea* for this offence. The Supreme Court noted that Hamilton had sent an e-mail "teaser" to various individuals in which he advertised software that could generate "valid working credit card numbers." Justice Fish noted that Hamilton "sought to make "a quick buck" by encouraging the intended recipients of his Internet solicitation to purchase a device that generated credit card numbers easily put to fraudulent use." Furthermore, the Supreme Court emphasized that Hamilton knew very well that "the use of false credit card numbers is illegal." Therefore, even if Hamilton had not actually wanted the purchasers of the files to commit the offences described in them, he was at the very least extremely reckless as to the risk that the files were likely to incite the purchasers to commit the offence of fraud.

Do you agree with the Supreme Court of Canada's decision to expand the scope of the *mens rea* for counselling an offence to include extreme recklessness? Should this decision have been left to Parliament or was it appropriate for the Supreme Court to modify the existing law to meet the challenge posed by the use of the Internet to communicate information that is likely to incite individuals to commit potentially serious crimes? Do you think Parliament should amend the *Criminal Code* to make it easier to obtain convictions in such cases? For example, should individuals such as Hamilton be made criminally liable for the *negligent* transfer of files that turn out to contain information as to how to commit offences even though they may not have actually read the files in question?

## Criminal Attempt

The offence of **criminal attempt** is focused on an accused person's intention to commit a crime that is never realized. Section 24(1) of the *Criminal Code* provides that "everyone who, having an intent to commit a crime, does or omits to do anything for the purpose of carrying out his intention is guilty of an attempt to commit the offence whether or not it was possible under the circumstances to commit the offence." Clearly, the *mens rea* of criminal attempt is nothing short of an actual intent to commit an offence. The *actus reus* of attempt is any step taken by the accused toward the completion of the offence, provided that this step goes beyond "mere preparation" and is not considered to be "too remote" from the completed offence. For example, buying a train ticket with a view to travelling to another city in order to rob a bank would be considered "mere preparation" and "too remote" from the completed robbery to justify convicting the accused of a criminal attempt. However, if the accused person actually reaches the front doors of the bank before being arrested by the police, it is clear that the *actus reus* of the offence

**criminal attempt**

A criminal attempt occurs when an individual does—or omits to do—anything for the purpose of carrying out a previously formed intention to commit a crime. The conduct in question must constitute a substantial step toward the completion of the crime that is intended.

of attempted robbery has been established. Unfortunately, it is often very difficult to predict exactly where the court will draw the line between mere preparation and an act that warrants conviction for a criminal attempt. It should also be emphasized that a criminal attempt may be committed even though it would be impossible for the accused to commit the complete offence that he or she has in mind. For example, if someone tries to steal a motor vehicle that has been totally disabled by its owner, this person would be guilty of attempted theft even though it would have been impossible for that person to take the vehicle from the spot where it had been parked. Similarly, if an accused person mistakenly shoots a wax dummy, believing it is an enemy, that person will be guilty of attempted murder. What is important to recognize is that the accused person seriously intended to commit murder and that there is a very real likelihood that, having failed on this particular occasion, the accused will try again and, perhaps, be more successful on that subsequent occasion.

## Conspiracy

**conspiracy**

An agreement by two or more persons to commit a criminal offence.

The crime of **conspiracy** is established when two or more individuals form a common intention to commit a crime. In addition, the Crown must prove that each individual who is charged with conspiracy actually intended to put the common design into effect. The *actus reus* of conspiracy is the agreement to engage in criminal conduct, while the *mens rea* component consists of the intent not only to enter into this agreement but also to implement it. Suppose two individuals apparently agree to kidnap a third party. However, it later turns out that one of these individuals was actually an undercover police officer who never had any intention to act on this supposed agreement. In this case, neither of the individuals may be convicted of conspiracy. The police officer lacks the necessary *mens rea* for conspiracy and the other individual cannot be convicted of this offence because the Crown must prove that there are at least two persons who seriously intended to implement the plan to commit murder. On the other hand, if there are two or more individuals who agree to commit murder and who fully intend to carry out their homicidal plans, they would be convicted of conspiracy even if an undercover officer is also part of this group. As long as there is a minimum number of two individuals who intend to carry out an agreement to commit a crime, there is a conspiracy. Conspiracy is a crime that provides the Crown with a number of distinct advantages. For example, certain types of evidence may be accepted at the joint trial of a group of alleged co-conspirators that would never be admitted against specific members of that group if they were tried separately. In effect, there is always the danger of "guilt by association" in conspiracy trials.

# Defences to a Criminal Charge

Conviction of a "true crime" should not occur unless the accused person is considered blameworthy. Merely because individuals engage in conduct that, from an objective point of view, is either actually or potentially harmful does not mean that they should be punished under the provisions of the criminal law. Indeed, the requirement of *mens rea* ensures that the Crown must first prove a culpable mental state or the prosecution will fail. However, in addition to the *mens rea* requirement, there are a number of distinct defences that may be raised by an accused person in a criminal trial. When analyzed carefully, some of these defences, such as mistake of fact, basically amount to a denial that the Crown has proved the necessary *mens rea*, but there are other defences, such as duress, that may be raised successfully even though the accused possessed the necessary *mens rea* for the offence that has been charged. Essentially, the patchwork of defences has evolved as a means of ensuring that those individuals who have a justification or excuse for their conduct are either acquitted of criminal charges or treated more leniently (for example, by conviction of a less serious offence).

## Mental Disorder as a Defence to a Criminal Charge

In the Supreme Court of Canada's decision in the case of *Winko* (1999), Justice McLachlin said:

> In every society, there are those who commit criminal acts because of mental illness. The criminal law must find a way to deal with these people fairly, while protecting the public against further harms. The task is not an easy one.

In Canada, this difficult task is undertaken through the application by the courts of the special defence of **not criminally responsible on account of mental disorder (NCRMD)**. The current test that must be used in deciding whether an accused should be found NCRMD is articulated in section 16(1) of the *Criminal Code:*

> No person is criminally responsible for an act committed or an omission made while suffering from a mental disorder that renders the person incapable of appreciating the nature and quality of the act or omission or of knowing that it was wrong.

The first requirement of the NCRMD defence is that the accused was suffering from a "mental disorder" at the time of the alleged offence(s). In fact, the Supreme Court of Canada has adopted an extremely broad definition of mental disorder but it is only those individuals who are suffering from very serious forms of mental disorder (such as schizophrenia) who will meet the other criteria specified in section 16(1), namely, that the accused has been rendered incapable either of appreciating the physical nature and quality of the act or omission in question or of knowing that the act or omission is considered morally wrong by the everyday standards of the ordinary Canadian. These criteria ensure that only the most severely mentally disordered individuals can raise the defence successfully. Most mentally disordered people understand the physical nature of their conduct (for example, most would realize that stabbing someone in the heart will cause death). Similarly, the majority of mentally disordered persons are capable of knowing that their conduct would be "morally condemned by reasonable members of society" [as Justice Arbour of the Supreme Court of Canada put it in the *Molodowic* case (2000)]. Significantly,

**NCRMD**

The special verdict of "not criminally responsible on account of mental disorder." In order to be found NCRMD, it must be proved on the balance of probabilities that, because of mental disorder, the accused lacked the capacity to appreciate the nature and quality of the act or omission in question or of knowing that it would be considered morally wrong by the average Canadian.

section 16(1) does not extend the benefit of the NCRMD defence to mentally disordered persons who claim that—as a consequence of mental disorder—they succumbed to an irresistible impulse to commit a crime; provided such individuals were capable of understanding what they were doing and that it was wrong, they are not considered to be NCRMD in Canadian criminal law.

The very narrow scope of the NCRMD defence ensures that relatively few accused persons may raise it successfully at their trials. In addition, it is significant that section 16 places the burden of proving the NCRMD defence on the shoulders of the accused person if he or she raises it at trial; in this situation, the accused person has to prove the defence on the balance of probabilities. Although this provision infringes the presumption of innocence, enshrined in section 11(d) of the Charter, the Supreme Court of Canada ruled, in the *Chaulk* case (1990), that this infringement of the accused person's right was justified as a reasonable limitation under section 1. The Court took the view that it would be impractical to require the Crown to prove beyond a reasonable doubt that the accused was not mentally disordered—particularly, in light of the fact that an accused person may refuse to cooperate with a psychiatrist nominated by the Crown to report to the court on the accused's mental condition.

Accused persons who are found NCRMD are not acquitted in the technical sense of that word. Indeed, section 672.1 of the *Criminal Code* states that a verdict of NCRMD constitutes a finding that "the accused committed the act or omission that formed the basis of the offence with which the accused is charged but is not criminally responsible on account of mental disorder." NCR accused may be granted (1) an absolute discharge, (2) a conditional discharge, or (3) an order holding them in custody in a psychiatric facility. Section 672.54(a) of the *Criminal Code* provides that, unless a court or review board determines that an NCR accused person constitutes a "significant threat to the safety of the public," then it *must* order an absolute discharge. In *Winko* (1999), the Supreme Court of Canada ruled that the threshold for justifying the imposition of restrictions on the liberty of a person who has been found NCRMD is very high:

> A "significant threat to the safety of the public" means a real risk of physical or psychological harm to members of the public that is serious in the sense of going beyond the merely trivial or annoying. The conduct giving rise to the harm must be criminal in nature.

In recent years, two cases have drawn attention to the treatment of NCR accused persons. In 2008, Vince Li brutally killed a young man on a Greyhound bus in Manitoba (see Chapter 10). Li was found NCRMD and sent to the Selkirk Mental Health Centre. Shortly after he arrived at the Centre the Criminal Code Review Board authorized escorted walks outside his secure living unit. Many Manitobans were upset that Li was going to be allowed out and the Manitoba government responded by upgrading security measures at the Centre and by requiring Li to be escorted by two trained special constables and a Centre staff member. Also, in 2008, Allen Schoenborn killed his three young children and was found NCRMD. In 2011, the B.C. Review Board approved his request for escorted community leaves. However, after widespread community protests Schoenborn withdrew his leave request. These cases show some of the difficulties people have understanding that decisions about the release of NCR accused persons cannot be based on punitive considerations but rather on a determination that they have recovered from their mental disorder and no longer pose a significant threat to the safety of the community.

## General Defences to a Criminal Charge

**Mistake of fact** may constitute a defence to a criminal charge if it causes the accused to erroneously believe that the circumstances facing him or her did not render his or her actions criminal. For example, if a woman participates in a marriage ceremony with a man erroneously believing that her first husband is dead, she would not be guilty of the crime of bigamy. The central element of the *actus reus* of bigamy is that one of the parties to a marriage ceremony is already married. If the accused honestly believed that she was a widow, then—in the circumstances as she perceived them to be—she was not committing a prohibited act because she was no longer married to her first spouse. When the accused operates under a mistake of fact, he or she is really stating that the Crown has failed to prove the necessary *mens rea* of the offence.

One of the most controversial uses of the defence of mistake of fact used to occur when an accused person who was charged with sexual assault claimed that he honestly believed in the complainant's consent, even though he was mistaken. However, section 273.2(b) of the *Criminal Code* (enacted in 1992) states that mistaken belief in consent will not be a valid defence to a charge of sexual assault unless the accused took "reasonable steps, in the circumstances known to the accused at the time, to ascertain that the complainant was consenting." By requiring the accused person to act reasonably, this amendment to the *Code* has considerably reduced the opportunities for abuse of the defence of honest belief in consent. For example, in *Crangle* (2010) the accused had initiated sexual intercourse with his twin brother's sleeping girlfriend. The victim initially thought that the accused was her boyfriend but, as soon as she realized his true identity, she strongly objected to his actions. The accused claimed that he had an honest—albeit mistaken—belief that the victim had consented. The trial judge rejected this defence because Crangle had done nothing to make his identity perfectly clear to the victim; undoubtedly, he had failed to take reasonable steps to ascertain whether there was consent. Box 3.3 illustrates that Parliament has enacted other provisions which are designed to encourage the victims of sexual offences to take their cases to the criminal courts.

**mistake of fact**

Mistake of fact may be a defence where the accused person acts under the influence of an honest mistake in relation to any of the elements of the *actus reus* of the offence charged.

# Criminology and the Media  Box 3.3

## PUBLICATION BANS AS A MEANS TO ENCOURAGE THE REPORTING OF SEXUAL OFFENCES

In the past, one of the main deterrents to the reporting of sexual offences was that victims feared that a court trial would lead to their names being published in the media. Despite being the innocent victims of a serious crime, they might well be profoundly concerned that they would suffer humiliation and embarrassment if details of the crime were to be published. Therefore, one of the ways in which victims may be encouraged to report sexual offences is to guarantee

*(continued)*

them anonymity by imposing a ban on publication of any information that might cause them to be identified. However, some might argue that imposing a publication ban infringes on the freedom of the press, which is guaranteed by section 2(b) of the *Canadian Charter of Rights and Freedoms* and considered a cornerstone of democratic traditions.

Section 486.4 of the *Criminal Code* provides that when an accused person is charged with a sexual offence, a human trafficking offence, and certain offences against public morals or disorderly conduct, the trial judge "may make an order directing that any information that could identify the complainant or a witness shall not be published in any document or broadcast or transmitted in any way." This order may be made at the judge's own initiative or in response to an application by one of the parties involved in the case. The *Criminal Code* states that, "at the first reasonable opportunity," the judge must inform any witness under the age of 18 and the complainant of their right to apply for a publication ban. If the complainant, the prosecutor (Crown Counsel), or the witness makes such an application, the trial judge has no discretion but to issue the publication ban—in effect, the party who applies has an absolute right to the ban.

Does the "automatic" imposition of such a publication ban violate the freedom of the press? The Supreme Court of Canada did indeed find that a publication ban infringes the freedom of the press contrary to section 2(b) of the *Charter* but ruled that it was justified under section 1 as a reasonable limitation in a free and democratic society (*Canadian Newspapers Co. v. Canada (Attorney General)*, 1988). The Court held that there was no dispute that "freedom of the press is indeed an important and essential attribute of a free and democratic society, and measures which prohibit the media from publishing information deemed of interest obviously restrict that freedom." However, the Court stated that publication bans in relation to sexual offences were justified because "encouraging victims to come forward and complain facilitates the prosecution and conviction of those guilty of sexual offences." The Court concluded that the overall objective of the publication ban is to "favour the suppression of crime and to improve the administration of justice."

Once a publication ban has been imposed with respect to a sexual or similar offence, the judge may only revoke it if the person who applied for the ban asks the judge to terminate it. The judge has no independent authority to revoke it, even if the accused person is ultimately acquitted. In *R. v. Adams (1995)*, the Supreme Court of Canada held that the fact a publication ban is mandatory encourages the reporting of sexual offences. If this objective is to be achieved successfully, then the victims must be certain that their names will not be published. If a publication ban could be revoked, it would "fail to provide the certainty that is necessary to encourage victims to come forward." Indeed, if the trial judge were to be granted the power to set aside a publication ban, a victim would "never be certain that her anonymity would be protected" and the ban would "serve as little more than a temporary guarantee of anonymity." Once a ban has been imposed, the witness or victim may not talk to the press about the case or communicate with the media in any manner that might identify her or him. Should he or she wish to do so, an application must be made to the Court to lift the ban.

To what extent does the public have a right to know what happens in criminal cases involving charges of sexual or similar offences? How important is freedom of the press when weighed against the interests of victims of crime? Finally, can publication bans be effective in the age of social media (including blogs, *Facebook*, and *Twitter*)?

For further reading, see Department of Justice Canada (2011). Publication Ban. Online at http://www.justice.gc.ca/eng/pi/pcvi-cpcv/ban-inter.pdf.

While honest mistake of fact constitutes a valid defence to a criminal charge, a mistake concerning the nature or scope of the criminal law does not absolve an accused person of criminal liability. Indeed, section 19 of the *Criminal Code* makes it very clear that ignorance of the law is no excuse. This is a harsh rule but an inevitable one since it would be impossible for the Crown to prove actual knowledge of the relevant legal principles. There are some exceptions to this rule. One of the more important exceptions arises when an official who is charged with the administration of certain types of regulatory legislation gives erroneous legal advice. If the accused person reasonably relies on this advice, he or she may take advantage of the defence of "officially induced error." For example, if a factory inspector tells a manufacturer that it is acceptable to modify a certain safety device, it would clearly be unfair to convict that manufacturer of a violation of the relevant occupational safety legislation. If the manufacturer reasonably relied on the advice of the factory inspector and committed what a court later concludes is a regulatory offence, then the defence of officially induced error will come to the rescue of the manufacturer.

**Intoxication** is a complex and highly problematic defence. A high proportion of violent crimes are committed by individuals who have abused alcohol and/or other drugs, and the great majority of the inmates in Canada's prisons have been diagnosed as having suffered from a substance abuse disorder. If the scope of a defence of intoxication were drawn too broadly, many violent offenders would escape criminal liability even though they were considered to have ingested alcohol and/or other drugs voluntarily. One of the main effects of alcohol (and some other drugs) is to cause disinhibition—a condition in which the accused may be rendered less able to control his or her conduct. However, the courts have consistently ruled that intoxication may not be raised as a valid defence by accused persons who simply claim that alcohol and/or other drugs impaired their ability to control their conduct. Instead, the intoxication defence focuses on whether the accused's state of intoxication (from alcohol and/or other drugs) prevented him or her from forming the necessary *mens rea* for the crime in question.

The defence of intoxication is primarily a "common law" defence in the sense that it was developed by the courts in the absence of any legislation that defined its nature and scope. Traditionally, the defence has applied only to those offences that required proof of a complex form of *mens rea* known as "specific intent." Therefore, the defence of intoxication may reduce the severity of a charge (for example, from murder to manslaughter or from robbery to assault). On the other hand, it has been a longstanding principle that intoxication is not a valid defence to a charge of such "basic intent" offences as assault, sexual assault, or damage to property (mischief). The legal rationale for maintaining the distinction between crimes of specific and basic intent is that intoxication does not normally impair people to the extent that they do not even have the minimal degree of *mens rea* required to assault someone or to damage property. Even extremely intoxicated people have some degree of awareness of what they are doing and the acts of committing an assault or damaging property require only a very minimal degree of intent. On the other hand, assaulting someone with the specific intent to kill (murder) or forcefully taking something from another individual with the specific intent to steal (robbery) are acts that require a considerably more complex pattern of thought, and intoxication may well prevent

**intoxication**
Intoxication caused by alcohol and/or other drugs may be a defence if it prevents the accused from forming the intent required for a specific intent offence, such as murder or robbery.

**necessity**

Necessity may be a defence to a criminal charge when the accused person commits the lesser evil of a crime in order to avoid the occurrence of a greater evil.

**duress**

Duress may be a defence to a criminal charge when the accused was forced to commit a crime as a consequence of threats of death or serious bodily harm made by another person.

the accused from forming the necessary specific intent that is required for conviction of these serious crimes. The defences of **necessity** and **duress** are based on the notion that it would be unfair to convict individuals of a criminal offence if they did not have a genuine choice at the time that they committed it. These defences are conceptualized by the courts as being "excuses"; as Justice Dickson said, in the Supreme Court of Canada's decision in *Perka* (1984), "An 'excuse' concedes the wrongfulness of the action but asserts that the circumstances under which it was done are such that it ought not to be attributed to the actor." Necessity is a common-law defence that arises when the accused person can avoid some disaster or calamity only by breaking the law. In these circumstances, the accused person is considered to act involuntarily from a "moral or normative" point of view. As Justice Dickson stated in the *Perka* case (1984),

> The lost Alpinist who, on the point of freezing to death, breaks open an isolated mountain cabin is not literally behaving in an involuntary fashion. He has control over his actions to the extent of being physically capable of abstaining from the act. Realistically, however, his act is not a "voluntary" one. His "choice" to break the law is not true choice at all; it is remorselessly compelled by normal human instincts.

The "evil" that the accused person seeks to avoid must be greater than the "evil" involved in the breaking of the law, and the accused must have no reasonable legal alternative but to break the law. Take the case of a surgeon who is contemplating the surgical separation of conjoined twins who share vital organs, such as the heart or the lungs. Without an operation to separate the babies, both of them will ultimately die. However, the operation will save one of the twins, while inevitably killing the other. Is the surgeon justified in killing one twin in order to save the other? In these particular circumstances, one can assume that the defence of necessity would be available to the surgeon should he or she ever be charged with murder.

When claiming the defence of necessity, defendants may point to any circumstances that constitute a threat to life or limb; however, where the defence of duress is raised, defendants are really asserting that their power of choice is being overborne by another human being. In the *Hibbert* case (1995), the Supreme Court of Canada ruled that duress, like necessity, was a defence that was based on the concept of "normative involuntariness." Section 17 of the *Criminal Code* sets out the requirements for the defence of duress; however, in the case of *Ruzic* (2001) the Supreme Court of Canada ruled that these requirements were so restrictive that they could result in the denial of the defence to an individual who was not blameworthy. As a result the court struck down these requirements as being invalid under the *Charter*. The Supreme Court then held that the courts should apply the "common law" defence of duress. The main elements of this defence are that the accused had been subjected to a threat of death or serious bodily harm that is directed either toward the accused or toward another person (such as a child or spouse). The threat must be so serious that the accused believes it will be carried out and the court must also be satisfied that it would have caused a reasonable person, placed in exactly the same position as the accused, to act as he or she did. Finally, it should be established that the accused had no obvious "safe avenue of escape." After all, if the accused had the option to escape from the person who was making threats, he or she cannot now claim that he or she was acting involuntarily.

In the *Ruzic* case, for example, the accused was charged with importing a narcotic and use of a false passport. Two kilograms of heroin had been found strapped to her body when she arrived at Pearson Airport in Toronto. Ruzic admitted the offences but asserted that she had acted under duress. Her story was that she lived with her mother in Belgrade (in the former Yugoslavia) and that she had been persistently threatened by a "paramilitary" man who physically assaulted and sexually harassed her. The man had a reputation for extreme violence and he informed Ruzic that she must take a consignment of heroin to Toronto. When the accused protested, the man threatened to harm her mother. At the time of these threats, law and order had largely broken down in Belgrade and Ruzic said that she did not inform the Belgrade police of the threats against her mother because they were "corrupt and would do nothing to assist her." The jury acquitted Ruzic on both charges and the Supreme Court of Canada ultimately upheld the acquittal. Ruzic had met all the requirements contained in the common-law defence of duress. She clearly believed that she had absolutely no alternative to bringing the heroin into Canada; if she had not done so, her mother might have been seriously harmed or killed, and seeking the assistance of the local police would have been a futile gesture given the particular circumstances that existed in Belgrade at that time.

Other important defences are provocation and self-defence. **Provocation** is only a partial defence; it may be raised only when the accused is charged with murder. If provocation is raised successfully by the accused, he or she is convicted of manslaughter rather than murder. The defence is available even though the accused undoubtedly possessed the *mens rea* for murder. Under the terms of section 232 of the *Criminal Code*, murder may be reduced to manslaughter if the accused killed "in the heat of passion caused by sudden provocation." Before the defence may be raised successfully, it must be established that the provocation was of a kind that would be "sufficient to deprive an ordinary person of the power of self-control." This would appear to establish an objective test; however, the Supreme Court of Canada has effectively watered down the objective requirements of the defence by ruling that the issue is whether an ordinary person with the particular characteristics associated with the accused would have lost the power of self-control if confronted with the specific situation that confronted him or her. As Justice Cory stated in the *Thibert* case (1996), "If the test is to be applied sensibly and with sensitivity, then the ordinary person must be taken to be of the same age, and sex, and must share with the accused such other factors as would give the act or insult in question a particular significance." It also has to be established that the accused acted in the heat of the moment "before there was time for his or her passion to cool."

The *Stone* case (1999), discussed earlier in connection with automatism, constitutes a typical case of provocation insofar as the accused killed the victim immediately following a series of hurtful insults (which included raising doubts about the paternity of his children and denigrating his sexual prowess). Clearly, the jury believed that an ordinary husband would be likely to lose the power of self-control in such circumstances and that Stone must be considered to have responded to sudden provocation before there had been time for his passion to cool.

**provocation**

Provocation may be a partial defence to a charge of murder (if successful, it reduces the offence from murder to manslaughter). The required elements of provocation are (i) that the accused responded to a wrongful act or insult that was of such a nature that an ordinary person would have been likely to lose the power of self-control and (ii) that the accused acted "on the sudden and before there was time for his (or her) passion to cool."

**self-defence**

The *Criminal Code* permits the use of force in self-defence in certain circumstances where the individual concerned becomes the object of an unlawful assault. Where the individual acted in self-defence without intending to inflict death or grievous bodily harm on the assailant, it must be shown that no more force was used than was necessary in the circumstances. Where the individual concerned inflicted death or grievous bodily harm, then it must be shown that he or she acted under a reasonable apprehension of death or grievous bodily harm and under a reasonable belief that he or she had no alternative but to employ lethal force.

The **self-defence** provisions of the *Criminal Code* are extraordinarily complex and, in certain respects, contradictory. However, the central provision is section 34 of the *Criminal Code*. Section 34(1) applies where an accused person has used force in self-defence but did not do so with the intent to inflict death or grievous bodily harm. The accused must demonstrate that he or she was unlawfully assaulted and did not provoke the assault. In addition, it must be shown that the force used was "no more than is necessary to defend him(her) self"; this requirement is significant because it means that there must be a degree of objective proportionality between the force used by the assailant and the force used in self-defence in response to the assailant. This principle has been encapsulated in the phrase "One cannot use a tank against a chariot."

When an accused who has acted in self-defence has either killed the assailant or inflicted grievous bodily harm, he or she will rely on section 34(2) of the *Criminal Code*. Under this provision, an accused person who is unlawfully assaulted is justified in using lethal or potentially lethal force if

(a) he causes it under reasonable apprehension of death or grievous bodily harm from the violence with which the assault was originally made or with which the assailant pursues his purposes, and

(b) he believes, on reasonable grounds, that he cannot otherwise preserve himself from death or grievous bodily harm.

It would appear that Parliament intended to impose an objective test for self-defence in these circumstances; indeed, section 34(2) clearly refers to "reasonable apprehension" and belief "on reasonable grounds." However, the Supreme Court of Canada has consistently softened the objective nature of the requirements for self-defence under section 34(2) by emphasizing that the real question is whether the particular accused acted reasonably in the specific circumstances that faced him or her at the time of the assault upon him or her. For example, the Supreme Court of Canada has emphasized the need to ensure that women who are the victims of domestic violence are judged by the standards of "reasonable women" who face the same circumstances of ongoing abuse and not by the standards of "reasonable men" brawling in a bar. In the *Lavallee* case (1990), the accused had shot her abusive male partner (Rust) in the back of the head. Rust was leaving Lavallee's room just after he had physically assaulted her and threatened her with death.

At Lavallee's trial for murder, a psychiatrist gave expert testimony concerning the so-called battered wife syndrome in order to help the members of the jury to determine whether the accused woman's beliefs and actions were reasonable in light of her experience of chronic abuse at the hands of her partner. The psychiatrist asserted that Lavallee "had been terrorized by Rust to the point of feeling trapped, vulnerable, worthless and unable to escape the relationship despite the violence." This witness concluded that Lavallee's shooting of Rust should be viewed as "a final desperate act by a woman who sincerely believed that she would be killed that night." The jury acquitted Lavallee. The Supreme Court of Canada later upheld the acquittal and ruled that the trial judge had acted appropriately in permitting an expert witness to testify about the "battered woman syndrome" as a means of assisting the members of the jury to assess the reasonableness of Lavallee's beliefs and actions.

In a later case, *Malott* (1998), the Supreme Court of Canada suggested that this type of evidence should be presented to the jury in order to assist them in understanding at least four separate issues: (1) why an abused woman might remain in an abusive relationship, (2) the nature and extent of the violence that may exist in an abusive relationship, (3) the woman's ability to perceive when her partner was dangerous, and (4) whether she believed on reasonable grounds that she could not otherwise preserve herself from death or grievous bodily harm. Furthermore, the Supreme Court has held that there is no requirement in section 34(2) that the accused person must actually be under attack or even that the accused must be in imminent danger of such an assault. Indeed, in the *Pétel* case (1994), the Supreme Court held that imminence is "only one of the factors which the jury should weigh in determining whether the accused had a reasonable apprehension of danger and a reasonable belief that she could not extricate herself otherwise than by killing the attacker." This means that a woman who is in acute fear for her life does not have to wait until she is actually being attacked or until such an assault is imminent, before she uses lethal force in self-defence.

While this concludes our brief survey of Canadian criminal law, it is important to recognize that one of the most significant developments in recent years has been the evolution of a body of international criminal law. The establishment in 2003 of the permanent International Criminal Court (ICC) in The Hague, the Netherlands, heralds an age in which certain horrendous crimes may be tried outside of the courts and tribunals of individual nation-states (see Box 3.4). Significantly, Canada has been one of the foremost supporters and promoters of the ICC. The relatively recent experience of "ethnic cleansing" in parts of the former Yugoslavia and of genocide in Rwanda suggests that the ICC is an institution that is sorely needed in the modern age.

# FOCUS BOX 3.4

## THE INTERNATIONAL CRIMINAL COURT

Crimes may be committed not only against the laws of individual states, such as Canada, but also against international law. Indeed, serious crimes, such as genocide, crimes against humanity (including all forms of sexual violence and exploitation involving significant numbers of victims), and war crimes, may be prosecuted under the provisions of public international law. On March 11, 2003, the International Criminal Court (ICC) was officially opened at The Hague, in the Netherlands. This Court is the first permanent tribunal to try cases under international criminal and it has the power to order that reparations be paid to the victims of crimes that fall within its jurisdiction. There are 18 judges organized into the Pre-Trial Division, the Trial Division, and the Appeal Division. A Canadian, Philippe Kirsch, was elected the first president of the Court.

The establishment of the ICC was rendered possible when 60 nations ratified the Rome Statute, a treaty that was signed at the Rome Diplomatic Conference in 1998. To date, 114 countries, including Canada, have ratified the Rome Statute. The ICC is a "court of last resort"; it will try cases involving grave crimes only when the national courts are unable or unwilling to do so themselves. For example, a country's court system may have collapsed following an armed conflict or a state may refuse to prosecute an individual who has the power or influence to escape

*(continued)*

justice within his or her own country. Canada played a major role in implementing the Rome Statute. However, the United States has refused to become a party to the Rome Statute and has indicated that it will not permit the Court to try an American citizen for a crime under international law. Similarly, Indonesia, China, and Russia have declined to submit to the jurisdiction of the ICC.

How active has the ICC been in its first decade? To date, Uganda, the Democratic Republic of the Congo, and the Central African Republic have referred "situations occurring on their territories" to the ICC. The Security Council of the UN also exercised its power to refer "the situation" in Darfur (Sudan) to the International Criminal Court. The Prosecutor of the Court has pursued investigations with respect to all of these referrals. In addition, the Prosecutor, on his own initiative, opened an investigation into "the situation" in Kenya (March 2010). Most recently (February 2011), the Security Council of the UN referred "the situation" in Libya to the ICC and the Prosecutor commenced an investigation into allegations of possible crimes against humanity. As of April 2011, there were five cases being tried at various stages before the ICC.

Do you think that there is a real need for a permanent international criminal court? In what circumstances, should an individual be brought before the ICC? Why has the United States insisted on remaining a non-party to the Rome Statute? Can the ICC be truly effective when such major states as China, Indonesia, Russia, and the United States have not become parties to the Rome Statute? Can the ICC achieve any tangible benefits for the victims of genocide, crimes against humanity, or war crimes? How should the ICC use the funds that have been set aside for victims?

For further information, see the website of the International Criminal Court: http://www.icc-cpi.int/Menus/ICC/Home.

## Summary

- A crime consists of a prohibition against certain conduct and a penal sanction (such as imprisonment or a fine).

- The sources of criminal law are (i) legislation and (ii) judicial decisions.

- Under the terms of the Canadian Constitution, the Parliament of Canada has the exclusive authority to enact "criminal law and the procedures relating to criminal matters."

- There is a significant difference between "true crimes" that arise under the *Criminal Code* and regulatory offences that arise under regulatory legislation enacted both by the various provinces and territories and by the Parliament of Canada.

- The enactment of the *Canadian Charter of Rights and Freedoms* has given judges the power to invalidate criminal law that unjustifiably infringes on an accused person's *Charter* rights.

- Each criminal offence can be analyzed in terms of its *actus reus* and *mens rea* elements.

- The *actus reus* generally consists of three components: conduct, circumstances, and consequences.

- *Mens rea* may be subjective or objective.

- Subjective *mens rea* may consist of intention and knowledge; recklessness; or wilful blindness.

- Objective *mens rea* is based on the requirement that there be a marked departure from the standard expected of the reasonable person acting prudently.

- An individual may become a party to a criminal offence in a number of different ways: actually committing an offence, aiding and/or abetting an offence, becoming a party to an offence by way of common intention, and counselling an offence that is committed.

- There are three inchoate offences that permit the police to intervene before a particular crime is committed: counselling an offence that is not committed, criminal attempt, and conspiracy.

- A successful defence of not criminally responsible on account of mental disorder (NCRMD) is not an acquittal; instead, it is a finding that the accused person has committed the act or omission in question but may not be held criminally responsible on account of mental disorder.

- The most important defences to a criminal charge include mistake of fact; intoxication; necessity; duress; provocation; and self-defence.

## QUESTIONS FOR CRITICAL THINKING

1. Why does Canadian criminal law place such importance on the requirement that the Crown prove the relevant *mens rea* elements of a criminal offence? Would it not make more sense for the state to intervene and deal with offenders solely on the basis of the fact that they have committed the *actus reus* of an offence (a harmful or potentially harmful act or omission)?

2. Pluto is driving his car down a steep hill in a large Canadian city. He discovers that his brakes are not functioning properly and the vehicle starts to gain speed. In the near distance, Pluto notices that there is a group of schoolchildren who are crossing the road. Worried that he may collide with these children, Pluto decides to steer his speeding car onto the sidewalk. Pluto is aware that there is an elderly man on the sidewalk but he is confident that he can avoid hitting him. Tragically, at that moment, Pluto suffers a fainting spell and, while he is unconscious, his car not only strikes and kills the man on the sidewalk but also returns to the road and injures five of the schoolchildren who are on the clearly marked crossing. There is some evidence that Pluto had experienced brief fainting spells before but he did not consider them to be serious. After the accident, it is discovered that Pluto probably suffers from a mild epileptic condition. Is Pluto guilty of dangerous driving causing death and dangerous driving causing bodily harm?

3. Should the criminal law be used as a preventative tool? Should the police be able to intervene and bring individuals to the criminal courts before those individuals have actually committed the crime(s) that they are planning to carry out? Do the existing inchoate offences in the *Criminal Code* strike an acceptable balance between the demands of public security and the civil rights of accused persons?

4. It has been suggested that the defence of provocation should be abolished because it is frequently raised in the context of family violence [see, for example, the *Stone* case (1999) in this chapter]. Do you think that there is any place for a defence of provocation in a modern criminal code?

5. Do you think self-induced intoxication should ever be a defence to a crime of violence? What are the arguments for and against permitting defendants to raise a defence of intoxication? For example, is it fair that an intoxicated person may kill someone and be sentenced to two years' imprisonment while a sober person who deliberately kills another will be convicted of first- or second-degree murder and be sentenced automatically to life imprisonment?

6. Daphne has lived with Apollo for 10 years, during which he has, on various occasions, subjected her to physical assaults, some of which have inflicted serious injuries (such as extensive bruising to the body, a broken nose, and concussion). One night, Daphne returns home late from an evening meeting and Apollo becomes furious with her. He yells that he is "going to fix her once and for all." However, Apollo is so drunk that he passes out on the couch. Daphne goes to the kitchen and picks up a sharp knife. She then returns to the room where Apollo is sleeping and stabs him to death. Would Daphne be able to raise a successful plea of self-defence if she were charged with murder or manslaughter?

## NET WORK

Increasingly, basic legal research is being conducted online. The federal government and the governments of the various provinces and territories in Canada operate websites that offer swift access via the Internet to the full text of legislation and the decisions of the courts. In addition, a number of commercial electronic database services, such as *BestCase*, *CriminalSource*, *Criminal Spectrum*, *QuickLaw*, and *LawSource* provide information concerning legislation, cases, and legal literature (journal articles and textbooks). You should be able to gain access to these data bases through your university or college. If you have such access, a useful exercise might be to search for Canadian criminal cases in which the courts have discussed the defence of duress.

You can start to explore the powerful electronic tools that are available for research into Canadian criminal law by visiting the website of the Canadian Legal Information Institute. This website provides easy access to federal and provincial/territorial legislation and court decisions. In addition, the website provides access to the decisions of various federal and provincial/territorial boards and tribunals (such as the Canadian Human Rights Tribunal and the Human Rights Tribunal of Ontario) and it also contains links to various external websites that may be of particular value to students (for example, the debates of the House of Commons *Hansard* or the *Canada Gazette* which provides "Canadians with their rightful access to the laws and regulations that govern their daily lives"). The website address for the Canadian legal Information Institute is **http://canlii.org/**. Using this website, find the report of the following case: *R. v. Charles*, 2011 ONCA 228, decided by the Ontario Court of Appeal on March 24, 2011.

Another general website that provides you with access to legislation and case law is LawNetCanada. It is of particular value as a means of searching federal and provincial legislation. In addition, it contains up-to-date news concerning law and justice issues and provides links to external websites that are of great value to researchers in the fields of criminal law and criminal justice. Log on to **http://www.lawnetcanada.ca/LawNetCanada/default.aspx**.

The website operated by the Department of Justice Canada is particularly useful. This site provides not only detailed information about the activities of the Department of Justice and federal developments concerning criminal law but also access to all federal legislation and regulations. The website address for the Department of Justice Canada is **http://www.canada.justice.gc.ca**. In order to locate legislation and regulations, click onto "The Laws Site" on the home page.

Using the Department of Justice Canada or the LawNetCanada websites, see what information is available concerning Bill C-21, the *Standing Up For Victims of White Collar Crime Act*, which received Royal Assent in March 2011.

Find the relevant website for the courts in your own province or territory (for example, in Ontario, log on to **http://www.ontariocourts.on.ca/en/sitemap.htm**, or, in British Columbia, log on to **http://www.courts.gov.bc.ca/**). It may be useful to know that both the Ontario and B.C. websites provide links to all of the other provincial and territorial court websites in Canada. As an exercise, find out if, during the period 2000 to 2011, your own provincial or territorial court of appeal decided any cases concerning the offence of fraud (section 380 of the *Criminal Code*).

## KEY TERMS

*actus reus*; pg. 74

*Charter*; pg. 73

common law; pg. 73

conspiracy; pg. 86

counselling; pg. 84

crime; pg. 68

criminal attempt; pg. 85

criminal law; pg. 70

criminal procedure; pg. 71

duress; pg. 92

inchoate crime; pg. 83

intoxication; pg. 91

*mens rea*; pg. 76

mistake of fact; pg. 89

necessity; pg. 92

not criminally responsible on account of mental disorder (NCRMD); pg. 87

objective *mens rea*; pg. 77

party to a crime; pg. 82

provocation; pg. 93

regulatory offences; pg. 72

self-defence; pg. 94

subjective *mens rea*; pg. 77

"true crime"; pg. 72

## CASES CITED

*Canadian Newspapers Co. v. Canada (Attorney General)*, [1988] 2 S.C.R. 122. Available at http://www.canlii.org/en/ca/scc/doc/1988/1988canlii52/1988canlii52.html.

*R. v. Adams*, [1995] 4 S.C.R. 707. Available at http://www.canlii.org/en/ca/scc/doc/1995/1995canlii56/1995canlii56.html.

*R. v. Beatty*, [2008] 1 S.C.R. 49. Available at http://www.canlii.org/en/ca/scc/doc/2008/2008scc5/2008scc5.html.

*R. v. Briscoe*, [2010] 1 S.C.R. 411. Available at http://www.canlii.org/en/ca/scc/doc/2010/2010scc13/2010scc13.html.

*R. v. Chaulk*, [1990] 3 S.C.R. 1303. Available at http://canlii.org/en/ca/scc/doc/1990/1990canlii34/1990canlii34.html.

*R. v. Crangle* (2010), 256 C.C.C. (3d) 254 (Ont.C.A). Available at http://www.canlii.org/en/on/onca/doc/2010/2010onca451/2010onca451.html.

*R. v. Creighton*, [1993] 3 S.C.R. 3. Available at http://canlii.org/en/ca/scc/doc/1993/1993canlii61/1993canlii61.html.

*R. v. Daviault*, [1994] 3 S.C.R. 63. Available at http://canlii.org/en/ca/scc/doc/1994/1994canlii61/1994canlii61.html.

*R. v. Hamilton*, [2005] 2 S.C.R. 432. Available at http://www.canlii.org/en/ca/scc/doc/2005/2005scc47/2005scc47.html.

*R. v. Hibbert*, [1995] 2 S.C.R. 973. Available at http://canlii.org/en/ca/scc/doc/1995/1995canlii110/1995canlii110.html.

*R. v. Hydro-Québec*, [1997] 3 S.C.R. 213. Available at http://canlii.org/en/ca/scc/doc/1997/1997canlii318/1997canlii318.html.

*R. v. Lavallee*, [1990] 1 S.C.R. 852. Available at http://canlii.org/en/ca/scc/doc/1990/1990canlii95/1990canlii95.html.

*R. v. Malmo-Levine; R. v. Caine*, [2003] 3 S.C.R. 571. Available at http://www.canlii.org/en/ca/scc/doc/2003/2003scc74/2003scc74.html.

*R. v. Malott*, [1998] 1 S.C.R. 123. Available at http://canlii.org/en/ca/scc/doc/1998/1998canlii845/1998canlii845.html.

*R. v. Martineau*, [1990] 2 S.C.R. 633. Available at http://canlii.org/en/ca/scc/doc/1990/1990canlii80/1990canlii80.html.

*R. v. Molodowic*, [2000] 1 S.C.R. 420. Available at http://canlii.org/en/ca/scc/doc/2000/2000scc16/2000scc16.html.

*R. v. Morgentaler, Smolig and Scott*, [1988] 1 S.C.R. 30. Available at http://canlii.org/en/ca/scc/doc/1988/1988canlii90/1988canlii90.html.

*R. v. Olan, Hudson and Hartnett*, [1978] 2 S.C.R. 1175. Available at http://canlii.org/en/ca/scc/doc/1978/1978canlii9/1978canlii9.html.

*R. v. Perka*, [1984] 2 S.C.R. 232. Available at http://canlii.org/en/ca/scc/doc/1984/1984canlii23/1984canlii23.html.

*R. v. Pétel*, [1994] 1 S.C.R. 3. Available at http://canlii.org/en/ca/scc/doc/1994/1994canlii133/1994canlii133.html.

*R. v. Pickton*, [2010] 2 S.C.R. 198. Available at http://canlii.org/en/ca/scc/doc/2010/2010scc32/2010scc32.html.

*R. v. Ruzic*, [2001] 1 S.C.R. 687. Available at http://canlii.org/en/ca/scc/doc/1994/1994canlii133/1994canlii133.html.

*R. v. Sault Ste. Marie (City of)*, [1978] 2 S.C.R. 1299. Available at http://canlii.org/en/ca/scc/doc/1978/1978canlii11/1978canlii11.html.

*R. v. Sharpe*, [2001] 1 S.C.R. 45. Available at http://canlii.org/en/ca/scc/doc/2001/2001scc2/2001scc2.html.

*R. v. Stone*, [1999] 2 S.C.R. 290. Available at http://canlii.org/en/ca/scc/doc/1999/1999canlii688/1999canlii688.html.

*R. v. Théroux*, [1993] 2 S.C.R. 5. Available at http://canlii.org/en/ca/scc/doc/1993/1993canlii134/1993canlii134.html.

*R. v. Thibert*, [1996] 1 S.C.R. 37. Available at http://canlii.org/en/ca/scc/doc/1993/1993canlii134/1993canlii134.html.

*R. v. Wholesale Travel Group Inc.*, [1991] 3 S.C.R. 154. Available at http://canlii.org/en/ca/scc/doc/1991/1991canlii39/1991canlii39.html.

*Winko v. British Columbia (Forensic Psychiatric Institute)*, [1999] 2 S.C.R. 625. Available at http://canlii.org/en/ca/scc/doc/1999/1999canlii694/1999canlii694.html.

# Counting Crime

**4**

**John Evans**

**Alexander Himelfarb**

YORK UNIVERSITY

This chapter is about statistics on crime and criminal justice. Over the past century, those who have tried to understand crime have relied heavily on statistical descriptions of criminal behaviour, criminals, and the criminal justice response. What we know about crime depends on the quality, coverage, reliability, and validity of our measures of crime.

This chapter describes how social scientists count crime. After discussing the problems of the validity and reliability of our measures of crime, we introduce the long-standing debate over whether crime statistics accurately reflect the amount of crime in Canada or whether they merely reflect the activities of the criminal justice system. To help you to understand the strengths and weaknesses of Canadian crime statistics, we describe how the administrative records of the police, courts, and prisons are turned into measures describing the amount of crime and the characteristics of offenders and victims. This process involves developing clear procedures concerning units of count, levels of data aggregation, definitions, data elements, and counting procedures. Particular attention will be paid to the most commonly used measure of crime: the Uniform Crime Report system (UCR). The UCR is based on crimes reported to the police across the country. Finally, the chapter describes victimization surveys and self-report studies. These provide data that are complementary to those produced by the UCR.

## Learning Objectives

After reading this chapter, you should be able to

- Describe how the administrative records collected in the criminal justice system are turned into statistics about crime and the characteristics of offenders and victims.
- Understand the problems of reliability and validity associated with measures of crime and offenders.
- Understand the system that produces Canadian crime and criminal justice statistics.
- Describe the trends in Canadian crime rates over the past five decades.
- Describe the strengths and weaknesses of victimization and self-reported criminality surveys and understand how these two methods enhance our understanding of the problem of crime in Canada.

# Controversies Over Counting Crime

**methodology**

Refers to the study or critique of methods.

**reliability**

Identifies one of the standards (another being validity) against which the tools used to measure concepts are judged. Reliability refers to consistency of results over time.

**validity**

The extent to which a tool or instrument (questionnaire, experiment) actually measures the concept the researcher claims to be interested in and not something else.

**crime rate**

Criminologists calculate crime rates (or rates of incarceration, conviction, or recidivism) by dividing the amount of crime by the population size and multiplying by 100 000. This produces the standard rate per 100 000; occasionally it is useful to calculate a rate per million or some other figure when looking at less frequently occurring offences.

The first concern of those who first sought to measure crime was coverage: how can one obtain data about the amount and nature of crime in a society? As the official sources of statistics have increased, and as creative **methodologies** for data collection have advanced, the questions of **reliability** and **validity** have become the most pressing concern. In simple terms, are the methods and techniques involved in gathering statistics strong enough that anyone following the procedures would produce the same counts (reliability)? And do the statistics collected count what they purport to count (validity)?

Imagine a situation in which you wished to test a theory of crime causation. For example, what aspects of communities create pressures to greater criminality? Let us say that your theory predicts higher **crime rates** in big cities than in small towns. You are then going to need statistical data on the amount of crime in these two types of settings. How do you get these counts? You could consult police statistics. Police gather vast amounts of information on suspects, incidents, arrests, and charges. These are the data often used by criminologists to test their ideas. However, there have always been problems with police statistics. When police officers are dispatched to a call, each officer must use his or her own judgment to decide whether a crime has been committed or whether the call is unfounded. If the officer determines that there has been an offence, a report will be filled out by the officer and processed by police department staff. Most police departments then send the data from each incident to the Canadian Centre for Justice Statistics (CCJS), a division of Statistics Canada. Police are supposed to follow a uniform set of rules (the Uniform Crime Reporting Rules) in recording criminal incidents or calls for service. Yet it has been discovered that different police departments often use different rules for recording their information. In fact, individual police officers exercise a good deal of discretion in what they decide to record and how they record it. There may be doubts, then, about the reliability of the statistics derived from police records. However, there is perhaps an even more fundamental problem. Are suspects criminals? Are those arrested and charged criminals? Are all incidents that are recorded actual crimes, and are these incidents a complete count of crimes? Do the data provide a valid count of crime?

A particular difficulty arises in crime counts because as the reliability of a statistical measure increases, its validity as a count of crime frequently decreases. Thus, while the police certainly never detect or become aware of all crimes and despite enormous problems of reliability, their counts of crime are likely to be a far more valid reflection of the amount of criminal behaviour than are counts of convictions or counts of prisoners. The criminal justice system operates as a funnel: only some fraction of incidents result in a police record of a criminal incident, only a portion of recorded incidents result in suspects identified, only a portion of suspects are arrested or charged, only a portion of charges result in conviction, and only a portion of convictions result in incarceration (see Figure 4.1). The farther you go into the system, the more confident you can be that the count is accurate and reliable and that it is a decreasingly valid representation of all criminal behaviour. Also, there are built-in biases

**FIGURE 4.1**   The Crime Funnel: Break-and-Enter Offences Processed through the Canadian Criminal Justice System, 2009

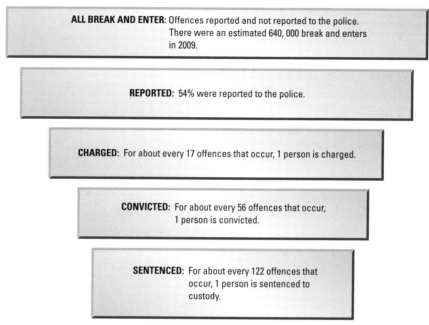

Note: This diagram illustrates the processing of break-and-enter offences through various stages in the criminal justice system. For cautions about these data, see Box 4.3, Summary and Cautions: Using Victimization Survey Data and Data from the UCR and the Court Surveys.

Sources: Perreault, Samuel and Shannon Brennan. From Statistics Canada publication JURISTAT—Criminal Victimization in Canada, 2009, Vol. 30, no. 2. The Court data are from Adult and Youth Court Surveys done by Statistics Canada.

because some crimes (and some criminals) are more likely than others to be reported and to result in arrest, charge, conviction, and a sentence to incarceration. For example, murderers are more likely to be arrested and to go to jail than are corporate criminals or shoplifters. The farther you go into the system, the more obvious it becomes that you are counting something about how the system itself operates; you are counting official decisions about crime and criminals. Statistical descriptions of the prison **population** may provide valid indicators of one way that a society responds to crime. These descriptions, however, do not provide a valid measure of the amount and the nature of crime.

How have criminologists handled these problems? For a long time, they acknowledged the problems and then, when they needed data, they pretended the problems away. Kaplan's "law of the hammer" holds that if you give a small child a hammer, he or she discovers that everything needs pounding. Similarly, social scientists have often been accused of letting their methods or the most readily available statistics dictate their theories. Social scientists will often find out what they are able to discover most easily and build their theories around this limited information. Many of the early theories of criminology discussed elsewhere in this text were built upon a rather uncritical acceptance of official

**population**

The term population refers to all members of a given class or set. For example, adult Canadians, teenagers, Canadian inmates, or criminal offenders can each be thought of as populations.

sources of statistics. Many early criminologists used prisoners to study the differences between criminals and non-criminals. Some used police records of arrest or charge; some used court records. These criminologists rarely asked the following questions: Are all criminals equally likely to get arrested? To be charged? To be put in prison? Even when criminologists recognized the limits of the available information, they used these unreliable and often invalid measures because this was all they had.

In the 1960s and the 1970s, a number of sociologists and criminologists focused their attention on the systematic biases of past theories built on official records. New theories suggested that official records showed us how the criminal justice system operated to create crime and criminals. The statistics revealed information about the police, about the courts, and about whom they selected for their attention and worst punishments. Arrest, charge, and conviction were parts of a formal labelling process, a ceremony of degradation in which a person was formally stigmatized. These labelling or social reaction theories (see Chapter 13) asked why certain people were more often selected for this process and then studied the consequences of this process for these people. The same "crime statistics" that had been used to describe the behaviour of criminals were now being used to describe the official agents of social control. More recently, criminologists are increasingly becoming polarized. Many seem to be returning to the conservative criminology of the past, to the acceptance of official records as a reasonable indicator of crime, and focusing on explaining crime for the purpose of controlling it. Others, influenced by some variant of "critical" criminology (see Chapters 11 and 12), see crime statistics as simply part of the government's control mechanism, a way of characterizing the crime problem, a means of self-justification, and a reflection of more fundamental structural inequalities.

Are crime statistics whatever one makes of them? Are statistics simply a resource to tell lies or support one's own favoured position? Yes, sometimes. But they need not be. **Theories** about crime and facts about crime are built simultaneously, are mutually dependent, and shape one another. Theory without facts is indistinguishable from **ideology**; facts without theory are often implicit ideology; statistical facts without theory are numerology, often bent to ideological ends. Theorists and policy-makers have often been guilty of using statistics to their own ideological ends, using crime counts to show that we are going through a crime wave, or using the same counts to show how we are living through a wave of repression. We live in an age when numerical values have a certain magic and a power to convince us, to make arguments seem true. Statistics can be dangerous if we do not know how to consider them critically.

For example, imagine that you read, in some credible source, that violence in Canadian society has risen by 100 percent over the past decade. Before you set off to explain this "fact," or before you turn your home into a fortress, you should ask just what is being counted as violence? Crimes? Some crimes? Political dissent? Violence by the state? Domestic violence? What theory or ideological assumptions have guided this choice of "fact"? And how good are the facts? How well and consistently have they been counted? Are they reliable and valid?

**theory**

A theory consists of a set of concepts and their nominal definition or assertions about the relationships between these concepts, assumptions, and knowledge claims.

**ideology**

A linked set of ideas and beliefs that act to uphold and justify an existing or desired situation in society.

What have social scientists and policy-makers done about the lack of good crime information? Over 40 years ago, the American sociologist Ned Polsky (1967) argued that our understanding of crime would never be significantly advanced if we relied on statistical data. He was concerned that sociologists and criminologists relied too heavily on remote sources of information. They remained too distant from the criminals they wished to understand. He advocated field research through which social scientists live among, and learn from, the criminals themselves. Not surprisingly, few have followed Polsky's lead. Rather, most have worked to improve the quality of statistics based on official sources, to specify the valid uses of these statistics, and to develop innovative methodologies to complement official data and to fill gaps. Despite the problems, criminological theory and criminal justice policy remain heavily dependent on statistics about crime and the criminal justice system. This is not to say that there are not many other ways to advance our understanding of crime. This, however, is not a methods chapter. Qualitative techniques and other methods of studying crime should be examined elsewhere.

One can distinguish three broad types of criminal justice statistics: statistics about crime and criminals, statistics about the criminal justice system and its response to crime, and statistics about perceptions of crime and criminal justice. Theory and policy require statistics about the decisions of those who break the law, about the decisions of those who maintain it, and about what people think of all of this.

# Statistics on the Criminal Justice System

The criminal justice system produces an enormous amount of raw data in the form of police reports and records, the recorded decisions of prosecutors and judges, the **administrative records** of prisons and penitentiaries, and the recorded decisions of parole boards and probation and parole services. From these administrative records the Canadian Centre for Justice Statistics (CCJS) has developed a sophisticated system of statistics on the criminal justice system.

**administrative record**
A collection of information about individual cases.

## From Records to Statistics

Administrative records are not statistics. Records are concerned with individual cases and are intended primarily to help practitioners make decisions about these individual cases. Statistics are aggregated; they are concerned with what is common among individual cases. Statistics are meant to provide information about larger questions: planning and evaluation, policy and program development, and theory building and testing. While good records are the base, the conversion of records into statistics requires a number of conceptual decisions. The potential clients or users of the statistics must decide what it is they want to know and how they plan to use the information. Statistical systems should be built to address the enduring theoretical and policy concerns.

Specifically, the following issues must be addressed before records can be converted into statistics: unit of count, **levels of aggregation**, definitions, **data elements**, and **counting procedures**.

**levels of aggregation**
This refers to how data are to be combined. Do we want city-level, provincial, or national data?

**data element**
Specification about what, exactly is to be collected?

**counting procedure**
A consensus on how to count units and data elements.

**Unit of Count: Consensus about What It Is That We are Counting** In the course of everyday activities police may count many different things: suspects, offences, charges, or calls for service. Typically, they work with occurrences. An occurrence may involve several offenders, several victims, and several offences. The unit we wish to count in a statistical system will depend on whether we are trying to learn something about police workload or productivity, or whether we are seeking to learn something about crime or victims. Recently, for example, there has been a growing awareness among policymakers and criminologists that victims have been an ignored unit of count, and we know little about their characteristics. Some units of count are specific to a particular sector. For example, the prison sector can count inmates; the court sector, convictions; and the police, suspects.

**Levels of Aggregation: Consensus about How to Combine Data** A crucial decision is the level at which we want our statistics. For example, do we want to combine police records for a city? Do we want to combine statistics for an entire province? Or region? Or the nation? To the extent that we want to generalize our theories or develop or evaluate national policies, we are likely to want national statistics. But several criminologists have warned that the further you move from those who produce the data and the more you try to combine data from different sources, the more questionable is the result. They prefer the richer and more detailed information available from local police to the abstracted, less complete data available about national policing.

**Definitions: Consensus about How to Define What is Being Counted** While the Criminal Code provides a common set of definitions for counting crime, there remains a good deal of discretion about when an incident of crime is truly an incident, or even what, for example, constitutes "inmate." If one wishes to count inmates, should one count those who are temporarily absent, or those on remand, or those in community correctional facilities, or those who have committed criminal acts and have been assigned to mental institutions? Common definitions are essential. This is not merely a technical issue. Depending on how the terms are defined, you can inflate or deflate the statistics; you can make it appear that crime is higher or lower, or that there are more or fewer prisoners.

**Data Elements: Consensus about What Specific Information Should be Collected** While the police will need certain kinds of information to help them in their investigative activities, this information will be far more detailed than, and sometimes quite different from, what is needed as aggregated statistics. Similarly, the police in one jurisdiction may, for their own good reasons, maintain records quite different from those of other police departments. As understandable as this is, it is extremely difficult to build aggregated statistics out of different types of records that may be incompatible.

**Counting Procedures: Consensus on How to Count Units and Elements** If an offender goes on a break-and-enter spree and hits six houses in an evening, how many offences should be counted—six (one offence per house) or one (a singular spree)? Or if, during a break and enter, an offender is confronted by the home owner and assaults him or her, is this one or two offences? If one, which offence should be counted? If we agree that the most serious should be counted, how do we determine seriousness?

## Canadian Criminal Justice Statistics

The questions or issues of unit of count, levels of aggregation, definitions, data elements, and counting procedures are at the base of much of the technical and critical literature on criminal justice statistics. Within Canada, attempts to answer these questions have traditionally been the responsibility of our national statistical agency, Statistics Canada. More recently, the federal and provincial governments have created a national institute—the **Canadian Centre for Justice Statistics (CCJS)**—which is a division of Statistics Canada and is governed by a board of directors of senior officials responsible for justice.

A major difficulty confronting the Centre is achieving agreement on priorities such as whose needs should be met. Crime statistics are used by different people and for different purposes: criminologists and researchers want to build and test theories, policy-makers and analysts want to identify problems and develop and test solutions, and administrators and program managers want to plan and run their operations and to monitor and evaluate their programs. Most important, statistics serve the public interest by keeping people informed and by providing some measure of public accountability. Good statistics are important, but they are important in different ways for different users.

At the present time, Canada has reasonably good national data on criminal justice inputs such as resources and expenditures. The data are now far better when it comes to outputs such as incidents, arrests, charges, convictions, and dispositions. The CCJS has developed and improved the Adult Criminal Court Survey, a census of courts in Canada. As of 2009, the survey collects data from jurisdictions that represent about 95 percent of the national criminal court caseload. Correctional statistics are the most accurate because we can count the number of prisoners in Canada and provide some information on their social characteristics. This can be quite useful for projecting future inmate populations and for planning future facilities and services. When linked to other data, it can also be useful for developing correctional policy. For example, how much are we using incarceration and are we doing so in the most useful and appropriate ways?

Data on prisoners, however, do not tell us much about crime and criminal behaviours. They tell us about the criminal justice system. The confusion comes when people equate "criminal" with "prisoner." Some people are more likely to be caught; some people are more likely to be charged; some people are more likely to be convicted; and some people are more likely to be sentenced to prison or to a penitentiary. We know too much about how people get selected for incarceration to assume that prison statistics tell us very much about crime.

But what can such data show? Figure 4.2 shows the growth in number of adults incarcerated in Canada between 1978/79 and 2008/09. In this

**Canadian Centre for Justice Statistics**

A division of Statistics Canada, formed in 1981, with a mandate to collect national data on crime and justice.

"Justice and Crime" Statistics Canada

http://www5.statcan.gc.ca/
subject-sujet/theme-theme.
action?pid=2693&lang=eng&more=0

**FIGURE 4.2   Average Daily Count of Adults in Custody**

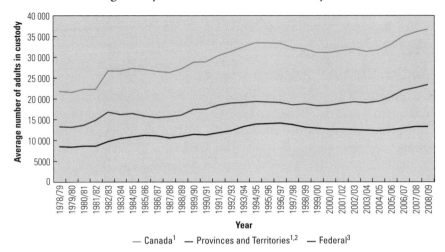

Notes: 1. Province/Territory and Canada totals exclude Prince Edward Island, Northwest Territories, and Nunavut for comparison between years. 2. Provincial and territorial counts may include federal sentenced offenders in a provincial or territorial facility. 3. Federal counts may include provincial/territorial offenders in a federal facility and those temporarily detained in a federal facility.

Source: Statistics Canada, Canadian Centre for Justice Statistics, Correctional Services Surveys, Adult Key Indicators Report.

period, the adult inmate population increased from 21 834 to 36 713. In addition, in 2008/09 there were 19 631 youths in custodial supervision; a rate of 82 per 10 000 youths aged 12 to 17. This rate is down 10 percent from 2004/05.

Obviously, these figures are important for administrative and planning purposes. But do these figures tell us something about growing crime in Canada? No. Do they tell us something about harsher or more punitive sentencing practices? No. In fact, if we look at the rate of incarceration (per 100 000 adult Canadians), we see that much of the growth in penitentiary population can be accounted for by the growth of the Canadian population (Figure 4.3).

International comparisons are difficult and problematic, but they show that Canada incarcerates people at a much higher rate than most western European nations but at a much lower rate than the United States, where nearly 2.4 million people were incarcerated in 2008. This is an incarceration rate of 504 per 100 000 U.S. residents, up from 411 in 1995 (Bureau of Justice Statistics, 2010) and 3.6 times the Canadian rate of 141 per 100 000 in 2008–2009. When compared to the rates of western European nations, some have argued that this is proof that Canada is too punitive, that too many people are being put behind bars and put there for too long. Others have argued that it simply means that Canada has more serious crime than many other nations. The debates flourish. Canadian statistics do not provide the answers; they indicate only where problems may exist.

**FIGURE 4.3** **Adult Incarceration Rates**

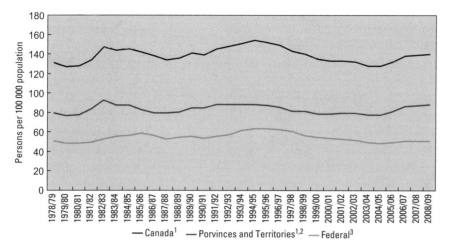

Notes: 1. Incarceration rates for Provinces/Territories and Canada exclude Prince Edward Island, Northwest Territories, and Nunavut for comparisons between years. 2. Provincial and territorial counts may inlcude federal sentenced offenders in a provincial or territorial facility. 3. Federal counts may include provincial/territorial offenders in a federal facility and those temporarily detained in a federal facility.

Source: Statistics Canada, Canadian Centre for Justice Statistics, Correctional Services Surveys, Adult Key Indicators Report.

## How Much Crime?

It should come as no surprise that criminologists have had difficulty counting crime. Crime is typically a secretive activity. When people commit crimes, they try to avoid becoming part of the count of criminals. (They do not want to become a statistic!) The "best" crime is one that no one knows about, and no criminal justice system will ever be able to ferret out all the crimes and criminals. Some crimes are harder to detect than others, and some criminals are harder to apprehend and convict. Criminologists have long recognized that the major problem of counting crime is the so-called **dark figure of crime** that remains unreported, unrecorded, and largely unknown. In response to the problem, criminologists have developed a variety of ways of counting crime, or at least to describe crime patterns and trends. They have tried to rationalize and improve official statistics, but they have also developed approaches that do not depend on official counts of crime. In the next section, we look at official records, victimization surveys, and self-report studies as sources of data about crime.

**dark figure of crime**
The amount of crime that is unreported or unknown.

## Official Statistics: Canadian Uniform Crime Reports

Despite their problems, we rely heavily on official counts of the amount of crime. Until 45 years ago, we were dependent on local police records collected for police purposes and handled differently in each locale. For nearly five

## Uniform Crime Reports (UCR)

Since 1962, Statistics Canada has published the Uniform Crime Reports based on a standardized set of procedures for collecting and reporting crime information.

decades Canada has had in place a system called the Canadian Uniform Crime Reports (UCR), designed to provide uniform, comparable, and national statistics. However, just what this system counts has been the subject of an almost endless debate within criminology.

While the Canadian Uniform Crime Report drew heavily from a similar system in the United States, it is an improvement over the American system. First, common crime classifications and definitions are easier to arrive at in Canada than in the United States because Canada operates under a common criminal code while each American state has a separate code. Second, the coverage of police departments is far more complete in Canada than in the United States. But both systems share some fundamental problems. Some of these problems are being addressed by ongoing improvements to the Uniform Crime Report survey; however, some of the problems are more fundamental because they are built into all official statistics.

In Canada two versions of the UCR collection instrument operate simultaneously: the UCR Aggregate (UCR1.0) Survey and the UCR2 Incident-based Survey, which is made up of two versions, UCR2.0 and UCR2.1. The UCR Aggregate Survey (UCR1.0) collects summary data for nearly 100 separate criminal offences and has been in place since 1962.*

The UCR2 Survey was developed in the mid-1980s as a method of collecting more detailed information on each incident, the victims, and the accused persons. This method of data collection, in which a separate statistical record is created for each criminal incident, is known as an incident-based reporting system.

A revised version of the UCR2 survey, known as UCR2.1, was introduced in 1998. This survey introduced certain efficiencies for police services and lowered the response burden by eliminating or simplifying UCR2 variables (Statistics Canada, 2010). In 2004 another version, UCR2.2, was introduced to add new violations and other variables.

Let us look more closely at the "seriousness rule." A number of studies (Nettler, 1974; Silverman and Teevan, 1975; Silverman, 1980; de Silva and Silverman, 1985) have documented some of the problems in the recording and scoring rules and how these rules are applied. Specifically, the studies have examined the implications of the "**seriousness rule**," which holds that only the most serious crime is scored in an incident involving several crimes. The concerns this rule creates are threefold: First, this rule deflates the total crime count since less serious crimes are not counted separately; second, it inflates serious crimes as a proportion of the total; and third, the way in which seriousness is scored is problematic because not enough qualitative data about the crimes are recorded to use a sophisticated scale of seriousness. See Box 4.1 for a discussion of the main UCR categories and the most serious offence rule.

## seriousness rule

If there are several crimes committed in one incident, only the most serious crime is counted. UCR1.0 uses the seriousness rule.

*The description of the UCR is based on the CCJS website: http://www.statcan.ca Search for UCR.

# FOCUS BOX 4.1

## UCR CATEGORIES AND THE MOST SERIOUS OFFENCE RULE

**Violent incidents** involve offences that deal with the application, or threat of application, of force to a person. These include homicide, attempted murder, various forms of sexual and non-sexual assault, robbery, and abduction. Traffic incidents that result in death or bodily harm are included under Criminal Code traffic incidents.

**Property incidents** involve unlawful acts with the intent of gaining property but do not involve the use or threat of violence against an individual. Theft, breaking and entering, fraud, and possession of stolen goods are examples of property crimes.

**Other Criminal Code incidents** involve the remaining Criminal Code offences that are not classified as violent or property incidents (excluding traffic). Examples are mischief, bail violations, disturbing the peace, arson, prostitution, and offensive weapons.

**Total Criminal Code incidents** is the tabulation of all violent, property, and other Criminal Code incidents reported for a given year.

### Most Serious Offence

The UCR1.0 Survey classifies incidents according to the most serious offence (MSO) in the incident. In categorizing incidents, violent offences always take precedence over non-violent offences. Within violent and non-violent categories, offences are then sorted according to the maximum sentence under the Criminal Code. The UCR Survey scores violent incidents differently from other types of crime. For violent crimes, a separate incident is recorded for each victim (categorized according to the most serious offence against the victim). If, for example, one person assaults three people, then three incidents are recorded. If three people assault one person, only one incident is recorded. For non-violent crimes, one incident (categorized according to the most serious offence in the incident) is counted for every distinct or separate occurrence. Robbery is one exception to the above scoring rule. Robbery is categorized as a violent offence. Unlike all other violent offences, one occurrence of robbery is equal to one incident, regardless of the number of victims. The reason for this exception is that robbery can involve many people who could all be considered victims. In a bank robbery with five tellers and 20 customers present, 25 incidents of robbery would be counted if the normal scoring rule for violent incidents were applied. This would seriously overstate the occurrence of robbery. Thus, the total number of incidents recorded by the UCR Survey is not a census of all violations of the law that come to the attention of police. Rather, it is equal to the number of victims of violent (other than robbery) plus the number of separate occurrences of non-violent crimes (and robberies).

### Actual Incidents

When a crime is reported to the police, the incident is recorded as a "reported" incident. Police then conduct a preliminary investigation to determine the validity of the report. Occasionally, crimes reported to the police prove to be unfounded. Unfounded incidents are subtracted from the number of reported incidents to produce the number of "actual incidents." Numbers and rates of crime are calculated on the basis of "actual incidents" categorized according to the most serious offence.

Source: Adapted from Statistics Canada, special tabulation, unpublished data, Uniform Crime Reporting (UCR1) Survey, Canadian Centre for Crime Statistics, 1998 to 2009.

Concerns have also been expressed that the crime categories used are too general, allowing too many different kinds of acts to be recorded in the same way. For example, thefts and attempted thefts are recorded under the same category.

**gross counts of crime**

A count of the total amount of
crime in a given community,
making no distinction between
crime categories.

Furthermore, as previously indicated, it is not always entirely clear just what it is we want to count. In Canada, the count of crimes includes violations of the Criminal Code, violations of other federal and provincial statutes, and violations of some municipal by-laws. Many of these criminal and quasi-criminal laws are not what most Canadians think of as crime. When most people think of crime they are thinking about particular offences. They are not thinking about the Criminal Code and the full range of behaviours legally defined as criminal. When we seek to count crime, we are invariably struck with a complex mix of these two sets of definitions. For this reason, **gross counts of crime** may be very misleading. For example, in 1969 the Ouimet report pointed out that total convictions for all criminal offences in Canada increased by an alarming 2500 percent between 1901 and 1965. The report added, however, that 98 percent of the increase was accounted for by summary convictions—less serious crime—particularly traffic offences. Thus much of the apparent increase in crime actually reflected the increased use of automobiles in Canada during this period. With the report of the gross crime counts alone, most people would no doubt have had horrific visions of violent predators preying on innocent victims, rather than the more accurate vision of careless motorists abusing one another and pedestrians. For these reasons, UCR programs count offences within particular offence categories so that each offence can be examined separately.

Another often-cited problem is that the Canadian UCR treats property crimes and personal crimes differently. Several property crimes, even if they involve different victims, may be recorded as a single offence if they are considered to be part of the same incident. This is not the case for personal offences. However, even for personal offences, the UCR1 survey collects very little information about victims and offenders. The CCJS has sought to rectify this by developing the richer UCR, the UCR2, which as we saw above collects data on characteristics of the victim and the accused as well as characteristics of the incident itself. As a result of the most serious offence scoring rule, less serious offences are under-counted by the aggregate survey. However, the incident-based survey allows up to four violations per incident, permitting the identification of lesser offences.

By 2009 the response rate from police respondents to the UCR surveys was virtually 100 percent. UCR2 data provide a rich source of information for the nation. Continuity with the UCR aggregate survey data is maintained by a conversion of the incident-based data to aggregate counts at year-end.

The question remains, however, whether the new and improved Canadian UCR will provide us with an accurate count of crime or even a reasonable indicator of crime and crime trends. Can official statistics ever tell us about total crime? Are official statistics useful only for understanding the criminal justice system?

We might have discussed the Canadian UCR under the heading of criminal justice statistics because these official data may tell us more about police activities than about crime. "Official violations" statistics are, in part, a product of policy decisions within the criminal justice system, that is, decisions about which criminal infractions deserve the most police attention and resources. Furthermore, crime statistics are the product of individual police decisions made in the exercise of police discretion about what crimes are serious enough to attend to, record, and pursue. In fact, the ways in which police and police departments apply crime recording and scoring procedures reflect, to some extent, the policing style and policy of the particular police department. Because combining or comparing statistics from different departments is highly problematic, the CCJS has developed elaborate rules and procedures for collecting and verifying data.

Police statistics are also shaped by public perceptions, concerns, and fears. The police are dependent on the accounts of victims and witnesses. In other words, victims and witnesses must recognize an act as a criminal justice matter, must believe it to be of sufficient seriousness to warrant a report to the police, and must believe that reporting the act is worthwhile—all this before the police make their decisions about how to respond to and record an act (see, for example, Shearing, 1984).

Official crime statistics, then, are shaped by both common-sense and legal definitions of what constitute crime. These statistics reflect the decisions of many people, not simply the behaviours of criminals. Official counts of crime will change as legal definitions change, as common-sense definitions change, and as the priorities of agents of law enforcement change. For example, if Parliament made premarital sex illegal, we could well expect a rather sharp increase in crime. Would this be reflected in official crime counts? To the extent that there are no direct victims to bring these offences to police attention, the answer is probably no. Much would depend on the priority attached to enforcement of this offence.

Consider two less hypothetical examples. As official statistics reveal to us increasing rates of family violence, theoretical explanations of the crisis in the nuclear family abound. But has the incidence truly increased, or have Canadians become less tolerant of such behaviour and more willing to bring such incidents to police attention? Have police become more sensitive to the seriousness of the problem and more likely to record the incidents as crimes? In other words, has the incidence of family violence increased, or have the definitions and reporting and recording behaviours changed? For those students wanting more statistical and substantive information on this topic, the CCJS website has a wealth of excellent studies on family violence and victimization of women.

Now consider drug offences. During the period 2000–2010, total drug offences increased by 10 percent; cannabis offences were up by 13 percent; cocaine offences were up by 32 percent. Other drug offences, reflecting the increased popularity of ecstasy, methamphetamines, and other "designer drugs," were up 91 percent (Brennan and Dauvergne, 2011).

Why has there been such an increase in "other" drug offences? Has their use really increased that much or have the priorities of law enforcement agencies shifted as well? One factor contributing to the increase in cannabis offences may be the effort to shut down marijuana-growing operations across the country as hydroponics have enabled Canadian growers to supply an increasing share of the domestic market and to export to the United States, frequently in exchange for cocaine for the Canadian market. Because statistics for victimless crimes such as drug use are as much a result of police priorities and budgets as they are of the amount of criminal behaviour, official statistics may not tell us much about the actual prevalence of these behaviours.

What, then, can the UCR tell us? From the inception of the Uniform Crime Reports in 1962, the total Criminal Code offence rate nearly tripled from 2771 offences per 100 000 Canadians to 7224 in 2009. Figure 4.4 shows the trend line during this period. During this period, both violent and property crime rates increased steadily until 1992. They continued to decline or to be stable through 2009. Violent crimes (1314 per 100 000 in 2009) were consistently much lower than property crimes (4081 per 100 000) (see Figure 4.4).

Those who work with crime statistics generally refer to crime **rates** when they wish to take into account the size of the population. The crime rate is simply the number of incidents for every 100 000 Canadians. Reference to rate, then, rather than incidence, makes sure that comparisons from jurisdiction to jurisdiction, or over time, do not reflect changes in population size rather than differences in criminal behaviour.

In 2010 Canada had 554 homicides (first- and second-degree murder, manslaughter, and infanticide) and 693 attempted murders. Together these crimes account for less than half of one percent of reported violent incidents. The 2010 rate (1.6 homicides per 100 000 population) is the lowest rate since 1966 (see Figure 4.5).

Crime has been declining during recent years. Although the crime rate rose from 1962 to 1991, it has generally declined since then (see Figure 4.6, which shows the levels of all recorded offences for the period 2000 to 2010). The overall crime rate is down 19 percent from a decade ago.

## Crime Severity Index

To address the problem of the crime rate being driven by high volume but less serious offences the CCJS developed crime severity indexes. These were first

**FIGURE 4.4**   **Total Criminal Code Offences Reported to Police by Most Serious Offence, Rate per 100 000 Canadians, 1962–2010**

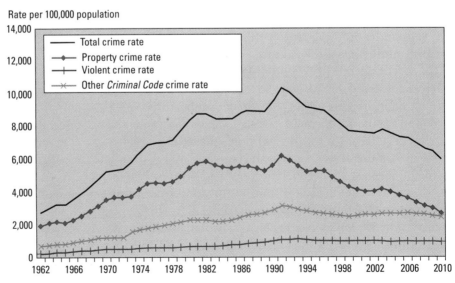

Source: From Shannon Brennan and Mia Dauvergne. (2011). "Police-reported CrimeStatistics in Canada, 2010." Juristat 30 (4): 18, http://www.statcan.gc.ca/pub/85-002-x/2011001/article/11523-eng.pdf.05_

**FIGURE 4.5**   Homicide Rate per 100 000 Canadians, 1961–2010

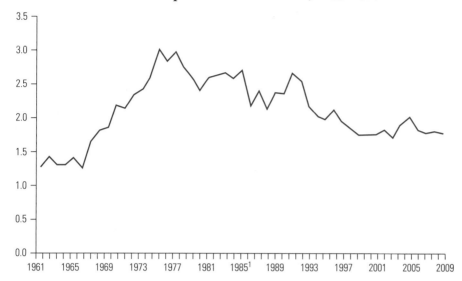

[1] Excludes 329 victims killed in the Air India incident.

Source: 2010 data from Shannon Brennan and Mia Dauvergne. (2011). "Police-reported Crime Statistics in Canada, 2010." Juristat 30 (4): 18, http://www.statcan.gc.ca/pub/85-002-x/ 2011001/article/11523-eng.pdf.05_

released in April 2009. The crime severity index is calculated by assigning each offence a weight derived from actual sentences given by the criminal courts. The more serious the average sentence, the greater the weight. Thus, more serious offences have a greater impact on the severity index. Figure 4.6 shows the crime severity indexes from 2000–2010.

**FIGURE 4.6**   Police-Reported Crime Severity Indexes, 1999–2009

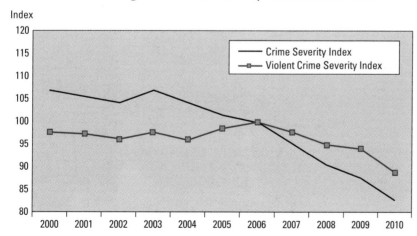

Note: Indexes have been standardized to a base year of 2006 which is equal to 100.

Source: From Shannon Brennan and Mia Dauvergne. (2011). "Police-reported CrimeStatistics in Canada, 2010." Juristat 30 (4): 18, http://www.statcan.gc.ca/pub/85-002-/2011001/ article/11523-eng.pdf.05_

The crime severity index has decreased by 23 percent from 2000–2010. (For a full account of these new indexes, including a youth crime severity index, see Dauvergne and Turner, 2010.) Table 4.1 shows the both the crime rate and the crime severity values for most of Canada's largest cities for 2010. The city rankings on the two measures are very similar.

**TABLE 4.1**   Crime Rate and Crime Severity Index Values, by Census Metropolitan Area, 2010

| Census Metropolitan Area | Crime Rate | Crime Severity Index |
|---|---|---|
| Regina | 9813 | 131.4 |
| Kelowna | 9548 | 113.1 |
| Saskatoon | 9384 | 128.1 |
| Thunder Bay | 8713 | 111.3 |
| Winnipeg | 8405 | 122.3 |
| St. John's | 7960 | 101.9 |
| Edmonton | 7853 | 102.0 |
| Vancouver | 7484 | 101.2 |
| Saint John | 7450 | 91.9 |
| Halifax | 7379 | 96.8 |
| Abbotsford | 7254 | 99.8 |
| Brantford | 7226 | 99.1 |
| Victoria | 7130 | 83.7 |
| London | 6213 | 82.4 |
| **Canada** | **6145** | **82.7** |
| Moncton | 5744 | 96.8 |
| Sudbury | 5717 | 84.2 |
| Barrie | 5290 | 60.1 |
| Kingston | 5108 | 62.3 |
| Montreal | 5099 | 83.7 |
| Calgary | 5047 | 76.5 |
| Windsor | 5027 | 66.1 |
| St. Catharines | 5284 | 69.8 |
| Hamilton | 4954 | 70.9 |
| Kitchener | 4950 | 68.0 |
| Peterborough | 4864 | 67.8 |
| Trois-Rivieres | 4861 | 69.4 |
| Ottawa | 4257 | 60.1 |
| Guelph | 4241 | 50.4 |
| Quebec | 3898 | 56.1 |
| Toronto | 3563 | 57.8 |

Source: Brennan, Shannon and Mia Dauvergne. (2011). "Police-reported Crime Statistics in Canada, 2010." *Juristat* 30(4): 18, http://www.statcan.gc.ca/pub/85-002-x/2011001/article/11523-eng.pdf.05_

Remember that all these data are based on reports to the police. But what can we say about crime rates given all the cautions with which we began this chapter? How much crime remains hidden to the police? Which crimes? How much do police recording practices shape the UCR figures? How much do these practices change over time? Are these data useless? The answer to the last question is no. For example, the homicide statistics collected by the Canadian Centre for Justice Statistics reflect the actual number of homicides fairly accurately. It is also probable that certain other offences that are of high priority within the criminal justice system, and which victims are likely to report, are relatively well captured by the UCR program. Motor vehicle theft is the best example of this type of offence. In sum, we can learn something about the incidence of crime from these data, but we are not sure how much.

We can be more confident that if police departments across Canada are recording and reporting crimes relatively consistently, then the UCR data give us a picture of what crimes the police are processing. For example, in the 1980s changes in policy limited police discretion in laying charges when handling domestic violence incidents. This policy has produced more official incidents of such assaults, reflecting changes in police practice if not changes in criminal behaviour. Some optimists would argue that the UCR gives an indication of trends in crime. The less optimistic say no, there is too much we do not know about victim reporting behaviour, about the exercise of police discretion in deciding what is criminal and what is not, about police recording and reporting practices, and about the nature and seriousness of the offences captured by the UCR. Out of these concerns have emerged attempts to develop other ways of counting crime. The most important of these is the victimization survey.

## Victimization Surveys

**Victimization surveys** are based on the idea asking people whether they have been victims of acts that the Criminal Code defines as criminal; to describe the nature and consequences of their victimization experiences; to describe the criminal justice response; to indicate whether victims or others brought the incidents to official attention, and, if not, why not; and to indicate their perceptions and attitudes about crime and criminal justice in Canada. The first large-scale victimization survey in Canada was carried out in 1982 by the Ministry of the Solicitor General of Canada and Statistics Canada. Those interested in the methodological developments for the first large-scale victimization surveys can read Catlin and Murray (1979), Evans and Leger (1978), and Skogan (1981).

Since 1988 Statistics Canada has conducted a victimization survey about every five years (1988, 1993, 1999, 2004, and 2009) as part of the General Social Survey. For the 2009 survey telephone interviews were conducted with a random **sample** of approximately 19 500 people, aged 15 and older, living in the 10 provinces. The three territories were also covered, using a different sampling design.

**victimization survey**

A survey of a random sample of the population in which people are asked to recall and describe their own experience of being a victim of crime.

**sample**

A group of elements (people, offenders, inmates) selected in a systematic manner from the population of interest.

Respondents were asked for their opinions concerning the level of crime in their neighbourhood, their fear of crime, and their views concerning the performance of the justice system. They were also asked about their experiences with criminal victimization. Respondents who had been victims of a crime in the previous 12 months were asked for detailed information on each incident, including when and where it occurred, whether the incident was reported to the police, and how they were affected by the experience.

Not all crimes can be captured through this survey method. One need not be a methodologist to recognize that murder cannot be included in such a survey. Nor can consensual crimes for which there are no direct victims—drug use, gambling, and the like. These consensual crimes are not captured very well through official data or through victimization surveys. Similarly, those crimes designed to keep victims unaware that they have been victimized cannot be captured accurately in victimization surveys (or official data sources). Fraud, embezzlement, employee pilferage, price fixing, and the wide range of consumer, corporate, and white-collar crimes were not included in the survey. The eight categories of crime included were sexual assault, robbery, assault, break and enter, motor vehicle theft, theft of household property, theft of personal property, and vandalism. The major findings of the 2009 survey are outlined in Box 4.2.

# FOCUS BOX 4.2

## CRIMINAL VICTIMIZATION IN CANADA, 2009: HIGHLIGHTS

- The 2009 General Social Survey (GSS) found that just over one-quarter of Canadians aged 15 years and older reported being the victim of a crime in the preceding 12 months. This proportion was similar to that in 2004, when the previous victimization survey was conducted.

- Seven in 10 self-reported victimizations were non-violent in nature. Of the eight offences measured by the GSS, theft of personal property was the most common.

- Overall rates of self-reported violent victimization remained stable between 2004 and 2009, as did the rates of sexual assault, physical assault, and robbery.

- Overall rates of self-reported household victimization also remained stable between 2004 and 2009. However, motor vehicle thefts declined 23 percent while break-ins increased 21 percent.

- Self-reported rates of violent and household victimization in 2009 were higher in western Canada, particularly Manitoba and Saskatchewan, than in the eastern part of the country.

- Younger Canadians reported higher rates of violent victimization than older Canadians. The rate of violence reported by 15-to-24 year olds was almost 15 times higher than the rate for individuals 65 years or older.

- Just under one-third of Canadians (31 percent) who had been victimized reported their victimization to police, down slightly from 2004 (34 percent). Break-ins and motor vehicle thefts were more likely than other types of victimizations to be brought to the attention of authorities.

- In 2009 the vast majority (93 percent) of Canadians felt somewhat or very satisfied with their personal safety from crime, similar to the GSS findings from 2004.

Source: Perreault, Samuel and Shannon Brennan. Summer 2010. "Criminal Victimization in Canada 2009." Adapted from Statistics Canada Catalogue no. 85-002-X, Vol. 30, no. 2, page 5.

Note that of the incidents identified, just under one-third (31 percent) had been reported to the police or had otherwise come to police attention. Recognizing that the victimization survey cannot capture the entire "dark" figure missed by the UCR, the survey data do reveal that many more Canadians are victimized by crime than is revealed by official statistics.

As most would guess, a large proportion of the unreported crime is relatively trivial, the kinds of incidents that most of us would not expect the police to devote time or resources to resolving. For example, a few dollars stolen by somebody within the household, a toy stolen from the porch, or an umbrella stolen from a restaurant are the kinds of common incidents that are rarely reported. Nonetheless, as Table 4.2 shows, more serious incidents may often go unreported. For example, in the 2004 Victimization Survey, 92 percent of those who had been sexually assaulted did not report the incident to the police. Women assaulted by people they knew indicated that fear of revenge was one of the reasons they failed to report. Figure 4.7 presents the major reasons for failing to report to the police in the 2009 survey.

Where incidents produced great financial loss to the victim, reporting was far more likely, even more likely than for those incidents that resulted in pain or injury but no loss. Reporting property crimes, particularly when the loss was over $1000, is less an act of justice (or even revenge) than a far more utilitarian act—seeking redress, recompense, or recovery. On the other hand, 83 percent of victims of violent crime felt it was their duty to report to the police. Figure 4.8 displays the data on reasons for reporting from the 1999 survey.

The survey data confirm many of the concerns about official sources of crime data. Some crimes are more likely to come to police attention than others. Some categories of victims are more likely to report their victimizations, and some categories of offenders (for example, family members) are less

**TABLE 4.2    Incidents Reported to Police, 1993, 1999, 2004, and 2009**

| Incidents | 1993 | 1999 | 2004 | 2009 |
|---|---|---|---|---|
| Theft personal property | 42 | 35 | 31 | 28 |
| Robbery | 46 | 46 | 46 | 43 |
| Physical assault | 33 | 37 | 39 | 34 |
| Break and enter | 68 | 62 | 54 | 54 |
| Motor vehicle/parts theft | 50 | 60 | 49 | 50 |
| Theft household property | 43 | 32 | 29 | 23 |
| Vandalism | 46 | 34 | 31 | 33 |

Source: For 1993–2004 data: Gannon, Maire and Karen Mihorean. "Criminal Victimization in Canada, 2004." Adapted from Statistics Canada Catalogue no. 85-002-XPE, Vol. 25, no. 7, Figure 11, page 17. http://www.statcan.gc.ca/bsolc/olc-cel/olc-cel?catno=85-002-X20050078803&lang=eng; 2009 data: adapted from Statistics Canada Catalogue no. 85-002-X, Summer 2010, Chart 3, page 15. http://www.statcan.gc.ca/pub/85-002-x/2010002/article/11340-eng.htm.

**FIGURE 4.7** Reasons for Not Reporting Victimization Incidents to Police, 2009

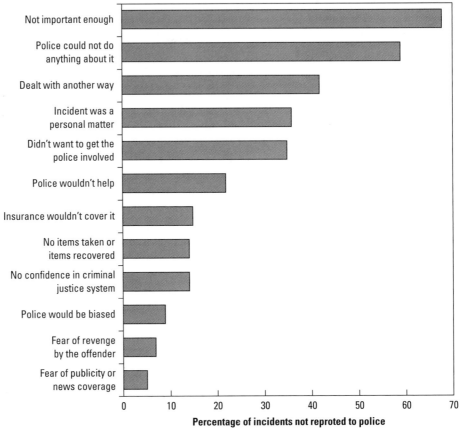

Note: Excludes all incidents of spousal sexual and physical assault. Excludes data from the Northwest Territories, Yukon, and Nunavut, which will be published at a later date.

Source: "Reasons for not reporting victimization incidents to police, 2009", adapted from Statistics Canada publication JURISTAT—Criminal victimization in Canada, 2009, Vol. 30, no. 2, page 16, http://www.statcan.gc.ca/pub/85-002-x/2010002/article/11340-eng.pdf.

likely to be reported. In general, it is only through such knowledge that we can begin to understand the UCR data and the dark figure of crime. Because victimization surveys are based on victims' perceptions and experiences, and because they collect information about the victims of crime, they are useful in identifying those categories of people most at risk of criminal victimization. For example, victimization surveys show that, contrary to conventional wisdom, the risk of victimization is lowest for older Canadians, especially those 65 years of age or older. In fact, the victimization data provide a profile of the victim of crime that explodes many popular myths. The typical victim of crime is young, single, male, not employed full-time, and living an active social life. The number of evenings spent outside the home is one of

**FIGURE 4.8   Reasons Given for Reporting Incidents to Police**

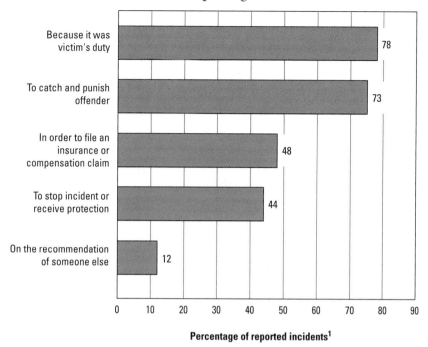

Percentage of reported incidents[1]

1 *Total exceeds 100% due to multiple responses. Excludes incidents that were not classified by crime type and incidents of spousal sexual and physical assault.*

Source: "Victims report incident because "it is my duty," adapted from Statistics Canada publication JURISTAT—Criminal victimization in Canada, 1999, Catalogue 85-002, Vol. 20, No. 10, page 12, http://www.statcan.gc.ca/pub/85-002-x/85-002-x2000010-eng.pdf.

the best predictors of whether a person has been victimized or not. Some of the reasons for these patterns of victimization are discussed in Chapter 15. Perhaps most important, victimization surveys allow us to go beyond merely counting crime. They provide data on the costs of victimization, the financial losses, the physical injuries, and the concern and fear victimization may produce. In addition, these data allow the exploration of various dimensions of seriousness. Clearly, victimization hits some harder than others. Nonetheless, and contrary to most people's expectations, women and men experience similar levels of violent victimization. Seniors have very low rates of victimization: "Households with only senior residents experienced household crimes (such as a break-in, property theft, motor vehicle theft or vandalism) at a rate of 87 incidents for every 1,000 senior households in Canada, nearly three times lower than the rate for all Canadian households (248 incidents per 1,000 households)" (Ogrodnick, 2007, 15). This is reflected in their perceptions of safety, as the survey also found that "seniors' satisfaction with their personal safety improved slightly between 1999 and 2004. The vast majority (92%) of seniors reported feeling satisfied with their overall level of safety from crime in 2004, compared to 89% reported in 1999. This increase closes the gap between seniors and younger Canadians, resulting in fairly consistent levels of satisfaction with their personal safety (92% compared to 94%)" (Ogrodnick, 2007, 17).

Victimization surveys cannot measure all crimes. They are dependent on the vagaries of human memory and are subject to the kinds of criticisms levelled against any survey, including the fact that some people may not tell interviewers the truth. Victimization surveys are dependent on respondents' ability not only to recall incidents and their details, but also to place the incidents correctly in time. We know that respondents are fallible. And, as Skogan (1978) suggests, well-educated, articulate respondents are more likely than others to talk to interviewers and to give rich and full accounts of their victimization experiences, thus perhaps biasing the data. There is reason as well to be cautious about interpreting data on domestic and sexual assaults that have been collected through surveys. Respondents may well be reluctant to discuss such experiences with an interviewer. Also, the methodology is still relatively young. Special methods will be needed to get data about rural victimization and victimization of Aboriginal Canadians. A good start was made in the 2004 survey (see the Box 4.3 "Violence Among Diverse Populations").

Special methodologies are also required to measure white-collar crime, consensual crime, and what has come to be called enterprise crime—organized crime and the crimes of organizations and the state. More information is also required on the psychological and emotional impact of victimization.

Despite the limitations, these data provide us with the opportunity to go beyond counting incidents and to gain some understanding of what it is we are counting. The data are an essential, complement to other sources of crime statistics.

## Self-Report Studies

Yet another approach to generating data on the nature and distribution of crime is the self-report study. The people who know the most about crime are those who break the law. Rather than relying on police data that will inevitably be incomplete or on the knowledge of victims, why not just ask criminals what they do and how often they do it? Many sociologists have done this, most commonly through questionnaires given to students in junior and senior high schools. A classic study done by Travis Hirschi (1969) in the San Francisco area is typical of self-report studies (you will read about some of the results of this study in Chapter 14, "Social Control Theory"). Hirschi took a random sample of all the junior and senior high school students in Richmond, California, and administered questionnaires to 5545 students. The survey was a very lengthy one, and we will consider here only the questions measuring delinquent behaviour. The students were asked six questions about their illegal conduct and for each were asked to check off one of the following responses: "A. No, never"; "B.

# FOCUS BOX 4.3

## VIOLENCE AMONG DIVERSE POPULATIONS

Through the 2004 GSS, it is possible to examine rates of violent victimization experienced by visible minorities, immigrants, including recent immigrants, and Aboriginal people, and to assess whether these segments of the population are at increased risk of being victimized.

Aboriginal people reported higher rates of violent victimization than other minority populations and the rest of the non-Aboriginal population. Those who self-identified as being Aboriginal were three times more likely than the non-Aboriginal population to be the victim of a violent incident (319 people per 1000 versus 101 per 1000). Even when controlling for other factors such as age, sex, and income, Aboriginal people remained at greater risk of violent victimization.

Aboriginal women appeared particularly at risk of victimization. Rates for Aboriginal women were 3.5 times higher than the rates recorded for non-Aboriginal women, while rates for Aboriginal men were 2.7 times higher than those for non-Aboriginal men.

The risk of violent victimization of visible minorities did not differ significantly from that of their non-visible minority counterparts (98 versus 107 per 1000 population) (see the accompanying figure). This was true for both men and women. However, in the case of immigrants, overall rates were lower than that of non-immigrants (68 versus 116 per 1000 population). The reduced likelihood of victimization was even more pronounced when only those who had immigrated to Canada since 1999 were excluded. For example, 71 per 1000 population of those who immigrated prior to 1999 were the victims of a violent crime, compared to 53 per 1000 population of those who had immigrated in the past five years. Again, these patterns were similar for immigrant women and men.

One possible explanation for lower rates within the immigrant population may be due to the fact that the immigrant population tends to be older, a factor which reduces risk of victimization. According to the Census of the

Rates per 1000 population 15 years and over

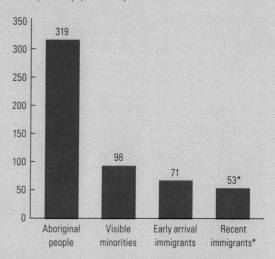

Source: Adapted from Statistics Canada, ""Victims don't report to police because "incident not important enough"[1]", Juristat - Criminal victimization in Canada, 1999, Catalogue 85-002, Vol. 20, No. 10, page 12, http://www.statcan.gc.ca/pub/85-002-x/85-002-x2000010-eng.pdf.

Population, compared to immigrants, a higher proportion of non-immigrants were under the age of 25 years, the most at-risk group for violent victimization.

Notes: Includes incidents of spousal sexual and physical assault.

[E]Use with caution.

1. Included are immigrants arriving between 1999 and 2004.

Source: Adapted from Statistics Canada, "Criminal victimization in Canada, 2004," Juristat, 85-002-XIF2005007, vol. 25 no. 7, November 2005; http://www.statcan.gc.ca/bsolc/olc-cel/olc-cel?catno=85-002-XIE&lang=eng.

# FOCUS BOX 4.4

## SUMMARY AND CAUTIONS: USING VICTIMIZATION SURVEY DATA AND DATA FROM THE UCR AND THE COURT SURVEYS

### Victimization Surveys

These surveys provide rich data but remember that they collect information on a limited set of crimes—eight in the Statistics Canada surveys. The Uniform Crime Reports (UCR) survey covers more than 100 offence types. When considering these data use caution. Refer back to Figure 4.1, The Crime Funnel. The 2009 victimization survey estimated that there were 630 000 break and enters in Canada. Note that these are break and enters of households. Break-and-enter offences against businesses are not included. Thousands of break and enters are therefore excluded from the victimization survey but they will be included in police and court data. This in turn affects each subsequent item in the funnel. The figure is an illustration only.

### Defining Courts-Based Data and Police Incident-Based Data

### Police

The Canadian Centre for Justice Statistics conducts the Uniform Crime Reporting (UCR) survey. This survey collects data on the crimes reported to the police. Coverage of the UCR Survey in 2005 was at 99.9 percent of the caseload of all police services in Canada. Currently there exists both an aggregate UCR survey and an incident-based UCR2 survey. The latter replaces the former as respondent police services become capable of providing the level of detail required by the incident-based survey.

The basic unit of count selected to report crimes to the incident-based UCR survey is the "criminal incident." The fundamental characteristic of an incident is that it may involve several victims, several accused persons, and several different violations of the law. All these different elements will be grouped together into one incident if they meet specified conditions (or rules). These rules are outlined in the Uniform Crime Reporting Incident-Based Survey, Reporting Manual, March 2006, Canadian Centre for Justice Statistics, Statistics Canada.

### Most Serious Offence and Scoring Rules

The UCR survey classifies incidents according to the most serious offence in the incident. Generally, this is the offence that carries the longest maximum sentence under the Criminal Code. However, in categorizing or ranking incidents, violent offences always take precedence over non-violent offences.

Furthermore, for violent crime, a separate incident is recorded for each victim. For example, if one person assaults three people, then three incidents are recorded. For non-violent crime, one incident is counted for every distinct or separate occurrence. For example, a fraudulent offence involving three victims would only result in one incident being recorded.

"Persons cleared by charge" refers to persons who have been formally charged or recommended to be charged by police.

### Courts

The purpose of the Adult Criminal Court Survey (ACCS) and the Youth Court Survey is to provide a national database of statistical information on the processing of cases through the adult and youth criminal court systems. The surveys consist of a census of Criminal Code and other federal statute charges dealt with in adult criminal courts and youth courts. In 2008–2009, the ACCS represented approximately 95 percent of the national adult criminal court caseload. The Youth Court Survey has 100 percent coverage.

### Counting Procedures

The basic unit of count for the Court Surveys is a case. A case is one or more charges against an accused person or corporation, where the charges receive a final disposition on the same date. Charges are linked to a case on the basis

*(continued)*

### Most Serious Offence and Decision Rules

When a case has more than one charge, it is necessary to decide which charge will be used to represent the case (since a case is identified by a single charge). In such multiple-charge cases, the "most serious decision" rule is applied. Decisions are ranked from the most to the least serious as follows: (1) guilty, (2) guilty of a lesser offence, (3) acquitted, (4) stay of proceeding, (5) withdrawn, dismissed, and discharged, (6) not criminally responsible, (7) other, and (8) transfer of court jurisdiction.

In cases where two or more offences have resulted in the same decision (e.g., guilty), the "most serious offence" rule is applied. All charges are ranked according to an offence seriousness scale, which is based on the average length of prison sentence and rate of incarceration. If two charges are tied according to this criterion, information about the sentence type (e.g., prison, probation, and fine) is considered. If a tie still exists, the magnitude of the sentence is considered.

### Comparisons Between Courts and Police UCR Survey Data

Counts from the UCR survey for offences cleared by charge are not comparable to the Adult Criminal Court Survey (ACCS) figures for charges disposed of. There are many reasons for this. In part, it is the result of scoring rules used by the UCR survey. The UCR survey counts violent offences by the number of victims in the incident; non-violent offences are counted by the number of separate incidents.

For example, two persons break into a house and subsequently commit vandalism and theft. This would be considered as one police incident. Assuming the charges were laid and the matter proceeded to court, there would be a minimum of six charges—three charges for each accused.

In addition, the differences in the "most serious offence" rule between the courts and police surveys can result in court cases and police incidents being represented by different offences even though they may have been part of the same crime.

Furthermore, the published UCR figures include offences involving youths, while the ACCS case counts include only the very few youth offences that have been transferred to adult court (less than 100 per year).

Moreover, information is captured in the UCR with the laying of a charge, while in the ACCS information is captured upon the court rendering a decision. This time lag in data collection between the two surveys further affects comparability.

of the accused identifier and the date of the last court appearance.

---

More than a year ago"; "C. During the last year;" and "D. During the last year and more than a year ago." The delinquency questions were:

- Have you ever taken little things (worth less than $2) that did not belong to you?
- Have you ever taken things of some value (between $2 and $50) that did not belong to you?
- Have you ever taken things of large value (worth over $50) that did not belong to you?
- Have you ever taken a car for a ride without the owner's permission?
- Have you ever banged up something that did not belong to you on purpose?
- Not counting fights that you may have had with a brother or sister, have you ever beaten up on anyone or hurt someone on purpose?

**self-report study**

A method for measuring crime involving the distribution of a detailed questionnaire to a sample of people, asking them whether they have committed a crime in a particular period of time. This has been a good method for criminologists to determine the social characteristics of offenders.

# FOCUS BOX 4.5

## "IF IT BLEEDS, IT LEADS": THE MEDIA AND PUBLIC PERCEPTIONS OF CRIME

Most Canadians learn about crime through the media rather than from first-hand experience. Stories portrayed on television and radio, and in newspapers, magazines, and books, shape our views about crime and criminals. But the media do not simply "report" the news. Editors and reporters select the crime news and construct the way this news is presented to us.

Unfortunately, the picture of crime we receive from the media is not always accurate. For example, most crime is property crime but most media stories deal with violent crime. Gabor (1994) reviewed all the crime-related stories reported over two months in an Ottawa newspaper. More than half the stories focused on violent crimes, particularly murders. However, violent crimes made up only seven percent of reported crimes in Ottawa, and the city averaged just six murders per year. While violent crimes were over-reported, property crimes received little attention, and white-collar and political crimes were almost never discussed.

Why do the media misrepresent crime? The primary goal of the media is to make profits by selling advertising. Stories about violent crime boost ratings and circulation. The informal media rule "if it bleeds, it leads" reflects the fact that the public is fascinated by sensationalized, bloody stories. Commenting on his experience with the media, the executive director of the Nova Scotia Bar Society said, "If there's no blood and gore, or there's no sex, it's not newsworthy. And if it falls into the category of being newsworthy, then they have to show the dead body. They've got to show the corpse" (McCormick, 1995, 182).

The media's misrepresentation of crime has several consequences. First, Canadians greatly over-estimate the amount of violent crime and have a fear of crime that is disproportionate to the real risk of victimization. One survey found that the vast majority of Canadians (75 percent) felt that more than half of all crimes are accompanied by violence. The true figure is less than 10 percent (Doob and Roberts, 1983). Crime stories lead us to see Canada as a violent and dangerous place.

The media also provide a distorted stereotype of offenders. Violent crimes are most often committed by relatives, friends, and acquaintances, and not by the anonymous stranger that so many of us fear. Our fear of crime and our image of the criminal have an impact on government policy toward crime. Actual crime trends are irrelevant—if the public feels crime is out of control, it will demand that government do something about it. While crime rates are in reality on the decline, a combination of increasing media coverage of crime and pressure from a variety of interest groups has led the federal government to tighten several laws, including those concerning immigration, young offenders, credit for time served, and firearms.

Source: Jane Lothian Murray, Rick Linden, and Diana Kendall. 2011. *Sociology in Our Times,* 5th edition. Toronto: Nelson.

Hirschi looked at responses to these delinquency questions and compared them with other measures, including such things as students' reports of their friends' behaviour, and their family and school relationships, in order to try to shed some light on what caused some students to become delinquent while others did not. Like victimization surveys, self-report studies were used to try to overcome some of the weaknesses of police data. In most cases the results have supported the view that there are systematic biases.

Because self-report studies supposedly avoid these biases, they have been particularly important in research and theory on the causes of crime and delinquency, especially the relationship between social class and crime. For a long time, these studies were not very carefully scrutinized. A major work to determine the reliability of self-report studies was carried out by Hindelang, Hirschi, and Weis (1981). They concluded that the self-report method does demonstrate that people are willing to report crimes, both those known and not known to officials, and that respondents' reports are internally consistent. A difficulty arises in that it appears that different populations answer self-report questions in different ways. Lower-class males and black males in the United States study are more likely to underreport their own criminal behaviour than are middle-class white males. Similarly, in Canada, Fréchette and LeBlanc (1979; 1980) confirm that while self-report studies do uncover much hidden delinquency and raise questions about the biases in official statistics that show the preponderance of lower-class crime, previous self-report studies have also masked the fact that lower-class crime is typically more serious and persistent.

In 2006 Canada participated in the International Self-reported Delinquency Study conducted in over 30 countries. Canada's study was conducted in Toronto schools, sampling youth in Grades 7 to 9. According to the International Youth Survey, over one-third (37 percent) of students in Grades 7 to 9 in Toronto reported having engaged in one or more delinquent behaviours in their lifetime, through either acts of violence, acts against property, or the sale of drugs. The lifetime prevalence was higher among boys (41 percent) than among girls (32 percent) (Savoie, 2007).

There are two related problems with self-report studies. First, it would appear that those who are typically law abiding are more likely to report completely their occasional infractions than are the more committed delinquents to report their more serious and frequent infractions. Second, differences between official statistics of delinquent behaviour and self-report data may reflect not simply biases in official data, but biases in the self-report method as well. The official data are likely to include more serious offences, and self-report data are more likely to include more minor infractions, as you can see from the items used in Hirschi's studies.

There are a number of other more technical problems with self-report studies. For example, there are sampling problems—it is difficult to get "hard-core criminals" in a sample for several reasons including the fact that they are less likely than other youth to be in school where most of these surveys are administered. There are also disagreements about which offences to select and which produce the most reliable and valid data, and which scoring procedures best suit the uses of the data (see Hindelang et al. 1981; Thornberry and Krohn, 2000). Although self-report studies are never likely to be an instrument for counting crimes, recent methodological refinements have enhanced their potential for addressing fundamental questions about crime and the correlates of crime.

Self-report data can be used for other purposes as well. By using formal self-report surveys such as Hirschi's or by interviewing criminals in prison or in other, less restrictive situations we can learn a great deal about their motivations for committing crimes and the techniques they use to commit crimes. This information can help us to understand the causes of crime and to prevent it. In later chapters of the book you will read about many of the lessons that criminologists have learned from talking to criminals.

# The Future of Crime and Criminal Justice Statistics

The importance of good statistics for planning, policy-making, and administration has long been recognized within the criminal justice system. The existence of the Canadian Centre for Justice Statistics is a recognition—in a country with shared jurisdiction for criminal justice—of the importance of developing national commitment and national strategies for producing and sharing criminal statistics.

New information technology holds great promise for improving the official records that form the basis of most criminal justice statistics on prisons, courts, and police. It is only through a nationally coordinated effort that we can avoid the danger of developing incompatible systems in each province (or worse, each municipality) that feed many different criminal justice systems and inhibit the continued development of a coordinated national system of justice.

The methods for counting crimes are still in their formative stages. Some, like the UCR, will be derived from official records (designed in accordance with UCR rules) and will, therefore, suffer the limitations of all such official statistics. Nevertheless, recent advances in police management information systems and crime classification systems hold great promise for providing us with a measure of calls for police service, police caseloads, and police activity. The richer information from the UCR2 will help here. Other methods, like victimization surveys, will draw on people's experiences and will, therefore, suffer the limitations of all such surveys. Significant progress has been achieved in Canada in the development and refinement of victimization surveys and self-report studies.

How much crime is there in Canada, and what are the trends? Is it bad and getting worse? Do we have cause for alarm? Are things good and getting better? Do we have cause for complacency? Depending on your bias and prejudices, the state of the art allows you to find some evidence and numbers to justify either extreme. But with the improvements in our knowledge about crime and the development of new methods, we are coming to recognize the complexity of the questions. When taken together, the UCR and the victimization surveys encourage neither alarm nor complacency. Overall, there is certainly less serious crime than most Canadians assume based on media accounts and the high visibility of sensational incidents. At the same time, we are starting to uncover some particular kinds of serious incidents that have remained hidden for too long. Sexual assault and family violence are two important examples. Much more work is needed. Only through an integrated program of criminal justice statistics that recognizes the limits of any one source of information will we be able to build powerful theories of crime and sound policies and programs for crime prevention and control.

## SUMMARY

- Statistics can help us to better understand the nature and extent of crime in Canada. However, in order to interpret these crime statistics properly, we must understand their strengths and weaknesses.

- The quality of official statistics varies depending on their sources. Corrections data are the most reliable and valid because the task of counting prisoners can be done accurately. On the other hand, crimes known to the police, the most commonly used statistics, will always be biased by inconsistencies in reporting and recording, although the CCJS is very stringent about verifying data.

- Administrative records can be the basis of statistics if clear procedures are developed about units of count, levels of data aggregation, definitions, data elements, and counting procedures.

- The Canadian Uniform Crime Report (UCR) system is designed to provide uniform and compatible national statistics. There is much debate about just what is counted. Some hold that the UCR provides a reasonable estimate of crime rates. Others hold that what is being measured is criminal justice processing.

- The crime rates provided by the UCR, based on crimes reported to the police, have declined since the peak year of 1991. Both violent and property crimes have declined. The overall decline from 1999 to 2009 is about 17 percent.

- Victimization surveys provide an alternative and complementary method of measuring crime. These surveys ask random samples of the population about their victimization experiences. They also provide data on such important issues as reasons for reporting and not reporting crimes to the police.

- Self-report studies are not serious rivals of either the UCR or victimization surveys as a method of measuring crime. However, they do have a useful place in answering specific questions related to understanding the causes and correlates of crime.

- Developing Canada's national statistics will take continued effort and commitment from all the actors in the system. The CCJS has made great progress and the statistics now available are much better than they were 10 or 20 years ago.

## QUESTIONS FOR CRITICAL THINKING

1. Crime rates in Canada declined between 1999 and 2009. How would you account for this decline? You might wish to read ahead in Chapter 5 to help you find some possible answers to this question.
2. The media do not provide an accurate portrayal of the nature and extent of crime in Canada. Can you find examples in your own community of media distortions of crime? Why do the media behave in this way? What are the consequences of these distortions?
3. Victimization surveys reveal that many crimes, including serious violent crimes, are not reported to the police. Why not? What is the significance of this for society?
4. To what extent do official statistics measure the amount of crime in society? What are the major biases in official statistics?
5. How are self-report studies used in criminology? Can you find examples of the use of self-report data in later chapters of this book?

## NET WORK

Canadian crime statistics are compiled by the Canadian Centre for Justice Statistics, which reports the annual number of crimes reported to the police. Go to the Statistics Canada website at **http://www5.statcan.gc.ca/subject-sujet/index.action?&lang=eng** and go to "Crime and Justice." Using the information on "Crimes, by type of offence," identify the trends in the crimes reported in Figure 4.4 of this text. Look at the information on "Homicide offences, number and rate." Have homicide rates gone up or down in the past five years? Which provinces and territories have the highest rate of homicide? Do the actual crime figures reported by Statistics Canada correspond with your perception of crime rates reported by the mass media?

## KEY TERMS

administrative record; pg. 105
Canadian Centre for Justice
    Statistics; pg. 107
counting procedure; pg. 105
crime rate; pg. 102
dark figure of crime; pg. 109
data element; pg. 105
gross counts of crime; pg. 112
ideology; pg. 104
levels of aggregation; pg. 105
methodology; pg. 102

population; pg. 103
reliability; pg. 102
sample; pg. 117
self-report study; pg. 126
seriousness rule; pg. 110
theory; pg. 104
Uniform Crime Reports (UCR);
    pg. 110
validity; pg. 102
victimization survey; pg. 117

## BIBLIOGRAPHY

Beattie, S., and A. Cotter. (2010). "Homicide in Canada, 2009." *Juristat* 30(3). http://www .statcan.gc.ca/pub/85-002-x/2010003/article/11352-eng.htm.

Besserer, S., and C. Trainor. (2000). "Criminal Victimization in Canada, 1999." *Juristat* 20 (10). http://www.statcan.gc.ca/pub/85-002-x/85-002-x2000010-eng.pdf.

Brennan, Shannon and Mia Dauvergne. (2011). "Police-reported CrimeStatistics in Canada, 2010." Juristat 30(4): 18, http://www.statcan.gc.ca/pub/85-002-x/2011001/ article/11523-eng.pdf.05_

Bureau of Justice Statistics. (2010). *Prison Statistics*. Washington, DC: Department of Justice. http://www.ojp.usdoj.gov/bjs/prisons.htm.

Catlin, G., and S. Murray. (1979). *Report on Canadian Victimization Survey Methodological Pretests*. Ottawa: Statistics Canada.

Dauvergne, M., and J. Turner. (2010). "Police-Reported Crime Statistics in Canada, 2009." *Juristat* 30 (2). http://www.statcan.gc.ca/pub/85-002-x/2010002/article/11292-eng.htm.

de Silva, S., and R.A. Silverman. (1985). "New Approaches to Uniform Crime Reporting in Canada." Paper presented at the annual meeting of the American Society of Criminology, San Diego (November).

Doob, A., and J.V. Roberts. (1983). *An Analysis of the Public's View of Sentence*. Ottawa: Department of Justice Canada.

Evans, J., and G. Leger. (1978). "The Development of Victimization Surveys in Canada." *Public Data Use* 6 (November).

Fréchette, M., and Marc LeBlanc. (1979). "La délinquance cachée à l'adolescence." *Inadaptation juvénile* Cahier 1. Montreal: Université de Montréal.

———. (1980). "Pour une pratique de la criminologie: configurations de conduites délinquantes et portraits de délinquants." *Inadaptation juvénile Cahier 5*. Montreal: Université de Montréal.

Gabor, T. (1994). *Everybody Does It: Crime by the Public*. Toronto: University of Toronto Press.

Gannon, M. (2006). "Crime Statistics in Canada, 2005." *Juristat* 26 (4). http://www.statcan. gc.ca/bsolc/olc-cel/olc-cel?catno=85-002-X20060049251&lang=eng.

Hindelang, M.J., T. Hirschi, and J.G. Weis. (1981). *Measuring Delinquency*. Beverly Hills: Sage.

Hirschi, Travis. (1969). *Causes of Delinquency*. Berkeley: University of California Press.

McCormick, C. (1995). *Constructing Danger: The Misrepresentation of Crime in the News*. Halifax: Fernwood Publishing.

Murray, Jane Lothian, Rick Linden, and Diana Kendall. (2011). *Sociology in Our Times: The Essentials* (5th edn). Toronto: Nelson

Nettler, G. (1974). *Explaining Crime*. New York: McGraw-Hill.

Ogrodnick, Lucie. (2007). *Seniors as Victims of Crime, 2004 and 2005*. Ottawa: Statistics Canada Catalogue Number 85F0033MIE20-014.

Perreault, S., and S. Brennan. (2010). "Criminal Victimization in Canada, 2009." *Juristat* 30 (2). http://www.statcan.gc.ca/pub/85-002-x/2010002/article/11340-eng.htm.

Polsky, Ned. (1967). *Hustlers, Beats, and Others*. Chicago: Aldine.

Savoie, J. (2006). "Youth Self-reported Delinquency, Toronto, 2006." *Juristat* 27 (6). http:// www.statcan.gc.ca/pub/85-002-x/85-002-x2007006-eng.pdf.

Shearing, Clifford D. (1984). "Dial-A-Cop: A Study of Police Mobilization." Report for the Centre of Criminology, University of Toronto.

Silverman, R.A. (1980). "Measuring Crime: More Problems." *Journal of Police Science and Administration* 8 (3): 265–74.

Silverman, R.A., and J. Teevan. (1975). *Crime in Canadian Society*. Toronto: Butterworths.

Skogan, W. (1978). "Review of Surveying Crime." *Journal of Criminal Law and Criminology* 69: 139–40.

———. (1981). *Issues in the Measurement of Victimization*. Washington, DC: U.S. Department of Justice, Bureau of Justice Statistics.

Statistics Canada. (2003). *Canadian Crime Statistics*. Ottawa: Canadian Centre for Justice Statistics, chapter 6. Catalogue No. 85-205-XIE.

———. (2010). *Uniform Crime Reporting Survey (UCR)*. Ottawa: Statistics Canada.

Thornberry, Terence P., and Marvin D. Krohn. (2000). "The Self-Report Method for Measuring Delinquency and Crime." *Criminal Justice 2000*, Vol. 4. National Institute of Justice, Washington, DC.

# Correlates of Criminal Behaviour

**5**

## Timothy F. Hartnagel

**UNIVERSITY OF ALBERTA**

Which Canadians are most likely to commit crimes? Are older people more likely to commit crimes than younger people? Are men more likely to commit crimes than women? Are upper-class people more or less likely to break the law than their lower-class counterparts? Which provinces have the highest rate of crime? Each of these questions asks about a **correlate** of crime. A correlate is a phenomenon that accompanies another phenomenon and is related in some way to it. Correlates of crime are those phenomena that are associated with criminal activity. While a list of such phenomena would include any number of conditions, the discussion in this chapter will be limited to some of the social conditions that are correlated with crime. We will describe and discuss the relationship between criminal behaviour and age, sex, race, drug abuse, social class, and region.

**correlate**

Any variable that is related to another variable. Age and sex are the two strongest correlates of crime.

---

After reading this chapter, you should be able to

- Distinguish between correlates and causes of criminal behaviour.
- Identify and describe the major social correlates of criminal behaviour in Canada.
- Describe and explain trends in the age and sex distribution of criminal behaviour.
- Describe the relationship between race and criminal behaviour and explain the over-representation of Aboriginal people in the Canadian criminal justice system.
- Understand the relationship between drug misuse and criminal behaviour.
- Discuss and reconcile the apparently conflicting evidence regarding the correlation between social class and criminal behaviour.
- Describe how crime rates vary by geographic region.

**Learning Objectives**

## Correlates Defined

Before turning to the details of these specific correlates, the concept of correlation itself should be considered briefly. **Correlation** refers to a relationship between at least two phenomena that are related, or occur, or vary together.

**correlation**

A relationship that exists when two or more variables, such as age and crime, are associated or related to one another.

For example, some criminologists have claimed that delinquent behaviour is correlated with physique or body type. They claim that adolescent males with an athletic, muscular body build commit more delinquent acts than those whose physique is lean and fragile. Other criminologists have shown that some types of crime occur more frequently in larger cities than in smaller towns and rural areas. They argue that city size and crime vary together. These examples give measurements on two variables (for example, city size and crime) for a number of individuals or aggregates (for example, cities). The task is to determine whether and how these two sets of measurements go together—that is, whether and how they're correlated. When we analyze the relationship between two variables, we may find that they are positively correlated, negatively correlated, or unrelated to each other. A positive relationship means that as one variable increases, the other also increases. For example, the more deviant friends we have, the more likely we are to be deviant ourselves. A negative relationship means that as one variable increases, the other decreases. For example, as we get older, we are less likely to be involved in criminal behaviour. Discovering such correlations or relationships is an important first step for any scientific discipline such as criminology. Thus, a good deal of the early work in criminology was devoted to the task of identifying and describing the correlates of crime.

Having identified and described a correlate of crime—a relationship—it is natural to want to know why it exists. How might this relationship be explained? What might have produced it?

One explanation for a correlation or relationship between two variables is causal. The concept of causation has been debated by philosophers and social scientists. At the very least, the idea of causation has proven to be a useful way of thinking about the natural and social world. A causal explanation refers to the inference that a change in one variable results from or is produced by change in another variable. A common mistake is to confuse correlation with causation and so to infer that one variable causes another from the fact that they are correlated. However, correlation means only that two variables are related. They are associated but a change in one does not necessarily produce a change in the other. Criminologists are frequently interested in establishing causal explanations. They are not usually satisfied, for example, with knowing that poverty and crime are correlated; they want to know if crime results from poverty, and if it does, how? However, it would be a mistake to conclude from their correlation alone that poverty causes crime. So correlation between two variables is a necessary first step toward causal explanation but is not in itself sufficient for inferring such an explanation.

The second element of a causal explanation is a *theory* linking the variables. Events may occur together, but one will not be viewed as causing the other unless we have some explanation of how they are linked. We look for correlates of crime to help us to explain criminal behaviour, and our explanatory theories must be tested against what we know about crime. For example, we may have a theory that the movement of the planets causes criminality. However, when we test this explanation, we find that there is no correlation between planetary movements and crime rates. Thus, we will reject the theory, at least until some evidence supporting it can be found. Much of the attention of criminologists has been devoted to developing and testing theories of crime, and these theories must explain the facts about crime. Therefore, the correlates discussed in this chapter set the stage for the theories that follow.

Human beings have a tendency to simplify their perceptions of the world. This tendency can lead to a distortion of the understanding of correlates and causes. There is a temptation to assume that an effect can have only one cause that is both necessary and sufficient. There is also the temptation to assume that causes must be perfectly correlated with their effects and that no other variables are necessary for interpreting how the cause operates or for specifying the particular conditions or circumstances under which it has its effect(s) (Hirschi and Selvin, 1966). But reality is substantially more complicated than this, and it would be wise to develop the habit of thinking of crime as the consequence of multiple causes that combine in complicated ways to produce their effects. Nettler (1982) uses the image of a dense web to communicate the meaning of this view of causation. He describes this as a multiplicity of tightly packed causes that interact strongly and non-uniformly. As selected correlates of crime are examined, then, the urge to reach hasty conclusions concerning the causal character and significance of these correlations should be resisted.

# Age

## Peak Ages for Crime

Without much exaggeration, crime can be said to be a young man's game. To put this into more technical terms, age and sex are strong correlates of criminal behaviour. Any number of criminologists has singled out these two variables for their strong relationship with crime. For example, Sutherland and Cressey (1978) state that sex status is of greater importance in differentiating criminals from non-criminals than any other trait, and that statistics from a variety of years and jurisdictions uniformly indicate a higher prevalence of crime among young persons compared with other age groups.

Figure 5.1 shows the distribution of persons accused of crime by age for 2010. The percentage of persons accused of crime increases from early adolescence to young adulthood and then generally declines. In 2010, age-specific rates for those accused of crime were highest among 15-to-20-year-olds, with the peak age at 18 years (Brennan and Dauvergne, 2011). This pattern is stronger for property crimes (Bunge et al., 2005).

Data for 2008–09 from the Adult Criminal Court Survey (Thomas, 2010) also show that younger adults are over-represented among accused persons when comparing the age distribution of offenders to the age distribution of the general adult population. For example, 18-to-24-year-olds made up 12 percent of the adult population but accounted for 31 percent of all cases in adult criminal court in 2008–09. Similarly, persons 25 to 34 represented 17 percent of the adult population and 28 percent of the adult criminal court cases. This age distribution is stronger for property crimes (33 percent of accused were 18 to 24) than for violent crimes (26 percent were 18 to 24).

Shelly Milligan. (2010). "Youth Court Statistics, 2008/09." *Juristat* 30 (2). To find this and other interesting research papers, go to www.statcan.ca/bsolc/english/bsolc?catno=85-002-XI

**FIGURE 5.1    Persons Accused of Crime, by Age, Canada, 2010**

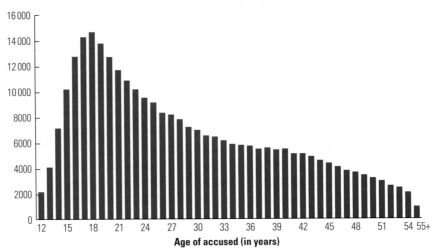

Source: Adapted from Statistics Canada, Police-reported Crime Statistics in Canada, 2010, Juristat, 85-002-XIE2011001, July 2011; http://www.statcan.gc.ca/bsolc/olc-cel/olc-cel?catno=85-002-XIE&lang=eng#formatdisp

Different crimes peak at different ages, and rates of some types of crime decline much more slowly with increasing age (Steffensmeier et al., 1989). Offences where the accused in 2008/09 was 35 years of age or older in the majority of cases included criminal harassment (59 percent), other sexual offences (59 percent), prostitution (59 percent), and sexual assault (57 percent) (Thomas, 2010). Some crimes, including embezzlement, fraud, and gambling, do not conform to the general pattern and peak later in the life cycle (Steffensmeier and Allan, 1995). Braithwaite (1989) has pointed out that white-collar crimes, which are committed by persons of respectability and high status in the course of their occupation, peak later in life because these crimes require the opportunities provided by occupations that most people under 25 have yet to attain.

Self-report data also support the age–crime relationship, though such research has generally limited its attention to juveniles and is, therefore, of only limited usefulness for examining the full range of the age–crime relationship. The self-report results from a national survey of adolescents in the United States by Ageton and Elliott (1978) only partially agree with the official data concerning age and crime. Their results suggest that the peak ages for youthful crime are somewhat younger than the official data indicate, with the highest incidence for many property and violent offences occurring between the ages of 13 and 15. Juvenile diversion programs and hesitancy to formally process adolescents through the criminal justice system may play some role in explaining the higher peak ages in official data on arrests and convictions. Osgood et al. (1989) compared offence rates based on arrests and on self-reports and found that both methods show substantial declines from ages 17 through 23 for virtually all offences, with the major exception of arrests for assault.

Canadian self-report research in Montreal by LeBlanc (1983) found that in a sample of adolescents aged 12 to 18, self-reported delinquency increased progressively until age 16 or 17 and then diminished, though this pattern varied with the nature of the delinquency. Serious delinquency tended to diminish with increasing age, while drug and status offences increased.

Since younger age categories are over-represented among criminal offenders, it's quite likely changes over time in the crime rate reflect, at least in part, changes in the age composition of the total population. Several researchers have shown that a significant amount of the rise and fall of U.S. crime rates can be explained by the changing age composition of the American population, primarily the aging of the "baby boomers" (Cohen and Land, 1987; Sagi and Wellford, 1968; Steffensmeier and Harer, 1991; Wellford, 1973). Overall crime rates rose as this group reached their late teens in the 1960s and then fell as they began to reach their 30s a decade later (Carrington, 2001). Similarly in Canada, baby boomers—those born between 1947 and 1966—reached 15 years of age in the 1960s and 1970s, a time when violent and property crime rates were rising. Figure 5.2 shows the trend in overall crime and in the number of 15-to-24-year-olds as rates per 100 000 population. The rate of 15-to-24-year-olds began dropping in the early 1980s. The general decline in crime rates since the early 1990s coincided with a decrease in the proportion of persons aged 15 to 24 during the same time period (Savoie, 2002). Ouimet (2002) examined the drop in crime in the 1990s in both the United States and Canada and attributed it primarily to these shifts in the age composition of the population, as well as improved employment opportunities. Carrington (2001) has forecast that all types of crime in Canada should decline to the year 2041 because of the

**FIGURE 5.2**   Crime Rate and Population Aged 15–24, per 100 000 Population, Canada 1962–2003[1]

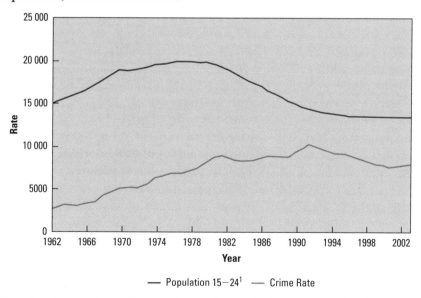

[1]Note that the population 15–24 refers to changes in the population for these age groups and not changes in crime rates.

Source: Wallace, Marnie. "Crime Statistics in Canada, 2003," adapted from Statistics Canada Catalogue no. 85-002-XIE, Vol. 24, no. 6, page 3.

continuing aging of the population, ignoring all other factors that might affect crime rates.

However, other researchers have found the changing age structure of the population to have only a limited impact on crime rates (Levitt, 1999; Steffensmeier and Harer, 1991). This may depend on the type of crime. For example, two Canadian studies reported the changing age composition had a significant impact on the decline in Canadian homicide rates (Leenaars and Lester, 2004; Sprott and Cesaroni, 2002). But an examination of the relationships between changes in crime rates for the four major crime types of homicide, robbery, break and enter, and motor vehicle theft and a number of socio-demographic and economic trends during the period 1962 to 2003 found only a positive relationship between the proportion of the population aged 15 to 24 and rates of break and enter (Bunge et al., 2005). These authors conclude that shifts in the age composition of the population are only one of many factors contributing to crime rate changes.

## Maturational Reform

To conclude this discussion on age and its relation to crime, the ways in which criminologists have attempted to explain this correlation should be briefly noted. Factors such as bias in the criminal justice system in favour of the very young or the much older offender, increased skill in avoiding detection with advancing age, and the decline in physical strength and agility associated with aging have all been mentioned as possible causes. However, the social position of youth in urban, industrial society has been seen as the major contributor to "**maturational reform**" or the rapid decline in crime as adolescents move into young adulthood. Various authors have argued that adolescence is a time of transition, a period between childhood and adulthood, and that the ambiguities and marginality of the social position of youth in modern societies create a variety of tensions and problems, of which crime is but one example (Nettler, 1984). Adolescents tend to be excluded from participation in adult roles such as marriage, work, and adult leisure activities. At the same time, they experience emancipation from the constraints and demands of childhood and are encouraged to aspire to adult status (Bloch and Niederhoffer, 1958; West, 1984). As Nettler (1984, 217) remarks, "[S]tructures of modern states encourage crime and delinquency. They lack institutional procedures for moving people smoothly from protected childhood to autonomous adulthood." But as youth move into the adult ages and their social status and integration increase, the personal costs of crime to the individual also increase—they now have more to lose—while at the same time, crime becomes somewhat redundant to their improved social position. Youth acquire added stakes in conforming behaviour (see Chapter 14) as they occupy social roles and acquire material goods that would be jeopardized by criminal behaviour. They become more socially integrated into relationships, groups, and organizations and, therefore, more dependent on the social rewards of conformity (Rowe and Tittle, 1977). New rewards and costs associated with their new adult status replace those that sustained delinquency in adolescence; new satisfactions replace those previously provided by delinquency (Trasler, 1980).

**maturational reform**

The observation that involvement in crime tends to decrease as people age.

Greenberg (1979) has offered the most elaborate version of this type of explanation. He argues that adolescents in North American society are particularly vulnerable to the expectations and evaluations of their peers because of the increased age segregation resulting from the exclusion of young people from adult work and leisure activity. At the same time, money is necessary for participation in this youth culture, but the deterioration of the teenage labour market has resulted in adolescents being less able to finance their costly social life. Greenberg regards theft as a way of financing participation in activities with peers in the absence of legitimate sources of income. With increasing age, both the dependence on peers and the lack of legitimate sources of funds are reduced for many of these young people; consequently, theft declines. Greenberg also discusses how the extended requirements for schooling restrict adolescent autonomy and how public humiliation of some students by teachers undermines self-esteem and produces embarrassment before peers. This can result in non-utilitarian crime, such as vandalism and violence, as an attempt to assert independence and enhance self-esteem before a sympathetic audience of peers. These motivations to crime are removed when young people leave the restrictive and sometimes degrading school setting. Greenberg also claims that the cost of crime for youth through legal penalties increases as they progress from early to later adolescence, as do opportunities for establishing stakes in conforming behaviour, particularly employment. These social controls, or costs, increase with age and therefore also contribute to the decline in crime.

Hirschi and Gottfredson (1983) present evidence that the relationship of age to crime has been similar in earlier historical times and in other types of society, thus challenging the premise that the nature of modern, urban, industrialized society is crucial for explaining this age–crime correlation. Hirschi and Gottfredson cite research suggesting that the effects of age on crime do not depend on such life-course events as leaving school, finding gainful employment, getting married, and so forth: "Age affects crime whether or not these events occur" (1983, 580). Some research (Tittle and Ward, 1993) also supports the Hirschi–Gottfredson hypothesis that the correlates and causes of crime do not significantly vary by age. Furthermore, Tanner and Krahn (1991) report a small *positive* effect of part-time work on illegal behaviour among Canadian high school seniors, although other variables were more strongly linked to this self-reported delinquency. Teenagers with part-time jobs while in school were more likely than those not working to report illegal behaviour, a finding somewhat at odds with Greenberg's (1979) argument. These findings undermine the maturational reform type of explanation, though other research questions this interpretation.

Research examining crime over the life course suggests that such salient life events as leaving school, entering the labour market, and getting married influence the likelihood of criminal behaviour (Loeber and LeBlanc, 1990; Sampson and Laub, 1990, 1992). Maturational reform among males may be accelerated by such events as completion of education, marriage, and parenthood, and delayed by events such as joining a gang or experiencing unemployment (Rand, 1987). A longitudinal study of Canadian high school graduates, which followed them during the transition into young adulthood, found that those who had delinquent friends reported more criminal behaviour (Hartnagel, 1998).

Furthermore, the combination of longer amounts of unemployment and having delinquent peers during this time of transition also led to increased crime. So, despite evidence of continuity in deviant behaviour over the life course, certain social transitions help explain the decline in crime in young adulthood. Finally, Warr (1993) has recently shown that the age–crime relationship is modified by the amount of exposure to delinquent peers, casting additional doubt on Hirschi and Gottfredson's claim that the age distribution of crime cannot be explained by social variables. Although the correlation of age with crime is one of the most undisputed facts of criminology, its interpretation and explanation still remain open to a good deal of debate.

## Sex

### Sex Differences and Crime Trends

As has already been indicated, sex is strongly correlated with crime. The crime rate for men greatly exceeds the rate for women. Of all adult criminal court cases in 2008/09 in Canada, 77 percent involved a male accused, while 17 percent involved a female accused. Sex was not reported in six percent of cases (Thomas, 2010). This sex difference in crime varies somewhat by type of crime. Offences for which males had their highest involvement included sexual assault (98 percent), other sexual offences (97 percent), being unlawfully at large (91 percent), weapons offences (91 percent), and break and enter (90 percent). Violent crime, in particular, is correlated with being male. In contrast, the highest representation of females was found in cases of prostitution (31 percent), fraud (31 percent), and theft (30 percent) (Thomas, 2010).

Data from victim surveys parallel arrest statistics in demonstrating that offenders are disproportionately male. Victimization data from the 2009 General Social Survey in Canada (Perreault and Brennan, 2010) estimated that males represented 88 percent of the perpetrators of all violent crime, 87 percent of sexual assault, 94 percent of robbery, and 88 percent of physical assault—figures reasonably similar to those provided by the official data on males charged with these offences.

Self-report research with juveniles has also generally substantiated this sex difference in delinquency, though the gap is not as great as in the official data on adults. Hagan (1985) noted that the sex ratio in a number of self-report surveys conducted in the United States in the 1970s showed males exceeding females in self-reported delinquency by more than two to one, compared to the 1975 official arrest ratio of 3.72 to one for those younger than 18. Yet LeBlanc's (1983) research in Montreal showed a much smaller gap between male and female delinquency (three to one) than the official statistics indicated (eight or 10 to one). This may, at least in part, reflect differences in police handling of juvenile offenders. Furthermore, Hindelang et al. (1979) have argued sex differences found in self-report studies are highly contingent upon the content of the specific items asked. They concluded that once the typically limited seriousness of these items is taken into account, apparent discrepancies between self-report and official data prove to be illusory; they don't measure the same domain of behaviour. Fitzgerald (2003) examined sex differences in delinquency among

Roxan Vaillancourt. (2010). *Gender Differences in Police-reported Violent Crime in Canada, 2008*. Statistics Canada: Canadian Centre for Justice Statistics.

www.statcan.gc.ca/pub/85f0033m/85f0033m2010024-eng.pdf

Canadian youth aged 12–15 surveyed in the National Longitudinal Survey of Children and Youth. As expected, the females reported lower rates of delinquency than did the males for each of the property and violent acts. While 29 percent of males reported committing violent and property-related delinquency, only 19 percent of females said they committed property crimes and 10 percent reported involvement in violent acts. The ratio of male to female delinquency was greater for the more serious acts.

These official statistics and self-report studies are static and don't give any indication of historical trends. For instance, it is *possible* that sex differences in crime have varied over the years such that, at certain times, females may have approached equality with males in a broad spectrum of offences. In fact, some criminologists have argued that a new female criminal has arisen in the past few years. Adler (1975) argues that not only has the participation of women in crime increased, but they have moved into areas of lawbreaking that were formerly the exclusive domain of men. The data on trends through time in the criminality of men and women should be considered, then, to see whether the gap between them has expanded and/or narrowed over the years.

A number of researchers have examined and attempted to interpret trends in male and female contributions to crime in the United States (Simon, 1975; Hagan, 1985; Steffensmeier, 1978; Steffensmeier et al., 1979; Austin, 1993). The general consensus of this research is that the gender gap in crime, particularly serious and violent crime, remains substantial. O'Brien (1999) examined the trends in selected arrest rates for males and females in the United States over a longer time period (1960–1995). He reported that the rates appeared to be converging for robbery, burglary, and auto theft and diverging for homicide, with no significant overall trends in either direction for aggravated assaults or larceny. This shows the importance of examining male and female trends in specific crimes, some of which appear to be converging. In Canada there has been a definite narrowing of the gender gap in crime overall, and for both violent and property offences (Campbell, 1990). But the speed of convergence has not been constant, depending upon the time period examined, and most Canadian female crime still consists of petty property offences such as shoplifting (Boritch, 1997).

Fisher (1986) replicated Steffensmeier's U.S. research with Canadian data on trends in persons charged by sex between 1962 and 1978. Like Steffensmeier, she found a narrowing of the relative gap between males and females in property crime charge rates, with the greatest increases in the rate at which females are charged with petty property crime—the crimes with which women have traditionally been associated. However, the absolute gap widened for all property crimes except for theft over $200 such that female property crime levels continue to lag behind those of males despite large increases in the rate at which females are charged for property crime. The relative gap between the sexes in violent crime remained about the same, while the absolute gap widened. Violent crime remained predominantly the domain of males. Fisher also documented the much lower base rates from 1962 for females. Therefore, large percentage increases resulted from relatively small absolute increases in female crime. Fisher's Canadian results are generally quite comparable to those of Steffensmeier for the United States, though the Canadian crime rates for both men and women are lower, particularly for violent crime.

Figure 5.3 shows the changes from 1986 to 2005 in the number of adult females and adult males charged by police for violent offences relative to their number in the general population, that is, the charge rate. For females, charge rates for serious violent crimes have increased since the mid-1980s although their rates remain substantially lower than the rates for males. Between 1986 and 2005 the rate of serious violent crime among female adults grew from 25 to 46 per 100 000 population, with most of this change occurring before 1994. The rate at which women were charged with common assault more than doubled from 1986 to 2005, from 44 to 93 per 100 000 population. Rates among adult males have taken a very different path during the last decade and a half with declining rates of both serious violent crime and common assault since the early 1990s. Consequently, the gap between the number of adult males and females charged with violent crime has narrowed from nine to one in 1986 to five to one in 2005 (Kong and AuCoin, 2008).

Figure 5.4 presents the adult female and male charge rates for serious property crime. Adult female charge rates for serious property crimes have decreased slowly since the mid-1990s, from 137 per 100 000 population to 101

**FIGURE 5.3   Rate of Males and Females Charged with Violent Offences 1986–2005**

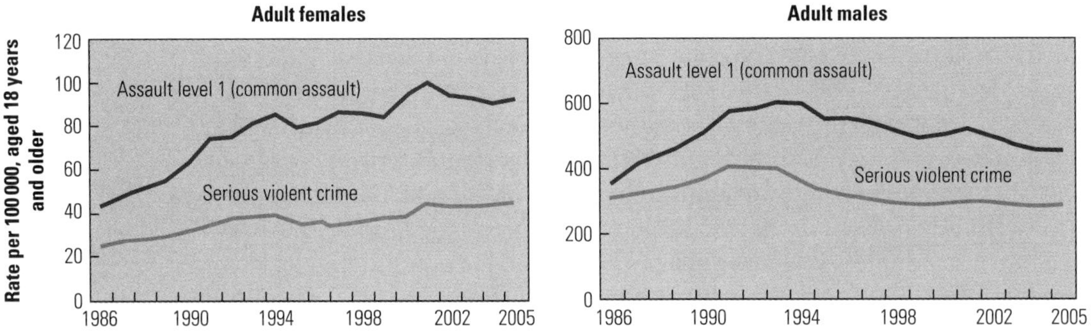

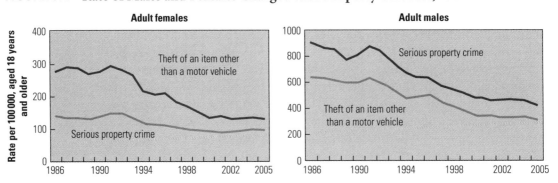

Source: Kong, Rebecca and Kathy AuCoin. "Female Offenders in Canada", adapted from Statistics Canada publication JURISTAT, Catalogue no. 85-002-XIE, Vol 28, no. 1, page 8.

**FIGURE 5.4   Rate of Males and Females Charged with Property Offences, 1986–2005**

Source: Kong, Rebecca and Kathy AuCoin. "Female Offenders in Canada", adapted from Statistics Canada publication JURISTAT, Catalogue no. 85-002-XIE, Vol 28, no. 1, page 9.

per 100 000 in 2005, a 26 percent decline. Their rates for the more prevalent offence of theft of an item other than a motor vehicle have fallen more drastically than rates for serious property crime. However, these thefts are more likely to be under-reported to the police. The adult male charge rates have declined to a greater degree but still remain substantially higher than the female rates (Kong and AuCoin, 2008).

Conclusions about trends in female crime that are based on official data sources, such as arrest rates or charge rates, are vulnerable to the claim that such official data reflect changes in the response to female crime by the criminal justice system as much as or more than they do real changes in criminal behaviour. Therefore, it would be desirable to have trend data from alternative sources such as self-report research. But self-report data are generally very time-bound, having been conducted in a particular location at a given point in time, and they are, therefore, limited in their usefulness for examining trends in crime. However, Smith and Visher (1980) analyzed 44 different self-report and official data studies that reported on the relationship between sex and deviance and found that the year the data were gathered was an important factor in explaining the magnitude of the sex-deviant behaviour correlation. They found that this correlation has been decreasing in size over time—meaning less gender disparity in deviant behaviour—and has declined more rapidly according to self-report studies than to research based on official sources of data. This narrowing of the gap is mainly for minor acts of deviance rather than for serious criminal behaviour and more for youths than for adults.

These various data on sex differences and crime trends lead to the conclusion that sex, like age, remains strongly correlated with criminal behaviour. Males are much more involved in criminal acts than females. Women have increased their participation in crime, including violent crime, although the increase has been greatest for minor property crimes such as theft and fraud. These two categories include offences such as shoplifting, credit card fraud, and passing bad cheques that women have commonly committed in the past. While the gender gap in crime has narrowed somewhat, it remains substantial, particularly for the most serious offences.

## Role Convergence?

Criminologists have offered various explanations for the sex difference in criminal involvement, as well as for the changes in female participation in crime through time. Early theories of female criminality emphasized biological and psychological factors (Smart, 1976). More recently, greater emphasis has been placed on the importance of socially structured differences in gender roles. This line of reasoning argues that males and females are subjected to differing expectations and demands regarding appropriate behaviour, as well as being subject to different mechanisms of social control (see Chapter 6).

Changes in gender role expectations should have consequences on the actual behaviour of males and females, including their criminal behaviour. More specifically, the convergence hypothesis suggests that as the social roles of the sexes become more equal or begin to converge, differences in their

**role convergence**

Explanation for the rising crime rate among women has been that their roles have become similar to (converged with) those of men.

criminal behaviour should diminish (Nettler, 1984; Fox and Hartnagel, 1979). In one version of this thesis, Simon (1975) suggested that increases in property crimes committed by women could be attributed to the expansion of employment opportunities for women. This apparent emancipation of women from domestic roles may bring with it increased opportunities to commit property crime as well as subjecting women to greater pressures for achievement, which may create pressures or strains toward crime (Merton, 1938). Fox and Hartnagel (1979) tested the **role convergence** hypothesis by examining the relationship between changes in the Canadian conviction rate for females from 1931 to 1968 and three measures of women's changing gender role. Women's participation in the labour force over these same years and the rate at which females were granted post-secondary degrees were used as measures of the convergence of gender roles, while the total fertility rate indicated the degree of persistence of women's domestic role. The convergence hypothesis was generally supported by this analysis, particularly for the female conviction rate for theft. As the female labour force participation rate and the rate at which females were granted post-secondary degrees increased and the fertility rate declined, the female conviction rate for theft increased. However, the authors note that they were unable to introduce measures to control for an alternative hypothesis. Changes in the treatment of females by the police or courts may better account for any changes in the female conviction rate. Less preferential treatment for women by the criminal justice system could explain rising female crime rates.

Other criminologists have questioned the role convergence hypothesis. Steffensmeier (1980), for example, has argued that most of the increase in female property crime is for the traditional female crimes of petty theft and fraud. These crimes are more related to the traditional female domestic roles of shopper and consumer. He questioned the degree to which gender roles have really changed by pointing to women's restricted labour market participation. Most women work in jobs with limited access to illegitimate opportunities. Furthermore, women still have primary responsibility for home and child care. "Female experiences are not moving beyond traditional roles, either legitimate or illegitimate" (1980, 1102). As Holly Johnson (1987) has reminded us, the high proportion of women offenders charged with theft or fraud is consistent with women's traditional role as consumers and, increasingly, as low-income, semi-skilled, single parents. Female offenders tend to be young, poor, undereducated, and unskilled, suggesting that female crime is at least partly the product of women's subordinate socio-economic position (Boritch, 1997; Johnson, 1987). The typical crimes of women may be symptomatic of their economic deprivation and marginality. Steffensmeier and Streifel (1992) tested alternative explanations for changes in the female share of property crime arrests in the United States. Their findings did not support the gender equality–role convergence argument. Instead, increases in the female share of property crime were largely a function of more formal, bureaucratic policing and, to a lesser extent, the greater economic marginality of women. Further research on this topic should include attention to the relation between gender roles and patterns of social control.

# Race

## Race and Crime

While not as strongly related to crime and delinquency as age and sex, race has been found to be a good predictor of criminality, at least in the United States (Tonry, 1995). However, Canadian research on race and crime is much more limited since race information is generally not collected by the criminal justice system. The question of whether race and crime data should be routinely collected in Canada has been the subject of some debate (Johnston, 1994; Roberts, 1994). In 1990, Statistics Canada decided to collect police data on the race of crime suspects on a trial basis but had to reverse this decision when only a minority of police forces were willing or able to provide such data and because of criticism from various minority organizations and academics (Roberts and Doob, 1997). Thus our information on the relationship between race and crime in Canada is very limited. The information that is available suggests that certain racial minorities are over-represented in the Canadian correctional system.

Specifically, the data in Figure 5.5 reveal that in combination visible minorities account for approximately 11 percent of those incarcerated and 16 percent of those serving time in the community. Since they constituted 13 percent of the total population in 2001, visible minorities as a category are not over-represented among incarcerated offenders although they are slightly over-represented among those serving time in the community. But differences

**FIGURE 5.5   Racial Distribution of Offenders in Federal Correctional System, Canada, November 2002**

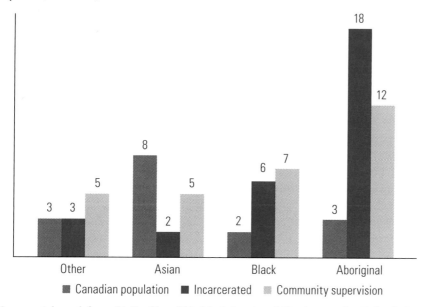

Source: Adapted from "A Profile of Visible Minority Offenders in the Federal Canadian Correctional System, 2004." Reproduced with the permission of the Minister of Public Works and Government Services Canada, 2011.

emerge when specific groups are examined. While they make up only about two percent of the population, Blacks represent six percent of the federally incarcerated and seven percent of those serving time in the community. Asian offenders, on the other hand, are under-represented relative to their share of the Canadian population; "other" minorities are not over-represented among the incarcerated but are slightly over-represented among those serving time in the community. Caucasians are under-represented among both categories of offenders. Aboriginal offenders, on the other hand, are significantly over-represented among both categories. While they made up approximately three percent of the population in 2001, they accounted for 18 percent of offenders in federal prisons in 2002 and 12 percent of those under community supervision.

Controversy has surfaced in recent years on the topic of alleged racial profiling by police. Much of this debate has been focused on the Toronto police due in part to a series of articles by the *Toronto Star* newspaper and subsequent discussion in academic journals (see, for example, Melchers, 2003; Wortley and Tanner, 2003, 2005; Gold, 2003; Gabor, 2004). The focus of this discussion has been on the treatment of Blacks by the Toronto Police Service. The series of *Toronto Star* articles alleging the racial profiling of Blacks was based on the newspaper's analysis of arrest data obtained under a freedom of information request and interviews with Black community leaders and advocates. The Toronto Police Service denied these claims and commissioned an independent review of the *Star*'s analysis that concluded that the conclusions of the *Star*'s articles were completely unjustified and irresponsible (quoted in Melchers, 2003, 347). But the bases for this conclusion have, in turn, been severely critiqued on methodological and interpretive grounds (Melchers, 2003; Wortley and Tanner, 2003). Since police in Canada are not required to report on the race of the people they target for field investigations (Wortley, 2003), it is difficult for Canadian researchers to determine whether racial minorities received greater police surveillance than people from other racial backgrounds, although there is some evidence from field studies suggesting this is the case (James, 1998; Neugebaur, 2000). If racial minorities are subject to greater police surveillance, they are also more likely to be caught when they break the law than are white people who engage in the same forms of criminal behaviour. So arrest statistics, particularly for certain crimes, may have more to do with police surveillance practices than actual racial differences in criminal behaviour. Thus racial profiling may help explain the over-representation of minorities in arrest statistics (Wortley, 2003), as well as contributing to their over-representation in subsequent stages of the criminal justice system.

Social surveys are an alternative method for gathering data to address this issue. As part of their response to the controversy in Toronto, Wortley and Tanner (2005) reported on some results from their Toronto Youth Crime and Victimization Survey conducted in 2000 with a random sample of 3393 Toronto high school students. Students who self-identified as Black were much more likely to self-report being stopped and searched by the police than students from other racial backgrounds, with white students more likely to report being stopped and searched than Asians, South Asians, or West Asians. Black students also scored significantly higher on a self-report deviant behaviour scale than white or Asian students. Black youths were also more likely to report gang membership while white students reported the highest levels of drug and alcohol use. These authors also conducted a multivariate analysis to estimate the impact of race on self-reported police stops and searches while controlling for deviant activity, leisure routines, and demographic variables. While the results suggested that youths who reported more deviant activity and those who reported more public leisure activities such as riding in cars with friends and partying and hanging out in public spaces were more likely to report being stopped and searched by the police, black racial identity was the strongest predictor of being stopped and searched. In additional analyses these racial differences in self-reported police stop-and-search experiences were greatest among the low-deviance youths. Wortley and Tanner concede that research on racial profiling in Canada is still in its infancy. Additional work on race, crime, and criminal justice should focus, among other things, on how race intersects with other important identity markers such as social class, gender, age, immigration status, religion, language, and sexual orientation (Wortley, 2003).

While the circumstances of Aboriginal Canadians in the criminal justice system—particularly in correctional institutions—have received a fair amount of attention, this is much less so in the case of the black population and other visible minorities. Therefore, the remainder of this section will focus on Aboriginal over-representation in the criminal justice system.

## Over-Representation of Canadian Aboriginal People in the Criminal Justice System

As early as 1967 the report *Indians and the Law* (Canadian Corrections Association, 1967) showed the disproportionate presence of Aboriginal people in the Canadian criminal justice system (Nielsen, 1992). Subsequently, a number of commissions and task forces have recognized this **over-representation** and made numerous recommendations to respond to it (see, for example, LaPrairie, 1996; Manitoba Public Inquiry into the Administration of Justice and Aboriginal People, 1991; Task Force on the Criminal Justice System and Its Impact on the Indian and Métis People of Alberta, 1991). Although the over-representation of Aboriginal people is widely recognized (LaPrairie, 1983), implementation of recommendations to change this situation has been slow (Blackburn, 1993), and the over-representation persists.

Currently, the only available data on offenders in the Canadian criminal justice system are in correctional statistics. Additional data concerning Aboriginal offenders can be found in various reports and special studies and in the homicide database. These data sources document various aspects of the disproportionate involvement of Aboriginal offenders in the criminal justice system. For example, while Statistics Canada projected the Aboriginal population at approximately three percent of the Canadian adult population, Aboriginal offenders accounted for 27 percent of all sentenced admissions to provincial custody in 2008/09, 21 percent of admissions to remand, and 18 percent of admissions to federal prisons (Calverley, 2010). Based on the 11 jurisdictions that have reported consistently over time, the representation of Aboriginal people among sentenced custody admissions has increased by two percentage points since 2004/05 (Calverley, 2010).

While Aboriginal people are generally over-represented in admissions to correctional services throughout Canada, Table 5.1 demonstrates that there

**over-representation**

A group that has a number of its members in some condition in greater numbers than their population would suggest.

**Indian and Northern Affairs Canada**
www.ainc-inac.gc.ca

**Table 5.1   Characteristics of Adult Offenders Admitted to Correctional Services, 2008–2009**

Standard table symbols

| Jurisdiction | Sentenced custody | | | Remand | | | Probation | | | Conditional sentence | | Total adult Aboriginal population in 2006 |
|---|---|---|---|---|---|---|---|---|---|---|---|---|
| | Female | Aboriginal | Median age[1] | Female | Aboriginal | Median age[1] | Female | Aboriginal | Median age[1] | Female | Aboriginal | |
| | percent | percent | years | percent | percent | years | percent | percent | years | percent | percent | percent |
| Newfoundland and Labrador | 9 | 19 | 31 | 11 | 22 | 28 | 18 | .. | 31 | 24 | 14 | 4 |
| Prince Edward Island | 10 | .. | .. | 10 | .. | .. | 15 | .. | .. | .. | .. | 1 |
| Nova Scotia[2] | 10 | 9 | 32 | 13 | 10 | 30 | 20 | 6 | 32 | 18 | 7 | 2 |
| New Brunswick[2] | 11 | 10 | 32 | 11 | 10 | 30 | 19 | 9 | 30 | 22 | 8 | 2 |
| Quebec | 9 | 3 | 37 | 9 | 4 | 34 | 15 | 6 | 33 | 15 | 5 | 1 |
| Ontario | 11 | 10 | 33 | 14 | 10 | 31 | 18 | 8 | 32 | 22 | 13 | 2 |
| Manitoba | 9 | 71 | 28 | 14 | 68 | 28 | 20 | 56 | 29 | 21 | 45 | 12 |
| Saskatchewan | 15 | 80 | 30 | 10 | 78 | 28 | 23 | 71 | 28 | 19 | 74 | 11 |
| Alberta[3] | 14 | 40 | .. | 14 | 36 | .. | 18 | 25 | 30 | 20 | 17 | 5 |
| British Columbia | 11 | 25 | 33 | 14 | 23 | 33 | 19 | 21 | 33 | 18 | 17 | 4 |
| Yukon | 12 | 80 | 34 | 14 | 80 | 33 | 20 | 65 | 34 | 31 | 58 | 22 |
| Northwest Territories[4] | 10 | 88 | 29 | 9 | 86 | 28 | .. | .. | .. | .. | .. | 45 |
| Nunavut | 6 | 98 | .. | 8 | 96 | .. | .. | .. | .. | .. | .. | 78 |
| **Provincial and territorial total** | **12** | **27** | **..** | **13** | **21** | **..** | **18** | **18** | **..** | **19** | **20** | **3** |
| Federal total | 6 | 18 | 33 | .. | .. | .. | .. | .. | .. | .. | .. | .. |
| Total | 11 | 26 | .. | .. | .. | .. | .. | .. | .. | .. | .. | .. |

... not available for a specific reference period

... not applicable

1. The median age at admission is the age where, if all the people are ordered by age, half of the people are younger and half are older.

2. Sentenced custody excludes intermittent sentences.

3. Alberta uses a different counting methodology whereby an admission to custody is counted once, regardless of change in status. As such, in 2008/2009 Alberta reported 13,767 remand admissions; 10,203 remanded later sentenced admissions, and; 8,306 sentenced only admissions. CCJS methodology counts an admission as movement from one status in correctional services to another. For instance, an individual who moves from remand to sentenced custody will be counted as one admission to remand and one admission to sentenced custody. This report has included Alberta's remanded later sentenced admissions in both the number of admissions to remand and then again in the number of admissions to sentenced custody, resulting in a higher number of admissions than that reported by the jurisdiction.

4. Sentenced and remand counts include residents of Nunavut held under an exchange of service agreement.

Source: Calverly, Donna. "Adult Correctional Services in Canada, 2008/2009", adapted from Statistics Canada publication JURISTAT, Catalogue no. 85-002-X, Fall 2010, Vol. 30, no. 3, page 23

are considerable differences across the country. For example, in 2008/09 Aboriginal people made up 80 percent of those admitted to adult custodial facilities in Saskatchewan, compared to their representation of 11 percent of the adult population. In Manitoba, Aboriginal people represented 71 percent of admissions to provincial custody compared to their makeup of 12 percent of the population; and in Alberta 40 percent of admissions to provincial facilities were Aboriginal persons compared to their five percent makeup of the adult population. Similar patterns exist for community correctional services such as probation and conditional sentences (Calverley, 2010).

Similar to their representation in the general population, Aboriginal adults in correctional services were younger, had lower levels of education, and were less likely to have been employed compared to their non-Aboriginal counterparts (Brzozowski et al., 2006).

This over-representation of Aboriginal people in prison has persisted for some time. The report of the Task Force on Aboriginal Peoples in Federal Corrections (1989) concluded that the rate of growth of the Aboriginal offender population has exceeded that of the general inmate population since at least 1982–83.

LaPrairie's (1996) review of research dealing with Aboriginal inmates also indicated that they were generally younger, had more prior contact with the criminal justice and correctional systems, and came from more dysfunctional backgrounds than non-Aboriginal offenders. Proportionately, more Aboriginal than non-Aboriginal offenders were serving time for fine defaults, and Aboriginal women were particularly over-represented in correctional institutions. While use of incarceration as a sentence was greater for federal Aboriginal offenders after controlling for type of offence (but without information on prior record), they also received shorter sentences on average than non-Aboriginal offenders in both federal and provincial institutions (LaPrairie, 1996). Aboriginal persons were also more likely than non-Aboriginals to be re-admitted to the correctional system after being released (Johnson, 2005). A recent comparison of the developmental progression of criminal behaviour of Aboriginal and non-Aboriginal offenders from early adolescence to middle adulthood found that, while only a small proportion of these offenders showed persistent and serious offending behaviour over their life course, the size of this group was higher among the Aboriginal group (18.7 percent) than among the non-Aboriginals (12.3 percent). The chronic high offending Aboriginal offenders were more likely to come from an impoverished background characterized by an unstable family environment, substance use, and negative peer associations. These risk factors contributed to their serious and persistent pattern of criminality (Yessine and Bonta, 2009).

There is only limited evidence concerning the over-representation of Aboriginal peoples at earlier stages of the criminal justice system. Two studies of urban Aboriginal crime (in Calgary, Regina, Saskatoon, and Vancouver) concluded that for those offences with an identified accused, Aboriginal persons were more likely than non-Aboriginals to be accused of a property or violent offence or to have been the victim of a violent crime (Griffiths et al., 1994; Trevethan, 1993). In these four cities, Aboriginals constituted from two to six percent of the population but represented from nine to 43 percent of those accused of a crime, depending on the type of crime and on the city.

For homicides in which Aboriginal status of the accused is known, Aboriginal persons represented 23 percent of all those accused of committing a homicide between 1997 and 2004. Aboriginal people were 10 times more likely to be accused of homicide than were non-Aboriginal people, with Aboriginal males particularly highly over-represented (Brzozowski et al., 2006). One factor that may contribute to this over-representation is the age composition of the Aboriginal population. The high-risk age group for homicide and other violent crime is 15 to 24, and this age group accounted for 17 percent of the Aboriginal population in 2001 compared to 13 percent for the rest of the population. A detailed analysis of homicides involving Aboriginal people in Ontario between 1980 and 1990 revealed that the rate of homicides among Aboriginal people on reserves was approximately the same as the rate off reserve, although in both settings, the suspect and victim rates were considerably higher than the rates for non-Aboriginal people (Doob et al., 1994). On most comparisons, on- and off-reserve Aboriginal homicides and homicides involving Aboriginal victims were more likely to have occurred after a non-violent social encounter, a verbal argument, or a fight that escalated. This pattern of results suggests that the causes of Aboriginal homicides are likely to be different from those of non-Aboriginal homicides (Doob et al., 1994).

Crime rates on reserves are higher than those outside reserves, and the nature and extent of crime on reserves differ compared to crimes committed elsewhere in Canada. On-reserve crime rates were about three times higher in 2004 than crime rates elsewhere. For certain types of offences, the differences were greater still. Just over half (55 percent) of on-reserve incidents were classified as "Other Criminal Code" offences, such as mischief and disturbing the peace, while 25 percent were violent and 21 percent were property offences. In off-reserve areas, in contrast, property crimes were the most frequently recorded (51 percent), followed by "Other Criminal Code" (38 percent) and violent offences (11 percent) (Brzozowski et al., 2006).

Although the level of crime among Aboriginal people, particularly violent crime, is considerably higher than that for non-Aboriginals, there is still a great deal of variation in the rates of both violent and property crimes among Aboriginal communities and Aboriginal populations across Canada (Wood and Griffiths, 1996). This variation in recorded crime is probably at least partly due to differences in the nature of policing in these communities and jurisdictions, as well as differences in the likelihood of the police recording incidents reported to them (Roberts and Doob, 1997). A comparison of several research studies conducted in different jurisdictions revealed that the mean of the rates for violent crimes varied between 19 and 70 per 1000 population, while for property crime the rates ranged from 22 to 108 per 1000 population (Wood and Griffiths, 1996). This means that at least some Aboriginal communities have rates of crime below the Canadian average.

## Explanations of Aboriginal Over-Representation

There are a number of potential explanations for this over-representation of Aboriginal people in the Canadian criminal justice system. These include: conflict between the values of Aboriginal culture and the dominant Canadian culture; the social and economic deprivation experienced by many Aboriginal peoples stemming from their colonization and oppression and resulting in higher Aboriginal offending rates and/or their discriminatory treatment by the criminal justice system; the commission by Aboriginals of types of offences more likely to result in a justice system response; and a decline in interdependency in Aboriginal communities, resulting in cultural dislocation and the decline of informal mechanisms of social control (see, for example, LaPrairie, 1983, 1996).

Verdun-Jones and Muirhead (1979–80) distinguish between cultural and structural explanations. **Cultural explanations** emphasize the lack of certain traits in Aboriginal culture that are valued by the dominant white culture. James (1979), while claiming that the core values of Aboriginal and white cultures may be essentially the same, argues that there is conflict in the ways in which these values are expressed behaviourally in society. "Native values are placed under stress by the pressures of expressing them acceptably in a complex urban society" (1979, 455). For example, James suggests that the sharing of material possessions among Aboriginal people implies a potentially reciprocal action rather than a permanent transfer of ownership. However, when such sharing of belongings is practised without permission in the dominant culture, it is called theft. The Native Counselling Services of Alberta (1982) has identified a number of areas of conflict between Aboriginal and non-Aboriginal cultures related to the legal system and it has suggested that many Aboriginal people have only a limited understanding of the dominant Canadian legal and justice system. Similarly, Dumont (1993) describes a number of conflicts between Aboriginal responses to the law and the expectations of the Canadian legal system. For example, while Aboriginal culture emphasizes mediation and negotiation to resolve disputes and reconcile offenders with victims, the Canadian legal system is based on retributive justice with punishment set by legislation. Furthermore, Aboriginal defendants are reluctant to testify and often plead guilty on the basis of honesty or the avoidance of confrontation; in contrast, the Canadian system is adversarial and assumes innocence until proven guilty. So cultural explanations emphasize conflicting values. The over-representation of Aboriginals results from the imposition of a somewhat alien set of values and rules on Aboriginal culture, as well as from the higher rate of commission by Aboriginals of acts called crime by Canadian law but regarded as normative or expected behaviour in the context of Aboriginal culture.

**cultural explanation**

An explanation for crime that is phrased in terms of the values and beliefs of a society or its component subgroups.

**Structural explanations** of Aboriginal over-representation emphasize the economically and socially dependent position of Aboriginals in Canadian society. Thus Hylton (1982) claims that the over-representation of Aboriginal people is a symptom of the underlying social and economic inequality of Canadian society, while LaPrairie (1983) states that the suggestion of a link between the living conditions of Aboriginals and their over-representation in the criminal justice system is compelling. She views over-representation as an effect of structural disadvantage. She documents examples of such disadvantage with comparisons between Aboriginals and non-Aboriginals in federal penitentiaries. Only 12 percent of Aboriginal inmates, compared to 26 percent of non-Aboriginal inmates, had more than a Grade 9 education; 31 percent of Aboriginal inmates but only 19 percent of non-Aboriginal inmates had either no education or education of only Grade 6 or less. The Métis and Non-Status

**structural explanation**

An explanation for crime that focuses on social structure (usually this refers to inequality, poverty, or power differentials). For example, the patriarchal structure of the family might help explain the abuse of women and children within the family.

Indian Crime and Justice Commission (1978) report also attributed the high rate of Aboriginal imprisonment to their deprived social situation, illustrated by the report's findings from a survey of Aboriginal inmates in federal penitentiaries. Fifty-seven percent of the inmates said they were unemployed at the time of their offence, 49 percent had spent time in skid row areas of cities, and 49 percent had less than a Grade 9 education. The final report of the Task Force on Aboriginal Peoples in Federal Corrections (1989) concluded that any reduction in Aboriginal crime must address the correlated socio-economic conditions among Aboriginals—conditions that, compared to those of other Canadians, are discouraging. Generally, Aboriginals continue to have a lower average level of education, fewer marketable skills, a higher rate of unemployment, an infant mortality rate twice the national rate, a higher degree of family instability, and a rate of violent death three times the national average. Aboriginal inmates, then, are even more disadvantaged in some respects than other inmates.

LaPrairie (2002) explored the impact of socio-demographic characteristics of Aboriginal populations living in nine Canadian cities and found regional disparities with higher levels of social disadvantage in the Prairie cities of Saskatoon, Regina, and Winnipeg and in Thunder Bay, compared to cities in British Columbia, southern Ontario, and Nova Scotia. These disadvantaged populations live predominantly in the regions with the highest levels of over-representation of Aboriginal people in the criminal justice system. Furthermore, the three Prairie cities had three to four times as many Aboriginal people living in extremely poor neighbourhoods of these cities. LaPrairie suggests that this concentration of poor, single parent, and poorly educated Aboriginal people in the inner core of cities weakens social cohesion and informal social controls, resulting in more disorder and crime. Fitzgerald and Carrington (2008) reported that a substantial part of the elevated level of police-reported Aboriginal crime in Winnipeg was explained by the structural characteristics of the disadvantaged neighbourhoods in which Aboriginal people tended to live. An earlier study of Aboriginal residents of the inner-city areas of four Canadian cities (Edmonton, Regina, Toronto, and Montreal) explained the over-representation of Aboriginal people by their marginalization and alienation resulting from unstable and violent childhoods, as well as their lack of opportunity and dependency on alcohol (LaPrairie, 1995).

Verdun-Jones and Muirhead (1979–80), moreover, argue that the structurally deprived position of Aboriginals in contemporary Canadian society is rooted in a history of exploitation by the dominant white society through what was, in essence, a colonial system based on the fur trade. From this perspective, the criminal justice system functions today primarily to control subjugated groups such as Aboriginals—to keep them in their dominated, powerless position—in order to protect the interests of the dominant, powerful segment of society. This dominant segment of society is made up of the white majority generally and, more particularly, its leading, economically powerful segments. The criminal justice system specifically, and the state generally, are both seen by these authors as agents of the economically powerful who control the underclasses. The criminal justice system mirrors the socio-economic organization and operation of society. Hence, over-representation of Aboriginals within the criminal justice system is merely a reproduction of the basic socio-economic inequalities present in the surrounding society. Furthermore, the criminal justice system functions to support and maintain that structure of inequality. Thus the Canadian justice system has been seen as the central institution that reinforces colonial relationships against Aboriginal people, with over-representation a systemic problem of a society structured on discriminatory values, beliefs, and practices (Monture-Angus, 1996).

LaPrairie (1996) has argued that a decline in traditional interdependency in Aboriginal communities has resulted from their colonization and the creation of the reserve system, as well as their cultural dislocation and the decline of informal mechanisms of social control. "The end result is socially stratified communities where limited resources and resource distribution create large groups of disadvantaged people, a growing youth sub-culture with few legitimate outlets or opportunities, decontextualized exposure to the mass media, and the lack of cultural and social resources to assist in identity formation which support pro-social values" (LaPrairie, 1996, 63). The result is a large group of marginalized and non-integrated people in many Aboriginal communities who have few tools for survival or integration into mainstream society when they leave reserves for urban areas. Their lack of skills, coupled with substance abuse problems and dysfunctional family life, leads to negative peer associations and the adoption of pro-criminal attitudes. Structural explanations, then, regard higher Aboriginal crime rates as a product of the social and economic oppression of Aboriginals by the dominant white society. The majority of Aboriginals are kept poor and dependent, and this breeds crime, violence, and other social disorders to which the criminal justice system responds, thereby furthering Aboriginals' exploitation by the existing system of inequality.

Discriminatory treatment of Aboriginal people by the criminal justice system has also been offered as an explanation of over-representation by several task forces (Manitoba Public Inquiry, 1991; Task Force on the Criminal Justice System, 1991) and some criminologists (Havemann et al., 1985; Monture-Angus, 1996). The Manitoba inquiry, for example, pointed out that Aboriginal people were more likely to face multiple charges, to be held in jail before their court appearance, to spend a longer time in custody before their trials, to see their lawyers less frequently and for less time, to enter guilty pleas, to be sentenced to jail terms, to receive longer sentences, and to receive absolute or conditional discharges less frequently.

Several Canadian research studies that investigated this hypothesis of differential treatment by the criminal justice system included race as a variable in their analysis. The most relevant of these studies for the present discussion is no doubt Hagan's (1974) early research in five Alberta correctional institutions. He examined the sentences received by Indian and Métis inmates, who were represented at least four times as often among newly incarcerated offenders as among the general population. Hagan discovered that Aboriginals were primarily charged with minor offences and, as a result, received shorter sentences. Incarceration resulting from failure to pay a fine was nearly twice as common for Aboriginals as for non-Aboriginals. Almost two-thirds of Aboriginal inmates were serving sentences resulting from such default. Race, therefore, played no *direct* role in influencing the over-representation of Aboriginals in these institutions. The sentences imposed conformed to legal requirements and reflected the disproportionate involvement of Aboriginals in minor offences, particularly involving alcohol abuse, for which they received a fine. However, because of their poverty, many were unable to pay these fines and ended up serving time in jail for minor offences. In a subsequent analysis, Hagan (1977) found that Aboriginals were more likely to be sent to jail in default of fine payments in rural than in urban Alberta communities, a finding he attributed to the trend toward greater uniformity of treatment in the more bureaucratic urban criminal justice system. Other research has suggested that limited sentencing options in remote Aboriginal communities may explain some of the disproportionate use of incarceration for convicted Aboriginals (LaPrairie, 1990).

Several other studies have examined the hypothesis of selective enforcement against Aboriginal people in different parts of the criminal justice system. Hagan (1977), for example, found that probation officers in rural jurisdictions in Alberta were more likely to recommend more severe sentences for Aboriginal offenders in their presentence reports, without the justification of legally relevant considerations such as prior record, seriousness of offence, or number of charges. But Boldt et al. (1983) found no racial effect on presentence recommendations in the Yukon. In general, Hagan (1975a, 1975b) failed to discover evidence of differential treatment due to race itself in presentence recommendations or sentencing, though probation officers took a dimmer view of Aboriginal defendants' prospects for success on probation, which in turn affected their sentence recommendations and the final disposition of the case by the judge. But those judges characterized by Hagan as less concerned about the maintenance of a conservative notion of "law and order" used part of their discretion to sentence Aboriginal defendants more *leniently* (Hagan, 1975c). Since there is evidence that Aboriginal offenders sentenced to incarceration receive shorter sentences for certain offences than comparable non-Aboriginal offenders, over-representation of Aboriginals in prisons cannot be simply explained by racial discrimination (LaPrairie, 1990). Research on parole decision making by Demers (1978) supported Hagan's conclusion that Aboriginal candidates were less likely to receive favourable recommendations from parole officers. This was probably due to a variety of factors, but indirectly produced racial inequality in parole release decisions made by the Parole Board, which is dependent on parole officers for information and advice. Wynne and Hartnagel (1975) found evidence from a study of Crown prosecutors' files that Aboriginals were less likely than whites to successfully engage in plea bargaining, though this depended on certain conditions, such as being represented by defence counsel and the presence of repetitious counts and/or multiple charges in the indictment.

Unfortunately, there is little evidence on how the police exercise their discretion with respect to Aboriginal people. It has been suggested that in cities, Aboriginal people may tend to attract police attention by their physical appearance and/or location in run-down, skid row areas (Canadian Corrections Association, 1967). Aboriginals may have a greater public visibility, particularly when drinking, and this may result in more frequent arrests (Bienvenue and Latif, 1974). Some criminologists (Giffen, 1966; Greenaway, 1980; Frideres, 1988) have even argued that the police "find" crime where they look for it, at least with respect to public-order offences such as public drunkenness. Therefore, police initiative and discretion in seeking out the poor and disadvantaged may be implicated to some extent in the higher frequency of Aboriginal arrests for certain types of crime. But there is also some evidence that the police may be called by Aboriginal people in some communities to deal with problems that would not be seen as police business in non-Aboriginal communities, due in part to the fact that the police may be the only service available in the community to deal with such problems (Roberts and Doob, 1997).

While it is clear that Aboriginal people are over-represented in the criminal justice system, the explanation for this over-representation remains somewhat in doubt. Furthermore, little research has been done in Canada on the ways in which crime may be produced by the relations between indigenous Aboriginal society and culture and the dominant white society and its culture. However, the disproportionately high rates of Aboriginal crime and violence suggest "a serious rupture of traditional control mechanisms in contemporary aboriginal communities" (LaPrairie, 1992, 285).

## Drug Misuse and Criminal Behaviour

The 2004 Canadian Addiction Survey (Canadian Centre on Substance Abuse, 2004) of how Canadians aged 15 years and older use alcohol, cannabis, and other drugs indicates that while nearly 80 percent drink, most drink in moderation. Seventeen percent of past-year drinkers are considered high-risk drinkers; they are predominantly male and under the age of 25. While 45 percent reported using cannabis at least once, only 14 percent reported use in the past year; males and younger people are again more likely to be past-year users. Among past-year users, 16 percent report use monthly, 20 percent weekly, and 18 percent daily. Although about 1 in 6 Canadians had used an illicit drug other than cannabis in their lifetime, few (one percent or less, except 1.9 percent for cocaine use) have used these drugs during the past year; both lifetime and past-year use was highest among males and those aged 18 to 24. More recent data from the 2009 Canadian Alcohol and Drug Use Monitoring Survey (Health Canada, 2009) indicate that while   past year cannabis use declined to 10.6 percent for those aged 15 years and older, the level of use of other illicit drugs was comparable to that of 2004. This survey suggests that while alcohol and other drug use is fairly widespread, misuse or serious abuse in the general population is limited to a smaller proportion.

**Canadian Centre on Substance Abuse CCSA**
www.ccsa.ca

The picture is quite different when we examine the offender population. The misuse of serious drugs is particularly widespread in the criminal population (Bennett and Holloway, 2005). This suggests that the misuse/abuse of drugs and crime are linked in some fashion. The concept of drug-related crime includes a number of crime types, including drug offences such as possession of illegal substances, crimes committed as part of the functioning of drug markets (e.g., trafficking, money laundering, violent crime to "protect" markets), and crimes committed as a result of drug use, or drugs consumed as a result of crime (Bennett and Holloway, 2005). The link between drug abuse and crime refers to this latter type. Research from a number of countries indicates a strong association or correlation between crime and the use and abuse of alcohol and illicit drugs: there are high rates of prevalence of drug use among offenders, and a large number of drug abusers are involved in criminal activities (Pernanen, et al., 2002; see also the literature reviews in Bennett and Holloway, 2005, and Bean, 2004).

While drug abuse and crime may be related to one another, they may not be causally linked but merely occur together among some individuals or groups. For example, crime and drug abuse may both be part of a deviant street lifestyle but not be causally linked. Furthermore, they may both be effects of a common cause or causes. There is some evidence, for example, that drug effects may be confounded with pre-addiction psychiatric conditions; in such cases this could be a common factor to explain both the abuse of alcohol/drugs and the criminal behaviour (Pernanen et al., 2002). Social circumstances of disadvantage and exclusion could lead to both drug abuse and crime. Of course, misuse of alcohol/drugs may cause some criminal conduct, although this would likely depend on the type of drug, frequency and extent of the drug misuse, ability to support a drug habit through conventional means, and specific crime types. The most common drugs investigated in the drugs–crime relationship are heroin, crack, and cocaine, and the most common offences are burglary, theft, and robbery (Bennett and Holloway, 2005). So, for example, heavy dependence on heroin may lead to acquisitive crimes such as theft, shoplifting, or burglary to pay for further drug use. Criminal behaviour may also act as a cause of alcohol/drug abuse when, for example, prior involvement in criminal activity results in economic proceeds that are used to finance a lifestyle involving heavy use of alcohol and other drugs.

While it is clear, then, that alcohol/drug misuse is correlated with criminal behaviour, their relationship is complex and contingent on a number of factors. At a minimum, it is necessary to determine two things before assuming a causal link between them: which came first, the alcohol/drug (mis)use or the criminal behaviour, and whether both are merely effects of a common cause that results in their correlation. In the case of recreational drugs like cannabis, the majority of research findings indicates the drug use preceded any crime; for the more serious drugs (typically heroin, crack, or cocaine), the majority of findings show that crime preceded drug use (Bennett and Holloway, 2005).

The Canadian Centre on Substance Abuse (Pernanen et al., 2002) conducted a series of studies to estimate the strength of the association between different types of crime and the use and abuse of drugs, and the share of crimes in Canada that can be attributed to the use and abuse of alcohol and drugs. Data were obtained from self-report surveys and interviews of federal and provincial prison inmates and from the observations of arresting police officers in 14 cities. A large proportion of inmates reported using illicit drugs while free. Many used frequently, with 30 percent reporting use at least a few times a week. Inmates scored higher on psychometric scales measuring alcohol and drug dependency when compared to the general population. Alcohol-dependent federal inmates were much more likely to have committed a violent crime than were drug-dependent inmates, while the latter were more likely to have committed a gainful crime. The inmates who were dependent upon drugs and/or alcohol committed the most crimes—averaging about seven crimes per week. Slightly more than half (54 percent) of offenders entering federal custody reported having been under the influence of a psychoactive substance when they committed the most serious crime on their current sentence, with alcohol intoxication more common than drug intoxication (24 percent versus 19 percent). The arresting police reported 51 percent of arrestees were under the influence of a psychoactive substance at the time of arrest, with alcohol indicated more often than illicit drugs. A significant proportion of crimes were reported to have been committed in order to obtain psychoactive substances for personal use. The authors estimated that between 40 and 50 percent of the crimes committed by federal and provincial inmates were attributable to the use of alcohol and/or illicit drugs in Canada. Between 10 and 15 percent were attributed to illicit drugs only, between 15 and 20 percent to alcohol only, and 10 to 20 percent to both alcohol and illicit drugs.

Fischer et al. (2001) conducted a survey of a cohort of untreated illicit opiate drug users in Toronto. Self-report interview data illustrated that criminal involvement is a prevalent and frequent occurrence in this sample, with very few reporting no involvement in illegal activities. The majority of crimes were non-violent income-generating offences to obtain the substantial funds required to finance their addiction. A large part of the sample also participated in illicit drug market activities, engaging in small-scale dealing. However, a more recent study conducted in five Canadian cities found significant variations among the cities for three types of self-reported criminal activity—drug dealing, sex work, and property crime—engaged in by untreated drug users (Manzoni et al., 2007).

There is strong evidence for an association between alcohol use and crime—particularly aggression and violent crime—although it is unclear whether this correlation also implies a causal relationship (Mosher and Jernigan, 2001; Parker and Auerhahn, 1998). A sizeable presence of alcohol is found in almost all studies of assaults and homicides, with 40–45 percent of perpetrators in Canadian studies drinking (Pernanen et al., 2002). Data from adolescents in Finland suggested that the relationship between drinking and petty theft was almost completely spurious while alcohol had a causal effect on violence, vandalism, car theft, and graffiti writing (Felson et al., 2008). Fagan's (1990) research review found that that people who become aggressive after consumption of intoxicants often have a long history of aggression; there is only limited evidence that ingestion of intoxicants is a direct pharmacological cause either stimulating or disinhibiting aggression. Although intoxication may not directly cause aggression, there is evidence that in situations that become violent, substance use may increase the severity of the violence (Wolff and Reingold, 1994). Immediate situational influences as well as various social and cultural variables are likely important mediating factors in the alcohol–violent crime link.

Alcohol abuse has had a severe impact on Aboriginal people. The survey *Indian Conditions* (Indian and Northern Affairs Canada, 1980) estimated that between 50 and 60 percent of Indian illnesses and deaths were alcohol related. Alcohol also plays a major role in Native American criminal behaviour (Lester, 1999). Havemann et al. (1985) have reviewed a number of Canadian studies that identify alcohol as a major contributor to the crimes Aboriginal people commit. This contribution can be direct, through the violation of liquor laws, as well as indirect, as when other crimes are committed under the influence of alcohol. Surveys of Aboriginal inmates (Irvine, 1978; Métis and Non-Status Indian Crime and Justice Commission, 1978) found that a large percentage admitted alcohol played a role in the commission of their crimes. According to data from the Homicide Survey, between 1997 and 2004, while the consumption of an intoxicating substance was common among many accused persons, it was much more prevalent among Aboriginal accused.  In incidents where it was known that intoxicants were involved, 89 percent of Aboriginals had consumed an intoxicant at the time of the homicide compared to 61 percent of non-Aboriginal accused. Furthermore, while substance abuse was assessed to be at a medium or high level for a majority of adults involved in correctional services, it was particularly prevalent among Aboriginal persons (9 in 10 compared to 7 in 10 non-Aboriginals) (Brzozowski et al., 2006).

However, the link between alcohol abuse and Aboriginal criminality is not well understood or agreed on. Some have suggested that heavy drinking has become a regular, normal occurrence within some Aboriginal communities, associated with family and group activities and, therefore, accorded a good deal of tolerance (Brody, 1971; Jensen et al., 1977). Highly visible group drinking may be socially accepted and expected, without the development of corresponding informal social controls to regulate or limit the extent of such drinking. An additional possibility is that alcohol abuse and its associated criminal consequences may be a response to, or reaction against, the poverty and deprivation experienced by so many Aboriginal people. Alcohol may provide some respite, however temporary, from their oppressive life circumstances, whether on reserves, in impoverished rural areas, or in the city slums. Havemann et al. (1985) expand on this argument by linking alcohol and involvement with the criminal justice system with the social impact of the underdevelopment of Aboriginal communities. They argue that alcohol is used as a means to modify moods and escape real-life situations and that it is a way for Aboriginal people to manage the alienation created by the destruction of their culture and the economic exploitation of their land resources for the benefit of southern Canada and the corporate structure. Thus these authors locate the use of alcohol by Aboriginal people and their consequent over-representation in the criminal justice system in the structure of socio-economic relations between Aboriginal people and the dominant white society, rather than in some disease model or other individualistic-type explanation that ends up blaming the victim.

# Social Class

## Conflicting Evidence?

Few issues have been in greater dispute among criminologists in recent years than the correlation between social class and criminal behaviour. Thus Gordon (1976), for example, regards the crime or delinquency relationship with social class status as one of the most thoroughly documented, while Tittle and Villemez (1977) conclude that the purported relationship between class and criminality is problematic and Tittle et al. (1978) refer to such a relationship as a myth. Hindelang et al. (1979) state that illusions of discrepancies in the research evidence abound, while Braithwaite (1981) concludes from his review of over 100 studies that class is one of the very few correlates of criminality, a conclusion persuasively supported by a large body of empirical evidence. Clearly, this is a controversial question among criminologists, and there are disagreements over what the research literature reveals.

Official data appear to support an inverse or negative relationship. Those arrested, convicted, and/or incarcerated are more likely to come from lower socio-economic categories of the population as measured by such variables as income, education, and occupational status. Tittle and Villemez (1977) report that of the 23 studies on this relationship they could locate that used official police or court data, 65 percent found a negative relationship, while another eight percent detected class variation in crime but only for some subcategories of individuals. Twenty-six percent of these studies found no consistent class variation. Of course, these official records may underestimate the amount of crime committed by those in the higher socio-economic positions. Nettler (1984) states that official statistics on serious crimes from a variety of countries show that people with less money, lower occupational status, and less schooling are disproportionately represented. But it could be immediately asked: what qualifies as a serious crime? Some would argue that bank embezzlement, for example, is at least as serious as bank robbery or that corporate crimes are more seriously harmful than many of the crimes typically committed by lower-class individuals.

Additional evidence, using official crime statistics, on the class–crime relationship comes from the long history of research on poverty, economic inequality, and crime. While the argument that crime is one of a number of undesirable consequences of poverty can be traced far back into antiquity, the first empirical research examining the relationship between poverty and crime can be found in the mid-19th-century work of Guerry and of Quetelet in Europe (Vold and Bernard, 1986). Anticipating later developments, this early work showed that wealthier provinces had higher property crime rates and suggested that the greater opportunities for theft and other property offences offered by these wealthier regions might explain this unexpected pattern. Quetelet also suggested that great inequality between wealth and poverty in the same place, rather than absolute poverty, might be a critical factor. While poverty refers to the lack of that level of income necessary for mere survival, economic inequality signifies the size of the income gap between those who have the least income and those who have the most income (Vold and Bernard, 1986).

Since this early research, criminologists have continued to analyze and interpret various data relating economic conditions and crime at different levels of ecological aggregation ranging from city neighbourhoods to nation-states. Summarizing this large body of research is complicated by this variation in units of analysis, as well as by such factors as varying measures of poverty and inequality, the inclusion of a variety of crime types, and the use of differing sets of control variables. However, there appears to be some consensus that the degree of economic inequality rather than the amount of poverty is the more important variable (Braithwaite, 1979; Box, 1987; Vold and Bernard, 1986). More specifically, nations with greater economic inequality have higher homicide rates, particularly under conditions of political democracy (Krahn et al., 1986). Cross-national comparisons of property crime rates are more inconsistent, perhaps as a result of the effect of varying opportunities for property crime in different nations (Stack, 1984). Economic inequality and crime rates, with the possible exception of homicide, are fairly strongly and consistently related in studies of U.S. cities and Standard Metropolitan Statistical Areas, but less so at the level of states. Daly et al. (2001) reported a strong, positive relationship between the income inequality and homicide rates of the 10 Canadian provinces, averaged across a period of 15 years, a relationship that persisted when controlling for provincial median household income levels. So this body of work suggests that the degree of contrast between economic classes—poverty amid affluence—is more strongly correlated with rates of crime than the proportion of the population in the poorest class. The limited Canadian research on this topic also supports this interpretation (Kennedy et al., 1991).

Evidence from self-report research seems to challenge this conclusion of a negative relationship between class and criminal behaviour. It was Short and Nye's (1957) use of the self-report measurement of delinquency that stimulated much of the later debate concerning the class and delinquency correlation, since they reported no relationship between self-reports of delinquency and parental socio-economic status. However, they did find a moderately strong relation between social class and incarceration in a training school. Fifty percent of the institutionalized boys studied came from the lowest socio-economic status category, compared to only 13 percent of the high school boys. But Hindelang et al. (1979) have shown how Short and Nye over-estimated the strength of the relationship between official delinquency and socio-economic status because the institutionalized boys did not constitute a representative sample.

Tittle et al. (1978) examined 35 studies in which the relationship between a measure of individual class position and a measure of crime or delinquency was reported and found, on average, only a very slight, negative correlation (–0.09). These authors claim that studies using official data show a more marked negative correlation (average of –0.25) than do those based on self-report data (–0.06). They argue that the average correlation between class and crime or delinquency showed a steady decline in strength from the 1940s (–0.73) to the 1970s (–0.03), a trend they believe is largely the result of a decline in the relationship between class and official measures of crime because the correlation for self-report measures remained relatively constant and low. Tittle et al. interpret these findings as a reflection of changes in the way in which criminal justice agencies deal with members of the various social classes. Their interpretation implies that the true correlation between class and crime "has remained consistently near zero and has only appeared to be greater because official data reflected biases in the law enforcement process which have now been ameliorated" (1978, 652).

Of course, researchers have attempted to account for the apparent discrepancy between self-report and official measures of delinquency in their relationship to socio-economic status by examining the hypothesis of official discrimination against lower-class adolescents in the enforcement of the law (see Nettler, 1984, for a review of many of these studies). However, after legally relevant factors such as seriousness of the offence and prior record of the suspect or accused are taken into account, the evidence for such class bias in law enforcement is weak and is, therefore, unlikely to substantially affect the official statistics.

Two other self-report studies found a negative relationship between class and crime once certain refinements in measurement and analysis were introduced. Elliott and Ageton's (1980) research, which involved a national sample with a large number of respondents and a self-report measure covering the full range of delinquent and criminal acts with a true measure of frequency, discovered class differences on an overall delinquency scale as well as for predatory crimes against persons, but not for other types of offences. Lower-class respondents reported close to four times as many predatory crimes against persons (for example, assault and robbery) as did middle-class respondents. But these differences were largely the result of the high-frequency offenders. Lower-class youths were found disproportionately among high-frequency offenders; they reported more than one and a half times as many offences overall as middle-class youths in the high-frequency category, and nearly three times as many predatory crimes against persons. So Elliott and Ageton seem to have demonstrated a behavioural basis for the class differences observed in the official data since the more frequent and serious offenders are more likely to be arrested and the class differences in self-reported delinquency are greater at the high end of the frequency continuum and for serious, predatory crimes.

In the second study, Farnworth et al. (1994) argued that criminological theories imply that it is the sustained experience of deprivation and poverty among the underclass that creates a greater risk of crime and delinquency. Furthermore, these authors claimed that most theories that incorporate class as an important predictor of delinquency are concerned with explaining a serious, frequent, and persistent pattern of offending. Therefore, measures of class and crime should be consistent with these theoretical concerns. In this study, the strongest and most consistent class–crime relationships were found between measures of continuing underclass membership and sustained involvement in street crimes.

These two studies, then, support the conclusion of a negative correlation between social class and crime under certain conditions, specifically for more serious offences and among more frequent and adult offenders, particularly those most disadvantaged educationally, racially (Blacks), and in employment status.

There is comparatively little Canadian research on the class and crime relationship. The studies that do exist illustrate some of the same problems and apparently conflicting conclusions as discussed. In 2008/09 45 percent of adults age 25 and over in provincial custody in reporting provinces had not completed high school and 47 percent were unemployed at admission to custody (Calverley, 2010). To the extent that educational attainment and occupational status can be taken as a measure of socio-economic status, these official data generally support the negative correlation between class and crime.

Canadian self-report studies raise the same issues as the U.S. studies discussed. LeBlanc (1975) found no difference in the self-reported delinquency of adolescents from working-class areas compared to those from upper-class neighbourhoods, using a standard set of self-report delinquency items, even though adolescents from the working-class neighbourhoods were more likely to be officially labelled as delinquent by the police. Gomme's (1985) analysis of self-reported delinquency among younger adolescents (Grades 7 to 10) in a small urban centre in southern Ontario found no direct relationship between socio-economic status, measured by father's occupation, and participation in delinquent behaviour. But in a study in New Brunswick, Tribble (1972) concluded that the higher the status of the father's occupation, the lower was the probability that the son would be involved in delinquency. Furthermore, among the delinquents, the higher the status, the fewer the number of offences reported. Statistics Canada's Violence Against Women Survey supported the view that domestic violence is greatest in the lower class (Johnson, 1996). The study found that men who were out of work committed assaults at twice the rate of men who were employed and that men who earned less than $15 000 per year assaulted their wives at twice the rate of men with higher incomes. Above this $15 000 level, there was no relationship between income and wife assault. This again suggests that the highest crime rates can be found at the very bottom of the economic ladder.

## Reconciling the Apparent Conflicts

There are several methodological and substantive issues in the research on class and crime that, once understood, should help clarify and reconcile the apparently conflicting conclusions of different studies. First, most of these studies of the relationship between class and crime are not very representative of the population at large. This severely limits the degree to which one can generalize from them. Almost all of the self-report research has focused on juveniles rather than adults and, more specifically, on white male adolescents in small towns to medium-sized cities (Elliott and Ageton, 1980; Tittle et al., 1978). Poor adults in large cities—precisely those whom many criminologists would expect to have higher crime rates—have been very under-represented in the research on socio-economic status and crime (Clelland and Carter, 1980).

Second, serious crime is a relatively rare event. The typically small sample sizes, restricted time frame, and crude measurement of frequency of crime commission in self-report studies make it extremely difficult to identify class differences in serious crime, given its low prevalence in the general or adolescent population (Hindelang et al., 1979).

Third, it is inappropriate to compare most self-reports with official data on crime because they only rarely refer to the same domain of conduct (Hindelang et al., 1979). The usual set of self-report items is weighted in favour of less serious acts, particularly those trivial acts for which middle-class adolescents report higher prevalence (Elliott and Ageton, 1980). So the typical self-report delinquency scale overlaps only in part with the crimes in official statistics, particularly those predatory, interpersonal crimes most often officially reported. Therefore, one should be cautious about generalizing from the failure to find class differences in the self-reports of the less serious forms of delinquency to *any* conclusion concerning predatory criminal acts by adults (Farnworth et al., 1994).

Fourth, it should be recognized that official statistics are limited and give only a partial picture of the class distribution of crime. In particular, official data are notorious for understating the frequency of certain crimes, some of which are characteristically committed with greater frequency by members of the middle class (for example, occupationally related theft) and representatives of the powerful segments of society (such as consumer fraud). And, of course, class position may also influence the likelihood of official intervention (Tittle and Villemez, 1977), particularly for those crimes more typically committed by those higher in status.

Criminologists have not paid sufficient attention to the many meanings and measures of class. Class position has most often been equated by criminologists with occupational status or prestige, at least for purposes of measurement. Class is thereby reduced to a handful of occupational categories, such as blue-collar, white-collar, or professional/managerial. These categories lump together some quite diverse positions in the labour market on questionable grounds, while at the same time excluding those not in the labour force, such as the unemployed.

Those most marginal to the labour market—rather than those in less skilled occupations, with less education or fewer financial resources—are more at risk for turning to conventional, predatory crime. This is precisely the population segment typically ignored in criminological research on class and crime, partly because this segment is difficult for researchers to locate and survey (Clelland and Carter, 1980), and partly on account of the fuzzy thinking that has characterized much of the empirical research on this topic. Quinney (1977) and others argue that the negative correlation between class and crime found in official statistics applies only to the crimes of the underclass or marginalized segment of the population. So class position may be related to crime in something of a curvilinear fashion— high crime at both the bottom and the top of the class hierarchy—depending on how one defines and measures both class position and criminal behaviour. In fact, Tittle et al. (1978) have gone so far as to suggest that it is *only* at the extremes of the class hierarchy that class is a significant factor in crime in a mass society with a mass culture such as that found in North America. It's a bit paradoxical, then, that these same authors conclude their paper by stating that criminology should shift away from class-based theories. Rather, what seem to be required "are class-based theories which explain why certain types of crime are perpetrated almost disproportionately by the powerless, while other forms of crime are almost exclusively the prerogative of the powerful" (Braithwaite, 1981, 49).

## Region

Criminal behaviour is correlated with geographic region. That is, crime rates are higher in certain nations of the world, regions within a country, communities, and urban neighbourhoods (Brantingham and Brantingham, 1984).

It is difficult to compare the crime rates of different countries. There are major differences in criminal codes, in police practices, in the willingness of

**UNODC (United Nations Office on Drugs and Crime)**
www.unodc.org

citizens to report crime, and in record keeping that make most international comparisons meaningless. The only figures that can be compared with any degree of confidence are homicide statistics, and even these are not completely reliable for many countries. Figure 5.6 shows the homicide rates for selected countries in recent years. Although Canada's homicide rate is about one-third the U.S. rate, it is still higher than rates in many European countries, such as England and Wales, Germany, and France, as well as Australia (Beattie and Cotter, 2010). The highest rates of murder are generally found in the less economically developed countries. This conclusion is consistent with the pattern of high levels of violent crime in the less-developed nations and high levels of property crime in the economically more developed nations evident in Interpol statistics for several decades. While a number of variables are no doubt involved in the explanation of this pattern, income inequality and economic opportunity seem particularly relevant. Countries with greater inequality in the distribution of income have higher homicide rates (Krahn et al., 1986), but economic development creates many more opportunities for property crime (Brantingham and Brantingham, 1984; Hartnagel, 1982).

Crime has a definite regional pattern within Canada, with the highest rates in the territories and the west (see Figure 5.7). As in past years, in 2010 the severity of police-reported crime in the three territories far surpassed that recorded by the provinces (Brennan and Dauvergne, 2011). In 2010

**FIGURE 5.6**   **Homicide Rates for Selected Countries**

Note: * Figures reflect 2004–05 data
** Figures reflect 2005–06 data

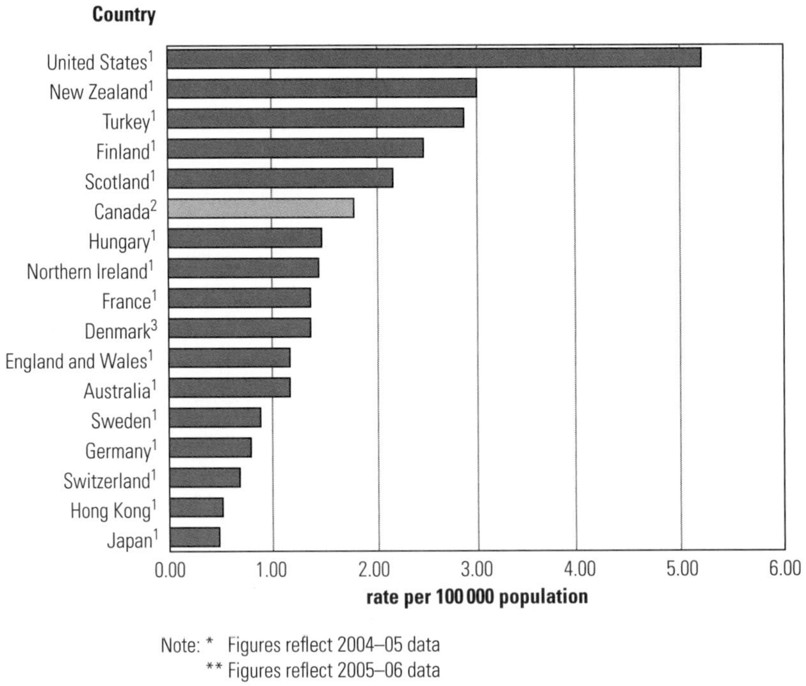

Source: Adapted from Statistics Canada, Homicide in Canada, 2009, Juristat, 85-002-XIE2010003, vol. 30 no. 3, October 2010; http://www.statcan.gc.ca/bsolc/olc-cel/olc-cel?catno=85-002-XIE&lang=eng#formatdisp.

**FIGURE 5.7**  **Police-Reported Crime Severity Indexes, by Province and Territory, 2010**

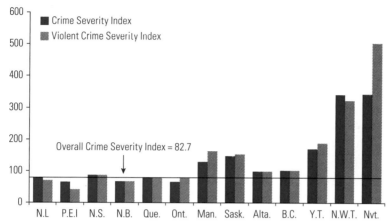

Source: Adapted from Statistics Canada, Police-reported Crime Statistics in Canada, 2010, Juristat, 85-002-XIE2011001, July 2011; http://www.statcan.gc.ca/bsolc/olc-cel/olc-cel?catno=85-002-XIE&lang=eng#formatdisp

provincial/territorial crime severity indices varied from a low of 65 in Ontario to a high of 346 in Nunavut. Among the provinces, Saskatchewan reported the highest crime severity index (148) followed by Manitoba (127). The violent crime severity index showed a similar trend, but with Saskatchewan and Manitoba switching their positions and with Prince Edward Island having the lowest level. The non-violent crime severity index also follows the same regional pattern. Victim survey data for 2009 indicate that residents of Western provinces, particularly Manitoba and Saskatchewan, generally reported higher rates of victimization than those living in central and eastern Canada, although comparisons with police-recorded crime are limited by crime coverage and definition (Perreault and Brennan, 2010).

These regional differences have not received much research attention to date. Provincial differences in the age and sex composition of populations and degree of urbanization may contribute to the crime rate differences. Provinces with a higher proportion of young males and urban residents could be expected to have higher crime rates, but the evidence does not suggest that these variables are of major importance (Hartnagel, 1978; Giffen, 1965; 1976). A recent examination of trends in unemployment rates, age composition, and education levels did not reveal any discernable pattern that would distinguish Manitoba, Saskatchewan, and the Yukon Territory from eastern Canada. Rates of inflation, on the other hand, tended to be somewhat higher in Manitoba and Saskatchewan. Saskatchewan and Manitoba are also home to a larger proportion of Aboriginal people who have higher levels of social disadvantage than Aboriginal people in other parts of the country (LaPrairie, 2002). Kennedy et al. (1991) attributed regional variation in homicide rates to differences in economic inequality and social disorganization. They found a convergence of murder rates among eastern, central, and western Canada in Census Metropolitan Areas where there were higher levels of inequality and disorganization. Provincial differences in crime rates are at least partly a function of differences in the amount of geographic mobility experienced in different provinces (Hartnagel, 1997). Provinces with higher migration of population from other provinces have higher rates of both violent and property crime, controlling for urbanization, age composition, police per capita, and percentage of the provincial population with low income.

Crime rates also vary by community size: rates of many crimes are higher in larger-sized communities than in smaller towns and rural areas. The correlation between community size and crime is stronger for property crime than violent crime (Hartnagel and Lee, 1990). However, crime is not necessarily a large urban phenomenon: overall crime rates as well as total violent and total property crime rates in Canada in 2005 were highest in small urban areas. Smaller cities like Winnipeg, Saskatoon, and Regina had higher total, violent, and property crime rates than the larger cities of Toronto and Montreal. Rural areas had the lowest overall and property crime rates but reported higher violent crime rates than large urban areas (Francisco and Chenier, 2007). Urban residents report higher rates of both personal and, in particular, household victimization than do rural residents (Mihorean et al., 2001).

There are several potential explanations for the differences in crime rates in communities of different size (Hartnagel and Lee, 1990). Social disorganization theory (see Chapter 14) proposes that urbanization—the increasing size, density, and heterogeneity of a community—leads to a weakening of community cohesiveness and normative consensus, thereby undermining informal mechanisms of social control and increasing crime (Wirth, 1938; Skogan, 1977). Economic deprivation arguments locate the causes of urban crime in poverty and/or the degree of inequality in the distribution of income (Braithwaite, 1979; Blau and Blau, 1982). Routine activities theory (see Chapter 15) (Cohen and Felson, 1979) suggests that features of urban locations, such as the density of potential targets, increased potential for social interaction, greater anonymity, and ease of transportation, are particularly conducive to crime. Finally, the demographic composition of cities may affect their crime rates. Since urban populations are disproportionately young and childless, behaviours such as crime to which they are especially at risk should be more evident in urban areas (Fischer, 1976). Hartnagel and Lee (1990) tested these arguments with data from 88 Canadian cities with a population of 25 000 and over. The results provided strong support for routine activities theory, although the authors qualify this conclusion by noting some of the study's limitations. Cities with a greater dispersal of work and leisure activities away from households offer more opportunities for direct contact, predatory crimes of violence, and crimes against property. However, Schulenberg et al. (2007), using data from 374 municipal police jurisdictions, found support for a social disorganization explanation of municipal crime rates rather than criminal opportunity with the exception of the indicator of female employment. The structure of urban opportunities for crime deserves further investigation as an explanation for differences in community crime rates.

Within urban centres, crime rates vary by neighbourhood (Brantingham and Brantingham, 1984; Bursik and Grasmick, 1993). Criminal areas where many criminals reside exist in most cities and persist for long time periods (Brantingham and Brantingham, 1984). These areas tend to be located adjacent to the central business district, although this can vary depending upon local land-use patterns (Shaw and McKay, 1969). The early research of Shaw and McKay (1942) in Chicago found these areas to be characterized by physical deterioration, low income, a heterogeneous population, high density, population mobility, and the presence of many renters in multiple-family dwellings. Later studies have generally replicated these findings (Kornhauser, 1978; Stark, 1987; Byrne and Sampson, 1986). There have been several Canadian studies on urban neighbourhoods and crime. Jarvis and Messinger (1974) examined delinquency rates in the census tracts of London, Ontario. Their findings were consistent with the U.S. research. The 1985 survey of crime victims in Edmonton found that reports of violent victimization were twice as high for residents of the downtown area as for residents of suburban areas (Solicitor General Canada, 1987). However, reports of property crime victimization were not greatly different in the two areas (Solicitor General Canada, 1988). A recent series of spatial analyses of crime in seven Canadian cities found that crime is concentrated in a limited number of neighbourhoods, mainly in the core areas. The highest rates of property crime were concentrated in the city centres, although hot spots of lesser intensity were also found near shopping centres and superstores or power centres. Violent crime rates were also highest in the core neighbourhoods, but a few cities had several areas of moderate crime intensity in residential neighbourhoods. Multivariate analyses indicated that access to socio-economic resources and land use characteristics (i.e., commercial use) were the risk factors most closely associated with differences in crime rates among neighbourhoods (Savoie, 2008). Charron's (2009) spatial analysis of crime in Toronto found that violent crime rates were also more concentrated in neighbourhoods with limited access to socio-economic resources, but also in neighbourhoods with higher population densities and higher residential mobility. Property crime rates were associated with areas of high commercial activity, such as shopping centres, and neighbourhoods close to the city centre.

Neighbourhood variation in crime rates has most often been interpreted from a social disorganization perspective. Neighbourhoods of low economic status, ethnic heterogeneity, and residential mobility experience a disruption of local social organization and informal control since residents have few stakes in the local area and experience difficulty in forming primary relationships and groups to solve common problems (Kornhauser, 1978). Although Shaw and McKay (1942) and early replications of their work did not directly test this model of social disorganization, more recent research has examined indicators of neighbourhood structure and control with generally favourable results (Sampson and Groves, 1989; Bursik and Grasmick, 1993). However, the neighbourhood distribution of criminal opportunities may also affect the distribution of criminal acts within cities (Bursik and Grasmick, 1993). For example, Sampson and Wooldredge (1987) discovered that high levels of target attractiveness were related to neighbourhood burglary rates, and individuals were most at risk of personal theft in areas with high levels of street activity. Ouimet

(2000) tested the ability of the social disorganization and criminal opportunities perspectives to explain juvenile offender rates (where delinquents live) and juvenile crime rates (where crimes are committed) at both the census tract (495) and neighbourhood (84) levels of aggregation in the city of Montreal. Social disorganization variables predicted offender rates fairly well while opportunity variables were generally unimportant. On the other hand, opportunity variables helped explain juvenile crime rates, along with the social disorganization variables. More of the variation in both offender rates and crime rates was explained at the neighbourhood rather than the census tract level. As yet, however, there has been little investigation of the dynamics involved in the convergence of offenders and suitable targets at the neighbourhood level (Bursik and Grasmick, 1993).

## Summary

- Correlates of crime are those phenomena that are associated with, or related to, criminal behaviour. Among the most important correlates of crime are age, sex, race, drug abuse, social class, and region.

- Crime is strongly associated with age. After peaking in late adolescence/early adulthood, crime decreases with age.

- Sex is also strongly associated with crime. Males are much more likely to be involved in criminal behaviour than females, particularly for violent crimes and for serious property offences. However, in the past three decades, women have increased their involvement in both violent and property crime, although their highest rates continue to be found among the less serious property crimes.

- Blacks and Aboriginal people are greatly over-represented in our criminal justice system. This is most evident when looking at the population of jails and prisons. Alcohol plays a major role in the crimes of Aboriginal people and, directly or indirectly, contributes to this over-representation. Both cultural and structural explanations have been given for the disproportionate involvement of Aboriginal people in crime, as has the possibility of biased enforcement of the law.

- There is a strong correlation between criminal behaviour and the use and abuse of alcohol and illicit drugs. However, their relationship may not be causal but is complex and contingent on a number of other factors.

- Finally, crime varies by region. Violent crime rates are higher in less economically developed countries, while property crime is higher in more developed nations. Crime in Canada varies by region, with the highest rates occurring in the west and the north. Crime rates are also correlated with community size. Larger communities generally have higher crime rates, particularly for property crime, than do small towns and rural areas, although small urban areas had the highest rates in 2005. Neighbourhoods within cities differ in their rates of crime, with high-rate neighbourhoods tending to be located near the city centre. A combination of theories stressing economic inequality, social disorganization, and opportunities for crime has been used to explain these regional patterns.

## QUESTIONS FOR CRITICAL THINKING

1. Define correlation, distinguish it from causation, and illustrate the difference with a criminological example.
2. Describe maturational reform and discuss its application to the age distribution of criminal behaviour.
3. Summarize the trends in the sex differences in criminal behaviour and discuss the concept of role convergence as applied to these trends.
4. Should data on the race of criminal offenders be routinely collected by criminal justice agencies in Canada?
5. Discuss and evaluate several possible explanations of Aboriginal over-representation in the Canadian criminal justice system.
6. Discuss the ways in which the correlation between drug abuse and crime could be explained.
7. Describe and evaluate the evidence concerning the relationship between social class and criminal behaviour.
8. Discuss how provincial variation in crime rates could be explained.

## NET WORK

Statistics Canada provides a great deal of information about crime and its correlates over the Internet. To learn more about correlates of crime, first go to the Statistics Canada home page at **http://www.statcan.ca/start.html**. Under "Browse by Subject," click on "Crime and Justice," then "Crimes and Offences," then "Summary Tables." Then click on the table "Crimes by Type of Violation, by Province and Territory." Using the data in this table, answer the following question:

1. How do the provincial and territorial crime incidents and rates vary across the country when you compare all Criminal Code violations, violent Criminal Code violations, and property crime violations? How do drug violations vary across the country?

Then click on the table "Homicide Offences, Number and Rate, by Province and Territories." Using the data in this table, answer the following question:

2. How do the provinces rank in terms of the number of homicide offences in 2009? Does their rank vary depending on the year?

Then click on the table "Victims and Persons Accused of Homicide, by Age and Sex." Using the data in this table, answer the following question:

3. Look at homicide victims; what is the five-year trend for male and female victimization? Is the trend the same for male and female victims under the age of 12? What about for male and female victims ages 18 to 24? Other age categories?

## KEY TERMS

correlate; pg. 133
correlation; pg. 133
cultural explanation; pg. 151
maturational reform; pg. 138

over-representation; pg. 147
role convergence; pg. 144
structural explanation; pg. 151

## BIBLIOGRAPHY

Adler, F. (1975). *Sisters in Crime*. New York: McGraw-Hill.

Ageton, Suzanne S., and Delbert S. Elliott. (1978). *The Incidence of Delinquent Behavior in a National Probability Sample of Adolescents*. Boulder, CO: Behavioral Research Institute.

Austin, R.L. (1993). "Recent Trends in Official Male and Female Crime Rates." *Journal of Criminal Justice* 21: 447–66.

Baron, S.W. (1994). "Street Youth and Crime: The Role of Labour Market Experiences." Unpublished Ph.D. dissertation, Department of Sociology, University of Alberta.

Bean, Philip. (2004). *Drugs and Crime*. Portland, OR: Willan Publishing.

Beattie, K. (2005). "Adult Correctional Services in Canada, 2003/04." *Juristat* 25 (8).

Beattie, S., and A. Cotter. (2010). "Homicide in Canada, 2009." *Juristat* 30 (3).

Bell-Rowbotham, B., and C.L. Boydell. (1972). "Crime in Canada: A Distributional Analysis." In C.L. Boydell, C.F. Grindstaff, and P.C. Whitehead (eds.), *Deviant Behavior and Societal Reaction* (pp. 93–116). Toronto: Holt, Rinehart and Winston.

Bennett, Trevor, and Katy Holloway. (2005). *Understanding Drugs, Alcohol and Crime*. Maidenhead, Berkshire UK: Open University Press.

Bienvenue, R.M., and A.H. Latif. (1974). "Arrests, Disposition and Recidivism: A Comparison of Indians and Whites." *Canadian Journal of Criminology and Corrections* 16 (2): 105–16.

Blackburn, C. (1993). "Aboriginal Justice Inquiries, Task Forces and Commissions: An Update." In *Royal Commission on Aboriginal Peoples, Aboriginal Peoples and the Justice System* (pp. 15–41). Ottawa: Minister of Supply and Services Canada.

Blau, J.R., and P.M. Blau. (1982). "The Cost of Inequality." *American Sociological Review* 47: 114–29.

Bloch, H.A., and A. Niederhoffer. (1958). *The Gang*. New York: Philosophical Library.

Boldt, E.D., L.E. Hursh, S.D. Johnson, and K.W. Taylor. (1983). "Presentence Reports and the Incarceration of Natives." *Canadian Journal of Criminology* 25: 269–76.

Boritch, H. (1997). *Fallen Women*. Toronto: ITP Nelson.

Box, S. (1987). *Recession, Crime and Punishment*. London: Macmillan Education.

Box, S., and C. Hale. (1984). "Liberation/Emancipation, Economic Marginalization, or Less Chivalry." *Criminology* 22 (4): 473–97.

Brennan, S., and Mia Dauvergne. (2011). "Police-reported Crime Statistics in Canada, 2010." *Juristat* 30 (4).

Braithwaite, J. (1979). *Inequality, Crime, and Public Policy*. London: Routledge.

———. (1981). "The Myth of Social Class and Criminality Reconsidered." *American Sociological Review* 46: 36–57.

———. (1989). *Crime, Shame and Reintegration*. New York: Cambridge University Press.

Brantingham, P., and P. Brantingham. (1984). *Patterns in Crime*. New York: Macmillan.

Brody, H. (1971). *Indians on Skid Row*. Ottawa: Information Canada.

Brzozowski, Jodi-Anne, Andrea Taylor-Butts, and Sara Johnson. (2006). "Victimization and Offending among the Aboriginal Population in Canada." *Juristat* 26 (3).

Bunge, Valerie Pottie, Holly Johnson, and Thierno A. Balde. (2005). *Exploring Crime Patterns in Canada*. Ottawa: Statistics Canada.

Bureau of Justice Statistics. (1993). *Highlights from 20 Years of Surveying Crime Victims*. Washington, DC: U.S. Department of Justice.

Bursik, R.J., and H.G. Grasmick. (1993). *Neighborhoods and Crime*. Toronto: Maxwell Macmillan.

Byrne, J.M., and R.J. Sampson (eds.). (1986). *The Social Ecology of Crime*. New York: Springer-Verlag.

Calverley, Donna. (2010). "Adult Correctional Services in Canada, 2008/09." *Juristat* 30 (3).

Campbell, G. (1990). "Women and Crime." *Juristat* 10 (20): 1–14.

Canadian Centre on Substance Abuse. (2004). *Canadian Addiction Survey*. Ottawa: Canadian Centre on Substance Abuse.

Canadian Corrections Association. (1967). *Indians and the Law*. Ottawa: Canadian Corrections Association.

Carrington, P.J. (2001). "Population Aging and Crime in Canada, 2000–2041." *Canadian Journal of Criminology* 43: 331–56.

Charron, Mathieu. (2009). *Neighborhood Characteristics and the Distribution of Police-reported Crime in the City of Toronto*. Ottawa: Canadian Centre for Justice Statistics.

Clelland, D., and T.J. Carter. (1980). "The New Myth of Class and Crime." *Criminology* 18 (3): 319–36.

Cohen, L.E., and M. Felson. (1979). "Social Change and Crime Rate Trends." *American Sociological Review* 44: 588–608.

Cohen, L.E., and K.C. Land. (1987). "Age Structure and Crime." *American Sociological Review* 52: 170–83.

Daly, M., M. Wilson, and S. Vasdev. (2001). "Income Inequality and Homicide Rates in Canada and the United States." *Canadian Journal of Criminology* 43: 219–36.

Dauvergne, Mia, and John Turner. (2010). "Police-reported Crime Statistics in Canada, 2009." *Juristat* 30 (2).

Dauvergne, Mia, and Geoffrey Li. (2006). "Homicide in Canada, 2005." *Juristat* 26 (6).

Demers, D.J. (1978). "Discretion, Disparity and the Parole Process." Unpublished Ph.D. dissertation, University of Alberta.

Doob, A.N., M.G. Grossman, and R.P. Auger. (1994). "Aboriginal Homicides in Ontario." *Canadian Journal of Criminology* 36 (1): 29–62.

Dumont, J. (1993). "Justice and Aboriginal People." In *Royal Commission on Aboriginal Peoples, Aboriginal Peoples and the Justice System* (pp. 42–85). Ottawa: Minister of Supply and Services Canada.

Elliott, D.S., and S. Ageton. (1980). "Reconciling Differences in Estimates of Delinquency." *American Sociological Review* 45 (1): 95–110.

Fagan, J. (1990). "Intoxication and Aggression." In M. Tonry and J.Q. Wilson (eds.), *Drugs and Crime* (pp. 241–320). Chicago: University of Chicago Press.

Farnworth, M., T.P. Thornberry, M.D. Krohn, and A.J. Lizotte. (1994). "Measurement in the Study of Class and Delinquency." *Journal of Research in Crime and Delinquency* 31: 32–61.

Felson, Richard, Jukka Savolainen, Mikko Aaltonen, and Heta Moustgaard. (2008). "Is the Association between Alcohol Use and Delinquency Causal or Spurious?" *Criminology* 46 (3): 785–808.

Fischer, Benedikt, Wendy Medved, Maritt Kirst, Jurgen Rehm, and Louis Gliksman. (2001). "Illicit Opiates and Crime: Results of an Untreated User Cohort Study in Toronto." *Canadian Journal of Criminology* 43 (2): 197–217.

Fischer, C.S. (1976). *The Urban Experience*. New York: Harcourt Brace Jovanovich.

Fisher, J. (1986). "Canadian Trends in Selected Female Crimes." Unpublished M.A. thesis, University of Alberta.

Fitzgerald, Robin. (2003). "An Examination of Sex Differences in Delinquency." Ottawa: Statistics Canada.

Fitzgerald, Robin T., and Peter J. Carrington. (2008). "The Neighborhood Context of Urban Aboriginal Crime." *Canadian Journal of Criminology and Criminal Justice* 50 (5): 523–57.

Fox, J., and T. Hartnagel. (1979). "Changing Social Roles and Female Crime in Canada." *Canadian Review of Sociology and Anthropology* 16 (1): 96–104.

Francisco, Joycelyn, and Christian Chenier. (2007). "A Comparison of Large Urban, Small Urban and Rural Crime Rates, 2005." *Juristat* 27 (3).

Fréchette, M. (1983). "Delinquency and Delinquents." In R.R. Corrado et al. (eds.), *Current Issues in Juvenile Justice* (pp. 49–60). Toronto: Butterworths.

Frideres, J.S. (1988). *Native Peoples in Canada*. Scarborough: Prentice Hall.

Gabor, Thomas. (2004). "Inflammatory Rhetoric on Racial Profiling Can Undermine Police Services." *Canadian Journal of Criminology and Criminal Justice* 46: 457–66.

Giffen, P.J. (1965). "Rates of Crime and Delinquency." In W.T. McGrath (ed.), *Crime and Its Treatment in Canada*. Toronto: Macmillan.

———. (1966). "The Revolving Door." *Canadian Review of Sociology and Anthropology* 3 (3): 154–66.

———. (1976). "Official Rates of Crime and Delinquency." In W.T. McGrath (ed.), *Crime and Its Treatment in Canada* (pp. 66–110). Toronto: Macmillan.

Gold, Alan D. (2003). "Media Hype, Racial Profiling, and Good Science." *Canadian Journal of Criminology and Criminal Justice* 45 (3): 391–99.

Gomme, I.M. (1985). "Predictors of Status and Criminal Offences among Male and Female Adolescents in an Ontario Community." *Canadian Journal of Criminology* 27 (2): 147–59.

Gordon, R.A. (1976). "Prevalence: The Rare Datum in Delinquency Measurement and Its Implications for the Theory of Delinquency." In M.W. Klein (ed.), *The Juvenile Justice System* (pp. 201–84). Beverly Hills: Sage.

Greenaway, W.K. (1980). "Crime and Class: Unequal Before the Law." In J. Harp and J.R. Hofley (eds.), *Structured Inequality in Canada* (pp. 247–65). Scarborough: Prentice Hall.

Greenberg, D. (1979). "Delinquency and the Age Structure of Society." In S.L. Messinger and E. Bittner (eds.), *Criminology Review Yearbook* (pp. 586–620). Beverly Hills: Sage.

Griffiths, C.T., D.S. Wood, E. Zellerer, and J. Simon. (1994). *Aboriginal Policing in British Columbia*. Victoria: Ministry of Attorney General.

Hagan, J. (1974). "Criminal Justice and Native People." *Canadian Review of Sociology and Anthropology* Special Issue (August): 220–36.

———. (1975a). "The Social and Legal Constitution of Criminal Justice." *Social Problems* 22 (5): 620–37.

———. (1975b). "Parameters of Criminal Prosecution." *Journal of Criminal Law and Criminology* 65 (4): 536–44.

———. (1975c). "Law, Order and Sentencing." *Sociometry* 38 (2): 374–84.

———. (1977). "Criminal Justice in Rural and Urban Communities." *Social Forces* 55 (3): 597–612.

———. (1985). *Modern Criminology: Crime, Criminal Behavior, and Its Control.* New York: McGraw-Hill.

Hagan, J., and B. McCarthy. (1990). "Streetlife and Delinquency." Paper presented to American Society of Criminology.

Hagan, J., J. Simpson, and A. R. Gillis. (1979). "The Sexual Stratification of Social Control." *British Journal of Sociology* 30: 25–38.

Hartnagel, T.F. (1978). "The Effect of Age and Sex Compositions of Provincial Populations on Provincial Crime Rates." *Canadian Journal of Criminology* 20 (1): 28–33.

———. (1982). "Modernization, Female Social Roles, and Female Crime." *Sociological Quarterly* 23: 477–90.

———. (1997). "Crime Among the Provinces: The Effect of Geographic Mobility." *Canadian Journal of Criminology* 39 (4): 387–402.

———. (1998). "Labour Market Problems and Crime in the Transition from School to Work." *Canadian Review of Sociology and Anthropology* 35 (4): 435–59.

Hartnagel, T.F., and G.W. Lee. (1990). "Urban Crime in Canada." *Canadian Journal of Criminology* 32: 591–606.

Havemann, P., K. Couse, L. Foster, and R. Matonovich. (1985). *Law and Order for Canada's Indigenous People.* Regina: Prairie Justice Research, School of Human Justice, University of Regina.

Health Canada. (2009). *Canadian Alcohol and Drug Use Monitoring Survey, 2009.* Available at http://www.hc-sc.gc.ca/hc.ps/drugs-drogues/stat/index-eng.php; accessed December 27, 2010.

Hindelang, M.J., T. Hirschi, and J.G. Weis. (1979). "Correlates of Delinquency." *American Sociological Review* 44 (6): 995–1014.

Hirschi, T., and M. Gottfredson. (1983). "Age and the Explanation of Crime." *American Journal of Sociology* 89 (3): 552–84.

Hirschi, T., and H. Selvin. (1966). "False Criteria of Causality in Delinquency Research." *Social Problems* 13 (3): 254–68.

Hylton, J.H. (1982). "The Native Offender in Saskatchewan." *Canadian Journal of Criminology* 24 (2): 121–31.

Indian and Northern Affairs Canada. (1980). *Indian Conditions.* Ottawa: Minister of Indian Affairs and Northern Development.

Irvine, M.J. (1978). *The Native Inmate in Ontario.* Toronto: Ministry of Correctional Services, Province of Ontario.

James, C. (1998). "Up to No Good: Black on the Streets and Encountering Police." In V. Satzewich (ed.), *Racism and Social Inequality in Canada* (pp. 157–76). Toronto: Thompson.

James, J.T.L. (1979). "Toward a Cultural Understanding of the Native Offender." *Canadian Journal of Criminology* 21 (4): 453–62.

Jarvis, G.K., and H.B. Messinger. (1974). "Social and Economic Correlates of Juvenile Delinquency Rates." *Canadian Journal of Criminology and Corrections* 16: 361–72.

Jensen, G.F., J.H. Stauss, and V.W. Harris. (1977). "Crime, Delinquency, and the American Indian." *Human Organization* 36 (3): 252–57.

Johnson, H. (1987). "Getting the Facts Straight." In E. Adelberg and C. Currie (eds.), *Too Few to Count* (pp. 23–46). Vancouver: Press Gang Publishers.

———. (1996). *Dangerous Domains: Violence Against Women in Canada*. Scarborough: Nelson Canada.

Johnson, S. (2005). "Returning to Correctional Services After Release: A Profile of Aboriginal and non-Aboriginal Adults Involved in Saskatchewan Corrections from 1999/00 to 2003/04." *Juristat* 25 (2).

Johnston, P. (1994). "Academic Approaches to Race–Crime Statistics Do Not Justify Their Collection." *Canadian Journal of Criminology* 36: 166–73.

Kennedy, L.W., R.A. Silverman, and D.R. Forde. (1991). "Homicide in Urban Canada." *Canadian Journal of Sociology* 16: 397–410.

Kong, Rebecca, and Kathy AuCoin. (2008). "Female Offenders in Canada." *Juristat* 28 (1).

Kornhauser, R. (1978). *Social Sources of Delinquency*. Chicago: University of Chicago Press.

Krahn, H., T.F. Hartnagel, and J.W. Gartrell. (1986). "Income Inequality and Homicide Rates." *Criminology* 24: 269–95.

LaPrairie, C.P. (1983). "Native Juveniles in Court." In T. Fleming and L.A. Visano (eds.), *Deviant Designations* (pp. 337–50). Toronto: Butterworths.

———. (1990). "The Role of Sentencing in the Overrepresentation of Aboriginal People in Correctional Institutions." *Canadian Journal of Criminology* 32: 429–40.

———. (1992). "Aboriginal Crime and Justice." *Canadian Journal of Criminology* 34: 281–97.

———. (1995). *Seen But Not Heard: Native People in the Inner City*. Ottawa: Minister of Public Works and Government Services Canada.

———. (1996). *Examining Aboriginal Corrections in Canada*. Ottawa: Supply and Services Canada.

———. (2002). "Aboriginal Over-representation in the Criminal Justice System: A Tale of Nine Cities." *Canadian Journal of Criminology* 44 (2): 181–208.

LeBlanc, M. (1975). "Upper Class vs. Working Class Delinquency." In R.A. Silverman and J.J. Teevan Jr., *Crime in Canadian Society* (pp. 102–18). Toronto: Butterworths.

———. (1983). "Delinquency as an Epiphenomenon of Adolescence." In R.R. Corrado et al. (eds.), *Current Issues in Juvenile Justice* (pp. 31–48). Toronto: Butterworths.

Leenaars, A., and D. Lester. (2004). "Understanding the Declining Canadian Homicide Rate: A Test of Holinger's Relative Cohort Size Hypothesis." *Death Studies* 28: 263–65.

Lester, D. (1999). *Crime and the Native American*. Springfield, Ill.: Charles Thomas.

Levitt, S. (1999). "The Limited Role of Changing Age Structure in Explaining Aggregate Crime Rates." *Criminology* 37 (3): 581–97.

Loeber, R., and M. LeBlanc. (1990). "Toward a Developmental Criminology." In M. Tonry and N. Morris (eds.), *Crime and Justice*, Vol 12. Chicago: University of Chicago Press.

Manitoba Public Inquiry into the Administration of Justice and Aboriginal People. (1991). *Report of the Aboriginal Justice Inquiry of Manitoba*. Winnipeg: The Inquiry.

Manzoni, Patrik, Benedikt Fischer, and Jurgen Rehm. (2007). "Local Drug-Crime Dynamics in a Canadian Multi-Site Sample of Untreated Opioid Users." *Canadian Journal of Criminology and Criminal Justice* 49 (3): 341–73.

Melchers, Ron. (2003). "Do Toronto Police Engage in Racial Profiling?" *Canadian Journal of Criminology and Criminal Justice* 45 (3): 347–66.

Merton, R. (1938). "Social Structure and Anomie." *American Sociological Review* 3: 672–82.

Métis and Non-Status Indian Crime and Justice Commission. (1978). *Report*. Ottawa: Minister of Supply and Services.

Mihorean, K., S. Besserer, D. Hendrick, J.A. Brzozowski, C. Trainor, and S. Ogg. (2001). *A Profile of Criminal Victimization: Results of the 1999 General Social Survey.* Ottawa: Minister of Industry.

Monture-Angus, P.A. (1996). "Lessons in Decolonization." In D.A. Long and O.P. Dickason (eds.), *Visions of the Heart* (pp. 335–54). Toronto: Harcourt Brace and Company.

Mosher, J., and D. Jernigan. (2001). "Making the Link: A Public Health Approach to Preventing Alcohol-Related Violence and Crime." *Journal of Substance Use* 6: 273–89.

Native Counselling Services of Alberta. (1982). "Native People and the Criminal Justice System." *Canadian Legal Aid Bulletin* 5 (1): 55–63.

Nettler, G. (1982). *Explaining Criminals.* Cincinnati: Anderson Publishing.

———. (1984). *Explaining Crime.* New York: McGraw-Hill.

Neugebauer, R. (2000). "Kids, Cops and Colour." In R. Neugebauer (ed.), *Criminal Injustice: Racism in the Criminal Justice System* (pp. 46–59). Toronto: Canadian Scholars' Press.

Nielsen, M.O. (1992). "Introduction." In R.A. Silverman and M.O. Nielsen (eds.), *Aboriginal Peoples and Canadian Criminal Justice.* Toronto: Butterworths.

O'Brien, R.M. (1999). "Measuring the Convergence/Divergence of 'Serious Crime' Arrest Rates for Males and Females: 1960–1995." *Journal of Quantitative Criminology* 15: 97–114.

Osgood, D. W., P.M. O'Malley, J.G. Backman, and L.D. Johnston. (1989). "Time Trends and Age Trends in Arrests and Self-Reported Illegal Behaviour." *Criminology* 27: 389–417.

Ouimet, M. (2000). "Aggregation Bias in Ecological Research." *Canadian Journal of Criminology* 42: 135–56.

———. (2002). "Explaining the American and Canadian Crime 'Drop' in the 1990s." *Canadian Journal of Criminology* 44: 33–50.

Parker, R.N., and K. Auerhahn. (1998). "Alcohol, Drugs, and Violence." *Annual Review of Sociology* 24: 291–311.

Pernanen, Kai, Marie-Marthe Cousineau, Serge Brochu, and Fu Sun. (2002). *Proportions of Crimes Associated with Alcohol and Other Drugs in Canada.* Ottawa: Canadian Centre on Substance Abuse.

Perreault, Samuel, and Shannon Brennan. (2010). "Criminal Victimization in Canada, 2009." *Juristat* 30 (2).

Pollak, O. (1950). *The Criminality of Women.* Philadelphia: University of Pennsylvania Press.

Quinney, R. (1977). *Class, State and Crime.* New York: David McKay Company.

Rand, A. (1987). "Transitional Life Events and Desistance from Delinquency and Crime." In M.E. Wolfgang and T.P. Thornberry (eds.), *From Boy to Man: From Delinquency to Crime* (pp. 134–62). Chicago: University of Chicago Press.

Roberts, J. (1994). "Crime and Race Statistics: Toward a Canadian Solution." *Canadian Journal of Criminology* 36: 175–85.

Roberts, J.V., and A.N. Doob. (1997). "Race, Ethnicity, and Criminal Justice in Canada." In M. Tonry (ed.), *Ethnicity, Crime, and Immigration* Vol. 21 (pp. 469–522). Chicago: University of Chicago Press.

Rowe, A.R., and C.R. Tittle. (1977). "Life Cycle Changes and Criminal Propensity." *The Sociological Quarterly* 18: 223–36.

Sagi, P.C., and C.F. Wellford. (1968). "Age Composition and Patterns of Change in Criminal Statistics." *Journal of Criminal Law, Criminology and Police Science* 59: 29–36.

Sampson, R.J., and W.B. Groves. (1989). "Community Structure and Crime." *American Journal of Sociology* 94: 774–802.

Sampson, R.J., and J.H. Laub. (1990). "Crime and Deviance over the Life Course." *American Sociological Review* 55: 609–27.

———. (1992). "Crime and Deviance in the Life Course." *Annual Review of Sociology* 18: 63–84.

Sampson, R.J., and J. Wooldredge. (1987). "Linking the Micro- and Macro-Level Dimensions of Lifestyle-Routine Activity and Opportunity Models of Predatory Victimization." *Journal of Quantitative Criminology* 3: 371–93.

Savoie, J. (2002). "Crime Statistics in Canada, 2001." *Juristat* 22 (6): 1–22.

———. (2008). *Analysis of the Spatial Distribution of Crime in Canada: Summary of Major Trends 1999, 2001, 2003 and 2006.* Ottawa: Canadian Centre for Justice Statistics, Statistics Canada.

Schelenberg, Jennifer L., Joanna C. Jacob, and Peter J. Carrington. (2007). "Ecological Analysis of Crime Rates and Police Discretion with Young Persons: A Replication." *Canadian Journal of Criminology and Criminal Justice* 49 (2): 261–77.

Shaw, C.R., and H.D. McKay. (1942). *Juvenile Delinquency and Urban Areas.* Chicago: University of Chicago Press.

———. (1969). *Juvenile Delinquency and Urban Areas* (2nd ed.). Chicago: University of Chicago Press.

Short, J.F., Jr., and F.I. Nye. (1957). "Reported Behavior as a Criterion of Deviant Behavior." *Social Problems* 5: 207–13.

Simon, R.J. (1975). *Women and Crime.* Lexington, Mass.: D.C. Heath.

Skogan, W.G. (1977). "The Changing Distribution of Big-City Crime." *Urban Affairs Quarterly* 13: 33–48.

Smart, C. (1976). *Women, Crime and Criminology.* London: Routledge and Kegan Paul.

Smith, D.A., and C.A. Visher. (1980). "Sex and Involvement in Deviance/Crime." *American Sociological Review* 45 (4): 691–701.

Solicitor General Canada. (1987). *Patterns in Violent Crime: Canadian Urban Victimization Survey*, Bulletin No. 8. Ottawa: Ministry of Solicitor General.

———. (1988). *Patterns in Property Crime: Canadian Urban Victimization Survey*, Bulletin No. 9. Ottawa: Ministry of Solicitor General.

Sprott, Jane, and C. Cesaroni. (2002). "Similarities in Homicide Trends in the United States and Canada: Guns, Crack, or Simple Demographics?" *Homicide Studies* 6 (4): 348–59.

Stack, S. (1984). "Income Inequality and Property Crime." *Criminology* 22: 229–57.

Stark, R. (1987). "Deviant Places." *Criminology* 25: 893–909.

Statistics Canada. (2007). "Crime Statistics, 2006." *The Daily*, July 18, 2007. Ottawa: Statistics Canada.

Steffensmeier, D. (1978). "Crime and the Contemporary Woman." *Social Forces* 57 (2): 566–83.

———. (1980). "Sex Differences in Patterns of Adult Crime, 1965–77." *Social Forces* 58 (4): 1080–1108.

Steffensmeier, D., and E. Allan. (1995). "Criminal Behavior: Gender and Crime." In J.F. Sheley (ed.), *Criminology: A Contemporary Handbook* (2nd ed.), (pp. 83–113). Belmont, Calif.: Wadsworth.

Steffensmeier, D.F., E.A. Allan, M.D. Harer, and C. Streifel. (1989). "Age and the Distribution of Crime." *American Journal of Sociology* 94: 803–31.

Steffensmeier, D.J., and M.D. Harer. (1991). "Did Crime Rise or Fall During the Regan Presidency?" *Journal of Research in Crime and Delinquency* 28: 330–59.

Steffensmeier, D., and C. Streifel. (1992). "Time-series Analysis of the Female Percentage of Arrests for Property Crimes, 1960–1985." *Justice Quarterly* 9 (1): 77–103.

Steffensmeier, D., R.H. Steffensmeier, and A.S. Rosenthal. (1979). "Trends in Female Violence, 1960–1977." *Sociological Focus* 12 (3): 217–27.

Sutherland, E., and D. Cressey. (1978). *Criminology*. New York: J.P. Lippincott.

Tanner, J., and H. Krahn. (1991). "Part-Time Work and Deviance among High-School Seniors." *Canadian Journal of Sociology* 16: 281–302.

Task Force on Aboriginal Peoples in Federal Corrections. (1989). *Final Report*. Ottawa: Minister of Supply and Services.

Task Force on the Criminal Justice System and Its Impact on the Indian and Métis People of Alberta. (1991). *Report of the Task Force on the Criminal Justice System and Its Impact on the Indian and Métis*. Edmonton: The Task Force.

Thomas, D. (1993). "The Foreign Born in the Federal Prison Population." Canadian Law and Society Association Conference, Ottawa, June 8.

Thomas, J. (2010). "Adult Criminal Court Statistics, 2008/09." *Juristat* 30 (2).

Tittle, C.R., and W.J. Villemez. (1977). "Social Class and Criminality." *Social Forces* 56 (2): 474–502.

Tittle, C.R., W.J. Villemez, and D.A. Smith. (1978). "The Myth of Social Class and Criminality." *American Sociological Review* 43 (5): 643–56.

Tittle, C.R., and D.A. Ward. (1993). "The Interaction of Age with the Correlates and Causes of Crime." *Journal of Quantitative Criminology* 9: 3–53.

Tonry, M. (1995). *Malign Neglect: Race, Crime and Punishment in America*. New York: Oxford University Press.

Trasler, G. (1980). "Aspects of Causality, Culture, and Crime." Paper presented at the 4th International Seminar at the International Centre of Sociological, Penal and Penitentiary Research and Studies, Messina, Sicily.

Trevethan, S. (1993). *Police-Reported Aboriginal Crime in Calgary, Regina and Saskatoon*. Ottawa: Canadian Centre for Justice Statistics.

Tribble, S. (1972). "Socio-Economic Status and Self-Reported Juvenile Delinquency." *Canadian Journal of Criminology and Corrections* 14: 409–15.

Verdun-Jones, S.N., and G.K. Muirhead. (1979–80). "Natives in the Canadian Criminal Justice System." *Crime and Justice* 7/8 (1): 3–21.

Vold, G.B., and T.J. Bernard. (1986). *Theoretical Criminology*. New York: Oxford University Press.

Wallace, M. (2004). "Crime Statistics in Canada, 2003." *Juristat* 24 (6).

Warr, M. (1993). "Age, Peers, and Delinquency." *Criminology* 31: 17–40.

Wellford, C.F. (1973). "Age Composition and the Increase in Recorded Crime." *Criminology* 11: 61–70.

West, W.G. (1984). *Young Offenders and the State*. Toronto: Butterworths.

Wirth, L. (1938). "Urbanism as a Way of Life." *American Journal of Sociology* 44: 3–24.

Wolff, L., and B. Reingold. (1994). "Drug Use and Crime." *Juristat* 14 (6): 1–19.

Wood, D.S., and C.T. Griffiths. (1996). "Patterns of Aboriginal Crime." In R.A. Silverman, J.J. Teevan, and V.F. Sacco (eds.), *Crime in Canadian Society* (5th ed.), (pp. 222–33). Toronto: Harcourt Brace and Company.

Wortley, Scot. (2003). "Hidden Intersections: Research on Race, Crime and Criminal Justice." *Canadian Ethnic Studies* 35 (3): 99–117.

Wortley, Scot, and Julian Tanner. (2003). "Data, Denials, and Confusion: The Racial Profiling Debate in Toronto." *Canadian Journal of Criminology and Criminal Justice* 45 (3): 367–91.

———. (2005). "Inflammatory Rhetoric? Baseless Accusations? A Response to Gabor's Critique of Racial Profiling Research in Canada." *Canadian Journal of Criminology and Criminal Justice* 47 (3): 581–609.

Wynne, D.F., and T.F. Hartnagel. (1975). "Race and Plea Negotiation." *Canadian Journal of Sociology* 1 (2): 147–55.

Yessine, Annie K., and James Bonta. (2009). "The Offending Trajectories of Youthful Aboriginal Offenders." *Canadian Journal of Criminology and Criminal Justice* 51 (4): 435–72.

# Feminism and Criminology

## 6

**Elizabeth Comack**

UNIVERSITY OF MANITOBA

Like other academic disciplines, criminology has been a male-centred enterprise. Despite the use of generic terms such as "criminals," "defendants," and "delinquents," most of criminology has really been about what men do. As a consequence, women have been rendered invisible in much criminological inquiry. When women are looked at as offenders, their small numbers relative to men have typically been used to justify or rationalize this neglect. In 2005, for instance, only one in five persons accused by Canadian police of a Criminal Code offence was female (Kong and AuCoin, 2008). And more recent court statistics suggest this ratio has not changed since then (Thomas, 2010). When women were looked at as victims, violence against them was traditionally not a major area of concern. Official statistics on crime indicated that offences such as rape were relatively infrequent, and victim surveys reported young males to be the group most at risk from crime. Perhaps even more significant is that even though the subject matter of criminology has been men, criminologists have done very little work on men as men. In short, they have neglected to consider the "maleness" of their subjects. Over the past three decades, there has been a growing awareness of the implications that these omissions hold for the discipline. This has come about largely through the feminist engagement with criminology: the efforts of feminist criminologists to move women—and an analysis of gender—from the periphery to the centre of criminological inquiry. The purpose of this chapter is to recount this history with a view to clarify the kinds of issues and questions that are now commanding criminologists' attention.

## Learning Objectives

After reading this chapter, you should be able to

- Explain the various theories that have been developed to understand women's involvement in crime.
- Understand the social, cultural, and legal factors that pertain to the issue of male violence against women.
- Appreciate some of the connections between a woman's law violations and her history of abuse.
- Evaluate the claim that women are "men's equals" in violence and some of the problems raised with using the Conflict Tactics Scale to research violence between intimate partners.
- Appreciate the gains to be made in addressing the connections between masculinity and crime.

# The Invisibility of Women

The feminist engagement with criminology began over 30 years ago when pioneers in the discipline, such as Marie-Andrée Bertrand (1967) and Frances Heidensohn (1968), first called attention to criminology's amnesia when it came to women. Heidensohn (1968, 171), for instance, described the analysis of women and crime as "lonely uncharted seas" and stated the need for a "crash programme of research which telescopes decades of comparable studies of males." In its initial phases, however, the feminist engagement with criminology consisted of a critique of the existing approaches to explain crime. This critique took two paths. Initially, writers like Dorie Klein (1973) and Carol Smart (1976, 1977) focused attention on the **sexism** of the small body of theories that had been developed to explain women's crime. Other writers soon broadened the focus to include the invisibility of women in the mainstream theories within the discipline.

## Theories of Women's Crime

**The Conservative Approach** Historically, a particular pathway can be followed when tracing the initial attempts to explain women's criminality. It begins with the publication of Lombroso and Ferrero's *The Female Offender* in 1895 and is followed by Thomas's *The Unadjusted Girl* in 1923, Glueck and Glueck's *Five Hundred Delinquent Women* in 1934, and Pollak's *The Criminality of Women* in 1950. Each of these works reflects a **conservative approach** to understand differences between men and women. Specifically, "difference" is rooted in biology. Women are viewed as "naturally" inferior to men, and it is this inferiority that is used to explain women's criminality.

For example, in applying the concepts of atavism and social Darwinism (see Chapter 8), Lombroso and Ferrero suggested that women possessed limited intelligence. They were also less sensitive to pain than men, full of revenge and jealousy, and naturally passive and conservative. Women's natural passivity, for instance, was caused by the "immobility of the ovule compared to the zoosperm" (Lombroso and Ferrero, 1895, 109). Atavistically, women were seen as displaying fewer signs of degeneration than men. The reason, according to Lombroso and Ferrero, was that women (and nonwhite males) had not advanced as far along the evolutionary continuum as (white) males and so could not degenerate as far. Given that women were relatively "primitive," the criminals among them would not be highly visible. However, those women who were criminal were cast as excessively vile and cruel in their crimes. They combined the qualities of the criminal male with the worst characteristics of the female: cunning, spite, and deceitfulness. Lacking the "maternal instinct" and "ladylike qualities," criminal women were seen as genetically more male than female.

First published in 1923, Thomas's (1967) work on female delinquency was premised on a similar kind of biological determinism. Thomas suggested that human behaviour was based on four "wishes": for adventure, security, response, and recognition. These wishes corresponded to features in the nervous system, which were expressed as biological instincts of anger, fear, love, and the will to

**sexism**

Attributing to women's socially undesirable characteristics that are assumed to be intrinsic characteristics of that sex.

**conservative approach**

An approach that understands "difference" between men and women as biologically based sex differences. Women are viewed as "naturally" inferior or unequal to men.

gain status and power, respectively. However, Thomas asserted that men's and women's instincts differed both in quantity and quality. Since women had more varieties of love in their nervous systems, their desire for response was greater than men's. According to Thomas, it was the need to feel loved that accounted for women's criminality, and especially prostitution.

Glueck and Glueck (1934) continued in this same tradition with *500 Delinquent Women*. The Gluecks described the women in their study as a "sorry lot. Burdened with feeblemindedness, psychopathic personality, and marked emotional instability, a large proportion of them found it difficult to survive by legitimate means" (299). The view of criminal women as "Other" is clearly evident in the Gluecks' work: "This swarm of defective, diseased, anti-social misfits . . . comprises the human material which a reformatory and a parole system are required by society to transform into wholesome, decent, law-abiding citizens! Is it not a miracle that a proportion of them were actually rehabilitated?" (303).

Pollak's (1961) work attempted to account for what he described as the "masked" nature of women's crime. Skeptical of the official data on sex differences in crime, Pollak suggested that women's crime was vastly under-counted. He put forward the view that female criminality was more likely to be hidden and undetected. Women were more often the instigators than perpetrators of crime. Like Eve in the Garden of Eden, they manipulated men into committing offences. Women were also inherently deceptive and vengeful: they engaged in prostitution, blackmailed their lovers, as domestics they stole from their employers, and as homemakers they carried out horrendous acts on their families (like poisoning the sick and abusing children). According to Pollak, woman's devious nature was rooted in her physiology. While a man must achieve erection in order to perform the sex act, and hence will not be able to conceal orgasm, a woman can fake orgasm. This ability to conceal orgasm gave women practice at deception. Pollak also suggested that female crime was caused by the vengefulness, irritability, and depression women encountered as a result of their generative phases. For example, menstruation drove women to acts of revenge by reminding women of their inferior status (and their ultimate failure to become men) (see Box 6.1). The concealed nature of their crimes, the vulnerability of their victims, and their chivalrous treatment by men who could not bear to prosecute or punish them, all combined to "mask" women's offences. When these factors are taken into account, according to Pollak, women's crimes are equal in severity and number to those of men.

As Heidensohn (1985, 122) notes, these early approaches to explain women's crime lent an aura of intellectual respectability to many of the old folk tales about women and their behaviours. They reflected the widely held assumptions about "women's nature," including the good girl/bad girl duality and a double standard that viewed sexual promiscuity as a sign of "amorality" in women but "normality" in men. Relying on "common-sense," anecdotal evidence and circular reasoning—that is, "things are as they are because they are natural, and they are natural because that is the way things are" (Smart, 1976, 36)—the early theorists failed to call into question the structural features of their society and the gendered nature of the roles of men and women. Instead, sex (a biological difference) and gender (a cultural prescription) were equated as one and the same, with the "ladylike qualities" of the middle- and upper-class white woman used as the measuring rod for what was inherently female. In the process, the theories constructed were not only sexist, but classist and racist as well.

While we can look back on these early theories of women's crime with some amusement, it bears noting that the kinds of assumptions and beliefs reflected in them have not disappeared. As Klein (1973, 7) comments, "The road from Lombroso to the present is surprisingly straight." Throughout the 1960s, researchers continued to rely on the assumptions and premises of the earlier approaches (see, for example, Cowie et al., 1968; Konopka, 1966). Following in the footsteps of Pollak, a more contemporary version of this conservative approach to understand the difference between men and women links hormonal changes associated with women's menstrual cycles to their involvement in crime.

Premenstrual syndrome (PMS) has been described as a condition of "irritability, indescribable tension" and a "desire to find relief by foolish and ill-considered actions" that is thought to occur during the preceding week or two prior to the onset of menstruation (Frank cited in Osborne, 1989, 168). There have been some 150 different symptoms (behavioural, psychological, and physiological) associated with PMS, and estimates of its incidence vary from 20 to 95 percent of the female population. There are no biomedical tests for determining the existence of PMS; it is the only "disease" not dependent on a specific type of symptom for its diagnosis. Nevertheless, PMS has been argued to be a cause of violent behaviour in women who suffer from it. It gained popularity as a cause of women's criminality in the 1980s, when PMS was introduced in two British court cases as a mitigating factor in homicide, enabling the women to receive more lenient sentences (Luckhaus, 1985). Sandie Smith was convicted on a reduced charge of manslaughter and given three years probation plus mandatory progesterone treatments. Christine English pleaded guilty to manslaughter with diminished responsibility and received a one year conditional discharge and was banned from driving for a year (she had run her boyfriend over with a car).

While research linking PMS to women's criminality has been criticized for its methodological deficiencies (Morris, 1987), feminist criminologists have questioned the validity of framing explanations for women's criminality that isolate the source of the problem in women's bodies, thereby ignoring the cultural meanings (especially with regard to menstruation) and social contexts that are at play (Kendall, 1991, 1992). So long as women are pathologized as "sick" or "diseased," the broader structural factors that impinge upon women's lives—and are thereby implicated in their offending behaviours—will be ignored.

**The Liberal Approach** In the 1970s, theories of women's crime began to shift toward a more sociological orientation. Rather than focusing on biology, attention shifted to culture. In this **liberal approach**, differences between men and women are not necessarily innate or inborn, but are learned by individuals through the process of socialization. It is the culture that marks off the differences between men and women by proscribing certain roles and behaviours

**liberal approach**

Distinguishes sex (biological) from gender (cultural) and sees differences between men and women as resulting from gender roles and socialization patterns.

# FOCUS BOX 6.1

## THE "WOMEN PROBLEM"

In the following passage, Otto Pollak offers us an illustration of a male-centred view of what has been traditionally referred to as the "woman problem" and its relationship to female criminality.

> The student of female criminality cannot afford to overlook the generally known and recognized fact that [women's] generative phases are frequently accompanied by psychological disturbances which may upset the need satisfaction balance of the individual or weaken her internal inhibitions, and thus become causative factors in female crime. Particularly because of the social meaning attached to them in our culture, the generative phases of women are bound to present many stumbling blocks for the law-abiding behaviour of women. Menstruation with its appearance of injury must confirm feelings of guilt which individuals may have about sex activities which they have learned to consider as forbidden. As a symbol of womanhood, it must also, because of its recurrent nature, aggravate any feeling of irritation and protest which women may have regarding their sex in a society in which women have had, and still
>
> have, to submit to social inequality with men. In both instances, it must lead to a disturbance of the emotional balance of the individual and this becomes potentially crime-promoting. Pregnancy in a culture which frowns upon illegitimacy and fosters in large sectors of society limitation in the number of children or even childlessness must become a source of irritation, anxiety, and emotional upheaval in many instances. The menopause in a society which makes romance and emotional gratification the supreme value in a monogamous marriage system must be experienced, at least by married women, frequently as a threat to the basis of their emotional security if not to their general marital existence. In view of these cultural implications of the generative phases and their psychological consequences, it is difficult to understand why the existing literature contains so little discussion of their possible crime-promoting influence.

Source: Otto Pollak. (1961). *The Criminality of Women*. New York: A. S. Barnes, pp. 157–58. Originally published by University of Pennsylvania Press (Philadelphia) in 1950.

as "male appropriate" and "female appropriate." "Gender" was therefore separated from "sex" and made the key focus of inquiry. This liberal approach to understand difference took the form of role theory as an explanation for female criminality. Hoffman-Bustamante (1973), for example, suggested that the lower rate of delinquency of girls can be accounted for by differential socialization and child-rearing practices. Whereas boys are encouraged to be aggressive, outgoing, and ambitious and are allowed greater freedom, girls are taught to be passive and domesticated and are more closely supervised. Since girls are taught to be non-violent, they do not acquire the skills, technical ability, or physical strength to engage in violent acts such as gang fighting. When women do engage in violent behaviour, their actions reflect their greater domesticity. For example, women who murder are more likely to use kitchen knives than guns. The finding that women are more likely to be charged with shoplifting offences was similarly explained with reference to their gender roles and social-ization. Women are traditionally the consumers in society and, when they steal, girls are more likely to take small items like make-up. Role theory, then, offered an explanation in terms of the differential gender socialization for both the types and nature of offences that females commit.

Another version of role theory was put forward by Hagan and his col-leagues (Hagan et al., 1979, 1985, 1987) in the form of a power-control theory of sex and delinquency. Power-control theory is designed to explain the sex differences in delinquency by drawing linkages between the variations in par-ental control and the delinquent behaviour of boys and girls. More specific-ally, Hagan and his colleagues suggest that parental control and adolescents' subsequent attitudes toward risk-taking behaviour are affected by family class relations. They distinguish two ideal types of family: the patriarchal family in which the husband is employed in an authority position in the workforce and the wife is not employed outside the home, and the egalitarian family in which both husband and wife are employed in authority positions outside the home. Hagan and his colleagues suggest that in the former, a traditional gender division exists whereby fathers and especially mothers are expected to control their daughters more than their sons. Given the presence of a "cult of domesticity," girls are socialized to focus their futures on domestic labour and consumption activities while boys are prepared for their participation in production activities. In the latter form, parents redistribute their con-trol efforts so that girls are subject to controls more like those imposed on boys. "In other words, in egalitarian families, as mothers gain power relative to husbands, daughters gain freedom relative to sons" (1987, 792). As such, the authors predict that these different family forms will produce differing levels of delinquency in girls: "Patriarchal families will be characterized by large gender differences in common delinquent behaviours, while egalitarian families will be characterized by smaller gender differences in delinquency" (1987, 793).

Smart (1976) has commented that role theory can offer only a partial explanation of women's crime. Because of a failure to situate the discussion of gender roles in broader structural terms, little attention is devoted to why socialization patterns are gender differentiated and how they have come to be that way. In the absence of a structural analysis, it is too easy to fall back on explanations that view such differences as biological, and not social, in their origins: "role is destiny" can therefore act as a ready substitute for "biology is destiny" (Morris, 1987, 64). While Hagan and his colleagues endeavour to place role theory in a broader structural context (by attending to the labour force participation of parents), they make an important assumption: if a woman is working for wages, there will be "equality" within the household. Their formu-lation does not pay enough attention to the nature of women's paid work and to other variables that might be in operation (such as how power and control may be exercised between males and females within the household).

In addition to engaging in critical evaluations of the specific theories that had been developed to explain women's involvement in crime, feminist criminologists drew attention to the invisibility of women in the mainstream approaches within the discipline.

## The Mainstream Theories of Crime

Since the 1970s, mainstream approaches to explain crime have come under increasing scrutiny. Writers such as Leonard (1982),  Heidensohn (1985), Morris (1987), and Naffine (1987) have highlighted the general failure of mainstream theories in criminology to adequately explain or account for women's involvement in crime; "mainstream" was, in effect, "malestream."

For example, in explaining crime in relation to the strain that results from the disjunction between culture goals (like monetary success) and institutionalized means (education, jobs), Merton's anomie theory (see Chapter 10, "Strain Theories") reflected a sensitivity to the class inequalities that exist in society. The same could not be said, however, with regard to an awareness of gender inequalities. If lower-class individuals were more likely to engage in crime because of a lack of access to the institutionalized means for achieving monetary success, then it follows that women—who as a group experience a similar lack of access—should also be found to commit crime as a consequence of this strain. This is not the case.

Like strain theory, Sutherland's differential association theory is presented as a general theory of crime (see Chapter 13, "Interactionist Theories"). In focusing on the processes by which individuals learn definitions of the legal codes as either favourable or unfavourable, Sutherland posited the existence of a "cultural homogeneity" in society with regard to pro- and anti-criminal associations. While this cultural heterogeneity accounted for men's involvement in crime, women were the anomaly or exception in that they displayed a "cultural homogeneity." In Sutherland's view, women were more altruistic and compliant than men. As Naffine (1987) has noted, Sutherland missed a great opportunity when he neglected to explore this apparent cultural homogeneity in females. Given his critical outlook on the individualism and competition that he felt characterized American society, an examination of women's conformity could have provided Sutherland with clues to better understand crime and its causes.

Hirschi's work on social control theory is also characterized by a neglect of the female (see Chapter 14, "Social Control Theory"). While other criminologists focused their attention on explaining deviance, Hirschi set out to explain conformity. In this regard, since women appear to be more conformist than men, it would have made sense to treat women as central to his analysis. Nevertheless, despite having collected data on female subjects, Hirschi set these data aside and—like his colleagues—concentrated on males.

With the advent of the labelling and conflict theories during the 1960s and 1970s, the potential for a more inclusive approach to crime increased. Yet, while Becker's labelling perspective raised the question of "Whose side are we on?" and advocated an approach to deviance that gave a voice to those who were subject to the labelling process, it was never fully realized in the case of women. Similarly, Taylor, Walton, and Young's *The New Criminology* (1973), which offered up a devastating critique of the traditional criminological theories, failed to give any mention to women.

In general, when sex differentials in crime are considered by the mainstream theorists, the tendency has been to rely on stereotypical constructions of masculinity and femininity: men are aggressive, independent, daring, and adventurous; women are submissive, dependent, and compliant. In the process, female law violators are classed as a rather "dull lot." Even in their deviance, they are less interesting than men. Moreover, such stereotypical depictions of women have been considered "so obvious" that they require no further discussion (see, for example, Cohen, 1955, 142)—let alone theoretical or empirical concern.

We have seen in Chapter 5 that females commit less serious offences, in smaller numbers, and with less frequency than males. Criminologists have typically responded to these findings by formulating their theories to account for only male crime and delinquency. The ramifications of this tendency have been spelled out by Gelsthorpe and Morris:

> Theories are weak if they do not apply to half of the potential criminal population; women, after all, experience the same deprivations, family structures and so on that men do. Theories of crime should be able to take account of both men's and women's behaviour and to highlight those factors which operate differently on men and women. Whether or not a particular theory helps us to understand women's crime is of fundamental, not marginal importance for criminology. (Gelsthorpe and Morris, 1988, 103, emphasis added)

## The Generalizability Problem

**generalizability problem**

Raises the issue of whether mainstream theories of crime—which have largely been developed with men in mind—can be made to "fit" women.

One issue raised by this problem with the mainstream theories of crime is referred to by Daly and Chesney-Lind (1988) as the **generalizability problem**: can theories generated to explain male offending be modified to apply to women? Several criminologists responded to this problem by attempting to make the mainstream theories of crime "fit" women. For example, Leonard (1982) reformulated Merton's strain theory, suggesting that females may be socialized to aspire to different culture goals than males, in particular, relational ones concerning marriage and having children. If this is the case, then women's low rate of criminality would be explained by the relatively easy manner in which females can realize their goals. Nevertheless, as Morris (1987) notes, such a formulation relies on an idealized and romanticized version of women's lives. Not only does it display an insensitivity to the strains and frustrations associated with women's familial role, but it also fails to acknowledge the economic concerns that women confront. Such efforts to revise mainstream theories of crime to include women have been referred to as the "add women and stir" approach. Part of the difficulty with this endeavour is that women are presented as afterthoughts, not as integral to the arguments being developed (Gelsthorpe and Morris, 1988). A more significant problem with this effort is captured by Naffine (1997, 32): "The point of these exercises has been to adapt to the female case, theories of crime which purported to be gender-neutral but were in fact always highly gender specific. Not surprisingly, the results have been varied and generally inconclusive."

## The Gender-Ratio Problem

**gender-ratio problem**

Poses the question of why are there sex differences in rates of arrest and types of criminal activity between men and women.

A second issue raised by the feminist critique of mainstream criminology is one which Daly and Chesney-Lind (1988, 119) refer to as the **gender-ratio problem**. Why are women less likely than men to be involved in crime? What explains the sex difference in rates of arrest and in the variable types of criminal activity between men and women? Attention to the gender-ratio problem sparked a plethora of studies in the 1970s and 1980s on the processing of men and women by the criminal justice system (see, for example, Scutt, 1979; Kruttschnitt, 1980–81, 1982; Steffensmeier and Kramer, 1982; Zingraff and Thomson, 1984; Daly, 1987, 1989). The main question that guided much of this research stemmed from Pollak's assertion of the "chivalry" on the part of criminal justice officials: are women treated more leniently than men? Like the generalizability problem, the results have been mixed. For instance, research that supports the chivalry hypothesis indicates that when it does exist, chivalry benefits some women more than others, in particular, the few white middle- or upper-class women who come into conflict with the law. It also appears to apply only to those female suspects who behave in a stereotypical fashion, that is, "crying, pleading for release for the sake of their children, claiming men have led them astray" (Rafter and Natalizia, 1981, 92). In this regard, Rafter and Natalizia have argued that chivalrous behaviour should be seen as a means of preserving women's subordinate position in society, not as a benign effort to treat women with some special kindness. Naffine (1997, 36), however, points to a larger problem with this research. By turning on the question of whether women were treated the same as or different than men, the chivalry thesis (and its rebuttal) took men to be the norm: "Men were thus granted the status of universal subjects, the population of people with whom the rest of the world (women) were compared."

## The Women's Liberation Thesis

While research on the chivalry thesis drew the attention of criminologists in the 1970s and 1980s, another thesis was attracting considerable attention. The women's liberation thesis posits that women's involvement in crime will come to more closely resemble men's as differences between men and women are diminished by women's greater participation and equality in society. As reflected in the work of Simon (1975) and Adler (1975), the thesis suggests that changes in women's gender roles will be reflected in their rates of criminal involvement. Simon suggested that the increased employment opportunities that accompanied the women's movement would also bring an increase in opportunities to commit crime (such as embezzlement from employers). Adler linked the apparent increase in women's crime statistics to the influence of the women's movement and suggested that a "new female criminal" was emerging: women were becoming more violent and aggressive, just like their male counterparts.

Naffine (1997, 32) refers to the thesis that "women's liberation" causes crime in women as "perhaps the most time-consuming and fruitless exercise" in criminology. The numerous empirical difficulties with the thesis were discussed at some length in Chapter 5. For feminist criminologists, the main difficulty with the women's liberation thesis—similar to the chivalry thesis—was that it posed a question that took males to be the norm: were women becoming more "liberated" and thus more like men, even in their offending?

Given the difficulties encountered in the efforts to respond to the generalizability and gender-ratio problems, many feminist criminologists saw the need to "bracket" these issues for the time being in order to understand better the social worlds of women and girls (Daly and Chesney-Lind, 1988, 121). Cain (1990) took this suggestion further. She noted that while feminist criminologists needed to understand women's experiences, there were no tools in existing criminological theory with which to do this. Cain therefore advocated a "transgressive" approach, one that started from outside the boundaries of criminological discourse.

## Criminalized Women

For many feminist criminologists, starting from outside criminology has meant resisting the temptation to fashion theories of women's involvement in crime that take crime categories (such as crimes against the person or crimes against property) as their starting point. As writers such as Smart (1989), Laberge (1991), and Faith (1993) have pointed out, "crime" is not a homogenous category. There are notable differences between women in the nature and extent of both their criminal involvement and their contacts with the criminal justice system. As well, crime categories are legal constructions, the end result of a lengthy process of detection, apprehension, accusation, judgment, and conviction. They represent one way of ordering or making sense of social life. Crime categories are also premised on a dualism between "the criminal" and "the law-abiding," which reinforces the view of criminal women as "Other" and thereby misses the similarities that exist between women. In this respect, criminal women are in very many ways no different from the rest of us. They are mothers, daughters, sisters, girlfriends, and wives, and they share many of the experiences of women collectively in society. Since crime is the outcome of interactions between individuals and the criminal justice system, writers like Laberge (1991) have proposed that we think not in terms of "criminal women" but "criminalized women."

In these terms, women may commit a variety of crimes for a variety of reasons; there is no single or special theory for their criminality. As Carlen (1985, 10) has emphasized, "The essential criminal woman does not exist." In contrast to the conservative and liberal approaches that have dominated criminologists' thinking about the "difference" between men and women, a **feminist approach** understands "difference" as rooted in the structure of society. More specifically, the lives of criminalized women are located within a broader social context characterized by inequalities of class, race, and gender.

With regard to their class location, criminalized women tend to be young, poor, undereducated, and unskilled. They are most likely to be involved in property crimes. Johnson and Rodgers (1993, 98) suggest that "women's participation in property offences is consistent with their traditional roles as consumers and, increasingly, as low income, semi-skilled, sole support providers for their families. In keeping with the rapid increase in female-headed households and the stresses associated with poverty, greater numbers of women are being charged with shoplifting, cheque forging and welfare fraud."

In contrast to the women's liberation thesis, feminist criminologists have suggested that increases in women's involvement in crime are more directly connected with the "feminization of poverty" than with women's emancipation. Indeed, several writers have called attention to how government cutbacks to social assistance have left increasing numbers of women and children at risk

**feminist approach**

Understands "difference" between men and women as structurally produced by inequalities of class, race, and gender that condition and constrain women's lives.

(Chunn and Gavigan, 2006; Mosher, 2006; Crocker and Johnson, 2010). In the province of Ontario, for example, social assistance payments were cut by 21.6 percent in 1995, "workfare" programs were implemented, and a zero-tolerance policy on welfare fraud was put in place. The feminization of poverty has been accompanied by the "criminalization of poverty." Next to homicide, individuals convicted of welfare fraud now have the greatest likelihood of receiving a sentence of incarceration. A 1997 study of 50 cases of welfare fraud convictions found that 80 percent were sentenced to time in prison (Martin, 1999). One individual caught up in this process was Kimberly Rogers (see Box 6.2).

Justice with Dignity—includes articles and information on the inquest on the death of Kimberly Rogers
http://dawn.thot.net/Kimberly_Rogers/

# FOCUS BOX 6.2

## INQUEST TO PROBE HOUSE-ARREST DEATH

SUDBURY—If Hazel St. has seen better days, the evidence of that era is long gone.

The short street where Kim Rogers lived and died in destitution is a mix of warehouses and run-down old homes just south of the courthouse where an inquest into her death begins today.

The 40-year-old woman lived for three years on the top floor of a red brick house across the road from a parking lot. When she moved in, the west-facing window might have seemed like a bonus, flooding the small bedroom with bright light.

But by August, 2000, she was eight months pregnant. As temperatures soared to 30°C and the sun's unforgiving rays bounced off the unshaded street, she must have longed each day for the respite of nightfall.

Because this apartment—its living room with a view of a wall, its narrow kitchen with a peeling gray linoleum and rusting appliances, its tiny bathroom windowless—was her prison.

In April, she was put under house arrest after pleading guilty to defrauding the welfare system of $13,000, which she drew in 1996–99 while also collecting $49,000 in student loans.

A few years earlier, this would not have been considered an offence.

"The whole concept of being on welfare and getting a student loan—that didn't used to be illegal until this government came in," said Janet Gasparini, executive director of the Sudbury Social Planning Council. "There are many success stories that came out of people who did what she did."

By 1996, it was a crime.

"I'm very sorry it happened," Rogers said as she pleaded guilty in the Ontario Court of Justice on April 25, 2001. Mr. Justice Greg Rodgers sternly pointed out that she had engaged in "almost four years of deception and dishonesty."

"I am satisfied you did not lead an opulent lifestyle, even with these two sources of income, but welfare is there for people who need it, not for people who want it, who want things and who want money."

Rodgers sentenced her to a jail term in her home of six months, followed by 18 months probation. She would be allowed to leave for medical or religious reasons, to report to a supervisor, and to shop for the necessities of life, to be done only on Wednesdays between 9 a.m. and noon.

Rogers was also ordered her to pay back the full amount to the Ontario Works program, which was already "clawing back" $52 a month from her $520 monthly cheque.

But the criminal conviction triggered an automatic three-month suspension of benefits, a penalty introduced by the Harris government

*(continued)*

and subsequently stiffened in April 2000, when a "zero-tolerance policy on welfare cheats" raised the penalty to lifetime suspension.

These are among the policies that will go under the microscope at the five-week inquest, presided over by coroner David Eden.

"We cannot live in a society where we say at some point we would stop supporting people," said Gasparini, whose organization has been granted standing but denied legal aid.

The Social Planning Council has been told to piggy-back on the resources of two national coalitions with standing—one headed by the Canadian Association of Elizabeth Fry Societies, the other by the Ontario Social Safety Network. Gasparini said her organization offers the only community perspective and should have been granted separate legal representation.

"Two government ministries, the municipality and the police department will all be represented by lawyers paid with taxpayers' dollars," she said. "It's imperative to have a local voice to tell about the impact of these policies."

Rogers' family has chosen not to participate. Her mother, Meryl Caetano, said she knows she's going to be upset by the public airing of personal details of her daughter's life.

"To me, she's my daughter and I loved her," she said.

Still, she said, she can't argue with the need to examine what led to Rogers' death. "I think it should be taken seriously. These things shouldn't happen to anyone."

Reports on the physical cause of death will be among the first evidence to be led by coroner's counsel Al O'Marra. It points to a suicide, sources told *The Star* soon after the tragedy.

Rogers had attempted suicide before, in 1996, before enrolling at Cambrian College, from which she graduated in 2000 with a social services diploma. Her most recent employment was with a call centre, chasing people who had defaulted on their long-distance charges—a job she quit in January 2001, because of the stress of dealing with abusive customers.

By early May, Rogers had no food. The local food bank would allow only one visit a month, and she had been there just before Easter. She was behind on her $450 monthly rent, and her drug card had been suspended so she could not obtain medication prescribed for depression and nausea.

"I am unable to sleep because of my situation," she said in a May 23 affidavit. "I am very upset and I cry all the time."

Some responded. Her landlord agreed to reduce her rent to $300 a month until her circumstances improved. The estranged father of her unborn child came up with a "one-time" payment of $300 for her rent. Friends gave her food.

Workers for the Elizabeth Fry Society and the Social Planning Council scrounged for help, with limited success. Her family doctor intervened to get her drug card reinstated.

Toronto lawyer Sean Dewart launched a constitutional appeal on her behalf and persuaded Madam Justice Gloria Epstein to reinstate her benefits in the interim.

In a May 31 ruling, Epstein found that "for a member of our community carrying an unborn child" to be homeless and deprived of basic sustenance is a situation that would adversely affect the public—"its dignity, its human rights commitments and its health care resources."

Rogers still had five months of house detention. She would last only two. Residents of a downstairs apartment said she had been dead several days when her body was found Aug. 9 in her bed, a little more than a month before her baby was due.

Last week, neighbours said they felt the treatment she received was harsh.

"She would have been better off in jail," said Mary Lou Fabbro, owner of a nearby stained-glass business.

The death reflects poorly on our society, she said. "We need to take care of each other."

Source: Kate Harries. "Inquest to probe house-arrest death," *The Toronto Star* (October 15, 2002). Reprinted with permission—Torstar Syndication Services.

Locating women's involvement in crime in its broader social context also involves attending to racial inequality. Aboriginal people in Canada are disproportionately represented in crime statistics, but the over-representation of Aboriginal women in Canadian prisons is even greater than that of Aboriginal men (Correctional Service of Canada, 2006; Perreault, 2009). Aboriginal women are incarcerated for more violent crimes than non-Aboriginal women. And alcohol has played a role in the offences of twice as many Aboriginal women in prison than Aboriginal men (La Prairie, 1993; Comack, 1996). The historical forces that have shaped Aboriginal communities—the processes of colonization, of economic and political marginalization, and of forced dependency on the state—have culminated in a situation where violence and drugging and drinking have reached epidemic proportions in many Aboriginal centres (Hamilton and Sinclair, 1991; Royal Commission on Aboriginal Peoples, 1996). As Monture Angus (1999, 27) has noted, "Aboriginal people do not belong to communities that are functional and healthy (and colonialism is significantly responsible for this fact)."

Attention to gender inequality—and its interconnections with race and class—helps to explain prostitution or sex trade work (Brock, 1998; Bruckert and Parent, 2006). According to Johnson and Rodgers, women's involvement in prostitution is a reflection of their subordinate social and economic position in society: "Prostitution thrives in a society which values women more for their sexuality than for their skilled labour, and which puts women in a class of commodity to be bought and sold. Research has shown one of the major causes of prostitution to be the economic plight of women, particularly young, poorly educated women who have limited legitimate employment records" (Johnson and Rodgers, 1993, 101, emphasis in original).

The structured inequalities in society that contour and constrain the lives of criminalized women provide an important backdrop for understanding their involvement in crime. As Carlen (1988, 14) notes, women set about making their lives within conditions that have certainly not been of their own choosing. Indeed, in their efforts to transgress criminology, feminist criminologists have become increasingly aware that to understand women's lives we must bring into view women's experiences of violence at the hands of men. This violence needs to be understood as a manifestation of **patriarchy** or the systemic and individual power that men exercise over women (Brownmiller, 1975; Kelly, 1988).

**patriarchy**

A system of male domination that includes both a structure and an ideology that privileges men over women.

# Violence Against Women

At the same time that feminist criminologists were criticizing criminology for its neglect of women, feminists in the women's movement were raising the issue of male violence against women. This is an issue that historically has not been a matter of societal, legal, or academic concern.

## The Cultural Construction of Rape

With regard to the lack of societal concern about male violence against women, feminists questioned the kinds of assumptions and beliefs that have dominated

**cultural construction**

A perspective on a subject that is shaped by cultural assumptions rather than having a natural or objective basis.

the public's understanding of sexual violence. The **cultural construction** of rape, for example, was riddled with certain myths or misconceptions about the nature of the act itself, and with stereotypical images of "true" rape victims and offenders. These myths and stereotypes—and their limitations—include the following:

- Women "ask for it" by their dress or their behaviour. The absurdity of this claim is revealed when we apply the same logic to victims of robbery (see Box 6.3).

- Rape is a sexual act brought on by a man's uncontrollable sexual urges that cannot be halted once a woman has "turned him on." Such a view not only depicts male sexuality in a distorted way, it ignores the element of physical coercion and the effects of fear and threats on the woman.

- When women say no they really mean yes. This belief suggests that women are expected to be coy and flirtatious, and men are encouraged not to take no for an answer. In these terms, it legitimates the act of rape.

- If a woman has had sexual relations in the past, she will be less credible when she says she didn't consent to sex. This myth suggests that "bad girls" or "loose women" deserve to be raped.

- Women cannot be trusted. For instance, they will make false accusations against innocent men. Casting all women as inherently untrustworthy acts to silence survivors and exonerate rapists.

- The act of rape really has little long-term impact on the woman. So long as the harm of rape is denied, society can continue to ignore the issue and its effects on women's lives.

- Men who commit "real" rape are an "abnormal" group in society. Attributing rape to the actions of a small, disturbed minority in society effectively lets men as a group off the hook. Rape is thus cast as an isolated problem for psychologists and psychiatrists to deal with or is narrowly defined as a "women's issue"—not an issue that all of us need to confront.

# FOCUS BOX 6.3

## WAS HE ASKING FOR IT?

In 1975, *Harper's Weekly* carried the following response to an American Bar Association finding that few rapists are punished for their crime. The article asks us to imagine a male complainant in a robbery case undergoing the same sort of cross-examination that a female complainant in a rape case does.

"Mr. Smith, you were held up at gunpoint on the corner of First and Main?"

"Yes."

"Did you struggle with the robber?"

"No."

"Why not?"

"He was armed."

*(continued)*

"Then you made a conscious decision to comply with his demands rather than resist?"

"Yes."

"Did you scream? Cry out?"

"No. I was afraid."

"I see. Have you ever been held up before?"

"No."

"Have you ever given money away?"

"Yes, of course."

"And you did so willingly?"

"What are you getting at?"

"Well, let's put it like this, Mr. Smith. You've given money away in the past. In fact, you have quite the reputation for philanthropy. How can we be sure you weren't contriving to have your money taken by force?"

"Listen, if I wanted—"

"Never mind. What time did this holdup take place?"

"About 11 p.m."

"You were out in the street at 11 p.m.? Doing what?"

"Just walking."

"Just walking? You know it's dangerous being out on the street that late at night. Weren't you aware that you could have been held up?"

"I hadn't thought about it."

"What were you wearing?"

"Let's see—a suit. Yes, a suit."

"An expensive suit?"

"Well—yes. I'm a successful lawyer, you know."

"In other words, Mr. Smith, you were walking around the streets late at night in a suit that practically advertised the fact that you might be a good target for some easy money, isn't that so? I mean, if we didn't know better, Mr. Smith, we might even think that you were asking for this to happen, mightn't we?"

Source: Reprinted with permission from the 197 issue of ABA Journal. Copyright 1975, ABA Journal. All rights reserved. License # ABA21721

Smart (1989, 28) has described this cultural construction of rape as "phallocentric," by which she means "the prevailing dominance of the masculine experience of, and meaning of, sexuality. Sexuality is comprehended as the pleasure of the Phallus, and by extension the pleasures of penetration and intercourse—for men." Clearly, the more prevalent such phallocentric myths and stereotypes about sexual violence are in society, the more far-reaching will be their consequences. For perpetrators of sexual violence, they can translate into less chance of detection, higher acquittal rates, and lighter sentences. Studies show, for example, that most rapists do not even believe that they have done anything wrong (Clark and Lewis, 1977; Scully and Marolla, 1985; Messerschmidt, 1986). For survivors of sexual violence, rape myths can mean a "double victimization." Survivors not only endure the humiliation and degradation inherent in the act itself, but may experience further humiliation if they choose to report the case to the authorities. Also, since phallocentric cultural beliefs suggest that rape is the woman's fault, survivors may feel responsible for their own victimization. As Smart (1989, 35) has argued, "The whole rape trial is a process of disqualification (of women) and celebration (of phallocentrism)." For women generally, the cultural construction of rape can produce feelings of fear and vulnerability that impose restrictions on their daily activities. One study, for example, reported that 24 percent of women (compared with only three percent of men) stay at home at night because they are afraid to go out alone (Johnson, 1996). Another study (Statistics Canada, 2005) found that 27 percent of women worried for their personal safety when they were home alone at night, compared with only 12 percent of men. And twice the proportion of female as compared to male night-time transit users worried when taking it alone at night (58 percent versus 29 percent).

## The Law's Role in Condoning Male Violence Against Women

Recognition of the pervasiveness of these phallocentric myths and stereotypes led to a questioning of the role that law has played in condoning male violence against women. Feminists noted, for example, that women have historically been viewed as the "property" of men. The law upheld this view by granting husbands certain legal rights, in particular, the "right to consortium" and the "right to chastise" their wives.

Consortium generally refers to the companionship, affection, and assistance that one spouse in a marriage is entitled to receive from the other. According only husbands the right to consortium meant that wives had a legal obligation with respect to the "consummation of marriage, cohabitation, maintenance of conjugal rights, sexual fidelity, and general obedience and respect for his wishes" (Dobash and Dobash, 1979, 60). The husband's right to consortium was reflected in Canadian law until 1983. Under the old rape law, a rape was defined to have occurred when "[a] male person has sexual intercourse with a female person who is not his wife, (a) without her consent, or (b) with her consent if the consent (i) is extorted by threats or fear of bodily harm, (ii) is obtained by impersonating her husband, or (iii) is obtained by false and fraudulent representations as to the nature and quality of the act" (s. 143, emphasis added). It made no sense, under law's logic, to prevent men from "consorting" with their own property; wives did not have the legal right to say no.

In addition to granting a husband's immunity from rape charges, the rape law also reinforced the cultural construction of rape. For instance, reflecting the belief that "women cannot be trusted" when they claim they have been raped, the legislation included a corroboration requirement, whereby the accused could not be found guilty in the absence of corroborating evidence (such as cuts and bruises) that would support the testimony of the complainant. As well, under the doctrine of recent complaint, it was assumed that a woman who complained at the first reasonable opportunity was more credible or believable than one who complained some time after the rape had taken place. Because the key element in establishing the guilt of the accused in rape cases was consent, the focus of the trial rested on the credibility of the woman. Her moral character came under the scrutiny of the court in the attempt to determine whether she could be believed when she said she did not consent. Defence lawyers were permitted to ask questions about the past sexual history of the complainant, reinforcing the belief that women who have had sexual relations in the past are "less credible" when they say they didn't consent to sex.

With regard to the right to chastise, law historically has given a husband the authority to use force in order to ensure that his wife fulfilled her obligations. The only restraint law placed upon a husband was that he did so in a moderate manner. As English jurist Sir William Blackstone explained in 1765, since the husband was obliged under law to answer for his wife's misbehaviour (as she was his property), "the law thought it reasonable to intrust him with his power of restraining her, by domestic chastisement, in the same moderation that a man is allowed to correct his apprentices and children, for whom the master or parent is also liable in some cases to answer" (Blackstone, cited in Dobash and Dobash, 1979, 61). When husbands went too far, and their wives died as a result, the British courts were inclined to leniency. On the other hand, if a wife killed her husband, it was considered a "species of treason" akin to killing the king, as she was going against his authority (Edwards, 1985). Law, in essence, reflected and reinforced patriarchal relations between men and women. This view continued to inform legal practice into the latter part of the 20th century. Because police officers were inclined to view violence in the home between intimate partners as a "private trouble" that was not the law's business, they were reluctant to intervene or to define the situation as a criminal matter.

## Criminology's Complicity

Within criminology, male violence against women was similarly not seen as a social problem. Official statistics suggested that crimes like rape were relatively infrequent in their occurrence. Victim surveys—which asked respondents whether they had been victimized by crime—indicated that the group most at risk of victimization was young males, and not women. When criminologists' attention did turn to crimes like rape, the focus was on the small group of men who had been convicted and incarcerated for the offence, and these men were typically understood as an abnormal and pathological group. Much of traditional criminology, then, tended to mirror the cultural construction of rape. In his "classic" study of rape, for example, Amir (1971) introduced the notion of "victim precipitation." The concept suggests that some women are "rape prone" or invite rape, and Amir's work essentially blamed the woman for the violence she encountered.

**Canadian Association of Sexual Assault Centres**
www.casac.ca

## Breaking the Silence

In combination, the absence of societal, legal, and academic concern about the issue of male violence against women had the effect of silencing women. One of the main goals of the women's movement as it gained momentum in the 1970s was to break this silence. As women came together to share their stories, and with increasing efforts devoted to provide support and services to women (such as rape crisis centres, crisis lines, and shelters for abused women), it soon became evident that the incidence of sexual violence far exceeded what was reported in the official crime statistics. In 1980, for example, the Canadian Advisory Council on the Status of Women (CACSW) estimated that one in every five Canadian women will be sexually assaulted at some point in her life, and one in every 17 will be subjected to forced sexual intercourse. Yet only one in 10 sexual assaults was ever reported to the police (Kinnon, 1981). That same year, the CACSW released its report, *Wife Battering in Canada: The Vicious Circle*. MacLeod (1980), the author of the report, estimated that every year, one in 10 Canadian women who is married or in a relationship with a live-in partner is battered. Yet when this finding was reported in the House of Commons (on May 12, 1982), it was met with laughter from members of Parliament. Public outrage ensued and, over the next decade, wife abuse was gradually transformed from a "private trouble" into a "public issue."

The growing awareness of male violence against women led to pressures for legislative reform. Two major changes occurred in 1983. First, the old rape law was repealed and three new categories were added to the offence of assault: sexual assault (s. 246.1); sexual assault with a weapon, threats to a third party, and bodily harm (s. 246.2); and aggravated sexual assault (s. 246.3). Under this new legislation, husbands could now be charged with sexually assaulting their wives, limitations were placed on the ability of the defence to ask questions about the past sexual history of the complainant, the corroboration requirement was dropped, the doctrine of recent complaint was formally removed, and there was provision for a publication ban on any disclosure of the identity of the complainant. These changes were designed to redress the apparent gender inequities in the law and to reduce the trauma experienced by the complainant during the trial in an attempt to encourage the reporting of cases. Second, a national directive was issued to encourage police to lay charges in wife assault cases (previously, the decision was left to the wishes of the complainant) and police training was upgraded to stress sensitive interventions in cases of wife assault. These reforms led to increases in the number of charges for domestic assaults. In Winnipeg, for instance, there were 629 domestic assault charges laid in 1983; by 1989, the number had increased to 1137 charges laid (Ursel, 1994).

## The Montreal Massacre

The reality of violence against women was made most evident on December 6, 1989, when a gunman entered a classroom at the École Polytechnique in Montreal, separated the men from the women students, proclaimed, "You're all a bunch of feminists," and proceeded to gun them down. Fourteen women were killed that day and 13 others wounded. The gunman's suicide letter explicitly identified his action as politically motivated: he blamed "feminists" for the major disappointments in his life. Police also found a "hit list" containing the names of prominent women (see Box 6.4). The Montreal Massacre served to reinforce what women's groups across the country had been arguing for decades: that violence against women is a widespread and pervasive feature of our society. It takes many forms, including sexual harassment in the workplace, date rape, violent sexual assaults, incest, and wife abuse.

While the murder of 14 women in Montreal has understandably received the attention it deserves, it is also noteworthy that the violence that women encounter at the hands of men has become "routine." In 1993, Statistics Canada released the findings of the Violence Against Women Survey (VAWS). The first national survey of its kind anywhere in the world, the VAWS included responses from 12, 300 women (see Johnson, 1996). Using definitions of physical and sexual assault consistent with the Canadian Criminal Code, the survey found that one-half (51 percent) of Canadian women have experienced at least one incident of physical or sexual violence since the age of 16. The survey also confirmed the results of other research in finding that women face the greatest risk of violence from men they know. "Almost one-half (45%) of all women experienced violence by men known to them (dates, boyfriends, marital partners, friends, family, neighbours, etc.), while 23% of women experienced violence by a stranger (17% reported violence by both strangers and known men)" (Statistics Canada, 1993, 2). The VAWS also found that 29 percent (or three in 10) of ever-married women had been assaulted by a spouse.

# FOCUS BOX 6.4

## A TIME FOR GRIEF AND PAIN

### Montreal

Fourteen women are dead for one reason: they are women. Their male classmates are still alive for one reason: they are men. While gender divides us in thousands of ways every day, rarely are the consequences of misogyny so tragic.

I found out about the murders early yesterday morning. I came home from dinner with friends about 1 a.m., and listened as usual to my answering machine. It was the last message that gave me a jolt. It was a good friend telling me that there would be a vigil last night for the 14 women who had been killed at the University of Montreal.

Not believing my ears and desperate for news, I turned on the radio. I ended up listening to an open-line show. The talk was about relationships between young men and women these days.

Most of the callers were men. They blamed the murders on everything from drugs and condom distributors in high schools to women who have made men feel insecure. Many callers said they did not understand what had happened. It's all very well and fine to be misogynous, said one caller, but you can't lose your head.

I realized, as I was listening to this show, that I was trembling. So were the voices of the female callers. I felt something I had not experienced in a long time: fear of being alone in my apartment.

There were sounds at the window I would normally ignore. Now I could not. Immobilized, I was afraid to stay alone and afraid to go out.

It does not matter that the man who decided to kill 14 women—and he clearly did decide to do that—killed himself afterward; it is not of him I am afraid. I am afraid of what he represents, of all the unspoken hatred, the pent-up anger that he expressed. Hatred and anger that is shared by every husband who beats his wife, every man who rapes his date, every father who abuses his child, and by many more who would not dare.

It happened at the École Polytechnique in Montreal but it could have been anywhere.

It would be a great mistake, I think, to see this incident as some kind of freak accident, the act of a madman that has nothing to do with the society in which we live. The killer was angry at women, at feminism, at his own loss of power. He yelled: "You're all a bunch of feminists" on his way to killing 14 women.

Now there is little that is comforting to say to women. It is a time for grief for all of us; grief for those who have died, and pain at being reminded of how deep misogyny still runs in our society.

Source: Diana Bronson. "A Time for Grief and Pain." *The Globe and Mail* (8 December 1989), A7. Reprinted with permission of the author.

## Missing and Murdered Women

In addition to its gendered nature, the racialized nature of violence has become more of a public issue as attention has been fixed on the numbers of missing and murdered women in Canada. In 2004, Amnesty International published its report, *Stolen Sisters*, which called attention to the violence encountered by Aboriginal women and pointed to the role that cultural and systemic discrimination played in perpetuating this violence, thereby impeding their basic human right to be safe and free from violence. The report noted that Aboriginal women are five times more likely to die as a result of violence (Amnesty International, 2004, 23). It also documented many of the cases of missing and murdered women—including the disappearance of women from the streets of

Native Women's Association
of Canada

www.nwac.ca

Vancouver's Downtown Eastside. In 2005 the Native Women's Association of Canada (NWAC) launched the *Sisters in Spirit* initiative, which was aimed at addressing the root causes, circumstances, and trends of missing and murdered Aboriginal women and girls. By March, 2010 NWAC had gathered information about the disappearance or death of more than 580 Aboriginal women and girls across Canada (NWAC, 2010).

Between 1978 and 1992 some 60 women, many of them Aboriginal and involved in the street sex trade, were reported to have vanished from Vancouver's Downtown Eastside—known as Canada's "poorest postal code." As Hugill (2010) notes, however, Vancouver's crisis of missing and murdered women generated very little interest on the part of the media and criminal justice system prior to 1998, and it was not until 2001 that police formed a Missing Women Joint Task Force to investigate these cases. In February 2002 this new unit raided the Port Coquitlam pig farm of Robert Pickton. Pickton was eventually charged with the murder of 27 women. In December 2007 he was convicted of second-degree murder of six women and sentenced to life imprisonment.

Events such as these confirm that male violence against women continues to be a serious social problem in Canadian society. They also raise concerns about the effectiveness of the criminal justice system in responding to this pressing problem.

## Recent History of Law's Response to Violence Against Women

As the 1990s unfolded, many feminists became uncertain as to whether engaging with the criminal justice system to combat male violence against women was having the desired outcome. With respect to sexual assault, it appeared that the phallocentric myths and stereotypes surrounding rape were continuing to invade the practice of law. Some judges, for instance, were making statements in court that suggested their decisions were being influenced by these myths. In a British Columbia case heard in 1991, the judge made the following statement in his written decision: "The mating practice, if I may call it that, is less than a precise relationship. At times no may mean maybe, or wait awhile" (Letendre, cited in Boyle, 1994, 141). In June 1998, an Alberta Court of Appeal judge upheld a lower court's acquittal of a man charged with sexually assaulting a 17-year-old girl. In his decision, the judge commented on the clothing worn by the young woman (a T-shirt and shorts), noting, "It must be pointed out that the complainant did not present herself to [the accused] in a bonnet and crinolines" (Laghi, 1998). Several decisions by the Supreme Court of Canada also raised concerns over the law's treatment of sexual assault cases.

In a 1991 ruling on the cases of Seaboyer and Gayme, the Supreme Court struck down section 276 of the Criminal Code. Known as the "rape shield" provision, section 276 was included in the 1983 sexual assault law with the aim of preventing a woman's sexual conduct from being used to discredit her testimony. The Supreme Court ruled that, while laudable in its intent, the provision went too far and could deny the accused the right to a fair trial. Critics took exception to this decision because it left the question of whether evidence of the complainant's past sexual history would be admissible in court to the discretion of the trial judge. In response, Parliament introduced Bill C-49 in 1992, which was designed to amend the 1983 sexual assault legislation.

Under this new legislation, rules of evidence now state that evidence that the complainant has engaged in sexual activity, whether with the accused or with any other person, is not admissible to support an inference that the complainant is either more likely to have consented to the sexual activity in question or is less worthy of belief. A new test for judges is also provided for determining whether a complainant's sexual history may be admitted at trial. Bill C-49 also provided a definition of "consent" as it applies to sexual assault cases—"the voluntary agreement of the complainant to engage in the sexual activity in question" [s. 243.1 (1)]—and specified the conditions under which "no consent" is obtained (for instance, where the complainant is incapable of consenting to the activity by reason of intoxication or where the complainant expresses, by words or conduct, a lack of agreement to engage in the activity). As well, restrictions were placed on the defences available to men accused of sexual assault; the onus was now on the accused to show that he took "reasonable steps" in the circumstances to ascertain that the woman was consenting [s. 273.2 (b)].

The Supreme Court's ruling in the O'Connor case in 1995 had even more profound implications for survivors of sexual assault. Bishop O'Connor was a priest and principal at a residential school near Williams Lake, British Columbia, where four Aboriginal women attended and worked. In 1991, the women laid charges of rape and indecent assault against O'Connor for incidents that occurred at the school between 1961 and 1967. The charges were stayed by the trial judge in 1992 when the Crown failed to release to the defence counsel the women's residential school records and all therapy and medical records since the time they had left the school (none of these records were in the Crown's possession). When the case reached the Supreme Court, the Court overturned the stay and ordered a new trial for O'Connor, but gave exceptionally large scope to defence access to complainants' records held by third parties. Subsequent to the Court's decision, women's shelters and rape crisis centres were being subpoenaed to turn over all files and counselling records relating to cases before the courts, and criminal defence lawyers were being advised by their association that they would be "negligent" if they did not subpoena complainant's files (Busby, 1997).

The Supreme Court's ruling in O'Connor meant that confidential records, as well as personal diaries, letters, and the like, could now all be accessed. The ruling also had special implications for the work of therapists and rape crisis counsellors because they could now be required to hand over any and all records or notes relating to a complainant in a sexual assault case. Critics noted that such materials are not designed to be a written record of allegations; they are maintained for therapeutic, not evidentiary, purposes. For example, one of the issues regularly dealt with in therapy sessions is the need to explore feelings of guilt or shame that a woman may experience after a rape. In the hands of the court, this could be taken as evidence of "consent" or "complicity" on the part of the woman. To this extent, the O'Connor decision supports the old rape myths: that women lie or make false allegations, and that they cannot be trusted. One of the main effects of the ruling was the silencing of women. Women who were sexually assaulted had to decide whether they would seek counselling or initiate criminal prosecution of their assailant (Busby, 1997, 2006).

In response to concerns raised over the O'Connor decision, Parliament passed Bill C-46 in May 1997 to limit the access of defendants to confidential records of complainants in sexual assault cases. The bill established more restrictive grounds for access, required that the defence establish that the records are relevant to the case at hand, and restricted the disclosure only to those parts that are important to the case. Only a few months after its passage, the legislation was constitutionally challenged as a violation of the fair trial guarantees of the Charter and struck down by two lower courts. In 1999 the Supreme Court rendered its decision on this question in *Mills* (1999). While the Court held that the legislation governing the disclosure of records did not violate an accused's constitutional rights, some commentators, such as Gotell (2001, 340), argued that the decision did tame the meaning of the legislation: "To the extent that this decision eases the statutory test for disclosure put in place by *Bill C-46*, Canada remains a jurisdiction where women's claims of sexual violation can be discounted through records production."

More recently, a Manitoba judge came under heavy criticism in February 2011 for his decision to sentence a man convicted of sexual assault to a conditional sentence of two years less a day. The assault by the 40-year-old man against a 26-year-old woman had occurred along a darkened highway near Thompson, Manitoba in 2006. While the Crown had argued for a three-year prison sentence, the judge disagreed, saying that the man's actions "had the characteristics of a clumsy Don Juan" and that "this is a case of misunderstood signals and inconsiderate behaviour" (*Rhodes*). The judge also described the situation as one in which "sex was in the air," as the man and his friend had met the woman and her girlfriend that night outside a bar under "inviting circumstances." He also made the point of noting that the women were wearing tube tops with no bra, high heels, and make-up. The announcement of the decision, which came just one week after a Toronto police officer apologized for telling a crowd of university students at a safety session not to "dress like sluts" if they wanted to avoid being raped, led critics to suggest that the cultural construction of rape was still very much in operation.

This recent history of the law's treatment of sexual assault highlights a number of tensions. For one, there appears to be tension between the courts—whose decisions become binding as case law—and Parliament—which, in passing statute law, has endeavoured to be sensitive to the concerns raised from women's constituencies across the country. For another, there is a tension within the law with regard to competing rights, in particular, the right of a defendant to a fair trial compared with the right of a complainant to privacy. Clearly, the extent to which the legal system will be able to resolve these tensions and thereby offer both women and men equal protection and treatment under the law is a matter of ongoing debate.

Although the national directive to police forces in 1983 resulted in increasing numbers of domestic assault charges entering the criminal justice system, several provinces took further steps to respond to the problem of wife assault. In the city of Winnipeg, for example, a specialized Family Violence Court was established in 1990. The number of spousal assault cases dealt with by this court rose from 1302 in 1990–91 to 3543 in 1993–94, a

172 percent increase (Ursel, 1998). A large part of this increase can be attributed to the implementation of a zero-tolerance policy on domestic violence by the Winnipeg Police Service in 1993. Under this policy, police are instructed to lay a charge when there are reasonable grounds to believe that a domestic assault has occurred, whether or not the victim wishes to proceed with the matter and even in circumstances where there are no visible injuries or independent witnesses. The zero-tolerance policy resulted in increasing numbers of men—and women—being charged. However, a high proportion of charges resulted in a dismissal or stay of proceedings. One Winnipeg study, for instance, found that 80 percent of charges against women and 51 percent of those against men were subsequently stayed by the Crown (Comack et al., 2000). While the underlying intent of this more rigorous charging protocol was to assist victims of domestic violence (who are predominantly women), zero tolerance opened the way for "double-charging" to occur, whereby both partners end up being charged with an offence when police are called to the scene. Comack et al. (2000) found that double-charging occurred in 55 percent of the cases they studied involving women accused and in 10 percent of those cases involving men. Stays of proceedings were even higher in these cases (88 percent and 70 percent, respectively). In sum, while the changes that have occurred within the criminal justice system have a symbolic value—they carry a strong message of society's unwillingness to tolerate wife abuse—feminists have questioned whether the traditionally punitive and adversarial nature of the system is the most effective means for combating the problem (see, for example, Snider, 1991, 1994).

## Blurred Boundaries: Women as Victims and Offenders

Breaking the silence around male violence against women has had an impact on how feminist criminologists understand the lives of criminalized women. Violence against women is clearly a gender-related factor; it both reflects and reinforces women's inequality in society in relation to men. As the *War Against Women* report (1991, 9) noted, "The vulnerability of women to violence is integrally linked to the social, economic and political inequalities women experience as part of their daily lives." How, then, does this gender-based violence figure in the lives of criminalized women?

**Canadian Association of Elizabeth Fry Societies**
www.elizabethfry.ca

Several studies carried out in the 1990s revealed the extent of abuse experienced by criminalized women. Research conducted for the Task Force on Federally Sentenced Women, for instance, found that 68 percent of women serving a federal term of imprisonment in Canada had been physically abused as children or adults, and 53 percent were sexually abused at some point in their lives. Among Aboriginal women, the figures were considerably higher: 90 percent said that they had been physically abused and 61 percent reported sexual abuse (Shaw et al., 1991, vii and 31). Another study of women in a provincial jail found that 78 percent of the women admitted over a six-year period reported histories of physical and sexual abuse (Comack, 1993).

Qualitative research conducted by feminist criminologists explored women's accounts of their law breaking and its connections to abuse (see, for example, Gilfus, 1992; Adelberg and Currie, 1993; Sommers, 1995; Ritchie, 1996). Women in Trouble (Comack, 1996) was built around the stories of 24 women who were incarcerated in a provincial jail. The women's stories revealed the connections between a woman's law violations and her history of abuse to be complex. Sometimes the connections are direct, as in the case of women who are criminalized for resisting their abusers. Janice, for instance, was serving a sentence for manslaughter. The offence occurred at a party:

> I was at a party, and this guy, older guy, came, came on to me. He tried telling me, "Why don't you go to bed with me. I'm getting some money, you know." And I said, "No." And then he started hitting me. And then he raped me. And then [pause] I lost it. Like, I just, I went, I got very angry and I snapped. And I started hitting him. I threw a coffee table on top of his head and then I stabbed him. (Janice, cited in Comack, 1996, 96)

Sometimes the connections become discernable only once a woman's law violations are located in the context of her struggle to cope with the abuse and its effects. Merideth, for example, had a long history of abuse that began with her father sexually assaulting her as a young child, and extended to several violent relationships with the men in her life. She was imprisoned for writing cheques on her bank account when she didn't have the money to cover them. The cheques were used to purchase "new things to keep her mind off the abuse":

> I've never had any kind of conflict with the law. [long pause] When I started dealing with all these different things, then I started having problems. And then I took it out in the form of fraud. (Merideth, cited in Comack, 1996, 86)

Sometimes the connections are even more entangled, as in the case of women who end up on the street, where abuse and law violation become enmeshed in their ongoing, everyday struggle to survive. Brenda had this to say about street life:

> Street life is a, it's a power game, you know? Street life? You have to show you're tough. You have to beat up this broad or you have to shank this person, or, you know, you're always carrying guns, you always have blow on you, you always have drugs on you, and you're always working the streets with the pimps and the bikers, you know? That, that alone, you know, it has so much fucking abuse, it has more abuse than what you were brought up with! . . . I find living on the street I went through more abuse than I did at home. (Brenda, cited in Comack, 1996, 105–6)

This kind of work subsequently became known as pathways research—a term that has been applied to a variety of different studies, all of them sharing the effort to better understand the lives of women and girls and the particular features that helped lead to their criminal activity (see, for example, Chesney-Lind and Rodriguez, 1983; Miller, 1986; Arnold, 1995; Heimer,

1995; Chesney-Lind and Shelden, 1998). In drawing the connections between women's law violations and their histories of abuse, pathways research led to a blurring of boundaries between "offender" and "victim" and raised questions about the legal logic of individual culpability and law's strict adherence to the victim/offender dualism in the processing of cases (for not only women, but also poor, racialized men; see Comack and Balfour, 2004). It also had a decided influence on advocacy work conducted on behalf of imprisoned women. For instance, *Creating Choices*, the 1990 report of the Canadian Task Force on Federally Sentenced Women, proposed a new prison regime for women that would incorporate feminist principles and attend to women's needs (see Shaw, 1993; Hannah-Moffat and Shaw, 2000; Hannah-Moffat, 2001; Hayman, 2006). The near-complete absence of counselling services and other resources designed to assist women in overcoming victimization experiences (see Kendall, 1993) figured prominently in the Task Force's recommendations.

As Snider (2003, 364) notes, feminist criminologists succeeded in reconstituting the criminalized woman as the "woman in trouble." Less violent and less dangerous than her male counterpart, she was more deserving of help than punishment. When women did engage in violence, it was understood as a self-defensive reaction typically committed in a domestic context (Browne, 1987; Dobash and Dobash, 1992; Jones, 1994). Nevertheless, while the concept of blurred boundaries and the construct of the woman in trouble were important feminist contributions to criminology, they had particular ramifications for the ability of feminist criminologists to counter competing knowledge claims—ones founded on representations of women not as victims but as violent and dangerous.

## The Violent Woman

One decisive event that challenged the blurred boundaries between victim and offender was the Karla Homolka case. In July 1993 Karla Homolka was sentenced to 12 years in prison for her part in the deaths of two teenage girls, Kristen French and Leslie Mahaffy. Homolka's sentence was part of a plea bargain reached with the Crown in exchange for her testimony against her husband, Paul Bernardo. The Crown had entered into this plea bargain prior to the discovery of six homemade videotapes that documented the sexual abuse and torture of the pair's victims—including Homolka's younger sister, Tammy. Bernardo was subsequently convicted of first-degree murder, kidnapping, aggravated sexual assault, forcible confinement, and offering an indignity to a dead body. He was sentenced to life imprisonment in September 1995 (McGillivray, 1998, 257).

During Bernardo's trial the real challenge came in trying to explain the role of Homolka, the prosecution's key witness. As Boritch (1997, 2) notes, "Among the various professionals who commented on the case, there was a general agreement that, as far as serial murderers go, there was little that was unusual or mysterious about Bernardo. We have grown used to hearing about male serial murderers." Homolka, however, was the central enigma of the drama that unfolded, transforming the trial into an international, high-profile media event.

The legal documents and media accounts of the case offered two primary readings of Homolka. The first reading constructed her as a battered wife, one of Bernardo's many victims (he had also been exposed as "the Scarborough rapist"). A girlish 17-year-old when she first met the 23-year-old Bernardo, Homolka had entered into a relationships that progressed into a fairytale wedding (complete with horse-drawn carriage) and ended with a severe battering (complete with darkened and bruised racoon eyes). According to this first reading, Homolka was under the control of her husband, having no agency of her own. Like other women who find themselves in abusive relationships, she was cast as a victim and diagnosed as suffering from the Battered Woman Syndrome, a psychological condition of "learned helplessness" that ostensibly prevents abused women from leaving the relationship (Walker, 1979, 1987). The representation of Homolka as a battered wife and compliant victim of her sexually sadistic husband (see Hazelwood et al., 1993) was meant to bolster her credibility as a prosecution witness and validate her plea bargain. This first reading was met with strong resistance in the media and public discourse, leading to the second reading. Journalist Patricia Pearson (1995), for one, vigorously countered the picture of "Homolka as victim" and instead demonized her as a "competitive narcissist" willing to offer up innocent victims (including her own sister) to appease the sexual desires of her sociopathic husband. Despite their divergent viewpoints, both of these readings relied on the discourse of the "psy-professions" (psychology, psychotherapy, and psychiatry) to make sense of Homolka.

Feminist criminologists countered both of these readings, for instance, by pointing out that women are seldom charged with the offence of murder and, when they do kill, women are most likely to kill their male partners—and that while Homolka's middle-class background and lifestyle set her apart from the vast majority of women charged with criminal offences, her efforts to conform to the standard feminine script (dyed blonde hair, fairytale wedding) put her in company with a host of other women. But these claims were seldom heard. Instead, the cry that "Women are violent, too!" grew louder, even to the point of arguing that women's violence was quantitatively and qualitatively equal to that of men's.

In a widely publicized book, *When She Was Bad: Violent Women and the Myth of Innocence*, Pearson (1997; see also Dutton, 1994; Laframboise, 1996) argued not only that "women are violent, too" but also that their violence can be just as "nasty" as men's. Following on the footsteps of the 1950s criminologist Otto Pollak, Pearson (1997, 20–21) suggested that women's violence is more masked and underhanded than men's violence: women kill their babies, arrange for their husbands' murders, beat up on their lovers, and commit serial murders in hospitals and boarding houses. Nevertheless, argued Pearson (1997, 61), when their crimes are discovered, women are more likely to receive lenient treatment from a chivalrous criminal justice system. In a fashion that hearkened back to other early criminologists, Pearson (1997, 210) also stated: "Female prisoners are not peace activists or nuns who were kidnapped off the street and stuck in jail. They are miscreants, intemperate, wilful and rough."

Pearson drew support for her position from studies that use the Conflict Tactics Scale (CTS) to measure abuse in intimate relationships. Developed by U.S. researcher Murray Straus and his colleagues (Straus, 1979; Straus et al., 1980), the scale is a quantitative instrument that consists of 18 items and measures three different ways of handling interpersonal conflict in intimate relationships: reasoning, verbal aggression, and physical violence. The scale categorizes items on a continuum from least to most severe (for example, "discussed an issue calmly" and "cried" to "threw something," "hit with a fist," and "used a knife or a gun"). Respondents in a survey are asked how frequently they perpetrated each act in the course of conflicts or disagreements with their partners within the past year, and how frequently they had been on the receiving end. These self reports of perpetration and victimization are then used to construct estimates of the rate of violence used by male and female partners. Most criminologists who have employed the CTS have found equivalent rates of violence by women and men (Steinmetz, 1981; Straus and Gelles, 1986; Brinkerhoff and Lupri, 1988; Kennedy and Dutton, 1989). Such findings have led to the conclusion that there is a sexual symmetry in intimate violence; that is, that women are just as violent as men.

Despite the scale's popularity, however, it has been subject to extensive critiques (see, for example, DeKeseredy and Hinch, 1991; Dobash et al., 1992; Schwartz and DeKeseredy, 1993; Johnson, 1996). Criminologists have noted that the CTS is an incomplete measure of intimate violence because

- it measures only incidents of violence and thus ignores the social context of the violence (such as whether a woman is acting in self-defence);

- it situates items only in the context of settling quarrels or disputes and thus misses assaults that "come out of the blue" or are motivated by the desire to control another person;

- it relies on self-reports of violence and may thereby underestimate the incidence of violence by males (who, it has been found, are more likely to under-report);

- it fails to make adequate distinctions between the severity of different forms of violence (for example, "tried to hit with something" is defined as "severe" while "slapped" is defined as "minor"); and

- it does not capture the outcome of the violence (for example, the degree of injury incurred by the participants).

Pearson, however, argued that these methodological concerns amount to unwarranted attacks by feminists and their supporters, who were invested in a gender dichotomy of men as evil/women as good. In this regard, unlike earlier conservative-minded criminologists, Pearson asserted that women were no different than men. While feminists were intent on gendering violence by drawing its connections to patriarchy, Pearson (1997, 232) was adamant that violence be de-gendered: violence was simply a "human, rather than gendered, phenomena," a conscious choice, a means of solving problems or releasing frustration by "a responsible actor imposing her will upon the world" (1997, 23).

The claims made by writers like Pearson, in combination with the difficulties encountered with using the CTS as a measure of violence between intimate partners, led feminist criminologists to seek alternative strategies for determining whether, in fact, women are "men's equals" in violence. To explore qualitative differences in men's and women's violence, for example, Vanessa Chopyk, Linda Wood, and I drew a random sample of 1002 cases from police incident reports involving men and women charged with violent crime in the city of Winnipeg over a five-year period at the beginning of the 1990s. While studies that use the CTS have concluded that a sexual symmetry exists in intimate violence (men are as likely as women to be victims of abuse, and women are as likely as men to be perpetrators of both minor and serious acts of violence), we found that a different picture emerged in police incident reports (Comack et al., 2000, 2008). First, the violence tactics used by men and women differed in their seriousness. Men were more likely to use physical strength or force against their female partners, while women were more likely to resort to throwing objects (such as TV remote controls) during the course of a violent event. Second, female partners of men accused of violence used violence themselves in only 23 percent of the cases, while male partners of women accused of violence used violence in 65 percent of the cases. This finding suggests that the violence that occurs between intimate partners is not "mutual combat." Third, almost one-half (48 percent) of the women accused—as opposed to only seven percent of the men accused—in partner events were injured during the course of the event, adding weight to the argument that violent events between men and women are not symmetrical.

Finally, in incidents involving partners, it was the accused woman who called the police in 35 percent of the cases involving a female accused (compared with only seven percent in those involving a male accused). If we interpret calls to the police as a form of "help-seeking behaviour" on the part of someone in trouble, this finding suggests that in more than one-third of the cases involving a woman accused, she was the one who perceived the need for help. Nevertheless, the woman ended up being charged with a criminal offence.

These findings are supported by data from the General Social Survey conducted by Statistics Canada (2005), which show the nature and consequences of spousal violence to be more severe for women than for men. Female victims of spousal violence were more than twice as likely to be injured as were male victims. Women were also three times more likely to fear for their lives, and twice as likely to be the targets of more than 10 violent episodes. In countering the arguments made by writers like Pearson, then, feminist criminologists placed the issue of women's violence and aggression in a different context (see also Chan, 2001; Mann, 2003; Morrissey, 2003; Comack and Brickey, 2007).

While women are certainly capable of violence, these findings suggest that they are not "men's equals." Writers like Pearson are to be credited for pointing to the "culture of victimhood" that is produced when feminists rest their understandings on dualistic constructions such as "victim versus offender." Yet, in her efforts to call attention to women's capacity for violence, Pearson goes to the other extreme. By casting women as scheming, underhanded manipulators who engage in violence "to defend their aspirations, their identity

**TABLE 6.1**   Theories of Women's Crime

| Theory | Theorists | Key Elements |
|---|---|---|
| Early theorists | Lombroso/Ferrero, Thomas, Glueck/Glueck, Pollak | Women's "inherent nature" and their natural inferiority to men account for the nature and extent of their criminality. |
| Sex role socialization | Hoffman-Bustamante | Differential socialization of females is reflected in the types of offences they commit and the nature of their participation in crime. |
| Power-control theory | Hagan/Simpson/Gillis | Gender differences in delinquency can be explained by variations in parental control. Girls in patriarchal families will be less free to deviate than those in egalitarian families. |
| Women's liberation thesis | Adler, Simon | Women's changing gender roles are reflected in the nature and extent of their criminal involvement. Women are becoming "more like men"— more aggressive and violent— and have greater opportunities to commit crime. |
| Feminist theories | Carlen, Chesney-Lind, Comack, Daly, Gilfus, Morris, Naffine | Structured inequalities of class, race, and gender (including experiences of male violence) condition and constrain the lives of criminalized women. |

and their place on the stage" (Pearson, 1997, 20), she effectively replaces the "men as evil" image that she so roundly criticizes feminists for with a "woman as evil" imagery.

# Gendering Crime

The feminist critique of criminology and the effort to draw attention to the gendered nature of women's lives led to a call to "gender" crime more broadly. Women, it was argued, were not the only ones with a gender; men's lives too needed to be understood in gendered terms. In this regard, while criminology had been traditionally characterized by its neglect of the female, critics pointed out that the discipline's ability to explain male patterns of criminal activity were just as troublesome. Since the 1990s, various criminologists have responded to this challenge by initiating studies of men, masculinity, and crime.

One criminologist to take up this project has been Messerschmidt (1993, 1997, 2004). In his endeavour to contribute to a "feminist theory of gendered crime" (1993, 62), Messerschmidt designed a theory that situates men's involvement in crime in the context of "doing" masculinity. Following on the work of West and Zimmerman (1987), gender is viewed as a "situated accomplishment." While sex is the social identification of individuals as man or woman, gender is the accomplishment of that identification in social interaction: "we coordinate our activities to 'do' gender in situational ways" (1993, 79). In the process, individuals realize that their behavior is accountable to others and so construct their actions "in relation to how they might be interpreted by others in the particular social context in which they occur" (1993, 79). In a culture that believes there are but two sexes—male and female—this accountability will involve living up to the gender ideals that have been tied to each sex; that is, behaving "as a man" or "as a woman" would in a given social situation. Because we accomplish masculinity and femininity in specific situations (although not necessarily in circumstances of our own choosing), these are never static or finished products.

Messerschmidt borrows the concept of "hegemonic masculinity" from the work of Connell (1987, 1995, 2000). Connell was interested in how a particular gender order—a "historically constructed pattern of power relations between men and women and definitions of femininity and masculinity" (Connell, 1987, 98–99)—comes to be reproduced in society. Connell suggested that male dominance in the gender order is achieved by the ascendancy of a particular idealized form of masculinity that is culturally glorified, honoured, and exalted. **Hegemonic masculinity** therefore references not just a set of role expectations or identity; it is a "pattern of practice" (Connell and Messerschmidt, 2005, 832). Different from a male sex role, this cultural ideal may not correspond with the actual personalities of the majority of men, and may well not be "normal" in a statistical sense as only a minority of men may enact it. In these terms, exemplars such as sports heroes, movie stars, and even fantasy figures (such as Rambo or the Terminator) offer representations of masculinity that come to be normative in the sense that they embody "the currently most honored way of being a man" and require all other men to position themselves in relation to these representations (Connell and Messerschmidt, 2005, 832).

Messerschmidt argues that it is in the process of "doing" masculinity that men simultaneously construct forms of criminality. He explains: "Because types of criminality are possible only when particular social conditions present themselves, when other masculine resources are unavailable, particular types of crime can provide an alternative resource for accomplishing gender and, therefore, affirming a particular type of masculinity" (1993, 84). Messerschmidt subsequently put his theory to work to understand varieties of youth crime, street crime, corporate crime, sexual harassment in the workplace, wife beating, and rape (Messerschmidt, 1993). Key to his analysis is the thesis that gendered power is central to understanding why men commit more crimes and more serious crimes than women: crime is one practice in which and through which men's power over women can be established, and the different types of crime men may commit are determined by the power relations among them (1993, 84).

**hegemonic masculinity**

A particular idealized form of masculinity that is culturally glorified, honoured, and exalted. For example, associating 'the masculine' with physical strength, aggression, independence, ambition, lack of emotion, and heterosexuality.

## Summary

- One of the primary aims of the feminist engagement with criminology has been to bring women into view. This has involved a re-evaluation of the accumulated knowledge about criminalized women, the nature of their offending, and the claims made about their "differences" from males. In the process, mainstream criminologists have been forced to consider how their traditional subject matter—men and male criminality—has influenced their theories and research.

- Feminist criminologists have argued that understanding women's involvement in crime requires an awareness of the larger social context, specifically, the structured inequalities of class, race, and gender that condition and constrain the lives of criminalized women.

- Breaking the silence around male violence against women has meant questioning the ways in which societal and legal responses reinforce and reproduce the problem.

- Making women more visible in criminology requires not simply letting women into the mainstream of the discipline but developing alternative ways of conceptualizing and studying the social world so that the interests and concerns of both men and women are included. In the process, the criminological enterprise is itself transformed.

## QUESTIONS FOR CRITICAL THINKING

1. How does the way in which the "difference" between men and women is understood influence our understanding of women's involvement in crime?
2. To what extent is the "cultural construction of rape" evident in films, music videos, advertising, and other aspects of Canadian culture? To what extent does it influence your own thinking about sexual violence?
3. In what ways have rape myths and stereotypes been evident in law and legal practice?
4. Is the criminal justice system the most effective strategy for responding to the problem of domestic violence?
5. How does making gender a central focus of criminological inquiry affect the ways in which criminologists study men's involvement in crime?

## NET WORK

Are you interested in finding more information about the issues of domestic violence and sexual assault? To find a variety of sites that deal with these issues, first visit the Canadian Women's Virtual Information Centre home page at **www.Womencan.ca**. Here you will find various links to domestic violence sites and sites dealing with sexual assault.

Using these links or any of the links found throughout this chapter, answer the following questions:

1. Describe some of the programs that are offered in Canada to serve survivors of domestic violence and sexual assault.
2. Identify some of the controversies concerning domestic violence. Can you find sites on the Internet that present different perspectives on this problem? How can you assess the validity of the information presented on different websites?

## KEY TERMS

conservative approach; pg. 180
cultural construction; pg. 192
feminist approach; pg. 188
gender-ratio problem; pg. 186
generalizability problem; pg. 186

hegemonic masculinity; pg. 208
liberal approach; pg. 182
patriarchy; pg. 191
sexism; pg. 180

## BIBLIOGRAPHY

Adelberg, Ellen, and Claudia Currie. (1993). "In Their Own Words: Seven Women's Stories." In E. Adelberg and C. Currie (eds.), *In Conflict with the Law: Women and the Canadian Justice System*. Vancouver: Press Gang Publishers.

Adler, Freda. (1975). *Sisters in Crime*. New York: McGraw-Hill.

Amir, Menachem. (1971). *The Patterns of Forcible Rape*. Chicago: University of Chicago Press.

Amnesty International. (2004). *Stolen Sisters: A Human Rights Response to Discrimination and Violence Against Indigenous Women in Canada*. Available at http://www.amnesty .ca/stolensisters/amr2000304.pdf.

Arnold, R. (1995). "The Proceses of Victimization and Criminalization of Black Women." In B. R. Price and N. Sokoloff (eds.), *The Criminal Justice System and Women*. New York: McGraw-Hill.

Bertrand, Marie-Andrée. (1967). "The Myth of Sexual Equality before the Law." Fifth Research Conference on Delinquency and Criminality. Montreal, Centre de Psychologies et de Pédagogie (pp. 129–61).

Boritch, Hellen. (1997). *Fallen Women: Female Crime and Criminal Justice in Canada*. Toronto: Nelson.

Boyle, Christine. (1994). "The Judicial Construction of Sexual Assault Offences." In J. Roberts and R. Mohr (eds.), *Confronting Sexual Assault: A Decade of Social and Legal Change*. Toronto: University of Toronto Press.

Brinkerhoff, Merlin, and Eugen Lupri. (1988). "Interspousal Violence." *Canadian Journal of Sociology* 13(4):407–34.

Brock, Deborah. (1998). *Making Work, Making Trouble: Prostitution as a Social Problem*. Toronto: University of Toronto Press.

Bronson, Diana. (1989). "A Time for Grief and Pain." *The Globe and Mail*, December 8, p. A7.

Browne, Angela. (1987). *When Battered Women Kill*. New York: Free Press.

Brownmiller, Susan. (1975). *Against Our Will: Men, Women and Rape*. New York: Bantam Books.

Bruckert, Chris, and Colette Parent. (2006). "The In-Call Sex Industry: Reflections on Classed and Gendered Labour on the Margins." In G. Balfour and E. Comack (eds.), *Criminalizing Women: Gender and (In)justice in Neo-liberal Times*. Halifax: Fernwood Publishing.

Busby, Karen. (1997). "Discriminatory Uses of Personal Records in Sexual Violence Cases." *Canadian Journal of Women and the Law* 9(1):149–77.

———. (2006). "'Not a Victim until a Conviction Is Entered': Sexual Violence Prosecutions and Legal Truth." In E. Comack (ed.), *Locating Law: Race/Class/Gender/Sexuality Connections*. (2nd ed.). Halifax: Fernwood Publishing.

Cain, Maureen. (1990). "Towards Transgression: New Directions in Feminist Criminology." *International Journal of the Sociology of Law* 18:1–18.

Carlen, Pat (ed.). (1985). *Criminal Women.* Cambridge: Polity Press.

———. (1988). *Women, Crime and Poverty.* Milton Keynes: Open University Press.

Chan, Wendy. (2001). *Women, Murder and Justice.* London: Palgrave.

Chesney-Lind, Meda, and N. Rodriguez. (1983). "Women Under Lock and Key." *The Prison Journal* 63:47–65.

Chesney-Lind, Meda. and R. Sheldon. (1998). *Girls, Delinquency and Juvenile Justice.* California: Wadsworth.

Chunn, Dorothy E., and Shelley A.M. Gavigan. (2006). "From Welfare Fraud to Welfare as Fraud: The Criminalization of Poverty." In G. Balfour and E. Comack (eds.), *Criminalizing Women: Gender and (In)justice in Neo-liberal Times.* Halifax: Fernwood Publishing.

Clark, Lorenne, and Debra Lewis. (1977). *Rape: The Price of Coercive Sexuality.* Toronto: Women's Press.

Cohen, Albert. (1955). *Delinquent Boys.* Glencoe, Ill.: The Free Press.

Comack, Elizabeth. (1993). "Women Offenders' Experiences with Physical and Sexual Abuse: A Preliminary Report." Criminology Research Centre, University of Manitoba.

———. (1996). *Women in Trouble: Connecting Women's Law Violations to Their Histories of Abuse.* Halifax: Fernwood Publishing.

Comack, Elizabeth, and Salena Brickey. (2007). "Constituting the Violence of Criminalized Women." *Canadian Journal of Criminology and Criminal Justice* 49(1):1–36.

Comack, Elizabeth, Vanessa Chopyk, and Linda Wood. (2000). "Mean Streets? The Social Locations, Gender Dynamics and Patterns of Violent Crime in Winnipeg." Winnipeg: Canadian Centre for Policy Alternatives (Manitoba) (www.policyalternatives.ca).

———. (2008). "Aren't Women Violent Too? The Gendered Nature of Violence." In B. Schissel and C. Brooks (eds.), *Marginality and Condemnation: An Introduction to Critical Criminology.* (2nd ed.). Halifax: Fernwood Publishing.

Connell, R. W. (1987). *Gender and Power.* Cambridge: Polity Press.

———. (1995). *Masculinities.* Cambridge: Polity Press.

———. (2000). *The Men and the Boys.* Berkeley: University of California Press.

Connell, R. W., and James Messerschmidt. (2005). "Hegemonic Masculinity: Rethinking the Concept." *Gender & Society* 19(6):829–59.

Correctional Service of Canada. (2006). *Ten-Year Status Report on Women's Corrections, 1996–2006.* Ottawa: Correctional Service of Canada.

Cowie, John, Valerie Cowie, and Eliot Slater. (1968). *Delinquency in Girls.* London: Heinemann.

Crocker, Diane, and Val Marie Johnson. (2010). *Poverty, Regulation & Social Justice: Readings on the Criminalization of Poverty.* Halifax: Fernwood Publishing.

Daly, Kathleen. (1987). "Discrimination in the Criminal Courts: Family, Gender, and the Problem of Equal Treatment." *Social Forces* 66(1):152–75.

———. (1989). "Rethinking Judicial Paternalism: Gender, Work-Family Relations, and Sentencing." *Gender and Society* 3(1):9–36.

Daly, Kathleen, and Meda Chesney-Lind. (1988). "Feminism and Criminology." *Justice Quarterly* 5(4):101–43.

DeKeseredy, Walter, and Ronald Hinch. (1991). *Woman Abuse: Sociological Perspectives.* Toronto: Thompson.

Dobash, R. Emerson, and Russell Dobash. (1979). *Violence against Wives: A Case against Patriarchy*. New York: Free Press.

————. (1992). *Women, Violence and Social Change*. London: Routledge.

Dobash, Russell, R. Emerson Dobash, Margo Wilson, and Martin Daly. (1992). "The Myth of Sexual Symmetry in Marital Violence." *Social Problems* 39(1) (February):71–91.

Dutton, Donald. (1994). "Patriarchy and Wife Assault: The Ecological Fallacy." *Violence and Victims* 9.

Edwards, Susan. (1985). "Gender Justice? Defending Defendants and Mitigating Sentence." In S. Edwards (ed.), *Gender, Sex and the Law* (pp. 129–54). Kent: Croom Helm.

Faith, Karlene. (1993). *Unruly Women: The Politics of Confinement and Resistance*. Vancouver: Press Gang Publishers.

Frenschkowski, Joanne. (2002). "We've Learned Little from Kimberly Rogers's Death." *Globe and Mail*, August 9:A13.

Gelsthorpe, Lorraine, and Allison Morris. (1988). "Feminism and Criminology in Britain." *British Journal of Criminology* 23:93–110.

Gilfus, Mary. (1992). "From Victims to Survivors to Offenders: Women's Routes of Entry and Immersion into Street Crime." *Women and Criminal Justice* 4(1):63–89.

Glueck, Eleanor, and Sheldon Glueck. (1934). *Five Hundred Delinquent Women*. New York: Alfred A. Knopf.

Gotell, Lise. (2001). "Colonization through Disclosure: Confidential Records, Sexual Assault Complainants and Canadian Law." *Social and Legal Studies* 10(3):315–46.

Hagan, J., A. R. Gillis, and J. Simpson. (1985). "The Class Structure of Gender and Delinquency: Toward a Power-Control Theory of Common Delinquent Behavior." *American Journal of Sociology* 90:1151–78.

Hagan, J., J. Simpson, and A. R. Gillis. (1979). "The Sexual Stratification of Social Control: A Gender-Based Perspective on Crime and Delinquency." *British Journal of Sociology* 30:25–38.

————. (1987). "Class in the Household: A Power-Control Theory of Gender and Delinquency." *American Journal of Sociology* 92(4) (January):788–816.

Hamilton, A. C., and C. M. Sinclair. (1991). *The Justice System and Aboriginal People: Report of the Aboriginal Justice Inquiry of Manitoba*. Vol. 1. Winnipeg: Queen's Printer.

Hannah-Moffat, Kelly. (2001). *Punishment in Disguise: Penal Governance and Federal Imprisonment of Women in Canada*. Toronto: University of Toronto Press.

Hannah-Moffat, Kelly, and Margaret Shaw (eds.). (2000). *An Ideal Prison? Critical Essays on Women's Imprisonment in Canada*. Halifax: Fernwood Publishing.

Harries, Kate. (2002). "Inquest to Probe House-Arrest Death," *The Toronto Star*, October 15.

Hayman, Stephanie. (2006). *Imprisoning Our Sisters: The New Federal Women's Prisons in Canada*. Montreal and Kingston: McGill-Queen's University Press.

Hazelwood, R., J. Warren, and P. Dietz. (1993). "Compliant Victims of the Sexual Sadist." *Australian Family Physician* 22(4):474–9.

Heidensohn, Frances. (1968). "The Deviance of Women: A Critique and an Enquiry." *British Journal of Sociology* 19(2):160–75.

————. (1985). *Women and Crime*. London: Macmillan.

Heimer, K. (1995). "Gender, Race and Pathways to Delinquency." In J. Hagan and R. Peterson (eds.), *Crime and Inequality*. Stanford: Stanford University Press.

Hoffman-Bustamante, Dale. (1973). "The Nature of Female Criminality." *Issues in Criminology* 8:117–36.

Hugill, David. (2010). *Missing Women, Missing News: Covering Crisis in Vancouver's Downtown Eastside*. Halifax: Fernwood Publishing.

Johnson, Holly. (1996). *Dangerous Domains*. Toronto: Nelson.

Johnson, Holly, and Karen Rodgers. (1993). "A Statistical Overview of Women in Crime in Canada." In Ellen Adelberg and Claudia Currie (eds.), *In Conflict with the Law: Women and the Canadian Justice System* (pp. 95–116). Vancouver: Press Gang Publishers.

Jones, Anne. (1994). *Next Time She'll Be Dead: Battering and How to Stop It*. Boston: Beacon Press.

Kelly, Liz. (1988). *Surviving Sexual Violence*. Minneapolis: University of Minnesota Press.

Kendall, Kathleen. (1991). "The Politics of Premenstrual Syndrome: Implications for Feminist Justice." *Journal of Human Justice* 2(2) (Spring):77–98.

———. (1992). "Dangerous Bodies." In D. Farrington and S. Walklate (eds.), *Offenders and Victims: Theory and Policy* (pp. 45–61). London: British Society of Criminology.

———. (1993). *Program Evaluation of Therapeutic Services at the Prison for Women*. Ottawa: Correctional Services Canada.

Kennedy, Leslie, and Donald Dutton. (1989). "The Incidence of Wife Assault in Alberta." *Canadian Journal of Behavioural Science* 21:40–54.

Kinnon, Dianne. (1981). *Report on Sexual Assault in Canada*. Ottawa: CACSW.

Klein, Dorie (1973). "The Etiology of Female Crime: A Review of the Literature." *Issues in Criminology* 8(3):3–30.

Kong, Rebecca, and Kathy AuCoin. (2008). "Female Offenders in Canada." *Juristat* 28(1).

Konopka, Gisella. (1966). *The Adolescent Girl in Conflict*. Englewood Cliffs, NJ: Prentice Hall.

Kruttschnitt, Candace. (1980–81). "Social Status and Sentences of Female Offenders." *Law and Society Review* 15(2):247–65.

———. (1982). "Women, Crime and Dependancy." *Criminology* 195:495–513.

Laberge, Danielle. (1991). "Women's Criminality, Criminal Women, Criminalized Women?: Questions in and for a Feminist Perspective." *Journal of Human Justice* 2(2): 37–56.

Laframboise, Donna. (1996). "Men and Women are Equals in Violence." *National Post*, July 10.

Laghi, Brian. (1998). "Alberta Judge Stirs Outrage in Sex Case." *Globe and Mail*, February 23:A1, A11.

La Prairie, Carol. (1993). "Aboriginal Women and Crime in Canada: Identifying the Issues." In Ellen Adelberg and Claudia Currie (eds.), *In Conflict with the Law: Women and the Canadian Justice System* (pp. 235–46). Vancouver: Press Gang Publishers.

Leonard, Eileen. (1982). *Women, Crime and Society: A Critique of Theoretical Criminology*. New York: Longman.

Lombroso, C., and W. Ferrero. (1895). *The Female Offender*. London: Fischer Unwin.

Luckhaus, Linda. (1985). "A Plea for PMT in the Criminal Law." In S. Edwards (ed.), Gender, *Sex and the Law* (pp. 159–81). Kent: Croom Helm.

MacLeod, Linda. (1980). *Wife Battering in Canada: The Vicious Circle*. Ottawa: CACSW.

Mann, Ruth. (2003). "Violence against Women or Family Violence? The 'Problem' of Female Perpetration in Domestic Violence." In L. Samuelson and W. Antony (eds.), *Power and Resistance: Critical Thinking about Canadian Social Issues*. Halifax: Fernwood Publishing.

Martin, Dianne. (1999). "Punishing Female Offenders and Perpetuating Gender Stereotypes." In Julian V. Roberts and David P. Cole (eds.), *Making Sense of Sentencing*. Toronto: University of Toronto Press.

McGillivray, Anne. (1998). "'A Moral Vacuity in Her Which is Difficult if not Impossible to Expalin': Law, Psychiatry and the Remaking of Karla Homolka." *International Journal of the Legal Profession* 5(2/3):255–88.

Messerschmidt, James. (1986). *Capitalism, Patriarchy and Crime: Toward a Socialist Feminist Criminology*. Totowa, NJ: Rowman and Littlefield.

———. (1993). *Masculinities and Crime: A Critique and Reconceptualization of Theory*. Landham, MD: Rowman and Littlefield.

———. (1997). *Crime as Structured Action: Gender, Race, Class, and Crime in the Making*. Thousand Oaks, CA: Sage.

———. (2004). *Flesh and Blood: Adolescent Gender Diversity and Violence*. Landham, MD: Rowman and Littlefield.

Miller, E. (1986). *Street Woman*. Philadelphia: Temple University Press.

Monture Angus, Patricia. (1999). "Women and Risk: Aboriginal Women, Colonialism, and Correctional Practice." *Canadian Women's Studies* 19(1) (Spring/Summer):24–29.

Morris, Allison. (1987). *Women, Crime and Criminal Justice*. Oxford: Basil Blackwell.

Morrissey, Belinda. (2003). *When Women Kill: Questions of Agency and Subjectivity*. London: Routledge.

Mosher, Janet E. (2006). "The Construction of 'Welfare Fraud' and the Wielding of the State's Iron Fist." In E. Comack (ed.), *Locating Law: Race/Class/Gender/Sexuality Connections*. (2nd ed.) (pp. 207–29). Halifax: Fernwood Publishing.

Naffine, Ngaire. (1987). *Female Crime: The Construction of Women in Criminology*. Sydney: Allen and Unwin.

———. (1997). *Feminism and Criminology*. Sydney: Allen and Unwin.

Native Women's Association of Canada (NWAC). (2010). *What Their Stories Tell Us: Research Findings from the Sisters in Spirit Initiative*. Ottawa: NWAC. Available at: http://www.nwac.ca/sites/default/files/imce/2010_NWAC_SIS_Report_EN.pdf.

Osborne, Judith. (1989). "Perspectives on Premenstrual Syndrome: Women, Law and Medicine." *Canadian Journal of Family Law* 8:165–84.

Pearson, Patricia. (1997). *When She Was Bad: Violent Women and the Myth of Innocence*. Toronto: Random House.

Perreault, Samuel. (2009). "The Incarceration of Aboriginal People in Adult Correctional Services." *Juristat* 29(3).

Pollak, Otto. (1961). *The Criminality of Women*. New York: A. S. Barnes.

*R. v. Mills*, [1998] 3 S.C.R. 688.

Rafter, N. H., and E. M. Natalizia. (1981). "Marxist Feminism: Implications for Criminal Justice." *Crime and Delinquency* 27 (January):81–98.

Ritchie, Beth. (1996). *Compelled to Crime: The Gender Entrapment of Battered Black Women*. New York: Routledge.

Royal Commission on Aboriginal Peoples. (1996). *Report of the Royal Commission on Aboriginal Peoples*. Ottawa: Department of Indian and Northern Affairs.

Schwartz, Martin, and Walter DeKeseredy. (1993). "The Return of the 'Battered Husband Syndrome' through the Typification of Women as Violent." *Crime, Law and Social Change* 20:249–65.

Scully, D., and J. Marolla. (1985). "'Riding the Bull at Gilly's': Convicted Rapists Describe the Rewards of Rape." *Social Problems* 32:251–63.

Scutt, Jocelyn. (1979). "The Myth of the 'Chivalry Factor' in Female Crime." *Australian Journal of Social Issues* 14(1):3–20.

Shaw, Margaret. (1993). "Reforming Federal Women's Imprisonment." In E. Adelberg and C. Currie (eds.) *In Conflict with the Law: Women and the Canadian Justice System.* Vancouver: Press Gang Publishers.

Shaw, Margaret, Karen Rogers, Johannes Blanchette, Tina Hattem, Lee Seto Thomas, and Lada Tamarack. (1991). *Survey of Federally Sentenced Women: Report on the Task Force on Federally Sentenced Women: The Prison Survey.* Ottawa: Ministry of the Solicitor General of Canada. User Report No. 1991-4.

Simon, Rita. (1975). *Women and Crime.* Lexington, MA: D. C. Heath.

Smart, Carol. (1976). *Women, Crime and Criminology: A Feminist Critique.* London: Routledge and Kegan Paul.

———. (1977). "Criminological Theory: Its Ideology and Implications Concerning Women." *British Journal of Sociology* 28(1):89–100.

———. (1989). *Feminism and the Power of Law.* London: Routledge.

Snider, Laureen. (1991). "The Potential of the Criminal Justice System to Promote Feminist Concerns." In E. Comack and S. Brickey (eds.), *The Social Bias of Law: Critical Readings in the Sociology of Law.* (2nd ed.) (pp. 238–60). Halifax: Fernwood Publishing.

———. (1994). "Feminism, Punishment and the Potential of Empowerment." *Canadian Journal of Law and Society* 9(1):74–104.

———. (2003). "Constituting the Punishable Woman: Atavistic Man Incarcerates Postmodern Woman." *British Journal of Criminology* 43(2):354–78.

Sommers, Evelyn. (1995). *Voices from Within: Women Who Have Broken the Law.* Toronto: University of Toronto Press.

Statistics Canada. (1993). "The Violence against Women Survey." *The Daily*, November 18.

———. (2000). "Family Violence." *The Daily*, July 25. Available at http://www.statcan.ca/Daily/English/ 000725/d000725b.htm; accessed July 14, 2011.

Statistics Canada. (2005). "General Social Survey: Victimization." *The Daily*, July 7. Available at http://www.statcan.ca/Daily/English/050707/d050707b/htm; accessed February 2, 2007.

Steffensmeier, Darryl, and J. Kramer. (1982). "Sex-based Differences in the Sentencing of Adult Criminal Defendants." *Sociology and Social Research* 663:289–304.

Steinmetz, Suzanne. (1981). "A Cross-cultural Comparison of Marital Abuse." *Journal of Sociology and Social Welfare* 8:404–14.

Straus, Murray, and Richard Gelles. (1986). "Societal Changes and Change in Family Violence from 1975 to 1985 as Revealed by Two National Surveys." *Journal of Marriage and the Family* 48:465–80.

Straus, Murray, Richard Gelles, and Suzanne Steinmetz. (1980). *Behind Closed Doors: Violence in the American Family.* New York: Doubleday.

Taylor, I., P. Walton, and J. Young. (1973). *The New Criminology.* London: Routledge and Kegan Paul.

Thomas, J. (2010). "Adult Criminal Court Statistics, 2008/09." *Juristat* 30(2).

Thomas, W. I. (1967). *The Unadjusted Girl.* New York: Harper and Row.

Ursel, Jane. (1994). "The Winnipeg Family Violence Court." Juristat 14(12).

———. (1998). "Eliminating Violence Against Women: Reform or Co-Optation in State Institutions." In L. Samuelson and W. Antony (eds.), *Power and Resistance: Critical Thinking about Canadian Social Issues.* (2nd ed.). Halifax: Fernwood Publishing.

Walker, Lenore. (1979). *The Battered Woman.* New York: Harper and Row.

_____. (1987*). Terrifying Love: Why Battered Women Kill and How Society Responds.* New York: Harper Collins.

Wallace, Marnie. (2004). "Crime Statistics in Canada, 2003." *Juristat* 24(6).

The War Against Women. (1991). *Report of the Standing Committee on Health and Welfare.* Ottawa: Social Affairs, Seniors and the Status of Women (June).

West, Candace, and Don Zimmerman. (1987). "Doing Gender." *Gender & Society* 1(2): 125–51.

Zingraff, M., and R. Thomson. (1984). "Differential Sentencing of Women and Men in the U.S.A." *International Journal of the Sociology of Law* 12:401–13.

# Victimology, Victim Services, and Victim Rights in Canada

**Irvin Waller**

UNIVERSITY OF OTTAWA

For centuries, the traditional system of law enforcement, criminal justice, and corrections has focused on catching, convicting, and, in some cases, fining or incarcerating offenders. The role of the victim has been limited to calling the police, collaborating with the police investigation when asked, and acting as a witness in the court case. Many criminologists blame pressure from victims of crime for the increases in incarceration that politicians implemented, particularly in the United States, in the last four decades.

Ironically, advancing services and rights for victims of crime, including stopping victimization, is best achieved by reinvesting government expenditures away from ineffective and costly responses to crime such as mass incarceration. Victims of crime are often described as the orphans of criminal justice and even as the orphans of social policy. They are also the orphans of criminology. Many criminology students still graduate without having learned what we know about victims and so may perpetuate many myths about victims and victimization.

## Learning Objectives

After reading this chapter, you should be able to

- Discuss the risk of being a victim of crime, comprehend the key components of the harm to victims of crime, and understand the ways of measuring these components.

- Outline the way that the traditional system of police, courts, and corrections limits the role of the victim to complainant and witness.

- Identify the key laws and international standards that provide the vision for the shift from the traditional criminal justice system to a system which embraces the needs and human rights of victims.

- Propose specific and basic ways for police to meet the needs of victims, including victims of gender-related crimes.

- Show how services for victims in general, as well as for specific types of victims, can reach international standards.

- Specify the ways in which restitution from the offender, civil remedies, restorative justice, and compensation from the state will repair damage to victims.

- Debate ways for victims of crime to have their basic human rights respected in criminal courts without being unnecessarily trumped by rights for defendants.
- Understand the key components of system-wide strategies for stopping violence and repeat victimization.
- Justify actions likely to shift crime policy from the traditional system to one that embraces reducing victimization and providing services and rights for victims of crime.

# FOCUS BOX 7.1

## A SNAPSHOT OF VICTIMIZATION IN CANADA

On average, each year in a Canadian city of 1 000 000 persons the combination of all interpersonal crime will cause victims $2.5 billion in costs and pain and suffering, including 60 000 adult victims of assault, 16 000 adult victims of sexual assault, and 18 000 adult victims of thefts from or of cars. Additionally, it is important to recognize that

- Fewer than one in three will call the police to report the crime and an even lower number will report the offense of sexual assault.
- Fewer than three percent of victims will see "their" offender convicted.
- Victims who do not cooperate as witnesses may be arrested.
- Police services will cost $400 million out of local taxes and correctional services will cost $180 million out of federal and provincial taxes. Expenditures on victim services and rights are often paid out of fines and may be less than $10 million.

- Police are unlikely to inform victims of the availability of services. such as property repair, volunteer victim support, restitution, or compensation
- Those working with victims are paid less than half the salary of police officers.
- Most eligible victims will not receive restitution or compensation.
- Victim impact statements do not impact sentences.
- Victims do not have remedies for their rights.

Sources: Adapted from Institute for the Prevention of Crime. (2009). *Making Cities Safer: Action Briefs for Municipal Stakeholders*, Number 3, University of Ottawa; Irvin Waller. (2010). *Rights for Victims of Crime: Rebalancing Justice*. New York: Rowman and Littlefield, Chapters 1 and 3; Irvin Waller. (2008). *Less Law, More Order: The Truth about Reducing Crime*. Ancaster: Manor House, 2008, pp. 10–14; Perreault, Samuel, and Shannon Brennan. (2010). "Criminal Victimization in Canada, 2009." *Juristat* 30 (2); Ting Zhang. (2011). *Costs of Crime in Canada, 2008*. Ottawa, ON: Department of Justice Canada.

# Prevalence, Impact, and Needs of Victimization

Criminologists, knowledgeable about the flaws in the data collection of crime statistics from the police, have begun to measure the prevalence of victimization. The two main flaws found in the data on crime from the police are that (1) many victims do not report crime to the police and (2) many reported crimes are not recorded by the police. To investigate victimization, criminologists began large-scale surveys of adults to find out who had been a victim of crime and whether the victim had reported the offense. These surveys are known as **victimization surveys** (see Chapter 4).

These surveys have been undertaken on an annual basis in other countries for many years and so have become accepted by policy makers and the media in countries such as the United Kingdom and the United States. However, Canada has only done these surveys intermittently over the last 40 years. Even today, the surveys by Statistics Canada are only done every five years and do not get the attention that they deserve. A brief summary of the data uncovered by these Statistics Canada victimization surveys is outlined in Box 7.1.

The main source of data about the prevalence of victimization in Canada is the General Social Survey (GSS). This survey shows that

- Over one-quarter of adult Canadians are victimized by some type of the theft, assault, and sexual assault crimes included in the survey.

- This rate of victimization has not changed significantly over the last 15 years.

- Adult victims of violent crimes are young (the age group of 15–24 has reported being victimized over 15 times more than the 65 and older age group); more likely to be male, except for sexual assault; and more likely to be Aboriginal (Perrault and Brennan, 2010).

Table 7.1 shows the rates of victimization for seven of the offenses included in the Statistics Canada GSS for the last three years in which the survey was undertaken—1999, 2004, and 2009. These rates confirm small increases in sexual assault, robbery, and physical assault. They also show some increases and decreases for property crime in terms of the various types of theft and vandalism; specifically, they detail a a significant increase from 1999–2004 with a small decrease from 2004–2009.

**victimization surveys**

Surveys of the general public to identify who has been a victim of crime, whether they reported the crime to police, and other related aspects of victimization.

**TABLE 7.1** **Rates of Victimization in Canada**

| *Rates of Victimization (per 1000 population age 15 years and older)* | | | |
|---|---|---|---|
| *Year* | *Sexual Assault* | *Robbery* | *Physical Assault* | *Subtotal* |
| 1999 | 21 | 9 | 81 | 111 |
| 2004 | 21 | 11 | 75 | 107 |
| 2009 | 24 | 13 | 80 | 117 |

| *Rates of Victimization (per 1000 households)* | | | | |
|---|---|---|---|---|
| *Year* | *Break and Enter* | *Motor Vehicle/ Parts Theft* | *Theft of House- hold Property* | *Vandalism* | *Subtotal* |
| 1999 | 48 | 41 | 62 | 66 | 217 |
| 2004 | 39 | 44 | 88 | 77 | 248 |
| 2009 | 47 | 34 | 83 | 74 | 238 |

Sources: Statistics Canada General Social Survey 2004, Statistics Canada General Social Survey 2009, and Statistics Canada General Social Survey 1999.

**repeat victimization**

The phenomenon of a person being a victim of a crime more than once.

**Repeat victimization** of the same victim (or victim's household) has been frequently observed in victimization surveys. According to the 2004 Statistics Canada Survey, of those who stated that they had been victimized by a crime during the preceding 12 months, 40 percent reported that they had been victimized more than once. As in other countries, these surveys show victimization to be concentrated in certain areas, families, and individuals. For example, males aged from 15–25 who are not married and who go out from their residence are much more likely to be victims of most crimes. In Canada, Aboriginal peoples are much more at risk.

## Impact of Victimization

It is now widely accepted that crime causes financial loss, injury, and emotional pain and trauma to victims. These harms can also be suffered by persons who have relationships with the victim such as the spouse, parents and friends. Some of the consequences of victimization include injury, such as cuts and broken bones, diseases (STDs, AIDS, etc.), and pain; emotional trauma, which can manifest as anger, fear, shock, depression, or post-traumatic stress disorder, or trauma caused by the loss of objects of sentimental value; and financial loss, often seen in terms of stolen or damaged property, medical care costs, loss of wages, and the financial costs of "pain and suffering."

**harm to victims**

The direct impact of crime on victims includes harm, such as loss, injury, pain, and emotional trauma. These can be exacerbated by the experience with the police, courts, corrections, and others.

In 2011 Justice Canada released a report showing the tangible costs, and pain and suffering to victims of crime (Zhang, 2011). This report concluded that the total annual cost of **harm to victims** in 2008 was $83 billion (Table 7.2).

**TABLE 7.2   Estimates of Costs of Crime for Victims, 2008**

| Victim Costs—Tangible Costs | Costs $ (millions) |
| --- | --- |
| Health Care | 1443 |
| Productivity Losses | 6734 |
| Stolen/Damaged Property | 6143 |
| Total Tangible Victim Costs | 14 320 |
| **Selected Services—Tangible Costs** | **Costs $ (millions)** |
| Victim Services and Compensation Programs | 451 |
| Shelters for Victims | 254 |
| Other Expenditures Related to Crime | 238 |
| Total Selected Services Costs | 943 |
| **Victim Costs—Intangible Costs** | **Costs $ (millions)** |
| Pain and Suffering | 65 100 |
| Productivity Losses | 3055 |
| Total Intangible Victim Costs | 68 155 |
| Grand Total | 83 418 |

Source: *Costs of Crime in Canada, 2008, http://www.justice.gc.ca/eng/pi/rs/rep-rap/2011/rr10_5/index.html*. Department of Justice Canada, 2008. Reproduced with the permission of the Minister of Public Works and Government Services Canada, 2011.

**TABLE 7.3**  Costs of Criminal Justice in Canada, 2008

| Criminal Justice System Costs | Costs $ (millions) |
|---|---|
| Police | 12 000 |
| Court | 1000 |
| Prosecution | 528 |
| Legal Aid | 373 |
| Corrections | 5630 |
| Total Criminal Justice System Costs | 19 531 |

Source: *Costs of Crime in Canada, 2008, http://www.justice.gc.ca/eng/pi/rs/rep-rap/2011/rr10_5/index.html*. Department of Justice Canada, 2008. Reproduced with the permission of the Minister of Public Works and Government Services Canada, 2011.

While tangible costs exceeded $14 billion, the intangible costs of pain and suffering exceeded $68 billion. This study estimated annual expenditures on services for victims at less than a $1 billion.

Expenditures on police, courts, and corrections are rising and have now reached nearly $20 billion in Canada (Table 7.3). It is estimated that between 50–60 percent of police costs are used to respond to 911 calls made by or on behalf of crime victims (Skogan and Frydl, 2004; Waller, 2008).

## Needs of Crime Victims

International organizations such as the International Association of Chiefs of Police (IACP, 2008), researchers working on needs of victims, and victim organizations have identified eight core needs or **rights of crime victims**. These have been articulated under three broader categories of support, justice and governance in Table 7.4.

**Right to Recognition**  Victims need to be recognized. Crimes are committed against people—they are not just an affront to the state. Human faces are associated with every crime; every robbery, rape, and assault has harmed a citizen, not the state. These are the faces of persons suffering loss, injury, and trauma at the hands of an offender who was responsible for inflicting the harm.

**Right to Information**  Victims need to be provided with information. They need to know which services are available to them and what rights they have to recover reparation. They also need information regarding the process of the police investigation, prosecution, and criminal court if an offender is caught.

**Right to Assistance**  Victims—whether in a large or small city or in a rural, isolated area—need to be informed of services, to be given access to these services, and to have them adequately funded. Specific services are required for victims of specific crimes; for example, rape victims, child abuse victims, and robbery victims will require different types of services. Different types of services are also needed as the victims' needs evolve over time.

**rights of crime victims**
Legislators in different countries and intergovernmental agencies such as UN have recognized various fundamental principles of justice and rights for victims of crime, such as the right to be informed, to receive restitution, or to be present in court.

**TABLE 7.4    Core Rights for Victims of Crime and Likely Responses**

| Support | Core Needs for Victims of Crime | Right to Legislation and Implementation to Provide |
|---|---|---|
| 1 | Recognition and emotional support | Trained informal and professional crisis support and counselling |
| 2 | Information on criminal justice, their case, services, and personal developments | Timely information on : law enforcement, criminal justice and corrections; case; assistance; and expected developments |
| 3 | Assistance to access practical, medical, and social services | Advocacy and assistance with repair, practical, social, and other services |
| **Justice** | | |
| 4 | Help to pay bills caused by victimization | Emergency funds and restitution from offender, compensation from state, and paid medical and mental health care |
| 5 | Personal safety and protection from accused | Prevention of revictimization and protection from accused |
| 6 | Choice to voice in justice | Choice to participate and be represented to defend safety, reparation, truth, and justice |
| **Good Government** | | |
| 7 | Best public safety | Modern strategies that reduce crime and prevent victimization |
| 8 | Implementation | Performance measures and surveys of victims as clients |

Source: Irvin Waller. (2010). *Rights for Victims of Crime: Rebalancing Justice*. New York: Rowman and Littlefield, pp. 28–33.

**restitution from the offender**

Victims of any type of crime may request that the offender pay the victim money as reparation for financial or other losses caused by the crime.

**compensation from the state**

Victims of crimes that suffered physical or other injuries may apply to a provincial agency to receive lump sum or monthly payments according to provincial legislation.

**Right to Reparation** Victims need help to recover financially from their crime victimization. Some of this recovery should be done through **restitution from the offender**. Some may be paid in **compensation from the state**. Some may come from civil suits against the offender or a third party.

**Right to be Protected from the Accused** Victims need to be protected from the accused, and not just through incarceration of the offender. Victims of domestic abuse or child victims are prone to be re-victimized by the offender. The state needs to intervene to ensure this does not happen.

**Right to Participation and Representation** Victims need to be able to participate and to be represented in the legal process, and the legal process should be geared to defending their interests. Under Canadian law, the victim impact statement does not go far enough in providing this right.

**Right to Effective Policies to Reduce Victimization** Governments need to implement those programs known to be effective in preventing the first victimization and any repetition, not simply to punish offenders after the fact.

**Right to Implementation** A victim does not have a right unless there is a remedy. Many of the principles of justice and bills of rights have not been adequately implemented and the provisions for a remedy are very limited or non-existent.

# The Origins of Victimology and International Standards

In the 1960s, pioneers of what would become victimology and victim rights started to seek changes in the ways that victims of crime are treated. The motivations of these people centred on a concern for victims. Some started rape crisis centres and refuges for battered wives because they were shocked by the lack of appropriate attention to victims of violence against women. The first organizations formed by crime victims, and particularly by the parents of murdered children, began to demand reforms (Amernic, 1984). Others had different motivations. Some pioneers started victim–witness assistance programs to support the traditional system of criminal justice by increasing the proportion of crime victims going to police and collaborating with prosecutors. Some promoted victim offender mediation and restorative justice programs in an effort to make the traditional system less harsh on offenders. Some undertook the first victimization surveys while seeking better data on the extent of crime.

Whatever their motivation, these disparate groups became part of an international movement which brought together advocates for victim services and rights, some of whom work in the trenches with victims and some of whom are in academe. Soon they discovered that the problems of victims had many similarities in different countries.

In 1979, the World Society of Victimology (WSV) was formed to allow all the various researchers, policy makers, and service providers to pursue their common interests and to exchange knowledge and experiences. Since then, they have organized a major international symposium every three years. They have also sponsored graduate courses, such as the renowned annual two-week course in Dubrovnik, Croatia, which has celebrated its 26th consecutive year and which has become the starting point for many students to learn about victimology and victim rights.

## *Magna Carta* for Victims

The WSV quickly began to put social science knowledge, human rights principles, and international collaboration to work by influencing the UN. In 1985 the UN General Assembly adopted a landmark resolution that called for a major shift from the traditional criminal justice system approach to an approach that emphasises both prevention of victimization and respect for the human rights of victims of crime. Every government in the world is part of the UN General Assembly and so every government endorsed this resolution. This is technically known as UN General Assembly Resolution 1985 A/30/44 on the Declaration of Basic Principles of Justice for Victims of Crime and Abuse of Power.

The resolution committed every government in the world to a transformative shift from traditional criminal justice by recognizing that crime does damage to victims and families (not just against the state), as well as difficulties that victims of crime experience with police, justice, and health services. The governments agreed to (1) implement basic principles of justice for victims of crime and abuse of power (the UN Declaration) and (2) prevent victimization by a series of comprehensive measures, including attacking social causes and fostering individual responsibility.

The UN Declaration principles include:

1. Information on criminal justice, their case, and services
2. Assistance to access practical, medical and social services
3. Guidelines and training for police, health and other services
4. Reparation through restitution and state compensation
5. Right and access to justice (voice in justice)

The UN Declaration of Basic Principles of Justice for Victims of Crime and Abuse of Power has become the benchmark for basic services and rights for victims. It is often referenced as the *magna carta* for victims of crime because it is the first time that the UN General Assembly endorsed a set of basic human rights for victims which were designed to shift the traditional system from its obsession with the courtroom battle of the state versus the offender to comprehensive efforts to stop victimization and to provide services and rights to victims of crime.

However, the shift from the traditional system to a balance between a focus on offenders and the needs of victims is happening extremely slowly. The investment in the traditional system of police, courts, and corrections with their focus on catching, convicting, and incarcerating offenders is immense and resistant to change. In part, criminology has perpetuated this by focusing on the negative aspects of sentencing and prisons without providing alternatives. Criminologists blame the victim movement for increases in punishment because populist politicians claim that victims of crime are helped by increasing expenditures on the traditional system, particularly on longer sentences in prisons. The most unfortunate aspect is that, in part, criminologists overlook the needs of victims without realizing that meeting those needs would reduce some of the victim frustration with the traditional system.

## Origins of Victims Rights Policies in Canada

The first seeds of policies to help victims in Canada were sown in the 1960s. In 1967 Saskatchewan joined jurisdictions such as New Zealand, the United Kingdom, and California in creating a scheme to provide compensation to victims of violent crime. In the 1970s the first criminological monographs on crime victims were published on burglary victims (Waller and Okihiro, 1978) and rape victims (Clarke, 1977). These studies remain models of what criminology could do as it influenced efforts to focus on the prevention of crime, including violence against women, and to change the response to victims.

In 1981 the US National Organization for Victim Assistance and the Canadian Council for Social Development organized a major international conference in Toronto to discuss the topic of assistance to victims of crime.

This conference led to a federal–provincial task force of public servants who made recommendations for justice for victims in 1983. Its recommendations included some positive suggestions, including

1. Gathering survey data on numbers of victims
2. Providing information for victims
3. Providing services for victims
4. Providing restitution, compensation, and property return
5. Protecting victims from intimidation and in-camera hearings
6. Providing victim impact statements to assist with restitution and holding trials within a reasonable time
7. Paying for services using a fine surtax on offenders
8. Monitoring the implementation of recommendations

However, the report was produced behind closed doors by public servants working for the traditional system without the open meetings that took place in other countries, such as Australia or the USA, and without using the social science knowledge about victims. The committee's lack of attention to participatory justice and to the emotional trauma experienced by victims meant that the report neglected the importance of both victim participation in justice processes, prevention of victimization, and mental health services.

In stark contrast, the U.S. President's Task Force (1982) followed a much more scientific and transparent procedure to arrive at a much broader and more comprehensive set of recommendations, in addition to recommendations that combined using the traditional system to help meet the needs of crime victims. It included major sections on mental health and a draft constitutional amendment to provide victims with standing equivalent to an offender at critical stages such as bail and sentencing.

In an attempt to better serve the needs of victims of crime, the Ontario Secretary of Justice organized a transparent consultation to review the task force recommendations with groups representing victims of crime including parents of murdered children and victims of sexual assault (Ontario, 1984). The consultation recommendations included calls for prevention and for providing legal standing for victims in the criminal justice system. Unfortunately, the Attorney General of Ontario—Roy McMurtry—followed the advice of his officials from the traditional system to avoid implementing these additional recommendations that would have moved government policy more in line with the needs of crime victims than the needs of the traditional system.

## Tensions Between the Traditional and Human Rights for Victims

Canada supported the efforts in 1985 to get the UN General Assembly to adopt the Declaration discussed earlier by organizing a preparatory meeting. However, two tensions have slowed down a full respect for the basic human rights for victims of crime. One is the gap that remains between what is identified in that declaration and the resistance to change within the traditional system. The other is the gap between social science research and the legal training of those responsible for the traditional system. Unfortunately, the groups responsible for proposing and implementing reforms are part of the legal bureaucracy that is committed to the status quo and  the traditional system. This gap is sustained and exacerbated in Canada because there is also a lack of transparency in the development of policies to meet victim needs. This contrasts with developments in the United Kingdom and in the United States, particularly at the national level.

Manitoba was the first province to adopt legislation to provide services and some limited rights for victims of crime in 1986. This was inspired by pioneering legislation in Massachusetts which showed how to supplement the compensation program with a statement of standards for services and a central office to implement services to meet those standards. These and later federal legislative initiatives started a system of fine surcharges to provide funding for some victim services. Some assessments of these services suggest that they are a patchwork and often judges do not order the **victim fine surcharge**. Unfortunately, there have not been social science surveys to measure the exact extent of the gap between what was promised and what was delivered. For example, while it is known that judges do not always order the fine surcharges, there is no remedy to get judges to follow the law.

**victim fine surcharge**
A monetary penalty similar to a fine, which can be assessed at sentence or added to a fine such as in a traffic violation, but can only be used by the government to fund services for victims.

In 1988 the federal and provincial ministers agreed to a Canadian Statement of Principles of Justice in an effort to "Canadianize" the UN Declaration. Though inspired by the UN resolution, the federal, provincial, and territorial ministers' agreement fell far short of the UN human rights. At that time, the provinces joined Manitoba's earlier initiative to pass legislation to create new services, but even these are often weak and they do not create a strong responsibility centre to implement them. This is particularly true of Ontario. On June 11, 1996, *An Act Respecting Victims of Crime—Victims' Bill of Rights* was proclaimed law in Ontario. The Act is described by the Ministry of the Attorney General (of Ontario) as "a set of principles that guide how justice system officials should treat victims at different stages of the criminal justice process." The Act also created an Office for Victims of Crime but its role is limited to advising the Attorney General on victim issues. As a result, there are no rights because there is no remedy. The government has made promises but it has not provided a way for victims to ensure that these promises are kept, for instance by allowing appeals to a judge who would review the situation and if necessary order the government or a judge to act appropriately.

Though the intentions were good, these initiatives have done little to guarantee rights for victims. A Canadian parliamentary committee reviewed progress on victim services and published 17 recommendations to improve the situation (Canada, 1998). The committee held town hall meetings in different constituencies across Canada and listened to both crime victims and experts. Their report, entitled *Victims: A Voice not a Veto*, made significant recommendations for reform, including the creation of an adequately funded, high-level leadership centre and reforms to the basic principles.

When called to task by the Parliamentary Committee (Canada, Standing Committee, 2000), the federal, provincial, and territorial governments revised their principles in 2003. to those set out in Box 7.2. While they include some obvious principles and so are good, as far as they go, they still do not include effective ways to implement them as requested by the Parliamentary Committee. They also overlook such basic issues as assistance to access services (other than information); help obtaining reparation, such as restitution and compensation (other than information); providing victims with a voice in justice; effective policies to prevention victimization; and ways of ensuring and monitoring implementation. Once again the results are disappointing, as the process was not open to victim groups. There was no involvement of social science experts and no apparent effort to look at the UN resolution, which included specific ways to achieve implementation. The Declaration also overlooked many basic principles of justice.

## FOCUS BOX 7.2

### CANADIAN STATEMENT OF BASIC PRINCIPLES OF JUSTICE FOR VICTIMS OF CRIME

In honour of the United Nations' Declaration of Basic Principles of Justice for Victims of Crime, and with concern for the harmful impact of criminal victimization on individuals and on society, and in recognition that all persons have the full protection of rights guaranteed by the Canadian Charter of Rights and Freedoms and other provincial Charters governing rights and freedoms; that the rights of victims and offenders need to be balanced; and of the shared jurisdiction of federal, provincial, and territorial governments, the federal, provincial, and territorial Ministers Responsible for Criminal Justice agree that the following principles should guide the treatment of victims, particularly during the criminal justice process.

The following principles are intended to promote fair treatment of victims and should be reflected in federal/provincial/territorial laws, policies and procedures:

- Victims of crime should be treated with courtesy, compassion, and respect.
- The privacy of victims should be considered and respected to the greatest extent possible.
- All reasonable measures should be taken to minimize inconvenience to victims.
- The safety and security of victims should be considered at all stages of the criminal justice process and appropriate measures should be taken when necessary to protect victims from intimidation and retaliation.
- Information should be provided to victims about the criminal justice system and the victim's role

and opportunities to participate in criminal justice processes.
- Victims should be given information, in accordance with prevailing law, policies, and procedures, about the status of the investigation; the scheduling, progress and final outcome of the proceedings; and the status of the offender in the correctional system.
- Information should be provided to victims about available victim assistance services, other programs and assistance available to them, and means of obtaining financial reparation.
- The views, concerns and representations of victims are an important consideration in criminal justice processes and should be considered in accordance with prevailing law, policies and procedures.
- The needs, concerns and diversity of victims should be considered in the development and delivery of programs and services, and in related education and training.
- Information should be provided to victims about available options to raise their concerns when they believe that these principles have not been followed.

Source: *Canadian Statement of Basic Principles of Justice for Victims of Crime, 2003, http://www.justice.gc.ca/eng/pi/pcvi-cpcv/pub/03/princ.html.* Department of Justice Canada, 2003. Reproduced with the permission of the Minister of Public Works and Government Services Canada, 2011.

Some modifications have been made to the Criminal Code and to the Youth Criminal Justice Act to protect the privacy of victims, enable restitution orders in criminal courts, and allow victim impact statements. However, the lack of attention to social science research measuring the impact of these changes means that little is known about the extent to which these provisions are, or indeed ever likely to be, used extensively.

Ontario has only recently started to use the victim justice fund—the fund to which victim surcharges are paid—to expand victim services. In 2007 the Ontario provincial ombudsman undertook an inquiry into compensation for victims of violent crime. His report labelled the system as "Adding Insult to Injury" just before an election. In response, the Ontario Attorney General appointed the retiring Chief Justice of Ontario, Roy McMurtry, to investigate and to make recommendations. His report measured the current services and compensation for victims of crime against the internationally agreed standards of the UN Declaration on Basic Principles of Justice. It made several practical recommendations for improvements such as getting police to provide victims with information about victim services, using surveys of victims to measure gaps in the delivery of services and so on. Ironically, Justice McMurtry is the same person who more than 20 years earlier had resisted basic changes to fundamental rights for victims. However, his more enlightened and informed views in the recent report have still not been implemented by the current Attorney General of Ontario.

**Victims Matter**
http://www.victimsmatter.gc.ca/
index.html

In 2007, the federal government created the office of the Ombudsman for Victims of Crime. This is a public office created to defend the rights of victims and to bring about systemic change. However, this office was not established by legislation and two of its annual reports have not even been released. Justice Canada launched an awareness campaign in 2010 called Victims Matter which includes a tool to identify services for victims by postal code. While it is certainly a start, these improvements fall far short of developments in comparable jurisdictions as we will see in the next section.

## A Comparison of Canada to Other Jurisdictions

In Table 7.5, the Canadian principles are compared to some of the developments in other countries.

In the United States, the federal Victims of Crime Act was adopted in 1984 to increase victim assistance services and criminal injuries compensation across the country. This legislation included the creation of the independently funded and powerful Office for Victims of Crime (OVC) which allocates close to $1 billion every year to multiply victim assistance and compensation. In 1994 the Violence against Women's Act was passed and subsequently re-authorized in 2000 and 2005. This Act resulted in the creation of the Office on Violence Against Women as part of the U.S. Department of Justice. This office focuses on gendered victimization issues, specifically mandated to improve services for female victims, tailoring the programs to issues of gender and protecting the victim from the accused. It includes a requirement to evaluate the implementation of the Act.

In 2004 Japan established a task force to review victim services and then implemented the 10 key recommendations, including providing information, services, restitution, compensation, and standing in criminal courts. It also provides significant funding for these activities.

**TABLE 7.5**    **Comparison of International Rights for Victims of Crime with FPT Principles and Ontario Bill of Rights**

| Core Need | 2006 Draft Convention (article) | 1985 UN Declaration | 2001 EU Framework Decision | 2004 Int. Crim. Court | 2006 UK code of Practice | 1995 Victims Bill of Rights | 2003 Federal/ Territorial/ Provincial Principles |
|---|---|---|---|---|---|---|---|
| **Support** | | | | | | | |
| 1 | Recognition of victims, co-victims, good samaritans (1) | Yes | Yes | Yes | Yes | Yes | Yes |
| 2 | Information (7) | Yes | Yes | Yes | Yes | Yes | Yes |
| 3 | Assistance (8)—referral by police | No | Yes | Yes | Yes | Yes | Yes |
| | Assistance (8)—short term | Yes | Yes | Yes | Yes | Yes | Yes |
| | Assistance (8)—medium term | Yes | Yes | Yes | Yes | No | No |
| | Special assistance because of age, gender, disability, race (3) | No | No | Yes | No | No | Yes |
| **Justice** | | | | | | | |
| 4 | Restitution from offender (10) | Yes | Yes | Yes | No | No | No |
| | Restorative Justice (9)—respecting victim rights | Yes | Yes | No | No | No | Yes |
| | Compensation from state (11) | Yes | No | Yes | Yes | No | No |
| 5 | Protection of victims, witnesses, and experts | Yes | Yes | Yes | No | No | No |
| 6 | Access to justice and fair treatment | Yes | Yes | Yes | No | No | No |
| **Good Government** | | | | | | | |
| 7 | Commitment to reduce victimization | Yes | No | Yes | No | No | No |
| 8 | Implementation | Yes (res) | Yes | Yes | Yes | No | No |

Source: Irvin Waller. (2010). *Rights for Victims of Crime: Rebalancing Justice*. New York: Rowman and Littlefield, Figure 2.1, page 37.

The National Association of Victim Support Schemes (NAVSS) established victim service standards across England and Wales. In the 1990s, the government introduced a victim's charter to establish performance standards for what victims should receive (in terms of both services and compensation). The government adapted this Charter in 2006 into the more specific Code of Practice for Victims of Crime to better govern the services provided to victims: it defines what victims of specific types of crimes would receive from police, victim services, prosecutors, and several other key agencies. In 2010 the government integrated NAVSS into its National Victim Service so that the government ensures that all victims of crime do in fact receive the specified standard of support service. Now the United Kingdom has a one-stop system with a national victim commissioner to oversee the implementation of the Code of Practice.

In 2001 all the member governments of the European Union (EU) adopted standards for services for victims of crime. These standards cover information, services, mediation, and more. The implementation of the standards has been evaluated by the International Victimology Institute and Victim Support Europe with EU funds. As a result, the EU has initiated new actions to implement the services and rights across Europe.

In sum, we see that the tension between the needs of crime victims and the needs of the traditional system, and the tension between social science and the traditional legal culture have left Canada with some principles and laws but with few legal remedies for so-called rights. Transparent assessments of the current situation, such as the Parliamentary Committee in 1998 and the Ontario Ombudsman in 2007, show Canada lagging in legislation and implementation. Ironically the political figure who stopped progress in the 1980s chaired the McMurtry task force in 2008. This task force did hold public hearings and recommended key initiatives for Ontario that include a victim advocate or ombudsman, better implementation, and social science research to evaluate outcomes. Implementation of McMurtry's report in Ontario, and likely in most provinces, would bring Canada closer to international standards and fair treatment of crime victims.

# Policing, Victim Services, Reparation, Courts, and Prevention

## Victim Services and the Police

An increasing number of victims in Canada no longer go to the police. If they do, most will not get information on services, assistance, and support. If the police start an investigation, few victims will obtain reparation, protection, or go on to a criminal court—let alone get what they consider justice.

The proportion of victims of crime reporting their victimization to the police in Canada has been dropping. In 2009 only 31 percent reported to the police, down from 37 percent in 1999 and more than 40 percent earlier. The details of this decline are shown in Table 7.6 and are taken from the last three victimization surveys. The drop in reporting rates experienced in Canada has not occurred in the United States or in England. Furthermore, the proportion of sexual assault victims going to police in Canada is even worse at less than 10 percent.

**TABLE 7.6**   **Percentage of Crime Victims Reporting to Police by Offense (1999, 2004, and 2009)**

*Violent Victimization*

| Year | Sexual Assault | Robbery (%) | Physical Assault (%) | Total (%) |
|------|----------------|-------------|----------------------|-----------|
| 1999 | Unavailable | 46 | 37 | 31 |
| 2004 | 8% | 46 | 39 | 33 |
| 2009 | Unavailable | 43 | 34 | 29 |

*Household Victimization*

| Year | Break and Enter (%) | Motor Vehicle/Parts Theft (%) | Household Property Theft (%) | Vandalism (%) | Total (%) |
|------|---------------------|-------------------------------|------------------------------|---------------|-----------|
| 1999 | 62 | 60 | 32 | 34 | 44 |
| 2004 | 54 | 49 | 29 | 31 | 37 |
| 2009 | 54 | 50 | 23 | 35 | 36 |

| Year | Theft of Personal Property (%) | Total Victimization (%) | |
|------|--------------------------------|-------------------------|---|
| 1999 | 35 | 1999 | 37 |
| 2004 | 31 | 2004 | 34 |
| 2009 | 28 | 2009 | 31 |

Sources: Statistics Canada, Criminal Victimization in Canada, 2009. Juristat 30, no. 2. Ottawa, ON: Canadian Centre for Justice Statistics, 2010; Statistics Canada, Criminal Victimization in Canada, 2004, Juristat 25, No. 7. Juristat. Ottawa, ON: Canadian Centre for Justice Statistics, 2005; Statistics Canada, Criminal Victimization in Canada, 1999, Juristat 20, No. 10. Juristat. Ottawa, ON: Canadian Centre for Justice Statistics, 2000.

In the 2004 and 2009 victimization surveys, adult Canadians who are victims of crime are asked only why they did not report the crimes to the police. The assumption of the question is that everyone would want to report their crime to the police. The most frequent reasons for not reporting include that the crimes did not seem important enough, that the police could not do anything about it, that the crimes would be dealt with in another way, that the incident was a personal matter, or that they did not want the police involved at all.

Surveys in other countries ask why victims *do* call the police, which does not assume that everyone wants to report. The annual and extensive National Crime Survey in the United States shows that victims report to police because (1) victims of violence want to ensure their personal safety and ensure that others aren't victimized and (2) property crime victims want to recover stolen property, get damages repaired, and collect insurance. Punishment of the offender is the least frequent reason that victims contact the police (Waller, 2010, 60–62).

The Canadian surveys confirm a common finding in countries similar to Canada: most women who are victims of sexual assault or rape do not report their victimisation to the police. Specialized surveys exist to measure violence against women and violence against children but these are not undertaken regularly in Canada (Waller, 2010, 59–60). In the United States these surveys have shown that approximately 800 000 adult women are victims of forcible rape each year, and only 18 percent will report to the police. A disproportionate number of these rapes victimize college and university students; as many as one in five female students will graduate from university after being a victim of rape while on the university campus, typically by a male student in the same university (Fisher and Sloan, 2007).

Another common finding from government surveys in similarly situated countries is that most victims who report to the police will not see their offender identified or arrested (Waller, 2008, 14; Waller, 2010, 60). Overall, less than four percent of victims in Canada will see "their" offender convicted (Figure 7.1).

Police services in Canada are proud of their orientation to provide service to their communities; however, they have not focused on services to victims in any significant way. A major reason for the loss of confidence in the police in Canada is the lack of existing protocols detailing how the officer responding to a 911 call should respond (see McMurtry, 2008 for a recommendation on a protocol).

The Ontario Police Services Act sets out six principles that structure 911-call responses, but only one of the principles refers specifically to respect for victims of crime. This has not yet been accompanied by the sort of procedures and assessments that the International Association of Chiefs of Police (IACP) sees as essential to putting crime victims at the zenith of policing. The Ontario Police Services Act (Ontario, RSO, 1990) requires police services to be delivered

**FIGURE 7.1**   **Proportion of Victimizations that are Reported to Police, Cleared by Charge, and Where the Offender is Found Guilty, Canada 2004**

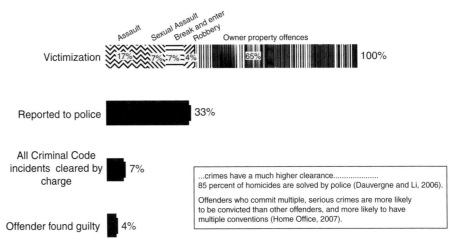

*Homicides do not include suicides or death crimed by begigener, accidents, or self defence.

Sources: Adapted from: Statistics Canada, Criminal Victimization in Canada, 2004, Juristat 25, No. 7. Ottawa, ON: Canadian Centre for Justice Statistics, 2005.; Statistics Canada, Adult Criminal Court Survey, 2003/2004, Juristat 24, No. 12. Ottawa, ON: Canadian Centre for Justice Statistics, 2005; and Statistics Canada, Crime Statistics in Canada, 2004, Juristat 25, No. 5. Ottawa, ON: Canadian Centre for Justice Statistics, 2005.

in accordance with the following principles. It is the fourth principle that is most relevant to our discussion.

1. The need to ensure the safety and security of all persons and property in Ontario.
2. The importance of safeguarding the fundamental rights guaranteed by the Canadian Charter of Rights and Freedoms and the Human Rights Code, 1981.
3. The need for cooperation between the police and the communities they serve.
4. The importance of respect for victims of crime and understanding of their needs.
5. The need for sensitivity to the pluralistic, multiracial, and multicultural character of Ontario society.
6. The need to ensure that police are representative of the communities they serve.*

Several police services in Ontario have established crime victim services units. The nature of each unit varies from municipality to municipality. Some units are crisis units with mental health workers who sometimes work in teams with police officers, while others are victim service units staffed by workers with mental health training. Still other units are composed of a professional executive and trained volunteers. There is no systematic data available on how many victims of what offenses are serviced by these units or on the results of their efforts.

Another reason for the drop in confidence in the police is the failure of police to improve the way that they respond to female victims of sexual assault despite many high profile failures. In Ontario, the Bill of Rights for Victims includes a right that a victim of sexual assault should be able to get an officer of the same gender but there is no evidence that this is ever implemented. Despite the IACP guidelines and the laws in Ontario, victims of sexual assault continue to miss out on basic respect from the police. The Jane Doe case is only one well-known example where a woman was not warned of a serial rapist operating near her residence and then was not well-treated by the investigators with the Toronto Police Service (Waller, 2010, 148–149). Recently, the Toronto Police Service sent an officer to talk to students at York University where he told them that they were more likely to be raped if they dressed like sluts. This led to such outrage that people took to the streets of both Toronto and Ottawa to protest.

Many senior Canadian police officers are members of the International Association of Chiefs of Police (IACP), which is the largest professional body for police leadership in North America. It has had a sustained interest in spelling out what police services should do to enhance their response to victims of crime. As early as 1983 the IACP developed its own guidelines which, among other things, drew attention to the need to respond to female victims of sexual assault with female officers.

In an effort to overcome the lack of leadership and implementation, the IACP worked with the U.S. Office for Victims of Crime to develop and implement the "21st Century" strategy (see Box 7.3) to enhance the police response to victims of crime (IACP, 2008; Waller, 2010, chapter 3). In 2008 the IACP developed a full set of tested procedures that are ready for implementation and that could be used in Canada (Waller, 2010, 55–76). They have proposed

---

*This is an unofficial version of Government of Ontario legal materials. http://www.e-laws .gov.on.ca/html/statutes/english/elaws_statutes_90p15_e.htm#BK0

some very simple, obvious, and practical ways of improving services to victims. Every officer responding to a 911-call should make the victim aware of which services are available to them with a short and simple informational brochure or wallet card (already a practice in England and Wales). Officers should be trained to listen to a victim with sensitivity and to provide emotional support. The guide was field tested both in Charlotte-Mecklenburg, North Carolina with a population of 800 000 and in other smaller police departments.

The IACP strategy places an emphasis on police leadership to enforce implementation by all police officers and of police support for victim assistance agencies outside the police service. The proposals include simple, non-time consuming services that the responding police office can provide to victims. In Canada some police services ask the officer to check a form if they provided information to a victim, but it is well known that this is not enough to get victims routinely the information they need. The IACP strategy shows how to use social science surveys to monitor performance of responding officers and of police services with which the victim interacts. While there are small victim service groups in police agencies in Canada, the mainstreaming of an appropriate response by police to victims falls far short of what is needed and what is possible.

A significant shift is needed in the way that Canadian police respond to victims of crime. This better way of meeting the needs of victims and encouraging more reporting of crime need not be costly. Waller (2010, 75–76) proposes the following four steps for Canadian police to reach international standards in their response to victims of crime:

1. Improve the proportion of victims reporting to police and assess progress by holding officers accountable for providing information in a timely manner to victims.
2. Develop and follow protocols to better meet the needs of victims who are women, children, Aboriginal, or disabled.
3. Develop a timetable to implement the IACP strategy package to make victims a primary concern of law enforcement.
4. Ensure independent surveys of victims who report to the police to monitor the extent to which their core needs for information, referral to services, and protection among others are being met.[*]

## Services for Victims of Crime

Canadian provinces provide health services without charge to all residents of Canada. As a result, health services for physical injuries, disease, or pregnancy incurred as a result of crime are provided to all victims in Canada. While this is similar to countries such as the United Kingdom, it is markedly different from the United States, where victims can incur significant medical and hospital costs which may or may not be reimbursed by state compensation programs.

However, crime victims also need emotional and psychological support following their victimization. Victims are likely to turn to their friends and family immediately following the crime to ask for advice: where should they turn? who should they call? what should they do?

---

[*]Irvin Waller. (2010). *Rights for Victims of Crime: Rebalancing Justice.* New York: Rowman and Littlefield.

# FOCUS BOX 7.3

## INTERNATIONAL ASSOCIATION OF CHIEFS OF POLICE GUIDE TO RESPECT VICTIMS OF CRIME

The Strategy Package includes an implementation strategy, toolkit, and training so that police can enhance their response to victims of crime. It emphasises leadership, partnering, training, and performance monitoring. Here are the seven stages:

- *Safety:* Protection from perpetrators and assistance in avoiding re-victimization
- *Support:* Assistance to enable participation in the criminal justice system processes and repair of harm
- *Information:* Concise and useful information about victims' rights, criminal justice system processes, and available victim services
- *Access:* Ability to participate in the justice system process and have ready availability to support services
- *Continuity:* Consistency in approaches and methods across agencies through all stages of the criminal justice process
- *Voice:* Opportunities to speak out and be heard on specific case processing issues and larger policy questions
- *Justice:* Receiving the support necessary to heal and seeing that perpetrators are held accountable.

Source: Adapted from International Association of Chiefs of Police. (2008). *Enhancing Law Enforcement Response to Victims: A 21st Century Strategy*. Alexandria, VA: International Association of Chiefs of Police.

The most universally recognized mental health issue surrounding victimization is post-traumatic stress disorder (PTSD). Following a crime, it is normal to feel shock, numbness, and disorientation. PTSD is diagnosed when such post-traumatic symptoms persist. Sufferers of PTSD usually have difficulty sleeping, mentally relive the experience, and feel a need to avoid normal situations that trigger memories of the original trauma. While research needs to continue on definitive solutions to PTSD, it is not clear to what extent the current state of services in Canada are adequately equipped to handle victims who suffer PTSD, neither in the adequacy of these services nor in the financial resources needed to pay for such treatment. If they have private insurance, for instance, through a large employer such as a university or government, they may be able to get a limited number of sessions with a therapist but most victims with PTSD or other emotional trauma require much more.

Victim assistance services are expanding in Canada but it is not known to what extent victims are aware of these services. It is also unknown if the services are adequate to meet all the needs and what proportion of victims with needs access these services. Victims of domestic violence and sexual assault are in a similar situation. There are a few child advocacy clinics. Child protection is generally available through provincial social services.

Statistics Canada attempted to do a complete census of victim service providers in Canada and estimated that there were 884 providers. This may sound extensive but it reflects the reality that there is a patchwork of services with many gaps. The study found that 40 percent of the service providers were based in police agencies,

23 percent were based in the community, 8 percent were based in the courts, and 17 percent were sexual assault crisis centres. These agencies had more than 3000 paid employees who, along with volunteers, served more than 400 000 victims annually. This represents about 10 percent of adults known to have been victimized, according to the Statistics Canada victimization survey. Remember, though, that we do not know how many others were not informed who could also have benefited from these services. Table 7.7 provides an overview of the services in Ontario.

**TABLE 7.7**   **Services for Victims of Crime in Ontario**

| Core Need | 2006 Draft Convention (article) | Services |
|---|---|---|
| **Support** | | |
| 1 | Recognition of victims, co-victims, good Samaritans (1) | |
| 2 | Information (7) | Victim Assistance & Referral Services (VCARS), Victim Quick Response Program (VQRP), SupportLink |
| 3 | Assistance (8)—referral by police | |
| | Assistance (8)—short term | Victim Support Line (VSL) |
| | Assistance (8)—medium term | Sexual Assault/Rape Crisis Centres (SACs) |
| | Special assistance because of age, gender, disability, race (3) | Sexual Assault/Rape Crisis Centres (SACs), Domestic Violence Court (DVC) Program, Partner Assault Response (PAR) Programs, Internet Child Exploitation (ICE) Counselling |
| **Justice** | | |
| 4 | Restitution from offender (10) | |
| | Restorative Justice (9)—respecting victim rights | |
| | Compensation from state (11) | Victim Quick Response Program (VQRP), Criminal Injuries Compensation Board (CICB) |
| 5 | Protection of victims, witnesses, and experts | Victim/Witness Assistance Program (VWAP), Child Victim/Witness Program |
| 6 | Access to justice and fair treatment | |
| **Good Government** | | |
| 7 | Commitment to reduce victimization | |
| 8 | Implementation | |

Source: http://www.attorneygeneral.jus.gov.on.ca/english/ovss/programs.asp

The City of London, Ontario has long been at the forefront of services for victims of domestic violence, such as child abuse and wife battering. Starting in 1972 the London Police Service implemented, in collaboration with the University of Western Ontario, police–social worker teams to respond to family violence—the police officer to control the situation and the social worker to work on solving the problems. After forming an inter-agency team to look at other complementary programs, the city has pioneered a battered wife advocacy clinic, world renowned innovations in its court systems, and recently an effective program called the 4th R to stop violence against women (Crooke et al., 2008; Institute for Prevention of Crime, 2009).

From a 2008 survey we know there were 3179 residents in battered wife shelters in Ontario: 51 percent (1634) were women and 49 percent (1545) were dependent children. Unlike the annual domestic violence census in the United States, there are no recent statistics on the number of women and children turned away. The U.S. survey shows that approximately one women and child are turned away every day for each woman and child in a shelter.

For victims of sexual assault, there are a number of sexual assault or rape crisis centres scattered across Canada, mainly in urban areas. Though there is little systematic research on these centres, they likely provide services as good as similar centres in other countries where research has shown their importance to victims (Waller, 2010). What is known is that they are typically not funded on a permanent basis and, despite the importance and effectiveness of their work, the salaries of staff are significantly lower than those of other professionals (police, lawyers, judges, etc.) working in criminal justice.

One interesting model for responding to victims of sexual assault is Nina's Place in Burlington, Ontario. Nina's Place provides specialized health care, police services, and agency referrals for women and men who have experienced sexual assault within the past 72 hours and recent domestic violence. The support is available whether the survivor has involved the police or not. It is named in memory of Nina de Villiers, the victim of a tragic assault in Burlington in 1991. Nina's Place is open 24 hours a day, seven days a week and the services are free (Nina's Place, 2011). The services offered by Nina's Place include a physical examination and treatment of any physical injuries, the collection and recording of evidence of the assault (forensic evidence within 24 hours) which could be used if the victim decides to involve the legal system, testing and counselling for possible pregnancy, risk assessment and safety planning, follow-up medical care and referral to community agencies, and counselling.

Basic responses to assist victims of crime in Canada lag behind services in other countries. In the United Kingdom, as mentioned above, victim support is available throughout the country and has now been changed into a National Victims Service by the United Kingdom, Ministry of Justice (2011). In New York City, Safe Horizons is the largest and most comprehensive victim service agency in the world. It annually advocates for more than 250 000 children, youth, and adults and fields 160 000 calls for help from victims. It has been providing shelter or transitional housing for women victims of domestic violence, rape crisis centres, child advocacy centres, court-based programs, homicide victim family services, and much more in five boroughs of New York city since 1978 (Waller, 2010, 85–93).

Waller (2010, 95–96) proposes the following priorities to bring Canada up to international standards:

1. Increase funding significantly, use general revenue, and pay professional salaries for the full range of victim support services, including sexual assault and domestic violence.
2. Develop and implement professional standards for support services along the lines of those in the United Kingdom.
3. Ensure that professional care for mental health trauma is available at no cost to the victim.
4. Schools and universities should teach citizens to provide emotional support to victims of crime.
5. Conduct surveys to measure the gaps between the core needs of victims and the services provided to them.*

## Restitution from the Offender, Compensation from the State, and Civil Remedies

Crime often involves direct financial loss, costs of services, and loss of quality of life. Victims have several potential ways of obtaining reparation to recover these losses:

1. An order of restitution made in a criminal court
2. A civil suit brought against the perpetrator of the crime
3. A civil suit brought against a third party whose negligence may have contributed to the crime
4. Restorative justice
5. A payment made by a state/provincial compensation board

**Restitution from the Offender** Though restitution is available though criminal and juvenile courts, it is not known how often it is considered appropriately, ordered, or paid. What we do know is that programs such as a model program in Saskatchewan (Box 7.4) and varied best practices in the United States do result in some restitution ordered and paid.

Experts have identified key steps to get restitution paid but these have not yet been applied in Canada. According to the U.S. National Crime Victim Centre (2009; Waller, 2010, 101–104), restitution would be paid if jurisdictions followed seven steps:

1. Victims must request restitution in writing.
2. Victims must demonstrate losses.
3. Identify assets, income, and liabilities of the offender at the beginning of the justice process.
4. Make restitution payments automatic.
5. Monitor payments.

---

*Irvin Waller. (2010). *Rights for Victims of Crime: Rebalancing Justice*. New York: Rowman and Littlefield.

# FOCUS BOX 7.4

## ADULT RESTITUTION AND CIVIL ENFORCEMENT PROGRAM, SASKATCHEWAN

Victims are helped to get payments from restitution orders by a unique provincial program in Saskatchewan which has two components—the Adult Restitution Program and the Restitution Civil Enforcement Program. The Ministry of Justice and Attorney General operates these programs to help victims receive restitution (Saskatchewan, 2007).

The Adult Restitution Program provides information to victims about restitution, monitors payments, works with offenders to help ensure payments are made, and works with Probation Officers and Prosecutors to enforce restitution orders. This program ensures the Crown is aware both that the victim has suffered financial loss as a result of the crime and the extent of the loss. A court will generally only order restitution if the amount of loss is "readily ascertainable."

The Restitution Civil Enforcement Program assists victims with the civil enforcement of restitution orders. The program pursues civil enforcement of the restitution order on the victims' behalf (when a supervised order has expired or in the case of stand-alone restitution orders) and this may include, but is not limited to, the garnishment of the offender's wages and bank accounts, and seizure of personal property.

There are pilot projects being funded by the Department of Justice. Nova Scotia is currently establishing a new Restitution Program which is modelled after Saskatchewan's Adult Restitution Program to assist victims in obtaining restitution payments.

Source: Adapted from Saskatchewan. (2011). *Restitution Civil Enforcement Program*. Regina, SK: Justice and Attorney General.

6. Enforce compliance.
7. Make restitution payments the priority over other government payments such as fines.*

**Civil Suits** Civil suits are available to victims in Canada but it is not known how often they are pursued. In the United States, there is a movement to increase their use because they can be an important way for victims to gain satisfaction in some cases. Victims of crime in the United States, are accessing legal assistance through the National Crime Victims Bar Association and National Crime Victims Law Institute.

The civil justice option may recover more reparations from the offender or other parties than both restitution and state compensation through the criminal justice system. In 2007 the National Crime Victims Bar Association—an affiliate of the National Centre for the Victims of Crime—published an easy-to-read booklet designed to give crime victims and those who work with victims a basic understanding of the potential for the civil justice system to meet some of their needs (Waller, 2010).

The National Crime Victim Law Institute mobilizes lawyers to fight for victim rights. It has created a database of hundreds of victims' rights case summaries, amicus curiae briefs, and more. It organizes an annual training

---

*Irvin Waller. (2010). *Rights for Victims of Crime: Rebalancing Justice*. New York: Rowman and Littlefield.

conference to foster enforcement of victim rights in criminal cases, and it has been remarkably successful in getting rights for victims of crime both under the federal and state legislation. In 2011 the Oregon Supreme Court in the Barrett case ordered a new sentencing hearing because the trial judge had not respected the rights of the victim, who had wished to be present for sentencing.

**Restorative Justice**  There are several models for restorative justice but the majority involve the basic elements of the victim and offender meeting with a professional coordinator or mediator. The goal is to reconcile the two parties.

Restorative justice was pioneered internationally in the area around Waterloo, Ontario by Mennonites in the 1970s. Indeed, in 1981, when the U.S. National Organization for Victim Assistance came to Toronto for their annual conference, Ontario was a leader in restitution and supported victim–offender reconciliation programs across the province. At that time, the Church Council on Justice and Corrections took up the challenge of spreading restorative justice models across Canada but these are more often pioneering projects rather than comprehensive policy. However, Nova Scotia had achieved one of the most extensive networks of restorative justice for juvenile offenders by 2010.

Though popular among criminologists, restorative justice models have not achieved their potential. As with many other victim innovations, the system has resisted these options. Furthermore, the victim movement has been quick to stress that victims are not always given the same attention as the offender. Restorative justice has become an international movement in which there is more often talk in university classrooms than action in practice in Canada.

Nevertheless, research by Strang and Sherman (2007) using random control trials has demonstrated in both Australia and United Kingdom that victims prefer restorative justice to the traditional system and that, on average, offenders who go through this process are less likely to reoffend.

**Compensation from Government**  Saskatchewan was the first province to provide compensation to victims of violence in 1967. Since then, many provincial governments have set up compensation programs to ensure that victims of violence are compensated for their loss; however, it seems that many victims are not aware of these programs. In Ontario for instance, only 4,000 victims apply each year, which is a relatively small proportion of those who are estimated to be eligible. When a person is injured or killed as result of a violent crime the maximum (lump sum) awarded is $25 000. Additionally, when a victim is unable to work due to their victimization, they may only be awarded a maximum of $1000 monthly to cover this loss. This is equivalent to $50 a day. Table 7.8 shows Ontario payments for 2009–2010.

Victims of violence in the United Kingdom are informed about compensation and can use a website (www.cica.gov.uk) to make a claim. The website provides instructions on how to make a claim, and it shows that the awards range from $1000 to $800 000. Because of the U.K. code of practice requiring the police to inform victims about services and the accessibility of victims to support services (police are required to inform the services that the person has been victimized), proportionately more victims get much more adequate awards than in most jurisdictions.

**TABLE 7.8**  **Criminal Injuries Compensation Board Awards 2009–2010**

| Awards (Lump Sums) | Amounts ($) | Average ($) claims awarded | |
|---|---|---|---|
| Pain and Suffering | 25,982,000.00 | 8,354.34 | |
| Loss of Wages | 754,000.00 | 767.82 | |
| Medical and Reports | 1,103,000.00 | 178.31 | |
| Funeral Expenses | 394,000.00 | 7,035.71 | |
| Legal Expenses | 70,000.00 | 409.36 | |
| Other Pecuniary Loss | 189,000.00 | 200.64 | |
| Other | 1,037,000.00 | 1,460.56 | |
| Total | 29,529,000.00 | Average Lump Sum Award: The average lump sum award was $7,800. This figure represents the total amount of compensation awarded as a lump sum divided by the total number of claims completed. When calculated against only those cases for which an award was granted, the average rises to $9,200. | Received: 4,031 applications<br><br>Heard: 3,792 claims<br><br>Completed: 3,548 claims |

Notes: Monetary amounts from CICB report reduced to no decimal points. Emergency funds paid out by VSS. First column in chart drawn from CICB data. Second column is obtained by permission from the CICB's Integrated Financial Information System (IFIS).

Source: © Queen's Printer for Ontario. Reproduced with permission.

To bring services and compensation up to international standards, some significant investment and rethinking is needed. After looking at what has been achieved in other jurisdictions, Waller (2010, 113–114) says there are several things Canada should do in order to establish a similar standard, including implementing seven key steps to collect restitution from offenders and paid to victims; ensuring that compensation paid by state meets costs and "pain" of victims from violent crime; providing mediation and restorative justice programs that respect the core needs of victims; and supporting research informing victims how to get restitution, civil suits orders, compensation, and restorative justice.

## Human Rights for Victims in Criminal Courts

In Canada's criminal and youth courts victims are still limited to the role of witness, although some will be allowed to submit a victim impact statement. The impact statement is usually a written statement, but in some cases it is a brief oral statement. Having said this, there are no data on the number of victims who are informed of this option or who take advantage of it.

Long standing arrangements in France as well as developments in the United States, some other countries, and the International Criminal Court (of which Canada is an active partner) provide a greater opportunity for victims to be empowered through representation and participation. For instance, France has provided victims a role in the court system for over 40 years. Victims have legal standing in the courtroom and they are represented as a civil party in the criminal justice system. This combination of criminal and civil proceedings allows for victims to defend their interests in the pursuit of truth, reparation, public safety, fair sentencing, and other issues simultaneously. Victims can raise concerns about personal safety and force a more thorough investigation of the offences against them.  Many cases in the French system result in restitution orders that are paid. By binding this measure to the courtroom, the victim has a more tangible and enforceable agreement to which both the accused and the victim can agree than is typically the case in restorative justice.

France is no longer alone in employing this civil/criminal combination system. Belgium, Germany, Japan, and Korea are some of the nations which have mobilized this system by providing legal assistance to victims in the last decade.

In the United States, the federal Justice for All Act passed in 2004 provides extensive rights to protect victims and facilitate restitution. In 2008, the State of California adopted Marsy's Law. Both of these provide models that will likely be adapted to Canada over the next few years; however, it should be noted that some people oppose these initiatives because of concerns that they compromise the rights of the accused.

The International Criminal Court, of which Canada is a signatory, provides even more extensive rights for victims in a system that continues to provide offenders with rights under an adversarial system (see Figure 7.2).

Table 7.9 provides a schematic of the current Criminal Code and Youth Criminal Justice Act and compares it to the U.S. Justice for All Act (Waller, 2010). The Canadian Corrections and Conditional Release Act provides some additional rights to victims.

It is striking to see the number of initiatives to support victims which have been implemented in other countries but which have not yet been addressed in Canada. There are six distinct stages during which victims in other countries

**FIGURE 7.2**  **Participation and Representation in the International Criminal Court**

| *Support* |
|---|
| Victims are protected and supported |
| Victims are given responses sensitive to gender, age, and other issues |
| *Justice* |
| Victim participation and representation (grouped) is paid by legal aid in adversarial trial and sentencing |
| Restitution is paid to victims through trust funds fed by offenders and others |
| *Good Government* |
| Trust funds contribute to awareness and prevention |
| Permanent infrastructure is paid for by governments with performance assessments |

Source: Irvin Waller. (2010). *Rights for Victims of Crime: Rebalancing Justice*. New York: Rowman and Littlefield, pp. 126–130, figure 6.4

**TABLE 7.9**   Comparison of Provisions for Victim Rights in the US Federal Justice for All Act with the Criminal Code and the Youth Criminal Justice Act

| Justice for All Act (U.S., 2004) | Criminal Code | Youth Criminal Justice Act |
| --- | --- | --- |
| 1. The right to be reasonably protected from the accused. | | |
| 2. The right to reasonable, accurate, and timely notice of any public court proceeding, or any parole proceeding, involving the crime or of any release or escape of the accused. | | |
| 3. The right not to be excluded any such public court proceeding, unless the court, after receiving clear and convincing evidence, determines that testimony by the victim would be materially altered if the victim heard other testimony at the proceeding. | | |
| 4. The right to be reasonably heard at any public proceeding in the district court involving release, plea, sentencing, or any parole proceeding. | Section 672.5 (14) | Section 50-1 |
| | Victim Impact Statements | Victim Impact Statements |
| | Right to have read at sentencing. | Right to have read at sentencing. |
| 5. The reasonable right to confer with the attorney for the Government in the case. | | |
| 6. The right to full and timely restitution as provided in law. | Section 83.17 (2) | Section 42-2-F |
| | Restitution | Restitution |
| | Judge has discretion | Judge has discretion |
| 7. The right to proceedings free from unreasonable delay. | | |
| 8. The right to be treated with fairness and with respect for the victims dignity and privacy. | | |

Source: Adapted from Irvin Waller. (2010). *Rights for Victims of Crime: Rebalancing Justice.* New York: Rowman and Littlefield, pp. 121–124

have some type of representation with their own lawyer and may be heard: the police investigation, the bail hearing, the case scheduling, the plea negotiation, the sentencing, and the review of prior convictions.

The European Union (EU) has gone an additional step to monitor performance that has lessons for Canada. In 2002 the EU adopted a comprehensive set of principles that were to be implemented over the next four years in every member country. To ensure that the legislation would be implemented, they set up a performance monitoring mechanism. One part of this mechanism included asking the governments whether everything had been implemented. However, it also included an independent monitoring—paid for by the EU—five years after the target dates for implementation had passed. This monitoring showed many gaps on which the EU is now working to correct with the individual governments. One important recommendation to improve the ways victims are treated at each of the different stages of the criminal justice process is that "the role of the victim throughout the criminal justice process should be respected and recognised as equal to that of the accused" (Victims Support Europe, 2010).

If there is one particular area in which Canada lags behind other countries, it is in providing victims of crime with ways to protect their interests in their safety, their search of the truth and justice in the judicial system. In order to reach international standards, Canada must make many more reforms and overcome the resistance in the traditional system. To make progress, Waller (2010, 132) has made a number of concrete propositions for Canada, including establishing a judicial system to provide remedies for victims who do not receive rights consistent with the law or accepted standards; providing funding for legal assistance so that victims can have their interests represented in court, request reparations, pursue payment of restitution and exercise their rights; paying for social science surveys to identify the extent to which victims get to realize their rights, and so identify systemic remedies; and experimenting with joint criminal and civil court proceedings to empower victims as well as legislation similar to the U.S. federal legislation.

## Stopping Violence against Victims and Preventing Repeat Victimization

By far the best way to reduce the $83 billion harm to victims which was highlighted at the beginning of this chapter (Zhang, 2011) is to prevent the victimization in the first place by investing in what is known to work. In a recent book written for (potential) victims, taxpayers, legislators, and indeed therefore for students, Waller (2008) draws upon research brought together by the World Health Organization, many leading criminologists, and government agencies to show that we have the knowledge to reduce violence against women, street violence, property crime and child abuse by 50 percent or more for a reinvestment of about 10 percent of what we are spending on reactive policies now (Waller, 2008, 131–136). As we saw earlier, expenditures on policing, courts, and corrections are at $20 billion and rising. If we can reinvest $2 billion smartly, it is likely that we could reduce losses to victims by $40 billion.

Several experimental projects have allowed sophisticated random control evaluations. They have demonstrated that it is indeed possible for government to tackle the negative life experiences of persons at-risk to offending in order to support them to live their lives without victimizing others (Waller, 2008, 21–36). For instance, programs such as Quantum Opportunities reach out to young men who are likely to drop out of school. As a result of mentoring, more of these at-risk youths are kept in school and the acts of violence perpetrated by those men are reduced. A Canadian initiative, Stop Now and Plan (SNAP), helps children and parents regulate youth aggression. This program has been subjected to rigorous evaluations, many of which have demonstrated positive outcomes among children under the age of 12. Every dollar spent on effective prevention programs saves at least seven dollars associated with incarcerating the individual in question (Waller, 2008, 21–36; Institute for Prevention of Crime, 2009, 2.1).

Equally scientific and impressive have been the testing of programs to prevent child abuse and subsequent adolescent offending. These programs have different names—Perry Pre-school Program, Public Health nurse visitation programs, and Triple P (Positive Parenting Program). These programs help parents in difficult situations to raise their children in a more consistent and caring way. In 2011 the U.S. Justice Department announced the creation of a new website, http://crimesolutions.gov, to help taxpayers judge the effectiveness of state and local anticrime programs. The selection and assessment is much more reliable because it is done transparently by experts rather than by public servants, as happens on a similar Canadian website.

The cost benefit analyses of the evaluation of these programs are very impressive and they show a huge return on investment. This is known as the prevention dividend (Waller, 2008). The work by the Washington State Institute on Public Policy, done directly for the legislature of the State of Washington, is an important and continuing source of additional and detailed updates. We can also look to England's Youth Inclusion Projects, a series of programs developed to reach the most difficult teenagers and significantly reduce their offending. The United Kingdom did not wait to test and re-test the Youth Inclusion Projects. Instead it multiplied them in 72 low-income housing estates with an evaluation. When they succeeded again, they doubled the projects. Canada's National Crime Prevention Centre still only funds limited replications of these projects, and the time is long overdue to make investment in a national program that draws from the successes achieved in other countries.

Youth are also involved in many of the sexual assaults occurring in elementary and secondary schools, universities and colleges, and neighbourhoods in Canada. Fortunately, Canadian research confirms that when we change male attitudes towards violence and women, we can expect to reduce most common types of violence against women. One strategy that stands out is the "4th R", which was tested in a large scale random control trial in Canada. It changes the attitudes of teenagers in high school regarding alcohol and drug abuse, violence, and sexual assault against women. This program was developed by the partnership of the University of Western Ontario and the City of London, Ontario described earlier in this chapter (Crooke et al., 2008, Institute for Prevention of Crime, 2009, 1.2; Waller, 2010, 144).

Some of the successful models to reduce crime focus on reducing the risk to victims. The first proven prevention of residential burglary occurred in Seattle in the 1970s with more than 50 percent of residential burglaries avoided.

A similar strategy in Kirkholt, England achieved similar results but focused on repeat burglary victims and showed more than an 80 percent reduction rate (Waller, 2008, 53–66).

The World Health Organization, the United Nations Commission on Crime Prevention and Criminal Justice, the U.S. National Research Council, and the 2007 Alberta Task Force on Reducing Crime have called for a three-pronged approach to reduce victimization. This approach combines: (1) enforcement, (2) community treatment for persons at risk of offending, and (3) prevention. All the organizations stress the importance of mobilizing key agencies such as schools, social services, housing, and policing to collaboratively diagnose the solutions to the problems, implement the solutions, and follow up with careful evaluation of the results.

One way to get the re-investment is to establish a task force that analyzes what we are currently doing, identifies the gaps with international knowledge, and then recommends the necessary actions. This is exactly what the Province of Alberta did in 2007 and as a result it became the leading jurisdiction in North America in implementing the best approaches for reducing crime. It implemented a three-pronged, evidence-based strategy of enforcement, treatment, and prevention while also committing an additional $500 million over three years as part of a long-term, comprehensive strategy. The program was implemented by a permanent leadership centre called the Community Safety Secretariat that is composed of senior officials assigned to the centre on a permanent basis. The program, which became permanent in 2011, will be evaluated using indicators of reduction in victimization and harm to victims. Another spectacular, but little known and non-replicated, Canadian example is the Winnipeg Auto-Theft Suppression strategy (see Chapter 15) which is saving Winnipeg residents about $40 million each year in auto insurance premiums.

A growing number of municipalities including Edmonton, Montreal, Ottawa, and the Waterloo Region have also established permanent leadership centres to diagnose problems and implement solutions. However, these cities have not made the financial investment that research shows is required to provide successful programs.

We now know a great deal about how to stop people from becoming victims of crime. Alberta, major Canadian cities, and other jurisdictions are aware of what can be achieved and are implementing policies consistent with the data on what works. Waller (2010, 149–151) identifies a number of ways through which we can do better to reduce the number of victims.

1. Shift crime policies to pre-emptive strategies orchestrated by a small secretariat to diagnose problems and to mobilise key sectors such as schools, housing, and policing, following the impressive evidence-based strategy of Alberta,
2. Invest adequately in programs that have demonstrated their effectiveness, such as repeat victimization programs, compulsory curricula, such as the 4th R to reduce sexual assault, Triple P to stop child abuse, and the strategies used in Winnipeg to reduce car theft.
3. Continue to tackle alcohol and drug abuse among younger adults.*

*Irvin Waller. (2010). *Rights for Victims of Crime: Rebalancing Justice.* New York: Rowman and Littlefield.

# Systemic Ways to Shift, Reinvest, and Rebalance Justice for Crime Victims

In the first section of this chapter, we saw the prevalence and impact of crime on victims. In the second section, we saw the origins of the victimology movement in Canada and the development of international standards. In third section, we saw areas where Canada could advance towards those standards to better meet the needs of crime victims.

Throughout this chapter, we have seen that the traditional criminal justice system has resisted the social science research and the shift that is needed. It has even resisted the implementation of the recommendations from the 1998 Parliamentary Report—*A Voice not a Veto*—and McMurtry's Report in Ontario in 2007. In 2010, Waller looked at the innovations in the EU and the U.S. that are making the shift comprehensively to effective prevention, services, and rights for victims of crime (2010, 154–164). He focused on five key components for a successful action plan that would ensure comprehensive implementation. These include an office for victims of crime, standards and training, evaluation and ombudspersons, social science surveys to foster success, and research and development.

In this section we will look at three key ways to successfully achieve the shift and re-investment—model legislation, an independently funded institute, and an amendment to the Charter of Rights and Freedoms. We will then discuss the key recommendations from a national symposium in 2011 that looked at ways to help Canada reach the international standards.

## Model Legislation

Fourteen international experts met in 2005 to prepare a draft report for a UN Convention that would speed up action by governments to follow through on the 1985 resolution to prevent victimization and to implement services and rights for victims. Waller has adapted this draft into a model law that could be adopted by either a U.S. state or a Canadian province (2010, 173–183).

The model law is divided into three major sections on support, justice, and good government. The support section includes subsections on recognition, information, and assistance. The justice section makes provisions for restitution and repayment, protection from the accused, participation, and representation. The good government section covers effective policies to reduce victimisation and the all-important issues of implementation.

## An Independently Funded Institute

An office for victims of crime responsible for pushing the victims' agenda, as well as a federal ombudsman for victims of crime is not enough. We need to create a permanently funded institute. Such an institute, while requiring contributions from legal professionals, social researchers, and victim's rights agencies, must be independent of them all. This institute would likely be based out of a Canadian university and would function as a central hub for education, research, and policy observation. It would work in close cooperation with service agencies in the community, the Federal Victim's Ombudsman, and legal practitioners.

One such institute has already been created in Europe and could serve as a best practices model for a Canadian institute. INTERVICT is the International Victimology Institute Tilburg. It was launched by Tilburg University in the Netherlands in 2005, and it is an institute that has continually expanded research on victimization and victim assistance within Europe. It has conducted extensive evaluations of the implementation of victim legislation in the European Union and has been leading the world on issues of victimization (identity theft, human trafficking, online victimization, and more).

## An Amendment to the *Canadian Charter of Rights and Freedoms*

The *Canadian Charter of Rights and Freedoms* includes a number of paragraphs protecting the rights of accused and convicted persons against the powers of the state. At this time, it does not include any rights for victims of crime. So the traditional rights of defendants "trump" the basic human rights of victims that have been recognized by the UN but not yet by Canada.

Crime victims need their rights to safety, reparation, and justice to be recognized by an amendment to the Charter. Waller proposes that such an amendment could include the following wording: "To have the rights of victims of crime to safety, reparation and justice respected" *and* "Balanced fairly, against rights of the accused or convicted offender" *and* "heard through participation and representation equal to that of the accused in all judicial and administrative proceedings" (Waller, 2010, 168–170).

## Key Actions

Every year, Justice Canada encourages a Crime Victim Awareness Week in April. In 2011 the Faculty of Social Sciences at the University of Ottawa organized a national symposium—Crime Victim Rights: Reaching for International Standards. Delegates were invited from the federal, provincial, and municipal governments as well as national associations.

The costs of implementing a national action plan that would include the proposals in this chapter were discussed based on estimates by Waller (2010, 164–168; 2008, 132–134). The order of the re-investment needed to implement all of the recommendations discussed in this chapter is approximately 10 percent of the expenditures on the traditional criminal justice system. Finding this 10 percent can be done gradually over a five-year period.

The Canadian Resource Centre for Victims of Crime and the International Organization for Victim Assistance were the principal partners for the National Symposium. Inspired by the debates, they have called for the creation of:

1. A **national action plan**, including standards such as those in the UK and the model law (see above), that would apply to policing, services, restitution, compensation, prosecution and courts; that would be sensitive to special needs such as those of women, children, and Aboriginal populations; and that would have leadership offices for victims of crime to implement
2. A **provincial victim advocate**, supported by **surveys** to provide better data and an **Institute** to focus on research and development

3. **Provincial and municipal prevention strategies** to effectively reduce crime and promote community safety
4. **Permanent funding** to be established that is equivalent to at least **10 percent** of the current expenditures on criminal justice to be used for prevention, victim services, and rights
5. An **amendment** to the Charter

In this chapter, we have seen that the needs of victims have been overlooked by the traditional system. Starting with the landmark UN Declaration—the *magna carta* for victims—we have seen that an increase in the awareness of the needs of victims internationally has led to some cautious steps in Canada. These steps have included improvements in policing, victim services and compensation, and courts and restitution, but there is still a long way to go. Rebalancing the justice system to respect victims' human rights requires more than ad hoc solutions. Instead, it requires a national action plan, serious investments in that plan, investments in effective prevention, and possibly an amendment to the Charter.

One of the most important steps for helping legislators to make the reinvestments is to get the knowledge out to voters, taxpayers, and (potential) victims of crime, while showing how the shift to stopping victimization and implementing victim rights is in the interest of (potential) victims and taxpayers. Social media are fast growing as a way to get these messages out, particularly in situations where the status quo is so resistant to change as it has been for victims of crime. Many leading think tanks, such as the Canadian Resource Centre for Victims of Crime (http://crcvc.ca/en/), the renowned Vera Institute for Justice in New York City (http://www.vera.org/), the National Crime Victim Law Institute (http://law.lclark.edu/centers/national_crime_victim_law_institute/), and academic experts such as Waller (http://www.irvinwaller.org) are using Twitter to share key reports with the general public.

## Summary

- About one in four adult Canadians is a victim of some type of common crime every year. Though relatively few are victims of serious crime, the cumulative harm to victims was estimated at more than $80 billion for 2008.

- Canada resolved at the UN General Assembly in 1985 to invest in preventing crime and guaranteeing human rights for victims of crime (Declaration of Basic Principles of Justice for Victims) but it has not implemented these promises.

- Canadians paid more than $20 billion in 2010 for a traditional system of police, courts, and corrections that still limits the role of the victim to complainant and witness. Few of these funds have been invested in preventing victimization, assisting victims, and protecting human rights of victims.

- The International Association of Chiefs of Police has developed strategic ways to enhance the police response to victims of crime but their Canadian members have done little to implement these proven strategies.

- Surveys for more than 30 years have shown that victims of sexual violence rarely report to police but little has been done to improve this situation.

- The personnel in victim assistance services, sexual assault crisis centres, and shelters for battered women are not paid salaries that are competitive with wages in the traditional criminal justice system. Unlike other criminal justice agencies, victims' organizations often have to re-apply for funding every year.

- Compensation to victims for criminal injuries varies from province to province and in most cases is inadequate.

- Restitution and restorative justice are popular discussion points for criminologists but have been losing ground in application in Canada despite the pioneering role played by Canadian groups in the 1970s and 1980s.

- Traditional criminal courts appear to ignore or find ways to overlook sections in the criminal code designed to protect victims, such as the victim fine surcharge, restitution, and victim impact statements.

- Canada is at the cutting edge of programs to stop victimization, such as the Alberta Crime Reduction Strategy, the Winnipeg Auto Theft Suppression Strategy, municipal crime prevention strategies and the 4th R program, but it lacks any overall action plan and funding to shift from over-reliance on the traditional criminal justice system;

- Ways of rebalancing the system to meet needs and human rights for victims of crime are well known but have not yet been applied in Canada. These include social science surveys, a research and training institute, national standards, and much more.

## QUESTIONS FOR CRITICAL THINKING

1. What are the needs of victims of crime and how do these differ from the desire for more punishment?
2. Which needs and human rights for crime victims are overlooked or made worse by the traditional criminal justice system?
3. What are the actions that would be needed by the police, services and compensation, and courts and restitution to meet the needs of victims of crime?
4. What is the role of social science in rebalancing criminal policy from over-reliance on the traditional criminal justice system to stopping victimisation and respecting human rights of victims of crime?
5. How would a victimology institute, social science surveys of victims, and national standards rebalance justice for victims of crime?

## NET WORK

1. What practical information exists on the Internet about your home town on
   (a) How to report a crime to the police?
   (b) What services are available in your community for different types of crime victims, including a break-in, an aggravated sexual assault, and a person killed by a drunk driver?

(c) How to assess harm to victims and apply for compensation from the state if you are injured in a crime and what are the key conditions, including the maximum award that can be provided?

(d) How to apply for restitution and get it paid?

(e) What is your right to a victim impact statement and how do you exercise it?

2. Compare your answers to these questions to the following:

(a) the information on the website of Justice Canada for crime victims (http://www.victimsmatter.gc.ca/index.html)

(b) help you can get from the Federal Ombudsman for Victims of Crime (http://www.victimsfirst.gc.ca/index.html )

(c) the British Code of *Practice for Victims of Crime* (http://www.direct.gov .uk/prod_consum_dg/groups/dg_digitalassets/@dg/@en/documents/ digitalasset/dg_073647.pdf) and the Criminal Injuries Compensation Authority(http://www.justice.gov.uk/guidance/compensation-schemes/ cica/index.htm)

3. Locate the victim services act or the bill of rights for victims of crime for your province and

(a) compare the provisions with those stated in the UN Declaration of Basic Principles of Justice for Victims of Crime and Abuse of Power (http://www.un.org/documents/ga/res/40/a40r034.htm).

(b) propose your best action to get them implemented.

## KEY TERMS

compensation from the state; pg. 222

harm to crime victims; pg. 220

repeat victimization; pg. 220

restitution from the offender; pg. 222

rights of crime victims; pg. 221

victim fine surcharge; pg. 226

victimization surveys; pg. 219

## BIBLIOGRAPHY

Amernic, Jerry. (1984). *Victims: Orphans of Justice*. Toronto: McClelland and Stewart-Bantam.

Besserer, Sandra, and Catherine Trainor. (2000). "Criminal Victimization in Canada, 1999." *Juristat* 20(10).

Campbell, Rebecca. (2006). "Rape Survivors' Experiences with the Legal and Medical Systems: Do Rape Victim Advocates Make a Difference?" *Violence Against Women* 12(1): 30–35.

Canada, Canadian Federal-Provincial Task Force on Justice for Victims of Crime. (1983). *Final Report*. Ottawa, ON: The Task Force.

Canada, Department of Justice. (2004). "Canadian Statement of Basic Principles of Justice for Victims of Crime, 2003." Ottawa, ON: Department of Justice Canada; available at http://www.justice.gc.ca/eng/pi/pcvi-cpcv/pub/03/princ.html, accessed April 4, 2010.

Canada, Standing Committee on Justice and Human Rights. (2000). *Victims' Rights—A Voice Not a Veto*. Ottawa, ON: Parliament of Canada, 2000.

Clarke, Lorenne, and Debra Lewis. (1977). *Rape: The Price of Coercive Sexuality*. Toronto: Women's Press.

Crooks, Claire, D., Wolfe, R. Hughes, P. Jaffe, and D. Chiodo. (2008). *Development, Evaluation and National Implementation of a School Based Program to Reduce Violence and Related Risk Behaviours: Lessons from the 4th R*. Ottawa, ON: Institute for the Prevention of Crime.

European Council. (2001). *Framework Decision of 15 March 2001 on the Standing of Victims in Criminal Proceedings* (2001/220/JHA). Brussels: Commission of the European Communities.

Fisher, Bonnie, and John J. Sloan. (2007). *Campus Crime: Legal, Social and Policy Perspectives*. Springfield, IL: Charles C. Thomas.

Gannon, Maire, and Karen Mihorean. (2005). "Criminal Victimization in Canada, 2004." *Juristat* 25(7).

Gaudreault, Arlène, and Irvin Waller. (2001). "Xe Symposium international de victimologie: Textes choisies du Symposium." Paper presented at the Association québécoise Plaidoyer-Victimes, Montréal, August.

Groenhuijsen, Marc, and Rianne Letschert (eds.). (2009). *Compilation of International Victims' Rights Instruments*. Nijmegen, The Netherlands: Wolf Legal Publishers.

Institute for the Prevention of Crime. (2009). *Making Cities Safer: Action Briefs for Municipal Stakeholders, Number 3*, March. Ottawa, ON: University of Ottawa.

International Association of Chiefs of Police. (2008). *Enhancing Law Enforcement Response to Victims: A 21st Century Strategy*. Alexandria, VA: International Association of Chiefs of Police.

International Victimology Institute Tilburg. (2006). "Towards Implementation of the UN Declaration on Basic Principles of Justice for Victims of Crime and Abuse of Power—Preparing a Draft Convention on the Rights of Victims of Crime, Abuse of Power and Terrorism." Report on Expert Group Meeting. Tilburg: University of Tilburg.

Kilpatrick, Dean, Heidi Resnick, Kenneth J. Ruggiero, Lauren Conoscenti, and Jenna McCauley. (2007). *Drug-facilitated, Incapacitated, and Forcible Rape: A National Study*. Washington, DC: U.S. Department of Justice, National Institute of Justice.

Mothers Against Drunk Driving Canada. (2010). "The Magnitude of the Alcohol/Drug-Related Crash Problem in Canada." *MADD Canada*; available at http://madd.ca/english/research/magnitudememo.html, accessed April 3, 2010.

McMurtry, Roy. (2008). "Report on Financial Assistance for Victims of Crime in Ontario." Toronto:OntarioMinistryoftheAttorneyGeneral;availableathttp://www.attorneygeneral.jus.gov.on.ca/english/about/pubs/mcmurtry/mcmurtry_report.pdf, accessed April 24, 2010.

Miller, Ted, Mark Cohen, and Brian Wiersema. (1996). *Victim Costs and Consequences: A New Look*. Washington, DC: National Institute of Justice, U.S. Department of Justice.

National Crime Victim Bar Association. (2007). *Civil Justice for Victims of Crime*. Washington, DC: National Center for Victims of Crime.

National Sheriffs' Association. (2008). *First Response to Victims of Crime: A Guide Book for Law Enforcement Officers*. Washington, DC: U.S. Department of Justice.

Newmark, Lisa. (2006). *Crime Victims' Needs and VOCA-Funded Services: Findings and Recommendations from Two National Studies*. Washington, DC: National Institute of Justice.

Newmark, Lisa, Judy Bonderman, Barbara Smith, and E. Blaine Liner. (2006). *The National Evaluation of State Victims of Crime Act Assistance and Compensation Programs: Trends and Strategies for the Future* (Full Report). Washington, DC: National Institute of Justice.

Nina's Place. (2011). Available at http://www.jbmh.com/Home.aspx?PageID=550&mid=_ctl0_MainMenu__ctl1-menu Item000, accessed April 10, 2011.

Ombudsman of Ontario. (2007). *Adding Insult to Injury: Investigation into the Treatment of Victims by the Criminal Injuries Compensation Board.* Toronto, ON: Ombudsman of Ontario.

Ontario, Criminal Injuries Compensation Board. (2010). *35th Annual Report—2009/2010;* available at http://www.cicb.gov.on.ca/en/about3.htm, accessed March 25, 2010. Ontario. (1984). Government Consultation on Victims of Violent Crime. Toronto: Secretary for Justice.

Perreault, Samuel, and Shannon Brennan. (2010). "Criminal Victimization in Canada, 2009." *Juristat* 30(2).

Safe Horizons. (2011). Available at http://www.safehorizon.org/index/about-us-1/who-we-are-52.html, accessed April 3, 2011.

Saskatchewan. (2011). *Restitution Civil Enforcement Program.* Regina, SK: Justice and Attorney General; available at http://www.justice.gov.sk.ca, accessed July 10, 2011.

———. (2007). *Victim Services Branch.* Regina, SK: Justice and Attorney General; available at http://www.justice.gov.sk.ca/victimsservices, accessed July 10, 2011.

Seymour, Anne, and Steve Derene. (2003). "An Oral History of the Crime Victim Assistance Field." University of Akron; available at http://vroh.uakron.edu/index.php, accessed April 3, 2010.

Skogan, W., and K. Frydl. (2004). *Fairness and Effectiveness in Policing: The Evidence.* Washington, DC: National Academies Press.

Statistics Canada. (2009). *Residents of Canada's Shelters for Abused Women, 2008.* Ottawa, ON: Canadian Centre for Justice Statistics.

———. (2009b). *Police Personnel and Expenditures.* Ottawa, ON: Canadian Centre for Justice Statistics; available at http://www.statcan.gc.ca/daily-quotidien/101215/dq101215c-eng.htm, accessed March 25, 2011.

Sauvé, Julie. "Victim Services in Canada: Results from the Victim Services Survey 2007/2008." Justice Canada Website, Victims of Crime Research Digest; available at http://www.justice.gc.ca/eng/pi/rs/rep-rap/rd-rr/rr07_vic4/p3.html, accessed March 30, 2010.

———. (2005). "Crime Statistics in Canada, 2004." *Juristat* 25(5).

Sherman, Lawrence W., and Heather Strang. (2007). *Restorative Justice: The Evidence.* London: The Smith Institute.

Thomas, Mikhail. (2004). "Adult Criminal Court Statistics, 2003/2004." *Juristat* 24(12).

United States, U.S. Department of Justice, Bureau of Justice Statistics. (2010). "Criminal Victimization in the United States, 2007 Statistical Tables." Available at http://bjs.ojp.usdoj.gov/content/pub/pdf/cvus07.pdf, accessed April 8, 2010.

———. (2009). *Criminal Victimization, 2008.* Washington, DC: Office of Justice Programs.

United States, U.S. Department of Justice, Office for Victims of Crime. (1999). *International Crime Victim Compensation Directory.* Washington, DC: U.S. Department of Justice.

———. (2002). *Restitution: Making it Work.* Washington, DC: U.S. Department of Justice.

———. (2009). "Nation Wide Analysis—Performance Reports." *U.S. Department of Justice, Office of Justice Programs, 2009.* Available at http://www.ojp.usdoj.gov/ovc/fund/vocanpr_va08.html, accessed April 7, 2010.

United States, U.S. Department of Justice, Office on Violence Against Women. (2007). *2006 Biennial Report to Congress on the Effectiveness of Grant Programs Under the Violence Against Women Act.* Washington, DC: U.S. Department of Justice.

———. (2006) *S.T.O.P. Program Services, Training, Officers, Prosecutors, Annual Report 2006.* Washington, DC: U.S. Department of Justice.

United States, U.S. Government Accountability Office. (2009). *Crime Victim Rights Act: Increasing Victim Awareness and Clarifying Applicability to the District of Columbia Will Improve Implementation of the Act.* Washington, DC: U.S. Government Accountability Office.

United Nations, General Assembly. (1985). *Declaration of Basic Principles of Justice for Vvictims of Crime and Abuse of Power* (GA/res/40/34). New York: United Nations; available at http://www.un.org/documents/ga/res/40/a40r034.htm, accessed July 8, 2011.

United Nations, Office for Drugs and Crime. (1999). *Guide for Policy Makers on the Implementation of the Declaration of basic principles of justice for victims of crime and abuse of power.* New York: United Nations.

———. (1999). *Handbook on Justice for Victims on the Use and Application of the Declaration of Basic Principles of Justice for Victims of Crime and Abuse of Power.* New York: United Nations.

———. (2005). *Guidelines on Justice for Child Victims and Witnesses.* New York: United Nations.

United States. (1982). *President's Task Force on Victims of Crime Final Report.* Washington, DC: U.S. Government's Printing Office.

van Dijk, Jan, Robert Manchin, John van Kesteren, and Gergely Hideg. (2007). *The Burden of Crime in the EU: A Comparative Analysis of the European Survey of Crime and Safety.* Brussels: Gallup Europe.

Victim Support Europe. (2010). *Victims in Europe: Implementation of the EU Framework Decision on the Standing of Victims in the Criminal Proceedings in the Member States of the European Union.* Lisbon: Associação Portuguesa de Apoio à Vítima.

Waller, Irvin. (2010). *Rights for Victims of Crime: Rebalancing Justice.* New York: Rowman and Littlefield.

———. (2008). *Less Law, More Order: The Truth about Reducing Crime.* Westport, CT: Praeger Imprint Series, 2006/Ancaster, Manor House.

———. (2004). "Harnessing Criminology and Victimology Internationally." In John Winterdyk and Liqun Cao (eds.), *Lessons from International/Comparative Criminology/ Criminal Justice* (pp. 233–48). Toronto, ON: De Sitter.

Waller, Irvin, and Norm Okihiro. (1978). *Burglary, the Victim and the Public.* Toronto: University of Toronto Press.

Wang, Ching-Tung, and John Holton. (2007). "Total Estimated Cost of Child Abuse and Neglect in the United States." *Prevent Child Abuse America*; available at http://www.preventchildabuse.org/about_us/media_releases/pcaa_pew_economic_impact_study_final.pdf, accessed April 4, 2010.

Wemmers, Jo-Anne. (2003). *Introduction a la victimologie.* Montreal: Les Presses de l'Université de Montreal.

Wing-Cheong Chan (ed). (2008). *Support for Victims of Crime in Asia.* London: Routledge.

World Health Organization. (2002). *World Report on Violence and Health.* Geneva: World Health Organization.

———. (2004). *Economic Dimensions of Interpersonal Violence.* Geneva: World Health Organization.

———. (2009). *Violence Prevention: The Evidence.* Geneva: World Health Organization, 2009.

———. (2010). *Preventing Intimate Partner and Sexual Violence against Women: Taking Action and Generating Evidence.* Geneva: World Health Organization.

Zhang, Ting. (2011). *Costs of Crime in Canada, 2008.* Department of Justice Canada; available at http://www.justice.gc.ca/eng/pi/rs/rep-rap/2011/rr10_5/index.html, accessed March 25, 2011.

# Explanations of Crime

The field of criminology is multidisciplinary. Lawyers, sociologists, political scientists, psychologists, biologists, physicians, historians, and philosophers all may consider the study of crime as part of their discipline. Nowhere is this diversity more apparent than in the development of theories of the causes of crime. Why some people commit crime while others do not has been addressed from a variety of perspectives and we review some of the major ones in the chapters in Part 2.

Part 2 covers many of the most popular explanations of crime. The debate over which of these explanations is "best" has often become heated, and no attempt is made to resolve this issue here. It would be premature to impose such a judgment on a field that has been described as consisting of "a number of fitful leads from one partially examined thesis to another."* Instead, each theory is presented by an author who has had experience (and some sympathy) with it, and who presents the theory's strengths and weaknesses. A number of researchers are now trying to synthesize several of the different approaches, and some of the authors discuss this integrative work.

Part 2 illustrates how theories of crime causation have developed over time. In Chapter 8, several of the earliest approaches to the explanation of crime are discussed. The most important point made in this chapter is that explanations of crime arise from particular historical milieus and reflect the social and intellectual fashions of the day. Chapter 9 presents theories that focus on the traits of individuals. The psychological perspective has been with us for many years and is still popular today. Chapters 10 to 15 are concerned with the sociological explanations of crime. They illustrate the diverse ways in which social structure and social processes may promote or restrain criminal behaviour.

---

* Paul Rock. (1980). "Has Deviance a Future?" In Hubert M. Blalock (ed.), *Sociological Theory and Research* (pp. 290–303). New York: Free Press.

# Early Theories of Criminology

## 8

**Tullio Caputo**

CARLETON UNIVERSITY

**Rick Linden**

UNIVERSITY OF MANITOBA

W e begin this chapter by exploring the context within which modern criminology developed. Societal beliefs relating crime to superstition and sin were slowly replaced during the Enlightenment by naturalistic explanations based on the idea that people are free and rational beings. This development was consistent with the struggle for individual rights and freedoms that was gaining prominence during this period and the view that the social order reflected a social contract between the individual and the state. These changes were based on the growing power of the rising merchant classes and the reduced influence of the feudal aristocracy, whose power rested on the ownership of the land and the loyalty of the peasants who lived and worked on it.

Next we discuss the rise of the Classical School of criminology during this era. The principle of "let the punishment fit the crime" represents the core of the philosophy of the Classical School and its belief in people's ability to reason and to act rationally. Although this reform provided the basis for our modern Criminal Code, it was found to be too inflexible in practice. The argument of later Positive criminologists that mitigating circumstances had to be considered when dealing with crime and criminals led to further reforms in the manner in which we dealt with criminals. The chapter concludes with an examination of the early theories that searched for the causes of crime in the biological make-up of individual offenders.

## Learning Objectives

After reading this chapter, you should be able to

- Discuss the context within which modern explanations of crime and criminality were developed.
- Identify the founders of the Classical School of criminology, the key principles of this approach, and the impact of this school on our legal system.
- Outline the criticisms of the Classical approach and the changes in the legal process that were influenced by the Positive criminologists.
- Describe the basic features of the Positive School of criminology, and outline their approach and key principles.

- Show how the ideas advanced by the Positive School influenced other researchers to search for the biological causes of crime.
- Discuss how biological explanations of criminality influenced the development of this field at the beginning of the 20th century.

Prior to the 18th century, theories about crime were inspired primarily by religious beliefs and superstition. As Zilborg (1969, 11) notes,

> [F]rom the most primitive beginnings of human history, man [sic] believed in the existence of spirits and magic, and . . . from the earliest days of his existence on earth, he began to ascribe various unusual phenomena of nature to the activities of evil spirits. This naturally led him to believe that any pathology in human behavior must be due to an evil spirit.

The link between evil spirits and wrongdoing is an important one for many religions. For example, Judeo-Christian teachings provide two powerful explanations outlining the role of evil spirits in sinful behaviour: temptation and possession. The idea of temptation is based on the belief that people exercise their free will and choose to act in particular ways, even ways they know to be wrong. Indeed, the Devil is thought to be at work tempting people. Of course, righteous believers can resist the Devil's powerful allure by drawing strength from their faith. They are encouraged to do this by religious leaders who employ images of hell-fire and threats of eternal damnation to help steel the spines of the faithful who might otherwise waver. These images and beliefs about temptation imply that people who succumb are weak and morally inferior beings. In this way, the poor, the destitute, and other unfortunate members of society have been held responsible for their situations throughout much of history. Their misfortunes are seen as the result of their own moral failures. These beliefs also provide the basis for our ideas about deterrence. Thus most people believe that the threat of severe punishment should be enough to persuade people to avoid engaging in misdeeds.

The second, and equally powerful, Judeo-Christian imagery linking sin to evil spirits is that of possession. Wrongdoers were often suspected of being possessed by the Devil or some other malevolent spirit. These unfortunate individuals were thought to have little hope of recovering and were treated quite harshly. A host of horrifying tortures were used to drive the evil spirits from their bodies, and evidence of guilt was determined through a series of trials designed to differentiate between the righteous and the sinner. These included trial by battle, trial by ordeal, trial by fire, and trial by water. In most cases, the accused had little to look forward to, whether innocent or guilty, since these trials were extremely severe and often fatal.

These practices reflect a belief in the power of supernatural forces. They reached their zenith during the Middle Ages with the introduction of the notorious Inquisition and the witch craze it spawned. This was a period marked by tremendous social upheaval and rapid social change. Western Europe was in the midst of the transition from feudalism to capitalism. Confusion and fear followed the revolution that was underway in the material and intellectual worlds of the day. Those in power—the political and religious elites—used every means at their disposal to protect their positions and privileges. They sought to preserve the status quo and maintain the existing order. This included using both religious and civil laws. As Angell (1965, 118) notes,

> The development of a common criminal law was aided by the close connection between crime and sin. . . . [P]unishment meant expiation. It is only one step from the fear of gods' displeasure to the desire for reassurance concerning the integrity of the moral order.

Medieval society was forced to change because existing social arrangements did not meet the needs of a growing European population. Poverty, misery, wars, and sickness ravaged the masses. These problems led people to question and even to challenge longstanding practices and beliefs, including those related to civil and religious authority. For example, the Protestant Reformation shook the foundations of the Christian world by challenging the power and authority of the Catholic Church. Throughout Europe, those in power were increasingly being held to account for deteriorating material conditions and social problems. It is in this context that the Inquisition and the witch craze found fertile ground. The religious and political elites began to seek ways of diverting attention from themselves and of silencing the rebellious members of society. Blaming the existing social problems on the influence of the Devil and other evil spirits provided a means of meeting both objectives. First, this diverted the public's attention from the elites and helped to place blame for social problems on individuals who were identified as being possessed or otherwise in league with the Devil. Second, those in power made themselves indispensable by arguing that they alone had the knowledge and ability to deal with the threat of the Devil on earth (Harris, 1974).

Importantly, these developments helped to blur the distinctions between sin and crime and provided ideal conditions for the confluence of civil and religious authority. In medieval England, for example, there existed

> an almost paranoid concern for order in society, and a close association between crime and sin. The Reformation and the increased power of the Puritans changed perceptions of crime and justice both in government and in the popular mind. Religion and morality became matters of state law and potential sources of rebellion; although sin and crime were usually dealt with by different courts (crime by the civil court, sin by the ecclesiastical court), they were in some ways almost indistinguishable. (Best, 1998)

By linking morality to rebellion, the authorities were effectively preventing anyone from challenging the status quo. Those who did were likely to be accused of heresy and, as a result, subjected to extremely harsh punishments, including death. This is precisely what happened to those accused of witchcraft and offers a partial explanation of how more than half a million people could be put to death during the 300 years in which the witch craze flourished. Indeed, the plight of those accused of being witches illustrates how charges of heresy were used to silence critics and quash any rebellious inclinations in the population.

Witches had been active in Western Europe for centuries, although they were never prosecuted. This changed as a result of the growing challenge to both religious and civil authorities during the 15th century. Witches provided a convenient scapegoat against whom the masses could vent their anger. Importantly, it was usually the less powerful members of a community who were most susceptible to accusations of witchcraft. Although this group included the elderly, the infirm, and children, the witch craze mainly victimized women. As Pfohl (1985) points out, women made up 85 percent of the people executed for witchcraft throughout history. He suggests that "it is hardly surprising that during times in which the great male mastery over nature seemed least secure, times of economic hardship and political instability, the priestly finger of men often found bewitching women to blame" (39). He goes on to note that this led to horrific ritual punishments, including "baths in boiling water, crushing by heavy weights, tearing the flesh from the breasts with searing-hot pincers, and torture of the female sex organs" (39).

Economically independent women and women who lived alone and outside the protection of men were most susceptible to charges of witchcraft. Their presence in a community disrupted and threatened the male-dominated power structures. Charges of witchcraft and public executions served to reassert the authority of male leaders and remind community members of their subordinate positions in the social hierarchy. At the same time, however, the cruelty and sheer barbarism of the courts and their punishments fuelled the cries for reform across Western Europe.

Early theorizing about crime and the beginnings of our modern system of criminal justice began to emerge during this tumultuous period of European history. "It was an era of racing industrial revolution, enclosure movements, growing capitalism and growing cities" (Sylvester, 1972). These developments were hastened by a rapidly expanding population and by the growth of trade and manufacturing.

The feudal economy was based on agricultural production, with clearly established relations between the aristocracy, who owned the land, and the peasants, who worked it. A system of mutual rights and obligations bound these two classes together and when this relationship was challenged the entire system was threatened. Increasingly, feudalism was unable to meet the needs of the growing population. It is estimated that England's population soared from 2.8 million in 1500 to 8.9 million in 1800. Similar increases were reported for the rest of Europe (Pfohl, 1985). This surge in population fuelled a period of colonial expansion as European monarchs sought havens for their surplus population and access to the markets and raw materials that colonies could provide. Europe's merchant classes gained considerable power during this period, as their economic activities offset the mounting economic shortfall (see Chapter 2).

Changes in the economy were mirrored by changes throughout the society. Revolutionary developments had taken place in philosophy, art, music, literature, and other intellectual pursuits. Progressive thinkers of the day fought to usher Europe into a new era—"the age of reason" emerged during the period known as the Enlightenment (see Box 8.1). The Enlightenment thinkers argued against fanaticism and religious superstition, advocating "naturalistic" explanations of the world based on people's ability to reason.

The Enlightenment philosophers believed that people were free and rational beings. This belief led them to call for the establishment of individual rights and freedoms. In their view, society was based on a social contract under which people chose to relinquish a small portion of their individual autonomy in order to ensure their own safety and the well-being of the entire group. These ideas were clearly contrary to the collectivist orientation of feudalism and the notion of noble privilege held by its rulers. If realized, a system based on rights and freedoms could seriously undermine the bonds of fealty, which held feudalism together. At the same time, the feudal bonds restricted the availability of labour and hampered the development of manufacturing and industry. Herein lies the essence of the conflict between the aristocracy and the merchants. What was useful for one was detrimental to the other. Each group fought to advance its own interests.

# FOCUS BOX 8.1

## THE EUROPEAN ENLIGHTENMENT

Of all the changes that swept over Europe in the seventeenth and eighteenth centuries, the most widely influential was an epistemological transformation that we call the "scientific revolution." In the popular mind, we associate this revolution with natural science and technological change, but the scientific revolution was, in reality, a series of changes in the structure of European thought itself: systematic doubt, empirical and sensory verification, the abstraction of human knowledge into separate sciences, and the view that the world functions like a machine. These changes greatly changed the human experience of every other aspect of life, from individual life to the life of the group. This modification in world view can also be charted in painting, sculpture and architecture; you can see that people of the seventeenth and eighteenth centuries are looking at the world very differently . . .

It's hard to pinpoint the shift in these attitudes. The introduction of humanism in the fourteenth century was in large part based on the idea that human intellect and creativity were trustworthy, and human experience was, to some extent, a reliable base on which to hang knowledge. But the humanist revolution didn't happen all at once; the dichotomy between "experience" and "authority" was a vexed question throughout the fourteenth and fifteenth centuries. What should you believe? What your experience shows you? Or what authorities, including the church and the bible, tell you to believe?

While it's hard to pinpoint the shift in European attitudes, the first, unambiguous statement of this shift in values comes in Leonardo da Vinci's treatise on painting:

Here, right here, in the eye, here forms, here colors, right here the character of every part and every thing of the universe, are concentrated to a single point. How marvelous that point is! . . . In this small space, the universe can be completely reproduced and rearranged in its entire vastness! . . .

This new perspective expressed by Leonardo was a profound shift in the European world view. In a fundamental way, it postulated that human experience was and should be the central concern of human beings. It also postulated that human sensory experience, especially vision, was not only a valid way of understanding the universe, it also made it possible for humans to understand anything whatsoever about the universe.

Source: Richard Hooker. (n.d.). "The European Enlightenment." *World Civilizations*. Washington State University. Available at http://www.wsu.edu/~dee/ENLIGHT/ENLIGHT.HTM.

The merchant classes enjoyed little political influence despite their growing economic power because participation in the legislatures of the day was restricted to landowners. Importantly, land was not considered a commodity that could be bought and sold. Rather, it was held primarily for its immediate use in agricultural and other pursuits. So, even though they were financially wealthy, the merchants owned little land and were prevented from acquiring any more since they could not buy land. As a result, they were barred from gaining political power through landownership. In response, the merchants turned to the legal arena to have their interests served.

In an ironic twist, the merchant classes found an opportunity to strengthen their position in society by financing the costly wars being fought by European monarchs over new colonies. The European aristocracy was forced to turn to the merchants for funds as their own resources were depleted. In exchange for their financial assistance, the merchants were able to gain significant legal concessions. While many of these concessions were aimed specifically at enhancing mercantile activities, a number of important legal principles were established, which reflected the ideals of the Enlightenment philosophers. It was within this milieu that the **Classical School** of criminology made its most significant contributions to the establishment of our modern criminal justice system.

## The Classical School

In 1764, Cesare Beccaria published his major work, *An Essay on Crimes and Punishments*. Although this work contained little that was novel, "it captivated the attention of Europe, much more than did the voluminous lucubrations of theologians and publicists . . . for it summed up in a masterly, unanswerable manner the conceptions and aspirations of the progressive minds of the age" (Phillipson, 1970). Beccaria provided a focus for the humanitarian reform movement that was gaining momentum throughout Europe with his criticism of the cruelty and inhumanity that characterized the criminal justice system of his day.

Abuses in the administration of justice were routine. Practices established in the notorious Court of Star Chamber and the institutionalized terror of the Inquisition had become commonplace. "The existence of criminal law of eighteenth-century Europe was, in general, repressive, uncertain, and barbaric. Its administration encouraged incredibly arbitrary and abusive practices" (Mannheim, 1972). Few safeguards existed for the accused, and judicial torture was a routine method of securing confessions and discovering the identities of accomplices (Langbein, 1976).

The more popular forms of torture for these crimes included the rack, the ducking stool, thumbscrews, and other mechanical devices designed to inflict severe pain. The death penalty was administered in a number of ways, including burning at the stake, hanging, decapitation, and drawing and quartering. Hostetller describes the savage penalty for high treason under Britain's Bloody Code:

w(W)w

"Cesare Beccaria
(1738–1794)" The Internet
Encyclopedia of Philosophy
www.iep.utm.edu/b/beccaria.htm

**Classical School**

Considered to be the first formal school of criminology, Classical criminology is associated with 18th and early 19th century reforms to the administration of justice and the prison system. Associated with authors such as Cesare Beccaria (1738–1794), Jeremy Bentham (1748–1832), Samuel Romilly (1757–1818), and others, this school brought the emerging philosophy of liberalism and utilitarianism to the justice system, advocating principles of rights, fairness, and due process in place of retribution, arbitrariness, and brutality.

A man found guilty was drawn behind a cart to the place of execution, hanged and cut down whilst still alive, disembowelled and castrated, with his intestines burnt before his eyes and finally decapitated with the remainder of his body cut into quarters. (2011: 51)

In 18th-century England, as many as 350 offences were punishable by death. About 70 percent of death sentences were given for robbery and burglary (Newman, 1978). Practices in the colonies were similar in the early 1800s. The first person executed in Toronto was hanged for passing a bad cheque.

Clamour for the reform of such practices had started long before Beccaria's book was published. Humanitarian appeals were heard from jurists, writers, and philosophers of the era, including Hobbes, Locke, Montesquieu, and Voltaire. The administration of the criminal law, in particular, embodied practices that were in direct contrast to many of the principles advocated by the Classical theorists. It was contrary to the ideals of the social contract, as it denied the average citizen fair and impartial treatment at the hands of the state. European society was ripe for the liberating ideas of the Classical theorists and their humanitarian reforms. Beccaria's book served as a catalyst for these sentiments. The reform of a barbaric system of justice provided an excellent vehicle through which the ideas of the Classical theorists could be focused.

## The Classical Theory of Crime

The roots of Classical criminology lie in the philosophy of the Enlightenment. Social contract theory represented a new way of looking at the relationship

## FOCUS BOX 8.2

### WITCHCRAFT AND TORTURE

It is estimated that five hundred thousand people were convicted of witchcraft and burned to death in Europe between the fifteenth and seventeenth centuries. Their crimes: a pact with the Devil; journeys through the air over vast distances mounted on broomsticks; unlawful assembly at sabbats; worship of the Devil; kissing the Devil under the tail; copulation with incubi, male devils equipped with ice-cold penises; copulation with succubi, female devils.

Other more mundane charges were often added: killing the neighbor's cow; causing hailstorms; ruining the crops; stealing and eating babies. But many a witch was executed for no crime other than flying through the air to attend a sabbat. . . .

Torture was routinely applied until the witch confessed to having made a pact with the Devil and having flown to a sabbat. It was continued until the witch named other people who were present at the sabbat. If a witch attempted to retract a confession, torture was applied even more intensely until the original confession was reconfirmed. This left the person accused of witchcraft with the choice between dying once and for all at the stake or being returned repeatedly to the torture chambers. Most people opted for the stake. As a reward for their cooperative attitude, penitent witches could look forward to being strangled before the fire was lit.

Source: Marvin Harris. (1974). *Cows, Pigs, Wars and Witches*. New York: Vintage Books. Copyright © by Marvin Harris. Reprinted by permission of Random House, Inc.

between people and the state. To avoid living in a state of nature that was, to use Hobbes's famous description, "solitary, poor, nasty, brutish, and short" (1958, 107), people voluntarily entered into a social contract with the state. This involved giving up some of their freedom to the state. In return, the state agreed to protect the citizen's right to live in security. The social contract was made with the consent of both parties, and neither had the right to break it. The state had to provide protection but could not violate the rights of citizens. The citizen had to obey the rules or face punishment from the state. In the opening chapter of his book, Beccaria writes:

> Laws are the conditions whereby free and independent men unite to form society. Weary of living in a state of war, and of enjoying a freedom rendered useless by the uncertainty of its perpetuation, men will willingly sacrifice a part of this freedom in order to enjoy that which is left in security and tranquility. (quoted in Monachesi, 1972)

The reforms proposed by the Classical theorists were based on a very well-developed theory of the causes of crime, a theory that represented a significant break with earlier theories. The Classical theorists had a simple explanation for crime. People broke the law because they thought that doing so would advance their own interests. In other words, deviance is the natural result of our rational self-interest. If it suits us, and if we think we can get away with it, we will break the law. Crime was understood to be a rationally calculated activity and not the result of some supernatural force or demonic possession.

Having addressed the causes of crime, the Classical theorists turned to the problem of finding ways to control it. The solution was to set up a system of punishment that would deter people from breaking the law. The Classical theorists believed that humans were rational beings who carefully calculated the consequences of their behaviour. Thus a person who might be tempted to break the law would consider the positive and negative consequences of his or her actions. A well-crafted Criminal Code would ensure that most people would choose to be good rather than evil. One might think that the extremely brutal justice system of the time should have been an effective deterrent, but its excessive harshness was contrary to the Enlightenment view that citizens should not be treated unfairly by the state. Instead, Beccaria proposed that the punishment should fit the crime, that is, it should be proportional to the harm done to society. Beccaria argued this on two grounds: that this amount of punishment would be the most effective deterrent, and that this was the fairest way to punish those who were not deterred and who chose to break the law. Unfair punishment would be a violation of the social contract and would be perceived as unjust by the individual and by other members of society. In the following quotation, Beccaria describes how this would affect the social contract and reduce the deterrent effect of law:

> In proportion as torments become more cruel, the spirits of men, which are like fluids that always rise to the level of surrounding objects, become callous, and the ever lively force of the passions brings it to pass that after a hundred years of cruel torments the wheel inspires no greater fear than imprisonment once did. . . . The countries and

times most notorious for severity of penalties have always been those in which the bloodiest and most inhumane of deeds were committed, for the same spirit of ferocity that guided the hand of the legislators also ruled that of parricide and assassin. (1963, 43–44)

Crime would be reduced if these reforms were implemented in law because calculating criminals would see that they would not profit from their actions. The punishment would cost them more than they could gain from their criminal behaviour. Beccaria also proposed that punishment should be swift and certain. If punishment followed too long after the act, or if it was unlikely to happen at all, then the law would not be an effective deterrent to crime. Finally, the law would be most effective in preventing crime if it was clear and simple enough that people could understand it.

With regard to specific reforms, Beccaria felt that the brutality of torture and the practice of executing people for minor offences must be abolished, as they were abuses of state power. Criminal matters should be dealt with in public according to the dictates of the law. Beccaria wanted to restrict the power of judges, which had been exercised in an arbitrary manner, in private, and generally without recourse for the defendant. He sought to restrict this power by separating the lawmaking power of the legislature from the activities of the judges. In his view, the law should be determined by the legislature; it should be accessible to all; trials should be public; and the role of the judiciary should be restricted to the determination of guilt and the administration of punishment set out in law.

The reforms suggested by Beccaria represented a call for equality and for the establishment of due-process safeguards. The creation of graded punishments effectively restricted the arbitrariness and inequality that characterized the existing system. By arguing that the punishment should "fit the crime," Beccaria shifted the focus away from the actor and onto the act. In this way, both noble and peasant would be judged on the basis of what they did and not who they were. Moreover, the judiciary was stripped of its discretion in sentencing since judges were bound to give punishments that were fixed by law. This was a powerful directive for equality since the preferential treatment formerly accorded to those of wealth and power could no longer be granted. However, as you have read in Chapter 2, those with wealth and power had the most influence in shaping the law, so the reforms in the justice system did little to alter the fundamental inequalities based on ownership of property.

## Assessing the Contributions of the Classical School

**The Classical School and Legal Reform** The ideals of the social contract theorists were translated into progressive criminal justice policy in the reforms promoted by the Classical School. In the process, the excesses and injustices that existed were attacked, and the foundations of our modern legal system were established. The due-process safeguards, which are taken for granted today, as well as reforms such as the guarantee of individual rights, equality before the law, the separation of judicial and legislative functions, and the establishment of fixed penalties, remain as the legacy of the Classical School of criminology. Canada's Criminal Code and our modern criminal justice system still reflect the work of the Classical theorists.

**Limitations of the Classical School**  Despite this success, the influence of the Classical School was not all positive. A serious problem with Classical theory was Beccaria's insistence that the degree of punishment must be proportional to the degree of harm that was done to society. While at first glance this proposal seemed reasonable, it meant that the personal characteristics of the offender and the circumstances of the offence could not be considered when courts determined punishments (Roshier, 1989). Also, by removing the flexibility of judicial discretion, the reforms actually gave more power to the state, which was responsible for passing very specific sentencing laws (Newman and Marongiu, 1990).

Although punishments could be rationally determined on paper, their application in real life often resulted in gross injustices. The courts were bound to follow the letter of the law and could not use discretion to temper the justice being meted out. For example, the hardship that results from having to pay a $1000 fine varies dramatically depending on whether a person is wealthy or poor. The courts, however, could not take this into account. Further, they were unable to consider mitigating circumstances or factors such as motive or mental competence, which would alter the responsibility of the convicted person. In this way, attempts to enforce equality resulted in a system that produced a great deal of injustice.

Changing this rigid system was one of the goals of Neoclassical criminologists, including the French magistrate Gabriel Tarde. Tarde contributed a number of ideas to criminology, most notably his "laws of imitation," but his main contribution came from his criticism of the legal system established by proponents of the Classical School (Beirne, 1993). Tarde rejected the notion of free will and proposed a modification of the system of punishment to recognize that there must be some individual treatment of offenders. As a result of the work of Tarde and other Neoclassical writers, courts began to take into account factors such as age (children were held less accountable), mental competence, motive, and mitigating circumstances. For example, in France, the Penal Code of 1791, which reflected the views of the Classical School, was revised in 1810 and again in 1819. With each revision, the rigid nature of the code was modified to include more discretion for judges as well as consideration of extenuating circumstances.

**deterrence**

As used in criminal justice, it refers to crime prevention achieved through the fear of punishment.

Another problem with the Classical School is its emphasis on **deterrence**. The approach the Classical School advocated was based more on a theory of deterrence than on a theory of crime, and it can be assessed on these grounds. The issue of deterrence continues to be an important element of this approach as modern-day Classical theorists emphasize its message. The work of James Q. Wilson, for example, is a current example of Classical thinking. "He argues that penalties need not be long and severe as long as they are swift and certain" (Pfohl, 1985). However, for most offences, the likelihood of punishment is so small, and the time between the criminal event and any punishment that is given is so great, that the Classical theorists' hopes of reducing crime by changing the legal codes have not been met (see Chapter 15).

An additional problem with the Classical School is its overly simplified view of human nature and the theory of human behaviour that this supports (Thomas and Hepburn, 1983). The Classical theorists wholly accepted the image of the free and rational human being. This view completely ignores the objective realities faced by different individuals as they make their choices, the inequalities they experience, the state of their knowledge at any given time, and a multitude of other factors that may influence their decisions.

Finally, the emphasis on the rational dimension of human behaviour did not stem from the collection of empirical evidence but was based mostly on philosophical speculation. Little effort was made to examine these theoretical ideas in the real world. The notion of deterrence based on a rationally calculated set of punishments was assumed to work because it was felt that most reasonable people would follow the same logic.

In spite of the problems with the ideas of the Classical School, their contribution to our modern criminal justice system cannot be denied. Legal principles such as due process and equality before the law are fundamental to our legal system. Beccaria's work had a direct influence on the drafting of the legal code of France following the French Revolution and on the U.S. Bill of Rights, and Classical principles remain as part of the legal systems of many countries. For example, in section 15 of our Charter of Rights and Freedoms, Canadians are guaranteed the right to equal treatment before and under the law. We are protected from cruel and unusual punishment by section 12. In sections 7 through 11, a whole array of procedural safeguards are outlined that guarantee Canadians the right to due process of law. Clearly, modern criminal justice owes a great debt to the Classical theorists and the reforms that they introduced. However, our legal system also incorporates the changes suggested by the Neoclassical reformers.

**"Canadian Charter of Rights and Freedoms" Department of Justice Canada**
http://laws.justice.gc.ca/en/charter/

## The Statistical School: Social Structure and Crime

The first half of the 19th century saw the emergence of an approach to criminology that differed markedly from that of the Classical School. This was evident in the work of André-Michel Guerry (1802–1866) in France, Adolphe Quetelet (1796–1874) in Belgium, and Henry Mayhew (1812–1887) in England. These researchers believed that crime, like other human behaviour, was the result of natural causes. Once discovered, these causes could be altered through the application of scientifically derived knowledge. Guerry, Quetelet, and Mayhew's reliance on objective empirical data, as opposed to philosophical conjecture or speculation, identified them as positivists.

Members of the **Statistical School** did not share the image of the rational individual held by the Classical theorists. Instead, they saw behaviour as the product of a whole host of factors. They systematically analyzed the statistical information available to them and tried to find a relationship between this information and crime. They analyzed such things as population density, education, and poverty (Thomas and Hepburn, 1983). A great deal of their work was based on geographical or cartographic analysis, which involved the plotting of various crime rates onto maps.

These theorists went far beyond simply describing what they learned from their maps and graphs. Many of their ideas anticipated the work of modern sociologists as they addressed issues related to criminal careers, delinquent subcultures, and social learning theory. They provided a critical and insightful perspective, as well as a thorough statistical analysis of criminal behaviour in their work.

**Statistical School**

Associated with early social scientists such as Adolphe Quetelet (1795–1874) and André-Michel Guerry (1802–1866), who began to explore the structure of emerging European societies with the assistance of statistical methods. While their early use of statistics is important, they also developed a structural explanation of crime and other social problems.

Perhaps the most significant contribution of these theorists is their discovery of the remarkable regularity of phenomena such as crime. Countries, provinces, cities, and towns all had rates of crime that were remarkably stable from one year to the next. Even murder, a highly individualistic act, varied little over time. They attributed this stability to elements of the social structure. Quetelet, for example, argued that "rather than being the result of our individual free wills, [our behaviour] is the product of many forces that are external to us" (Thomas and Hepburn, 1983). The fact that these forces appeared in regular and recurring patterns prompted these theorists to believe that human behaviour was governed by certain laws akin to those found in the natural or physical sciences.

In a style that anticipated much of our contemporary thinking about crime, these theorists focused on inequalities and other structural features of their society. People in unfavourable social circumstances were seen to have few options open to them. In Quetelet's words, "The crimes which are annually committed seem to be a necessary result of our social organization . . . the society prepares the crime and the guilty are only the instruments by which it is executed" (Bierne, 1993, 88).

The influence of the Statistical School was, unfortunately, limited. This was not the result of any shortcomings on their part; rather, it reflected the wider appeal of the biological theories of Cesare Lombroso and his colleagues. Nevertheless, these early pioneers of statistical analysis of criminology provided a uniquely sociological contribution to this emerging field of inquiry and demonstrated the value of testing theoretical formulations with empirical observations.

**"Cesare Lombroso" Museo Criminologico**
www.museocriminologico.it/
lombroso_3_uk.htm

**Positive School**

The first scientific school, it consisted of the Italian criminologists Cesare Lombroso (1836–1909), Raffaelo Garofalo (1852–1934), and Enrico Ferri (1856–1929). They supported the assumptions of positivism and argued that criminality is determined—the effect in a cause–effect sequence—and that the mandate of criminology should be to search for these causes. It was believed that with the exception of those deemed to be born criminals, the discovery of the causes of crime would allow for effective treatment.

# Lombroso and the Positive School

The **Positive School** of criminology is also known as the Italian School because its most influential members were the Italian criminal anthropologist Cesare Lombroso (1836–1909) and his students Enrico Ferri (1856–1929) and Raffaelo Garofolo (1852–1934). Lombroso was influenced by the evolutionary theories of Charles Darwin, by the positivist sociology of Auguste Comte, and by the work of the sociologist Herbert Spencer, who attempted to adapt Darwin's theory to the social world.

Like the members of the Statistical School, Lombroso brought the methods of controlled observation to the study of criminals, comparing them with non-criminals in order to isolate the factors that caused criminality. His own research was badly flawed, and his work is remembered because of his use of the scientific method rather than because of the specific findings he reported. Despite their flaws, Lombroso's ideas were widely accepted at the end of the 19th century. Their popularity was partly due to the growing influence of science, particularly to the awareness of Darwin's theory of evolution. It was likely also due to the comfort of the ruling classes with the view that criminals were not produced by society's flaws, as Quetelet and his colleagues had shown;

rather, criminals were genetic misfits who were born to break the rules that governed the lives of civilized people (Radzinowicz, 1966).

The impact of Darwin's ideas on the Positive School cannot be overstated. As Lilly et al. (2007, 28) note,

> Darwin's evolutionary thesis represents one of the most profound theories of all times. It not only offered revolutionary new knowledge for the sciences but also helped to shatter many philosophies and practices in other areas. It commanded so much attention and prestige that the entire literate community felt "obligated to bring his world outlook into harmony with their findings" (Hofstadter, 1955b, 3). According to Hofstadter, (1955b) Darwin's impact is comparable in its magnitude to the work of Nicolaus Copernicus (1473–1543) the European astronomer; Isaac Newton (1642–1727), the English mathematician and physicist; and Freud, the Austrian psychoanalyst. In effect, all of the Western world had to come to grips with Darwin's evolutionary scheme.

The main ideas in Darwin's theory—"the struggle for survival" and "the survival of the fittest"—found fertile ground in the minds of the Positive School criminologists who incorporated these ideas into their thinking about criminals and the way society should deal with them. Identifying criminals became a matter of searching for those physical and moral traits that differentiated more developed human beings from those who were less advanced in evolutionary terms. Dealing with criminals became a matter of incapacitating them since little could be done for them because their criminality was based on their genetic make-up. As you will see, however, some interpretations of these ideas led to a far more drastic approach called "eugenics," which promoted the sterilization and even elimination of those deemed to be inferior.

Lombroso had worked as an army doctor and as a prison physician. He was interested in psychology and at one stage of his career was a teacher of psychiatry. These diverse interests are reflected in his theory of criminality. Lombroso's interest in physiology led him to note certain distinct physical differences between the criminals and soldiers with whom he worked. His thoughts on the subject came together during an autopsy he was performing on the notorious thief Vilella. He noted that many of the characteristics of Vilella's skull were similar to those of lower animals. In a remarkable description of the moment of discovery, Lombroso recalled:

> This was not merely an idea, but a revelation. At the sight of that skull, I seemed to see all of a sudden, lighted up as a vast plain under a flaming sky, the problem of the nature of the criminal—an atavistic being who reproduces in his person the ferocious instincts of primary humanity and the inferior animals. Thus were explained anatomically the enormous jaws, high cheek-bones, prominent superciliary arches, solitary lines in the palms, extreme size of the orbits, handle-shaped or sessile ears found in criminals, savages, and apes, insensibility to pain,

extremely acute sight, tattooing, excessive idleness, love of orgies, and the irresistible craving for evil for its own sake, the desire not only to extinguish life in the victim, but to mutilate the corpse, tear its flesh, and drink its blood. (Wolfgang, 1972)

This discovery led Lombroso to believe that criminals were throwbacks to an earlier stage of evolution, or **atavisms**. His theory has been succinctly described by Gould (1981):

These people are innately driven to act as a normal ape or savage would but such behaviour is deemed criminal in our civilized society. Fortunately, we may identify born criminals because they bear anatomical signs of their apishness. Their atavism is both physical and mental, but the physical signs, or stigmata as Lombroso called them, are decisive. Criminal behaviour can also arise in normal men, but we know the "born criminal" by his anatomy. Anatomy, indeed, is destiny, and born criminals cannot escape their inherited taint.

**atavism**

Cesare Lombroso (1836–1909) believed that some criminals were born criminals; they were atavistic. This suggested that they were throwbacks to an earlier stage of human evolution and that this limited evolutionary development meant that they were morally inferior. This inferiority could be identified through a series of physical stigmata.

The contrast between the primitive nature of the criminal and the more completely evolved contemporary man is shown in Lombroso's explanation of the use of professional slang, or argot, by criminals. Born criminals talk differently because they experience the world differently. "They talk like savages because they are veritable savages in the midst of this brilliant European civilization" (Parmelee, 1912).

To support his theory, Lombroso had to show that organisms lower on the evolutionary ladder were naturally criminal. Thus primitive humans were described as "savages." Even when evidence of their savagery was absent, Lombroso was able to save his theory by speculating that among honourable primitives, the conditions for criminality simply did not yet exist. For example, "it is not possible . . . to steal when property does not exist or to swindle when there is no trade" (Lombroso, 1912). Once these supposed savages take on a little civilization, their criminality is inevitable. Lombroso went even further down the evolutionary ladder, finding evidence of criminality in the behaviour of animals, insects, and even insectivorous plants.

**stigmata**

Physical signs of some special moral position. Cesare Lombroso (1836–1909) used the term to refer to physical signs of the state of atavism (a morally and evolutionary inferior person).

Lombroso tested his ideas by observing many imprisoned criminals. In one study, he compared the physical characteristics of a group of criminals with those of a group of soldiers and found that the criminals had many more of the atavistic **stigmata** than did the soldiers. In another piece of research, he found that stigmata were present in 30 to 40 percent of anarchists, but in less than 12 percent of members of other extremist movements (Taylor et al., 1973). He also concluded that different types of offenders were characterized by different physiological characteristics. For example, "robbers have . . . small, shifting, quick-moving eyes; bushy connecting eyebrows; twisted or snub noses, thin beards . . . and foreheads almost receding," while "habitual homicides have glassy, cold, motionless eyes, sometimes bloodshot and injected. The nose is often aquiline, or rather hawklike, and always voluminous" (Lombroso, 1972). Lombroso felt that women had fewer stigmata and lower crime rates than males because women were closer to their primitive origins. Although he concluded that women were vengeful, deceitful, and jealous, he said that their crime rates were relatively low because these negative traits were neutralized by their maternal instinct, piety, and lack of passion.

Lombroso initially postulated two types of offenders—born criminals and occasional criminals. However, in response to his critics, he later added several more categories, including the following:

1. Epileptics. In addition to their disability, epileptics also had the atavistic characteristics of criminals.
2. Criminal insane. This is the category of those whose insanity has led to their involvement in crime.
3. Criminals of passion. These are criminals who contrast completely with born criminals in that they lack any of the criminal stigmata. They commit crimes because of "noble and powerful" motives such as love or politics.
4. Criminaloids. This is a grab-bag category, which includes anyone who commits a crime but does not fall into one of the other classifications. Lombroso felt that precipitating factors other than biological ones caused criminality among this group.

Some have interpreted this expansion of categories as a softening of Lombroso's commitment to his biological theory. This view seems to be supported by his last major work, Crime: Its Causes and Remedies, in which he discusses social and environmental causes of crime along with biological causes. However, examination of these modifications suggests that this change was more apparent than real. While there were differences between atavistic criminals, the insane, and the epileptics, all three categories had elements of degeneration that stemmed from epilepsy, which he called the "kernel of crime" (Lombroso, 1912). Criminaloids may lack some of the stigmata, but they differ from born criminals only in degree, not in kind. After long periods in prison, criminaloids may even come to resemble born criminals. While those who commit crimes out of passion do not show any of the stigmata, they show some points of resemblance with epileptics. The only category that has no connection with atavism or epilepsy is that of the occasional criminals. Even these pose no threat to Lombroso's theory, however, for he suggests that they should not be called criminals at all.

## The Contribution of the Positive School

In its day, Lombroso's work attracted a large following among those interested in studying the causes of criminality. The stigmata were used as indicators of criminality in many trials, and Lombroso himself appeared as an expert witness on several occasions. In one case, the court had to decide which of two brothers had killed their stepmother. Lombroso's testimony that one of the men had the features of a born criminal helped secure the man's conviction.

However, Lombroso's theory of criminal anthropology has not stood up to empirical test. Lombroso's research was poorly done by today's standards. His comparison groups were chosen unsystematically, his statistical techniques were crude, his measurements were often sloppy, and he assumed that those in prison were criminals and those out of prison were non-criminals. Many of the stigmata he mentioned in his research, such as tattooing, were social factors that could not possibly have been inherited. Yet despite these weaknesses, his work did represent an attempt at providing a scientific explanation of the causes of criminality.

Perhaps the most lasting contribution of Lombroso was his discussion of the criminal justice system. The Classical theorists felt that crime could be controlled if society could design punishments to fit the crime. Positive theorists, on the other hand, felt that the punishment should fit the criminal. Radzinowicz and King (1977) have nicely outlined the difference between the two perspectives: "The Classical School exhorts men to study justice, the Positivist School exhorts justice to study men."

Because Lombroso believed that people became involved in criminality for different reasons, he felt that they should be treated differently by the criminal justice system. If a respectable man committed murder because of passion, honour, or political belief, no punishment was needed as that man would never repeat the crime. For other offenders, indeterminate sentences would best ensure rehabilitation. Born criminals should not be held responsible for their actions, though they needed to be incarcerated for the protection of society. However, this was to be done in a humane way. He recommended that "sentences should show a decrease in infamy and ferocity proportionate to their increase in length and social safety" (Lombroso-Ferrero, 1972).

Some born criminals could be channelled in a socially useful direction. For example, banishment and transportation to one of the colonies might allow their tendencies to be redirected toward the difficult business of building settlements in a hostile environment. For others, more severe sanctions were required. "There exists, it is true, a group of criminals, born for evil, against whom all social cures break as against a rock—a fact which compels us to eliminate them completely, even by death" (Lombroso, 1912).

# FOCUS BOX 8.3

## A "NOVEL" THEORY

Criminal anthropology reached the attention of novelists as well as theorists. Bram Stoker and Lombroso were contemporaries, but Stoker's *Dracula* was published almost 20 years after Lombroso's most famous work. Compare Stoker's description of Count Dracula with Lombroso's description of the born criminal:

Dracula: "His face was . . . aquiline, like the beak of a bird of prey."

Lombroso: "[The criminal's] nose on the contrary is often aquiline like the beak of a bird of prey."

Dracula: "His eyebrows were very massive, almost meeting over the nose . . ."

Lombroso: "The eyebrows are bushy and tend to meet across the nose."

Dracula: ". . . his ears were pale and at the tops extremely pointed . . ."

Lombroso: "with a protuberance on the upper part of the posterior margin . . . a relic of the pointed ear. . . ."

Source: Leonard Wolf. 1975. *The Annotated Dracula.* New York: C.N. Potter.

A number of features of our current criminal justice system stem from the concern of Lombroso and his followers with individualizing the treatment of offenders. Probation, parole, indeterminate sentences, and the consideration of mitigating circumstances by the court were all influenced by Lombroso's work as well as by the work of Neoclassical criminologists. The rational person of Classical theory now had a past and a future.

# Biological Theories in the Early 20th Century

## Crime and Physical Characteristics

During his lifetime, Lombroso's theories came under frequent attack. In 1889, he responded to his critics by challenging them to compare 100 born criminals, 100 people with criminal tendencies, and 100 normal people. He promised to retract his theories if the criminals did not turn out to be different from the other groups. His challenge was ultimately taken up by an English prison medical officer, Dr. G. B. Griffiths, and completed by his successor, Dr. Charles Goring, who succeeded Griffiths in 1903 shortly after the project began.

Goring carefully measured and compared the physical and mental characteristics of 3000 English convicts with those of diverse samples of "normals," including British university students, schoolboys, university professors, insane Scots, German Army recruits, and British Army soldiers (Goring, 1972). Based on his comparison of these groups on 37 physical and six mental traits, Goring concluded that there was no evidence of a distinct physical type of criminal. Lombroso's "anthropological monster has no existence in fact" (Goring, 1913). Criminals were no more or less likely to possess stigmata than were members of the control groups. Goring did find that criminals were physically inferior to normals, but attributed this fact to social selection processes.

Goring's most important finding was the high correlation between criminality and low intelligence. This led to his own explanation that crime was inherited and that the most important constitutional mechanism through which crime was genetically transmitted was mental inferiority. Unlike Lombroso, Goring did feel that hereditary predispositions could be modified by social factors such as education. However, he also supported eugenic measures, which would restrict the reproduction of the constitutional factors leading to crime.

In some respects, Goring's research represented a major advance over the work of Lombroso. His measurement was far more precise, and he had access to statistical tools that were not available to Lombroso. However, his work also contained a number of serious methodological flaws. Among them was the fact that he was comparing officially labelled criminals, who were not a representative sample of all criminals, with diverse groups of other people who did not represent the non-criminal population. While many of the other criticisms of Goring's research are quite technical, they are serious enough to cause doubt both about his own theories and about his refutation of Lombroso (Driver, 1972).

The search for individual differences as the cause of crime did not end with Goring. This theme was picked up again in the 1930s by Harvard anthropologist Ernest A. Hooton. He compared more than 13 000 criminals with a sample of non-criminals drawn from groups of college students, firemen, hospital outpatients, militiamen, mental hospital patients, people using the change house at a public beach, and others. On the basis of this comparison, Hooton concluded that "criminals as a group represent an aggregate of sociologically and biologically inferior individuals" (1939). Among the new stigmata he attributed to criminals were such characteristics as "low foreheads, high pinched nasal roots, nasal bridges and tips varying to both extremes of breadth and narrowness," and "very small ears" (1939).

While Hooton was not as concerned as some of his predecessors with the policy implications of his research, he did not hesitate to draw the obvious conclusion. Since "crime is the resultant of the impact of environment upon low grade human organisms . . . it follows that the elimination of crime can be effected only by the expiration of the physically, mentally, and morally unfit, or by their complete segregation in a socially aseptic environment" (1939). These ideas formed the basis of the "eugenics" movement that developed in the United States at the turn of the 20th century (see Box 8.4).

Hooton's work was controversial, and his findings were challenged on a variety of grounds. He was accused of using poor scientific methods and circular reasoning. For example, he used conviction of a crime as a method of separating criminals from non-criminals; he then examined the convicted groups and concluded they were inferior; finally, he used this finding of inferiority to account for their criminality (Empey, 1982). Only in this way could a trait such as thin lips be turned into an indicator of criminality.

Several other criticisms of Hooton's methods are worth considering. His control group did not represent the general population. Students, firefighters, and mental patients have particular characteristics that distinguish them from the rest of the population. Furthermore, his findings show tremendous differences within the various control groups he used. In fact, the differences between his control groups drawn from Boston and Nashville were actually greater than between prisoners and controls (Pfohl, 1985). As in the case of Lombroso, Hooton's attempt to link criminal behaviour to physical types was thoroughly discredited.

This kind of research has made periodic appearances in a variety of forms since the days of Lombroso and Hooton. In the 1950s, William Sheldon attempted to re-establish the link between body type and criminality in his elaboration of a "somatotype" theory. He described three basic body types, which, he argued, were related to particular types of personalities and temperament. These consisted of endomorphs, with fat, round bodies and easygoing personalities; ectomorphs, who are tall and lean individuals with introverted personalities and nervous dispositions; and mesomorphs, who have well-built, muscular bodies with aggressive personalities and who are quick to act and insensitive to pain. Sheldon related each of these types to particular kinds of criminal behaviour. He found that the muscular mesomorphs were the type most likely to become involved in delinquent or criminal behaviour.

# FOCUS BOX 8.4

## CRIMINOLOGY AND EUGENICS

The term "eugenics". . . . simply means "well born" and it connotes a sense of contributing to or improving the stock of the race or the nation. The term became one of some suspicion when the goal of genetics was embraced by various political regimes and enforced through the state's coercive power as an effective instrument for social engineering. In modern times, the first extended programs in state-sponsored eugenics were developed in the United States in the late nineteenth and early twentieth century. These eugenics programs grew from a constellation of ideas derived from evolutionary theory which embraced Social Darwinism, from contemporaneous criminology encouraged by a scientific hypothesis supported by post-mortem studies of brains of criminals and the findings of the famous Juke Report (1875) on inheritance and criminal behaviour, from demographic concerns about dysgenics—the growth of criminal population and the growth of the feeble-minded population because of their unrestrained breeding patterns—and from surgical advances, such as vasectomy and salpingectomy [female sterilization], in the practice of medicine. Involuntary sterilization became the instrument of this modern attempt at eugenics. The idea of genetic sterilization, the pursuit of this end as a national goal, and the procurement of means to attain their desired result were pressed by some of the most influential families, by some of the most prestigious societies and foundations, by some powerful lawyers, judges, scientists, and physicians, and by some of the most elite universities in the United States.

This central notion and clearest articulation of the goals of this movement are best recorded in the words of Mr. Justice Oliver Wendell Holmes who, writing for the majority in a 1927 United States Supreme Court decision, Buck v. Bell, found involuntary sterilization to be compatible with the guarantees found in the U.S. Constitution.

Holmes concluded:

We have seen more than once that the public welfare may call upon the best citizens for their lives. It would be strange if it could not call upon those who already sap the strength of the state for lesser sacrifices, often not felt to be such by those concerned, in order to prevent our being swamped with incompetence. It is better for all the world, if instead of waiting to execute degenerative offspring for crime, or to let them starve for their imbecility, society can prevent those who are manifestly unfit from continuing their kind. The principle that sustains compulsory vaccination is broad enough to cover cutting the Fallopian tubes (Jacobson v. Massachusetts, 197 U.S. 11). Three generations of imbeciles are enough (Buck v. Bell. United States Supreme Court. Report 274, 1927). (Canada also practiced involuntary sterilization and the practice remained legal in Alberta until 1972.)

Source: Margaret Monahan Hogan. (n.d.). "Medical Ethics: The New Eugenics: Therapy—Enhancement—Screening—Testing." International Catholic University. http://home.comcast.net/~icuweb/c04106.htm.

Sheldon fared no better than his predecessors, however, when his work was subjected to scrutiny. It was found that he had done an extremely poor job of measuring delinquency among the young people he had studied. He had used vague and inconsistent categories that have been described as scientifically meaningless.

These criticisms could not be levelled at the Gluecks, who followed up on Sheldon's ideas. They applied his somatotype theory to a study of 500 juvenile delinquents. In their study, they compared the bodies of 500 adjudicated delinquents with a matched sample of non-delinquents. The Gluecks concluded from their work that delinquents were more likely to be mesomorphs. However, this finding may have raised more questions than it answered. Putting aside a whole host of methodological criticisms levelled at the Gluecks, it may be that mesomorphs actually look more like stereotypical delinquents than either endomorphs or ectomorphs. As a result, people may respond to mesomorphs differently and they may be more likely to be labelled delinquent than those who are non-mesomorphs. Also, other social selection factors may have been involved. Youths who are athletic, muscular, and active may be better candidates for Little League baseball, hockey, or delinquency than their less athletic peers.

## Crime and Intelligence

Other biological theories have focused on a variety of factors that have been associated with individual differences. Goring suggested that instead of looking for defective body types, the focus should be on genetic weaknesses demonstrated by low intelligence.

In one famous study of family and heredity, the American psychologist Henry Goddard traced the legitimate and illegitimate offspring of an army lieutenant, Martin Kallikak. Young Martin fathered an illegitimate son with a feeble-minded barmaid before he settled down and married a "respectable" woman. The study compared the family trees of the descendants of Kallikak's feeble-minded mate to those of his "normal" wife. The offspring of the feeble-minded barmaid produced a collection of deviants and feeble-minded degenerates. By contrast, the family of his wife showed no such weakness (Goddard, 1912).

Even if the enormous methodological weaknesses of Goddard's study are ignored (Gould (1981) has shown that even the photographs showing the "depraved" Kallikaks had been retouched to make them look like defectives), little is left of scientific consequence. It is hardly surprising that children raised under difficult and impoverished circumstances should be less than model citizens. In fact, a requirement for life under these conditions may be that an individual learns a great deal of undesirable behaviour simply to survive. The absence of any consideration of the social factors involved in this comparison clearly undermines the findings of Goddard's research.

Goddard continued his work using the Binet-Simon intelligence test, which had recently been developed in France. This IQ test was based on the notion of "mental age." Goddard studied the residents of a New Jersey mental institution and, on the basis of this work, established the mental age of 12 as the cut-off point for determining feeble-mindedness. Goddard then applied this IQ test to the inmates of jails and prisons throughout the New Jersey area. He found that in approximately half of the institutions, 70 percent of the inmate population was at or below the mental age of 12. From these findings, he concluded that IQ was an important determinant of criminal behaviour. He also concluded that feeble-mindedness was directly inherited and could only be eliminated by denying those he called "morons" the right to reproduce (1914). Goddard also argued that "criminal imbeciles" should not be held criminally responsible for their actions. His expert testimony helped to acquit at least one murderer on the grounds of criminal imbecility (Rafter, 1997).

The acceptance of Goddard's position was short-lived. In 1926, Murchinson published the results of a study in which he compared IQ data from World War I army recruits with that of a group of inmates (Pfohl, 1985). He found that 47 percent of the recruits, compared with only 30 percent of the prisoners, had IQ scores that fell below the mental age of 12. This startling finding implied that almost half of a very large sample of normal American men could be considered mentally feeble. The absurdity of these findings forced Goddard to lower his cut-off point for feeble-mindedness from 12 years to nine. This reduction resulted in the disappearance of any significant differences between inmates and soldiers, or anyone else for that matter (Pfohl, 1985).

Despite evidence so convincing that even Goddard disavowed his earlier work, governments responded to their fear of those with low IQs by passing legislation controlling their behaviour. These laws resulted in thousands of mentally retarded people in North America being forced into institutions and, in many cases, being involuntarily sterilized.

In Canada, sterilization laws were passed in Alberta in 1929 and in British Columbia in 1933. The Alberta law was not repealed until 1972. As a child growing up in Alberta, Leilani Muir was incorrectly labelled as mentally retarded. She was kept in an institution and was sterilized without her knowledge or consent. In 1995 Muir, who actually had normal intelligence, successfully sued the Alberta government and was awarded substantial damages. This case shows the problems with developing policies based on notions of individual inferiority.

The controversy over IQ tests has continued. A number of serious flaws in the assumptions behind this approach have been realized. For example, it has been suggested that high scores on these tests may have more to say about test-taking ability than they do about intelligence. Furthermore, the composition of these tests has been found to be biased in favour of the cultural groups of the designers of the tests. In a dramatic demonstration, Adrian Dove, a black sociologist, devised an IQ test based on the cultural referents and language of the black ghetto (Pfohl, 1985). Black respondents who were familiar with this culture did well on the tests, but white middle-class respondents did poorly. The validity of IQ tests remains suspect and their use has often been linked with racist ideology and propaganda.

A number of other recent formulations have sought to re-establish a link between individual characteristics and criminal behaviour. These include a focus on such things as chromosomes, unusual EEG results, hypoglycemic disorders, and premenstrual tension. The results in many of these cases are similar. While it would be foolhardy to deny the biological or psychological dimensions of human behaviour, the evidence supporting a link between pathology and criminal behaviour is weak. Moreover, this approach ignores the essentially political nature of social control—what one society praises and rewards, another may condemn. Given this variability in what we define as crime, an assessment of the underlying social and political context is indispensable.

The continued search for individual differences and the erroneous identification of a normal "us" and a criminal "them" has sometimes had political overtones (see Box 8.5 for an extreme example). The emergence of a

# FOCUS BOX 8.5

## BAD SCIENCE OR BAD POLITICS? CRIMINOLOGY IN NAZI GERMANY

Throughout this chapter, we have tried to link the developments in criminology to the wider social, political, and intellectual contexts from which they emerged. For example, we noted the impact of the Enlightenment and humanistic thinking on the development of the Classical School and the reforms they struggled to make to the criminal justice system of the day. We also noted how Social Darwinism had a far-ranging influence on the type of thinking that began to gain prominence in a number of fields after Charles Darwin published his famous treatise on evolution. This included the field of criminology and the ideas promoted by the Positive School.

What happens to these ideas and theories once they become popularized depends in large part on how they are used to further particular agendas or views of the world. In the case of the eugenics movement, criminological-biological research was used to justify forced sterilizations, executions of habitual criminals, and even genocide as was the case in Nazi Germany. "Hitler himself, in a speech to the 1929 Nazi Party Congress in Nuremburg, called it outrageous that 'criminals are allowed to procreate' and demanded drastic eugenic measures" (Wetzell, 2000, 180). This pronouncement eerily foreshadowed what was to come. As Rosenhaft (2001) notes, "From 1935 on, certain categories of criminals were officially treated as racially undesirable. Prostitutes, vagrants, and other so-called asocials, including Roma, or Gypsies, were taken off the streets and sent to prisons or camps indefinitely and without the right to appeal. Homosexuals, whose lifestyle contradicted both criminal law and the racial duty to produce children, were hounded and arrested.... It was from managing these thousands of ordinary captives that the concentration camp system was set up right at the beginning of the regime in 1933."

However unconscionable the horrors perpetrated by the Nazis were, they could be attributed to the vicious and racist ideology of the Nazi regime. Their use of science and biological-criminological research to justify their actions, however, should serve as a cautionary tale to us all.

The conclusions drawn by Richard Wetzell (2000) after his extensive investigation of German criminology during the Nazi era provide a sobering view on the role of "science." He states:

> A more complex picture of science under the Third Reich also diminishes the distance that we often perceive between "Nazi science" and our own science. Contemporary scientists as well as the general public often assume that science under Nazism was "bad" or "perverted" science. This view is reassuring because it suggests that our own, more "advanced" science does not have the same dangerous implications that "Nazi science" had. But if science under the Nazis was in fact more sophisticated, the distance between "Nazi science" and science in our own day is diminished, and we are forced to ask ourselves whether the role of science and medicine under the Nazi regime might point to dangers inherent in scientific research in the present. My point here is not to suggest that research on the genetic causes of crime, for instance, is intrinsically evil and dangerous and will necessarily lead to inhumane and murderous state policies. Rather, my point is that much of the scientific research conducted during the Nazi years was not as different from current scientific research as we would like to think. Like science before and after the Third Reich, scientific research in Nazi Germany was characterized by continual tension between the internal dynamics of science and the intellectual and political biases of the scientists and their society. This argument should make us uncomfortable in salutary ways. For it makes us realize that the connection between scientific research and the Nazi regime was more complicated than we might have thought, and it gives us a more critical view of science in our own time.

Source: From *Inventing the Criminal: A History of German Criminology* by Richard F. Wetzell. Copyright © 2000 by the University of North Carolina Press.

**TABLE 8.1    Early Theories of Crime**

| Theory | Theorists | Key Elements |
|---|---|---|
| Classical theory | Beccaria | Humans were rational thinkers. Those who contemplated breaking the law considered the positive and negative consequences of their actions. |
| | Glueck/Glueck | |
| | Pollak | A measured system of punishments was needed to deter crime. |
| Neoclassical theory | Tarde | Helped to develop a more individualized system of criminal justice. |
| Statistical School | Guerry, Quetelet, | Explored the social causes of crime. |
| | Mayhew | Related structural factors such as inequality to crime. |
| Positive School | Lombroso | Criminals were born, not made. They were atavisms who were less evolved than the law-abiding. |
| Early 20th-century Biological | Goring, Hooton, Sheldon, Goddard | Related criminality to several types of theories of biological inferiority including intelligence and body shape. |

positive science coincided with the rise of a powerful capitalist class and expanded colonial activity. Both of these developments welcomed the ideological justification contained within the Darwinian notion of survival of the fittest. Social Darwinism and positive criminology flourished in this environment.

This biological-criminological approach of the Positive School offered a ready-made and "humane" way of dealing with the problems of social control. This was extremely important at a time when the population was being transformed into a disciplined industrial labour force. Rather than applying the harsh and barbaric punishments of the past, a scientifically designed technology of control could be used to "treat" troublesome individuals. This focus on the pathologies of individuals also serves to conveniently remove one's gaze from the social structure. If it is certain that problems like crime are the result of individual deficiencies, then it is not necessary to be concerned with the social structure. If, on the other hand, the structural sources of inequality, such as racism, sexism, and other social ills, are examined, the very nature of the society may be called into question.

## Summary

- Early theories of crime were based on superstition and religious beliefs.

- This view of crime changed when the Classical School of criminology became popular. Members of this school argued that people were free and rational actors and proposed that the key to preventing crime was the establishment of a Criminal Code based on the principle that the punishment should fit the crime.

- The Classical School had a major impact on legal systems in many countries. However, the resulting legal codes were rigid and inflexible. Other scholars proposed a series of Neoclassical reforms that have now been incorporated in the legal systems of many countries.

■ Lombroso and other members of the Positive School brought scientific methods to the study of crime. While Lombroso's biological theory has not stood up to scientific scrutiny, the application of science to criminology represented a major shift in the discipline.

■ Lombroso's work was followed by a number of other researchers who sought to blame crime on the biological inferiority of criminals. As with Lombroso's theory, research has not supported these early 20th-century biological theories. However, they did have a major impact on the legal system, as measures such as involuntary sterilization and lengthy incarceration for "defectives" were passed in many jurisdictions.

## QUESTIONS FOR CRITICAL THINKING

1. How did the development of the Classical School of criminology reflect the wider changes taking place in European society at the time? Consider how the social, economic, and ideological forces influenced the founders of the Classical School.

2. What changes did the Positive School of criminology introduce? How did these alter the existing explanations of crime and criminality? What are the implications of the Positive School for the way we treat people who break the law today?

3. What were the major biological explanations of criminality that emerged early in the 20th century? How were these explanations received by social scientists?

4. Discuss the social policy implications of the early biological theories. In other words, if the theories were correct, what should societies do to deal with crime?

5. In general, what have you learned in this chapter about the relationship between theories of criminality and social policy concerning the treatment of criminals?

## NET WORK

In this chapter, you learned about the way that classical theory and positivist theory have influenced the way western nations such as Canada and the United States address issues like sentencing.  The debates over sentencing continue to influence public opinion and criminal justice policy today. Should the punishment "fit the crime" or should we take other factors into account when sentencing someone and let the punishment "fit the offender"? The intensity of this debate is clearly visible in the competing points of view expressed over two sentencing policies: (1) "three strikes" and (2) "mandatory minimum sentences."

To learn more about these debates, follow the links below to some interesting articles and information about other useful sites.

- Three Strikes Policy: **http://www.idebate.org/debatabase/topic_details.php?topicID=193**
- Wiki on Sentencing in Canada: **http://en.wikipedia.org/wiki/Criminal_sentencing_in_Canada**
- Mandatory Minimum Sentencing in Canada: **http://www.justice.gc.ca/eng/pi/rs/rep-rap/2005/rr05_10/p2.html**; **http://www.parl.gc.ca/Content/LOP/researchpublications/prb0553-e.htm**; and **http://www.straight.com/article-203919/mandatory-minimum-sentences-are-sometimes-unconstitutional**

Review the discussion around sentencing in order to answer the following questions:

1. What is the "three strikes" policy in sentencing?
2. Which theory of criminology is most reflected in the "three strikes policy"?
3. Briefly summarize the current debates over this criminal justice policy.
4. What is "mandatory minimum sentencing"?
5. Which theory of criminology is reflected in "mandatory minimum sentencing" policy?
6. Briefly summarize the current debate in Canada over this criminal justice policy.

## KEY TERMS

atavism; pg. 270
Classical School; pg. 262
deterrence; pg. 266

Positive School; pg. 268
Statistical School; pg. 267
stigmata; pg. 270

## BIBLIOGRAPHY

Angell, Robert. (1965). *Free Society and Moral Crisis*. Ann Arbor: University of Michigan Press.

Archer, Dane, Rosemary Gartner, and Marc Beittel. (1983). "Homicide and the Death Penalty: A Cross-National Test of a Deterrence Hypothesis." *Journal of Criminal Law and Criminology* 74:991–1014.

Beccaria, Cesare. (1963). *On Crimes and Punishments*. Translated by H. Paolucci. Indianapolis: Bobbs-Merrill. (First published as Dei Delitti E Delle Pene in 1764.)

Beirne, Piers. (1993). *Inventing Criminology*. Albany: State University of New York.

Best, Michael. (1998). "What Did Elizabethans Consider a Crime?" Shakespeare's Life and Times Home Page. Internet Shakespeare Editions 2001. Available at http://web.uvic.ca/shakespeare/Library/SLTnoframes/history/crime.html; accessed July 14, 2003.

Driver, Edwin D. (1972). "Charles Buckman Goring." In Hermann Mannheim (ed.), *Pioneers in Criminology* (pp. 429–42). Montclair, NJ: Patterson Smith.

Empey, LaMar T. (1982). *American Delinquency: Its Meaning and Construction*. Homewood, IL: The Dorsey Press.

Gibbs, Jack R. (1975). *Crime, Punishment, and Deterrence*. New York: Elsevier.

Goddard, H. H. (1912). *The Kallikak Family: A Study in the Heredity of Feeble-Mindedness*. New York: Macmillan.

———. (1914). *Feeble-Mindedness: Its Causes and Consequences*. New York: Macmillan.

Goring, Charles. (1913). *The English Convict*. London: His Majesty's Stationery Office.

———. (1972). *The English Convict*. Montclair, NJ: Patterson Smith.

Gould, Stephen Jay. (1981). *The Mismeasure of Man*. New York: W. W. Norton.

Harris, Marvin. (1974). *Cows, Pigs, Wars and Witches*. New York: Vintage Books.

Hobbes, Thomas. (1958). *Leviathan, Parts I and II*. Indianapolis: Bobbs-Merrill. (First published in 1651.)

Hogan, Margaret Monahan. (n.d.). "Medical Ethics: The New Eugenics: Therapy—Enhancement—Screening—Testing." International Catholic University. Available at http://home.comcast.net/~icuweb/c04106.htm.

Hooker, Richard. (n.d.). "The European Enlightenment." *World Civilizations*. Washington State University. Available at http://www.wsu.edu/~dee/ENLIGHT/ENLIGHT.HTM.

Hooton, Ernest Albert. (1939). *The American Criminal: An Anthropological Study*. Cambridge, MA: Harvard University Press.

Hostettler, John. (2011). *Cesare Beccaria: The Genius of 'On Crimes and Punishment'*. Sherfield on Loddon: Waterside Press.

Langbein, John H. (1976). *Torture and the Law of Proof*. Chicago: University of Chicago Press.

Lilly, J. Robert, Frances T. Cullen, and Richard A. Ball. (2007). *Criminological Theory: Context and Consequences* (4th ed.). Thousand Oaks, CA: Sage Publications.

Lombroso, Cesare. (1912). *Crime: Its Causes and Remedies*. Boston: Little, Brown and Company.

———. (1972). "Criminal Man." In S. F. Sylvester (ed.), *The Heritage of Modern Criminology* (pp. 67–78). Cambridge, MA: Schenkman.

Lombroso-Ferrero, Gina. (1972). *Criminal Man According to the Classification of Cesare Lombroso*. Montclair, NJ: Patterson Smith.

Monachesi, Elio. (1972). "Cesare Beccaria." In Hermann Mannheim (ed.), *Pioneers in Criminology*. Montclair, NJ: Patterson Smith.

Newman, Graeme. (1978). *The Punishment Response*. New York: J. B. Lippincott.

Newman, Graeme, and Pietro Marongiu. (1990). "Penological Reform and the Myth of Beccaria." *Criminology* (May):325–46.

Parmelee, Maurice. (1912). "Introduction to the English Version." In Cesare Lombroso, *Crime: Its Causes and Remedies* (pp. xi–xxxii). Boston: Little, Brown and Company.

Pfohl, Stephen J. (1985). *Images of Deviance and Social Control*. New York: McGraw-Hill.

Phillipson, Coleman. (1970). *Three Criminal Law Reformers*. Montclair, NJ: Patterson Smith.

Radzinowicz, Sir Leon. (1966). *Ideology and Crime*. London: Heinemann.

Radzinowicz, Sir Leon, and Joan King. (1977). *The Growth of Crime*. London: Pelican Books.

Rafter, Nicole Hahn. (1997). *Creating Born Criminals*. Urbana: University of Illinois Press.

Rosenhaft, Eve. "The Nazi Persecution of Deaf People." Panel Presentation, United States Holocaust Memorial Museum, Tuesday, August 14, 2001. Available at http://www .ushmm.org/research/center/presentations/discussions/details/2001-08-14/details/.

Roshier, Bob. (1989). *Controlling Crime: The Classical Perspective in Criminology*. Philadelphia: Open University Press.

Sylvester, F. Sawyer, Jr. (1972). *The Heritage of Modern Criminology*. Cambridge, MA: Schenkman.

Taylor, Ian, Paul Walton, and Jock Young. (1973). *The New Criminology: For a Social Theory of Deviance*. London: Routledge and Kegan Paul.

Thomas, Charles W., and John R. Hepburn. (1983). *Crime, Criminal Law and Criminology*. Dubuque, Iowa: Wm. C. Brown Company Publishers.

Wetzell, Richard. (2000). *Inventing the Criminal: A History of German Criminology: 1880–1945*. Chapel Hill: The University of North Carolina Press.

Wolf, Leonard. (1981). In Stephen Jay Gould, *The Mismeasure of Man*. New York: W. W. Norton.

Wolfgang, Marvin E. (1972). "Cesare Lombroso." In Hermann Mannheim (ed.), *Pioneers in Criminology* (pp. 232–91). Montclair, NJ: Patterson Smith.

Zilborg, Gregory. (1969). *The Medical Man and the Witch During the Renaissance*. New York: Cooper Square Publishers.

# 9

# Psychological Perspectives on Criminality

**Patricia A. Zapf**

JOHN JAY COLLEGE OF CRIMINAL JUSTICE

**Nathalie C. Gagnon**

KWANTLEN UNIVERSITY COLLEGE

**David N. Cox**

SIMON FRASER UNIVERSITY

**Ronald Roesch**

SIMON FRASER UNIVERSITY

This chapter reviews different psychological perspectives on criminality. We begin with a discussion of the characteristics of psychological theories and then review various psychological theories that have been proposed to explain criminality. Next, antisocial personality and psychopathy are described, and the differences between the two are illustrated through the use of three case studies—Charles Manson, Vince Li, and Canada's most notorious criminal, Clifford Olson. We conclude with a discussion of crime and mental illness, including a review of research in this area and a discussion of the prevalence of mental illness in jail and prison populations.

## Learning Objectives

After reading this chapter, you should be able to

- Describe and critique the different psychological theories that have been used to explain criminal behaviour, including psychoanalytic theory, moral development theory, Eysenck's theory, social learning theory, and operant conditioning theory.
- Understand what is meant by the term "antisocial personality."
- Describe the difference between Antisocial Personality Disorder and psychopathy.
- Describe the most current theories linking crime and mental illness.

# Psychological Theories of Crime

There has been considerable debate over psychological explanations of criminal behaviour. Psychologists typically approach the problem of understanding, explaining, and predicting criminality by developing theories of personality or learning that account for an individual's behaviour in a specific situation. Over 30 years ago, an extensive review of a decade of published research on offenders (Reppucci and Clingempeel, 1978) found that nearly all the research could be characterized as reflecting one of two value assumptions. The first is the **assumption of offender deficit**, which asserts that theories and interventions are premised on the notion that there is something psychologically wrong with offenders. The second is the **assumption of discriminating traits**, which holds that criminals differ from non-criminals, particularly in such traits as impulsivity and aggression. Research based on this assumption would involve studies of offender and non-offender populations and would utilize a number of personality tests in an attempt to find traits that differentiate the two groups.

Critics have taken issue with psychology's reliance on these two assumptions. Reppucci and Clingempeel (1978) point to two major omissions in psychological research. One is that there is typically very little emphasis placed on studies of the strengths of offenders. Most of the research and interventions focus on the deficits rather than on the positive characteristics of individuals. While the concerns of Reppucci and Clingempeel continue to have validity today, the field has made a considerable shift with recent research and theory increasingly recognizing the importance of offender strengths (Webster et al., 2006; Hoge, Guerra, and Boxer, 2008). A second omission identified by Reppucci and Clingempeel is that psychological research tends to ignore the potential importance of situational and environmental factors on individual behaviour. Again, recent developments have stressed the importance of external factors in both explaining criminal behaviour and developing intervention programs designed to reduce recidivism (e.g., Haney, 2002; Moretti, Jackson, and Obsuth, 2010).

Others, such as Reid (2003), have been critical of psychological theories of crime that are based on the expectation that it is possible to classify individuals as criminals and non-criminals, arguing that this classification cannot be done reliably. Rather, evidence suggests that criminal behaviour is pervasive, as indicated by studies of self-reported delinquency, white-collar crime, and corporate crime (Thornberry and Krohn, 2000).

Conversely, the work of David Farrington (2002) illustrates the importance of understanding individual differences. Farrington views criminal behaviour as the outcome of several different social and psychological factors (see also Loeber et al., 2001a, 2001b). According to him, the motivation to commit delinquent acts arises primarily out of a desire for material goods or a need for excitement. If these desires cannot be satisfied in a socially approved manner, an illegal act may be chosen. The motivation to commit delinquent acts will be influenced by psychological variables, including the individual's learning history and the beliefs he or she may have internalized regarding criminal behaviour. Eysenck and Gudjonsson (1989) support this position, suggesting that "psychological factors and individual differences related to the personality are

**assumption of offender deficit**

The view that offenders who break the law have some psychological deficit that distinguishes them from normal law-abiding citizens.

**assumption of discriminating traits**

The view that offenders are distinguished from non-offenders by, for example, their high levels of impulsiveness and aggression.

of central importance in relation to both the causes of crime and its control." They contend that psychology, with its focus on individual differences, is the central discipline in the study of criminal behaviour and that "no system of criminology has any meaning that disregards this central feature of all criminology: the individual person whom we are trying to influence."

While the individual perspective is clearly the dominant one in psychology, there are other psychological perspectives, such as those of **community psychology** (Roesch, 1988), that are quite closely akin to sociological perspectives. Commonly, such psychologists view social problems from what Rappaport (1977) has termed a "levels of analysis" perspective. Briefly, the four levels are (1) *individual level*, in which social problems are defined in terms of individual deficit; (2) *small-group level*, which suggests that social problems are created by problems in group functioning, essentially problems in interpersonal communication and understanding; (3) *organizational level*, in which the organizations of society have not accomplished what they have been designed to accomplish; and (4) *institutional or community level*, in which it is suggested that social problems are created by institutions rather than by persons, groups, or organizations. At this level the emphasis is on the values and policies underlying institutional functioning.

An example that cuts across these four levels would be the way in which "victimless" crimes, such as drug abuse and prostitution, are defined. If the problem is defined at the first level, individuals would be examined to determine what psychological problems they have. Once this has been determined, direct interventions could be employed in changing these individuals so that they might fit into society better and conform to the existing laws. At the small-group level, the influence of peers, such as drug-abusing friends, could be viewed as influencing the individual's behaviour. At the next level, organizations such as law enforcement agencies would be seen as having insufficient resources to prevent or deter individuals from engaging in criminal behaviour. Finally, if this problem is defined at the institutional level, it might be said that the problems that individuals face are caused by the laws their society has created. Therefore, the focus would be on changing the laws so that they do not affect people negatively. If the problem is defined at the institutional level, therapy for an individual would be inappropriate if the cause of the problem was, for example, related to socio-economic factors (Seidman and Rabkin, 1983). Community psychologists tend to define social problems at the organizational and institutional levels and have a theoretical perspective that has much in common with that of sociologists.

Haney (2002, 34) builds on this perspective and makes a strong case for a situational approach to understanding criminal behaviour. He comments that:

> A more situation-centered legal system would concentrate less exclusively on defective properties of the person and more on situational pathologies. A modern, psychologically informed criminal law would more carefully weigh the effects of environmental stressors that may have significantly altered a defendant's psychological state, and it would take into explicit account those situational pressures that may have undermined or precluded the "mature reflection" that in the past has been presumed to precede action.

**community psychology**

A perspective that analyzes social problems, including crime, as largely a product of organizational and institutional characteristics of society. It is closely related to sociology.

These concerns and alternative perspectives should be kept in mind as different psychological theories of criminal behaviour are considered. These theories focus, for the most part, on individual-level variables and explanations. The remainder of this chapter will review psychological theories that can be directly related to understanding criminal behaviour.

## Psychoanalytic Theory

Although psychoanalytic theories as an explanation for criminal behaviour have fallen out of favour in recent decades as the field moves more and more toward a model of evidence-based practice, it is useful to examine the history of psychoanyaltic theory given its importance to the foundation of clinical psychology. Sigmund Freud is the figure most associated with psychoanalytic theory, but he did not make any significant attempts to relate his theory specifically to criminal behaviour. Other psychoanalysts have, however, attempted to explain criminal behaviour with psychoanalytic concepts (Alexander and Healey, 1935; Friedlander, 1947; Polansky et al., 1950; Bowlby, 1953; Redl, 1966).

A basic premise of psychoanalytic theory is that people progress through five overlapping stages of development. These are the oral, anal, phallic, latency, and genital stages. Freud believed that personality is composed of three forces: the **id** (biological drives), the **ego** (which screens, controls, and directs the impulses of the id and acts as a reality tester), and the **superego** (conscience). Psychoanalytic theory holds that the ego and superego are developed through the successful resolution of conflicts presented at each stage of development. It is believed that both biological and social factors are involved in the resolution of each stage (see Figure 9.1).

Psychoanalytic theory presents an elaborate, comprehensive view of the psychological functioning of individuals. It deals with all aspects of human behaviour but the discussion here will be limited to its impact on the study of criminal behaviour. Briefly, this theory suggests that criminal behaviour occurs when "internal (ego and superego) controls are unable to restrain the primitive, aggressive, antisocial instincts of the id" (Nietzel, 1979). Criminal behaviour is the consequence of an individual's failure to progress through the early stages of development, which leaves the superego inadequately developed or deficient. The individual is left susceptible to antisocial behaviour (Martin et al., 1981).

Warren and Hindelang (1979) have summarized five other interpretations of criminal behaviour that can be derived from psychoanalytic theory:

1. Criminal behaviour is a form of neurosis which does not differ in any fundamental way from other forms of neuroses (e.g., while some neurotics work too hard, others set fires).
2. The criminal often suffers from a compulsive need for punishment in order to alleviate guilt feelings and anxiety stemming from unconscious strivings.
3. Criminal activity may be a means of obtaining substitute gratification of needs and desires not met inside the family.
4. Delinquent behaviour is often due to traumatic events whose memory has been repressed.
5. Delinquent behaviour may be an expression of displaced hostility.

Source: Warren, M. Q., and M. J. Hindelang. (1979). "Current Explanations of Offender Behavior." In H. Toch (ed.), *Psychology of Crime and Criminal Justice* (pp. 166–82). New York: Holt, Rinehart and Winston.

**id**

A psychoanalytical term that denotes the most inaccessible and primitive part of the mind. It is a reservoir of biological urges that strive continually for gratification. The ego mediates between the *id* and the *superego*.

**ego**

A psychoanalytical term that denotes the rational part of the personality. It mediates between the *id* and the *superego* and is responsible for dealing with reality and making decisions.

**superego**

A psychoanalytical term that denotes the ethical and moral dimensions of personality; an individual's conscience. The *ego* mediates between the *superego* and the *id*.

**"Freud Net" The Abraham A. Brill Library of The New York Psychoanalytic Institute** www.psychoanalysis.org/ resources-library.html

**FIGURE 9.1**    Freud's Theory of Personality

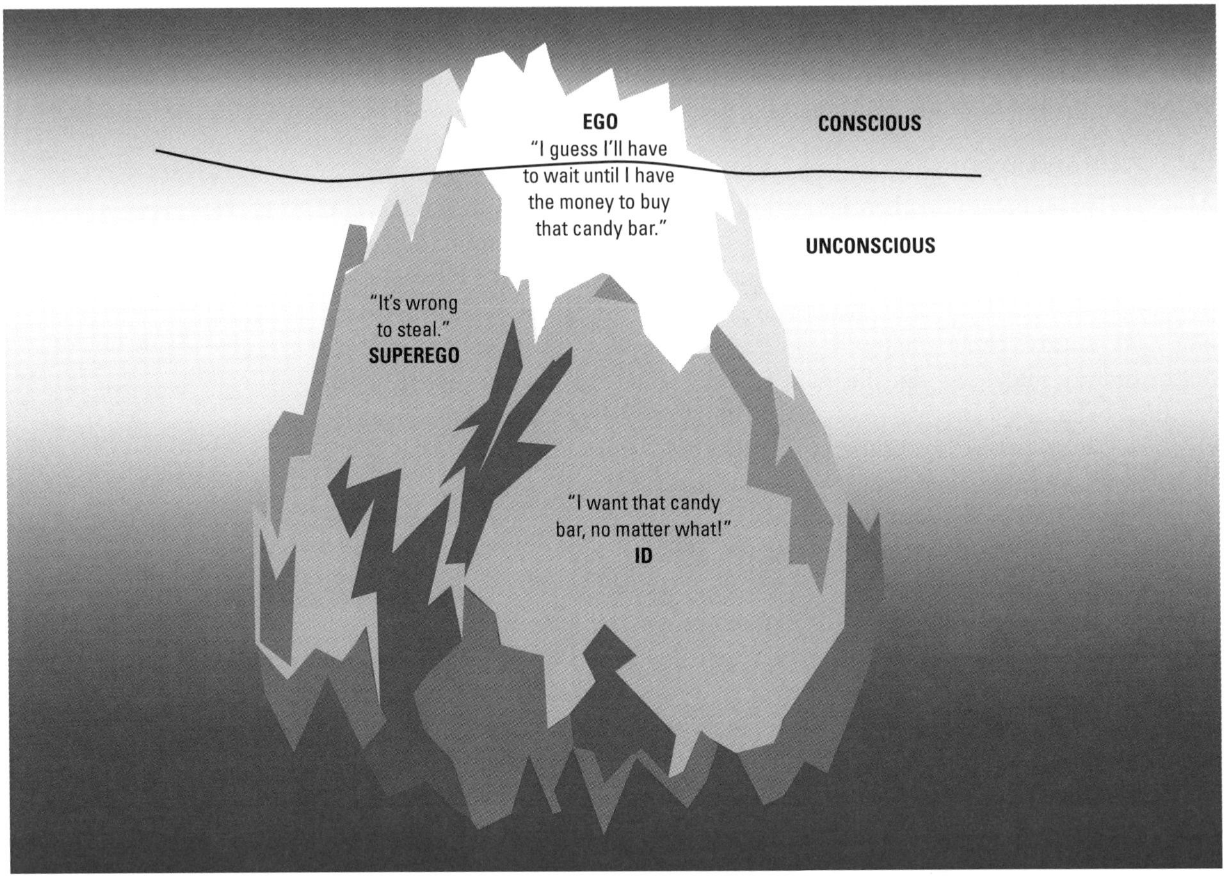

EGO
"I guess I'll have
to wait until I have
the money to buy
that candy bar."

CONSCIOUS

UNCONSCIOUS

"It's wrong
to steal."
SUPEREGO

"I want that candy
bar, no matter what!"
ID

This illustration shows how Freud might picture a person's internal conflict over whether to commit an antisocial act such as stealing a candy bar. In addition to dividing personality into three components, Freud theorized that our personalities are largely unconscious—hidden away outside our normal awareness. To dramatize this point, Freud compared conscious awareness (portions of the ego and superego) to the visible tip of an iceberg. Most of our personality—including the id, with its raw desires and impulses—lies submerged in our subconscious.

Source: From KENDALL. *Sociology In Our Times (with InfoTrac) 2E.* © 1999 Wadsworth, a part of Cengage Learning, Inc. Reproduced by permission. www.cengage.com/permissions.

Schoenfeld (1971) offered a theory of juvenile delinquency that illustrates psychoanalytic theory. Schoenfeld proposed that delinquent behaviour reflects a weak, defective, or incomplete superego that is unable to control the oral, anal, and phallic impulses that are resurrected at puberty. Schoenfeld believes that parental deprivation and lack of affection, especially during the first few years of a child's life, is the cause of a weak superego. Boys raised in a fatherless home, he adds, will be especially prone to deviant behaviour as they attempt to establish their male identity.

A number of studies support the view that family life is important in the process of **socialization**. Bowlby (1953) stressed that a stable attachment to a mother in the first few years of life allows the child to show affection toward others and to care for them. If this attachment does not occur, the child will

**socialization**

The interactive process whereby individuals come to learn and internalize the culture of their society or group.

be unable to show affection and, thus, may damage others without remorse through various forms of victimization.

One of the difficulties in assessing psychoanalytic theory is that many aspects of it are untestable because they rely on unobservable underlying constructs. As Ewen (1988, 55) has observed, "Psychoanalytic theory presents a formidable difficulty: the most important part of the personality, the unconscious, is also the most inaccessible." It is therefore the psychoanalyst who interprets the offender's behaviours and actions. Any attempt by the offender to refute the interpretation is seen as resistance and further evidence of its truth.

As Cohen (1966) points out, "Aggressive or acquisitive acts are often explained by underlying aggressive or acquisitive impulses." This explanation is a tautology in that aggressive acts are explained by aggressive impulses, but the only evidence of the aggressive impulses is the occurrence of aggressive acts. Many have suggested that psychoanalytic theory is empirically unverifiable, a necessary criteria for any scientific theory.

Another criticism of psychoanalytic theory is that studies have failed to demonstrate that criminals desire to be punished or suffer from guilt or anxiety, as one psychoanalyst (Abrahamsen, 1944) suggested. In fact, as Nietzel (1979) asserts, "criminals are very successful in their efforts to prevent detection or if detected, elude official prosecution and conviction. Most offenders do not appear unduly frustrated or further guilt-ridden by the fact that their 'crime pays' at least some of the time." Despite these problems, psychoanalytic theory is regarded by some as a useful conceptual framework for understanding the importance of early development on later behaviour of all types, including criminal behaviour.

## Theories of Moral Development

According to moral development theorists, if we wish to understand criminal and delinquent behaviour we need to ask how it is that individuals develop, or fail to develop, a sense of morality and responsibility. One of the first contemporary moral development theorists was the French psychologist Jean Piaget (1932), whose research focused on the moral lives of children. In order to determine how children developed their ideas about right and wrong, Piaget studied how children developed the rules to the games they played. He concluded that moral reasoning developed in stages. The thinking of young children was characterized by egocentrism. That is, they projected their own thoughts and wishes onto others because they were unable to take the perspective of those others. Through their interaction with others, by the ages of 11 or 12, children will normally have progressed to the stage of cooperation with others. Based on this research, Piaget concluded that the schools should teach moral reasoning by allowing students to work out the rules through problem solving in the classroom.

Kohlberg, expanding on Piaget's theory, has hypothesized that there are six stages of moral development (see Table 9.1). The stages are age related and progression through the stages occurs as "the developing child becomes better able to understand and integrate diverse points of view on a moral-conflict situation and to take more of the relevant situational factors into account" (Jennings et al., 1983). Kohlberg believes that all individuals go through the same sequence of stages, although the pace may vary and some individuals may never progress beyond the first few stages.

**TABLE 9.1    Kohlberg's Theory of Moral Development**

| Level | Stage | Description | |
|---|---|---|---|
| I. | Preconventional | 1. Punishment | Egocentric (What happens to me?) |
| | | 2. Instrumental hedonism | |
| II. | Conventional | 3. Approval of others | Social expectations (What do others expect of me?) |
| | | 4. Authority maintaining morality | |
| III. | Postconventional | 5. Democratically accepted law | Universality (What is best for all?) |
| | | 6. Principles of conscience | |

Source: Reprinted from *The Psychology of Criminal Conduct* with permission. Copyright 1994 Matthew Bender & Company, Inc., a member of the LexisNexis Group. All rights reserved.

Kohlberg categorizes the six stages into three levels of moral judgment development, each with two stages of moral reasoning.

The first is the *preconventional* level, characteristic of children under age 11 and of many adolescent and adult offenders. At this level, the morals and values of society are understood as "do's" and "don'ts" and are associated with punishment. The preconventional person is one for whom roles and social expectations are something external to the self.

The *conventional* level reflects the average adolescent and adult in our society and others. He or she understands, accepts, and attempts to uphold the values and rules of society. For a conventional person, the self is identified with or has internalized the rules and expectations of others, especially those of authorities.

The *postconventional* level is the one at which customs are critically examined with regard to universal rights, duties, and moral principles. It is characteristic of a minority of adults after the age of 20. The postconventional person has differentiated his or her self from the rules and expectations of others and defined his or her value by means of self-chosen principles (Jennings et al., 1983).

Carol Gilligan (1982) has criticized Kohlberg's theory of moral development, stating that it is biased in favour of males. Gilligan argues that there is variation in moral standards by gender, with females taking a more care-oriented approach to morality, while males typically use a more justice-oriented approach. She believes that Kohlberg's theory does not take into consideration the more care-oriented approach of females and that, as a result, females rarely obtain the higher stages of moral development in Kohlberg's theory. To support her argument, she points out that females were not taken into consideration when Kohlberg was developing his theory—the development of moral judgment was based on an empirical study of 84 males whom Kohlberg followed for a 20-year period. Gilligan states that females typically reach only the second level (third stage) in Kohlberg's theory, which is characterized by goodness being equated with helping and pleasing others and is consistent with the care-oriented approach of females to morality. She argues that Kohlberg and Kramer (1969) have looked at this concept of goodness and concluded that this level of moral reasoning would be adequate for women whose lives will take place in the home. They indicate that only when women enter the "traditional arena of male activity" do they realize that this level of moral reasoning is not sufficient, and therefore go on to progress toward the higher stages as men do. Gilligan points out that "herein lies a paradox, for the very traits that traditionally have defined the 'goodness' of women, their care for and sensitivity to the needs of others, are those that mark them as deficient in moral development" (1982, 18).

Considerable research has been done on the relationship between moral development and delinquency. Kohlberg believes that people with high moral development are more likely to make individual choices and be less influenced by friends or by consequences of actions. Thus there should be an inverse relationship between moral development and delinquency. Support for this relationship has been found in a number of studies. For example, Kiriakidis (2008) found that delinquents, compared to a non-delinquent sample, scored significantly higher on a moral disengagement scale. Jennings et al. (1983) reviewed a large number of studies on this relationship and concluded that "the overwhelming weight of the empirical data reviewed here supports the notion that juvenile delinquents' moral judgement is at a less advanced level than that of non-delinquent controls matched on a variety of variables." But they are careful to point out that a cause–effect relationship has not been established. Individuals at the same level of moral development may or may not become delinquent. They add that

> these studies lend support to the more modest claims that moral reasoning of increased maturity has an insulating effect against delinquency. Advanced stages of moral judgment cause one's moral orientation to be more integrated, stable and consistent. Higher reasoning makes one a more reliable moral agent and thus better able to withstand some incentives to illegal conduct postulated by a variety of sociological and psychological theories of the etiology of delinquency. (1983, 290)

This last statement suggests that moral development theory has considerable relevance for a sociological explanation of criminal behaviour. Indeed, Morash (1983) has discussed at length the possible integration of moral development and sociological theories, suggesting that it may be more fruitful to study the interaction of personal and situational variables. She concludes:

> Most serious delinquency would result from social conditions, primarily those that are enduring, that impinge on youths who possess the personality factors and the pre-conventional reasoning conducive to serious delinquent behavior. An advantage of this explanation is that it allows for the many pre-conventional individuals who do not break the law regularly or not at all, and it accounts for different patterns in delinquency—that is, the repeated serious delinquency and sporadic and/or less serious delinquency. (1983, 405)

**moral development theory**

Refers generally to theories of individual psychology that investigate how moral reasoning emerges in the individual and develops as the individual matures.

Research has supported the link between **moral development** and adult criminality. In a study examining the moral development of 72 adult male sex offenders participating in a community-based treatment, Buttell (2002) found that sex offenders employed a level of moral reasoning that was two standard deviations lower than the national norm. In addition, theories of moral development have important implications for offender rehabilitation programs (Blasi, 1980). Evidence suggests that education programs that focus on moral development have positive effects on inmates' moral judgments (MacPhail, 1989). However, future research will need to examine whether this increased morality leads to lower rates of criminal behaviour and recidivism.

In conclusion, there is evidence to suggest that level of moral reasoning is related to delinquent and criminal behaviour. However, the correlations reported in many studies are often quite low. Moral development may affect how an individual behaves in a given context, but it is clear that other characteristics of the individual, as well as the situation, will also be important determinants of behaviour.

"Hans Eysenck and Other Temperament Theorists"
C. George Boeree,
Shippensburg University of Pennsylvania
www.ship.edu/~cgboeree/
eysenck.html

## Eysenck's Theory of Crime and Personality

Hans Eysenck, a noted British psychologist, has developed an elaborate theory of how personality characteristics are related to criminal behaviour (Eysenck, 1977). This theory has generated considerable research, in large part because it lends itself quite readily to the identification of groups of offenders and to predictions about their behaviour.

Eysenck believes that illegal, selfish, or immoral behaviour is simple to explain. These behaviours are inherently reinforcing and, hence, it is more fruitful to try to explain why people do *not* commit crimes. Eysenck claims that children will naturally engage in such acts and only refrain from doing so if they are punished. Eysenck's theory is based on **classical conditioning**. Each time a child is punished, he or she may experience pain and fear. This pain and fear may be associated with the act itself. Thus whenever the child contemplates the act, he or she will experience fear, which will tend to inhibit the response. Eysenck equates this conditioned fear with conscience. Delinquents and criminals do not readily develop this conditioned response, either because of lack of exposure to effective conditioning practices by parents and others, or because they are less susceptible to conditioning. Eysenck (1990) states

**classical conditioning**

A basic form of learning whereby a neutral stimulus is paired with another stimulus that naturally elicits a certain response; the neutral stimulus comes to elicit the same response as the stimulus that automatically elicits the response.

> Depending on the frequency of pairings between the conditioned and unconditioned stimulus in the field of social behavior, and on the precise content of the conditioning program, children will grow up to develop appropriate types of behavior. Conditionability is a crucial factor on the social or environmental side. In a permissive society where parents, teachers, and magistrates do not take seriously the task of imposing a "conscience" which would lead them to behave in a socialized manner, a large number of individuals with poor or average conditionability will acquire a "conscience" too weak to prevent them from indulging in criminal activities, although had they been subjected to a stricter regime of conditioning, they might have grown up to be perfectly respectable and law-abiding citizens.

As Eysenck points out, the concept of "strictness" is not a function of excessive strength of the conditioning process, but a result of the certainty and frequency of pairings of the conditioned and unconditioned stimulus.

There are three dimensions of personality, according to Eysenck. **Extraversion** is a personality characteristic with highly sociable, impulsive, and aggressive people at one extreme of the continuum. Highly introverted, introspective, and inhibited people are the other extreme. *Neuroticism* is linked to the psychiatric concept of neurosis. People who are high on this dimension are characterized by such symptoms as anxiety, restlessness, and other emotional responses. The opposite extreme of neuroticism is referred to as stability. The third dimension is *psychoticism*. According to Eysenck and Eysenck (1976), a person who is high on this dimension is "cold, impersonal, hostile, lacking in sympathy, unfriendly, untrustful, odd, unemotional, unhelpful, antisocial, lacking in human feelings, inhumane, generally bloodyminded, lacking in insight, strange, with paranoid ideas that people are against him."

A number of hypotheses have been generated about the relationship of these dimensions to criminal behaviour. Extraverts, because of their high need for excitement, their impulsivity, and relatively weak conscience, are believed to be more prone to criminal behaviour. In addition, persons high on both neuroticism and extraversion would be predicted to be delinquents or criminals. Persons high on psychoticism would tend to be more serious offenders, with a propensity for violence. Hare (1982) investigated the relationship between these three dimensions and psychopathy. While neuroticism and extraversion did not correlate with measures of psychopathy, psychoticism did. It is concluded that this may be because each dimension taps a common element of psychopathy (criminal and antisocial tendencies) rather than those psychological features that are assumed in the diagnosis of psychopathy (for example, lack of remorse, lack of empathy).

Eysenck and others have developed psychological measures of each of these dimensions. Research in testing predictions about offenders has produced mixed results. In their extensive and excellent review of Eysenck's theory, Farrington et al. (1982) summarized data from 16 studies, most of which were conducted in Great Britain, and found that while some studies support the predictions of Eysenck's theory, other studies do not. Bartol (1980) comes to a similar conclusion.

Like other theories, personality theories such as Eysenck's have problems with tautology or circular reasoning. That is, in many measures of personality, the sub-scale that differentiates delinquents from non-delinquents includes items asking about antisocial behaviour (e.g., have you been in trouble with the law)—the very thing it proposes to explain. In addition, some have criticized personality theories for failing to adequately define its terms (Einstadter and Henry, 1995).

Eysenck's theory is important because it shows how psychological and social variables can be interrelated. Individuals who may have a psychological propensity to commit crime may be effectively socialized if they grow up in an environment that provides effective conditioning. Similarly, individuals with a low propensity for criminality may become criminal if their environment is too

**extraversion**
A personality characteristic associated with sociability, impulsiveness, and aggression.

permissive. Although Eysenck argues strongly for the importance of individual differences, he recognizes the importance of societal influences: "Crime . . . is essentially a function of the ethos of the society in which we live; it reflects the practices of positive and negative reinforcement, of reward and punishment, of teaching and conditioning, which are prevalent, and these in turn are mirrored and reflected by the types of films we see, television programs we watch, books and newspapers we read, and teaching and examples we receive at school." In the next section, it will be seen that social learning theory reflects this perspective more explicitly.

## Social Learning Theory

Another theory that lends itself to an integration of sociology and psychology is social learning theory. Although this theory focuses on individual behaviour, it takes into account the influence of the environment and of social conditions on the individual. Cognitive functioning—the ability to think and make choices—is central to social learning theory.

**modelling**

A form of learning that occurs as a result of watching and imitating others.

An important element of social learning theory is the role of **modelling**. Individuals can learn new behaviours through direct experience or by observing the behaviour of others. The latter, also referred to as vicarious learning, can be a most effective and efficient way to acquire new behaviours. Albert Bandura, a Stanford University professor of psychology, is a leading social learning theorist. He suggests that "virtually all learning phenomena resulting from direct experiences can occur on a vicarious basis through observation of other persons' behavior and its consequences for them" (Bandura, 1979).

Social learning theory has been used to explain how aggression is learned. Since this is of great concern to criminology theory, aggression will be used as an example of an application of social learning theory.

Bandura (1979) suggests that aggressive behaviour can be learned from three sources. The *family* is one source, with a number of studies showing that children of parents who respond aggressively to problems will tend to use similar tactics. Bandura also points to research on child abuse, which shows that many children who have been abused will later become abusers themselves. Another source of aggressive behaviour can be referred to as *subcultural influences*, or the influence of social models and peers. Bandura suggests that "the highest incidence of aggression is found in communities in which aggressive models abound and fighting prowess is regarded as a valued attribute." The third source of learned aggressive behaviour is through *symbolic modelling*. An example of this is violence on television, which provides models of aggressive behaviour (Skoler et al., 1994).

"Albert Bandura (1925– present)" C. George Boeree, Shippensburg University of Pennsylvania

www.ship.edu/~cgboeree/ bandura.html

Bandura's research on the role of film models reinforced existing concerns about the effects of television on aggressive behaviour. Geen (1983) reviewed the research on the relationship between viewing television violence and aggression. He first looked at the vast number of correlational studies, the majority of which support the conclusion that there is a positive relationship between viewing violence and aggressive behaviour. A typical study is the one by Teevan and Hartnagel (1976), which showed that high school students who described their favourite television shows as violent also reported committing more aggressive acts than students whose favourite shows were non-violent. More recently, Anderson and his colleagues (2010) have found evidence for a relationship between playing violent video games and aggressive behaviour.

The problem with correlational research, as Geen points out, is that the direction of causation is unknown. It is possible that people who are more likely to behave aggressively simply prefer more violent television shows. Thus it cannot be concluded through correlational studies alone that viewing violence is the cause of aggressive behaviour. Cook et al. (1983) re-analyzed data from several large-scale studies of the effects of television violence. They concluded that an association between television viewing and aggression by children can be found regularly, but the level of association is typically quite small and often not statistically significant. Nevertheless, they conclude that the association is most probably a causal one, that watching violence on television does have an effect on children's aggressive behaviour. The same can be said for violence in music videos (Smith and Boyson, 2002).

In addition to its direct effect on aggressive behaviour, it is also possible that exposure to television violence increases one's tolerance toward violence and decreases one's sensitivity to acts of violence. Thomas et al. (1979) found that both adult and child subjects showed less **autonomic reactivity** to a scene of real-life interpersonal aggression if they had first watched a violent scene from a television show. Malamuth and Check (1981) reported similar results in their study of the effects of film violence on attitudes toward violence. Male and female university students were randomly assigned to view either a violent-sexual or a control feature-length film. The films were shown as part of the regular campus film program, and subjects believed they were viewing the films as a film-rating task. Several days later, they were asked to respond to a number of attitude measures, but were unaware of any relationship between the film and the questionnaire. Malamuth and Check found that exposure to the film portraying violent sexuality was associated with a greater acceptance of interpersonal violence against women. This finding was true only for male subjects. Female subjects had a nonsignificant tendency in the opposite direction, as women exposed to violence tended to be less accepting of interpersonal violence than control females. It is important to realize, however, that this study does not provide any data on whether males exposed to violence would actually behave differently toward women. But the study does demonstrate that such exposure may have a significant effect on attitudes.

In his analysis of antisocial behaviour, Bandura (1986) suggests that the best deterrent to such activity is the provision of more attractive pro-social alternatives. However, he acknowledges that "when inducements to criminal acts are strong, when personal sanctions against such conduct are weak, and when people lack socially acceptable means of getting what they want, fear of punishment serves as a major deterrent to transgressive conduct." Deterrence may take two forms—direct or vicarious. In the former, punishment is used to discourage current transgressors of such activity in the future. In the latter, punishment serves as a general deterrent to others. Bandura identifies three major sources of deterrence against criminal activity: legal sanction, social sanction, and self-sanction. Legal sanctions derive from the belief that there

"Television Violence: A Review of the Effects on Children of Different Ages" Child and Family Canada

http://www.media-awareness.ca/english/resources/research_documents/reports/violence/tv_violence_child.cfm

**autonomic reactivity**
A measurement of the extent to which an individual's physical organism reacts to external stimuli.

are legal consequences to transgressions despite the reality that most crime goes unpunished. Bandura cites research by Clastner (1967) in stating that "people who are not in the habit of breaking the law share a distorted perception of legal threats, in which they greatly overestimate the risks of getting caught and punished for unlawful acts. In contrast, offenders judge personal risks to be lower and more in line with the actual probabilities." Social sanctions reflect the negative social consequences that criminal stigmatization can have for an individual and the powerful deterrent effect this risk has. Self-sanctions are self-imposed moral standards; they are seen as the most effective deterrent as they are operative even when there is no risk of detection involved. Bandura (1986) states, "In the absence of self-sanctions rooted in societal standards, whenever personal desires conflict with societal codes, external threats in the form of legal and social sanctions, and extensive social surveillance are needed to ensure that the rights and welfare of others are not completely disregarded."

The empirical status of social learning theory has recently been summarized by Akers and Jensen (2006, 37):

> Indeed, it is reasonable to propose that the theory has been tested in relation to a wider range of forms of deviance, in a wider range of settings and samples, in more different languages, and by more different people, has survived more "crucial tests" against other theories, and is the most strongly and consistently supported by empirical data than any other social psychological explanation of crime and deviance.

## Operant Conditioning

Another learning theory is based on the principle of operant conditioning. This involves the use of rewards and punishments to increase the probability or frequency of a given response. B. F. Skinner is the psychologist most identified with this theory, and his research forms the basis for both the theoretical and the applied applications of **operant conditioning**.

One way a response can be learned is through a process referred to as shaping. This involves rewarding approximations of some target behaviour until the behaviour gradually progresses to the desired response. Behaviour can also be learned through punishment, which can be either a withdrawal of a positive reinforcer or the introduction of a negative stimulus such as an electric shock. There have been a number of attempts to use operant conditioning theory to account for the acquisition of criminal behaviour. Notable among this work is that of Jeffery (1965) and that of Burgess and Akers (1966).

Burgess and Akers (1966) and Akers (1990) conceptualize criminal behaviour in terms of operant conditioning and imitation. The main component in Akers's (1990) social learning theory is differential reinforcement. This refers to the balance of rewards and punishments that govern behaviour. In this theory, operant conditioning is the basic process by which an individual's behaviour is shaped, and this can occur through both reinforcement and punishment. Reinforcement refers to any process that strengthens a behaviour while

**operant conditioning**

The basic process by which an individual's behaviour is shaped by reinforcement or by punishment.

"Operant (Instrumental) Conditioning" Bill Huitt, Valdosta State University
http://chiron.valdosta.edu/whuitt/col/behsys/operant.html

punishment is any process that weakens a behaviour. As applied to deviance and crime, Akers (1990, 655) states that

> social learning is a behavioral approach to socialization which includes individuals' responses to rewards and punishments in the current situation, the learned patterns of responses they bring to that situation, and the anticipated consequences of actions taken now and in the future in the initiation, continuation, and cessation of those actions. It is a "soft behaviorism" that allows for choice and cognitive processes. It views the individual's behavior as responding to and being conditioned by environmental feedback and consequences. It does not view the individual as unreasoning and only passively conditioned.

Considerable research has been conducted on the application of learning theory to the treatment of delinquents. The "teaching-family" group-home model begun in the late 1960s has been at the centre of group-home development. The approach

> rests on the view that an adolescent's behavior patterns, behavior discriminations, and skills are functions of past behavior-environment interactions (learning history), currently ongoing behavior-environment interactions, and genetic organismic variables (Braukman et al., 1980). In this conceptualization, inherited characteristics and environmental features in childhood, particularly parenting practices (relationship development, teaching, supervision, and discipline) affect later development. In adolescence, earlier developed antisocial patterns tend to persevere (indeed, are self-perpetuating) and can be maintained further by ongoing behavior-environment interactions associated with inappropriate parenting, deviant peers, and school failure. (Braukman and Wolf, 1987)

The group home provides the reinforcing environment designed to change existing behavioural interactions in the direction of functional and pro-social skills. The emphasis is on learning social and family life skills. The best known of these programs is Achievement Place, a program first implemented in a cottage-style treatment facility for delinquent youths in Lawrence, Kansas. (The name of the treatment facility was Achievement Place, hence the name of the program.) Youths in Achievement Place programs live in a residence with trained "houseparents." The heart of the program is a **token economy** system in which points can be earned (or lost). For example, residents can earn points for being at class on time, cleaning their bedroom, and engaging in other positive behaviours. Disruptive behaviour in the classroom, making aggressive statements or fighting, and being late for class can result in a loss of points. The points can be used to purchase privileges and material goods. Research on Achievement Place has demonstrated that "contingent token consequences could both establish behaviors basic to participation in lawful, productive intra- and extra-treatment activities, and eliminate behaviors likely to get the participants in further trouble" (Braukman and Wolf, 1987). A comprehensive outcome study on the teaching-family program (Braukman et al., 1985)

**token economy**

A behaviour therapy procedure based on operant learning principles. Individuals are rewarded (reinforced) for positive or appropriate behaviour and are disciplined (punished) for negative or inappropriate behaviour.

indicates that this approach has considerable short-term positive effects. However, the long-term implications are less positive since it is very difficult to control reinforcement following release from the institution. Because of this, increased emphasis has been placed on systematic aftercare to help maintain treatment effects.

# Antisocial Personality

**Antisocial Personality Disorder**

A personality disorder that involves disregard for the rights of others, as well as impulsive, irresponsible, and aggressive behaviour.

The study of antisocial personality provides a good example of how psychological theory can be applied to criminal populations. Some confusion has resulted from the variety of terms used to describe basically the same set of behaviours: sociopathy, psychopathy, moral insanity, antisocial personality, and **Antisocial Personality Disorder**. There has also been a tendency for some to use the term very loosely as a "wastebasket" category for antisocial individuals generally. There is, however, strong empirical evidence that the traits underlying this disorder form a valid, clinically meaningful cluster (Hare and Cox, 1978; Skilling et al., 2002). For many, this term is associated with images of violent and sadistic murderers as portrayed countless times on television or, all too often, demonstrated in real life. The brutal murders committed by Clifford Olson (see Box 9.3) and Charles Manson and his followers in California are frequently cited examples of psychopathy. Indeed, while there is some debate over the most appropriate diagnosis for Manson, many would argue that his behaviour best fits the clinical picture of psychopathy. As Nathan and Harris (1975) point out:

> Charles Manson acted upon society in an unbelievable variety of antisocial ways. At one time or another he robbed, deceived, assaulted, exploited, seduced—and murdered. But despite the extraordinary range of antisocial acts for which he had been responsible, perhaps his most surprising characteristic was that at no time did he show guilt or remorse about anything he had done. During his trial for the Tate murders, he said, "I've considered innocence and guilt and I know the difference between them and I have no guilt" (quoted from the *New York Times*, Dec. 25, 1969). A man who could be charming and captivating, brutal and ruthless, Manson could not be guilty, at least in his own eyes. What kind of human being feels no remorse over murder? Why would a person keep committing crimes despite repeated punishment? How can a man charm so many people and yet never relate with genuine feeling to anyone?

These questions are difficult to answer because the crimes Manson and Olson committed seem so senseless to society. However disturbing they may be, it is possible for most people to understand murders motivated by greed or passion, but the murder of Sharon Tate and others by Manson cannot be explained by either of these motivations. A recent Canadian case highlights the differences between psychopathy or antisocial personality disorder and more severe mental illnesses, such as schizophrenia, which might have a significant impact on one's ability to choose between right and wrong (see Box 9.1).

# FOCUS BOX 9.1

## VINCE LI: GROTESQUE KILLING ABOARD BUS 1170

Vince Weiguang Li was born in Dandong, China on April 30, 1968. He graduated from University with a Bachelor of Science in 1992. Mr. Li immigrated to Canada in 2001 and became a Canadian citizen in 2005. He was unable to find work in his field and so he worked a number of menial jobs including as a caretaker in a church, a sales assistant in a store, and as a newspaper carrier. His final employer described him as a good worker albeit somewhat unusual. Despite his largely uneventful past with no criminal arrests or convictions, Mr. Li brutally and savagely killed a fellow bus passenger in July 2008 in a fashion that is reminiscent of the gruesome movie *Silence of the Lambs*.

According to witnesses and as documented in the Agreed Statement of Facts, on July 30, 2008 Mr. Li boarded greyhound bus number 1170 destined for Winnipeg in Erickson, Manitoba at 7 PM. He sat near the back of the bus. He was described as a tall man in his 40s, with a shaved head and sunglasses. Approximately 90 minutes later, shortly after a rest stop, Mr. Li suddenly produced a large hunting knife and began stabbing his sleeping seatmate in the neck and chest. While most passengers quickly fled out of the bus, the driver and three other male passengers attempted to help the victim. They were chased away by Mr. Li who slashed wildly at them with a knife.

Mr. Li persisted to brutalize his victim by decapitating him and displaying his severed head to those gathered outside. Mr. Li continued to dismember the corpse and then proceeded to perform acts of cannibalism.

The rear door was barricaded with a snipe bar to prevent Mr. Li from escaping. In addition, the power to the bus was cut off to render the vehicle inoperable. Several minutes later, the Royal Canadian Mountain Police (RCMP) arrived. They encouraged Mr. Li to drop his weapon out of a small bathroom window but he refused while indicating, in addition to some unintelligible words, something to the effect that he had

to stay on the bus forever. Two hours later the province's Emergency Response Team took over from the RCMP. Mr. Li refused to give himself up. Instead, he continued pacing the length of the bus, defiling and eating the corpse. At approximately 1:30 AM, five hours after the attack began, Mr. Li was arrested when he attempted to escape through a broken back bus window. He was tasered several times, handcuffed, and placed in the back of a police cruiser. The victim's nose, tongue, and ear were found in a plastic bag in Mr. Li's pockets. The victim's eyes and parts of his heart were never recovered and are presumed to have been eaten by Mr. Li.

To many, this brutal crime might conjure images of Hannibal Lecter, the psychopath killer played by Anthony Hopkins in the famous movie *Silence of the Lambs*. However, there is one important difference. In *Silence of the Lambs*, Hannibal Lecter was acutely aware of his actions and knew that what he was doing was wrong. As is explained below, this was not the case with Mr. Li. In fact, Mr. Li was suffering from a mental disorder which rendered him unable to appreciate the nature and quality of his actions and to know that they were wrong.

At Mr. Li's second-degree murder trial, which began nearly a year after the crime on March 5, 2009, the Crown and defence attorneys agreed to a number of facts. Among them was the fact that Mr. Li had few friends and those he did have described him as having had mental problems. In addition, his former wife described him engaging in bizarre behaviours including sudden and unexplained absences, bus trips to unusual locations, and rambling talk. Despite his unusual behaviour, neither his friends nor his former wife had known him to be violent. One episode of unusual behaviour resulted in the Ontario Provincial Police (OPP) picking him up on a busy highway. He was hospitalized briefly in the fall of 2005 before being released with medication. Both before and after this incident, friends and family were unable to convince him to seek medical help.

*(continued)*

At his trial, psychiatric assessments of Mr. Li were put into evidence. In particular, the assessments suggested that Mr. Li was suffering from schizophrenia, a mental illness whose symptoms can include hallucinations, delusions, and paranoia. According to the psychiatrists' assessments, the voice of God had directed Mr. Li to move from Edmonton to Winnipeg. Moreover, the voice had led Mr. Li to believe, under a paranoid delusion, that the deceased victim was a threat to his own life, both before and after the deceased victim's death.

The judge accepted the assessments that Mr. Li was suffering from a mental disorder. In his decision, he said

> These grotesque acts are appalling. However, the acts themselves and the context in which they were committed are strongly suggestive of a mental disorder. He did not appreciate the actions he committed were morally wrong. He believed he was acting in self-defence. (McIntyre, 2009)

Moreover, the judge stated,

> Persons who are profoundly ill do not have the mental capacity to intentionally commit a crime. The goal of criminal law is to punish criminals, not persons who have a mental illness. Moreover, a person who is driven to act by severe psychotic delusions cannot be deterred by the fear of punishment, or public denouncement. In such cases, the only way to change the behaviour of a person who is driven to act by psychotic delusions is through treatment, and where the person poses an ongoing risk to society, through treatment in a secure institution. (Pritchard, 2009)

As a result of these findings, the judge found Mr. Li Not Criminal Responsible on account of Mental Disorder (NCRMD).

Under Canadian law, no person is criminally responsible for an act committed while suffering from a mental disorder that rendered the person incapable of appreciating the nature and quality of the act or of knowing that it was wrong (Criminal Code of Canada, C-46, s. 16(1)).

However, not all individuals who are suffering from a mental disorder will be found NCRMD. Rather, an individual will only be found NCRMD if the mental disorder, which is defined in law as a disease of the mind, renders the person unable to differentiate between right and wrong. In *Winko v. British Columbia (Forensic Psychiatric Institute)* the Supreme Court of Canada put it this way: "people who commit criminal acts under the influence of mental illnesses should not be held criminally responsible for their acts or omissions in the same way that sane responsible people are. No person should be conceited of a crime if he or she was legally insane at the time of the offence... Criminal responsibility is appropriate only where the actor is a discerning moral agent, capable of making choices between right and wrong."

In cases where individuals are found NCRMD, they are not admitted to jail or prison. Rather, their disposition depends on a number of considerations including the protection of the public, the individual's mental condition, the reintegration of the individual into society, and the individual's other needs. Disposition decisions are made by specially constituted Review Boards whose duty it is to weigh these considerations. The disposition of Mr. Li was decided by the Manitoba Review Board on September 15, 2009. His disposition order required him to be detained in a locked ward of a psychiatric hospital in Manitoba. When the order was reviewed on May 31, 2010, the Review Board again ordered him to be detained in a locked ward of a psychiatric hospital in Manitoba. However, this time they allowed for the possibility of escorted access to the hospital grounds (e.g., outside yard). Disposition orders are reviewed by the Review Board at least annually. Mr. Li is currently being held at the Selkirk Mental Health Centre in Manitoba.

Sources: Queen's Bench, Winnipeg Centre. (n.d.). *Between Her Majesty the Queen and Vince Weiguang Li—Agreed Statement of Facts.* Winnipeg: Queen's Bench; Province of Manitoba Review Board. (2009). *A Disposition Hearing held in Winnipeg, Manitoba on Monday, June 1, 2009.* Winnipeg: Manitoba Review Board; Province of Manitoba Review Board. (2010). *A Disposition Review Hearing held in Winnipeg, Manitoba on Monday, May 31, 2010.* Winnipeg: Manitoba Review Board.

Similarly, it is difficult to understand the motivations of "Canada's Ken and Barbie Killers"—Paul Bernardo and Karla Homolka—who were responsible for the grotesque rape and murder of three young women, including Karla Homolka's own sister. Although the prevalence of female psychopaths is lower than that of males, we are especially intrigued by these women. In recent parole board reports, Karla Homolka has been deemed a psychopath (see Box 9.2), though the motivation for her actions remains unclear.

This section began with a discussion of Charles Manson because it is this image that best fits the common conception of persons with an antisocial personality. It is a misleading picture, however, because many individuals with diagnoses of antisocial personality do not have a history of violence and, even among those who do, very few would exhibit the extreme forms that Manson did. The term *sociopath* was later used instead of the term *psychopath* to convey this less violent picture. More recently, the use of the term *Antisocial Personality Disorder* has become common.

The current edition of the *American Psychiatric Association's Diagnostic and Statistical Manual of Mental Disorder* (DSM-IV-TR) defines Antisocial Personality Disorder in the following manner:

> The essential feature of Antisocial Personality Disorder is a pervasive pattern of disregard for, and violation of, the rights of others that begins in childhood or early adolescence and continues into adulthood. (2000, 701)

Lying, stealing, fighting, truancy, and resisting authority are typical early childhood signs. In adolescence, unusually early or aggressive sexual behaviour, excessive drinking, and use of illicit drugs are frequent. In adulthood, those kinds of behaviour continue with the addition of an inability to sustain consistent work performance or to function as a responsible parent and failure to accept social norms with respect to lawful behaviour. After age 30, the more flagrant aspects may diminish, particularly sexual promiscuity, fighting, criminality, and vagrancy. It is estimated that between 15–30 percent of the inmate population in Canadian prisons could be considered psychopathic (Ogloff et al., 1990).

In his book *The Mask of Sanity*, Cleckley (1976) provided a clinical description of the antisocial personality and described the psychopath using the following criteria: unreliability; insincerity; pathological lying and deception; egocentricity; poor judgment; impulsivity; a lack of remorse, guilt, or shame; an inability to experience empathy or concern for others and to maintain warm, affectionate attachments; an impersonal and poorly integrated sex life; and an unstable life plan with no long-term commitments.

Since the 1960s, Hare and his colleagues have devoted considerable attention to the development of a reliable and valid procedure for the assessment of psychopathy. This program has culminated in the Revised Psychopathy Checklist (PCL-R) (Hare, 1991), a 20-item checklist of traits and behaviours associated with psychopathy (see Table 9.2). Research has continued to support the use of this scale in prison populations. An excellent review of the use, and

**TABLE 9.2**   The 20 Items of the Psychopathy Checklist

| | |
|---|---|
| 1. Glibness/superficial charm[p] | 11. Promiscuous sexual behaviour |
| 2. Grandiose sense of self-worth[p] | 12. Early behavioural problems[ab] |
| 3. Need for stimulation/proneness to boredom[ab] | 13. Lack of realistic, long-term goals[ab] |
| 4. Pathological lying[p] | 14. Impulsivity[ab] |
| 5. Conning/manipulative[p] | 15. Irresponsibility[ab] |
| 6. Lack of remorse or guilt[p] | 16. Failure to accept responsibility for own actions[ab] |
| 7. Shallow affect[p] | 17. Many short-term marital relationships |
| 8. Callous/lack of empathy[p] | 18. Juvenile delinquency[ab] |
| 9. Parasitic lifestyle[ab] | 19. Revocation of conditional release[ab] |
| 10. Poor behavioural controls[ab] | 20. Criminal versatility |

The checklist is composed of two factors: [p] identifies the items that define personality traits, and [ab] identifies items descriptive of antisocial behaviour.

Sources: R. D. Hare. (1991). "The Hare Psychopathy Checklist—Revised." Multi-Health Systems, Inc. Adapted from R. D. Hare. (1980). "A Research Scale for the Assessment of Psychopathy in Criminal Populations." *Personality and Individual Differences* 1:111–19. Oxford: Pergamon Press. © 1990 R. D. Hare. Reprinted with permission from Elsevier Science Ltd.

misuse, of the PCL-R has been provided by Hare. In discussing the PCL-R and its screening version, the PCL-SV (Hart et al., 1995), he concludes that these checklists

> provide reliable and valid assessments of the traditional construct of psychopathy. They are used widely for research purposes and for making decisions in the mental health and criminal justice systems. They are strong predictors of violence and recidivism in offenders and psychiatric patients, form a key part of current risk assessment procedures, and play an important role in many judicial decisions. (Hare, 1998c, 99)

Other commentators and researchers have cautioned against the overreliance on the PCL-R (or any assessment instrument) when making legal determinations and against equating the construct of psychopathy with scores on the PCL-R (see DeMatteo and Edens, 2006; Skeem and Cooke, 2010).

DSM-IV estimates that the prevalence of Antisocial Personality Disorder is three percent for men and less than one percent for women. However, estimates of this diagnostic classification in prison populations are, not surprisingly, considerably higher. Indeed, depending on how one interprets the diagnostic criteria, virtually all inmates could be so classified. The differences in interpretation may partly account for the large disparity in prison studies of this disorder, reflecting, in part, changes in diagnostic procedures and criteria. In a Canadian study of the prevalence of Antisocial Personality Disorder, Hare (1983) had two clinicians examine a provincial and a federal prison inmate sample.

# FOCUS BOX 9.2

## PSYCHOLOGISTS SUGGEST BERNARDO AND HOMOLKA ARE PSYCHOPATHS

TORONTO—Prosecutors painted a picture of a battered woman and a controlling, abusive husband who forced her to take part in unspeakable crimes. But some experts suspect that both Karla Homolka and Paul Bernardo are psychopaths—people who aren't mentally ill but lack any conscience and single-mindedly pursue their own pleasure.

In Bernardo, they suggest, psychopathic qualities combined with sexual sadism to form an explosive mix. Some psychologists who have followed the Bernardo trial say the crimes Homolka and Bernardo admitted to committing, and their almost total lack of emotion in the witness box, suggest psychopathic tendencies.

"What bothers me about him, and her, too, is the casual way these horrific things are described on the witness stand," said psychologist Robert Hare of the University of British Columbia, one of the world's leading experts on psychopaths.

"When a psychopath commits a violent act, they're not doing it because they're malicious or malevolent or evil. They're doing it because they don't give a damn."

Bernardo was "such a good psychopath" that he found a woman who had a penchant for submissive sex that complemented his urge to dominate, said psychologist Marnie Rice of Ontario's Penetanguishene Mental Health Centre. Homolka may not have got into trouble with another man. But hooked up with Bernardo, it's possible she agreed to take part in three-way sex with kidnapped teenage girls as part of a willingly subservient role, said Rice, whose hospital houses some of the province's most dangerous offenders.

"It appears the two found each other."

Homolka testified Bernardo beat her into submission and blackmailed her over her role in the death of her sister, who was drugged and raped by the couple. Two psychologists called by the Crown suggested Homolka suffered from battered women's syndrome. Rendered helpless and hopeless by repeated beatings, someone in her shoes could feel obliged to take part in the most heinous crimes, they said. Hare is skeptical.

"We look for very simple explanations for complex behaviour," he said. "To me, battered women's syndrome does not explain what she did."

Even a psychiatrist retained by the prosecution—but not called as a witness at Bernardo's trial—said Homolka's role in the horrific crimes can't be fully explained by the abuse she suffered.

"Karla Homolka remains something of a diagnostic mystery," Dr. Angus McDonald wrote in his report, which the Bernardo jury never saw.

"Despite her ability to present herself very well, there is a moral vacuity in her which is difficult, if not impossible, to explain."

In Bernardo's case, it appears there were no ethical restraints to hold him back from sex that inflicted pain, terror and humiliation on his partner, psychologists say. Among evidence ruled inadmissible at his trail was a statement the Crown says Bernardo made to two witnesses.

"I have no conscience," prosecutors quoted him as saying. "I could kill anybody."

Experts also say his videotaping of the sexual assaults is typical of many rapists and sex killers, who keep souvenirs of their victims such as jewelry, clothing or hair. Serial killer Harvey Murray Glatman used photographs of the women he murdered in Los Angeles during the 1950s to relive his sexual fantasies.

"They're like stamp collectors," said psychologist Vern Quinsey of Queen's University in Kingston. "They look at them and think about them and try to do better next time."

Psychopaths tend to be egocentric, lack remorse or guilt and constantly seek excitement, said Hare. They're also unable to empathize with others and tend to be deceitful and emotionally shallow. Only a small percentage are physically violent, he said.

"They are predators—emotional and physical and sexual predators."

*(continued)*

Bernardo's cool, confident and sometimes condescending demeanor in the witness box was typical, Hare said.

"A psychopath who has committed a crime and is caught is now on stage. He doesn't see himself as any sort of pariah, he sees himself as a victim of the system.... He's on stage, he's enjoying it, he's loving it.

"What these people do is confuse fame and infamy."

Source: Tom Blackwell. (n.d.) "Psychologists Suggest Bernardo and Homolka Are Psychopaths." Printed with permission of *The Canadian Press*.

The clinicians found that approximately one-third of the provincial sample and 42 percent of the federal sample met the criteria for Antisocial Personality Disorder. Overall, 39 percent of the total prison sample received this diagnosis. However, in a previous study described in the same paper, Hare, using the initial criteria proposed in a draft of DSM-III-R, found that 76 percent of a sample of 145 white male criminals met the criteria for Antisocial Personality Disorder. The reason for the difference is that the published version of DSM-III-R required that more stringent criteria be met before a diagnosis of Antisocial Personality Disorder could be made. Hare's work was influential in the decision to change the criteria. The two studies provide a clear illustration of how changes in diagnostic criteria and procedures can influence the perceived prevalence of antisocial personality.

A leading theory about antisocial personality is that these individuals do not learn from negative experiences because they do not become anxious in circumstances that should elicit anxiety. Also, they do not have sufficient fear of the consequences of their behaviour (Hare, 1970; Brodsky, 1977). Applying Eysenck's model, reviewed earlier in this chapter, the psychopath can be viewed as an extravert who does not easily acquire conditioned responses or, if he or she acquires them, extinguishes them very rapidly. Given these characteristics, particularly the inability to learn from punishment or to experience fear or anxiety, it is understandable that Brodsky (1977) concludes that imprisonment is unlikely to have much effect on the post-release behaviour of such individuals. Newman (1998) reviews a position suggesting that psychopaths exhibit deficits in information processing that limit their ability to use contextual cues appropriately in the implementation of goal-directed behaviour and interfere with effective self-regulation. Hare (1998b) suggests that while a great deal remains to be done, there is a convergence emerging with regard to etiologic bases of psychopathy, which forms "a reasonably coherent conceptual/empirical package that helps us understand how and why psychopaths differ from others in the processing and use of semantic and affective information, and in their capacity for callous, predatory behaviour" (1998b, 131).

Raine and Yang (2006) indicate that there has been surprisingly little brain imaging research done on the neuroanatomical basis of psychopathy. They conclude that this is because the complexity of the clinical construct makes it "highly likely that the neuroanatomical basis to psychopathy is not simple, and that abnormalities to multiple brain mechanisms contribute to the behavioural, cognitive, and emotional characteristics that make up the psychopath" (2006, 279). In reviewing the existing literature they draw two conclusions. One is that the area is very much under-researched and basic research is still required. The second is that, with regard to psychopathy, questions regarding specific brain impairments and their causes are even further removed from being answered (2006, 291). Given these limitations several possible neuroanatomical impairments have been identified (Raine and Yang, 2006). One is that abnormalities in the prefrontal cortex would support the view that psychopaths are low arousal, fearless, impulsive, and disinhibited individuals. Impairments in the hippocampus may result in dysregulation in affect and fear conditioning. Dysfunction in the amygdala has also been suggested in psychopaths (Blair, 2006), resulting in a reduction in the individual's "responsiveness to the sadness and fear of potential victims" and "their ability to learn the stimulus–reinforcement associations that are necessary for moral socialization" (2006, 307). A concern expressed in the identification of possible pathophysiologies in psychopathy is whether or not they are fundamental to the disorder or are secondary consequences of it (Blair, 2006).

Heilbrun (1979) conducted an interesting study of the influence of intelligence on the relationships between psychopathy, violence, and impulsiveness. His sample of 76 white male prisoners was divided into psychopathic and nonpsychopathic groups ($n = 38$). Two personality measures were used (one of which, incidentally, was validated in a study by Craddick, 1962, using a Canadian prison sample). He further divided the groups into high-intelligence and low-intelligence subgroups. Heilbrun found that intelligence level does indeed have an influence on violence and impulsiveness among psychopaths. The more intelligent psychopaths were neither violent nor impulsive and were more likely to have attained educational goals. This study points to the importance of viewing persons with the label of psychopath, or antisocial personality, in multidimensional ways. Not all such individuals should be expected to be violent or impulsive.

The Heilbrun study should also serve as a reminder that studies of prison populations may present a misleading picture of antisocial personality. Most of the research on antisocial personality has used samples obtained from institutional populations. This may give a distorted view because the impressions one has about people with antisocial personalities are, thus, based on people who committed criminal acts but were not able to avoid apprehension. Furthermore, it is certainly true that not all persons with this label are criminals (Cleckley, 1976). An exception to the focus on institutionalized populations is the work of Cathy Spatz Widom (Widom, 1977; Widom and Newman, 1985). In one study, Widom placed an advertisement in a local newspaper asking for "charming, aggressive, carefree people who are impulsively irresponsible but are good at handling people and at looking after number one." Twenty-nine applicants were interviewed. The demographic and personality test data applied to these people revealed some interesting information about this noninstitutionalized population. Only two subjects had not finished high school, and most had some college. Nearly two-thirds had at least one arrest, but the conviction rate was quite low (18 percent), even though many of the charges were felonies. While 50 percent had been incarcerated, most had been in jail less than two weeks. The subjects scored high on the extraversion and neuroticism scale of Eysenck Personality

w w w

**Minnesota Multiphasic Personality Inventory (MMPI)**
www.umn.edu/mmpi/

Inventory, consistent with Eysenck's (1977) notions of psychopathy. Scores on the Minnesota Multiphasic Personality Inventory (MMPI), an objective personality test, fit the classic profile of psychopathy (high scores on the psychopathic deviate and manic scales). Subjects had low scores on the measure of socialization, and most also had low scores on the empathy scale.

While many of the results of Widom's study were similar to those found in institutional populations, it presents a picture of somewhat more successful antisocial persons. That is, they are better educated and more successful at avoiding conviction and lengthy incarceration. These results support the conclusion of Widom and Newman (1985) that research on the antisocial personality must avoid a primary focus on the incarcerated criminal. Her methodology seems to have been successful in drawing a sample of noninstitutionalized persons who meet the antisocial personality criteria. This is important as it is vital for us to become more aware of the prevalence of psychopathy within the general population and to begin to understand better the non-criminal manifestations of this personality.

Of direct relevance to this concern is the recent book by Babiak and Hare (2006), *Snakes in Suits: When Psychopaths Go To Work*, in which the authors examine the impact of the psychopath in the corporate working world. Whereas one might initially assume that many of the traits the psychopath displays would make it obvious to potential employers that they would not work well with others and would constitute an employment risk, this does not appear to be the case. They identify four possible reasons for this contradiction. One is that some of the traits associated with psychopathy provide these individuals with skills in social manipulation. Their ability to charm others will often make them initially seem attractive and even charismatic in job hiring interviews. It is only in retrospect that it becomes clear that the decision was not a good one. A second issue is that some of the traits associated with psychopathy may appear on the surface to indicate leadership and management skills whereas they actually represent a need for dominance and manipulative and coercive abilities that are, again, not initially obvious. A third concern reflects the evolution of today's business world in which large, stable bureaucratic organizations have adopted a faster more flexible and somewhat chaotic approach to information processing. This has resulted in a change in hiring policies towards acquiring individuals who can "stir things up" and effect change quickly. As Babiak and Hare (2006) state, "the general state of confusion that change brings to a situation can make psychopathic personality traits—the appearance of confidence, strength, and calm—often look like the answer to the organization's problems…Egocentricity, callousness, and insensitivity suddenly become acceptable trade-offs in order to get the talents and skills needed to survive in an accelerated, dispassionate business world" (2006, xxi). A fourth dilemma is that the decreased constraints and levels of accountability in this new fast-paced business climate create an environment that psychopaths find inviting. The personal gains available are very appealing to the psychopath who relishes the risks and thrills involved. The relentlessness of this drive is captured in the somewhat chilling comment: "Like all predators, psychopaths go where the action is, which means to them positions, occupations, and organizations that afford them the opportunity to obtain power, control, status, and possessions, and to engage in exploitative interpersonal relationships" (Babiak and Hare, 2006, 97).

Clearly the implications of corporate psychopathic behaviour for companies and their workers can be disastrous and the authors provide numerous examples of the devastating impact that such individuals have had in recent history. Of course, the most often cited media examples of psychopaths in the workplace are the investment bankers and mortgage brokers responsible for bringing down the U.S. economy in 2008 and men, such as Bernie Madoff, who created Ponzi schemes that stole billions from investors. A concern here is that the extensive forensic research literature on the psychopath needs to be presented in a manner that those so much affected by their behaviour can recognize and better understand. However, at this time, the fascination with such individuals continues to be mostly a consequence of the overwhelmingly antisocial nature of their acts. In *Without Conscience: The Disturbing World of the Psychopaths Among Us*, Hare (1998a) captures the essence of this in his description of Clifford Olson (see Box 9.3).

As theories of crime, antisocial personality disorder, and psychopathy do not completely avoid the tautology that results from failing to distinguish between the criterion (antisocial personality disorder) and the outcome (crime). However, as previously discussed, psychopathy not only identifies those that have committed past offences but also predicts *future* criminality—both general and violent recidivism (Hare, 1998c). The construct of psychopathy has also been criticized for its oversimplicity and disregard for the dynamic nature of human behaviour (Walter, 2004). Nonetheless many consider psychopathy to be "the single most important clinical construct in the criminal justice system" (Hare, 1998c, 99).

A final note on treatment seems appropriate. Losel (1998) reviews a position taken by Suedfeld and Landon (1978) that no effective treatments exist for this disorder. While acknowledging that our understanding of issues related to concerns such as assessment, etiology; prediction; and biological, cognitive, emotional, and behavioural correlates has advanced greatly in the past 20 years, he indicates that treatment of such individuals remains an area of uncertainty.

# FOCUS BOX 9.3

## CLIFFORD OLSON—THE PROTOTYPICAL PSYCHOPATH

Canada's most notorious and reviled criminal is Clifford Olson, a serial murderer sentenced in January 1982 to life imprisonment for the torture and killing of eleven boys and girls. These crimes were the latest and most despicable in a string of antisocial and criminal acts extending back to his early childhood. Although some psychopaths are not violent and few are as brutal as he, Olson is the prototypical psychopath.

Consider the following quotation from a newspaper article written around the time of his trial: "He was a braggart and a bully, a liar and thief. He was a violent man with a hair-trigger temper. But he could also be charming and smooth-tongued when trying to impress people.... Olson was a compulsive talker.... He's a real smooth talker, he has the gift of gab.... He was always telling whoppers.... The

*(continued)*

man was just an out-and-out liar.... He always wanted to test you to the limits. He wanted to see how far he could go before you had to step on him.... He was a manipulator.... Olson was a blabbermouth.... We learned after a while not to believe anything he said because he told so many lies" (Farrow, 1982). A reporter who talked with Olson said, "He talked fast, staccato.... He jumped from topic to topic. He sounded glib, slick, like a con trying to prove he's tough and important" (Ouston, 1982).

These reports by people who knew him are important, for they give us a clue to why he was able to get his young, trusting victims alone with him. They may also help to explain the Crown's decision to pay him $100 000 to tell them where he hid the bodies of seven of the eleven young people he had killed. Not surprisingly, public outrage greeted disclosure of the payment. Some typical headlines were: KILLER WAS PAID TO LOCATE BODIES; MONEY-FOR-GRAVES PAYMENT TO CHILD KILLER GREETED WITH DISGUST.

In the years since his imprisonment Olson has continued to bring grief to the families of his victims by sending them letters with comments about the murders of their children. He has never shown any guilt or remorse for his depredations; on the contrary, he continually complains about his treatment by the press, the prison system, and society. During his trial he preened and postured whenever a camera was present, apparently considering himself an important celebrity rather than a man who had committed a series of atrocities. On January 15, 1983, the *Vancouver Sun* reported, "Mass killer Clifford Olson has written to the *Sun* newsroom to say he does not approve of the picture of him we have been using ... and will shortly be sending us newer, more attractive pictures of himself" (Ouston, 1982). (Quotes are from articles by R. Ouston, *Vancouver Sun*, January 15, 1982; and M. Farrow, *Vancouver Sun*, January 14, 1982.)

At this writing Olson has written to several criminology departments in Canada offering to help them establish a course devoted to studying him.

Source: Robert D. Hare. (1998). *Without Conscience: The Disturbing World of the Psychopaths Among Us*. New York: Guilford Press, pp. 132–34. Reprinted with permission of the author.

## Crime and Mental Illness

We begin this discussion of crime and mental illness with a most extreme statement: all crime is symptomatic of mental illness. While this may seem a preposterous statement today, many mental health professionals previously held this belief. Hakeem (1958) has summarized these views:

> So powerful is the conviction of some psychiatrists that crime stems from mental disease, that they have held that the commission of crime in itself constitutes evidence of the presence of mental disease. Again, this aspect of the ideology usually draws on the medical analogy. The thesis runs as follows: just as fever is a symptom of physical disease, so crime is a symptom of mental disease.

Today, most would disagree with this position. Indeed, the current view is that while many criminals exhibit symptoms of mental illness, many do not (Freeman and Roesch, 1989; Corrado et al., 2000). In the remainder of this

"Mental Disorders and Crime: The Connection Is Real" Crime Times www.crimetimes.org/96c/ w96cp1.htm

section, the extent to which persons charged with crimes are in need of mental health intervention will be examined.

There is widespread consensus among researchers, administrators, and front line staff that the prevalence of mental disorder among those in the criminal justice system is greater than that of the general population. So high is the prevalence of mental disorder in jails and prisons that some have referred to them as "the new mental institution" (Arboleda-Florez et al., 1995, 123), the "new psychiatric emergency room" (Lev, 1998, 72), the "new asylum" (Shenson, Dubber, and Michaels, 1990), "America's new mental health hospitals" (Torrey, 1995), or as an "alternative shelter" for mentally ill individuals who find themselves homeless (Chaiklin, 2001).

Despite this consensus, there is a lack of agreement with respect to the precise prevalence of mental disorder in jails, prisons, and other parts of the criminal justice system. This, in part, is because of a lack of consistency with respect to the definition of mental disorder in the prevalence literature (Hodgins, 1995; Roesch, Ogloff, and Eaves, 1995; Corrado, Cohen, Hart, and Roesch, 2000b). In a systematic review of 62 surveys of correctional samples across 12 western countries researchers found considerable heterogeneity between studies in how mental disorder was defined (Fazel and Danesh, 2002; see also Andersen, 2004). For example, some studies examined only the most serious disorders such as schizophrenia, bi-polar disorder, and major depression (e.g., Teplin, 1989, 1990a) but many others employed broader definitions including less serious disorders such as dysthymia and anxiety disorders (e.g., Falissard et al., 2006), substance abuse disorders (e.g., Teplin, 1991) and/or personality disorders (e.g., Gunn, Maden, and Swinton, 1991). Other studies have not used disorder based definitions at all, instead focusing merely on the presence of symptoms (Corrado et al., 2000b).

A further consideration when examining prevalence across jurisdictions, both within and between countries, is that the true prevalence may differ markedly in different sites as a result of the availability of health care resources and the differing attitudes, practices, and policies of law enforcement agencies and legal institutions (Drewett and Shepperdson, 1995; Harris and Rice, 1997; Corrado, Cohen, Hart, and Roesch, 2000a). However, despite arguably substantial differences in health and criminal justice policies in Canada and the United States, Corrado and his colleagues (2000a) found similar rates of serious mental disorder across Canadian and U.S. jails and prisons. Nonetheless, even within the same metropolitan centres rates in different regions may reflect the varying characteristics of the neighbourhoods. For example, researchers in the metropolitan area of Vancouver, British Columbia found vastly different prevalence rates for substance misuse across two studies, differences largely attributable to the characteristics of the jails' catchment areas (Ogloff, 1996; Roesch, 1995).

Despite methodological and conceptual challenges, sufficient research exists to provide estimates of the prevalence of mental disorders in various correctional settings. The most often cited studies in the context of jail prevalence are those conducted by Teplin in the early 1990s (Teplin, 1990a, 1990b, 1991, 1994; Teplin and Voit, 1996). In her review of jail studies, Teplin found that among jail detainees, the estimated prevalence of *any* mental disorder ranged from 16–67 percent and the prevalence of *severe* mental disorder (defined

**Why Canada's Prisons Can't Cope with Flood of Mentally Ill Inmates**

http://www.theglobeandmail.com/news/national/why-canadas-prisons-cant-cope-with-flood-of-mentally-ill-inmates/article1879501/

largely as schizophrenia, bipolar disorder, and major depression) ranged from 5–12 percent (Teplin, 1991). Recent surveys and reviews have reported similar United States estimates (e.g., Ogloff, 2002; Andersen, 2004; James and Glaze, 2006).

There is relatively little research in Canada examining the rates of mental disorder in Canadian jails but the research that does exist suggests that the prevalence of mental disorder in Canadian jails is also high. For example, a British Columbia study found that the prevalence of major mental disorders was 15.6 percent (Roesch, 1995). As well, the prevalence of substance use disorders was exceptionally high, with over 77 percent considered to have alcohol use or dependence disorders, and over 63 percent with drug use disorders.

Consistent with the literature in the United States, Canadian research suggests that the prevalence of mental disorder may be lower in prisons than in jails (James and Glaze, 2006; Teplin, 1991). In a 2004 report profiling the health needs of federal prison inmates in Canada, researchers found that seven percent of inmates at intake had a mental health need that required immediate attention (NA, 2004). A higher proportion of inmates reported mental health problems (31 percent of females and 15 percent of males). Moreover, a substantial proportion of incoming inmates (21 percent of females; 14 percent of males) had admitted attempting suicide in the preceding five years.

These prevalence rates should not be taken to suggest that most inmates are healthy (Ogloff, 1996). To the contrary, most inmates have substantial mental health needs in both Canadian jails and prisons, particularly with respect to substance use disorders (Hodgins and Coté, 1995; Roesch, 1995; Lamb and Weinberg, 1998). Many of these individuals have co-occurring disorders (e.g., schizophrenia and substance abuse), further compounding the mental health and social problems these individuals experience. Canadian findings are consistent with American studies which found considerable overlap between mental disorders and drug or alcohol abuse in jail populations (Abram and Teplin, 1991; Abram, Teplin, and McClelland, 2003). This is referred to as co-occurring disorders.

In a unique study conducted in British Columbia, researchers extracted data from the records of three provincial agencies to get a better understanding of health care and social assistance use among those who were provincially incarcerated (Somers, Cartar, and Russo, 2008). This study included the records of all members of the provincial corrections population in British Columbia from 1997/98 to 2003/04. Over 30 percent of individuals who were incarcerated during the seven-year period had been medically diagnosed with a substance use disorder during this same period. An additional 26 percent were diagnosed with a mental disorder unrelated to substance use. Among those who had a substance use disorder, more than 75 percent had a co-occurring disorder. This combination (mental disorder plus substance use disorder) was found to be particularly hazardous resulting in significantly higher health and service costs as well as greater involvement in corrections.

The high rate of individuals with co-occurring disorders also suggests the need for treatment programs both within the jail and after release. Abram and Teplin (1991) suggested that these individuals might be particularly appropriate for alternatives to prosecution, such as pretrial diversion programs. Mental health courts are also an option for these individuals (Slinger and Roesch, 1995).

The prevalence of mental disorders in jails has prompted the American Psychiatric Association (2000) and the National Commission on Correctional Health Care (2003) to recommend, in their standards and guidelines for the delivery of mental health services in jails, that all institutions adopt a systematic program for screening individuals upon detention, a recommendation echoed by health-care providers and researchers (Roesch, 1995; Birmingham et al., 2000; Osher, Steadman, and Barr, 2003; Nicholls et al., 2005). Specialized screening tools devised specifically for mental health screening in jails have started to emerge in the literature. For example, in Canada, Nicholls and her colleagues (2005) developed the *Jail Screening Assessment Tool*, a semi-structured interview used to screen inmates for mental health concerns, risk of suicide and self-harm, and risk of violence and victimization. In the same year, researchers in the United States created the Brief Jail Mental Health Screen (Steadman et al., 2005), a screening tool for serious mental illness comprising eight yes-or-no questions.

The high prevalence of mental disorders in jails comes at a substantial cost, not only at a fiscal level, but also on a humanitarian basis for both the inmates themselves and for correctional staff. Mentally disordered offenders are perceived by jail staff as the most disruptive type of inmates (Kropp, Cox, Roesch, and Eaves, 1989; Ruddell, 2006). In addition, they are at an increased risk for suicide and self-harm, victimization, and institutional maladjustments (Ogloff, 2002; Nicholls, Roesch, Olley, Ogloff, and Hemphill, 2005; James and Glaze, 2006). These adverse events impact not only individuals entering the criminal justice system with mental health difficulties but also those who develop mental health problems during (and perhaps, as a result) of their stay (Andersen, 2004).

There is little question that individuals with mental health problems are increasingly involved with the legal system. The first contact is usually by police officers, and there is evidence that police are increasingly encountering mentally ill individuals. A recent study in Vancouver found that over one-third of their calls involved a mental health issue (Wilson-Bates, 2008).

The training provided to police officers on mental health related issues and the use of specialized responses for calls involving people with mental illnesses varies widely between departments. Hails and Borum (2006) found that some police agencies provided zero hours of training in handling calls involving people with mental illnesses while others provided as many as 41 hours of training. Most of the agencies provided no post-academy in-service training hours dealing with the topic of mental illness. Hails and Borum also found that only 21 percent of agencies had a special unit or bureau within the department to assist police in handling people with mental illness. This percentage is disappointing given findings that specialized teams composed of a police officer and a mental health professional have helped avoid the criminalization of the mentally ill in some jurisdictions (Lamb et al., 1995). Moreover, in those rare cases where the interaction between a mentally disordered individual and the police has resulted in a coronial or fatality inquest, the most often made recommendation is the increase in police training so that they may be better prepared to work with individuals with mental disorder (Cotton and Coleman, 2010).

w(w)w

"The Prison Careers of Offenders with Mental Disorders" Correctional Service of Canada

http://www.csc-scc.gc.ca/text/ pblct/forum/e093/e093gg-eng .shtml

There is some evidence that the discretionary powers of the police in dealing with the mentally ill have been affected by the deinstitutionalization movement. This movement resulted in the release of large numbers of patients from mental hospitals. At the same time, the civil commitment laws were changed so that commitment had to be based on findings of mental illness and dangerousness. As a consequence, police could no longer use the mental hospital as an alternative disposition to jail and were often forced to arrest a mentally ill person.

If this is true, does it suggest that there is a significant relationship between crime and mental disorder? In his study of the rates of mental disorder in prisons, Gunn (1977) answers this question with a note of caution, suggesting that, as other alternatives for the placement of mentally ill persons were blocked off, it would be expected that a greater number of persons previously detained in mental hospitals would now end up in prisons. As Roesch and Golding (1985) point out, the increased rate of mental disorder in prisons is the result of "institutional and public policy practices that have nothing to do with individual deviance *per se*. In fact, the individual behavior may not have changed at all. What has changed, however, is the manner in which institutions of our society react to that individual behavior."

With these cautions in mind, it will be instructive to review some studies on the extent to which persons considered to be mentally ill are arrested for criminal offences. Most of the research on arrest rates of the mentally ill has relied on police or court records. Such research is limited by the availability of information in the files, which are often incomplete and inaccurate. One of the few researchers to actually observe how the police dealt with the mentally ill was Linda Teplin (1984). She was interested in examining the probability of arrest for mentally ill persons as compared to persons who were not mentally ill.

Teplin's sample was 1382 police–citizen encounters involving 2555 citizens. Overall, the probability of arrest was low, occurring in only 12 percent of 884 encounters (traffic-offence and public-service incidents were deleted from the total). In individual terms, 506 of the 1798 citizens involved were considered suspect, but only 29 percent were arrested.

Does the presence of symptoms of mental illness affect the probability of arrest? Teplin's data suggest that it does. Of 506 suspects, 30 were considered by observers to be mentally ill. Nearly one-half (14) were arrested, compared to an arrest percentage of 27.9 percent for those not mentally ill. Furthermore, this difference was not accounted for by differences in type of charge. In other words, mentally ill suspects were not arrested more often because they were suspected of committing more serious crimes. The difference held up across types of crime.

Once arrested, do mentally disordered offenders recidivate at a high level? In a recent meta-analysis of a large number of empirical studies, Bonta et al. (1998) found that mentally disordered offenders on average showed lower recidivism rates than other offenders. A diagnosis of Antisocial Personality Disorder was found to be a more potent predictor than any other clinical diagnosis. However, with respect to violence after release from custody, Borum (1996) notes that mental disorder is now considered a robust and significant risk factor for predicting violent recidivism, as mentally disordered offenders have a greater probability of committing violent offences after release. But

Borum adds that most persons with mental disorders are not violent, so it is a relative rather than an absolute risk factor. It is important to keep in mind that most mentally disordered offenders are not violent and may have a decreased risk of general recidivism.

The high prevalence of mental disorders in jails comes at a substantial cost, not only at a fiscal level, but also on a humanitarian basis for both the inmates themselves and for correctional staff. Mentally disordered offenders are perceived by jail staff as the most disruptive type of inmates (Kropp, Cox, Roesch, and Eaves, 1989; Ruddell, 2006). In addition, they are at an increased risk for suicide and self-harm, victimization, and institutional maladjustments (Ogloff, 2002; Nicholls, Roesch, Olley, Ogloff, and Hemphill, 2005; James and Glaze, 2006). These adverse events impact not only individuals entering the criminal justice system with mental health difficulties but also those who develop mental health problems during (and perhaps, as a result) of their stay (Andersen, 2004).

In conclusion, it is likely that theories of criminal behaviour that rely on models of mental illness will not account for the behaviour of most criminals. It is certainly true that some people who commit crimes can be considered mentally ill, but these individuals make up only a small percentage of the total criminal population. In a legal sense, most criminals are responsible for their actions in that they are aware of their behaviour and can distinguish between right and wrong.

Each of the psychological theories reviewed in this chapter (Table 9.3) makes a contribution to the understanding of criminal behaviour. However, there is a need for greater integration of sociological and psychological perspectives

**TABLE 9.3    Psychological Theories**

| Theory | Theorists | Key Elements |
|---|---|---|
| Psychoanalytic theory | Freud | Crime results when the ego and superego cannot control the antisocial instincts of the id. This occurs because the individual has not been adequately socialized in early childhood. |
| Moral development theory | Piaget<br>Kohlberg | Each individual must go through a sequence of moral development. Those with a high level of moral development will be more likely to make responsible choices when faced with the opportunity to get involved in criminal behaviour. |
| Personality theory | Eysenck | Law-abiding people must develop a conditioned fear of deviance. Those who become delinquents and criminals do not develop this fear because of poor conditioning by parents or because they are less susceptible to conditioning. |
| Social learning theory | Bandura | Deviant behaviour such as aggression can be learned through direct experience or through modelling the behaviour of others. |
| Operant conditioning theory | Skinner | Individual behaviour is shaped through both reinforcement and punishment. Behaviour that is rewarded will tend to be continued; behaviour that is punished will cease. |
| Psychopathy | Cleckley<br>Hare | Psychopaths seem to lack empathy for their victims and do not feel guilty about their crimes. They do not learn from their experience or fear the consequences of their behaviour. |

so that both situational determinants and individual differences can be taken into account in attempts to explain criminal behaviour (Monahan and Splane, 1980). A study by Conger (1976) provides an excellent example of an attempt to integrate the two approaches. Conger examined the relationship between two models of delinquent behaviour: the social control model (which is discussed in Chapter 14) and a social learning model. Based on data collected from a sample of Grade 7 boys, Conger demonstrated how social learning theory, particularly the effects of differential reinforcement and punishment, can be used to explain how an individual's bonds to society can be strengthened or weakened. Conger argued that the combination of the two theories can provide a more comprehensive theory of delinquent behaviour than can either theory by itself. It is likely that the same arguments can be made for any of the theories reviewed in this chapter.

## Summary

- Psychological theory is primarily concerned with explanations of behaviour at the level of the individual. Some psychological theories have been criticized for relying too much on trying to explain crime at the level of the individual and for not placing enough emphasis on environmental and situational factors.

- Certain psychological perspectives, such as community psychology, view social problems from a "level of analysis" perspective. Such levels include individual, small-group, organizational, and institutional or community levels.

- The premise for psychoanalytic theory is a series of five stages of development (oral, anal, phallic, latency, and genital) and three components of personality (id, ego, and superego). Psychoanalytic interpretations of criminality suggest that criminal behaviour occurs when the ego and superego are unable to restrain the id.

- Kohlberg has proposed a six-stage theory of moral development, with two stages occurring at each of three levels (preconventional, conventional, and postconventional). This theory has been criticized from a feminist perspective for not adequately considering the different approaches of males (more justice-oriented) and females (more care-oriented) to morality.

- Eysenck's theory of crime and personality is based on the premise of classical conditioning. He has proposed three dimensions of personality (extraversion, neuroticism, and psychoticism), has developed measures of each of the three dimensions, and has generated a number of hypotheses about the relationship of these dimensions of personality to criminal behaviour. Eysenck's work offers a comprehensive model or theory of criminal behaviour that remains to be validated.

- Social learning theory integrates sociology and psychology in explaining criminal behaviour. Modelling is an important aspect of social learning theory. Family, subcultural influences, and symbolic modelling are all important sources from which an individual can learn aggressive behaviour. Deterrence, on the other hand, can occur through legal sanction, social sanction, and self-sanction.

■ Operant conditioning is a subset of learning theory that has been proposed to explain criminal behaviour. Reinforcement and punishment are theorized to play a large part in strengthening or weakening criminal behaviours. A token economy is one method that has been used to change existing behavioural interactions of individuals.

■ Antisocial Personality Disorder is a diagnostic label that refers to a cluster of traits that underlie a pervasive pattern of disregard for the rights of others. Such traits include lying, stealing, fighting, and truancy. Behaviours that may be characteristic of this disorder include excessive drinking or the use of illicit substances, aggressive sexual behaviour, inconsistent work performance, and a failure to accept social norms with respect to lawful behaviour.

■ Psychopathy is a term that is often confused with antisocial personality. Psychopathy refers to a pattern of behavioural features that are similar to those associated with Antisocial Personality Disorder. However, in addition to these behavioural features, psychopathic individuals also display certain attitudinal features such as grandiosity, glib and superficial charm, lack of empathy, and a lack of remorse, guilt, or shame.

■ The majority of criminals do not display any symptoms of mental illness. The prevalence of mental illness in jails and prisons is difficult to assess. However, some studies have estimated it to be between five and 12 percent for severe disorders and between 16 and 67 percent for any mental disorder.

## QUESTIONS FOR CRITICAL THINKING

1. Describe how each of the major psychological theories would explain criminal behaviour (i.e., psychoanalytic theory, theories of moral development, Eysenck's theory of crime and personality, social learning theory, and operant conditioning). What are the social policy implications of each of these theories?
2. Describe what is meant by Antisocial Personality Disorder and psychopathy, and discuss how these two disorders differ from each other.
3. Discuss the relationship between crime and mental illness, and describe the prevalence of mental illness in criminal populations. Is prison the most appropriate place to deal with people with mental illness?

## NET WORK

In this chapter, you have learned about theories of moral development. You can read more about these theories at **http://tigger.uic.edu/~lnucci/MoralEd/ overview.html.**

Go to the "Overview" section of this website to read more about the work of Piaget, Kohlberg, and Gilligan. Then do the following:

1. Go to the "Classroom Practices" section of the website. Describe one of the programs that has been used to teach moral development in the schools. How does this differ from the teaching program that you experienced when you were in school?

2. In the same section, you will see a link to a site called "Leading Moral Dilemma Discussions." Can you think of a moral dilemma from fiction or from real life that would be suitable if you were doing a moral development session with first-year university students?

3. Go to the "Featured Articles" section of the website. Using the featured articles can you find two different contexts to which proponents feel moral development should be applied? Do you think moral development training would be useful in these contexts?

## KEY TERMS

Antisocial Personality Disorder; pg. 298

assumption of discriminating traits; pg. 285

assumption of offender deficit; pg. 285

autonomic reactivity; pg. 295

classical conditioning; pg. 292

community psychology; pg. 286

ego; pg. 287

extraversion; pg. 293

id; pg. 287

modelling; pg. 294

moral development theory; pg. 292

operant conditioning; pg. 296

socialization; pg. 288

superego; pg. 287

token economy; pg. 297

## BIBLIOGRAPHY

Abrahamsen, D. (1944). *Crime and the Human Mind*. New York: Columbia University Press.

Abram, K. M., and L. A. Teplin. (1991). "Co-Occurring Disorders Among Mentally Ill Jail Detainees: Implications for Public Policy." *American Psychologist* 46:1036–45.

Abram, K. M., L. A. Teplin, and G. M. McClelland. (2003). "Comorbidity of Severe Psychiatric Disorders and Substance Use Disorders among Women in Jail." *American Journal of Psychiatry* 160:1007–10.

Akers, R. (1990). "Rational Choice, Deterrence, and Social Learning Theories in Criminology: The Path Not Taken." *Journal of Criminal Law and Criminology* 81:653–76.

Akers, R. L., and G. F. Jensen. (2006). "Empirical Status of Social Learning Theory of Crime and Deviance: The Past, Present, and Future." In K. Blevins, F. Cullen, and J. Wright (eds.), *Taking Stock: The Status of Criminological Theory* (pp. 37–76). Beverly Hills, CA: Sage.

Alexander, F., and M. Healey. (1935). *Roots of Crime*. New York: Knopf.

Allodi, F., H. Kedward, and M. Robertson. (1977). "Insane But Guilty: Psychiatric Patients in Jail." *Canada's Mental Health* 25:3–7.

American Psychiatric Association. (1994). *Diagnostic and Statistical Manual of Mental Disorders* (4th ed.). Washington, DC: American Psychiatric Association.

American Psychiatric Association. (2000). *Psychiatric Services in Jails and Prisons* (2nd ed.). Washington, DC: American Psychiatric Association.

Anderson, C. A., Shibuya, A., Ihori, N., Swing, E. L., Bushman, B. J., Sakamoto, A., Rothstein, H. R., and Saleem, M. (2010). "Violent Video Game Effects on Aggression, Empathy, and Prosocial Behavior in Eastern and Western Countries." *Psychological Bulletin* 136:151–73.

Bandura, A. (1979). "The Social Learning Perspective: Mechanisms of Aggression." In H. Toch (ed.), *Psychology of Crime and Criminal Justice* (pp. 198–236). New York: Holt, Rinehart and Winston.

———. (1986). *Social Foundations of Thought and Action: A Social Cognitive Theory*. Englewood Cliffs, NJ: Prentice Hall.

Bartol, C. R. (1980). *Criminal Behavior: A Psychosocial Approach*. Englewood Cliffs, NJ: Prentice Hall.

Birmingham, L., J. Gray, D. Mason, and D. Grubin. (2000). "Mental Illness at Reception into Prison." *Criminal Behaviour and Mental Health* 10:77–87.

Blair, R. J. R. (2006). "Subcortical brain systems in psychopathy." In C. J. Patrick (ed.), *Handbook of Psychopathy* (pp. 296–312). New York: The Guilford Press.

Blasi, A. (1980). "Bridging Moral Cognition and Moral Action: A Critical Review of the Literature." *Psychological Bulletin* 88:1–45.

Bonta, J., M. Law, and K. Hanson. (1998). "The Prediction of Criminal and Violent Recidivism among Mentally Disorders Offenders: A Meta-Analysis." *Psychological Bulletin* 123:123–42.

Borum, R. (1996). "Improving the Clinical Practice of Violence Risk Assessment: Technology Guidelines and Training." *American Psychologist* 51:945–46.

Borzecki, M., and J. S. Wormith. (1985). "The Criminalization of Psychiatrically Ill People: A Review with a Canadian Perspective." *Psychiatric Journal of the University of Ottawa* 10:241–47.

Bowlby, J. (1953). *Child Care and the Growth of Love*. Baltimore: Penguin Books.

Braukman, C. J., K. A. Kirigin, and M. M. Wolf. (1980). "Group Homes Treatment Research: Social Learning and Social Control Perspectives." In T. Hirschi and M. Gottfredson (eds.), *Understanding Crime: Current Theory and Research*. Beverly Hills, CA: Sage.

Braukman, C. J., and M. M. Wolf. (1987). "Behaviorally Based Group Homes for Juvenile Offenders." In C. J. Braukman and M. M. Wolf (eds.), *Behavioral Approaches to Crime and Delinquency*. New York: Plenum Press.

Braukman, C. J., M. M. Wolf, and K. K. Ramp. (1985). "Follow-Up of Group Home Youths into Young Adulthood." (Progress Report, Grant MA 20030). Achievement Place Research Project. Lawrence, KS: The University of Kansas.

Brodsky, S. L. (1977). "Crime and Dangerous Behavior." In D. C. Rimm and J. W. Somervill (eds.), *Abnormal Psychology*. New York: Academic Press.

Burgess, R. L., and R. L. Akers. (1966). "A Differential Association Reinforcement Theory of Criminal Behavior." *Social Problems* 14:128–47.

Buttell, F. P. (2002). "Exploring Levels of Moral Development among Sex Offenders Participating in Community-Based Treatment." *Journal of Offender Rehabilitation* 34:85–95.

Clastner, D. S. (1967). "Comparison of Risk Perception between Delinquents and Nondelinquents." *The Journal of Criminal Law, Criminology and Police Science* 58:80–86.

Cleckley, H. (1976). *The Mask of Sanity*. St. Louis: Mosby.

Cohen, A. K. (1966). *Deviance and Control*. Englewood Cliffs, NJ: Prentice Hall.

Conger, R. D. (1976). "Social Control and Social Learning Models of Delinquent Behavior: A Synthesis." *Criminology* 14:17–40.

Cook, T. D., D. A. Kendzierski, and S. V. Thomas. (1983). "The Implicit Assumptions of Television Research: An Analysis of the 1982 NIMH Report on Television and Behavior." *Public Opinion Quarterly* 47:161–201.

Corrado, R. R., I. Cohen, S. D. Hart, and R. Roesch. (2000). "Comparative Examination of the Prevalence of Mental Disorders among Jailed Inmates in Canada and the United States." *International Journal of Law and Psychiatry* 23:633–47.

Cotton, D., and T. G. Coleman. (2010). "Canadian Police Agencies and Their Interactions with Persons with a Mental Illness: A Systems Approach." *Police Practice & Research: An International Journal* 11:301–14.

Craddick, R. (1962). "Selection of Psychopathic from Non-Psychopathic Prisoners within a Canadian Prison." *Psychological Reports* 10:495–99.

Diamond, P. M., W. W. Eugene, C. E. Holzer, C. Thomas, and D. A. Cruser. (2001). "The Prevalence of Mental Illness in Prison." *Administration and Policy in Mental Health* 29: 21–40.

Einstadter, W., and S. Henry. (1995). *Criminological Theory: An Analysis of Its Underlying Assumptions*. Fort Worth: Harcourt Brace College Publishers.

Ewen, R. B. (1988). *An Introduction to Theories of Personality*. Hillside, NJ: Lawrence Erlbaum Associates.

Eysenck, H. J. (1977). *Crime and Personality*. London: Routledge and Kegan Paul.

———. (1990). "Crime and Personality." In N. Z. Hilton, M. A. Jackson, and C. D. Webster (eds.), *Clinical Criminology: Theory Research and Practice* (pp. 85–99). Toronto: Canadian Scholars' Press.

Eysenck, H. J., and S. B. Eysenck. (1976). *Psychoticism As a Dimension of Personality*. London: Hodder and Stoughton.

Eysenck, H. J., and G. H. Gudjonsson. (1989). *The Causes and Cures of Criminality*. New York and London: Plenum Press.

Farrington, D. P. (1978). "The Family Background of Aggressive Youths." In L. A. Hersov, M. Berger, and D. Shaffer (eds.), *Aggression and Antisocial Behavior in Childhood and Adolescence*. Oxford: Pergamon.

———. (1979). "Environmental Stress, Delinquent Behavior, and Conviction." In I. G. Sarason and C. D. Spielberger, (eds.), *Stress and Anxiety*, Vol. 6. Washington, DC: Hemisphere.

———. (2002). "Multiple Risk Factors for Multiple Problem Violent Boys." In R. R. Corrado, R. Roesch, S. D. Hart, and J. K. Gierowski (eds.), *Multi-Problem Violent Youth: A Foundation for Comparative Research on Needs, Interventions and Outcomes* (pp. 23–34). Amsterdam, Netherlands Antilles: IOS Press.

Farrington, D. P., L. Biron, and M. LeBlanc. (1982). "Personality and Delinquency in London and Montreal." In J. Gunn and D. P. Farrington (eds.), *Abnormal Offenders, Delinquency, and the Criminal Justice System*. Chichester, U.K.: Wiley.

Freeman, R. J., and R. Roesch. (1989). "Mental Disorder and the Criminal Justice System: A Review." *International Journal of Law and Psychiatry* 12:105–15.

Friedlander, K. (1947). *The Psychoanalytic Approach to Juvenile Delinquency*. New York: International Universities Press.

Geen, R.G. (1983). "Aggression and Television Violence." In R. G. Geen and E. I. Donnerstein (eds.), *Aggression: Theoretical and Empirical Reviews*. New York: Academic Press.

Gilligan, C. (1982). *In a Different Voice: Psychological Theory and Women's Development*. Cambridge, MA: Harvard University Press.

Gunn, J. (1977). "Criminal Behaviour and Mental Disorder." *British Journal of Psychiatry* 130:317–29.

Hails, J., and R. Borum. (2006). "Police Training and Specialized Approaches to Respond to People With Mental Illnesses." *Crime and Delinquency* 49:52–61.

Hakeem, M. (1958). "A Critique of the Psychiatric Approach to Crime and Correction." *Law and Contemporary Problems* 23:650–82.

Haney, C. (2002). "Making Law Modern: Toward a Contextual Model of Justice." *Psychology, Public Policy, and Law* 7:3–63.

Hare, R. D. (1970). *Psychopathy: Theory and Research*. New York: Wiley.

———. (1982). "Psychopathy and the Personality Dimensions of Psychoticism, Extraversion and Neuroticism." *Personality and Individual Differences* 3:35–42.

———. (1983). "Diagnosis of Antisocial Personality Disorder in Two Prison Populations." *American Journal of Psychiatry* 140:887–90.

———. (1991). *The Hare Psychopathy Checklist—Revised*. Toronto: Multi-Health Systems.

———. (1998a). *Without Conscience: The Disturbing World of the Psychopaths among Us*. New York: Guilford Press.

———. (1998b). "Psychopathy, Affect and Behavior." In D. J. Cooke, A. E. Forth, and R. Hare (eds.), *Psychopathy: Theory, Research and Implications for Society* (pp. 105–37). Dordrecht, The Netherlands: Kluwer Academic Publishers.

———. (1998c). "The Hare PCL-R: Some Issues Concerning Its Use and Misuse." *Legal and Criminological Psychology* 3:101–19.

Hare, R. D., and D. N. Cox. (1978). "Clinical and Empirical Conceptions of Psychopathy, and the Selection of Subjects for Research." In R. D. Hare and D. Schalling (eds.), *Psychopathic Behavior: Approaches to Research*. Chichester, England: Wiley.

Hart, S. D., D. N. Cox, and R. D. Hare. (1995). *The Hare Psychopathy Checklist: Screening Version*. Toronto: Multi-Health Systems.

Heilbrun, A. B., Jr. (1979). "Psychopathy and Violent Crime." *Journal of Consulting and Clinical Psychology* 47:509–16.

Hodgins, S., and G. Côté. (1990). "Prevalence of Mental Disorders among Penitentiary Inmates in Quebec." *Canada's Mental Health* (March):1–4.

Human Rights Watch. (2003). *Ill-Equipped: U.S. Prisons and Offenders with Mental Illness*. New York: Human Rights Watch.

Jacobsen, D., W. Craven, and S. Kushner. (1973). "A Study of Police Referral of Allegedly Mentally Ill Persons to a Psychiatric Unit." In J. R. Snibbe and H. M. Snibbe (eds.), *The Urban Policeman in Transition: A Psychological and Sociological Review*. Springfield, IL: C. C. Thomas.

Jeffery, C.R. (1965). "Criminal Behavior and Learning Theory." *Journal of Criminal Law and Criminology* 56:294–300.

Jennings, W. S., R. Kilkenny, and L. Kohlberg. (1983). "Moral-Development Theory and Practice for Youthful and Adult Offenders." In W. S. Laufer and S. M. Day (eds.), *Personality Theory, Moral Development, and Criminal Behavior* (pp. 281–94). Lexington, MA: Lexington Books.

Kiriakidis, S. (2008). "Moral Disengagement: Relation to Delinquency and Independence from Indices of Social Dysfunction." *International Journal of Offender Therapy and Comparative Criminology* 52:571–83.

Kohlberg, L., and R. Kramer. (1969). "Continuities and Discontinuities in Child and Adult Moral Development." *Human Development* 12:93–120.

Lamb, H. R., R. Shaner, D. M. Elliott, W. J. DeCuir, and J. T. Foltz. (1995). "Outcome for Psychiatric Emergency Patients Seen by an Outreach Police—Mental Health Team." *Psychiatric Services* 46:1267–71.

Loeber, R., D. P. Farrington, and M. Stouthamer-Loeber. (2001a). "Male Mental Health Problems, Psychopathy, and Personality Traits: Key Findings from the First 14 years of the Pittsburgh Youth Study." *Clinical Child and Family Psychology Review* 4: 273–97.

———. (2001b). "The Development of Male Offending: Key Findings from the First Decade of the Pittsburgh Youth Study." In R. Bull (ed.), *Children and the Law: The Essential Readings* (pp. 336–78). Malden, MA: Blackwell Publishers.

Losel, F. (1998). "Treatment and Management of Psychopaths." In D. J. Cooke, A. E. Forth, and R. Hare. (eds.), *Psychopathy: Theory, Research and Implications for Society* (pp. 303–54). Dordrecht, The Netherlands: Kluwer Academic Publishers.

MacPhail, D. D. (1989). "The Moral Education Approach in Treating Adult Inmates." *Criminal Justice and Behavior* 16:81–97.

Malamuth, N. M., and J. V. P. Check. (1981). "The Effects of Mass Media Exposure on Acceptance of Violence Against Women: A Field Experiment." *Journal of Research in Personality* 15:436–46.

Martin, S. E., L. E. Sechrest, and R. Redner (eds.). (1981). *New Directions in the Rehabilitation of Criminal Offenders*. Washington, DC: National Press Academy.

McIntyre, Mike. (2009). "Only One Verdict Possible: Judge, Killer Ruled Not Responsible for Grisly Deed." *Winnipeg Free Press*, March 6. Available at http://www.winnipegfreepress.com/local/only_one_verdict_possible_judge-40835637.html, accessed August 8, 2011.

Monahan, J., and S. Splane. (1980). "Psychological Approaches to Criminal Behavior." In E. Bittner and S. Messinger (eds.), *Criminology Review Yearbook*. Beverly Hills, CA: Sage.

Monahan, J., and H. J. Steadman. (1983). "Crime and Mental Disorder: An Epidemiological Approach." In M. Tonry and N. Morris (eds.), *Crime and Justice: An Annual Review of Research*. Chicago: University of Chicago Press.

Morash, M. (1983). "An Explanation of Juvenile Delinquency: The Integration of Moral-Reasoning, Theory and Social Knowledge." In W. S. Laufer and J. M. Day (eds.), *Personality Theory, Moral Development, and Criminal Behavior* (pp. 385–409). Lexington, MA: Lexington Books.

Nathan, P. E., and S. L. Harris. (1975). *Psychopathology and Society*. New York: McGraw-Hill.

National Commission on Correctional Health Care (2003). *Standards for Health Services in Jails*. Chicago: National Commission on Correctional Health Care.

Newman, J. P. (1998). "Psychopathic Behavior: An Information Processing Perspective." In D. J. Cooke, A. E. Forth, and R. Hare (eds.). *Psychopathy: Theory, Research and Implications for Society* (pp. 81–104). Dordrecht, The Netherlands: Kluwer Academic Publishers.

Nicholls, T. L., R. Roesch, M. C. Olley, J. R. P. Ogloff, and J. F. Hemphill. (2005). *Jail Screening Assessment Tool (JSAT): Guidelines for Mental Health Screening in Jails*. Burnaby, BC: Mental Health, Law and Policy Institute, Simon Fraser University.

Nietzel, M. T. (1979). *Crime and Its Modification: A Social Learning Perspective*. New York: Pergamon.

Ogloff, J. R. P., S. Wong, and A. Greenwood. (1990). "Treating Criminal Psychopaths in a Therapeutic Community Program." *Behavioral Sciences and the Law* 8:181–90.

Osher, F., H. J. Steadman, and H. Barr. (2003). "A Best Practice Approach to Community Reentry from Jails for Inmates with Co-occurring Disorders: The APIC Model." *Crime & Delinquency* 49:79–96.

Piaget, J. (1932). *The Moral Judgment of the Child*. New York: Free Press.

Polansky, N., R. Lippitt, and F. Redl. (1950). "An Investigation of Behavioral Contagion in Groups." *Human Relations* 3:319–48.

Pritchard, Dean. (2009). "Beheading Verdict No Surprise: Family." *Winnipeg Sun*, March 5. Available at http://www.winnipegsun.com/news/winnipeg/2009/03/05/8639531.html, accessed August 8, 2011.

Province of Manitoba Review Board. (2010). *A Disposition Review Hearing Held in Winnipeg, Manitoba on Monday, May 31, 2010.* Winnipeg: Manitoba Review Board.

———. (2009). *A Disposition Hearing Held in Winnipeg, Manitoba on Monday, June 1, 2009.* Winnipeg: Manitoba Review Board.

Queen's Bench, Winnipeg Centre. (n.d.). *Between Her Majesty the Queen and Vince Weiguang Li—Agreed Statement of Facts.* (n.d.). Winnipeg: Queen's Bench.

Raine, A., and Y. Yang. (2006). "The Neuroanatomical Basis of Psychopathy." In C. J. Patrick (ed.), *Handbook of Psychopathy* (pp. 278–95). New York: The Guilford Press.

Rappaport, J. (1977). *Community Psychology: Values, Research, and Action.* New York: Holt, Rinehart and Winston.

Reid, C. L. (2003). "Do Minority and Female Offenders Have Distinct 'Criminal Personalities'?: A Critique of Yochelson-Samenow's Theory of Criminality." *Criminal Justice Studies* 16:233–44.

Redl, F. (ed.). (1966). *When We Deal with Children: Selected Writings.* New York: Free Press.

Reppucci, N. D., and W. G. Clingempeel. (1978). "Methodological Issues in Research with Correctional Populations." *Journal of Consulting and Clinical Psychology* 46:727–46.

Roesch, R. (1988). "Community Psychology and the Law." *American Journal of Community Psychology* 16: 451–63.

———. (1995). "Mental Health Interventions in Pretrial Jails." In G. M. Davies, S. Lloyd-Bostock, M. McMurran, and C. Wilson (eds.). *Psychology and Law: Advances in Research* (pp. 520–31). Berlin: De Greuter.

Roesch, R., and S. L. Golding. (1985). "The Impact of Deinstitutionalization." In D. P. Farrington and J. Gunn (eds.), *Aggression and Dangerousness.* New York: Wiley.

Schoenfeld, C. G. (1971). "A Psychoanalytic Theory of Juvenile Delinquency." *Crime and Delinquency* 19:469–80.

Seidman, E., and B. Rabkin. (1983). "Economics and Psychosocial Dysfunction: Toward a Conceptual Framework and Prevention Strategies." In R. D. Felner et al. (eds.), *Preventive Psychology* (pp. 175–98). Elmsford, NY: Pergamon.

Skilling, T. A., G. T. Harris, M. E. Rice, and V. L. Quinsey. (2002). "Identifying Persistently Antisocial Offenders Using the Hare Psychopathy Checklist and DSM Antisocial Personality Disorder Criteria." *Psychological Assessment* 14:27–38.

Skoler, G. D., A. Bandura, and D. Ross. (1994). "Aggression." In W. A. Lesko (ed.), Readings in *Social Psychology: General, Classic, and Contemporary Selections* (2nd ed.) (pp. 296–326). Boston, MA: Allyn & Bacon.

Slinger, E., and R. Roesch. (2010). "Problem-solving Courts in Canada: A Review and a Call for Empirically-Based Evaluation Methods." *International Journal of Law and Psychiatry* 33:258–64.

Smith, S. L., and A. R. Boyson. (2002). "Violence in Music Videos: Examining the Prevalence and Context of Physical Aggression." *Journal of Communication* 52:61–83.

Steadman, H. J., D. W. McCarty, and J. P. Morrissey. (1988). *The Mentally Ill in Jail: Planning for Essential Services.* New York: Guilford.

Steadman, H. J., J. E. Scott, F. Osher, F., T. K. Agnese, and P. C. Robbins. (2005). "Validation of the Brief Jail Mental Health Screen." *Psychiatric Services* 56:816–22.

Suedfeld, P., and P. B. Landon. (1978). "Approaches to Treatment." In R. D. Hare and D. Schalling (eds.), *Psychopathic Behaviour: Approaches to Research* (pp. 347–76). Chichester, England: Wiley.

Teevan, J. J., and T. F. Hartnagel. (1976). "The Effects of Television Violence on the Perceptions of Crime by Adolescents." *Sociology and Social Research* 60:337–48.

———. (1984). "Criminalizing Mental Disorder: The Comparative Arrest Rate of the Mentally Ill." *American Psychologist* 7:794–803.

———. (1991). "The Criminalization Hypothesis: Myth, Misnomer, or Management Strategy." In S. A. Shah and B. D. Sales (eds.), *Law and Mental Health: Major Developments and Research Needs* (pp. 149–83). Rockville, MD: U.S. Department of Health and Human Services.

Thomas, M. H., R. W. Horton, E. C. Lippincott, and R. S. Drabman. (1979). "Desensitization to Portrayals of Real-Life Aggression as a Function of Exposure to Television Violence." *Journal of Personality and Social Psychology* 35:450–58.

Thornberry, T. P., and M. D. Krohn. (2000). "The Self-report Method for Measuring Delinquency and Crime." *Criminal Justice* 4:33–83.

Walter, G. D. (2004). "The Trouble with Psychopathy as a General Theory of Crime." *International Journal of Offender Therapy and Comparative Criminology* 48:133–48.

Warren, M. Q., and M. J. Hindelang. (1979). "Current Explanations of Offender Behavior." In H. Toch (ed.), *Psychology of Crime and Criminal Justice* (pp. 166–82). New York: Holt, Rinehart and Winston.

Webster, C.D., T. L. Nicholls, M. L. Martin, S. L. Desmarais, and J. Brink. (2006). "Short-Term Assessment of Risk and Treatability (START): The Case for a New Structured Professional Judgment Scheme." *Behavioral Sciences and the Law* 24:747–66.

Widom, C. (1977). "A Methodology for Studying Non-Institutionalized Psychopaths." *Clinical Psychology* 45:674–83.

Widom, C., and J. P. Newman. (1985). "Characteristics of Non-Institutionalized Psychopaths." In D. P. Farrington and J. Gunn (eds.), *Aggression and Dangerousness* (pp. 57–80). New York: Wiley.

Wilson-Bates, F. (2008). *Lost in Transition: How a Lack of Capacity in the Mental Health System Is Failing Vancouver's Mentally Ill and Draining Police Resources.* Vancouver: Vancouver Police Board.

# Strain Theories

**James C. Hackler**

UNIVERSITY OF VICTORIA

Explaining the criminality of individuals has been an age-old task, but with the growth of sociology, scholars began to look at the wider relationship between crime and social structure. Two broad theoretical perspectives guided this work. The **consensus perspective** maintains that the vast majority shares similar values regarding right and wrong. Morality is universal and important values are shared by all members of society. Customs persist and the law represents a codification of societal values.

The **conflict perspective** questions these assumptions and argues that the criminal law reflects the interests of the groups that create and enforce those laws. The character of laws, the kinds of conduct they prohibit, and the types of sanctions depend on powerful groups that influence legislation. The social values that receive the protection of the criminal law are ultimately those treasured by the dominant interest groups. It is not the *majority*, but rather the most *powerful*, whose values and concerns will be represented in the justice system. Some of these ideas are discussed in detail in the next chapter. This chapter reviews some historical traditions that reflect the consensus perspective. While authors differ in their use of terms, recent discussions of **strain theory** fit this general orientation.

Consensus theorists assume a reasonable degree of agreement on things that matter in society. They also assume that social institutions such as the family, education, government, religion, and the economy normally all contribute to the smooth running of society. Crime occurs when something unusual happens that affects these institutions. This results in strains, stresses, and frustrations that affect behaviour.

**consensus perspective**

Also known as *functionalism*, this perspective assumes that societies have an inherent tendency to maintain themselves in a state of relative equilibrium through mutually adjustive and supportive interaction of their principal institutions. It also assumes that effective maintenance of society is in the common interest of all its members.

**conflict perspective**

The focus on the inherent divisions of societies based on social inequality and the way these social divisions give rise to different and competing interests, with the central assumption that social structures and cultural ideas tend to reflect the interests of only some members of society rather than society as a whole.

## Learning Objectives

After reading this chapter, you should be able to

- Understand the differences between conflict and consensus perspectives of crime.
- Describe Durkheim's pioneering work on the relationship between crime and social structure and to understand the particular importance of his conception of anomie or normlessness.
- Discuss how Robert Merton modified Durkheim so that anomie theory became a theory of relative deprivation rather than a theory of a lack of social regulation.
- Note that strains can arise from features in the society or from situations surrounding individuals.

**strain theory**

The proposition that people feel strain when they are exposed to cultural goals they are unable to reach because they do not have access to culturally approved means of achieving those goals.

- Outline the role played by opportunities in Cloward's theory.
- Note how a *Code of the Streets* can evolve from strains arising in inner cities.
- Understand the strengths and weaknesses of strain theories.
- Describe the social policy implications of strain theories.

**The Emile Durkheim Archive**
**L. Joe Dunham**
http://durkheim.itgo.com/main.html

# Durkheim: The Functions of Crime and Anomie

In his book *Division of Labor in Society*, first published in France in 1893, Émile Durkheim argued that social solidarity—social groups working together toward agreed-upon goals—was an essential characteristic of human societies (1933). These agreed-upon goals led to a set of shared norms. Without norms to guide them, societies function poorly. Such "normlessness," or anomie, occurs during periods of rapid change when social solidarity or social cohesion is reduced. The lack of a sense of community and a collective conscience leads to a breakdown in society and increases in suicide and crime.

Although some crime is normal, even necessary, to define the boundaries of acceptable behaviour, there must be a balance between the functional and dysfunctional aspects of deviance (see Box 10.1). Excessive crime and deviance would destroy a society, but if there were no crime at all, then society would almost be compelled to create some. Even in a society of saints, someone would have to be defined as pushing the limits of proper behaviour. Behaviour may be restrained, but someone will violate the rules. For Durkheim, every society needs its quota of deviants.

## Anomie and Normlessness

**anomie**

A concept developed by Émile Durkheim (1858–1917) to describe an absence of clear societal norms and values. Robert Merton (1910–2003) used the term more narrowly to refer to a situation in which people would adopt deviant means to achieve goals beyond their means.

Durkheim popularized the concept of **anomie** to explain crime in more advanced and differentiated urban societies. Heterogeneity and increased division of labour weakened traditional societal norms, loosened social controls, and encouraged individualism. When social cohesion breaks down in society and social isolation is great, society loses its traditional social control mechanisms and eventually suffers from a high rate of crime.

Anomie is often defined as a "sense of normlessness," but in Durkheim's *Suicide* (1897/1951) he also refers to anomie as a condition in which individual desires, or self-interests, are no longer governed and controlled by society. In other words, self-interest, rather than norms, controls behaviour.

# Merton: The Gap Between Aspirations and Means

**social structure**

The patterned and relatively stable arrangement of roles and statuses found within societies and social institutions.

Merton applied this idea to crime by linking **social structure** and anomie (1938). Too much emphasis on the pursuit of self-interested goals and not enough on "legitimate means" to achieve those goals leaves society "normless" or anomic. People then use illegitimate, or criminal, means to achieve their desires. For Durkheim and Merton an anomic society places a higher priority on self-interested values like the acquisition of wealth, status, and power, but gives a lower priority to collective values like fairness, equality, and justice.

Crime is a symptom of the gap between **culturally prescribed aspirations** and the socially structured means for realizing those aspirations. The culturally prescribed aspirations are the goals held up for all members of society. Merton argues that in America, the accumulation of money and the status that results from material wealth are universal goals.

Socially structured avenues such as schooling are the accepted institutionalized means of reaching such goals. These avenues may not be a problem for certain members of the society; for example, if one comes from a family in which the mother or father is a medical doctor it may be realistic for the son or daughter to aspire to the same occupation and social status. The family may live in a nice neighbourhood, the children may attend schools that condition students toward thinking about a university education, and the home environment may encourage reading and getting good grades. Although individual characteristics, such as a certain level of intelligence may be required, the means to achieve culturally prescribed aspirations are available to many middle-class youths.

By contrast, the child of a poor family, especially a racial minority family, could find things a bit more difficult. If the father has abandoned the family, if an older sibling has already been in trouble with the law, if the mother has been on welfare, and if the local schools are ineffective, then the means to achieve success may not be readily available. A youth coming from such an environment may not respect the school system and may have poor grades and minimal likelihood of entering university or college. However, he or she might aspire to become a doctor and to have both the material and social rewards that accrue to that occupation.

The gap between goals and means is small for certain portions of the society but large for others. The strain resulting from the gap between goals and the means to achieve those goals could result in some sort of innovation, usually deviant in nature. In simpler terms, when society encourages people to want things but makes it difficult for certain groups to get them, members of these groups are more likely to steal or go into prostitution.

Not only is the society anomic but the individual is as well. This is the condition known as *microanomie*—where an individual places more value on self-interest than on collective values. An individual with these values is then motivated to seek out self-interested desires and not think about or be concerned with the effect such a pursuit has on the group. In a study of a sample of college students, Konty (2005) found that those students favouring "**self-enhancing**" values over "**self-transcending**" values were more likely to report having committed criminal and deviant acts. The effect of these values on self-reported behaviour was stronger than the effects of other sociological variables like race and social class. Surprisingly, Konty found that the gap between male and female offending was mostly explained by these different values. Males were more likely to have microanomie than females. But simply having self-enhancing values did not produce crime and deviance if the self-transcending values were also strong. It was when self-transcending, or collective, values were weak that crime and deviance became more likely.

**culturally prescribed aspiration**
A rejection of the notion that aspirations are entirely self-created; rather, they are defined by culture and transmitted by other members of the society.

**self-enhancing values**
Values that emphasize social status, prestige, dominance over others, and personal success.

**self-transcending values**
Values that emphasize appreciation, tolerance, protection, and the welfare of others.

# FOCUS BOX 10.1

## DURKHEIM'S GENERAL MODEL OF DEVIANCE

In his classic work on suicide, Durkheim argues that in contrast to community-oriented or collective thinking, individualism leads to a lack of social cohesion. Suicide, crime, and general deviance are inhibited in cohesive communities. His research showed that Protestant communities, which are more individualistic, had higher suicide rates than Catholic communities, which are more oriented toward collective thinking. From this, Durkheim concluded that individualism can cause deviant behaviour by reducing the strength of communities. One can generalize the argument from the specific act of suicide to deviance and crime in general, as illustrated in the sequence below:

**An Oversimplified Model of Durkheim's Explanation of Suicide as a General Explanation of Crime**

| Greater Individualism | → | Lack of Social Cohesion | → | Suicide and Crime |

These arguments also fit many forms of lower-class crime, particularly among marginally employed people. Robert Crutchfield (1995) points out that the lack of work influences crime. In addition, if these marginally employed people reside in concentrations of similarly underemployed people, the propensity to engage in crime is greater. This description fits certain ethnic groups in the United States and Canada.

The argument also fits certain upper-class crimes in which people in business, and others, aspire to great wealth. The legitimate avenues to success may not be sufficient because of severe competition; others may be "cutting corners" in a variety of ways. Thus, one can see that no matter what the situation, if there is a gap between the desired goals and the means, innovation or illegitimate tactics are more likely.

## Strain as a Feature of Society (Rather Than of Individuals)

Were Merton's ideas intended to explain the behaviour of individuals or, as Thomas Bernard (1987) argued, the behaviour of aggregates or groups? Bernard argued that it was not correct to interpret strain or anomie in psychological or social psychological terms; rather, these were properties of social structures. According to Bernard, Merton's theory would predict that societies whose cultures overemphasized the goal of monetary success and underemphasized adherence to legitimate means would have high rates of instrumental crime. If legitimate opportunities to achieve those monetary goals were unevenly distributed, instrumental crime would be unevenly distributed.

One must note the distinction between *cultural* factors and *structural* factors in society. In societies in which structural features create an uneven distribution of legitimate opportunities—that is, where there are many blocked opportunities—there will be pockets of instrumental crime, regardless of cultural values. When a culture emphasizes the ruthless pursuit of wealth, even if there is equal opportunity, crime will be widespread and such a society will

**Table 10.1**   **Strain Theories (Societal)**

| Theory | Theorists | Key Elements |
|---|---|---|
| Anomie: weak social regulation | Durkheim | When social cohesion breaks down, society loses its traditional mechanisms of social control and eventually suffers from a high rate of crime. |
| Anomie: the gap between aspirations and means | Merton | Crime occurs when there is a gap between culturally prescribed aspirations and socially structured means for realizing those aspirations. |
| Institutional-anomie | Messner, Rosenfeld | Strong pressures to succeed monetarily and weak restraints on the means to succeed in a society that emphasizes economics leads to crime. |

have a high rate of crime. The United States, and to a slightly lesser extent, Canada, fit this pattern. Other wealthy countries, like Denmark, Norway, and Sweden, seem to be less concerned with the individual pursuit of wealth. (See Table 10.1 for a summary.)

Steven Messner and Richard Rosenfeld (2007) extend this argument with their institutional-anomie theory. American culture emphasizes monetary success, but places less emphasis on *legitimate* means of achieving that success. This combination of strong pressures to succeed monetarily and *weak restraints on the means* is intrinsic to the "American Dream." It contributes to crime *directly* by encouraging people to use illegal means to achieve culturally approved goals, especially monetary goals. It also exerts an *indirect* effect on crime through its links with, and impact on, the institutional structure, or "the institutional balance of power." One institution—the economy—dominates all others. This emphasis has created a greater potential for crime.

The modern corporation may increase this tendency toward crime by splitting the production aspects from the financing. In the past, many companies were created by individuals who were primarily concerned with producing a product or service. Of course, they hoped to make a profit. Today, one can make money trading shares while disregarding the productive activities of a company. Shareholders play no part in daily operations, nor are they committed to the reputation of the product or the long-term success of the company. They are simply entitled to a share of the profits. Investors who "buy low and sell high" are admired. Nortel illustrated this mentality. A person selling Nortel stock at $125 in 2000 was deemed to be clever. However, an investor who bought Nortel at its peak only to watch it drop to nothing a few years later might be seen as stupid and greedy. Concern for those who lost their jobs was secondary.

The Enron and Worldcom trials (see Chapter 17), and the prison sentence served by Conrad Black were unique in that top leaders were actually punished for their criminal behaviour. Often, people in positions of power are not necessarily punished in the same way as those without influence would be.

Edgar Bronfman, Jr., heir to the Bronfman fortune, was convicted of insider training in 2011 and given a 15-month suspended prison sentence, meaning he will not be incarcerated (McGrath, 2011). These cases illustrate a pattern by those at the top that can be described as a *subculture of power abuse*. In addition to being criminogenic, such behaviour is generally antisocial and tears at the very fabric of society (Hackler, 2006).

Robber barons of the past ruthlessly exploited others to build railways, oil companies, or steel mills; modern entrepreneurs with deviant tendencies have new strategies which offer a faster way of achieving monetary goals. Stock markets, and the variety of ways that have been created for "investing," have created a new potential for crime. Vincent Lacroix, president of Norbourg Management, illustrates the rather complex way corporate leaders can cheat. He was convicted in 2007 of 51 fraud charges, sentenced to 12 years in prison, and fined a fee of 255 000. In 2008 Lacroix was released from prison but, as a result of further investigations, he almost immediately faced additional charges of fraud. He pleaded guilty in 2009 to 200 criminal charges of fraud, conspiracy to defraud, money laundering, and other illegal acts. His 13-year prison sentence is the longest ever received for white-collar crime in Canada. However, while other criminals spend longer in prison, and despite the fact that Lacroix did great social harm in embezzling the savings of 9000 people, he was released in January 2011 after serving only a small part of his sentence (Leblanc, 2011).

Vincent Lacroix, Conrad Black, and Edgar Bronfman Jr. illustrate the weak restraints on the means to achieve wealth described by Messner and Rosenfeld (2007). Today's white collar criminals are able to steal much faster than Leland Stanford and his railway could pillage California in the 19th century. Enron was able to use new strategies to manipulate the sale of energy in a manner that was not possible previously. Auto insurance and health insurance, particularly in the United States, offer modern opportunities for criminal entrepreneurs.

The 2008/09 recession was fuelled by fraudulent mortgages and irresponsible behaviour by powerful people (Chapter 17). As usual, however, those who are part of *the subculture of power abuse*—those who led us into the recession—have rarely suffered financially. "Fresh revelations emerge about unscrupulous behaviour by bankers in the run-up to the financial crisis. A spasm of outrage follows, along with talk of new investigations. Then, more often than not, nothing happens" (Slater, 2011: B11).

Occasionally, political leaders vow to crack down on corporate and white collar crime, but such tasks are often assigned to those who have close ties with the corporate world. After a spurt of publicity, the efforts to "crack down on corporate crime" tend to fade. If world leaders and lawmakers are part of a *subculture of power* abuse that condones, or at least tolerates, these activities, is it likely that corrective action will be taken in Canada or the United States? This may be particularly true of Canada where there is a greater overlap on boards of directors. Canada is also the only developed country that does not have a national securities regulator. One U.S. prosecutor has referred to our enforcement mechanism as "quaint." Some provinces are opposed to a national organization for the enforcement of corporate crime. Clearly, Alberta is not going to prosecute the oil giants operating in that province. Canada is the only G7 state listed among the worst offenders with little or no enforcement on bribery offences. Since the Corruption of the Foreign Public Officials Act in 1999, Canada has only recorded a single conviction on foreign bribery charges. In this case, an Alberta company (Hydro Kleen) was fined $25 000, an amount that was less than the bribe it paid (OECD, 2011).

## Responding to Opportunistic Crimes of the Powerful

Assuming that North America wishes to reduce the crime that results from the abuse of power by corporate leaders, traditional enforcement measures could be used more successfully. Our judicial system may not be particularly effective against family violence or juvenile delinquency, but courts and watchdog agencies can deter powerful people who break the law. While long sentences for corporate criminals have become more common in the United States, Canadian investigators have not been nearly as aggressive as their U.S. counterparts, and Canadian sentences remain light.

Prosecution might make corporate leaders rethink certain behaviour. In 2005, the Canadian Imperial Bank of Commerce (CIBC) paid $2.4 billion to resolve a lawsuit from the University of California alleging that CIBC "participated in an elaborate scheme to defraud investors." Both the Royal Bank of Canada and Toronto Dominion were also involved with Enron, but several years after CIBC paid their $2.4 billion lawsuit in California, the Canadian authorities decided not to proceed with charges against the other banks. This lack of enforcement sends a clear message to potential criminals. Weak restraints on the means to achieve monetary success plus the inability of watchdog agencies and our justice system to respond effectively increases the likelihood of white collar and corporate crime.

So far we have focused on corporate crime, but the *subculture of power abuse* is much broader. Do the same factors that encourage corporate crime increase unethical behaviour in government? According to the *Globe and Mail*, the three independent federal watchdogs created by the Conservative government—Karen Shepherd, Commissioner of Lobbying; Mary Dawson, Conflict of Interest and Ethics Commissioner; and Christiane Ouimet, Public Sector Integrity Commissioner—have done little to increase integrity in government (Galloway, 2010). Like lapdogs, "they don't bark, they don't bite and they don't hunt," Liberal MP Shawn Murphy, who chairs the Commons Ethics committee, said. "If they don't bite, it doesn't matter if they have teeth" (Galloway, 2010, A4). Ms. Ouimet was forced to resign in 2010 because of the public outcry over her lack of action.

Compared with other societies in the past, economic institutions dominate North America. Other important institutions—the family, education, and the political system—are secondary. Although these other institutions traditionally curbed criminal tendencies and imposed controls over the conduct of individuals, economic factors overwhelm those institutions that socialize people into pro-social behaviour. In other nations, such as Japan and India, the family appears to rank higher on the hierarchy of institutions and to be more influential relative to economics, than in North America. Thus, North America produces higher levels of serious crime than those countries in which the institutional balance of power leans toward non-economic institutions.

John Hagan (2010) argues that U.S. government policy has encouraged corporate crime. During what Hagan calls the age of Roosevelt (1933–1973), the Great Depression and World War II led politicians to focus more on corporate crime. During the age of Reagan (1974–2008) politics reversed course, demanding harsher treatment of street criminals while reducing scrutiny and enforcement in the financial sector. Financial crimes were seen as minor in importance.

Princeton historian Sean Wilentz (2008) argues that the Reagan White House established a pattern of disregard for the law. Laws that advanced the interests of the administration were passed and heeded; those that did not were ignored (2008, 286). With the world "at risk," the true believers must subordinate the rule of law to the rule of politics.

With government policies that believed free enterprise could do no wrong, a criminogenic environment was created. Merton argued that the gap between aspirations and means would lead to crime by "innovation." The new opportunities to "innovate" were certainly created during the Reagan era with new financial inventions, such as hedge funds, and sub-prime mortgages provided even more opportunities for unethical behaviour.

## Reducing Crime by Changing the Behaviour of the Elite

It is useful to broaden the discussion to unethical, not just criminal, behaviour. I suggest that reductions in the unethical behaviour of corporate executives and other powerful people would lead to a reduction in *all* crime, including street crimes. The fabric of society involves a wide range of moral and immoral behaviour. In Figure 10.1 the morality curve lumps all "immoral acts together." The skewed curve tapers to the right; that is, minor, nasty acts are more frequent than very serious unethical acts. Shoplifters are much more common than serial killers. Many people think in terms of the broken line, believing that corporate criminals and income tax evaders are somehow different from those really bad criminals who make up the bump on the right. Many apologists for corporate crime claim that there is only an occasional rotten apple in the barrel. Not so. Every study since Sutherland's classic study (*White Collar Crime*, 1949) shows that crime among large corporations is endemic.

The dotted line with two humps leads us astray. We deceive ourselves into believing that we can punish the few serious offenders while the rest continue as usual. Actually, the solid line represents reality. Furthermore, the shape stays the same. If we wish to create change, we must *move the entire curve to the left.* Therefore we must target the *frequent* acts of immorality which make up the bulk of this "morality curve."

Because the social fabric of society is broad, we must think beyond criminal behaviour and consider a broad range of antisocial behaviour. Because of the magnitude of unethical behaviour in commercial activities (e.g., insider trading, unethical mortgage lending, income tax evasion) it is worth considering legislation and enforcement that would diminish these frequent and also serious violations. We must also consider the structural conditions that encourage psychopathic behaviour.

Robert Hare of the University of British Columbia argues that individuals climbing the corporate ladder have higher levels of psychopathic traits (Babiak,

**FIGURE 10.1**  The Morality Curve

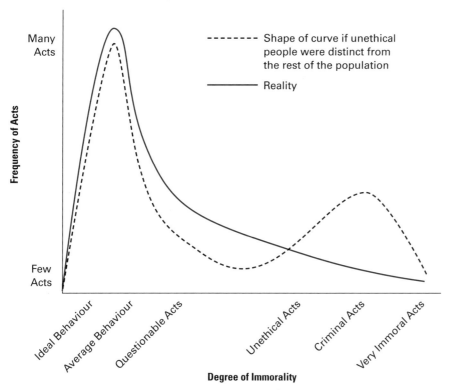

Source: James C. Hackler. (2006). *Canadian Criminology: Strategies and Perspectives (4th ed.).* Toronto: Prentice Hall Canada, page 327. Reprinted with permission by Pearson Canada Inc.

Neumann, and Hare, 2010). As a result, we should not be surprised that graduate students entering MBA programs have more psychopathic characteristics than those in other disciplines (Heinze, Allen, Magai, and Ritzler, 2010).

## Generalizing Merton's Strain Theory to Other Cultures

Hongming Cheng (2011) argues that Chinese academics pursue the "Chinese Dream" in the same way that corporate executives and those who face blocked opportunities pursue the "American Dream." The concept of "face" is important to the Chinese scholar, but "face" also involves wealth and power. A brilliant scholar who is poor does not receive the respect of a scholar who uses his academic base to earn money. Thus, there is a pressure to cheat. Unethical professors will become role models for unethical students and generally contribute to deviant behaviour to achieve the "Chinese Dream." Academic fraud moves the morality curve to the right. By contrast, honest professors who are content with the real satisfactions of an academic life and who take pride in seeing their students do well as ethical individuals may move the morality curve to the left. This demonstrates that Merton's basic argument fits more than economic institutions and provides clues as to how the world can be changed.

Michael Hellenbach (2006) provides a good illustration of how the capitalist economic model, responding as Merton would predict, increased crime in Eastern Germany. When the Berlin Wall came down in 1989 many people in the West assumed that capitalism would bring Communist East Germany a better material life. One incentive to bring modern industry to East Germany was to offer West German companies incentives to improve commercial operations; for example, a West German company could purchase a factory for one German Mark with the agreement that they would upgrade that factory. Instead, the western companies stripped the factories and closed them in order to avoid competition with their western enterprises.

A decade ago I stayed with a fisherman in an East German port that had been purchased by a West German firm. Instead of revitalizing the port they closed it and took all usable equipment. The fishermen were all out of work. Today there are fewer jobs in the East, salaries for the same work are lower, and young people must migrate to the West to find jobs. Unemployment is high and crime rates are rising. In other words, the unethical—if not downright criminal—behaviour of corporations has led directly to an increase in crime. The aspirations of young East Germans are high but the means to achieve monetary goals are low. The West German corporations also had monetary goals, but they also had access to unethical means.

While corporations offer obvious targets for unethical behavior, Merton's theory fits many situations. Medical doctors on salaries, when compared to doctors in private practice, may not aspire as much to greater wealth. Those in private practice may also have greater opportunities to "innovate" for profit.

The over-reaching argument I am making is that respect for the rule of law, ethical behaviour by the leaders of society, and societies that create just rules influence the potential for crime for everyone in that society. When Jim Shaw stepped down as CEO of Shaw Cable in his early 50s with a pension of $6 million dollars per year, it may not have been criminal but it was an abuse of power and privilege. It moves the morality curve to the right.

By contrast, passing and enforcing laws against white collar crime, prosecuting income tax violations more vigorously (perhaps publishing their names in the newspaper), and shaming CEOs into linking their bonuses with bonuses to all of their employees would move the morality curve to the left and reduce crime.

When two judges in Luzerne County, Pennsylvania accepted $2.6 million in kickbacks from the owners of two private juvenile correctional facilities for sending children to these places (Schwartz and Levick, 2010) was this a reflection of a capitalist system where the profit motive leads to greed that overwhelms other values? Or does a society that tolerates and creates a subculture of power abuse increase the likelihood that those placed in positions of trust will be corrupt? Or are both these ideas connected to each other?

Merton's theories provide us with ideas about how to reduce the harm caused by privileged predators. Figure 10.1 suggests that the successful reduction of crime and unethical behaviour among privileged predators would have far reaching impacts on the rest of crime.

## Strain as a Feature of Individuals

Perhaps Bernard is correct in arguing that Merton was applying his ideas to structures, but many of us find it useful to apply his ideas to individuals.

As one applies strain theory to individuals, one can see a convergence with differential association (Chapter 13) and control theory (Chapter 14). An attempt in this direction, using strain theory as a base, can be seen in the work of Robert Agnew (1992). Strain triggers negative emotions, which in turn requires that the individual cope with those emotions. Usually we are able to deal with our stresses. For example, strain could result from failing an exam. A legitimate coping strategy might be to accept the fact that one should have studied more. Another illustration: a boy develops a crush on a girl. She ignores him, so he works extra hard to become a top athlete. But if legitimate coping strategies are ineffective or unavailable, one may adopt illegitimate coping strategies.

Adolescents located in unpleasant environments from which they cannot escape, such as school, are more likely to be delinquent. Parental rejection, unfair or inconsistent discipline, parental conflict, and unsatisfactory relations with peers can all be sources of strain. Often adolescents have few means to cope. If the coercive treatment is perceived as unjust or arbitrary, the resulting anger can lead to the defiance of authority.

Agnew and others (Mazerolle and Piquero, 1997, 1998; Brezina, 1998) call attention to the intervening role of anger in the relationship between strain and delinquency. If the strain doesn't make you mad, you may simply endure it rather than search for illegitimate alternatives. If the strain does lead to anger that cannot be handled legitimately, because opportunities are not available or are ineffective, crime becomes more likely.

Strain has usually been defined in the past in terms of blocked opportunities in education and jobs, but Agnew reminds us that other negative experiences also lead to stress and hence a search for illegitimate alternatives. In addition, different types of strain are more relevant to different subgroups (Agnew, 1992). There is also empirical support for the interaction of strain variables and social psychological ones, such as having delinquent friends (Agnew and White, 1992). Bonds with both delinquent and non-delinquent friends can lead to other stresses.

As more sophisticated measures of strain/anomie are developed, these ideas are being applied to different populations (Agnew et al., 1996). Recent empirical studies suggest that strain, or anomie, theory is more complex than the simplified versions presented here. We are learning more about the sources of individual strain and the macro-level determinants of such strain (Jensen, 1995; Agnew, 1997). The nature of the relationships among these variables is probably more complex than even the elaboration of strain theory offered by Agnew.

# The Shift from Control to Opportunity Structures

Durkheim argued that human aspirations had to be regulated and channelled. Since human aspirations were boundless, and people could not always have what they want, they had to be persuaded to accept what they received. When people were not persuaded, the society became anomic. The moral guidelines were unclear. Social control broke down, and some people violated the norms established by those in power.

**opportunity structure**

Opportunity is shaped by the way the society or an institution is organized or structured.

**relative deprivation**

Deprivation in relation to others around you, rather than judged against an absolute standard of sustainability.

**absolute deprivation**

The inability to sustain oneself physically and materially.

While Durkheim emphasized the restraints that control crime, Merton focused on **opportunity structures**. He suggested that American society had an overriding dominant goal—material success—but the guidelines for achieving that success were not always clear. If this type of anomie was so widespread, however, why wasn't crime distributed evenly through society? Merton accepted the argument that crime was distributed unevenly—that it was higher in the urban slums, for instance. To explain this social-class-specific crime by anomie, he redefined anomie as the disjuncture between the cultural goal of success and the opportunity structures by which this goal might be achieved. Anomie was shifted from normlessness to **relative deprivation** (as opposed to **absolute deprivation**), whereby it was not the entire community that was anomic but rather specific individuals who were committed to the goal of wealth while being barred from the means that would realize that goal.

## Richard Cloward: Illegitimate Opportunity Structures

Just as there are differences between legitimate and illegitimate opportunities, there are different types of illegitimate opportunities. Cullen (1984) points out the importance of "structuring variables." Cloward (1960) asserts that simply being subjected to socially generated strain does not enable a person to deviate in any way he or she chooses. People can participate in a given adaptation only if they have access to the means to do so (Cullen, 1984, 40). Even though members of the lower class may be under a great deal of strain, they are unlikely to engage in violations of financial trust, political corruption, and other white-collar crimes in order to achieve their goals. In a book with Lloyd Ohlin entitled *Delinquency and Opportunity* (1960), Cloward extended the ideas of Merton by combining them with themes found in Sutherland's "differential association" (see Chapter 13). Sutherland argued that criminal behaviour is learned through associations with others who define criminal activity favourably. While Merton emphasized legitimate means, Sutherland concentrated on illegitimate means (Cullen, 1988). People under strain cannot become any kind of criminal they choose; they are limited by the opportunities available to them. Dealing in drugs is not automatically available to a "square" university professor as a means of supplementing her income; she probably lacks the skills and contacts to obtain a source of illegal drugs. In short, illegitimate means are not readily available to people simply because they lack legitimate means. While Durkheim and Merton developed plausible theories of structurally induced pressures, Cloward tried to explain that reasonable opportunities must exist. Illegal opportunities for fraud involving oil wells are more available in Alberta than in Toronto.

Opportunity theory fits many different types of deviance. Cloward and Ohlin applied these ideas to juvenile delinquency. Juveniles undergoing strain face different barriers to resolving that strain than adults do. The way they respond to social barriers for achieving goals could lead to three different types of gangs or **subcultures**: *criminal*, *conflict*, and *retreatist* gangs.

There are pressures toward conventional goals: achieving middle-class values, such as respectability and conventional success. When juveniles overcome those barriers, as most middle-class juveniles do, they commit little crime. However, lower-class males may actually have different goals. Instead of respectability, they may prefer money, a car, and showing off for their girlfriends.

**subculture**

A group of people who share a distinctive set of cultural beliefs and behaviours that differs in some significant way from that of the larger society.

**FIGURE 10.2**  Barriers to Legal and Illegal Opportunities Implicit in the Work of Cloward and Ohlin (1960)

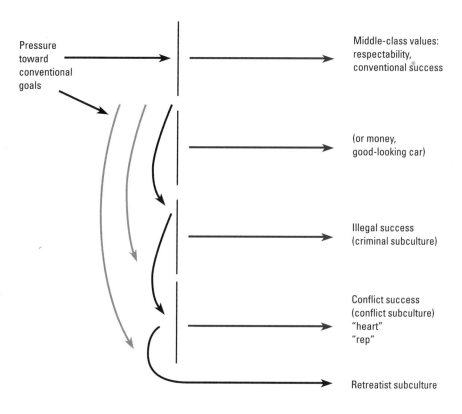

**SOCIAL BARRIERS TO ACHIEVING GOALS**

Pressure toward conventional goals

Middle-class values: respectability, conventional success

(or money, good-looking car)

Illegal success (criminal subculture)

Conflict success (conflict subculture) "heart" "rep"

Retreatist subculture

Under certain economic conditions, this might be achieved by working in areas in which their skills are scarce, working in a hazardous occupation, or possibly being fortunate as an athlete. In other words, it is possible to be successful in a working-class style of life. These ideas differ somewhat from Merton's in that aspirations are not universal. Striving for success can mean different things to different people.

However, there are barriers to lower-class goals as well (see Figure 10.2). Not only is there an opportunity structure for lower class goals, but crime also has an opportunity structure of its own. If legitimate opportunities are blocked, the next step may be to search for illegal success, but even here there are barriers. Without certain contacts, it may be difficult to get into illegal gambling or learn the skills of credit card fraud. Many juveniles will have difficulty learning the skills necessary to succeed in these areas. However, if there are barriers to profitable property crime, juveniles can still turn to conflict as a means of attaining status, at least among their peers.

Juveniles who are unskilled as thieves can show their bravery by fighting for their "turf." This will show others that they have "heart"; their courageous behaviour will give them a "rep." But even conflict success has barriers. Not every juvenile is keen on wielding a bicycle chain in a gang war. Some may lack strength or courage or both. These juveniles may employ a third delinquent alternative: the use of drugs. In the drug or retreatist subculture there are practically no barriers.

Individual characteristics, such as race, will be related to some of these barriers. Thus, Asian youths in Vancouver may have opportunities to work with Asian gangs who extort money from restaurant owners. Blacks who have lived in Nova Scotia since the American Revolution, Jamaican youths in Toronto, and Haitian immigrants in Montreal probably have a realistic view of the barriers to legitimate and illegitimate success. Violence and drugs may be the only things left. In Canada, the abuse of alcohol by First Nations people may also be influenced by barriers to both legitimate and illegitimate opportunities.

## Marginal Opportunity Structures

Francis Cullen (1988) believes the contributions made by Cloward are underappreciated because they focus primarily on the gap between aspirations and perceived opportunities. Other deviant styles of adaptation to illegitimate opportunities become apparent when one looks beyond traditional types of crime and at different settings. Fred Desroches describes the way some men adapt to pressures related to homosexual activity in public restrooms in Ontario (1995). The "tearoom," a public washroom where homosexual activity takes place, provides an opportunity structure for those under certain types of strain. Alternatives do not seem to fill the need; thus, this marginal opportunity structure is used with the risk that police action will create additional problems in their lives.

Street life in Vancouver offers another type of marginal or illegitimate opportunity structure (Hagan and McCarthy, 1997a). Youths in families that are functioning well perform better in school and are more successful in finding work. Negative family experiences increase the likelihood of "hanging out" on the street. The interactions among parental employment, weakened marital ties, neglect, and abuse increase the likelihood of crime directly, but they also expose such youths to additional new stresses when they leave one negative environment for another. While seeking food and shelter on the street, these vulnerable youths meet seasoned offenders who coach the newcomers in criminal activities. The police will also view them as criminally inclined.

Street life increases exposure to networks of seasoned offenders who offer tutelage in offending and a means of acquiring "criminal capital"—that is, information (e.g., where to sell stolen goods) and skills (e.g., how to use burglary tools). Physical and sexual abuse has conditioned them to respond to police confrontations with defiance and rage. Hagan and McCarthy show how employment, a source of social and **human capital**, in contrast to criminal capital, can reduce involvement in crime and street life (see Chapter 14).

Cloward's work may also offer an explanation of certain marginal activities, such as being an oil company spy. In Alberta, where many oil companies drill wells in the wilderness and try to keep their findings secret, spies from rival companies sometimes pose as hunters or wilderness trekkers to observe drilling operations without being detected. This often-hazardous activity highlights the presence of particular opportunities and barriers to potentially profitable tasks.

Opportunity structures, including illegitimate ones, pose an interesting policy question for society. Which is more desirable: having skid row alcoholics with no opportunities or having prostitutes and gamblers engaging in activities

**human capital**

The talents and capabilities that individuals contribute to the process of production. Companies, governments, and individuals can invest in human capital, just as they can invest in technology and buildings or in finances.

**TABLE 10.2**   **Strain Theories (Individual)**

| Theory | Theorists | Key Elements |
|---|---|---|
| General strain | Agnew | Adolescents in unavoidable unpleasant environments face strain leading to anger and delinquency. |
| Opportunity structures | Cloward | In addition to strains that create a pressure toward criminal behaviour, there are also different opportunity structures that may facilitate breaking the law. These structures are both legitimate and illegitimate. |
| Code of the Street | Anderson | Lack of employment opportunities leads to alternative ways of achieving respect: displaying toughness, taking another person's possessions, pulling a trigger. It helps build a reputation that prevents future challenges, but it also creates other problems. |

that are seen as deviant by society? While legitimate opportunities are clearly preferable to illegitimate ones, is it possible that the integration of some borderline, or even obvious, deviance would be better than the total breakdown represented by some of society's rejects? In a society that must sometimes choose between levels of evils, would policy-makers be wise to consider the nature of different opportunity structures and assess the impact of selected illegitimate opportunities on society? (See Table 10.2 for a summary.)

# Elijah Anderson: The Code of the Street

Elijah Anderson's *Code of the Street: Decency, Violence, and the Moral Life of the Inner City* (1999) describes the cumulative effects of structural changes in inner cities. During and after World War II, manufacturing jobs in the cities recruited many unskilled and semi-skilled workers. Many blacks, Hispanics, and other ethnic groups benefited from these opportunities. At the same time, more minorities were moving into middle-class jobs. However, with the exporting of manufacturing to countries paying low wages, the loss of these unionized jobs that paid reasonably well had a serious impact on those at the bottom of the social scale. Barriers to participate in mainstream society persisted for young blacks. Employers preferred white women and new immigrants to young blacks.

"The Code of the Street," according to Anderson, requires young males, and often females, to let others know how tough they are, how hard it would be for someone else to "roll on" them, how much "mess" they will take before they respond with a fist in the mouth. The most effective way of gaining respect is to manifest nerve. A man shows this by taking another person's possessions, messing with someone's woman, throwing the first punch, "getting in someone's face," or pulling a trigger. It helps build a reputation that prevents future challenges (Anderson, 1999, 92).

Many young blacks actively live their lives in opposition to whites and middle-class blacks. Lacking trust in mainstream institutions, many turn to "hustling" in the underground economy (1999, 108). To be self-respecting, young men and women must exhibit contempt for a system they are sure has contempt for them.

The drug trade offers economic opportunity, is organized around the code of the streets that employs violence for social control, and thus contributes significantly to the violence of inner-city neighbourhoods. For those with minimal success in the legal job market, illegal activities provide alternatives: the drug trade, prostitution, welfare scams, and other rackets.

Even though the majority of youths in school may be "decent," the street element dominates. It victimizes those who show weakness. Thus decent kids must take on the code of the street if they are to avoid being victimized. The lack of opportunity for legitimate employment leads to strain. To achieve respect, and the money that enhances respect, young people must display a willingness to use violence.

## Assessing Strain Theories

When Durkheim introduced his ideas, scholars were still explaining crime primarily by genetics and inner psychological forces. Durkheim focused attention on social forces, a radical idea at the time, but now the dominant methodology for explaining crime.

Durkheim was less accurate in his description of pre-modern nations as stable, crime-free societies. In fact, many had high levels of violence. Furthermore, Western countries seem to have experienced a long-term decline in crime over the past few centuries (Gurr, 1981). Despite the continual complaints we hear today, during the 17th century the average citizen in most cities in western Europe would rarely leave the security of a locked home after dark.

Merton's strain theory does not help us explain the lower crime rates of women. Merton takes into account differences in opportunity that arise out of social class, but he does not apply the same reasoning to blocked opportunities based on gender (Comack, 1992). Women, like disadvantaged lower-class males, might be expected to be more criminal as a means to achieve universal goals. While many conventional theorists have assumed that women experience less strain than men in the struggle to achieve through institutionalized means, many feminist scholars reject these statements as assumptions and biases rather than fact (Morris, 1987; Naffine, 1987). Although the strains women are subject to may differ from those experienced by men, they may be just as severe. Unless one assumes women have more modest goals, strain theory does not explain why women are less criminal.

Despite these criticisms strain theories seem to offer insights into the unethical behaviour of individuals, gangs, and corporations. Recent scholars have even used anomie theory to explain deviance in dictatorship countries which are now moving in the direction of democracy (Zhao and Cao, 2010; Hongming, 2011). Thus the ideas of Durkheim, Merton, and other strain theorists continue to be relevant.

CHAPTER 10 Strain Theories

## The Convergence of Strain Theory and Other Perspectives

There has been a convergence of ideas that permits strain theory, differential association, and control theory to complement one another. In addition, the policy implications of the different theories can be similar. For example, enabling the disenfranchised to participate more fully in what society has to offer is probably related to greater social bonding with others and a stronger belief in the rules that guide the larger society. However, if social bonds are primarily with people who condone or rationalize criminal behaviour, and with those who face similar blocked opportunities, criminal behaviour is likely. In such situations, control theory, differential association, and strain theory complement one another.

A vast oversimplification of these ideas might be as follows: (1) learning theories (Chapter 13), such as differential association, explain delinquency by *positive* relations with deviant others; (2) social control theories (Chapter 14) argue that delinquency occurs when juveniles have *little or no* attachment or social bonds to others; (3) Agnew's elaboration of strain theory emphasizes that *negative* relations and experiences in situations beyond their control lead juveniles to delinquency; and (4) all three conditions can reinforce one another and can have a reciprocal impact, increasing the likelihood of criminal behaviour.

# Uses of Strain Theory

Modern society creates many illegitimate opportunities for those wishing to take advantage of them. Credit cards, computers, and the flow of information across borders make new forms of theft possible. The terrorist attacks of September 11, 2001 on the World Trade Center created opportunities for fraud. More than 200 people have been arrested for defrauding agencies that were trying to help victims and relatives. A morgue manager, for example, was accused of stealing coffins and reselling them. However, most people do not avail themselves of the vast opportunities for theft in complex societies.

Messner and Rosenfeld (2007) argue that the emphasis on material wealth in North America encourages crime. Other countries may have a different value structure. In one informal study done by *Reader's Digest*, 1100 wallets were "lost" in about a dozen countries. Each wallet contained $50 in local currency and the name and phone number of the owner. About 44 percent of the wallets disappeared. However, in Norway and Denmark, every single wallet was returned (Felte, 2001). Do some societies create a climate that produces more good Samaritans and where illegitimate opportunities are ignored?

## John Braithwaite: Greater Class Mix and the Reduction of Crime

Braithwaite (1979) argues that one must look at the interaction between the social class of individuals and the social class of the neighbourhood in order to answer the question of whether an increase in class heterogeneity in neighbourhoods would reduce crime. He offers two propositions. The first is that crime is most likely when both exposure to illegitimate opportunities is high and exposure to legitimate opportunities is low. The second states that crime is unlikely either when legitimate opportunities are high or when illegitimate opportunities are low. In other words, in three out of the four possible combinations, there are factors that would inhibit crime. Only when *both* illegitimate opportunities and a lack of legitimate opportunities exist would there be a marked increase in crime.

Braithwaite also argues that belonging to the lower class has more effect on delinquency for youth in lower-class areas than for youth in middle-class areas. Consequently, cities with relatively large numbers of lower-class people living in predominantly middle-class areas and relatively large numbers of middle-class people living in predominantly lower-class areas have relatively low crime rates. That is, greater class mix results in less crime.

This implies that if the middle classes could keep together, they would be better off; on the other hand, if the lower classes stay together, they will be even worse off. Hence, it may be to the advantage of those with power and influence to keep themselves segregated. The quality of life for the society as a whole, however, would be improved if residential heterogeneity characterized the society.

Braithwaite's ideas seem more applicable to property crime, but another study shows that if there is a culture of violence, its roots are to be found in racial and economic inequalities (Blau and Blau, 1982). Spatial mixing in neighbourhoods would be more easily achieved with a reduction of racial and economic inequalities. Some observers have suggested that Canada has a lower crime rate than the United States in part because our housing policies have been less likely to "ghettoize" the poor in areas that could develop very high crime rates.

## Reducing Upper-Class Crime

Braithwaite also argues that "too little power and wealth creates problems of living, and this produces crime of one type; too much power corrupts, and this produces crime of another type" (1979, 200). This does not mean that upper-class people are more criminal than lower-class people. If lower-class people were exposed to the same vast opportunities as white-collar criminals, they, too, would engage in large-scale "power" crimes. Powerful people abuse their occupational power. It makes little sense to ask which social class commits more crime. Rather, opportunities differ by social class. If lower-class people commit crimes because of a lack of power and wealth, increasing their influence and well-being might help. Greater economic equality and a greater distribution of influence among people would modify to some extent those factors that lead to crime.

Lower-class crime may be caused by the failure to achieve success goals. By contrast, upper-class crimes arise from an unprincipled overcommitment to success goals. One study of college students found that those most dedicated to monetary success were those most likely to argue that they "can't afford to be squeamish about the means." Similarly, certain occupational structures can increase commitment to illegitimate success. Richard Quinney (1963) found that retail pharmacists tended to fall into two divergent categories with different role expectations: professional and business. The "professionals" were bound by guidelines for compounding and dispensing prescriptions. The "business oriented" believed that self-employment carries with it independence and freedom from control. For them, professional norms exercised less control. Prescription violations occurred more frequently among the business-oriented pharmacists. As both Quinney and Braithwaite would argue, the mutual support of like-minded individuals insulated them from the broader society, and from their professional colleagues, increased the likelihood of crime.

## Policy Implications

Five decades ago, crime-prevention projects used strain theories to change opportunity structures. In hindsight, the narrow focus of these projects made it difficult to obtain significant impacts, but they illustrate attempts to apply some of the ideas reviewed in this chapter.

Opportunities for Youth (OFY) in Seattle attempted to use work opportunities to reduce delinquency but the project met with little success (Hackler, 1966). One might argue that temporary job programs do not have a meaningful impact on the larger community. However, this same project had an impact on the attitudes of the adults living in the four communities in which the project was conducted (Hackler and Linden, 1970). Furthermore, parents of black children seemed particularly responsive to the idea of job opportunities for their children. Like so many programs launched during the 1960s, OFY attempted to use strain theories. Lower-class populations did respond and became involved. Although evidence of crime reduction in the short term is lacking, the opportunity structure was altered for some lower-class families. We should not be overly cynical or skeptical. Early childhood education programs implemented in the 1960s have demonstrated that they can have a significant effect on later school achievement and, eventually, success in the adult world (Schweinhart et al., 1993).

Unfortunately, opportunities for the lower classes may have decreased in North America in the past decade. While there has been a dramatic increase in the wealth of the upper classes, the frequent display of a luxurious lifestyle, especially on television, creates all the more strain for those who aspire to a share of that material wealth.

It may be difficult to alter the structure of society, but governments could support those institutions that ease some of the strains that arise from blocked opportunities. Public policies could provide visiting nurses, training and support for disadvantaged mothers, paid family leave, and universal health care. The work done by Richard Tremblay and his colleagues at the Université de Montréal on early childhood development is consistent with preschool "head start" programs that help reduce the strains caused by the challenges of education (Tremblay and Craig, 1995). Young people could be involved in national service programs, such as the Peace Corps, which lead to government funding for higher education or training in skilled occupations. Workplaces could offer continuing training and upgrading. In other words, some of the strains experienced in the family, school, and workplace do not have to lead to anger and attacks on society if institutions provide alternatives.

Disintegrative shaming pervades our current coercive criminal justice operations (Braithwaite, 1989). Social support is the key ingredient in "reintegrative shaming." Andrews and Bonta (1998) show that individuals can control their behaviour through rehabilitation programs that make use of cognitive and behavioural therapies. Given the right setting, this can lead to positive outcomes and legitimate ways of coping. In fact, most current crime control measures increase strain and anger. Unfortunately, moving toward a noncoercive, socially supportive criminal justice system does not seem likely at the present time.

Scholars do not have to be in complete agreement regarding strain theory before applying many of its principles to public policy in the important pursuit of reducing the gap between rich and poor. Nor should we ignore the warning Merton voiced in his 1938 article: *"The ruthless pursuit of profit creates a criminogenic society."* Increasing opportunities for the less privileged members of society makes a great deal more sense than rewarding the wealthy to encourage them to invest (for a profit, of course). The self-serving policies advocated by many powerful people in North America in recent years should, according to any version of strain theory, lead to more crime.

## Summary

- Two broad theoretical perspectives have guided sociological theories of crime. The consensus perspective maintains that the vast majority of the population share similar values regarding right and wrong. The law represents a codification of societal values. The conflict perspective questions such assumptions and argues that the criminal law does not necessarily represent the moral values of the majority but rather reflects the interests of the groups that are in a position to create and enforce those laws.

- Strain theory is part of the consensus tradition. Strain theorists assume that social institutions such as the family, education, government, religion, and the economy normally all contribute to the smooth running of society. Crime occurs when something unusual happens that affects some or all of these institutions. This results in strains, stresses, or frustrations that affect people's behaviour.

- Durkheim saw crime and other deviance as a consequence of modernity. Changes associated with modernity led to a weakening of social controls, and consequently rates of deviance increased.

- Merton began with Durkheim's concept of anomie but modified Durkheim's theory to account for what he felt were the realities of American society. In Merton's anomie theory, crime resulted from the gap between culturally prescribed aspirations and the socially structured means for realizing those aspirations.

- Messner and Rosenfeld argued that American culture emphasizes monetary success. When combined with weak restraints on illegitimate means, this encourages economic crimes.

- Agnew suggests that adolescents located in unpleasant and stressful environments, such as school, from which they cannot escape become frustrated and angry. If legitimate coping alternatives are not available, violent outbursts and delinquency are likely.

- Cloward pointed out that illegitimate opportunities were also not equally accessible to all. As a result, he hypothesized that there would be three different types of delinquent subcultures: criminal, conflict, and retreatist.

- Anderson notes that exporting manufacturing jobs overseas has made a bad situation worse in inner cities. With respect through traditional work not being available, young people have adopted a code of the street. One gains status by being tough and willing to use violence.

- Early strain theorists focused on lower class crime, but it also applies to white collar and corporate crime. Upper-class crimes can arise from an unprincipled overcommitment to success goals. Even successful people may feel pressure to make more money and may choose to break the law in order to achieve these financial goals.

## QUESTIONS FOR CRITICAL THINKING

1. In this chapter, you have read about the consensus and conflict perspectives to crime. Think of three different laws that prohibit behaviour most people would agree is wrong. Can you think of any circumstances under which these acts might be permissible? Now think of three different laws that prohibit behaviour that a significant number of Canadians think should be tolerated. Why do these behaviours remain against the law?

2. How would Merton's anomie theory explain the higher rates of deviance and crime among Canada's Aboriginal people? Does the theory help you to think of any possible solutions to this problem?

3. Researchers who have studied delinquent gangs have failed to find the three distinct criminal, conflict, and retreatist subcultures predicted by Cloward and Ohlin. Why do you think these distinct types of gangs do not exist?

4. Discuss some of the strengths and weaknesses of strain theory.

5. Merton (and those who followed him) developed strain theory to explain lower-class crime and delinquency. However, some might argue that strain theory actually provides a better explanation of white-collar and corporate crime. Describe how strain theory can be used to explain the crimes of the rich and powerful.

## NET WORK

Go to this website: **http://www.safecanada.ca/link_e.asp?category=2&topic=14.**
Look at the list of programs designed to prevent crime and delinquency and select a few. Which of these programs address issues raised by strain theorists? How likely do you think it is that these programs will have an impact on crime? Why?

## KEY TERMS

absolute deprivation; pg. 334

anomie; pg. 324

conflict perspective; pg. 323

consensus perspective; pg. 323

culturally prescribed aspiration;
   pg. 325

human capital; pg. 336

opportunity structure; pg. 334

relative deprivation; pg. 334

self-enhancing values; pg. 325

self-transcending values; pg. 325

social structure; pg. 324

strain theory; pg. 323

subculture; pg. 334

## BIBLIOGRAPHY

Agnew, Robert. (1992). "Foundation for a General Strain Theory of Crime and Delinquency." *Criminology* 30:47–87.

———. (1997). "The Nature and Determinants of Strain." In Nikos Passas and Robert Agnew (eds.), *The Future of Anomie Theory*. Boston: Northeastern University Press.

Agnew, Robert, and Helene Raskin White. (1992). "An Empirical Test of General Strain Theory." *Criminology* 30:475–99.

Agnew, Robert, Francis T. Cullen, Velmer S. Burton Jr., T. David Evans, and R. Gregory Dunaway. (1996). "A New Test of Class Strain Theory." *Justice Quarterly* 13:681–704.

Anderson, Elijah. (1999). *Code of the Street: Decency, Violence, and the Moral Life of the Inner City*. New York: W. W. Norton.

Andrews, Donald A., and James Bonta. (1998). *The Psychology of Criminal Conduct* (2nd ed.). Cincinnati, OH: Anderson.

Babiak, Paul, Craig Neuman, and Robert Hare. (2010). "Corporate Psychopathy: Talking the Walk." *Behavioral Sciences and the Law* 28(2):174–93.

Bernard, Thomas. (1987). "Testing Structural Strain Theories." *Journal of Research in Crime and Delinquency* 24:262–80.

Braithwaite, John. (1979). *Inequality, Crime and Public Policy*. London: Routledge and Kegan Paul.

Braithwaite, John. (1989). *Crime, Shame, and Reintegration*. Cambridge: Cambridge University Press.

Brezina, Timothy. (1998). "Adolescent Maltreatment and Delinquency: The Question of Intervening Processes." *Journal of Research in Crime and Delinquency* 35:71–99.

Cao, Liqun. (2004). "Is American Society More Anomic? A Test of Merton's Theory with Cross-National Data." *International Journal of Comparative and Applied Criminal Justice* 28(1):15–32.

Cloward, Richard, and Lloyd Ohlin. (1960). *Delinquency and Opportunity*. Glencoe, IL: Free Press.

Comack, Elizabeth. (2009). "Women and Crime." In Rick Linden (ed.), *Criminology: A Canadian Perspective* (6th ed.). Toronto: Harcourt Brace.

Crutchfield, Robert D. (1995). "Ethnicity, Labor Markets and Crime." In Darnell F. Hawkins (ed.), *Ethnicity, Race and Crime: Perspectives Across Time and Place*. Albany: State University of New York Press.

Cullen, Francis. (1984). *Rethinking Crime and Deviance Theory: The Emergence of a Structuring Tradition*. Totowa, NJ: Rowman and Allanheld.

———. (1988). "Were Cloward and Ohlin Strain Theorists? Delinquency and Opportunity Revisited." *Journal of Research in Crime and Delinquency* 25:214–41.

Desroches, Fred. (1995). "Tearoom Trade: A Law Enforcement Problem." *Canadian Journal of Criminology* 33(1):1–21.

Durkheim, Émile. (1893/1933). *The Division of Labor in Society.* New York: Free Press.

———. (1897/1951) *Suicide.* New York: The Free Press.

Farnworth, Margaret, and Michael Leiber. (1989). "Strain Theory Revisited." *American Sociological Review* 54:263–74.

Galloway, Gloria. (2010). "Tory-Appointed Watchdogs Reluctant to Probe Wrongdoing, Critics Charge." *The Globe and Mail*, January 28:A4.

Grabosky, Peter, and Neal Shover. (2010). "Forestalling the Next Epidemic of White Collar Crime: linking policy to theory." *Criminology & Public Policy* 9:641–54.

Gurr, Ted. (1981). "Historical Forces in Violent Crime." In Michael Tonry and Norval Morris (eds.), *Crime and Justice*, Vol. 3 (pp. 295–353). Chicago: University of Chicago Press.

Hackler, James C. (1966). "Boys, Blisters, and Behavior." *Journal of Research in Crime and Delinquency* 3 (July) 155–64.

———. (2006). *Canadian Criminology: Strategies and Perspectives* (4th ed.). Toronto: Prentice Hall Canada.

Hackler, James C., and Eric Linden. (1970). "The Response of Adults to Delinquency Prevention Programs: The Race Factor." *Journal of Research in Crime and Delinquency* 7 (January):31–45.

Hagan, John. (2010). *Who Are the Criminals?* Princeton and Oxford: Princeton University Press.

Hagan, John, and Bill McCarthy. (1997a). *Mean Streets: Youth Homelessness and Crime.* New York: Cambridge University Press.

Heinze, P., R. Allen, C. Magai, and B. Ritzler. (2010). "Let's Get Down to Business: A Validation Study of the Psychopathic Personality Inventory among a Sample of MBA students." *Journal of Personality Disorders* 24(4):487–98.

Hellenbach, Michael. (2006). *Arbeitsmotivation in Ost- und West Deutschland: Grundlagen und Vergleiche.* Saarbruecken: VDM. Verlag.

Hongming Cheng. (2011). "Academic Fraud in China: Assessing the Applicability of Merton's Strain Theory." Western Society of Criminology Conference, Vancouver, February 3–5.

Jensen, Gary F. (1995). "Salvaging Structure Through Strain: A Theoretical and Empirical Critique." In Freda Adler and William S. Laufer (eds.), *Advances in Criminological Theory*, Vol. 6: The Legacy of Anomie. New Brunswick, NJ: Transaction.

Konty, Mark. (2005). "Microanomie: The Cognitive Foundations of the Relationship between Anomie and Deviance." *Criminology* 43(February):107–31.

Leblanc, Daniel. (2011). "Bloc Takes Tories to Task on Fraudster's Release." *The Globe and Mail*, January 31. Available at http://www.theglobeandmail.com/news/politics/bloc-takes-tories-to-task-on-fraudsters-release/article1889541/, accessed August 23, 2011.

Mazerolle, Paul, and Alex Piquero. (1997). "Violent Responses to Strain: An Examination of Conditioning Influences." *Violence and Victims* 12:323–43.

———. (1998). "Linking Exposure to Strain with Anger: Investigation of Deviant Adaptations." *Journal of Criminal Justice* 26:195–211.

McFarland, Janet. (2010). "Drabinsky, Gottlieb Argue Appeals Judge Erred." *The Globe and Mail*, November 27. Available at http://www.globeinvestor.com/servlet/ArticleNews/print/GAM/20101127/RBLIVENTAPPEAL1127ATL, accessed August 22, 2011.

McGrath, John Michael. (2011). "The Son Also Stumbles: Edgar Bronfman Jr. Not Going to Jail After All (He's Just Been Slapped with a $6.7 million fine)." *Toronto Life*, January 24. Available at http://www.torontolife.com/daily/informer/march-of-crimes/2011/01/24/the-son-also-stumbles-edgar-bronfman-jr-not-going-to-jail-after-all-he%E2%80%99s-just-been-slapped-with-6-7-million-fine/, accessed August 22, 2011.

Merton, Robert K. (1938). "Social Structure and Anomie." *American Sociological Review* 3 (October):672–82.

Messner, Steven F., and Richard Rosenfeld. (2007). *Crime and the American Dream* (4th ed.). Belmont, CA: Thomson Wadsworth.

Morris, Alison. (1987). *Women, Crime, and Criminal Justice*. Oxford: Basil Blackwell.

Naffine, Ngaire. (1987). *Female Crime: The Construction of Women in Criminology*. Sydney: Allen and Unwin.

OECD. (2011). *Canada: Phase 3. Report on the Application of the Convention on Combating Bribery of Foreign Public Officials in International Business Transactions and the 2009 Revised Recommendations on Combating Bribery in International Business Transactions*. Paris: OECD Working Group on Bribery in International Business Transactions.

Quinney, Richard. (1963). "Occupational Structure and Criminal Behavior: Prescription Violation by Retail Pharmacists." *Social Problems* 11(Fall):179–95.

Schwartz, Robert G., and Marsha Levick. (2010). "When a 'Right' is Not Enough: Implementation of the Right to Counsel in an Age of Ambivalence." *Criminology and Public Policy* 9(20):365–73.

Schweinhart, L. L., H. V. Barnes, and D. P. Weikart. (1993). *Significant Benefits: The High/Scope Perry Preschool Study through Age 27*. Ypsilanti, MI: High/Scope Press.

Slater, Joanna. (2011). "After the Financial Crisis: A Dearth of Prosecutions." *The Globe and Mail*, April 19:B11.

Snider, Laureen. (2003). "Resisting Neo-Liberalism: The Poisoned Water Disaster in Walkerton, Ontario." *Social and Legal Studies* 5(2):27–47.

Sutherland, Edwin. (1949). *White Collar Crime*. New York: Dryden.

Thornberry, Terence P. (1987). "Toward an Interactional Theory of Delinquency." *Criminology* 25:863–91.

Tremblay, Richard E., and Wendy M. Craig. (1995). "Developmental Crime Prevention." In M. Tonry and D. P. Farrington (eds.), *Building a Safer Society: Strategic Approaches to Crime Prevention*, Vol. 19. Chicago: University of Chicago Press.

Wilkinson, Richard, and Kate Picket. (2009). *The Spirit Level: Why More Equal Societies Almost Always Do Better*. London: Allen Lane.

Zhao, Ruohui, and Liquin Cao. (2010). "Social Change and Anomie: A Cross Nation Study." *Social Forces* 85(3):1209–30.

# Conflict Theories

**11**

### Danica Dupont

n this chapter we will explore a number of conflict theories, including cultural conflict theory, group conflict theory, instrumental and structuralist Marxism, socialist feminism, and left realism. The conflict perspective assumes that societies are more divided by conflict than they are integrated by consensus. Whereas consensus theorists (see Chapter 10) view the law as the codification of mutually agreed upon societal norms and values, conflict theorists question the assumption that our laws represent the interests of society as a whole. Instead, the conflict perspective argues that the social norms and values codified into law are those endorsed by the more powerful or dominant groups in society.

## Learning Objectives

After reading this chapter, you should be able to

- Understand the differences between Sellin's culture group conflict theory and Vold's interest group conflict theory.

- Describe how Quinney's (1970) group conflict theory differs from both Vold and Sellin's conflict theories.

- Know the basic elements of Marx's mode of production, and what is meant by the economic base and the superstructure.

- Understand the differences between instrumental Marxism and structural Marxism, and the meaning of relative autonomy.

- Know how socialist feminism modified radical feminism and Marxism to arrive at a theory of capitalist patriarchy.

- Describe the basic elements of the left realist position.

## Cultural Conflict Theory

### Thorsten Sellin

Thorsten Sellin was one of the first criminologists to propose a conflict perspective for the analysis of crime. In *Culture Conflict and Crime* (1938), Sellin presented a criminological theory that focused on the role of "conduct norms" in explaining crime. For Sellin, modern society is composed of diverse cultural groups, each maintaining distinct "conduct norms" or cultural rules that govern appropriate conduct. Sellin suggests that in basic, culturally homogeneous societies the values and norms to which people subscribe will be fairly similar, so the conduct norms of the broader social group will tend to reflect

**conduct norms**

Specification of rules or norms of appropriate behaviour generally agreed upon by members of the social group to whom the behavioural norms apply.

**cultural conflict**

A theory that attempts to explain certain types of criminal behaviour as resulting from a conflict between the conduct norms of divergent cultural groups.

a societal consensus. However, in more complex societies characterized by cultural heterogeneity, urbanization, and industrialization, an overall societal consensus is less likely, and it is more likely that there will be conflict between the **conduct norms** of different cultural groups. In other words, the more complex a society becomes, the greater the probability of culture conflict.

According to Sellin, **cultural conflict** can arise when conduct norms clash on the border areas between distinct cultures; as a result of colonization, migration, or immigration; or when the laws of one cultural group are extended to cover the territory of another. Sellin was particularly interested in how the conduct norms of immigrant cultures could potentially come into conflict with the conduct norms of the established or dominant culture. One sphere where culture conflict appears is in the legal sphere, especially criminal law. Cultural practices in conflict with Canadian law include female genital mutilation, honour killings, marital rape, and forced marriage. While there are various ways in which social groups secure conformity of their members, the criminal law stands out because "its norms are binding upon all who live within the political boundaries of the state and are enforced through the coercive power of the state" (Sellin, 1938, 21).

Sellin felt that the criminal law "depends upon the character and interests of those groups in the population which influence legislation" (1938, 21). Ultimately, social values that receive the protection of the criminal law are those valued by dominant interest groups. Sellin uses the term *criminal norms* to describe the "conduct norms" embodied in the criminal law that represent the values of the dominant group. The criminal law will generally reflect the social values and conduct norms of the dominant cultural group. According to Sellin, then, crime is an expression of culture conflict when individuals who act based on the conduct norms of their own cultural group find themselves in violation of the conduct norms that the dominant group has enacted into law. Box 11.1 examines the murder of Ontario teenager Aqsa Parvez, and briefly surveys the Canadian literature on honour killings.

## Group Conflict Theory

### George Vold

**group conflict theory**

A theory that attempts to explain certain types of criminal behaviour as resulting from a conflict between the interests of divergent groups.

In *Theoretical Criminology* (1958), George Vold views **group conflict theory** as an explanation for certain types of criminal behaviour. Much like Sellin, Vold is interested in examining crime as it relates to conflict between groups. Unlike Sellin's explanation of crime as resulting from a conflict between the conduct norms of divergent cultural groups, Vold focuses on crime that occurs as a result of conflict between diverse "interest" groups. Vold begins with the assumption that humans are "group-involved" beings whose lives are oriented toward group associations. Groups form when members have common interests that are best furthered through collective action. Groups will come into contact with one another as their interests begin to overlap and become competitive. Vold sees society as a collection of groups existing in a constantly shifting, but more or less stable, equilibrium of opposing group interests.

# FOCUS BOX 11.1

## HONOUR CRIMES IN CANADA: THE MURDER OF AQSA PARVEZ

Sixteen-year-old Mississauga, Ont., resident Aqsa Parvez was, in many respects, a typical Canadian teenager. She wanted a part-time job; she wanted to choose her own clothing and be able to dress like the other kids at school; she wanted more privacy at home and more freedom to talk on the phone; and she wanted to attend the high school her friends went to, rather than the faith-based school her father wanted her to attend.

However, other aspects of Aqsa's life were far from that of a typical teenager. Despite her youth, Aqsa's parents had already chosen someone from her native Pakistan for her to marry. Aqsa had never been to see a movie in the theatre, and her life outside of school was tightly controlled. She was expected to go directly to and from school, she was not allowed to socialize outside of school hours, and she was not permitted to get a part-time job. Aqsa's wish to choose her own clothing caused a great deal of friction with her father, who expected her to conform to an Islamic dress code by wearing the hijab.

In September 2007 Aqsa told a school counselor she was afraid her father would kill her for disobeying his orders to tell Applewood High School officials she wanted to withdraw in order to attend an Islamic school. Aqsa was scared to go home and stayed in a shelter for three nights, after which she was persuaded to return to the family residence. By the middle of November, Aqsa told her closest friends that her father had sworn to her on the Koran that if she ran away again he would kill her.

On Thursday, November 29, 2007, Aqsa decided she would leave home for the second time. She was welcomed into the home of a friend and seemed determined to start a new life for herself. She went to school, reported her change of address, and asked a counselor for help with a resumé. She expressed her wish to get a part-time job and went to see a movie for the very first—and sadly—last time.

On Monday morning, December 10, 2007, Aqsa Parvez was strangled to death in her former family home. Her father Muhammad Parvez, 60, and her brother Waqas Parvez, 29, have since pleaded guilty to second-degree murder and were sentenced to life in prison with no chance of parole for 18 years. Eight other adults were at the family home at the time of the murder. All claimed to have heard nothing. When asked by police why her husband murdered their daughter, Mrs. Parvez said her husband told her "My community will say you have not been able to control your daughter. This is my insult. She is making me naked" ("*R. v. Muhammad Manzour Parvez (father) and Waqas Parvez (son)* AGREED STATEMENT OF FACTS," June 15, 2010).

The United Nations Population Fund has estimated that 5000 women and girls are killed each year in honour-related crimes (UNFPA, 2000). Some feel the actual number may be much higher. In a 10-month investigation of honour killings in Jordan, Pakistan, Egypt, Gaza, and the West Bank, journalist Robert Fisk reports that many women's groups in the Middle East and South-west Asia believe the number of honour killings is at least four times that of the United Nations estimate (*The Independent*, September 7, 2010). Researchers argue that it is almost impossible to accurately assess the true extent of honour killings because such crimes go unreported in many countries or are disguised as accidents or suicides (Warrick, 2005; Devers and Bacon, 2010).

While the number of honour killings committed in Canada is very small by comparison, it is nevertheless an issue of growing concern, according to Amin Muhammad, who suggests that honour killings are on the rise in Canada. Muhammad is researching honour killings in Canada for the Department of Justice and has estimated that at least 12 young women in Canada have died as the result of an honour killing over the past decade. "There are a number of organizations which don't accept the

*(continued)*

idea of honour killing; they say it's a Western-propagated myth by the media, but it's not true," Dr. Muhammad said. "Honour killing is there, and we should acknowledge it, and Canada should take it seriously." (*National Post*, June 17, 2010).

What, exactly, is an "honour killing"? Patel and Muhammad (2008, 684) have described this crime as "the cultural sanctioning of pre-meditated killings of women perceived to have brought dishonour to their families, often by engaging in illicit relations with men." In their analysis of honour killings in rural Turkey, a similar definition is offered by Sev'er and Yurdakul, who describe honour killing as "the premeditated murder of pre-adolescent, adolescent or adult women, by one or more male members of her immediate or extended family ... due to an allegation, suspicion or proof of sexual impropriety by the victim" (1999, 964).

While definitions of honour killings vary somewhat, certain features appear to be constant. First, honour killings almost always involve the murder of a woman or girl by her male family members. Second, the killer does not normally act alone, but with the approval or encouragement of other members of the family. Third, suspicion or rumour of an alleged impropriety is usually enough to justify an honour crime. Finally, most experts insist an essential characteristic of an honour killing is that it is premeditated (Terman, 2010, 10).

Shahrzad Mojab has written extensively on violence against women in patriarchal societies, with a particular focus on countries in the Middle East and Western Asia. She argues that while honour killing is part of the culture of the societies in which it is practiced, "reducing this crime to culture may readily lead to racist interpretations and appropriations" (2002, 2). Instead, she argues that honour killing should be viewed as a form of patriarchal violence against women and as "a means for the exercise of gender power, in this case male power" (ibid.). Sev'er and Yurdakul (1999, 964) offer a similar argument,

and suggest that honour killing should be dissociated from particular religious beliefs and instead located "within a continuum of patriarchal patterns of violence against women."

Aruna Papp takes a different view of this problem. Papp has been counselling South Asian immigrants and victims of violence for 30 years, and was herself in an abusive marriage when she immigrated to Canada from India in 1972. Papp argues that few researchers appreciate the distinction between Western patterns of domestic violence and culturally-driven abuse of girls and women in some immigrant communities. Among other differences, Western abuse is considered an aberration by kinship groups and society in general, whereas culturally driven violence "stems from culturally approved codes around collective family honour and shame, and is condoned and even facilitated by kinship groups and the community" (Papp, 2010, 7). Honour killing, Papp maintains, "is not the only crime committed in the name of honour, simply the most violent" (2010, 15).

Papp argues forcefully against a misguided multiculturalism that fails to denounce cultural abuse of women and girls in immigrant communities for fear of appearing racist or of perpetuating cultural stereotypes. She argues that when honour killings occur, a multiculturalism-inspired reluctance to "racialize" the crime by law enforcement and the media ultimately does a disservice to both the immigrant community and Canadian society more generally by ignoring "a cultural problem in dire need of acknowledgement and reform" (2010, 15).

Imagine that you have been asked to write a position paper on honour killings for the Department of Justice. Would you endorse Aruna Papp's argument that honour killings should be viewed as a specific form of culturally driven violence against women, or Shahrzad Mojab's argument that honour killings are a form of patriarchal violence against women? How might your policy recommendations differ, based on your choice of framework for analysis?

Vold is interested in the way the creation of law reflects the activities of antagonistic interest groups in the broader community. One interest group may seek the assistance of the state to enact a new law while an opposing interest group tries to resist the proposed legislation. The interest group marshalling the greater number of votes will have the most influence in determining whether the new law is enacted. Therefore Vold (1958, 209) argues that

> the whole political process of law making, law breaking and law enforcement becomes a direct reflection of deep-seated and fundamental conflicts between interest groups and their more general struggles for the control of the police power of the state. Those who produce legislative majorities win control over the police power and dominate the policies that decide who is likely to be involved in violation of the law.

For Vold, conflict between interest groups is a normal social process, and one of the fundamental principles of organized political society.

Vold describes two general classes of group conflict that can result in criminal behaviour. First, some crimes arise from a conflict between the behaviour of minority groups and the legal norms, rules, and regulations of the dominant majority, which are established in law. For example, Vold argues that the delinquent gang can be understood as a minority group whose interests are in opposition to the rules of the dominant majority—the adult world of regulations established in law and enforced by the police. A further example of a minority group whose interests are in opposition to the dominant majority is that of "conscientious objectors" during wartime who opt to serve prison sentences rather than participate in any form of compulsory wartime service.

Second, some crimes arise from a conflict between competing interest groups who are vying for power. For example, Vold argues that many crimes are the result of political revolution or protest movements whose aim is direct political reform. "A successful revolution," Vold argues, "makes criminals out of government officials previously in power, and an unsuccessful revolution makes its leaders into traitors subject to immediate execution" (Vold, 1958, 215). A further example of intergroup conflict that may result in criminal behaviour is that of the conflict of group interests between management and labour unions. In the case of strikes or lockouts, escalating tensions between management and striking workers may result in violence, property damage, or other crimes.

Vold argues that criminological theories that focus on notions of individual choice and responsibility may not be relevant in understanding criminal behaviour occurring as a result of conflict between interest groups. This is because individual criminal behaviour that results from intergroup conflict represents, for that same individual, a type of "loyal service" to the interest group. Group conflict theory is limited to instances where criminal behaviour arises from the conflict between interest groups and does not try to explain other types of criminal acts.

Conflict theory has been criticized for its narrow scope of explanation. Critics argue that it applies to a narrow range of crimes, where only politically or ideologically motivated crimes can be said to fit the model well. In addition,

**Educational Resource for Criminology**
www.crimetheory.com

others argue that most crime is intra-group, that is, committed by one member of a group against another member, rather than the inter-group crime upon which Vold focuses.

## Richard Quinney

Although Richard Quinney's theoretical perspective changed significantly in his later work, his 1970 book, *The Social Reality of Crime*, was widely viewed as an important contribution to group conflict theory. Following Sellin and Vold, Quinney's theory of crime explains criminality as the result of conflict between groups. Whereas Sellin focused on cultural group conflict and Vold on interest group conflict, Quinney's group conflict theory focused on the more broadly defined notion of "segments" of society, which he defined as types of "social groupings." For Quinney, the more powerful segments or social groups are able to secure and protect their own interests by influencing the formulation, enforcement, and administration of criminal law. Although both Sellin and Vold viewed criminal law as generally reflective of the values and norms of dominant groups in society, Quinney placed a much greater emphasis on the unequal distribution of power in society, especially as related to the formation of public policy. While Vold would view society as existing in a relatively stable equilibrium of opposing group interests where all groups are able to make themselves heard in policy decision making, Quinney argues that only some interest groups are sufficiently powerful to influence policy, because power is unequally distributed due to "the structural arrangements of the political state" (1970, 12).

Quinney outlines his conflict theory of crime in six propositions:

1. *Crime is a definition of human conduct that is created by authorized agents in a politically organized society.* For Quinney, crime is not inherent in behaviour, but rather is the product of legal definitions; it is a *definition* of behaviour imposed on some persons by others.
2. *Criminal definitions describe behaviours that conflict with the interests of segments of society that have the power to shape public policy.* Quinney argues that the more powerful segments of society can incorporate their interests, values, and norms into the criminal law, so these powerful segments can regulate the formulation of criminal definitions. These definitions are formulated because less powerful segments of society are in conflict with other more powerful segments.
3. *Criminal definitions are applied by the segments of society that have power to shape the enforcement and administration of criminal law.* The interests of powerful segments are not only represented in the formulation of criminal law, but also in its application. The enforcement and administration of the law is delegated to legal agents (e.g., police, prosecutors, judges) who represent the interests of these powerful segments.
4. *Behavioural patterns are structured in segmentally organized society in relation to criminal definitions, and within this context persons engage in actions that have relative probabilities of being defined as criminal.* For Quinney, it is not the quality of the behaviour that makes it criminal, but rather the action taken against the behaviour. The decision as to which acts are defined as criminal is made by the more powerful segments of society who formulate and apply

criminal definitions. Thus persons in less powerful social segments are more likely to have their behaviours defined as criminal, because their interests are not represented in the formulation and application of criminal definitions.

5. *Conceptions of crime are constructed and diffused in the segments of society by various means of communication.* The mass media play an important role in the diffusion of criminal conceptions throughout society. A particular conception of crime is diffused throughout society and subsequently becomes "the basis for the public's view of reality" (Quinney, 1970, 285). The more powerful segments of society are able to influence the mass media's portrayal of crime.

6. *The social reality of crime is constructed by the formulation and application of criminal definitions, the development of behavioural patterns related to criminal definitions, and the construction of criminal conceptions.* The sixth proposition is essentially a summation of propositions 2 to 5, and thus Quinney's model posits that the "social reality of crime" is a function of (2) the formulation of criminal definitions, (3) the application of criminal definitions, (4) the development of behaviour patterns in relation to criminal definitions, and (5) the construction of criminal conceptions. Quinney views the first proposition as a definition; thus the body of the theory comprises the middle four propositions.*

# Marxist Conflict Perspectives in Criminology

Beginning in the 1970s, Marxist theories began to gain prominence in the socio-legal and criminological literature. While Marx himself had very little to say about crime, many criminologists believed that aspects of Marx's work could help to analyze the relationship between crime and the broader social world. Similar to the conflict theories of Sellin, Vold, and Quinney, Marxist theories of crime and deviance do not look to the individual offender for explanations of crime. Thus, criminal behaviour is not viewed in isolation as an individual pathology. Marxist criminology takes the position that crime "must be analyzed in the context of its relationship to the character of the society as a whole" (Greenberg, 1993, 17). Marxists believe crime is best understood in relation to the social, political, and economic structures of the society in which it occurs.

You will recall that group conflict theorists, broadly speaking, view conflict as arising from opposing group interests, and crime as resulting from the ability of more powerful or dominant groups to criminalize the behaviour of other less powerful groups who find themselves in violation of the criminal norms and standards of the dominant majority. Marxist criminologists, on the other hand, view conflict as rooted in the very structure of capitalist society, particularly capitalist economic relations. The political and economic structures under capitalism promote conflict, in turn providing the precipitating conditions (such as unemployment) for crime to occur. Marxist criminologists focus on the relations between crime and the social arrangements of

---

*Quinney, Richard. *The Social Reality of Crime.* Copyright © 1970 by Transaction Publishers. Reprinted by permission of the publisher.

**Marxist Internet Archive**
www.marxists.org

society, especially the way in which societies organize their political, legal, and economic structures (Bohm, 1982). Generally speaking, Marxist criminologists take the position that the organization of capitalist society—both its way of producing material goods and its organization of political, legal, and economic structures—has important implications for the study of the amount and types of crime present in society (Greenberg, 1993).

Marx believed that the history of the development of human societies is best understood through the fundamental role played by production. Through production, we are able to satisfy our basic material needs, such as the need for food, clothing, and shelter. Marx was interested in examining the history of societies from the perspective of how production is organized, or what is described as the *mode of production*. The mode of production refers to the economic system whereby goods are produced, exchanged, and distributed in society. Marx identified several different modes of production throughout history, including the slave economies of ancient Greece and Rome, the agrarian economy of feudalism, and the wage-labour economy of capitalism.

The mode of production, in turn, is composed of the *forces of production* and the *social relations of production*. The forces of production refers to the tools, techniques, raw materials, and labour power used in production, while the social relations of production refers to the relationships that exist among humans with respect to the ownership of the means of production. For Marx, the social relations of production under capitalism—that is, under the capitalist mode of production—gave rise to two major groups or classes. The bourgeoisie are the economically dominant class who own the means of production (the land, machinery, and factories), and the proletariat are the economically subordinate class who are property-less. Because they neither own nor control the means of production, the proletariat have only their labour power to sell in exchange for their livelihood in the form of wages. It is important to note that class is *not* an attribute or characteristic of an individual or group in Marxist thought; rather it refers to a position in a relationship (Greenberg, 1993). For Marxists, capitalist society, like earlier societies, is based on class exploitation. The relationship between the capitalist class and the working class is inherently exploitative because the capitalist is able to extract the surplus labour of the worker in the form of profits. This surplus is based on the difference between the value the workers produce and what is received by the worker in wages.

Marx argued that because societies are always organized around the dominant mode of production "the mode of production of material life conditions the social, political, and intellectual life process in general" (Marx, in Cain and Hunt, 1979, 54). Marx made use of the metaphor of a building to describe the relationship between the mode of production and other aspects of society:

> The sum total of these relations of production constitutes the economic structure of society, the real foundation, on which rises a legal and political superstructure and to which correspond definite forms of social consciousness. (Marx, in Cain and Hunt, 1979, 54)

According to Marx, in Western societies the economic base of capitalism is the foundation upon which the various superstructural institutions of society are built, including political and legal institutions. Another way Marxists put this is that the economic base of capitalism has a *determining influence* on the superstructural institutions of society. Where one class is in a position of dominance over the other class (based on its ownership of the means of production) in the economic sphere, the other social institutions in society will be organized according to the interests of the dominant class (Comack, 1999a). The implication for Marxist approaches to law, crime, and criminology is that both the law and crime should not be studied in isolation, but rather in relation to the whole of society and particularly the economic sphere (Greenberg, 1993).

The Marxist approach provides criminologists and legal scholars with a theoretical framework that allows them to study the interrelationships between the capitalist mode of production, the state, law, crime control, and crime (Bohm, 1982). In addition, Marxist analysis typically involves a critical element (see also Chapter 12). It is a critique of the logic of the existing capitalist social order. In critiquing the existing society or social order, Marxian thought often begins with an analysis of the state. While Marx himself did not develop a systematic theory of the state, Marxist theorists have made use of aspects of Marx's writings to attempt to theorize the relationships between the state in capitalist society and class relations, law, crime, and crime control. It has become conventional in the criminological and socio-legal literature to distinguish between *instrumental* and *structural* Marxist theories of the state, law, and crime.

## Instrumental Marxism

Instrumental Marxists generally begin with the assumption that the state in capitalist societies broadly serves the interests of the ruling or capitalist class. A well-known passage from Marx and Engels' work, *The Communist Manifesto*, is often cited in support of **instrumental Marxism**: "The executive of the modern State is but a committee for managing the common affairs of the whole bourgeoisie" (Marx and Engels, 1992, 5). For Marx, the economic structure of society determines the nature of that society's political and legal superstructure. Instrumentalist Marxists interpret Marx's statement quite literally and argue that both the state and the legal and political institutions within the state are a direct reflection of the interests of the capitalist class. Law, then, is equated with class rule—the ruling class controls the formation of law, and the focus is on the coercive nature of the law. As Tierney (1996) points out, this approach was based upon an instrumentalist school of thought in political theory (Miliband, 1969; Domhoff, 1970), which argued that those who occupied powerful positions in the state apparatus were either capitalists themselves or they strongly identified with the interests of the capitalist class.

Instrumental Marxists therefore viewed the state and the legal system as instruments that could be directly manipulated by the capitalist class. For example, Miliband (1969, 22) argued that because the ruling class of capitalist society owns and controls the means of production, it is able to "use the state as its instrument for the domination of society." Early Marxist studies tended to focus on how the economic power of the capitalist class provided the opportunity to influence law and law formation. An example of an instrumental Marxist position is found in Richard Quinney's book, *Critique of the Legal Order* (1974). Recall that in Quinney's earlier work, he endorsed a conflict

**instrumental Marxism**

The state is viewed as the direct instrument of the ruling or capitalist class. Instrumentalism is based on the notion that the processes of the superstructure are determined by the economic base.

perspective on crime but his views changed over time. In the *Critique of the Legal Order*, Quinney (1974, 16) offers six propositions that summarize his critical Marxist theory of crime control:

1. American society is based on an advanced capitalist economy.
2. The State is organized to serve the interests of the dominant economic class.
3. Criminal law is an instrument of the state and ruling class to maintain and perpetuate the existing social and economic order.
4. Crime control in capitalist society is accomplished through a variety of institutions and agencies established and administered by a government elite, representing ruling class interests.
5. The contradictions of advanced capitalism . . . require that the subordinate classes remain oppressed by whatever means necessary, especially through the coercion and violence of the legal system.
6. Only with the collapse of capitalist society and the creation of a new society, based on socialist principles, will there be a solution to the crime problem.*

The instrumentalist Marxist position may be said to offer useful insights into the sociology of the capitalist class, the relationship between class power and state power, and the place of law in capitalist society. Critics, however, point out a number of flaws in the theory. First, instrumental Marxism has been critiqued for portraying the ruling class as a unified and homogeneous group, thus ignoring competing factions that may exist within the capitalist class itself. Second, instrumentalist accounts have been critiqued for ignoring how the actions of ruling class members are influenced or constrained by structural causes. For example, are there limits to any particular ruling class member's sphere of influence, such as shifting affiliations with the current party in power in a parliamentary democracy, the deep fluctuations of the stock market, political exigencies, and so on? Third, in its argument that the law represents only the interests of the ruling class, the instrumentalist position is unable to account for legislation that is not in the immediate interest of the ruling class, such as health and safety legislation, employment standards, and so on. Fourth, critics believe that instrumentalism draws upon an overly rigid interpretation of the base/superstructure metaphor. That is, the Marxist argument that the economic base is the foundation of the superstructure is said to be deterministic. By deterministic, we mean there is a form of causality where the superstructure is a necessary consequence of the economic base. In other words, the economic base under capitalism more or less wholly determines the political, economic, ideological, and cultural superstructure. This is why the instrumentalist position argues that the legal and political institutions in the state are a direct reflection of the capitalist class.

## Structural Marxism

**structural Marxism**

The state is viewed as acting in the long-term interests of capitalism as a whole, rather than in the short-term interests of the capitalist class.

During the 1970s and 1980s, Marxist theorists developed structuralist Marxist accounts of the state, law, and crime. **Structural Marxism** disputes the instrumentalist view that the state can be viewed as the direct servant of the capitalist or ruling class. Whereas the instrumentalist position argues that the

---

*Quinney, Richard. *Critique of the Legal Order*. Copyright © 1974 by Transaction Publishers. Reprinted by permission of the publisher.

institutions of the state are under the direct control of those members of the capitalist class in positions of state power, the structuralist perspective takes the position that the institutions of the state ensure the ongoing viability of capitalism more generally. Another way that Marxists put this is that the institutions of the state must function so as to reproduce capitalist society as a whole (Gold et al., 1975). Structuralists view the state in a capitalist mode of production as taking a specifically capitalist form, not because particular individuals are in powerful positions, but because the state reproduces the logic of capitalist structure in its economic, legal, and political institutions. We might say that a structuralist perspective would argue that the institutions of the state (including its legal institutions) function in the long-term interests of capital and capitalism, rather than in the short-term interests of members of the capitalist class. Structuralists would thus argue that the state and its institutions have a certain degree of *independence* from specific elites in the capitalist class.

The idea that the state is—to a certain degree—independent of the ruling class is known as **relative autonomy**. Structural Marxists have drawn from the work of Poulantzas (1975) and Althusser (1969) to argue that the relative autonomy of the state functions to preserve the long-term interests of capital, and the long-run stability of the capitalist structure as a whole. To begin with, we cannot assume the capitalist class is united in its interests and homogeneous in its beliefs. The state must therefore have the relative autonomy to mediate between divergent capitalist class factions in order to preserve the long-term interests of the capitalist class as a whole (Poulantzas, 1975). The relative autonomy of the state, therefore, provides a state structure "capable of transcending the parochial, individualized interests of specific capitalists and capitalist class factions" (Gold et al., 1975, 38). In addition, structural Marxists point to the relative autonomy of the state and its institutions to explain why many laws are enacted that do not represent the immediate interests of the capitalist class. That is, an instrumentalist Marxist position cannot account for the existence of minimum wage laws, laws against discrimination in employment, consumer protection laws, rent control, anti-trust legislation, and welfare legislation, in that these laws are not in the immediate interests of the capitalist class.

An interesting area that Canadian researchers have explored, with respect to law creation that does not seem to represent the immediate interests of the capitalist class as a whole, has been the development of anti-combines legislation in Canada (Goff and Reasons, 1978; Snider, 1979; Smandych, 1985). The aim of this legislation was to prevent corporations from monopolizing or cornering the supply of certain commodities or markets, and to fix prices. Goff and Reasons argue that Canada's first anti-combines legislation—the Combines Investigation Act of 1889—came about less from the desire to protect the general populace than from the complaints of small businessmen who "felt their firms were at the mercy of big business interests" (1978, 42). For the first decade, this legislation was unenforceable because of the weak wording of the act, which stipulated that combines had to be engaged in behaviour that *unlawfully* as well as *unduly* restricted trade. Snider examined the later revisions and amendments to the act in 1923, 1935, 1952, and 1960 and concluded that "at each stage proposals were weakened or eliminated in the face of business opposition" (1979, 110). Both Snider and Goff and Reasons concluded

**relative autonomy**

A term used in the structural Marxist perspective to indicate that the state has a certain amount of independence from the capitalist class and is therefore able to enact laws that are not in the immediate interests of the capitalist class.

that while reforms do occur, the state "is susceptible to the interests of powerful economic groups" (Goff and Reasons, 1978, 114), and thus reforms tend to be "resisted for as long as possible by the corporate elite" (Snider, 1979, 118).

Smandych argued that anti-combines legislation in Canada must also be considered in relation to the increasingly vocal trade unions of the late 19th century and the growing confrontations between capital and labour. He points out that the rise of militant trade unions in the late 1800s, such as the Knights of Labour in Toronto, "owed as much to labour's hatred of monopolistic companies as it did to labour's desire to improve working conditions" (1985, 45). In addition, the Knights of Labour and other trade unions had a great deal of influence on the working man's vote. Thus Smandych argued that the emergence of Canadian anti-combines legislation could be viewed as a pragmatic attempt by the government to find a "symbolic" solution to the confrontation between capital and labour, given the political influence of the more prominent trade unions. The solution was symbolic because the immense economic and political power of the monopolistic companies of the period influenced the state to enact what was ultimately an "ineffectual law that served only to foster the reproduction of combines activity in the late 19th century" (1985, 47). As Chambliss and Siedman (1982, 312) point out, "A great deal of state action concerns not the enhancement of profit for a particular faction of the ruling class, but the maintenance of relations of production that make capitalism possible." Thus the state ensures the reproduction of capitalism as a whole. In some instances, the state enacts laws that are ostensibly meant to curb the excesses of capital, yet are ineffective in their design and implementation.

In the structuralist perspective, then, the law cannot be said to exclusively represent the instrumental interests of the dominant capitalist class. Rather, structural Marxists argue that laws that benefit the less powerful reflect an ideological need to develop a widespread *consent* for the existing social order (Einstadter and Henry, 2006). On this view, consensus is generated for the established order by promoting law as an impartial system that protects the public rather than private interests, and where all are equal before the law. Structuralists argue that this notion of "equality before the law," also described as "the rule of law," masks or otherwise obscures the substantive inequalities of class, race, and gender that may exist between individuals who are nevertheless considered equal before the law. Stated differently, the formal equality of each individual in the legal sphere does not extend to the economic sphere (Brickey and Comack, 1989). For example, corporations and labour are treated in collective bargaining law as being on an equal footing, despite the structural inequalities between them, including the corporation's greater material and organizational resources (Bartholomew and Boyd, 1989). Structuralists therefore argue that law functions as an ideological means of domination. Ideological domination, as Hunt argues, "consists of those processes that produce and reaffirm the existing social order, and thereby legitimate class domination" (1993, 17). Law may be said to function as an ideological means of domination to the extent that it acts to legitimate the existing capitalist social order. Box 11.2 explores the relationship between law and ideology by using the example of the struggle for the vote by Canadian women.

# FOCUS BOX 11.2

## LAW, IDEOLOGY, AND THE STRUGGLE FOR THE VOTE BY CANADIAN WOMEN

The ideological character of the law, that is, the way in which the law produces and reaffirms the existing social order, can sometimes be easier to view from a distance, in times other than our own.

The struggle for the vote by Canadian women in the early 1900s is an example that helps to illustrate how the law served to reaffirm and legitimate the existing social order. As Hunt (1993, 25) has argued, "The most pervasive ideological effect of law is to be found in the fact that legal rules and their application give effect to existing social relations. The rules of law affirm the social and economic relations that exist within capitalist society."

Consider, for example, the following excerpt from a 1914 essay by Andrew Macphail, where he argues against the vote for women:

### Vote for Women—An Argument Against, 1914

The first equipment they demand is the right to vote. On the part of the gentler [sex], it is an appeal rather than a demand. They ask that they be allowed . . . to assume the privilege and undertake the duty of casting a ballot, so that they may work side by side with men, as comrades in social service for the uplift of humanity, if one may be permitted again to employ those flamboyant terms with which constant iteration has made us all so familiar. There is something pathetic in the appeal, and none but the most hardened can be insensible to it. If men have shown little alacrity in welcoming these volunteers to their ranks, it is because they are not convinced of the value of the work which is proposed to be done. . . .

What complicates the situation is that persons who are appealing for the vote are of higher intelligence, but with shallower instincts, than the average of the sex to which they apparently belong. They are not typical. They belong to a higher, a more masculine type. . . .

And this hesitancy to advocate so revolutionary a measure [as the vote] is increased by a lack of agreement amongst women themselves. It is a matter of common knowledge that the feminist propaganda is confined to a small number of persons.

Source: Andrew Macphail. (1976). "On Certain Aspects of Feminism," *University Magazine*, February 1914, in Cook and Mitchinson (eds.). *The Proper Sphere: Women's Place in Canadian Society*. Toronto: Oxford University Press. p. 301, 304.

For those who were against the enfranchisement of women, one typical argument was that women did not belong in public life; rather, as wives and mothers the proper sphere of women was the "domestic circle." For example, in 1916 Canadian economist and humorist Stephen Leacock expressed his opinion against the right of women to vote by arguing that a woman's only role was motherhood: "Women need not more freedom but less. Social policy should proceed from the fundamental truth that women are and must be dependent" (Leacock, quoted in Prentice et al., 1996, 222).

Hunt has also argued that "law is ideological in that it conveys or transmits a complex set of attitudes, values, and theories about aspects of society. Its ideological content forms parts of the dominant ideology because these attitudes, values, etc. are ones that reinforce and legitimize the existing social order" (Hunt, 1993, 25). In one sense, we can say that the laws that prevented women from having the legal right to vote also served to legitimate the existing social order of the early 20th century that understood the proper place of women to be in the home.

A similar position is taken in an even earlier article written in the *Queen's College Journal* in 1876, which argues that women should not be

*(continued)*

allowed to take a university degree, because a degree only has value for those in public life:

> The degrees of a University we consider inappropriate to ladies for this reason—that [degrees] have reference solely to public life. Their conferment implies that the objects of it are to go forth to push their way in the outside world, and there acquire *ipso facto* a certain acknowledged position. They only have value when considered with reference to public life, and their bestowal upon women would be a great step towards effectuating the views of the advocates to Women's Rights, and opening to them the professions and employments of public life, a consummation devoutly to be deprecated. If the conclusion arrived at be admitted, we are confident that among people who appreciate the delicate grace and beauty of women's character too much to expose it to the rude influences, the bitterness and strife of the world, few will be found to advocate her admission to universities. . . .
>
> Their proper sphere of action is the domestic circle. Their highest duties they owe to the family, which also calls forth their most shining virtues. Therefore her education should be practical, fitting her to govern her household with wisdom and prudence. For her own sake, her mind should be cultivated, but her mental culture should not be what is regarded as distinctively intellectual.

Source: (1976). "Sweet Girl Graduates," *Queen's College Journal*, December 16, 1876, in Cook and Mitchinson (eds.). *The Proper Sphere: Women's Place in Canadian Society*. Toronto: Oxford University Press. p 123.

As laws change, so do our attitudes, values, and beliefs. As our attitudes and beliefs change, so do our laws. The struggle for the enfranchisement of women gives us a window into an earlier time when the social order was very different, and the laws both reflected and legitimized this difference.

In 1916, Manitoba granted women the right to vote, the first province in Canada to do so. Later that same year, women were enfranchised in Alberta and Saskatchewan, with British Columbia and Ontario following in 1917. Women in Nova Scotia, New Brunswick, Prince Edward Island, Newfoundland, and Quebec were granted the right to vote in 1918, 1919, 1922, 1925, and 1940, respectively (Prentice et al., 1996, 234). Women were given the right to vote in federal elections in 1918.

By the end of the 1980s, a large body of critical work had been produced by Marxist scholars examining the relationships between the capitalist state, the economy, and the legal and political institutions of the state. Canadian Marxist theorists, in particular, contributed to a rich literature that explored the relationship between the Canadian state, its laws, and its legal institutions, as well as the relationship between the state and the criminal justice system (Hinch, 1983; West and Snider, 1985; Mandel, 1987; Brickey and Comack, 1989; Snider 1989). In addition, Canadian Marxist criminologists have also explored the broader area of corporate crime and social harm (Sargent, 1991; McMullan, 1992; Snider, 1993). We will examine two further areas of Marxist research to illustrate some of the work undertaken in Marxist criminology: first, research that focuses on the crimes of the powerless, and second, research that investigates the crimes of the powerful.

## Crimes of the Powerless

**Stephen Spitzer**　Spitzer (1975) made use of the Marxian notion of "surplus population" to formulate his "Marxian theory of deviance." Spitzer argued that the criminalization of much behaviour is directed toward those problem populations who are surplus to the labour market. These problem populations are created in two ways. First, they are created *directly* through the contradictions in the capitalist mode of production. For example, a surplus population is generated in capitalist economies as new technologies replace workers with machines, or when work is outsourced to other countries. Second, problem populations are created *indirectly* through contradictions in the institutions that help to reproduce capitalism, such as the schools. For example, Spitzer argues that while mass education provides a means of training future wage labourers, this schooling also provides youths with critical insight into the alienating and oppressive character of capitalist institutions. This, in turn, can lead to problem populations in the form of dropouts and student radicals. Problem populations become candidates for deviance processing when they disturb, hinder, or call into question any of the following (Spitzer, 1975, 642)*:

1. Capitalist modes of appropriating the product of human labour (for example, when the poor "steal" from the rich).
2. The social conditions under which capitalist production takes place (for example, those who refuse or are unable to perform wage labour).
3. Patterns of distribution and consumption in capitalist society (for example, those who use drugs for escape and transcendence rather than sociability and adjustment).
4. The process of socialization for productive and nonproductive roles (for example, youths who refuse to be schooled or those who deny the validity of family life).
5. The ideology that supports the functioning of capitalist society (for example, proponents of alternative forms of social organization).

**David Greenberg**　Another theorist who makes use of the Marxian notion of surplus population is Greenberg (1993). Greenberg explains juvenile delinquency from a Marxist perspective and argues that juveniles form a "class" of their own because they share a common relationship to the means of production. That is, young people are excluded from economically productive activity in a capitalist society, but are required to undergo training for their future productive role in the capitalist system. Juveniles can thus be considered a part of the surplus population, because they are excluded from lawful sources of income. This creates motivation toward delinquency, because juveniles' exclusion from the labour market means they cannot finance their leisure and social activities. If their parents are unable or unwilling to finance their social life to the required level, juveniles must seek out other sources of funding. Adolescent theft then occurs because of a conflict between the desire to participate in activities valued by peer culture and the lack of legitimate sources of funding to finance these activities (Greenberg, 1993).

---

*Spitzer, Steven. (1975). "Toward a Marxian Theory of Analysis." *Social Problems* 22(5): 638–51.

# Crimes of the Powerful

Whereas researchers who focus on the Marxian notion of "surplus population" are interested in the relationship between crime and those who are *outside* the sphere of production, Marxist research on corporate crime focuses on the socially harmful conduct of those who are *inside* the sphere of production in capitalist economies. Box 11.3 explores one instance of socially harmful conduct from a Marxist perspective by examining the tainted dog and cat food produced by Menu Foods Income Fund, a pet food manufacturing facility headquartered in southern Ontario. Canadian Marxist scholars argue that the study of corporate crime is important because the losses incurred as a result of corporate malfeasance—whether it is the total dollar amount, or the number of deaths, injuries, and illnesses—are far in excess of the losses incurred as a result of street crime (McMullan, 1992; Snider, 1993). In an early Marxist analysis of illegal activity of U.S. corporations, Pearce (1976) demonstrated that the dollar amount of corporate crime was much greater than the aggregate dollar amount of conventional crime. Similarly, both Snider (1993) and McMullan (1992) drew upon statistical evidence to argue that the total number of workers who died each year from both work-related accidents and occupationally induced diseases was far in excess of death rate statistics for homicide and manslaughter.

This branch of Marxist criminology attempts to situate law, the state, corporate crime, and social harm within the logic of the mode of production under capitalism. Marxist theorists argue that the structure of capitalist economies and the imperative of profit maximization create strong motivation for corporations to engage in criminal activities or other socially harmful behaviours (Henry, 1986; Snider, 1993). Accordingly, Marxist studies attempt to document both the nature and extent of corporate crime, and to analyze the relationship of corporate criminality to the capitalist mode of production (Goff and Reasons, 1978; Glasbeek, 1989; Pearce and Snider, 1995). Marxist criminologists are also interested in examining the contradictory role of the state in capitalist economies. That is, the state must create laws and regulate the criminal activities of corporations, but must also protect the overall interests of the capitalist economy by reproducing the conditions necessary for capitalism to continue (Sargent, 1991; McMullan, 1992; Snider, 1993; Gordon and Coneybeer, 1999).

Structural Marxism criminology has been criticized for its tautological character. This means that critics feel that it presents a circular argument. The theory begins with the assumption of class exploitation under capitalism in order to demonstrate that crime, in turn, is caused by capitalist class exploitation. Structural Marxism has also been critiqued for emphasizing structure at the expense of human agency, that is, at the expense of human action and ability to shape and direct the social world. A further critique has been that the exclusive focus on class relations has precluded other considerations from entering into analysis, such as gender oppression and race oppression. Socialist feminism, as we shall see below, represents one attempt to incorporate Marxist analysis into a framework that considers the relationship between class exploitation and gender oppression in capitalist societies.

# FOCUS BOX 11.3

## IS IT A CORPORATE CRIME? THE MENU FOODS PET FOOD RECALL

On March 16, 2007, Menu Foods, a pet food manufacturer headquartered in Mississauga, Ontario, announced a massive recall of 60 million cans and pouches of tainted dog and cat food. Something in its pet food—later identified as wheat flour contaminated with melamine and cyanuric acid—was causing acute kidney failure in dogs and cats. By May 3, 2007, the U.S. Food and Drug Administration (FDA) had received unconfirmed reports of 4150 cat and dog deaths due to the consumption of tainted food (*USA Today*, May 10, 2007).

The scope of the Menu Foods recall was unprecedented. By May 22, Menu Foods had issued eight separate recall notifications involving 67 brands of cat food and 64 brands of dog food, each sold in multiple varieties, sizes, and packaging formats—over 5300 products in total (Nestle, 2008). Brands identified in the recall ran the gamut from premium pet foods such as Hill's Prescription Diet, Iams, Eukanuba, and Science Diet, to discount labels such as Walmart's Ol' Roy, Costco/Kirkland Signature dog food, and Price Chopper cat food.

The news for consumers, however, went from bad to worse. The events that followed in the wake of the Menu Foods recall revealed not only how easily melamine contamination could enter the pet food supply, but also how the global sourcing of food ingredients has introduced dangerous vulnerabilities into our human food supply systems. Perhaps two of the most unsettling findings that arose from the pet food recalls were the ubiquity of the global sourcing of pet and human food ingredients and the magnitude of the outsourcing of production of branded pet food to contract manufacturers.

The Menu Foods recall revealed a little known fact about pet food production—namely, that many pet food companies, including the most trusted premium brands, do not make their own pet food but rather "outsource" this function to third party contractors, known as "co-packers". For example, in 2003 Menu Foods

signed a five-year exclusive contract with The Iams Company (purchased by Proctor & Gamble in 1999 for $2.3 billion) to manufacture all Iams and Eukanuba canned and pouch pet food in the U.S. and Canada (2004, Menu Foods Annual Report). At the time of the recall, Menu Foods was the largest co-packer of "wet" pet food—dog and cat food in cans and pouches—in North America (Nestle, 2008).

Pet owners may have been surprised to discover that well over 100 different brands of dog and cat food were made by just one company. A Marxist analysis would point to the structure of capitalist economies and the on-going pressure for companies to extract ever-increasing amounts of surplus value in the form of profits. Under this economic model, it makes good financial sense for pet food companies such as Iams, Hill's, Purina, and Nutro to seek lower costs of production—and hence greater profits—by outsourcing their pet food requirements to a third party contractor such as Menu Foods. The manufacture of wet pet food is a complicated process, after all, and requires significant investment in plant and machinery. By outsourcing production, pet food companies are able to rationalize their asset base and reduce expenses, for example by selling off excess manufacturing capacity and eliminating the associated labour costs.

In turn, a giant co-packer like Menu Foods is able to offer significant economies of scale to its pet food clients. More efficiencies can be exploited by a giant contract manufacturer producing 120 brands of pet food than from many individual manufacturing facilities each producing one or a few brands of dog or cat food. One such efficiency Menu Foods ostensibly could offer its clients was its bulk purchasing power and corresponding ability to purchase raw ingredients in the global marketplace for much lower cost than any single pet food company could do on its own. While the extensive global sourcing of lowest-cost raw ingredients is an industry norm for both pet and human food producers

*(continued)*

(Roth et al., 2008), the Menu Foods recall has helped to demonstrate the risks inherent in the globalization of animal and human food supply chains.

At the centre of the recall was Menu Foods' fateful decision to switch wheat gluten suppliers in December 2006, to Las Vegas importer ChemNutra, who in turn sourced the wheat gluten from an obscure Chinese manufacturer, Xuzhou Anying Biologic Technology Development Co. At the time, wheat gluten from China sold for 20 cents less per pound than that produced by U.S. manufacturers (*Maclean's*, April 30, 2007). Wheat gluten—used in pet food as a protein source and binding agent—is a derivative of wheat flour. FDA investigators were eventually able to determine that the product sold as wheat gluten by Xuzhou Anying was ordinary wheat flour intentionally adulterated with the nitrogen-rich industrial chemicals melamine and cyanuric acid (Kuehn, 2009, 473). Because nitrogen content has long been used as a surrogate for testing the amount of protein in food, the addition of melamine and cyanuric acid allowed unscrupulous suppliers to fraudulently sell the cheaper wheat flour (10 percent protein) as the more expensive wheat gluten (75 percent protein).

As disturbing as it was to discover how a toxic brew of melamine and cyanuric acid could so easily compromise the pet food supply, by the middle of May 2007 a series of announcements revealed surprising vulnerabilities in our human food supply chain. According to the FDA, between 2.7 and 3 million chickens were fed "salvaged" pet food—containing the melamine adulterated wheat flour—and subsequently sold to consumers. In addition, some 6000 hogs were fed the contaminated pet food—with the meat from 345 of the hogs entering into the human food supply before the remaining hogs could be quarantined (*Washington Post*, May 2, 2007). On May 8, 2007, the FDA announced that the melamine/cyanuric acid contaminated wheat flour had also been purchased by a Canadian manufacturer of fish pellets, and subsequently distributed to at least 60 fish farms in Canada and 200 fish farms in the United States (*Washington Post*, May 9, 2007).

It was soon to become tragically clear that melamine adulteration was not limited to pet food or feed for farm animals destined for human consumption. In September 2008, more than 294,000 infants and young children in China were sickened with kidney and urinary tract problems after consuming melamine contaminated infant formula. By the end of November, the Chinese Ministry of Health reported more than 50,000 hospitalizations and six infant deaths due to the consumption of tainted infant formula (Ingelfinger, 2008). Reported symptoms included acute renal failure, kidney and bladder stones, urinary tract infections, and other renal problems (Gossner et al., 2009; Sharma and Paradkar, 2010).

By the end of 2008, the hazards of our increasingly globalized food supply became apparent when an avalanche of food products imported from China were found to contain melamine. The long list of products included yogurts, frozen desserts, cereal products, confectionaries, cakes, biscuits, and protein powders. A variety of non-dairy products originating in China were also found to contain melamine—including ammonium bicarbonate, powdered eggs, fresh eggs, and nondairy creamer. In total, 47 countries, including Canada, received melamine-contaminated products (Gossner et al., 2009).

A Marxist criminologist might argue that at the same time the benefits of global food production accrue to multinationals, the risks of low-cost global sourcing of products and ingredients are offloaded to individual consumers. This unfair apportioning of surplus and risk is the crux of the Marxist critique of capitalism—that is, capitalism is inherently exploitative unless it is harnessed by the weight of government regulation and a corresponding willingness to detect and prosecute offenders. Currently, there is a lack of scientific data on the long-term health effects of melamine toxicity in humans, making prediction difficult for the health problems that might arise in the future (Ingelfinger, 2008; Sharma and Paradkar, 2010). Preliminary results from animal studies are not encouraging, however, with carcinogenic effects reported after high exposure to melamine (Gossner et al., 2009; Puschner et al., 2011).

*(continued)*

Is melamine adulteration a corporate crime? Marxist theorist Michalowski (1985, 314) defines crimes of capital as "socially injurious acts that arise from the ownership or management of capital or from occupancy of positions of trust in institutions designed to facilitate the accumulation of capital." There were certainly "sins of commission" committed by Chinese manufacturers who intentionally added melamine and cyanuric acid to pet and human food ingredients to fraudulently boost the apparent protein content. Were there also "sins of omission" committed by contract manufacturers such as Menu Foods and other human food purveyors? Did their collective lack of oversight in the global pursuit of low cost ingredients—thereby creating the economic vacuum quickly filled by unscrupulous suppliers—constitute criminal negligence? What do you think?

# Socialist Feminism

Socialist feminist perspectives on the law, state, and crime began to emerge in the late 1970s and early 1980s and can be considered as both a critique and an extension of traditional Marxist categories of analysis. In addition, socialist feminism can also be considered as a critique and extension of the radical feminist position. **Radical feminism** itself emerged in the early 1970s as a critique of the liberal feminist focus on rectifying gender inequality through legal reforms to the existing system. The liberal feminist concern with providing equal opportunities to women by altering aspects of existing social systems was critiqued by radical feminists, who argued that simply concentrating on "equal opportunities" for women would not address the fundamental structural inequalities between men and women. Instead, radical feminists locate the fundamental conditions of women's oppression in the institution of patriarchy, defined as "a systematic expression of male domination and control over women which permeates all social, political and economic institutions" (Boyd and Sheehy, 1989, 260).

While radical feminist theorists have made important contributions to the feminist literature, particularly in the critical analysis of laws governing sexual assault, pornography, and reproduction, this perspective has been criticized for assuming a universality of women's subordination, and thus failing to recognize power differentials among women themselves, particularly working class women and women of colour. In addition, the radical feminist position was also critiqued for its tendency to give primacy to gender oppression under **patriarchy**, at the expense of class oppression under capitalism. In other words, radical feminism replaced capitalism with patriarchy as the primary system of oppression.

Zillah Eisenstein (1979) was one of the first to articulate a socialist feminist position. Eisenstein argued that Marxist analysis, by giving priority class relations, does not adequately explain the unique position of women in relation to the capitalist mode of production. On the other hand, radical feminist analysis, by giving priority to patriarchy, does not adequately explain women's

**radical feminism**

A perspective that views the problem of gender inequality and of women's subordination in society as rooted in the institution of patriarchy.

**patriarchy**

A system of male domination and control whereby the structure of society privileges men over women. Stresses the systemic nature of the oppression of women.

relationship to the economic class structure. Thus Eisenstein argues that women's economic exploitation under capitalism and sexual oppression under patriarchy cannot be considered separately. These two systems support each other, and must be understood as "mutually dependent." What is needed, therefore, is a theory that integrates both Marxism and radical feminism (Eisenstein, 1979, 21). In socialist feminism, the major concepts in Marxism and radical feminism are jointly considered "to identify women's oppression as based in capitalist patriarchy" (Danner 1991, 52).

In this understanding of **socialist feminism**, the interconnections between capitalism (class) and patriarchy (gender) are examined, with a particular emphasis on the relationship between productive and reproductive labour. Marx was interested in examining society from the perspective of how production is organized and viewed the mode of production under capitalism as giving rise to exploitative class relations, because the capitalist class is able to extract surplus value or profit from the worker's labour. The worker's labour is also described as *productive labour*, or wage labour, because a wage is received. Socialist feminists are interested in examining society from the perspective of both productive labour and reproductive labour, also described as domestic labour because a wage is not received and the labour takes place in the home (Comack, 1999a). While socialist feminists disagree on the exact composition of reproductive labour, it is often thought to include the reproduction of the next generation of workers (childbirth and childrearing), and the work required to transform the labour wage received into a consumable form (cooking, cleaning, shopping) (Armstrong and Armstrong, 1985). The socialist feminist position is sometimes described as a synthesis of Marxism and radical feminism in that it does not give priority to either production (capitalism) or reproduction (patriarchy), but views them as equivalent concepts (Messerschmidt, 1986).

Canadian socialist feminist scholars have contributed to a rich literature, particularly in the area of the state, law, and crime (Snider, 1991, 1998; Ursel, 1991; Comack, 1999a; Gavigan, 1999). Feminist criminology in Canada dates back to the late 1960s and has made the concerns of women more visible within the "criminological enterprise." Canadian feminist criminologists have made major contributions to the study of violence against women. This research has documented the extent and nature of violence against women. The feminist research agenda, in its focus on women as victims of male violence, has helped to create the momentum for various initiatives to reform sexual violence laws and criminal justice policies in the area of wife abuse, including mandatory arrest and sentencing laws and specialized family violence courts (Comack, 1999b).

At the same time, feminist initiatives to reform the criminal law have not been universally endorsed (Currie, 1990; Snider, 1991; Busby, 1999). At issue is the question of whether criminal law reforms to address violence against women have been effective, as well as how "effectiveness" is to be measured, and finally, whether or not the feminist socialist project ought to engage at all with the state and the criminal justice system to further its goals of empowerment and transformation. Ursel (1991) maintains that it is,

**socialist feminism**

A perspective that views women's exploitation under capitalism and oppression under patriarchy as interconnected. Neither the class structure of capitalism nor patriarchal gender relations are given priority in socialist feminism, rather gender and class relations are viewed as mutually dependent.

**Biographies of Canadian Women in Science, Government, Music, Literature, and Sport**

www.collectionscanada.ca/women

in fact, possible for feminists to work with the "state" and the criminal justice system to improve the life conditions of women by lobbying for changes in the criminal law. For example, Ursel argues that a 1983 directive from the Attorney General of Manitoba that instructed police to lay charges in all reported cases of spouse abuse has effected real change with beneficial results for women. These changes include an increase in the number of men being charged with spousal assault, an increased percentage of offenders receiving court-imposed sanctions, and an increase in funding for wife abuse programs and services.

Snider (1994), on the other hand, argues that feminist attempts to engage with the state in the area of criminal law reform have failed to improve the life conditions of women, while directing attention away from strategies that have greater potential to ameliorate women's lives. Snider highlights some unintended consequences of mandatory arrest policies, such as an increase in the number of women arrested, often for using violence to defend themselves, as well as an increase in the number of women facing contempt charges for their subsequent refusal to testify against their abusers. Ultimately, Snider suggests that there is little evidence that mandatory response, arrest, and charging policies have ameliorated the lives of women (1998), and argues that the criminal law is an inappropriate means of achieving social transformation (1991). Feminist engagement with law reform should be limited to removing impediments that stand in the way of full legal equality for women, and establishing concrete rights such as universal medicare, daycare, or reproductive rights (Snider, 1994).

The debate over mandatory reporting laws highlights the complexity of legal reforms and the difficulty of establishing criteria for assessing whether or not a legal reform is judged as successful. For example, is the criterion whether mandatory arrest deters offenders (Faubert and Hinch, 1996)? How do we measure deterrence? Is the criterion an increase in arrest rates (Ursel, 1991)? If so, what benefits accrue from such an increase? Finally, is the feminist socialist project of improving the lives of working class and marginalized women in keeping with involving more people, both men and women, with the coercive power of the criminal justice system (Snider, 1994)? Can you think of other criteria for measuring the effectiveness of mandatory arrest policies in the case of spousal abuse? What are some other unintended consequences that might occur as a result of mandatory arrest policies?

## Left Realism

The final conflict perspective we will examine is left realism, which first emerged in Britain in the late 1970s and early 1980s (Young, 1979; Matthews and Young, 1992), and was subsequently taken up as an area of criminological inquiry by Canadian scholars (DeKeseredy, 1991; MacLean, 1991). In Britain, "left realism" was initially developed by Jock Young, John Lea, and Roger Matthews, who advanced a strong critique against what they described as "left idealism." Young (1979) coined the term left idealism to encompass both instrumentalist and structuralist Marxist accounts of the state, law, and crime. Left realists also criticize what they describe as conventional or orthodox criminology, and argue that both Marxist and conventional criminology are superficial accounts of crime. Specifically, left realists maintain that for conventional criminology, crime is "simply antisocial behaviour involving people who lack values," while for Marxist criminology, crime is "proto-revolutionary activity, primitive and individualistic, but praiseworthy all the same" (Lea and Young, 1984, 96).

Left realists emphasize the need to examine the "square of crime," that is, the relationship between the offender, the victim, the police, and the public (Matthews and Young, 1992; Young and Matthews, 1992). In Britain, left realism emerged in response to the perceived failure of other types of criminology, including Marxist criminology, to pay attention to the serious harm generated by street crime, also described as "working-class crime." Left realists such as Young, Lea, and Matthews have argued that Marxist critiques of capitalist society have not paid sufficient attention to the real suffering experienced by victims of street crime, particularly the poor and disadvantaged, who are typically the main victims of street crime. Street crime refers to some form of injury committed directly by one or more specific individuals against the body or property of the victim, such as murder, rape, robbery, theft, vandalism, and burglary. Left realists argue that the victims of most crimes tend to be those from the most vulnerable segments of the community, and that crime is disproportionately distributed among the working class, women, and racial minorities. In addition, the majority of working class crime is intra-class; that is, both the offender and the victim tend to be from the same socio-economic strata (Lea and Young, 1984; Lowman and MacLean, 1992).

The starting point for left realists is the observation that *crime really is a problem* for the working class and other marginalized groups in the community, and working class crime must therefore be "taken seriously" (Lea and Young, 1986). Taking crime seriously, for left realists, means developing a working class criminology that both examines and offers practical solutions to the street crime that marginalized people experience. The strategy employed to examine the problem of crime for the working class is the victimization survey (see Chapter 4). One of the first victimization studies, the Islington Crime Survey (ICS), was conducted in inner-city London in 1985. Employing self-report data, these types of surveys attempt to measure public attitudes, perceptions, and beliefs about the extent and nature of street crime in the community and the effectiveness of police in dealing with it (Jones et al., 1986). Left realists argue for concrete crime control programs, with the objective of offering non-repressive crime control policies (Lea and Young, 1986; MacLean, 1991). Crime control policies that have been endorsed by left realists include alternatives to prisons (community service, victim restitution, weekend prison sentences for working offenders); pre-emptive deterrence (encouraging citizens' groups to cooperate with the police); transforming the police force into a police service accountable to the public; and "harnessing the energies of the marginalized" to create a "politics of crime control" (Lea and Young, 1986, 360–63; Young, 1992, 41–42).

Left realism has made some valuable contributions to the criminology literature, including sensitizing us to the amount and kinds of street crime and domestic violence experienced by the most marginalized and vulnerable members of society. In turn, left realism has been subject to a number of critiques. For example, critics have argued that the left realist position is ahistorical; that is, left realism fails to take into consideration the political, economic, and cultural history of the society in which crime occurs. Can the square of crime (the relationship between victims, offenders, police, public) really be understood by analyzing responses to local victimization surveys undertaken at a particular point in time and space? O'Reilly-Fleming (1996, 10) suggests that the left realism's advocacy for greater crime control may ultimately have the effect of "widening the net of social control" and thus amount to little more than increasing state powers over the marginalized and disenfranchised groups under study. This has some interesting parallels with the feminist socialist debate described earlier that questioned whether engaging with the criminal justice system to strengthen criminal laws was in keeping with the feminist socialist project of ameliorating the lives of women. Finally, Mugford and O'Malley (1991, 23) argue that left realists make use of common sense notions (crime really is a problem), but neglect to transform these common sense notions into a defensible theoretical account.

**TABLE 11.1  Conflict Theorists**

| Theory | Theorists | Key Elements |
|---|---|---|
| Cultural Conflict | Sellin | Crime occurs when individuals acting on the conduct norms of their own group are in violation of the conduct norms the dominant group has enacted into law. |
| Group Conflict | Vold, Quinney | Interest groups (Vold) or social groupings (Quinney) attempt to protect their own interests by influencing the creation and enforcement of the criminal law. |
| Instrumental Marxism | Quinney | The state and the legal system are instruments that can be directly manipulated by the capitalist class. The capitalist class can thus directly influence law and law formation. |
| Structural Marxism | Althusser, Poulantzas | The relative autonomy of the state functions to preserve the long-term interests of the capitalist system. This helps to explain why many laws are enacted that do not represent the immediate interests of the capitalist class. |
| Socialist Feminism | Eisenstein, Comack, Snider, Ursel | Draws upon both radical feminist and Marxist categories of analysis to explore the relationship between capitalism (class) and patriarchy (gender). Violence against women has been a major issue studied by Canadian socialist feminists. |
| Left Realism | Young, MacLean, DeKeseredy | Argues that crime really is a problem for the working class and must be taken seriously. Most working class crime is intra-class. Major methodological tool is the victimization survey. Argues for a concrete crime control program; endorses crime control policies which are not repressive. |

# Summary

- Conflict theory views societies as more divided by conflict than they are integrated by consensus (see Box 11.1).

- According to Sellin's cultural conflict theory, crime can be viewed as an expression of cultural conflict when individuals who act based on the conduct norms of their own group are in violation of the conduct norms that the dominant group has enacted into law.

- According to Vold's group conflict theory, crime occurs as a result of conflict between diverse interest groups. Vold makes use of group conflict theory to explain two general classes of group conflict that can result in criminal behaviour: first, crime that arises as a result of minority group behaviour, and second, crime that results from direct contact between groups struggling for the control of power in the political and cultural organization of society.

- Richard Quinney's group conflict theory explains criminality as arising from conflict between "segments" of society, which he defined as types of social groupings. The more powerful segments or social groups in society are able to secure and to protect their own interests by influencing the formulation, enforcement, and administration of criminal law. Quinney places a greater emphasis than either Sellin or Vold on the unequal distribution of power in society.

- Instrumental Marxists view the state and the legal system as instruments that could be directly manipulated by the capitalist class. Instrumental Marxists thus maintain that laws are created and enforced in the interests of the ruling or capitalist class.

- Structural Marxists dispute the instrumentalist view that the state is the direct servant of the ruling or capitalist class and argue that the state and its institutions have a certain degree of independence from specific elites in the capitalist class. Structural Marxists point to the relative autonomy of the state to help explain why many laws are enacted that do not represent the immediate interests of the capitalist class.

- Socialist feminism offers a critique of both Marxism and radical feminism and offers a theory that attempts to integrate both class exploitation under capitalism and women's oppression under patriarchy. One major issue that Canadian feminist criminologists have studied has been violence against women.

- Left realists emphasize that crime really is a problem for the working class and other marginalized groups in the community, and that working class crime must be taken seriously. Left realists make use of victimization surveys to examine the problem of crime for the working class, with the objective of offering crime control policies that are not repressive.

## QUESTIONS FOR CRITICAL THINKING

1. In what way is Quinney's understanding of conflict, in his early work, different from that of Sellin and Vold? In what way is it similar?

2. How does structural Marxism address the critiques of instrumental Marxism? Describe what is meant by "relative autonomy."

3. How does socialist feminism address the critiques of radical feminism and Marxism?

4. In discussing the notion of the "rule of law" and "equality of all before the law," Marxist theorists sometimes make use of the following quote by social critic Anatole France (1894): "The law in its majestic impartiality forbids both the rich and poor alike to sleep under bridges, to beg in the streets or to steal bread." What contradiction does France point out? How might this quotation apply to the concept of law and ideology in Marxist thought?

5. The debate in the socialist feminist literature about the effectiveness of criminal law reform raises the issue of measurement criteria. Describe the different types of measurement criteria that might be employed to measure the effectiveness of reforms such as mandatory arrest for all reported cases of spousal abuse.

6. Left realists have argued for a concrete crime control program, with the objective of designing crime control policies that are not repressive. Is it possible to engage with the criminal justice system in the area of criminal law reform in a way that is not repressive for the groups that left realists study?

## NET WORK

Go to the website of the Canadian Encyclopedia at **www.thecanadianencyclopedia.com.** You can access the articles "Winnipeg General Strike," "Working-Class History," and "Nine-Hour Movement" by entering the name of the article in the search box at the top of the page.

1. As the link on "working class history" points out, "the consolidation of Canadian capitalism in the early 20th century accelerated the growth of the working class." What were some of the issues that the labour unions of the time were concerned about? What argument would structural Marxists make about the Industrial Disputes Investigation Act (1907)?

2. What was the nine-hour movement? Why was this movement considered to be unsuccessful? What would an instrumental Marxist argument say about the nine-hour movement?

3. When was the Winnipeg general strike and why is it considered a pivotal event in Canadian history? What was the Citizens' Committee of One Thousand, and how did it differ from the Central Strike Committee? What would an instrumental Marxist argument point out about the ensuing events?

## KEY TERMS

conduct norms; pg. 348
cultural conflict; pg. 348
group conflict theory; pg. 348
instrumental Marxism; pg. 355
patriarchy; pg. 365

radical feminism; pg. 365
relative autonomy; pg. 357
socialist feminism; pg. 366
structural Marxism; pg. 356

## BIBLIOGRAPHY

Althusser, L. (1969). *For Marx*. New York: Vintage Press.

Armstrong, Pat, and Hugh Armstrong. (1985). "Beyond Sexless Class and Classless Sex: Towards Feminist Marxism." In Pat Armstrong, Hugh Armstrong, Patricia Connelly, and Angela Miles (eds.), *Feminist Marxism or Marxist Feminism: A Debate* (pp. 1–37). Toronto: Garamond Press.

Bartholomew, Amy, and Susan Boyd. (1989). "Towards a Political Economy of Law." In Wallace Clement and Glen Williams (eds.), *The New Canadian Political Economy* (pp. 212–39). Kingston: McGill University Press.

Bohm, Robert M. (1982). "Radical Criminology: An Explication." *Criminology* 19(4): 565–89.

Boyd, Susan B., and Elizabeth A. Sheehy. (1989). "Overview: Feminism and the Law in Canada." In Tullio Caputo, Mark Kennedy, Charles E. Reasons, and Augustine Brannigan (eds.), *Law and Society: A Critical Perspective* (pp. 255–70). Toronto: Harcourt Brace Jovanovich.

Brickey, Stephen, and Elizabeth Comack. (1989). "The Role of Law in Social Transformation: Is a Jurisprudence of Insurgency Possible?" In Tullio Caputo, Mark Kennedy, Charles E. Reasons, and Augustine Brannigan (eds.), *Law and Society: A Critical Perspective* (pp. 316–30). Toronto: Harcourt Brace Jovanovich.

Busby, Karen. (1999). "Not a Victim until a Conviction Is Entered: Sexual Violence Prosecutions and Legal Truth." In Elizabeth Comack (ed.), *Locating Law: Race, Class, Gender Connections* (pp. 260–88). Halifax: Fernwood Publishing.

Cain, Maureen, and Alan Hunt. (1979). *Marx and Engels on Law*. London: Academic Press.

Chambliss, William, and Robert Siedman. (1982). *Law, Order and Power*. Reading: Addison-Wesley Publishing Company.

Comack, Elizabeth, and Stephen Brickey (eds.). (1991). *The Social Basis of Law: Critical Readings in the Sociology of Law*. Halifax: Garamond Press.

———. (1999a). "Theoretical Excursions." In Elizabeth Comack (ed.), *Locating Law: Race, Class, Gender Connections* (pp. 10–68). Halifax: Fernwood Publishing.

———. (1999b). "New Possibilities for Feminism 'in' Criminology? From Dualism to Diversity." *Canadian Journal of Criminology* 41(2):161–71.

Cook, Ramsey, and Wendy Mitchinson (eds.). (1976). "Sweet Girl Graduates." *The Proper Sphere: Women's Place in Canadian Society*. Toronto: Oxford University Press.

Currie, Dawn. (1990). "Battered Woman and the State: From the Failure of a Theory to a Theory of Failure." *Journal of Human Justice* 1(2):77–96.

———. (1991). "Realist Criminology, Women, and Social Transformation in Canada." In Brian D. MacLean and Dragan Milovanovic (eds.), *New Directions in Critical Criminology* (pp. 9–14). Vancouver: Collective Press.

Currie, Dawn, Walter S. DeKeseredy, and Brian D. MacLean. (1990). "Reconstructing Social Order and Social Control: Police Accountability in Canada." *The Journal of Human Justice* 2(1):29–53.

Danner, Mona J. E. (1991). "Socialist Feminism: A Brief Introduction." In Brian D. MacLean and Dragan Milovanovic (eds.), *New Directions in Critical Criminology* (pp. 51–54). Vancouver: Collective Press.

DeKeseredy, Walter S. (1991). "Confronting Woman Abuse: A Brief Overview of the Left Realist Approach." In Brian D. MacLean and Dragan Milovanovic (eds.), *New Directions in Critical Criminology* (pp. 27–30). Vancouver: Collective Press.

Devers, Lindsey, and Sarah Bacon. (2010). "Interpreting Honor Crimes: The Institutional Disregard towards Female Victims of Family Violence in the Middle East." *International Journal of Criminology and Sociological Theory* 3(1):359–71.

Domhoff, G. William. (1970). *The Higher Circles: The Governing Class in America.* New York: Random House.

Einstadter, Werner, and Stuart Henry. (2006). *Criminological Theory: An Analysis of Its Underlying Assumptions.* Lanham: Rowman & Littlefield Publishers Inc.

Eisenstein, Zillah. (1979). "Developing a Theory of Capitalist Patriarchy and Socialist Feminism." In Zillah Eisenstein (ed.), *Capitalist Patriarchy and the Case for Socialist Feminism* (pp. 5–40). New York: Monthly Review Press.

Faubert, Jacqueline, and Ronald Hinch. (1996). "The Dialectics of Mandatory Arrest Policies." In Thomas O'Reilly-Fleming (ed.), *Post-Critical Criminology* (pp. 230–51). Scarborough: Prentice Hall.

Fisk, Robert. (2010). "The Crimewave that Shames the World." *The Independent*, Tuesday, September 7.

France, Anatole. (1897). *The Red Lily.* London: John Lane Company.

Gavigan, Shelley. (1999). "Poverty Law, Theory, and Practice: The Place of Class and Gender in Access to Justice." In Elizabeth Comack (ed.), *Locating Law: Race, Class, Gender Connections* (pp. 207–30). Halifax: Fernwood Publishing.

Glasbeek, Harry. (1989). "Why Corporate Deviance Is Not Treated as a Crime: The Need to Make Profits a Dirty Word." In Tullio Caputo, Mark Kennedy, Charles E. Reasons, and Augustine Brannigan (eds.), *Law and Society: A Critical Perspective* (pp. 126–45). Toronto: Harcourt Brace Jovanovich.

Goff, Colin, and Charles Reasons. (1978). *Corporate Crime in Canada: A Critical Analysis of Anti-Combines Legislation.* Scarborough: Prentice Hall Canada.

Gold, David, Clarence Y. H. Lo, and Erik O. Wright. (1975). "Recent Developments in Marxist Theories of the Capitalist State." *Monthly Review* (October/November)27: 29–43/36–51.

Gordon, Robert, and Ian Coneybeer. (1999). "Corporate Crime." In N. Larsen and B. Burtch (eds.), *Law in Society: Canadian Readings* (pp. 101–27). Toronto: Nelson Thomson Learning.

Gossner, Céline, Jorgen Schlundt, Peter Embarek, Susan Hird, Danilo Wong, Jose Beltran, Keng Ngee Teoh, and Angelika Tritscher. (2009). "The Melamine Incident: Implications for International Food and Feed Safety." *Environmental Health Perspectives* 117(12):1803–08.

Greenberg, David F. (1993). *Crime and Capitalism: Readings in Marxist Criminology.* (2nd ed.). Philadelphia: Temple University Press.

Henry, Frank. (1986). "Crime—A Profitable Approach." In Brian D. Maclean (ed.), *The Political Economy of Crime* (pp. 182–203). Toronto: Prentice Hall.

Hinch, Ron. (1983). "Marxist Criminology in the 1970s: Clarifying the Clutter." Crime and Social Justice 19:65–74.

Humphreys, Adrian. (2010). "Canada Should Expect Rise in Honour Killings, Expert Says." *National Post*, Thursday, June 17.

Hunt, Alan. (1993). *Explorations in Law and Society: Towards a Constitutive Theory of Law.* New York: Routledge.

Ingelfinger, Julie. (2008). "Melamine and the Global Implications of Food Contamination." *The New England Journal of Medicine* 359:2745–48.

Jones, Trevor, Brian D. MacLean, and Jock Young. (1986). *The Islington Crime Survey: Crime, Victimization and Policing in Inner-City London.* Aldershot: Gower Publishing Company.

Kuehn, Bridget. (2009). "Melamine Scandals Highlight Hazards of Increasingly Globalized Food Chain." *JAMA* 301(5):473–75.

Lea, John, and Jock Young. (1984). *What Is to be Done About Law and Order?* Harmondsworth: Penguin Books.

Lea, John, and Jock Young (1986), "A Realistic Approach to Law and Order." In Brian D. MacLean (ed.), *The Political Economy of Crime: Readings for a Critical Criminology.* Ontario: Prentice Hall Canada.

Lowman, John, and Brian D. MacLean. (1992). "Introduction: Left Realism, Crime Control, and Policing in the 1990s." In John Lowman and Brian D. MacLean (eds.), *Realist Criminology: Crime Control and Policing in the 1990s* (pp. 3–29). Toronto: University of Toronto Press.

MacLean, Brian D. (1991). "The Origins of Left Realism." In Brian D. MacLean and Dragan Milovanovic (eds.), *New Directions in Critical Criminology* (pp. 9–14). Vancouver: Collective Press.

Mandel, Michael. (1987). "'Relative Autonomy' and the Criminal Justice Apparatus." In R. S. Ratner and John McMullan (eds.), *State Control: Criminal Justice Politics in Canada* (pp. 149–64). Vancouver: University of British Columbia Press.

Marx, Karl, and Friedrich Engels. (1992 [1848]). *The Communist Manifesto.* Oxford: Oxford University Press.

Matthews, Roger, and Jock Young. (1992). "Reflections on Realism." In Jock Young and Roger Matthews (eds.), *Rethinking Criminology: The Realist Debate* (pp. 1–23). London: Sage Publications.

McMullan, John. (1992). *Beyond the Limits of the Law: Corporate Crime and Law and Order.* Halifax: Fernwood Publishing.

Macphail, Andrew (1976). "On Certain Aspects of Feminism." In R. Cook and W. Mitchinson (eds.), *The Proper Sphere: Women's Place in Canadian Society* (pp. 301, 304). Toronto: Oxford University Press.

Messerschmidt, James. (1986). *Capitalism, Patriarchy, and Crime.* New Jersey: Rowman & Littlefield.

Michalowski, Raymond. (1985). *Order, Law and Crime: An Introduction to Criminology.* New York: Random House.

Miliband, Ralph. (1969). *The State in Capitalist Society.* London: Weidenfeld and Nicolson.

Mojab, Shahrzad. (2002). "'Honor Killing': Culture, Politics and Theory." *Middle East Women's Studies Review* xvii(1/2):1–7.

Mundell, E. J., and Steven Reinberg. (2007). "FDA: Millions of Chickens Fed Contaminated Pet Food." *Washington Post*, Wednesday, May 2.

Mugford, Stephen, and Pat O'Malley. (1991). "Heroin Policy and Deficit Models." *Crime, Law and Social Change* 15(1):19–36.

Nestle, Marion. (2008). *Pet Food Politics: The Chihuahua in the Coal Mine.* Berkeley: University of California Press.

O'Reilly-Fleming, Thomas. (1996). "Left-Realism as Theoretical Retreatism or Paradigm Shift: Toward Post-Critical Criminology." In Thomas O'Reilly-Fleming (ed.), *Post-Critical Criminology* (pp. 1–25). Scarborough: Prentice-Hall.

Papp, Aruna. (2010). "Culturally Driven Violence Against Women: A Growing Problem in Canada's Immigrant Communities." *Frontier Centre for Public Policy.* FCPP Policy Series No. 92:1–20.

Patel, Sujay, and Amin Muhammad. (2008). "Karo-Kari: A Form of Honour Killing in Pakistan." *Transcultural Psychiatry* 45(4):683–94.

Pearce, Frank. (1976). *Crimes of the Powerful.* London: Pluto

Pearce, Frank, and Laureen Snider. (1995). "Regulating Capitalism." In Frank Pearce and Laureen Snider (eds.), *Corporate Crime: Contemporary Debates* (pp. 19–47). Toronto: University of Toronto Press.

Poulantzas, N. (1975). *Classes in Contemporary Capitalism.* London: New Left Books.

Prentice, Alison, Paula Bourne, Gail Cuthbert Brandt, Beth Light, Wendy Mitchinson, and Naomi Black. (1996). *Canadian Women: A History.* (2nd ed.). Toronto: Harcourt Brace & Company.

Puschner, Birgit, and Renate Reimschuessel. (2011). "Toxicosis Caused by Melamine and Cyanuric Acid in Dogs and Cats: Uncovering the Mystery and Subsequent Global Implications." *Clinics in Laboratory Medicine.* In Press.

Quinney, Richard. (1970). *The Social Reality of Crime.* Boston: Little, Brown and Company.

———. (1974). *Critique of the Legal Order.* Boston: Little, Brown and Company.

Roth, Aleda, Andy Tsay, Madeline Pullman, and John Grey. (2008). "Unravelling the Food Supply Chain: Strategic Insights from China and the 2007 Recalls." *Journal of Supply Chain Management* 44(1):22–39.

*R. v. Muhammad Manzour Parvez (father) and Waqas Parvez (son).* (2010). "Agreed Statement of Facts." Available at http://www.nationalpost.com/multimedia/files/agreed_statement_of_facts.pdf.

Sargent, Neil. (1991). "Law, Ideology and Social Change: An Analysis of the Role of Law in the Construction of Corporate Crime." In Elizabeth Comack and Stephen Brickey (eds.), *The Social Basis of Law: Critical Readings in the Sociology of Law* (pp. 289–309). Halifax: Garamond Press.

Schmit, Julie. (2007). "Pet Food Probe: Who Was Watching Suppliers?" *USA Today,* July 5.

Sellin, Thorsten. (1938). *Culture Conflict and Crime.* New York: Social Science Research Council.

Sev'er, Aysan, and Gökçeçiçek Yurdakul. (1999). "Culture of Honor, Culture of Change: A Feminist Analysis of Honor Killings in Rural Turkey." *Violence Against Women: An International and Interdisciplinary Journal* 7(9):964–99.

Sharma, Kirti, and Manish Paradkar. (2010). "The Melamine Adulteration Scandal." *Food Security* 2:97–107.

Smandych, Russell. (1985). "Marxism and the Creation of Law: Re-Examining the Origins of Canadian Anti-Combines Legislation 1890–1910." In Thomas Fleming (ed.), *The New Criminology in Canada: State, Crime and Control* (pp. 87–99). Toronto: Oxford University Press.

Snider, Laureen. (1979). "Revising the Combines Investigation Act: A Study in Corporate Power." In Paul Brantingham and Jack Kress (eds.), *Structure, Law, and Power: Essays in the Sociology of Law* (pp. 105–19). Beverly Hills: Sage Publications.

Snider, Laureen. (1989). "Ideology and Relative Autonomy in Anglo-Canadian Criminology." *Journal of Human Justice* 1(1):27–42.

———. (1991). "The Potential of the Criminal Justice System to Promote Feminist Concerns." In Elizabeth Comack and Stephen Brickey (eds.), *The Social Basis of Law: Critical Readings in the Sociology of Law* (pp. 238–60). Halifax: Garamond Press.

———. (1993). *Bad Business: Corporate Crime in Canada*. Toronto: Nelson.

———. (1994). "Feminism, Punishment and the Potential of Empowerment." *Canadian Journal of Law and Society* 9(1):15–38.

———. (1998). "Towards Safer Societies: Punishment, Masculinities, and Violence against Women." *British Journal of Criminology* 38(1):1–39.

Spitzer, Steven. (1975). "Towards a Marxian Theory of Analysis." *Social Problems* 22(5): 638–51.

"Sweet Girl Graduates." (1976). In Ramsey Cook and Wendy Mitchinson (eds.), *The Proper Sphere: Women's Place in Canadian Society* (p. 123). Toronto: Oxford University Press.

Terman, Rochelle L. (2010). "To Specify or Single Out: Should We Use the Term 'Honor Killing?'" *Muslim World Journal of Human Rights* 7(1):1–39.

Tierney, John. (1996). *Criminology: Theory and Context*. London: Prentice-Hall.

United Nations Population Fund. (2000). "Ending Violence Against Women and Girls." *The State of World Population 2000*. Available at http://www.unfpa.org/swp/2000/english/ch03.html.

Ursel, Jane. (1991). "Considering the Impact of the Battered Women's Movement on the State: The Example of Manitoba." In Elizabeth Comack and Stephen Brickey (eds.), *The Social Basis of Law: Critical Readings in the Sociology of Law*. Halifax: Garamond Press.

Vold, George. (1958). *Theoretical Criminology*. New York: Oxford University Press.

Warrick, Catherine. (2005). "The Vanishing Victim: Criminal Law and Gender in Jordan." *Law and Society Review* 39(2):315–48.

Weiss, Rick. (2007). "Farm Raised Fish Given Tainted Food." *Washington Post* Wednesday, May 9.

West, W. Gordon, and Laureen Snider. (1985). "A Critical Perspective on Law and the Canadian State: Delinquency and Corporate Crime." In Thomas Fleming (ed.), The New *Criminology in Canada: State, Crime and Control* (pp. 138–70). Toronto: Oxford University Press.

Young, Jock. (1979). "Left Idealism, Reformism, and Beyond." In Bob Fine, Richard Kinsey, John Lea, Sol Picciotto, and Jock Young (eds.), *Capitalism and the Rule of Law* (pp. 11–28). London: Hutchinson.

———. (1992). "Ten Points of Realism." In Roger Matthews and Jock Young (eds.), *Rethinking Criminology: The Realist Debate* (pp. 24–68). London: Sage Publications.

Young, Jock, and Roger Matthews. (1992). "Questioning Left Realism." In Roger Matthews and Jock Young (eds.), *Issues in Realist Criminology* (pp. 1–18). London: Sage Publications.

# Contemporary Critical Criminology

## 12

**Bryan Hogeveen and Andrew Woolford**

UNIVERSITY OF ALBERTA AND UNIVERSITY OF MANITOBA

The downtrodden, the marginalized, and the impoverished make up the majority of individuals who are arrested by the police, represent the greatest number of inmates in our jails, and take up the bulk of spaces in the court docket. It seems that we inhabit an unjust world made up of enormous concentrations of wealth and power on one hand, and masses of powerless people on the other. This situation raises many questions: Is this the best Canadians can hope for? If so, does this indicate a diminishment of political dreams and the loss of hope for social justice? If it is not, how do we move to a more just state? As you read this chapter, keep in mind the *face* of suffering—whether it be that of the homeless person Canadians hurry by on their way to enjoying a $4 Starbuck's coffee or that of a news story about the starving East African child so easily flipped past on a 60-inch plasma screen television—and ask what you are willing to give up to ameliorate social, economic, and political suffering.

These are the dilemmas critical criminology forces us to face. As citizens fully socialized into the social order, we rarely critically engage with our world but rather take it for granted. Inspired by promises of "freedom" and "justice," critical criminology draws attention to hidden and overlooked injustices scattered throughout *our* world. Critical criminology attempts to highlight inequalities, discrimination, and suffering and to relate these to the discipline of criminology. Social problems abound but are easily dismissed as someone else's responsibility. Critical criminology attends to the processes through which the social world restricts human freedom and choice. It attempts to assemble and create more "just" worlds with less or no misery: "the possibility daily withheld, overlooked or unbelieved" (Bauman, 2000).

## Learning Objectives

After reading this chapter, you should be able to

- Explain what it means to be "critical" in critical criminology.
- Identify the origins of critical criminology in Canada in the New Criminology and the efforts of the Human Justice Collective.
- Understand Michel Foucault's approach to the concept of power and its importance to critical criminology.
- Describe how risk and actuarialism are prevalent in contemporary criminal justice practices and how this relates to the notion of the "risk society."

- Discuss cultural criminology and its contribution to critical criminology.

- Explain Pierre Bourdieu's "field theory" and its application to crime in the work of Loïc Wacquant.

- Define Giorgio Agamben's concept of the "state of exception" and explain its relationship to sovereignty.

- Describe Jacques Derrida's notion of "deconstruction" and how it is used in critical criminology.

# What Is *Critical* about Critical Criminology?

Contemporary *critical* criminology promises to offer something critical. But what does this mean? To be certain, everyone is critical—at least to a certain extent. We cast judgment on movies ("*Pirates of the Caribbean* was the greatest movie of all time!"), clothing (both our own and, especially, that which belongs to others), and music ("Britney Spears does not sing particularly well"). Is this the pursuit in which critical scholars are engaged? Certainly not. However, defining exactly what meets and what fails to meet the "critical" bar is far more difficult than it might seem. If everyone is critical and capable of critique, what sets critical criminology apart?

Some schools of criminology have adopted an administrative approach to the question of crime and have produced policy-oriented knowledge directed toward regulating disruptions and disorders (Young, 1998). The products of this mainstream criminology/criminal justice (programs such as zero tolerance and broken-windows policing) appeal to politicians who promise an eager electorate that they will be "tough on crime and the causes of crime." Such scholarship is critical to the extent that it challenges existing criminal justice orthodoxy by suggesting that we focus on minimizing criminal opportunities rather than explaining criminal motivations. However, governments and criminal justice organizations can safely adopt this brand of "critical scholarship" within their existing infrastructure without fear that these suggestions and programs will significantly change existing mandates or practices. Government agencies are now promoting and, in some cases, soliciting this type of administrative scrutiny of policy and programming, because they view it as a path toward more efficient governance and control.

By contrast, the promise implied by "critical criminology" ensures a type of critique that prefers "to take the system to task rather than tinker with its parts" (Ratner, 1971, n.p.). Hogeveen and Woolford (2006) maintain that critique should not fall into the trap of conceiving of programs that work well within the existing criminal justice system, but critical criminologists should extend critique and thought beyond these limits. Indeed, criminal justice institutions that receive critical criminological scholarship favourably would invite their own destruction (Pavlich, 2005). Critical criminologists, then, practise a transformative brand of critique that confronts inequalities and social suffering with promises of more just outcomes.

So "critical" in critical criminology implies transformation through promises of justice. But what does it mean to be "critical"? That is, if critical criminology is transformative, does this imply that transformation and critique are identical? No. Critique is a means to a transformative (just) end. Thus, while we now know that the goal of critical criminology is justice, we are yet unaware of what "critical" means. When attempting to understand a *thing*, etymology (the origins of words) is often a productive starting point. George Pavlich (2000, 25), notes that "criticism," "crisis and critique relate to the Greek word *Krinein* which is associated with images of judgment (judge, judging), but also with deciding, separating out, discerning, selecting, differentiating, and so on." Interestingly, early medical officials closely associated notions of critique with *Krises*, which involved the art of diagnosing crisis stages in the development of an illness. Traces of this image have survived in common medical diagnoses of patients said to be in a critical condition (Pavlich, 2000).

Over many years the broad meaning of the word *critical* has been reduced to such a degree that it is now almost exclusively associated with the act of judging. Take the television program *American Idol* as an example of how the Western understanding of *critical* and *critique* have become whittled down to judgment. The program masquerades as a singing competition that features three "experts" who have been tasked with cutting down the hundreds of thousands of applicants to a select few while providing feedback on individual performances. In many ways, Simon Cowell, the curmudgeon among the three judges in the earlier seasons of the show, embodied the modern vision of critique as judgment. His comments have included: "That's atrocious; that's simply not good enough," and "If your lifeguard duties were as good as your singing, a lot of people would be drowning."

Judgmental critique derives its critical ammunition from the veracity of the criterion (or critical standard). Continuing with the *American Idol* example, Cowell held the contestants up to a set of normative criteria for what counts as great singing. It is the *criterion* that allowed him to render judgment ("That was atrocious"). Mainstream criminologists engage in a similar critical enterprise. For instance, many criminologists employ criterion such as recidivism rates as the standard against which to assess programmatic and legislative success or failure. Such judgmental criterion can then be employed to evaluate policing, correctional, and court practices. However, as you have learned in Chapter 4, recidivism rates (the criteria) are not as robust and self-evident as once believed. Policing practices and a host of administrative conditions, including how long following their release offenders are tracked, are apt to artificially increase or reduce the criterion—the very foundation of much criminological judgment.

Critique typically implies that we are judging some *thing* against a normative standard held out as the epitome or the ultimate. Thus, when we claimed that Britney Spears does not sing particularly well, how did we render this assessment? We arrived at this judgment using Andrea Bocelli as our normative frame. Clearly, we must conclude—even if we prefer pop music to the operatic version—the latter can sing better than the former. This process and strategy fixes the critic as an expert judge who, because of a certain expertise (in music, in crime, etc.), is "deemed capable of authoritatively judging the true from the false, innocent from guilty, good from bad, progressive from regressive, and so on" (Pavlich, 2000, 74). Critique, as it is currently practised in criminology and elsewhere, is typically judgmental and reactive.

Forms of critique that seek to challenge the criminal justice status quo are not always appreciated. However, Pavlich (2000) claims that there was a time when critical genres in criminology had considerable influence among politicians and policy-makers, especially following the publication and subsequent dissemination of Taylor, Walton, and Young's (1973) highly touted *The New Criminology*. Disenchanted with administrative brands of social science, administrators for a time looked to more radical brands of criminology for inspiration. In the spirit of 1960s radicalism, insight derived from critical questioning of the status quo was evident in governmental discourse and practice. Pleas to abolish prisons, insight into the crime-producing tendencies of the modern criminal justice process, and prisoners' rights discourses were prominent (van Swaaningen, 1997). But these days were quite brief. Today, administrative and liberal strains figure most prominently in criminological conferences and scholarly journals.

The reason why "critical voices beyond the language of pragmatic technocracy are decidedly muted," especially when compared with critical debates from less than three decades ago, is that critics have "failed to address that which distinguishes their radical precepts from proponents of administrative criminology: critique" (Pavlich, 1999, 70). In recent years, drawing on the insights of philosophers such as Michel Foucault, Pierre Bourdieu, Jacques Derrida, and Giorgio Agamben (among others), critical criminologists have called for an approach that goes beyond judgment. Instead of employing one or another yard stick from which to judge the success and failure of criminal justice policies, these scholars employ an art of critique that involves destabilizing seemingly well-anchored relations into new patterns of being that do not pander to established social logics or rely upon reactive judgments (Hogeveen and Woolford, 2006). A nonjudgmental critical criminology would not render judgments about existing policy, programs, institutions, or societal structures. Rather, it would suggest "other" (just) ways of being in the world. "It would summon them, drag them from their sleep. Perhaps it would invert them sometimes—all the better" (Foucault, 1997).

Critical criminological critique attempts to move beyond complicity in government intrusion into the lives of the least powerful. It does not seek ways to better manage the poor and dangerous classes. Rather, it promises justice to those who are marginalized and discriminated against. Not justice that seeks to punish, however; instead, it promises justice through emancipation. How willing are you to address suffering in your social world?

As we hope you will learn from the rest of this chapter, following the notion of criticism set out in this section, the critical criminologist is not "critical" because he or she is bad-tempered or unconstructive; rather, the negativity of criticism is intended to open your mind to new ways of thinking about and being in the world.

# Critical Criminology in English Canada

Critical criminology in Canada was invigorated in 1973 with the arrival of *The New Criminology* by British criminologists Ian Taylor, Paul Walton, and Jock Young. In this wide-ranging critique of conventional criminology, Taylor, Walton, and Young identified starting points for a "new" criminology and criticized conventional criminology for supporting the political and economic status quo, for ignoring the structural causes of crime, and for focusing instead on biological and psychological factors. Taylor, Walton, and Young (1973, 270) recommended in contrast a "fully social" criminology that

1. *Understands crime within its wider socio-cultural context.* Crime is not merely an event that occurs between individuals, it takes place within broader social-structural and cultural conditions. Along these lines, a ghetto drug dealer is not just an individual seeking easy money—he may also be the product of a deindustrialized inner city that has been bled of all opportunities other than McJobs because capital investment has fled to the suburbs. He may also be immersed in patriarchal cultural conditions that associate masculinity with money, power, and violence, allowing him to obtain respect and credibility through drug dealing. These are just some of the structures that may influence his decision making.

2. *Examines the structural and political-economic dimensions that produce criminal behaviour.* Crime is not the result of "bad," abnormal, or poorly socialized people, but stems from structural conditions that produce unequal opportunities, stigmatized populations, real and relative deprivation, and other concepts criminologists often credit as motivations for crime. For example, stigma and labelling occur not only at the micro-level when authorities and significant others impose labels upon offenders and contribute to their secondary deviance (see Chapter 13), but also as the result of structural conditions that make certain individuals more likely to choose to commit crime, more likely to be caught, more likely to be punished, and therefore, more likely to be labelled. This is all part of what Taylor, Walton, and Young (1973, 274) call a "political economy of social reaction."

3. *Probes the relationship between crime and the prevailing mode of production.* Crime occurs within societies defined by specific systems of economic production. What is defined as a crime, and the way that crime is punished, will often depend on this mode of production. For example, vagrancy was criminalized in Britain during the 17th century, in part because cheap labour was required for the factory system (Chambliss, 1969) to feed the profits of the ruling class and sustain the capitalist mode of production.

4. *Questions the role of power and conflict in shaping crime and criminal justice.* Crime is not simply the reflection of a societal consensus but instead is defined by the powerful and punished in a manner that suits their interests. Therefore, criminologists must not simply accept state-defined crime as a given. They must question its origins and the ways in which power is implicit in its formation and application.

5. *Engages in a materialist analysis of the development of law in capitalist societies.* Law is not simply a matter of societal consensus but is a function of the material conditions that define our society. Therefore, the law will contain contradictions because it is a reflection of dominant material interests. For example, gambling is illegal in a private club, but not in a government-run casino. Other forms of gambling, such as betting on "futures" in the stock market, may be encouraged by the government. Similarly, certain drug habits, such as alcohol and coffee, are tolerated, if not encouraged. In contrast, others, such as marijuana, may be viewed as unproductive and criminalized.

6. *Takes a dialectical approach to analyzing how individuals both influence and are influenced by dominant social structures.* The New Criminology was not simply a shift to an objectivist standpoint holding that human action is fully determined by social structures. Instead, human agency and social structures each affect the other, meaning that although human actions are influenced by their cultural and political-economic conditions, humans can also act to change these conditions.

This approach inspired several Canadian criminologists to critically assess the liberal foundations of Canadian criminology. For example, R. S. Ratner (1984) argued that Canadian criminologists had not risen to the challenge of the New Criminology and were guilty of ignoring social structures, failing to challenge state definitions of crime, and naively believing the institutional apparatus of the criminal justice system could be easily adjusted to address systemic inadequacies and injustices.

Critical criminology soon spread to other venues. In 1985, Thomas O'Reilly-Fleming edited *The New Criminologies in Canada*, which was followed in 1986 by a special edition of the journal *Crime and Social Justice* dedicated to Canadian critical criminology (edited by R. S. Ratner) and a conference in Vancouver on the "Administration of Justice" organized by Brian MacLean and Dawn Currie. By the late 1980s Canadian critical criminologists had banded together to form the Human Justice Collective, a loose network of scholars assembled around their concerns with the narrow focus of mainstream criminology. Moreover, these scholars desired a criminology that was more sensitive to the criminogenic impacts of capitalism, patriarchy, racism, and other social structures (Dekeseredy and MacLean, 1993). Out of the Human Justice Collective was born the *Journal of Human Justice*. In the first issue of this journal R. S. Ratner (1989, 6) defined critical criminology as follows:

> Although varied conceptions abound, we are all united around those premises that underscore the central role of power and conflict in shaping "criminal" outcomes, the range of vested interests that influence "crime", the need for a dialectical analysis of crime and social control that integrates materialist and idealist factors, the crucial importance of the state and the equally important need to debunk state definitions of crime, and the necessity of devising a praxis that is not conditional on the imminent collapse of capitalist society.

This unity, however, was to be short-lived as funding challenges, personality conflicts, and scholarly differences made it difficult to sustain the Human

Justice Collective and its journal. Initially, it had been intended that the *Journal of Human Justice* would fund itself through members of the collective adopting it as required reading in their courses. However, classroom use diminished and the journal was in a difficult financial position. In addition, personality conflicts had erupted within the collective, leading to disputes among members. In 1995, under these conditions, one of the editors, Brian MacLean, transported the journal to the Division of Critical Criminology at the American Society of Criminology. This move allowed for the journal's continued survival but also marked the end of its Canadian identity.

The growing eclecticism of critical criminology has produced a group of scholars who are difficult to unify under a single label. Initially, a key rift developed between two groups defined as "left realists" and "left idealists" (Young, 1979). Left idealists were said to begin their inquiry into crime from abstract premises (e.g., Marxist theory) rather than empirical work. For this reason, they were criticized by realists for minimizing the harm crime causes to the working class and for romanticizing criminals as a potentially revolutionary force.

In contrast, left realists worked through local surveys of crime and victimization to try to move beyond partial criminological understandings that typically focused only on one aspect of crime: the offender, state, public, or victim. Their objective was to take the fear of crime among the working classes seriously, and to answer and oppose the work of "right realists," who under the Thatcher, Reagan, and Mulroney governments had spread the popularity of punitive sanctions and administrative approaches. However, left realism did not achieve a sustained following among critical criminologists. For some, the reform-based agenda of left realism was viewed to compromise the critical thrust of critical criminology by participating in and legitimating the discourses of conventional criminal justice (Pavlich, 1999).

The diversity of critical criminology in Canada would later expand with the popularity of neo-Marxist and post-structuralist theories imported from continental Europe. The perspectives discussed in the rest of this chapter all derive from these origins and represent a shift in critical criminological theorizing away from distinctly political-economic perspectives. Although the premise that state-defined law must be challenged rather than replicated through criminological study remains, a great diversity of methodology and conceptualization now defines the Canadian critical criminological scene, which also includes the work of several of the feminist scholars discussed in Chapter 6.

**Division on Critical Criminology, American Society of Criminology**

critcrim.org/node?page=1

## Governmentality and Power: Foucault and Criminology

Foucault did not regard himself as a significant contributor to the discipline of criminology. On the rare occasion when he did comment on criminology, he complained that its "garrulous discourse" and "endless repetitions" only served to relieve judges, police officers, and magistrates of their guilt for delivering pain and suffering on the guilty (Foucault, 1980, 47). Despite Foucault's

**Foucault Resources**
www.michel-foucault.com/

**governmentality**

The art of governing. It transcends and is considerably broader than the traditional understanding of government as a state-directed activity. Government, then, encompasses a wide array of techniques, within and outside of the state, intended to (re)shape and (re)direct human actions.

**power**

Power, for Foucault, extends beyond the state. It is not a quantity to hold or possess. It is, rather, relational, such that power is only ever evident in its exercise.

**micro-powers**

Small and mundane relations of governance, with an appreciable effect on human behaviour.

**discipline**

A meticulous manner or method of training. It intends to ensure constant subjection and obedience. It involves hierarchal observation, normalizing judgment, and examinations.

**surveillance**

The direct or indirect observation of conduct toward producing a desired outcome (i.e., conformity).

disdain for the discipline, many scholars have applied his work toward the understanding of crime and its control. His penological treatise on the "birth of the prison"—*Discipline and Punish*—continues to inspire fresh criminological theorizing. More recently scholars have used his work on **governmentality**.

Foucault was born in Poitiers, France, in 1926, and died in 1984 from complications of HIV/AIDS. A philosopher and historian who wrote about the history of sexuality, prisons, governance, psychiatry, and knowledge systems, he is heralded for his unique work on **power**. Power, for Foucault, is evident only when it is *exercised*. He did not see it as something states or individuals could hold, accumulate, possess, or monopolize. In other words, can you show us what power looks like? Some may claim, and they often do, that money or wealth *is* power. Foucault would argue otherwise. For Foucault, money becomes power only when it is used or otherwise put into effect.

A further characteristic of the Foucauldian notion of power is that it is not solely negative or repressive. He instead preferred a more *positive* theory of power: not in terms of good or beneficial, but rather as creative. He argues that

> we must cease once and for all to describe the effects of power in negative terms: it "excludes," it "represses," it "censures," it "abstracts," it "masks," it "conceals." In fact power produces; it produces reality; it produces domains of object and rituals of truth. (Foucault 1979, 194)

Thus, rather than viewing power in a manner that exaggerates its negative elements, Foucault urged scholars to focus on what is created when power is exercised. What is the outcome when power is employed?

A third characteristic of the Foucauldian understanding of power is the emphasis he placed on **micro-powers** that are disseminated throughout the social world. Almost everywhere we turn, everywhere we go, power operates on our bodies and souls. It seems power is perpetually influencing our behaviour, often without our awareness. Consider your daily trip to university or college. Assuming that you are driving a vehicle of some sort, think about all the ways your behaviour is controlled while you drive. Traffic lights, signs, painted lines, photo radar, and the presence or absence of police all affect how we go about our drive.

Foucault is convinced that to intimately understand the operation of power we must shift our focus from the state to the dispersed spaces in which power operates. This is the essence of what Foucault called discipline. **Discipline** operates at the smallest level of detail and attends to the intricacies of human behaviour through **surveillance** and observation of individual functioning so as to increase the efficiency and usefulness of human actions. When thinking about discipline, it is the everyday and the mundane that are important. Fully understanding power involves examining it at its main point of application: the body. Remember back to when you were learning how to write using a pencil. Recall the teacher standing over you correcting your finger placement. S/he would watch you (surveillance) and correct your mistakes to make certain that you used the implement in the most efficient manner possible (positive power). To maximize the utility of our bodies and to allow hierarchal control and correction, this meticulous exercise of power is infinitely multiplied throughout the social world. As such, discipline requires that individuals be organized in space and time. Consider the timetable from public school. It provided a general framework for activity and organized our days. The timetable structured not only our *use* of time, but also the *space* we were to occupy at certain points in the day. The bell organized our behaviour. What happened when the bell sounded? Being conditioned to move according to the sounding of the bell, students would get up to leave while the teacher attempted to quell the mass exodus. Thus time, space, and signals coexisted to discipline not only our minds but also our bodies (Hogeveen and Minaker, 2008).

Foucault's analysis of discipline was criticized for (a) abandoning the state in its analysis and (b) its supposed tendency to characterize human subjects as "docile" (inactive) bodies as opposed to active agents (Garland, 1997). Foucault's later work on governmentality addressed many of these concerns (see Box 12.1). For Foucault (1982, 221), governmentality

> must be allowed the very broad meaning which it had in the 16th century. Government did not refer only to political structures or the management of states; rather it designated the way in which the conduct of individuals or states might be directed; the government of children, of souls, of communities, of families, of the sick.

Therefore, the study of governmentality should cast its gaze widely and address such broad questions as "how to govern oneself, how to be governed, how to govern others, by whom the people will accept to be governed, and how to become the best possible governor" (Foucault, 1991, 45). Government(ality) entails "any attempt to shape with some degree of deliberation aspects of our behaviour according to particular sets of norms and for a variety of ends" (Dean, 1999, 10).

# FOCUS BOX 12.1

## RESTORATIVE JUSTICE AS GOVERNMENTALITY

Restorative justice is a broad term used to describe a range of justice practices designed to involve victims, offenders, and community members in directly resolving the harms caused by crime. For some of its proponents, restorative justice is intended to empower communities and individuals to creatively solve their own problems, to remove justice control from the hands of the state and professionals, and to allow for a justice tailored specifically to the needs of victims, offenders, and community members. All of this is to occur within informal settings such as community centres, with victims, offenders, and their families and friends, as well as community members sitting in a circle to discuss what led to the crime and how its harm might be repaired.

In contrast to this representation of restorative justice as a community-led activity separate from the formal practices of the state, George Pavlich (2005) has given two reasons why restorative justice is a form of governmentality. First, because the participants in restorative justice meetings are encouraged to examine and reshape their conduct in relation to their experiences of crime and justice. Offenders are asked to take responsibility for their actions, victims are asked to express how the crime has affected them and to present reasonable demands for

*(continued)*

repair, and community members are asked to participate in the reintegration of the offender and the healing of the victim. Moreover, it is hoped that participation in restorative justice will transform the way these participants deal with conflict in the future. All of these aspects of restorative justice encourage individuals to accept and internalize restorative values and practices through which they might better govern themselves and their communities, thus freeing the state of this responsibility.

Second, because restorative justice fashions a way of understanding the world (and crime in particular) that makes the pursuit of "restorative" justice appear more rational and understandable to those involved. If restorative justice is to govern our behaviour, it must first shift how we think about crime and criminal justice. It does this by reframing core components of criminal justice. For Pavlich, this involves providing different answers to the questions:

1. What is governed? Unlike formal criminal justice, restorative justice claims to govern "harm" rather than "crime" since it is not the violations of the state's law but rather the harms suffered by individuals and communities that are of primary concern.
2. Who is governed? Those who are to be governed are all of those who have a stake in the crime and its effects—victim, offender, and community members—rather than just the offender.
3. Who governs? Whereas judges and lawyers are the individuals empowered through the practice of criminal justice, restorative justice seeks to give greater agency to victims, offenders and community members.
4. What is appropriate governing? Instead of focusing on the past, restorative governance should be directed toward the future. It is therefore less a question of punishing a wrongdoer and more an issue of creating a dialogue among stakeholders so that they can work out how to avoid repetition of the crime.

For Pavlich, the problem with this restorative justice governmentality is that it does not represent a true alternative to the criminal justice system. Instead, restorative justice is fundamentally dependent on the criminal justice system and criminal law. For example, although restorative justice shifts our attention to the harm suffered by victims and community members, it nonetheless relies on criminal law to define the acts that are to be considered harmful. Therefore, it restricts itself from addressing harms that are not codified within criminal codes (such as suffering caused by industrial pollution), as well as structural harms (such as the gender inequalities that result from patriarchal systems of domination).

Source: Pavlich, George. 2005. *Governing Paradoxes of Restorative Justice*. London: Glasshouse Press.

Critical scholars have used Foucault's writings on governmentality to understand a wide range of state and non-state domains of governance. They have raised important insights about legal change and the centrality of law in the regulation of populations. They have also argued that critical criminology has been limited "by its emphasis on the state, and state-centred constructions of criminality, and by its failure to come to terms with how social injustices are reproduced through private institutions and modes of expertise that operate on the margins of the state and in the shadow of the law" (Lippert and Williams, 2006). For example, Lippert and Williams (2006) have looked to the margins of legal governance to explore how the rise of private security affects our social world. These authors maintain that critical scholarship should focus "less on how the machinery of the state is brought to bear on the production and control of individual subjects and offenders, and more on the myriad technologies of governance and their operation across diverse social fields" such as immigration and policing financial disorder (Lippert and Williams, 2006). Governmentality, then, draws scholarly attention to mechanisms *outside* the traditional state governmental machinery that structure and contour human behaviour. Recent years have witnessed the proliferation of private security firms that police a variety of venues, including the local mall, construction sites, and, as the upsurge in alarm companies continues, private dwellings. By attending to the growth of private security "the governmentality literature presents a unique opportunity to expand the theoretical range and conceptual reach of critical criminology, and to enhance its capacity to reveal and interrogate forms of injustice and domination crafted on the margins of the state" (Williams and Lippert, 2006).

## Actuarialism, Risk, and the Risk Society

Perhaps the greatest impact of Foucault's work on critical criminological studies has been on scholars' ability to understand how offenders' lives are increasingly organized around questions of **risk**. As we have seen already, Foucault was fundamentally concerned with understanding how individuals were normalized through government and discipline—that is, how they were corrected and brought into line with the needs of the larger society (O'Malley, 1996). In the field of crime control, recent years have witnessed the emergence and proliferation of actuarial or "insurance" based strategies of governance and control. It seems Western criminal justice systems have become somewhat preoccupied with managing risks as police, probation, prisons, and halfway houses seek to minimize the likelihood of future offending (Bosworth, 2004). Toward this end, many institutions employ a variety of risk prediction tools, which are all part of what has been dubiously christened "actuarial justice" (Feeley and Simon, 1994).

> **risk**
> The calculated probability of an eventuality.

Foucauldian-inspired theorists distinguish the everyday usage of the term *risk* from how it is construed as an **actuarial** (or insurance-based) technology. When we as citizens refer to risk it concerns the dangers and perils connected with an objective and often immediate threat—for instance, of being struck by lightning or having our house burglarized. However, this definition and understanding of risk has to be separated from its usage in actuarial terms where it indicates neither an "event nor a general kind of event occurring in reality, but a specific mode of treatment of certain events capable of occurring to a group of individuals" (Ewald, 1991). Risk, then, is the calculated probability of an eventuality. Think of the last time you purchased car insurance. The agent likely asked you a series of questions: What is your sex? How old are you? Where do you live? Where do you work? How far do you travel to work/school? These questions were then entered into a computer, which calculated your premium based on these factors. Agents ask these questions to derive a risk score. That is, by employing aggregated data (including accident reports and police statistics) collected over time and then comparing the aggregate to your indicators, insurance companies ascertain the probability of having to pay a claim on your

> **actuarial**
> Refers to statistical calculations of risk across time and groups.

behalf. If you are young, male and unemployed, your risk and insurance premium will be considerably higher than that of a married 40-year-old female who lives in the suburbs.

Events (car accidents) and populations (males, females, the elderly) are not inherent risks, but become constituted as "actuarial" risks through analyses and calculations of chance. Risk understood from a Foucauldian perspective, then, is constituted in relation to the aggregation of events over time and regulated through techniques such as higher insurance rates designed to contend with individual risk factors. Simon (1988) maintains that risk-based technologies of governance have become dominant largely because of their efficiency and their ability to intensify the effectiveness of disciplinary technologies (O'Malley, 1996). Probabilistic calculation is particularly evident in the youth correctional field where the Youth Level of Service/Case Management Inventory (YLS/CMI) is employed. Andrews and Bonta (1998, 245) maintain that this tool is premised on the four principles of risk, needs, responsivity, and professional discretion. First, the *risk* principle reflects the contention that criminal behaviour occurs in predictable patterns. Second, the *needs* principle implies that recidivism will be reduced through select targeting of criminogenic need through appropriate treatment programs. Third, given that many juvenile offenders suffer from attention deficit hyperactivity disorder, fetal alcohol spectrum disorder, or oppositional defiant disorder, responsivity is crucial to any "successful" treatment option and refers to the need for service providers to deliver treatment programs in a manner that is consistent with and appropriate to the offender's ability and learning style. Finally, *professional discretion* "strategically reasserts the importance of retaining professional judgment, provided that it is not used irresponsibly and is systematically monitored" (Hannah-Moffat and Maurutto, 2003, 3).

While at first blush actuarial strategies seem efficient and just, several factors raise questions about such assessments. Hannah-Moffat and Maurutto (2003, 7) have found that correctional officials and practitioners fail to conceptualize "the problems intrinsic to this kind of needs assessment and how a failure to distinguish between risk and need can result in increased surveillance of youth." Although blending of risk and need is a problem, the problems of risk-based governance are particularly troubling when applied to female and non-white populations (Minaker and Hogeveen, 2008). Notably, "female offenders are more often deemed higher risk because of their risk to themselves, whereas high-risk male offenders are more likely to pose a risk to others" (Hannah-Moffat and Shaw, 2001). Risk assessment tools typically do not account for gender and cultural variation in offending and recidivism. For example, the tests do not adequately capture histories of physical, mental, or sexual abuse prevalent among female youth. Moreover, risk assessment tools do not adequately address the broader socio-cultural and colonial context of Aboriginal youths (Hannah-Moffat and Shaw, 2001).

These Foucauldian notions of risk and actuarialism are occasionally combined with Beck's concept of the "**risk society**." Beck admits that characterizing the present as the "risk society" may seem odd in light of the daily risks and dangers faced by people in pre-industrial societies—such as plagues, famine, and natural disasters. However, there is a qualitative difference between the

**risk society**

An emerging societal form characterized by the production and increased awareness of human-made "risks," such as nuclear destruction and environmental devastation. More importantly, the risk society is organized around the management of such risks.

looming hazards of our industrial present and those of earlier times. Beck suggests that today's hazards are not forces outside of us, but instead internal creations, and their danger originates from our own decision making (Beck, 1992, 98). Our technological development and scientific rationality have provided us with the tools to construct the means of our own destruction—nuclear power, environmental pollution, climate change, and an assortment of life-threatening chemicals, just to name a few dangers. Moreover, Beck does not suggest that we have necessarily witnessed a quantitative increase in risk; rather, we have come to organize our societies more around the fact of risk.

This theoretical perspective comes to bear on critical criminology in at least two ways. First, social problems have increasingly come to be understood as "risks" to be *managed* rather than social "problems" to be *solved*. This shift in thinking is noticeable in criminological approaches that take crime to be inevitable and which, in response, prescribe various risk-reduction strategies to lessen crime's social costs. Along these lines, individuals are encouraged to become responsible for protecting themselves from opportunistic crimes through the techniques of "situational crime prevention" (O'Malley, 1992), whether by installing alarm systems in their homes or steering wheel locking mechanisms in their cars. As well, "three strikes" laws (see Box 13.1), which impose long-term prison sentences after a third criminal violation, are justified under a risk management logic as a means for warehousing repeat offenders who are perceived to pose too great a threat to the general public. This said, risk management techniques should not be painted solely as oppressive, since they can be used to establish more fair and efficient criminal justice processes under the current system, such as by providing a calculus for justifying the diversion of less risky offenders toward an alternative sentencing or community bail program, and thus away from the formal justice system. However, even with such seemingly benign applications of risk, critical criminologists remain skeptical of the individualizing and responsibilizing tendencies of risk-based approaches to crime.

Second, risk thinking transforms criminal justice practices. Risk management strategies infiltrate judicial, correctional, and law enforcement institutions, tasking criminal justice professionals with the collection of aggregated risk data and with administering risk assessments to their charges. For example, Ericson and Haggerty (1997) note how policing practices have been affected by the demands of the risk society. They cite the case of a modern police officer investigating a traffic accident. The officer must now not only gather information pertinent to the courts and police records, but also to the insurance companies, the public health system, provincial vehicle registries, and the automobile industry. Under these new demands, Ericson and Haggerty report that a simple traffic accident "took one hour to investigate, and three hours to write about it, to account for it, and to bureaucratically process it" (Ericson and Haggerty, 1997, 24).

In alerting us to these broader social changes, the "risk society" thesis serves a critical criminological function by demonstrating the effects broad societal shifts toward increased insecurity have upon the ways we think about and react to matters of criminal justice. In this sense, crime and its response are not taken as givens, but as socially constituted phenomena that can be better understood by locating them in their wider social context. And by identifying this wider social context, we are thus able to critically assess proposed criminal justice "solutions" through an understanding of their historical contingency.

Cultural Criminology
www.culturalcriminology.org/

# Cultural Criminology

The Social Reaction perspective (see Chapter 13) brings attention to crime as a process of social interaction involving victim, offender, bystanders, and criminal justice agencies in the construction of deviant meanings and identities. This insight has been absorbed and extended in the work of cultural criminologists who focus on crime as a cultural, rather than a legal, construct. These scholars turn their attention away from crime as a "real" phenomenon reflected in police data, victimization surveys, and other quantitative measures, and instead focus on "the debris of everyday life" (Morrison, 2007, 254) through an aesthetic and ethnographic engagement with their subject matter. In this manner, cultural criminologists do not accept crime simply as state-defined illegality; instead, they view it as a culturally negotiated phenomenon through which people create social meaning.

Hayward and Young (2004) identify five "motifs" of cultural criminology. First, cultural criminologists alert us to the importance of "adrenaline" in the commission of crime. In contrast, to rational choice theories that portray offenders as economic actors engaged in cost–benefit analyses of whether or not to break the law, cultural criminologists acknowledge that crime is *felt*. In other words, crime may be motivated by feelings of anger, insecurity, humiliation, or excitement. Moreover, the act of crime may produce a sensual and visceral rush that incites both panic and pleasure (Katz, 1988; Ferrell, 1998). Thus, although a potential car thief may make a *rational* choice not to steal your car because she or he is afraid that it might be a "bait car," the *attraction* of car theft may stem more from the desire to alleviate boredom through risk taking.

Second, cultural criminologists draw our attention to the "soft city" (Raban, 1974). This refers to the "underlife" of the city that hides beneath structured and rationally planned urban space. Whereas urban planning attempts to direct our everyday lives through policing strategies, the design of defensive urban space, and other modalities of social control, the "soft city" bubbles up as a realm of creativity and street-level possibility. While it may seem that we are free to go and do as we please in space, careful design contours our actions in very definite directions. Consider for example the layout of an IKEA store. The interior space has been mapped so that customers are forced to wander through all the showrooms before arriving at what they want to purchase. This is no accident. IKEA designers want us to see all their products on display, hoping this will make us want to purchase more than we intended. The "soft-city," by contrast, subverts planners' intentions. It is the space used, for example, by Critical Mass, to launch illegal bike rallies to confront our automobile culture and to illustrate how the daily commute is part of the depersonalized and routinized destruction of human sociability (Ferrell, 2004). As Ferrell (2004, 292) notes, "Critical Mass participants define their exuberantly collective bicycle rides not as traditional political protests, but as do-it-yourself celebrations enlivened by music, decoration and play." By resisting the boredom and repetition of the normal "protest march," Critical Mass seeks to reclaim the "soft city" of urban space through their theatrical rallies.

Third, cultural criminologists are interested in acts of "transgression" and rule-breaking that challenge the justness of laws. In this vein, a cultural criminologist might understand the spectacle of pro-cannabis protesters sparking joints on Parliament Hill not simply as individuals seizing the opportunity for public criminality, but rather as a collective act designed to challenge the criminalization of one leisure pursuit while others (e.g., alcohol, tobacco) go uncontested. Similarly, the Critical Mass cycle rallies expose the over-regulated nature of modern urban life and the ways in which this over-regulation denies freedom of movement (as well as dedicated traffic lanes) to slower and less expensive vehicles.

Fourth, cultural criminologists propose a methodology founded upon an **attentive gaze**. This requires that researchers do more than sit back in their offices and peruse quantified crime data. They must engage in "an ethnography immersed in culture and interested in lifestyle(s), the symbolic, the aesthetic, and the visual" (Hayward and Young, 2004, 268). This requires that they enter into the world where crime occurs and where it is represented to better comprehend the experiential and interpretive dimensions of crime. For example, O'Neill (2004) employs a methodology she refers to as "ethno-mimesis," which draws on media such as photography, film, performance, theatre, and text to illustrate the complexity of the emotional lives of individuals. In one such study, O'Neill and Campbell encouraged sex workers to use art and writing to represent their "issues, concerns, experiences, and ideas for change" (O'Neill, 2004, 226). The final result was not only a written report, but also an art exhibit and information pamphlet, which collectively combined to allow community members to express, reflect upon, and relate to pressing local issues in a variety of creative ways.

Finally, the knowledge produced by cultural criminology is argued to be **dangerous knowledge** because its purpose is to question all knowledge, including the status of criminology as an objective science. This might be achieved by drawing on unusual sources of knowledge. For instance, in his exploration of the crime of genocide, Morrison (2007) examines photographs snapped by Nazi police battalions, visits Belgian and Bangladeshi museums, and offers a reading of Joseph Conrad's novel *Heart of Darkness*. He uses these diverse sources to criticize criminology for its dependence on crimes defined and data generated by the state, and thereby its tendency to overlook crimes such as genocide that are perpetrated often by or beyond the state. In this sense, cultural criminology is a critical criminological project intended to relentlessly challenge the taken-for-granted assumptions of criminology and popular understandings of crime in order to expose how they are culturally constructed and delimited by a particular worldview.

**attentive gaze**
A methodological requirement that researchers immerse themselves where crime occurs in the everyday world in order to better understand the ways in which crime is experienced and interpreted by individuals.

**dangerous knowledge**
A form of knowledge that leaves no concept, notion, or idea un-touched by criticism. To achieve this relentlessly critical stance, cultural criminologists will often turn to diverse sources of information (e.g., novels and street-level observation) as means to reveal alternative perspectives that might shake the foundations of our taken-for-granted assumptions about crime.

# A "Field Theory" of Criminology

The sociology of Pierre Bourdieu also provides insight into the cultural and economic conditions in which crime and our understanding of crime are produced, although on a much broader scale. The grounding concept of Bourdieu's theoretical work is that of the **field** (DiMaggio, 1979). Bourdieu's notion of the field can be likened to a battlefield or sports field (Bourdieu, 1992). It is a space of conflict and competition wherein competitors, who each possess varying levels of social and economic power, vie for control. Nevertheless, the field is not level nor is it without pre-existing rules. Rather, participants encounter a field that is tilted to favour the already powerful (they will play downhill) and structured by predetermined rules that all must follow.

It is within a field of social activity, such as art, politics, or law, that a market defined by its own measures of value is established and it is in accordance with a field that actors seek the "profit of distinction" or, in other words, the awards associated with a display of competence (Bourdieu, 1991, 1990a, 1984). An actor's ability to display competence within a particular field depends, in part, upon his or her **habitus**. This is one's "feel for the game": that is, it refers to a set of "dispositions acquired through experience" (Bourdieu, 1990b, 9) that allow one to react to situations that arise within a particular field without the need to actively plot one's moves. Keeping with our sports analogy, imagine that in a game of hockey the skilled power forward Hogeveen finds a loose puck in a scrum in front of the net. In that instance, he automatically shifts the puck to his backhand and lifts it over the sprawling goalie, Woolford. Here, Hogeveen's dedication to his sport, and his practised experience of it, provide him the embodied knowledge necessary to succeed on the ice without needing to "overthink" his game (whereas Woolford's coach might advise him to work more on his hockey habitus).

The actor's "feel for the game" within the market relations of a specific field will vary, with those endowed with greater quantities of the forms of **capital** valuable within the field (e.g., economic, symbolic, cultural, or linguistic capital) more capable of transmitting an aura of competence (Brubaker, 1985). Thus, within a specific "game" or market situation actors come pre-equipped with differing amounts of capital, depending on their position(s) in the structural arrangements of society (e.g., level of education, occupation, age), and based on these factors are predisposed toward certain behaviours or practices. The valuational rules of the market ascribe these practices and behaviours with differing levels of profitability within the field, allowing some actors to feel more at home on their appointed terrain. To put this in simpler terms, if you are currently seeking a criminology degree this may be motivated by your desire to obtain employment in the legal or juridical field (e.g., as a police officer, lawyer, or probation worker). However, success in this field will depend on more than your possession of a criminology degree or your ability to extol Merton's strain theory. You will require possession of the forms of capital most valued within this field of activity. You will acquire some of this capital through your increased knowledge about the field of law, but you might also profit from the symbolic, linguistic, and cultural capital you have obtained through the

**field**
A basic unit of social activity. The social world is divided into many fields (e.g., the "artistic" field, the "academic" field, or the "economic" field). Each field of activity is defined by its own market through which certain practices or dispositions are valued more than others.

**habitus**
A set of durable dispositions acquired through experience that allow one to achieve a "feel for the game" within a specific field of activity. These are internalized practices that serve as a "second nature" responsive to the immediate demands of everyday life.

**capital**
Each person enters a field of activity already possessed of certain powerful qualities or "capital."

practice of writing essays, making public presentations, and reading "classic" works of literature and philosophy. These latter forms of capital equip you with an aura of competence that communicates to your future employer that you are a "capable" person (see—essays, presentations, and readings *are* important!). However, it should be noted that due to our inequitable social structures some people enter university already in possession of a great deal of the capital needed to get a job within the juridical field and therefore are at an advantage. For example, an individual who was raised by a father/lawyer and mother/judge, who habitually thinks of the world in terms of law and adversarial justice and who models his parents' ways of speaking and carrying themselves, is armed with a habitus that invests them with the capital needed to more easily navigate the legal profession.

In criminological analysis, Bourdieu's field theory has been most influentially used by Wacquant. In his studies of American prisons and ghettos, Wacquant (1998, 2000, 2001) examines the meshing of these two institutions in the project of excluding African Americans from American society. It is within these "peculiar institutions" that we see the spatial segregation of those who lack, or possess negative forms of, capital. Indeed, the economic deprivation of ghetto residents is readily apparent. The decline of industrial employment within the urban core and the change toward a service-sector economy resulted in a loss of income opportunities for African American ghetto residents. But ghetto residents also possess what Wacquant refers to as **negative *symbolic* capital** and **negative *social* capital**.

Negative symbolic capital refers to the ways in which the ghetto is marked by a stigma that automatically devalues its residents by dint of their association with this neighbourhood. Moreover, their spatial concentration within the ghetto enables their territorial confinement, constraint, and institutional regulation. In other words, the ghetto becomes a means for controlling and administering to a population that is viewed to be subordinate and outside the labour force. Here, similarities between prison and ghetto become more evident, since prisons (in particular, U.S. prisons) increasingly serve to warehouse "recidivist" offenders who are assessed to be "incurable" and therefore unlikely to ever play a productive role in society.

"Social capital" refers to the resources one has at his or her disposal by virtue of being located within "a durable network of more or less institutionalized relationships of mutual acquaintance or recognition—or, in other words, to membership in a group" (Bourdieu, 1986, 248). Social capital can be "informal" (i.e., based on family, neighbourhood, or friendship networks) or "formal" (i.e., based on private or public formal organizations). Wacquant's (1998) concern is with how state-based formal social capital in the ghetto, in the form of civic goods and services such as welfare and public housing, has been turned toward the tasks of surveillance and exclusion rather than social integration and trust-building. For ghetto residents, this amounts to "negative social capital" since they are no longer empowered by participation in programs such as welfare services, as these programs have come to be directed toward the tasks of gathering further data about welfare recipients, placing further restrictions on their day-to-day lives, and generally increasing the social regulation of the poor.

**negative *symbolic* capital**
The way in which stigma cast upon a neighbourhood might be symbolically transferred to the neighbourhood's residents, placing them in a deficit with respect to their ability to improve their social standing.

**negative *social* capital**
The way in which one's network of formal social resources (e.g., organizations designed to provide social services) can be used to more effectively regulate and control rather than empower an individual.

This approach fits the label of "critical criminology" because it does not simply accept "criminalized" identities as constructed through the criminal law and its application. Instead, it seeks to identify the symbolic, cultural, and economic factors (e.g., habitus and capital) that empower dominant actors to create and apply criminal categories while simultaneously disempowering subordinate groups from resisting this criminalization because they lack the necessary forms of "capital" to achieve "profit" within various arenas of social action (or "fields").

# Agamben: Sovereignty and the State of Exception

In political theory and public discourse the West is generally considered to be an asylum of human rights enmeshed within robust democracy (Ek, 2006). But this image has begun to erode in the wake of "exceptional" and seemingly extreme measures introduced after two planes piloted by terrorists slammed into the World Trade Center buildings in New York City on September 11, 2001. What are we to think about massive numbers of suspected terrorists being detained in Guantanamo Bay without ever being charged with an offence? To protect the public from similar future attacks, North American governments maintain that such practices are necessary. Moreover, in 2006, *USA Today* reported that the National Security Agency was "secretly collecting the phone call records of tens of millions of Americans," most of whom were not suspected of any crime. Typically wire taps and phone records are obtained by court order while gathering evidence against individuals suspected of crime. Why do Americans not vehemently protest such efforts? It seems that citizens have become stoic; that is, whatever measures the government implements in the name of national security and, perhaps more important, the prevention of future terrorist attacks, are considered not only appropriate but welcome. The wave of repressions and concessions since 9/11 are typically made in the name of safety and protection of self and country. And the phone call database is no exception.

Anything and everything (including torture?), it seems, is now permitted so long as the goal is the protection of the state and the public. Such a policy holds lethal implications. For example, after five suspected terrorist attacks left 54 dead and numerous wounded in the heart of London, England, an innocent man (Jean Charles de Menezes) was shot dead by police officers. Police Chief Sir Iain Blair, while disturbed by this tragedy, later admitted that more guiltless Londoners could lose their lives as police scoured the city for the suspected bombers. In effect, the police chief admitted that a mistake was made and stated that it could likely be made again in the future. How can we make sense of this? Giorgio Agamben, who has extended Foucault's work, has perhaps done more to assist scholars, activists, and the public in coming to terms with the post-9/11 world than any other academic.

Agamben's work is complex and not easily classifiable into a specific genre, although his writing has been heavily influenced by close readings of Foucault, Carl Schmitt, Walter Benjamin, and Saint Paul. Ek (2006) concludes that since the Italian philosopher tends to extract the most "useful" conclusions from prominent and influential scholars and assembles them in a meaningful way, it might be best to read Agamben as an eclectic scholar. That is, one who does not rigidly hold to a single philosophical tradition, but instead integrates many ideas, concepts, and styles into his work.

Much of Agamben's work is grounded in a concern for and about the modern conditions of sovereignty. He takes his leave from Schmitt, who defines political sovereignty in his now classic work *Political Theology*. For Schmitt and Agamben, the **sovereign** is the one who holds the power to declare a **state of exception** during which civil liberties (among other precautions) are suspended in the interests of defending and protecting the nation. That is, the sovereign is the one whom the juridical order grants the power to proclaim a state of exception. Declarations of this sort are typically issued after natural disasters, during wartime, and, especially, when the state is confronted by civil unrest. According to Schmitt (1985), the state of exception or emergency, as it is sometimes referred to, is declared when the sovereign deems suspension of the existing social order necessary in order that social order be restored. Typically, the state of exception is lifted once stability is returned.

Under Canada's National Emergencies Act (1988), which replaced the War Measures Act (1914), any national, provincial, or municipal government can declare a state of emergency. The Act defines an emergency as "an urgent and critical situation" that threatens Canadian citizens and the government's capacity to preserve Canadian "sovereignty, security and territorial integrity." Declaring a state of emergency empowers the government to, among other things, prohibit travel and remove people from their homes. The most egregious invocation of such powers can be seen in the imprisonment and confiscation of the property of German and Ukrainian Canadians during World War I and Japanese Canadians during World War II. But, a world war is not a necessary condition for a state of emergency to be declared. Indeed, in the hunt for terrorists from the Front de libération du Québec (FLQ) soldiers in full battle attire raided homes of Quebecers while tanks patrolled city streets in October 1970. Sparked by a seven-year-long series of bombings and kidnappings, Prime Minister Pierre Elliott Trudeau invoked the War Measures Act, which effectively suspended civil rights and afforded police wide-ranging powers of arrest and detention. After the dust settled, nearly 500 people had been arrested and detained but only 62 were ever formally charged.

How does this make sense? How can a government simply suspend your rights? The answer for Agamben lies in the fact that it is only by virtue of citizenship that modern states offer protections via human rights. At the same time, the nation's citizens are subordinated to the sovereign who could, at any time, decide to suspend these rights (Ek, 2006). That is, human rights are afforded by specific geo-political orders (e.g., Canada) and can be suspended only by the *de facto* sovereign. Thus, in the name of protection or defence of society and nation, the sovereign sets up the conditions under which he or she can abandon his or her subjects and return them to a state of **naked life**—unprotected by law and rights. When a state of emergency is declared, rights-bearing citizens can be deemed enemies of the state and subject to exceptional and extreme measures.

**sovereign**
One who holds supreme power in a territory or space. Agamben, following Carl Schmitt, claims the sovereign is the one who is empowered to declare a state of exception.

**state of exception**
A period of time where the sovereign declares civil liberties suspended: typically in a time of national crisis.

**naked life**
For Agamben, naked life is akin to Homo Sacer—an individual who is excluded from possessing human rights and can be killed by anyone but cannot be sacrificed during a religious ceremony.

We should "ask ourselves if we are today witnessing a definitive paradigmatic break in conceptions of the relationship between countries and their citizens" (Minca, 2006), if we are facing the creation of an enormous space of exception within which each and every one of us—through the temporary suspension of law and rights—can be potentially whisked away to a secret prison or camp. Do you think this cannot happen in Canada and that it is a horror tale confined to the United States, Britain, or some other nation? In Canada, Citizenship and Immigration can remove persons deemed threatening to the security and well-being of Canadians by issuing a Security Certificate under the Immigration and Refugee Act. Under this scheme both foreign nationals and permanent residents may be detained indefinitely without charge and without having full access to any evidence against them. Both detention and withholding evidence are justified, the Federal Court of Appeal ruled in 2004, in the interests of national security. Human rights are violated under this legislation, in a so-called haven of respect for humans—including the right to a speedy trial and innocence until a guilty finding.

Canadian Maher Arar's arrest as a suspected terrorist and his subsequent torture attests to the "paradigmatic break" described by Minca. Arar was born in Syria and immigrated to Canada in 1987. After earning a master's degree in computer engineering, he took a job as a telecommunications engineer in Ottawa. Supported by RCMP "intelligence," U.S. officials detained Arar in 2002 on a stopover in New York after a vacation in Tunisia, charging that he possessed links to the terrorist organization al-Qaeda. After intense questioning, during which he was denied legal representation and phone calls, his wrists and ankles were shackled and he was taken to a nearby building where he was detained in a cell. The next morning he was roused only to face more intense interrogation before being put on a flight to Zurich, where he was once again scrutinized about his suspected terrorist ties. After three months of this sort of interrogation, Arar was deported to Syria, where he was detained and subsequently tortured (O'Connor, 2006). Arar was eventually released but only after spending a year in custody under very difficult conditions (see Box 12.2). For much of Arar's stay in Syria, the Canadian government made few efforts to help him.

An egregious tragedy in all of this is that Arar was not working with al-Qaeda or any other terrorist group (O'Connor, 2006). But under a state of exception such considerations—the juridical order and human rights—are of little import when compared to national security interests. It seems the evidence that linked him to terrorism and resulted in an innocent man being denied liberty and tortured was provided by his own country's national police force (the RCMP). In the wake of months of public and media scrutiny and fervour, former RCMP Commissioner Giuliano Zaccardelli appeared before the House of Commons Committee on Public Safety and National Security to confess that he knew his officers passed on false information about Arar to U.S. authorities in 2002—he previously gave misleading testimony that he was only made aware of this information in the fall of 2006! Zaccardelli subsequently resigned from the RCMP.

# FOCUS BOX 12.2

## STATEMENTS FROM MAHER ARAR'S INTERVIEW WITH AMNESTY INTERNATIONAL

"I remember one of the immigration officers on the second day at the airport he asked me to voluntarily go to Syria—of course I refused—I explained to him why. And in one of the interviews at the embassy I explained at length that I would be tortured in Syria if I am sent back. They did not seem to care . . .

"I could not believe what I saw. I saw a cell almost the size of a grave. Three feet wide 6 feet deep and 7 feet high. And when I looked at him and said what is this he just did not say anything—he did this with his hands—so basically 'I have nothing to with that.' So I entered the cell and he locked the door. The cell had no light in it; it only had two thin mattresses (two thin blankets) on the ground. And I first thought they would keep me in that place, which I now call the grave, for a short period so that they could put pressure on me. But I was kept in that dark and filthy cell for about 10 months and 10 days. That was torture . . .

"The worst beating happened on the third day and they were trying to, you know, they were asking the same set of questions some times, some times more questions and they would beat me 3 or 4 times. They would stop, they would beat me again. They would ask questions; they would sometimes take me to another room where I could hear the other people being tortured. They would keep me there for a while. They would bring me back they would beat me again ask questions sometimes they would take me to the hallway and make me stand for a couple of hours blindfolded. That third day they wanted me, they kept telling me I had been to Afghanistan and I kept telling them no. And at the end of the day I could not take the pain any more and I falsely confessed of having been to Afghanistan. . . .

"In fighting this so-called war on terror what do we do with basic human rights? Do we throw them in the garbage and forget about our values that we pride ourselves with? Those are really the main points. And as I'm talking now, there are people, human beings being tortured...

"I think we have reached a point where we can confirm that these abuses, or this kind of torture is happening at different parts of the world at the behest of the CIA and the Bush Administration in general. So, there needs to be an action. Unless we do something about, it if we keep silent, if governments keep silent—in a way they are complicit."

Source: © Amnesty International, 1 Easton Street, London WC1X 0DW, UK http://www.amnesty.org

Maher Arar's handling by both Canadian and American officials prompted a commission of inquiry that was headed by Justice O'Connor (O'Connor, 2006). Confronted with nagging allegations of corruption and dereliction on the part of various government and police officials, in January 2007 Prime Minister Harper extended an official apology to Arar along with $10.5 million (plus legal fees) in compensation.

# Jacques Derrida: Deconstruction *Is* Justice

> Deconstruction, if such a thing exists, should open up. (Derrida, 1987, 261)

For Agamben and most others, sovereignty refers to a singular entity: to a head of state or some other similar type figure who can decide on the state of exception. Jacques Derrida (2005), in one of his last writings before his death in 2004, argued for a more open and wide-ranging definition. Keeping with the deconstructive ethic in which he worked throughout his life, Derrida attempted to open the concept of sovereignty up to other ways of thinking and relating. For him, sovereignty was intrinsic to each and all of us, insofar as the sovereign function is "anchored in a certain ability to do something" (Balke, 2005). Derrida was intent on undoing language and, in the process, peering behind discourse to reveal how it does not have a determinable meaning. He wanted to show that all language exceeds the boundaries of the taken-for-granted (e.g., sovereignty). **Deconstruction** attempts to reveal what is *really* going on in and through language. According to Derrida, we always say more than the surface of our language reveals.

But what is deconstruction? Derrida frequently defined deconstruction in negative terms by referring to what it was not rather than what it *is*. For example, he argued, "deconstruction is not a method or some tool that you apply to something from the outside" (Derrida, 1997, 9). But what is it? We might say that deconstruction has to do with opening up given linguistic arrangements to the mostly silent, background suppositions that give words and phrases their meaning. Given Derrida's reticence, perhaps showing deconstruction at work would aid us here. As an example let us consider the word *promise*. What does this mean to you? When you promise your mother you will be home tonight for dinner, what are you doing? On the face of things you are giving her an assurance that you will sit down with her to eat this evening. Unless you are truly irresponsible, there is no reason to doubt the truth of your assurance. Humans typically relate to presence, to what is uttered. Nevertheless, what is unspoken in language (the perversion of the promise) is as important to determining meaning as what we hear from another. What would happen if you did not show up? Your mother would be upset that you broke your promise and others would certainly feel let down by your absence. Such perversions of the promise are as fundamental to its meaning as carrying through with the promised event. For a promise to be such, the statement must have the potential of falling through. If it does not, if what is assured is already guaranteed, there is no promise, only perfect conjugation of the assertion ("I will be home for supper") and the event. Again using the above example, if you promised your mum to come to dinner while sitting at the table with fork and knife in hand, you have not promised anything.

If we had only to consider the presence of speech, we could take everyone at their word and there would thus be no need for contracts, warranties, or oaths. Typically, however, when we hear language we do not attempt to read into its hidden meaning, but instead relate to what is laid out before us. However, and

**deconstruction**

An opening up of seemingly closed "things." It intends to encounter the hidden and excluded elements of language, meaning, and experience.

this is the important part, when speaking and writing we say much more than what is present on the page or in conversation. Deconstruction, then, attends closely to the unspoken elements that enable the central, or privileged, structure of a given meaning formation (Pavlich, 2007).

Underlying all language is a **trace**: the silent or absent element of language that provides words with an essential part of their meaning (i.e., perversion in the promise). The trace can be likened to a footprint or a comet. That is, when we observe a comet in the sky we are struck by the *presence* of the comet and/or tail. However, what is absent here is the comet's nucleus and essence, which is composed of rock and ice. When we observe a comet we are not privy to its essence—the nucleus remains hidden. The same can be said of language. No element, no idiom can function as a sign without at the same moment referring to another that is simply not present, but gives meaning to it (Derrida, 1981). While we are at liberty to separate out presence and trace for the purposes of reducing the promise to constituents, we (obviously) do not typically perform this operation.

Opening language up to its silent constituents (the trace) is at deconstruction's core. However, before passing such analysis off as a banal play of words and of little utility to *real* social problems let us consider the implications of "community" under the Youth Criminal Justice Act. Community-based sanctioning and interventions occupy pride of place in the act. The preamble, for example, states that

> WHEREAS members of society share a responsibility to address the developmental challenges and the needs of young persons and to guide them into adulthood; WHEREAS communities, families, parents and others concerned with the development of young persons should, through multi-disciplinary approaches, take reasonable steps to prevent youth crime by addressing its underlying causes, to respond to the needs of young persons, and to provide guidance and support to those at risk of committing crimes. (YCJA, preamble)

Without the insights of deconstruction we are apt to quickly read over the term *community* and be off to the next of the Act's many sections. Calls for community responsibility for youth crime may be laudable. However, given that the very essence of community is exclusionary, perhaps such enthusiasm should be tempered. That is, we cannot have a community—a school, a neighbourhood, a class, a town, or whatever other configuration—without exclusion. Those who belong define themselves in opposition to the excluded. If everyone were included under this or that community rubric, the term *community* would cease to hold meaning. "Community" designates divisions between and among people. Under the YCJA it is the young offenders—their deviance and criminality—who provide impetus for the creation of community in the first instance. For example, Youth Justice Committees, which are made up of community members who hear and adjudicate relatively minor crimes committed by youths, find their meaning and definition in the wrong doings of young people. A crime committed by a young offender brings this community together. Because of his or her contravention, the young person becomes not only the rationale for the formation of community, but,

**trace**

The mark of absence in words that is the necessary condition of thought and experience (Derrida, 1976).

by virtue of the offence, its antithesis. Pavlich (2005) maintains that this is the very essence of community, wherein "communities are identified—implicitly or explicitly—by exclusion." Before proclaiming this a meaningless play of words, we should be reminded of the repulsive consequences that may accrue when exuberance for and devotion to community has spilled over its limits: ethnic wars of annihilation have been waged, genocide has been carried out, and prisons have become overcrowded with the residues of such intolerance (Hogeveen, 2006).

Communities may derive their *raison d'être* in relation to a particularly deviant and troubling other. A string of car thefts or a proliferation of graffiti in a geographical space may inspire previously disorganized citizens to band together against this provocation. "Recent efforts to rid (affluent) neighbourhoods of prostitutes, the use of CCTV on busy city streets, **broken windows policing**, and gated neighbourhoods are poignant examples of community inspired attempts to exclude the 'other' while shoring up a privileged lifestyle. This regulation of the 'other' may contribute to and assist in shoring up the creation of community, but it also holds the insidious possibility of contributing to exclusionary practices which limit, rather than encourage, wider and more inclusive patterns of harmony" (Hogeveen, 2006, 295; see also Pavlich, 2005).

Through the examples of promises and community we can see that deconstructive critique involves "opening up" things up to examine what lies behind and beyond presence. However, there is one word that is not deconstructable: **justice**. In common parlance we use the term *justice* in a variety of ways: we have a justice system; there are Justices of the Peace; Canada boasts a federal Department of Justice; it is used in law and legislation to imply the impartiality of the system (e.g., the Youth Criminal *Justice* Act), and it is even a village in Manitoba (located northwest of Brandon). Vengeance is by far the most commonplace understanding of justice (see Box 16.3). Here *justice* being done means an ethic of punishment that delivers obvious signs of unpleasantness to offenders. We live in an era where war, prison overcrowding, and vigilantism are justified in the name of justice. For example, the U.S. government constructed Osama bin Laden as a moral monster and a lunatic for crimes perpetrated upon the United States. All the while, the civilian and military death toll from the American campaign for "justice" mounts. The cost in dollars and human life are spiralling out of control, while domestic atrocities and oppressions are glossed over by a nation seeking justice.

If these are all instances of "justice," how can Derrida say that it does not exist? It is because Derrida seeks a different kind of justice, one that goes beyond "right, a justice finally removed from the fatality of vengeance" (Derrida, 1994, 21). One of Derrida's most faithful followers, John Caputo (1997), puts the situation this way: "Justice is not a present entity or order, not an existing reality or regime; nor is it even an ideal *eidos* towards which we earthlings down below heave and sigh while contemplating its heavenly form. Justice is the absolutely unforeseeable prospect (a paralyzing paradox) in virtue in which the things that get deconstructed are deconstructed" (Caputo, 1997, 131). For Derrida, then, "justice appears as a promise, beyond law, and is itself incalculable, infinite and undeconstructable" (Pavlich, 2007, 989). It is not a thing or a person that we

**broken windows policing**

Just as houses with broken windows indicate that nobody cares about the neighbourhood, proponents of this policing style feel that tolerating minor misbehaviour will mean that residents will be afraid to use their streets. They feel that police should quickly deal with minor incivilities such as panhandling, vandalism, and other behaviours that contribute to fear of crime. Critics feel this policing style potentially discriminates against the poor.

**justice**

For Derrida, since it is perpetually deferred, justice cannot be defined adequately. It is not contained in or constrained by law. It is infinite. It is "to come."

# FOCUS BOX 12.3

## CRIME PAYS OFF IN CANADA

Consider the assumptions made about "justice" in the following article: What are the sources of the reporter's dissatisfaction with the Canadian criminal justice system? What expectations does she have about justice and in what ways are they not being met? Also, note how she speaks as though her views represent taken-for-granted values that we all share and how she compares us (the "good" law-abiding and deserving) with youth offenders (the "bad," dangerous, and undeserving).

**By Michele Mandel**

Maybe this holiday weekend you're putting in another shift to help pay for your child's college tuition.

Maybe you are that student, worried about how you're going to put the cash together for school and your first apartment.

Or maybe you're a victim of crime, and you can't afford the counselling you so desperately need.

Too bad you're not a teen killer, because then you'd be showered—thanks to the Canadian government—with more than $100,000 a year.

It's called the Intensive Rehabilitative Custody and Supervision program or IRCS and for 24 of this country's worst youth offenders, the little-known federal justice program is akin to hitting the jackpot.

In return for accepting treatment for their mental issues, serious violent offenders can escape adult prison and do easy time instead in a youth facility, like Ontario's Sprucedale, while taxpayers spend $100,375 per inmate for academic courses, counselling, "life skills" and reintegration.

The theory is that these heavily damaged "kids" need intensive help if they are ever to find their way back into society.

What kind of help, you may ask?

Well, there was the $700 piece of wood we purchased for a killer who brutally beat and sexually assaulted 15-year-old Elisha Mercer under the Lorne Bridge in Brantford in 2001. According to a Sprucedale insider, the young murderer was given the lumber to fashion his very own home-made guitar.

"It makes us all want to vomit," says the employee, who doesn't want to be named. "The victims should be getting this money, not them."

When told by the *Sun*, Elisha's mom was outraged to learn what constitutes therapy for the killer of her only child. "It's ridiculous, absolutely ridiculous," Wilma Martin says. "These have been very hard years. My husband and I split up because of what happened, he took off and I was left to pay the mortgage and the bills. I came close to losing my home.

"I could have used $100,000."

Instead, Ottawa last year earmarked $3.4 million for the country's worst of the worst young murderers and rapists with psychological disorders.

In 2004, one of the first accepted into the new program was the 18-year-old Hamilton youth who had killed Jonathan Romero the year before. Romero, 18, had gone to Lime Ridge Mall to buy a Christmas present for his mom. Standing on the sidelines when his friend got involved in a fight, Romero was sucker punched by the youth and after falling to the ground, was savagely punched four more times in the head and neck. He died hours later in hospital.

A judge turned down the Crown's request for a 6½-year adult sentence for manslaughter and instead agreed to just 30 months in custody at Sprucedale. The young offender was deemed eligible for IRCS because—wait for it—he was diagnosed with attention deficit and hyperactivity disorder, post traumatic stress disorder and mood disorder.

If only every kid with ADD could get free one-on-one counselling and government-sponsored perks.

The Hamilton youth was assigned a "life coach" and various IRCS counselling programs. He was released four weeks ago to a six-month

*(continued)*

reintegration period, but according to the Sprucedale worker, none of the expensive rehabilitation seemed to have any impact at all. "He felt no remorse whatsoever for his crime and anyone who worked with him over the last three years will tell you the same thing," he says. "He was a poster child for everything that was wrong with the system."

"Danger to society"

"Do I think he still poses a danger to society? You bet I do. At that summer camp, he didn't learn a thing."

The youth, stung by a previous article slamming easy time at Sprucedale, insists he's a changed man in a letter published in the *Sun*. "Every achievement that I completed here is to the memory of that boy."

According to his former worker, the letter is just another demonstration of how he's learned to talk the talk as well as how to use the IRCS program to his advantage.

Now 20, the Hamilton killer was boasting to everyone that the federal government will now be paying for his college tuition, laptop computer and his living expenses. On his $16,000 IRCS wish list, he also requested a plasma screen TV and new designer clothing. The insider says he doesn't know if those goodies were granted as well.

"All of this stuff," says the angry youth worker, "an average family can't afford and these kids are getting it for murdering other kids? It's unbelievable. The public needs to know."

Oh Canada, why are we such gullible souls?

Source: Michele Mandel. "Crime Pays off in Canada," *Toronto Sun*, July 1, 2007: http://torontosun.com/News/ Columnists/Mandel_Michele/2007/07/01/4304140.html.

can hold up as exemplary or criterion for future generations. To maintain that Canada is a just nation or that we ourselves are just would be to conclude that our work is done. It would be the height of injustice to think that justice exists here in tolerant Canada in the midst of unimaginable suffering of Indigenous people, the tragic abuse of female partners, and the expanding extremes of poverty and wealth—and we could go on (Caputo, 1997). But, you may conclude, the law is just . . . right? On the contrary, there are situations in which the application of law was legal but unjust (e.g., Arar, Menezes). This is not to say that law is unnecessary and that it is wrong in its conception. Only that law can be unjust in its application and in its fundamental opposition to justice.

## Summary

- Critical criminology attempts to draw attention to hidden and overlooked injustices scattered throughout our world. Critical criminology seeks to highlight and genuinely grasp inequalities, discrimination, and suffering.

- Early critical criminology in Canada, inspired by Taylor, Walton, and Young's *The New Criminology*, maintained a focus on how economic power is implicated in the operations of criminal justice. Efforts to create a unified collective among Canadian critical criminologists were, however, cut short by several factors, including the growing diversity of critical criminology.

- Today's critical criminology does not maintain this dedication to a political economic approach to crime. Critique is less and less understood as a form of judgment gauged upon a fixed standard of evaluation and more as a means for disrupting and destabilizing taken-for-granted assumptions about and approaches to crime. The goal is not to prescribe a new social order but rather to create opportunities for unencumbered ideas and practices to arise and take form.

- Foucault has contributed to critical criminology through his work on power. For Foucault, power is not solely repressive—it is also productive. Through the tactics of discipline, surveillance, and governmentality, power shapes individuals so that they are transformed (or transform themselves) into more governable subjects.

- Actuarialism, risk, and the risk society are all terms used to understand the growing fixation on insurance-like evaluations of risk and harm in contemporary criminal justice practices. Through an understanding of the larger social context producing the "risk society," critical criminologists are able to challenge the logic of various risk-management approaches to criminal justice.

- Cultural criminology revives the ethnographic tradition in criminology and directs it toward discovering crime as a lived experience. Cultural criminologists investigate the cultural production of crime and our understandings of crime and thereby question popular notions about crime and criminal justice.

- Bourdieu's "field theory" alerts critical criminologists to the many forms of power that are amassed and the role they play in the domination over and definition of excluded and criminalized classes. Crime, therefore, is understood not only as a consequence of economic domination, but also of symbolic, cultural, and social domination.

- Giorgio Agamben points us to the power of the sovereign to define individuals as being outside of law. Thus built into law is the state of exception; that is, the sovereign's ability to suspend rights and protections. And through this concept criminal law is vividly revealed as a source of exclusion.

- Jacques Derrida's concept of deconstruction provides critical criminologists a tool for evaluating what is hidden or unspoken within social life and, in particular, criminal justice practices. It is a particularly powerful tool for unpacking the meanings hidden in fashionable criminal justice jargon, such as "community," "safety," and "security."

## QUESTIONS FOR CRITICAL THINKING

1. In your view, what does it mean to be "critical"? Does your understanding of criticism align with the practices of critical criminology?

2. Is it enough to criticize, to expose the limits placed on our thinking about crime, or is it incumbent on the critical criminologist to devise a "solution" to the "problem" of crime?

3. Some have criticized critical criminologists for using a complex, academic discourse. In your view, is it the responsibility of scholars to place their thoughts in terms that everyone can understand? Are there ever situations where complex ideas demand complex language?

4. How might a critical criminologist put some of the concepts described in this chapter into practice? For example, imagine that you are the executive director of a not-for-profit agency that advocates for offender rights. How might the theories listed above help guide you in your efforts to secure better treatment for offenders both within prisons and upon release into the community?

5. How does the project of critical criminology differ from the other theories you have learned about in this text?

## NET WORK

Visit the American Society of Criminology Divisions page at **http://www.asc41.com/divisions.htm.** Compare and contrast the description of the Critical Criminology Division to other Divisions of the ASC. What makes it 'critical' in contrast to the other Divisions?

## KEY TERMS

actuarial; pg. 387
attentive gaze; pg. 391
broken windows policing; pg. 400
capital; pg. 392
dangerous knowledge; pg. 391
deconstruction; pg. 398
discipline; pg. 384
field; pg. 392
governmentality; pg. 384
habitus; pg. 392
justice; pg. 400

micro-powers; pg. 384
naked life; pg. 395
negative *social* capital; pg. 393
negative *symbolic* capital; pg. 393
power; pg. 384
risk; pg. 387
risk society; pg. 388
sovereign; pg. 395
state of exception; pg. 395
surveillance; pg. 384
trace; pg. 399

## BIBLIOGRAPHY

Andrews, D. A., and J. Bonta. (1998). *The Psychology of Criminal Conduct.* (2nd ed.). Cincinnati, OH: Anderson Publishing Co.

Balke, Friedrich. (2005). "Derrida and Foucault on Sovereignty." *German Law Journal* 6(1): 71–85.

Bauman, Zymunt. (2000). *Liquid Modernity.* Cambridge: Cambridge University Press.

Beck, Ulrich. (1992). "From Industrial to Risk Society: Questions of Survival, Social Structure and Ecological Enlightenment." *Theory, Culture, and Society* 9:97–123.

Bosworth, Mary. (2004). "Gender, Risk and Recidivism." *Criminology & Public Policy* 3(2): 181–84.

Bourdieu, Pierre. (1984). *Distinction: A Social Critique of the Judgement of Taste.* Cambridge, MA: Harvard University Press.

———. (1986). "The Forms of Capital." In John Richardson (ed.), *Handbook of Theory and Research for the Sociology of Education* (pp. 241–58). New York: Greenwood Press.

———. (1990a). *The Logic of Practice*. Cambridge, MA: Polity Press.

———. (1990b). *In Other Words: Essays Toward a Reflexive Sociology.* Stanford, CA: Stanford University Press.

———. (1991). *Language and Symbolic Power*. Cambridge, MA: Harvard University Press.

———. (1992). *An Invitation to Reflexive Sociology*. Chicago: University of Chicago Press.

Brubaker, Rogers. (1985). "Rethinking Classical Theory: The Sociological Vision of Pierre Bourdieu." *Theory and Society* 14:745–75.

Caputo, John. (1997). *Deconstruction in a Nutshell: A Conversation with Jacques Derrida*. New York: Fordham.

Chambliss, William. (1969). "The Law of Vagrancy." In William Chambliss (ed.), *Crime and the Legal Process* (pp. 51–63). New York: McGraw-Hill.

Dean, Mitchell. (1999). *Governmentality: Power and Rule in Modern Society*. London: Sage.

Dekeseredy, Walter, and Brian D. MacLean. (1993). "Critical Criminological Pedagogy in Canada: Strengths, Limitations, and Recommendations for Improvements." *Journal of Criminal Justice Education* 4:361–76.

Derrida, Jacques. (1976). *Of Grammatology*. Trans. Gayatri Chakravorty Spivak. Baltimore: Johns Hopkins University Press.

———. (1981). *Positions*. Chicago: University of Chicago Press.

———. (1987). "Some Questions and Responses." In N. Fabb (ed.), *The Linguistics of Writing: Arguments between Language and Literature*. Manchester: Manchester University Press.

———. (1994). *Specters of Marx: The State of the Debt, the Work of Mourning and the New International*. London: Routledge.

———. (2005). *Rogues: Two Essays on Reason*. Stanford: Stanford University Press.

DiMaggio, Paul. (1979). "Review Essay: On Pierre Bourdieu." *American Journal of Sociology* 84:1460–474.

Ek, Richard. (2006). "Giorgio Agamben and the Spatialities of the Camp." *Geografiska Annaler: Series B, Human Geography* 88(4):363–86.

Ericson, Richard, and Kevin Haggerty. (1997). *Policing the Risk Society*. Toronto: University of Toronto Press.

Ewald, Francois. (1991). "Insurance and Risk." In Graham Burchell, Colin Gordon, and Peter Miller (eds.), *The Foucault Effect: Studies in Governmentality*. Chicago: University of Chicago Press.

Feeley, Malcolm, and Jonathan Simon. (1994). "Actuarial Justice: The Emerging Criminal Law." In David Nelken (ed.), *The Futures of Criminology*. New York: Sage.

Ferrell, Jeff. (1998). "Criminological Verstehen." In Jeff Ferrell and Mark Hamm (eds.), *Ethnography at the Edge*. Boston: Northeastern University Press.

———. (2004). "Boredom, Crime and Criminology." *Theoretical Criminology* 8(3): 287–302.

Foucault, Michel. (1979). *The History of Sexuality,* Vol. 1. New York: Vintage.

———. (1980). *Power/Knowledge: Selected Interviews and Other Writings*. New York: Pantheon.

———. (1982). "The Subject and Power." In Hubert Dreyfus and Paul Rabinow (eds.), *Michel Foucault: Beyond Structuralism and Hermeneutics*. Chicago: University of Chicago Press.

———. (1991). "Governmentality." In Graham Burchell, Colin Gordon, and Peter Miller (eds.), *The Foucault Effect: Studies in Governmentality*. Chicago: University of Chicago Press.

——. (1997). *The Essential Works, 1954–1985*, Vol. 1, Ethics, Subjectivity and Truth. New York: The New Press.

Garland, David. (1997). "Governmentality and the Problem of Crime: Foucault, Criminology, Sociology." *Theoretical Criminology* 1(2):173–214.

Hannah-Moffat, Kelly, and Paula Maurutto. (2003). *Youth Risk/Need Assessment: An Overview of Issues and Practices*. Ottawa: Department of Justice. Available at http://www.justice.gc.ca/en/ps/rs/rep/2003/rr03yj-4/rr03yj-4.html.

Hannah-Moffat, Kelly, and Margaret Shaw. (2001). *Taking Risks: Incorporating Gender and Culture into the Classification and Assessment of Federally Sentenced Women in Canada*. Ottawa: Status of Women.

Hayward, Keith J., and Jock Young. (2004). "Cultural Criminology: Some Notes on the Script." *Theoretical Criminology* 8(3):259–73.

Hogeveen, Bryan. (2006). "Memoir of a/the Blind." *Punishment and Society* 8(4):469–76.

Hogeveen, Bryan, and Andrew Woolford. (2006). "Critical Criminology and Possibility in the Neoliberal Ethos." *Canadian Journal of Criminology and Criminal Justice* 48(5): 681–702.

Katz, Jack. (1988). *Seductions of Crime: Moral and Sensual Attractions in Doing Crime*. New York: Basic Books.

Lippert, Randy, and James Williams. (2006). "Governing on the Margins: Exploring the Contributions of Governmentality Studies to Critical Criminology in Canada." *Canadian Journal of Criminology and Criminal Justice* 48(5):703–19.

Minaker, Joanne, and Bryan Hogeveen. (2008). *Youth, Crime and Society: Critical Reflections*. Toronto: Pearson.

Minca, Claudio. (2006). "Giorgio Agamben and the New Biopolitical Nomos." *Geografiska Annaler: Series B, Human Geography* 88(4):387–403.

Morrison, Wayne. (2007). *Criminology and the New World Order*. London: Glasshouse.

O'Connor, D. (2006). *Report of the Events Relating to Maher Arar: Analysis and Recommendations of the Commission of Inquiry in the Actions of Canadian Officials in Relation to Maher Arar*. Ottawa: Queen's Printer.

O'Malley Pat. (1992). "Risk, Power and Crime Prevention." *Economy and Society* 21: 252–75

——. (1996). "Risk and Responsibility." In Andrew Barry, Thomas Osbourne, and Nikoas Rose (eds.), *Foucault and Political Reason: Liberalism, Neoliberalism and Rationalities of Government*. Chicago: University of Chicago Press.

O'Neill, Maggie. (2004). "Crime, Culture, and Visual Methodologies: Ethno-Mimesis as Performative Praxis." In Jeff Ferrell, Keith Hayward, Wayne Morrison, and Mike Presdee (eds.), *Cultural Criminology Unleashed*. London: Glasshouse.

O'Reilly-Fleming, Thomas (ed.). (1985). *The New Criminologies in Canada: State, Crime and Control*. Toronto: Oxford University Press.

Pavlich, George. (1999). "Criticism and Criminology: In Search of Legitimacy." *Theoretical Criminology* 3(1):29–51.

——. (2000). *Critique and Radical Discourses on Crime*. Aldershot: Ashgate.

——. (2005). *Governing Paradoxes of Restorative Justice*. London: Glasshouse Press.

——. (2007). "Deconstruction." *Blackwell Encyclopedia of Sociology*. London: Blackwell.

Raban, Jonathon. (1974). *The Soft City*. London: Hamilton.

Ratner, R. S. (1971). "Criminology in Canada: Conflicting Objectives." Unpublished Manuscript.

————. (1984). "Inside the Liberal Boot: The Criminological Enterprise in Canada." *Studies in Political Economy* 13:145–64.

————. (1989). "Critical Criminology—A Splendid Oxymoron." *Journal of Human Justice* 1:3–8.

Schmitt, Carl. (1985). *Political Theology: Four Chapters on the Concept of Sovereignty.* Chicago: University of Chicago Press.

Simon, Jonathan. (1988). "The Ideological Effects of Actuarial Practices." *Law and Society Review* 22(4):772–800.

Taylor, Ian, Paul Walton, and Jock Young. (1973). *The New Criminology: For a Social Theory of Deviance.* London: Routledge and Kegan Paul.

van Swaaningen, Rene. (1997). *Critical Criminology: Visions from Europe.* London: Sage.

Wacquant, Loïc. (1998). "Negative Social Capital: State Breakdown and Social Destitution in America's Urban Core." *The Netherlands Journal of the Built Environment* 13(1): 25–40.

————. (2000). "The New 'Peculiar Institution:' On the Prison as Surrogate Ghetto." *Theoretical Criminology* 4(3):377–89.

————. (2001). "Deadly Symbiosis: When Ghetto and Prison Meet and Mesh." *Punishment & Society* 3(1):95–134.

Young, Jock. (1979). "Left Idealism, Reformism and Beyond: From New Criminology to Marxism." In B. Fine, R. Kinsey, J. Lea, S. Picciotto, and J. Young (eds.), *Capitalism and the Rule of Law* (pp. 11–28). London: Hutchinson.

————. (1998). "From Inclusive to Exclusive Society: Nightmares in the European Dream." In Vincent Riggiero, N. South, and Ian Taylor (eds.), *The New European Criminology: Crime and Social Order in Europe.* London: Routledge.

# 13 Interactionist Theories

## Robert A. Stebbins

**UNIVERSITY OF CALGARY**

Strain and conflict theories deal with causes of crime at the level of social structure. Strain theorists relate crime to variables such as cultural goals and the access to opportunities provided by society. For conflict theorists, cleavages between different groups in society and power relationships among these groups are critical in explaining criminality. **Interactionist theories**, alternatively, turn our attention to the smaller details of social life. They consider crime to be a consequence of interpersonal relationships and of the meaning of those relationships.

A central concept in interactionist theories of crime is the **deviant career**, or the passage of an individual through the stages of one or more related deviant identities. This idea is at the heart of labelling theory, which explains how the social response to initial, tentative acts of deviance can move a person toward a deviant identity and a deviant career. The other important interactionist theory discussed in this chapter—differential association—sets out how people learn to be criminals through interaction with other criminals and how they acquire a criminal identity.

## Learning Objectives

After reading this chapter, you should be able to

- Describe primary and secondary deviation and explain how primary deviation leads to secondary deviation.
- Understand the process of drift among juvenile delinquents.
- Explain how moral entrepreneurs create and enforce the law.
- Discuss the various contingencies that criminals encounter in their deviant careers.
- Understand how people are socialized into a life of crime.
- Outline the strengths and limitations of interactionist theories of deviance.

**symbolic interactionism**
A sociological perspective that focuses on the dynamics of how people interpret social situations and negotiate the meaning of these situations with others. It differs from more structurally focused perspectives in seeing individuals as actively creating the social world rather than just acting within the constraints of culture and social structure.

Interactionist theory in criminology centres on the interchanges people have with one another and on the meanings of these interchanges in the past, present, and future. Blumer (1986) notes that **symbolic interactionism**, the broader theory from which the interactionist theories of crime are derived, rests on three premises. First, people act toward the human and nonhuman objects in their lives according to the meanings those objects have for them. Second, these meanings emerge from interactions among people. Third, the meanings of objects learned in this manner are applied and occasionally modified as individuals interpret how objects and their meanings fit particular social situations, the people in them, and their reasons for being there.

Much of this chapter is about criminal interactions, meanings, interpretations, and situations. Before turning to these processes, however, let us set the stage for discussion with a brief illustration of the three premises operating on the scene of a crime. The following interview with Allen, about 20 years old, shows how the meaning of a situation changed through social interaction with other people present in an all-night drugstore:

> From what I understand from them, they didn't go in there with the intent to rob or beat anybody up or anything. I think they only really wanted to buy some gum and cigarettes, but by being drunk, they was talking pretty tough, and so the lady behind the counter automatically got scared. . . . The druggist . . . got a little pushy or ordered them out of the store, and by them being all fired up, naturally the next thing they did was jump on him.
>
> So now what do you have? You've got a drugstore. You've got a scared lady in the corner somewhere with her hands over her face. You've got a beat-up druggist laying on the floor. You've got three dudes that came in for chewing gum and cigarettes, but now they got two cash registers. So what do they do? They take the cash. Wasn't nothing to stop them, and it was there. Why would they leave it? They're thieves anyway and supposed to be hustlers. . . . There wasn't nothing to stop them, so they just took the money. (Katz, 1990)

## The Deviant Career

Interactionism centres chiefly on what happens to criminals once their deviant activities commence. Interactionists have observed, for example, that some groups or individuals have enough power to force the label of deviant on less powerful groups or individuals. The **labelling** process, however, is not always accurate. It is not even always fair. Some deviants escape public detection of their behaviour. Some who have not deviated are nonetheless labelled as having done so, despite their protests to the contrary. The application of the deviant label is sometimes subject to considerable negotiation between possibly deviant people and those in a position to label them deviant.

Thus, interactionist theory in criminology helps explain the establishment of moral rules, their application through labelling, and the long-term consequences of these two processes for deviants and for society. In interactionist theory, labelling and its consequences are viewed as unfolding within the deviant career.

A **career**, whether in deviance or a legitimate occupation, is the passage of an individual through recognized stages in one or more related identities. Careers are further composed of the adjustment to, and interpretations of, the contingencies and turning points encountered at each stage. For example, Short (1990) notes that careers in youth crime are likely to be prolonged after reaching

**labelling**

According to labelling theory, deviance is not a quality of the act but of the label that others attach to it. This raises the question of who applies the label and who is labelled. The application of a label and the response of others to the label may result in a person becoming committed to a deviant identity.

**career**

In common use, this refers to the sequence of stages through which people in a particular occupational sector move during the course of their employment. It has also been applied to the various stages of personal involvement with criminal activity.

certain turning points. One is an early interest in delinquent activities; another is an interest in drugs. The inability to find legitimate employment, a career contingency, also contributes to continued criminality. Type of offence, however, has been found to be unrelated to length of careers in youth crime, even to the rate at which it is perpetrated. During the careers of young offenders and other deviants, there is a sense of continuity. This sense is fostered by the perception of increasing opportunities, sophistication, and perhaps recognition among one's associates for skill in, or at least commitment to, the special endeavour.

## Primary Deviation

**primary deviation**

Occurs when an individual commits deviant acts but fails adopt a primary self-identity as a deviant.

**secondary deviation**

Occurs when an individual accepts the label of deviant. The result is adoption of a deviant self-identity that confirms and stabilizes the deviant lifestyle.

Lemert (1972) contributed two important concepts to the study of deviant careers: **primary deviation** and **secondary deviation**. Primary deviation produces little change in everyday routine or lifestyle. In general, this happens when the individual engages in deviance infrequently, has few compunctions about it, and encounters few practical problems when doing it. A person who occasionally smokes marijuana supplied by someone else exemplifies primary deviation.

Primary deviation occurs in the early stages of the deviant career, between the first deviant act and some indefinite point at which deviance becomes a way of life. Subsequently, at a still more advanced stage, secondary deviation (discussed later) sets in. According to Matza (2010), one precondition of deviance is a willingness to engage in it. That is, the individual must have an affinity—innate or acquired—for the intended act (for example, theft, homicide, drug use). The affinity helps him or her choose among existing options. By way of illustration, imagine someone who believes the rich cheat others to get their money. This person has an affinity for stealing from the rich. That affinity could lead the individual into crimes against the rich when faced with such unpleasant alternatives as poverty, unemployment, or tedious manual labour.

**drift**

A psychological state of weak normative attachment to either deviant or conventional ways.

Behind the willingness to engage in deviance lies a weak commitment to conventional norms and identities. Few young people have a strong value commitment to deviant norms and identities; instead, they **drift** between the world of respectability and that of deviance. They are "neither compelled to deeds nor freely choosing them; neither different in any simple or fundamental sense from the law abiding, nor the same; conforming to certain traditions in . . . life while partially unreceptive to other more conventional traditions" (Matza, 1990).

Matza was writing about American males who were young offenders. He found these youths firmly attached to certain marginal, masculine, *subterranean traditions* or ways of life. They found satisfaction in drinking, smoking, renouncing work, being tough, and enjoying the hedonistic pleasures of "real" men. Matza's subjects saw themselves as grown and mature, but their behaviour was hardly a true picture of adult life in general in the United States.

Lemert explains how this peculiar orientation can set one adrift toward deviance:

> While some fortunate individuals by insightful endowment or by virtue of the stabilizing nature of their situation can foresee more distant social consequences of their actions and behave accordingly, not so for most people. Much human behaviour is situationally oriented and geared to meeting the many and shifting claims which others make

upon them. The loose structuring and swiftly changing facade and content of modern social situations frequently make it difficult to decide which means will insure the ends sought. Often choice is a compromise between what is sought and what can be sought. . . . All this makes me believe that most people drift into deviance by specific actions rather than by informed choices of social roles and statuses. (Lemert, 1972)

Social control has failed for young offenders and young adults. This failure occurs because it is important for deviant individuals to enjoy good standing with their friends in the group. Good standing is attained by honouring and practising the marginal, or subterranean, traditions that Matza describes. The quest for honour among peers helps explain how entire groups of youth can drift toward deviance (Hirschi, 2001)

It appears that much, if not all, of this is applicable to Canada. For instance, a comparative study conducted in California and Alberta shows that ties to peers are important in the sample of delinquent youth, while being in touch with home and school are valued much less (Linden and Fillmore, 1981).

The young offender subculture (see Chapter 11) is composed of many elements, one of the most important being the **moral rhetorics** (Schwendinger and Schwendinger, 1985) used to justify deviant behaviour. Each rhetoric consists of a set of largely taken-for-granted guiding principles, sometimes logically inconsistent, and always selectively applied according to the social situations in which youths find themselves. The rhetoric of *egoism* is most often used by those who still feel guilty about their deviant acts. These are typically early offenders, who have learned various ways to neutralize the **stigma** that comes with their behaviour, such as claiming they steal in response to the greed and immorality of shopkeepers whose prices are unfair. Later young offenders are more likely to use the *instrumental* rhetoric to justify their acts. Here they stress the cunning and power they bring to bear against people who are otherwise more powerful and uncontrollable. Fraud, deceit, and violence are used to pursue deviant aims whenever they appear to pay off, whenever they can benefit from a weak moment in the lives of such people. The main point here is that young offenders, like people in many other walks of life, justify what they do. Though the law-abiding world sees it otherwise, offenders have their ways of defending their deviant acts as morally right.

During the primary deviation stages of their deviant career, young offenders and young adults drift, in part, because they lack value commitment to either conventional or deviant values. Value commitment is an attitude toward an identity, an attitude that develops when a person gains exceptional rewards from assuming that identity (Stebbins, 1970). Young men and women drifting between criminal and respectable pursuits have found few, if any, enduring benefits in either type of activity. Nonetheless, this pattern begins to change with more contact with agents of social control.

## Agents of Social Control

Those members of society who help check deviant behaviour are known as agents of social control. They include the police, judges, lawmakers, prison personnel, probation and parole officers, and ordinary citizens with an active

**moral rhetoric**

In the study of crime, this is the set of claims and assertions deviants make to justify their deviant behaviour. The moral rhetoric of a group is an important component of socialization into a deviant identity.

**stigma**

As used by Erving Goffman (1922–1982), a personal characteristic that is negatively evaluated by others and thus distorts and discredits the public identity of the individual. For example, a prison record may become a stigmatized attribute. The stigma may lead to the adoption of a self-identity that incorporates the negative social evaluation.

**moral entrepreneur**

Someone who defines new rules and laws or who advocates stricter enforcement of existing laws. Often such entrepreneurs have a financial or organizational interest in particular definitions or applications of law.

interest in maintaining law and order as they define it. Groups of ordinary citizens and lawmakers sometimes join hands as **moral entrepreneurs**:

> Rules are the products of someone's initiative, and we can think of the people who exhibit such enterprise as *moral entrepreneurs*. Two related species—rule creators and rule enforcers—will occupy our attention. (Becker, 1963)

The prototype of the rule creator, Becker observes, is the crusading reformer, whose dissatisfaction with existing rules is acute and who, therefore, campaigns for legal change (adding new laws or procedures and rescinding old ones) and, sometimes, for attitudinal change intended to lead to "proper" behaviour. Canadian society is replete with crusades, both past and present, such as those which seek to eliminate drug abuse, discourage use of alcohol, reduce availability of pornography, and stop exploitation of women in the workplace. Moral entrepreneurs are currently working to curb electronic crime (for a further example, see Box 13.1).

To conduct an effective crusade, moral entrepreneurs must construct an argument capable of convincing the community of a deep and genuine internal threat. This process of collective definition (Hewitt and Hall, 1973; Spector and Kitsuse, 2000) centres largely on the "claims-making activities" of entrepreneurs. They

1. assert existence of a particular condition, situation, or state of affairs in which human action is implicated as a cause;
2. define the asserted condition as offensive, harmful, undesirable, or otherwise problematic to the society but nonetheless amenable to correction by humans; and,
3. stimulate public scrutiny of the condition as the claims makers see it.

The claims are explained by quasi-theories that, unlike scientific theories, are selectively constructed to square with the claims makers' views, seldom responsive to **empirical evidence**, and contain simple explanations of complex, ill-defined problems.

**empirical evidence**

Evidence as observed through the senses; it can be seen, touched, heard, smelled, tasted, and, to some extent, measured. This is the only form of scientifically acceptable evidence.

Moral entrepreneurs also enforce legislated rules, applying them to people who misbehave. Such rules provide enforcers (police, security personnel) with jobs and justifications for them. Since the enforcers want to keep their jobs, they are eager to demonstrate that enforcement is effective. Yet they also realize there are more infractions than they can possibly prevent or respond to. Therefore, they must establish priorities. Thus,

> whether a person who commits a deviant act is in fact labelled a deviant depends on many things extraneous to his actual behaviour: whether the enforcement official feels that at this time he must make some show of doing his job in order to justify his position, whether the misbehaver shows proper deference to the enforcer, whether the "fix" has been put in, and where the kind of act he has committed stands on the enforcer's list of priorities. (Becker, 1963)

# FOCUS BOX 13.1

## CRACKING DOWN ON CRIME: COULD THIS MORAL ENTREPRENEURSHIP HAPPEN IN CANADA?

Moral entrepreneurs often seek to increase the penalties for particular offences. For example, Mothers Against Drunk Driving (MADD) has lobbied very effectively to force the justice system to treat drinking and driving more seriously. Whereas most people would probably support MADD's efforts, other initiatives to make laws tougher have been controversial. The most dramatic effort to increase penalties came in California with passage of a tough "three strikes you're out" law in 1994. It is far harsher than legislation in many other states or in Canada's dangerous offender legislation. The severity of this law can be traced to the powerful moral entrepreneurs responsible for its passage.

The events leading to the three strikes law began with the 1992 murder of Kimber Reynolds by a career criminal who was attempting to rob her (Vitiello, 1997). Her father, Mike Reynolds, worked with a judge in drafting the three strikes legislation and then lobbied the legislature to adopt it. Although the Justice Committee initially defeated the bill, the kidnapping and murder in 1993 of 12-year-old Polly Klaas by a repeat offender galvanized public support for it. After thousands of Californians signed an initiative supporting his proposal, Mr. Reynolds returned to the legislature and succeeded in getting the original bill passed with no modification. The legislation provides for a mandatory sentence of 25 years to life for a third felony conviction, with a doubled sentence for those with a second felony conviction.

The consequences of the three strikes legislation can now be seen. In 2010, approximately 8,500 offenders were serving time under the three strikes law. It costs billions of dollars to keep these people in prison, and these costs will escalate as the first three strikes offenders will not be released until 2019. By 2026, it is estimated that 30 000 three strikes offenders—a number that is close to the size of Canada's entire prison population—will be serving sentences of 25 years to life in California (King and Mauer, 2001).

As the following *Globe and Mail* editorial shows, many three strikes offenders have been sentenced for very minor offences:

Some convicted felons have the book thrown at them. Leandro Andrade had an entire library thrown at him. He was sentenced to life in prison with no hope of parole for 50 years for the crime of trying to steal several videotapes worth a total of $153.54 (U.S.) from two different stores in California.

This week, the U.S. Supreme Court upheld the sentence in a 5–4 decision. It reversed the ruling of the U.S. Court of Appeals for the Ninth Circuit, which had found the sentence unconstitutional because it amounted to "cruel and unusual punishment" under the Eighth Amendment of the U.S. Constitution.

You might suspect there is more to the story than that, and you would be right. The majority on the Supreme Court, including Chief Justice William Rehnquist, Justice Sandra Day O'Connor and Justice Clarence Thomas, found ways, inch by tenuous inch, to justify a sentence that is on the face of it absurd, because the judges deferred to California's right to adopt and enforce its "Three Strikes and You're Out" law.

The law says that someone convicted of a felony, who has previously committed two serious felonies, must automatically receive a sentence of 25 years to life. . . . To an extent, the law is similar to the Canadian law that permits serial criminals to be declared dangerous offenders, and held indefinitely in prison, if they pose a foreseeably high risk to society. The idea of Canada's rule is to protect the public by locking up predictably

*(continued)*

dangerous recidivists, and if that were the sole effect of the California law, few would object to it.

In practice, the law can run amok. In 1995, Mr. Andrade was detained while leaving a Kmart store with five videotapes. A few days later, he tried to steal four tapes from another Kmart. He had previously been in and out of prison for theft and burglary. He said he took the videos to pay for his heroin habit. His state probation officer wrote: "He says when he gets out of jail or prison he always does something stupid."

So, not an ideal citizen. But not an obvious candidate for 50 years in prison without hope of parole.

Enter the three-strikes law. The prosecutor decided to treat the tape thefts as felonies rather than misdemeanours. The jury found that his conviction on three counts of first-degree burglary in 1982 qualified as "serious felonies" under the law. He received 25 years to life for each of the two tape thefts.

On Wednesday, the Supreme Court ordered him to serve the time. After all, it said, it's not as though he has no chance of parole; he will be eligible after 50 years.

"The gross disproportionality principle reserves a constitutional violation for only the extraordinary case. . . ."

Justice David Souter, writing for his colleagues in the minority, had no problem with higher penalties for recidivists. However, he said, Mr. Andrade was a clear victim under the Eighth Amendment.

For a start, he received twice the sentence of a man who stole three golf clubs, though Mr. Andrade's offence was less serious and his criminal record less grave. "Andrade did not somehow become twice as dangerous to society when he stole the second handful of videotapes." And the judge wasn't impressed by the majority's note that Mr. Andrade will, after all, qualify for parole after 50 years—when he will be 87, if he lives that long.

"If Andrade's sentence is not grossly disproportionate," Judge Souter wrote, "the principle has no meaning."

---

Sources: Editorial. (2003). "Where Shoplifting Means Life in Prison." *Globe and Mail*, March 7, p. A14; Michael Vitiello. (1997). "Three Strikes: Can We Return to Rationality?" *Journal of Criminal Law and Criminology* 87 (Winter): 395–482; Ryan S. King and Marc Mauer. (2001). *Aging Behind Bars: "Three Strikes" Seven Years Later*. Washington: The Sentencing Project.

**ethnic group**

A group of individuals having a common, distinctive subculture. Ethnic group differ from races by implying that values, norms, behaviour, and language, not necessarily physical appearance, are important distinguishing characteristics.

It is no accident, then, that the least influential members of society (for example, the poor or certain **ethnic groups**) are often caught in the web of social control and labelled deviant out of proportion to their numbers. In other words, deviance is, in part, created by people in society. Moral entrepreneurs make certain laws, the infraction of which constitutes deviance. Moral entrepreneurs also apply these laws to particular people, labelling them as some kind of deviant. As Becker (1963) points out: "Deviance is not a quality of the act. . . . The deviant is one to whom that label has successfully been applied; deviant behaviour is behaviour that people so label."

But rules are applied to some people and not to others; application is sometimes biased. Hence, some people remain at large as secret, or potentially identifiable, deviants. Others go through life falsely accused of antisocial acts. To discover why only certain people are labelled deviant, labelling theorists also study those who make the laws that deviants violate and how those laws are applied.

Those publicly labelled "deviant" generally face some sort of community or societal reaction to their misdeeds (Lemert, 1951). Depending on the nature of the deviance, the deviant may experience one or more of the following: imprisonment, ostracism, fines, torture, surveillance, and ridicule. All labelled deviants soon learn they must cope with stigma.

A *stigma* is a black mark, or disgrace, associated with a deviant identity. It is part of the societal reaction, since it is a collective construction by agents of social control and ordinary members of the community of the supposed nature of the unlawful act and the person perpetrating it. As Goffman (1986) and Link and Phelan (2001) note, the collective image of stigma is constructed from social, physical, or psychological attributes the deviant is believed to possess. Here imputed possession of the attributes is far more important than actual possession.

Watson (1984) and Wolf (1991) found, after years of participation observation of outlaw motorcycle gangs, that members had a mentality and background noticeably different from that imputed to them by the general public. They were not especially hostile to most social institutions, including government, education, and the family. Most members had finished high school and had occasionally held jobs. Some had gone to college, some were military veterans. Nearly every member had been married at least once. They were, to be sure, not particularly successful in these areas of life, accounting thus for their tendency to live for the moment. And, although they were basically not violent men, they thought it important to be seen as "manly" in the most traditional sense of the term.

## Secondary Deviation

The existence of moral rules, societal reactions, and stigma that occurs when these rules are believed to have been violated sets the stage for secondary deviation. Deviation becomes secondary when deviants see that their behaviour substantially modifies their ways of living. A strong desire to deviate, or a feeling of extreme guilt, can foster this redefinition of one's deviant activities. But being accused of deviance is typically the most influential factor behind the redefinition. Being labelled by the authorities as a murderer, rapist, prostitute, or cheque forger and being sanctioned for such behaviour forces the deviant to change drastically his or her lifestyle. As Lemert (1972) puts it, "This secondary deviant . . . is a person whose life and identity are organized around the facts of deviance."

What does a lifestyle of secondary deviation actually consist of? Stebbins (1997) defines lifestyle as

> a distinctive set of shared patterns of tangible behaviour that is organized around a set of coherent interests or social conditions or both, that is explained and justified by a set of related values, attitudes, and orientations and that, under certain conditions, becomes the basis for a separate, common social identity for its participants.

For example, drug addicts regularly buy or produce their drugs, habitually follow certain practices designed to prevent discovery by the authorities, and routinely consume the illicit substance thus acquired. Some addicts, prostitutes

**FIGURE 13.1    Relationship of Primary Deviance, Societal Reaction, and Secondary Deviance**

among them, justify this lifestyle as an escape from intolerable working conditions. The identity of addict is pejorative, however, as the label "junky" clearly indicates. The relationship of primary deviance, societal reaction, and secondary deviance is portrayed in Figure 13.1.

Among the factors leading to secondary deviation is the tendency of society to treat someone's criminality as a **master status** (Becker, 1963). This status overrides all other statuses in perceived importance. Whatever laudable achievements the deviant might have, such as a good job or a successful marriage, this person is primarily judged in the community by the fact of deviance (see Box 13.2).

Lack, or a perceived low probability, of success in attaining respectability among non-deviants may lead to interaction with other deviants. Here we consider a special aspect of this sort of interaction that takes place between the labelled deviant and the organized deviant group. There are several characteristics of this type of group life that stimulate or maintain such behaviour. These characteristics are effective partly because the wider community has rejected the deviant.

As Becker (1963) observed, individuals who gain entrance to a deviant group often learn from the group how to cope with the problems associated with their deviance. This makes being a deviant easier. Furthermore, the deviant acquires rationalizations for his or her values, attitudes, and behaviour, which come to full bloom in the organized group. While these rationalizations vary greatly, note that the very existence of rationalizations seems to point to the fact that some deviants feel a need to deal with certain conventional attitudes and values they have also internalized.

Prus and Sharper (1991) quote one of their respondents, who was explaining how he developed the callous attitude prized by professional card hustlers:

> When I first got involved in hustling, my attitudes were less calloused [*sic*]. I might be at a stag of some sort and say some fellow is losing a little money. Through the course of the evening, talking back and forth, you find out that maybe he just got married, or that he has some kids and here he's writing cheques and I would slow down. If you pull something like this with a crew [of hustlers], the other guys will want to know what the hell you are doing! They're waiting for you to take him, and you're saying, "Well gee, the guy doesn't have much money." You would get the worst tongue lashing! The position they take is that "You can't have feelings on the road." And it's true, if you start saying to yourself, "Well, maybe I better not beat this guy or that guy," you would soon be out of business or at least you would really cut down on your profits."

**master status**

A status overriding all others in perceived importance. Whatever other personal or social qualities individuals possess, they are judged primarily by this one attribute. *Criminal* exemplifies a master status that influences the community's identification of an individual.

# FOCUS BOX 13.2

## THE MASTER STATUS OF AN INDIAN MENTAL PATIENT

### Stigma In Everyday Life

During my first incarceration, they labelled me "schizophrenic" and "psychopathic." I was forced to wear "baby dolls"—the kind many prisoners wear. They also gave me insulin shock and electroshock. In Selkirk, I refused to conform to what the white majority staff wanted. The attendants responded by ridiculing me. They'd say things like, "Indians are all alike." I finally exploded and tried to fight back. I paid the price.

To get back at me, the staff gave me the cold wet pack treatment. They tied me up like a mummy, held my nose while they poured water down my throat so I couldn't swallow. They'd ask me if I'd had enough, and when I said no, they'd just keep me in the pack. I was in the pack for an hour or an hour-and-a-half for many days. Then they put me in a warm pack. Why did they use the pack on me? "Indians are violent."

I still refused to co-operate. Whenever they asked me to do something, I said, "No, I don't want to." On the ward, there was no such thing as "I don't want to." They continued to ridicule me. "We looked after you before the Indians did," they sometimes told me. At this point, I knew I wasn't welcome in white society. I stood alone.

Sometimes the guards beat me when I refused to cooperate. . . .

Then they gave me twelve or more shock treatments. When I asked them why, they told me I had a "schizophrenic complex" or "schizophrenic tendencies." But I knew I wasn't "schizophrenic" and never was. They also gave me shock to forget: "We'll give him shock treatment so he'll forget he's an Indian."

Source: Lionel Vermette. "The 33 years of the Lost Indian Walk." In Bonnie Burstow and Don Weitz (eds.), *Shrink Resistant: The Struggle against Psychiatry in Canada* (pp. 117–120). Vancouver: New Star Books.

Because group forces operate to maintain and even promote deviance, it should not be assumed, as Goffman (1986) apparently does, that full-fledged deviants are always members of groups. There are those who reject the label of deviant during certain phases of their career, although they may be forced into that status. Some of these individuals spend part of their career trying to re-enter conventional life, often without success. Yet the fact that they refuse to identify themselves as deviant leads them to avoid others labelled thus (for example, shoplifters and embezzlers). There are, moreover, some forms of deviant behaviour that, whatever the reason, are enacted alone, as in rape and some cheque forging. It is probably true, nevertheless, that deviance has collective support in most instances.

The amount and kinds of interaction that take place between individuals suspected of deviant behaviour and agents of social control are extremely important for the future course of their deviant careers. In fact, the interaction that takes place here constitutes a major set of deviant career contingencies. A **career contingency** is an unintended event, process, or situation that occurs by chance; that is, it lies beyond the control of the individual pursuing the career. Career contingencies emanate from changes in the deviant's environment or personal circumstances or both. Movement through the career is affected by the contingencies the deviant meets along the way.

**career contingency**

An unintended event, process, or situation that occurs by chance, beyond the control of the person pursuing the career.

Cohen (1965) has presented this process most clearly: Alter (the agents of social control) responds to the action of ego (the deviant). Ego, in turn, responds to alter's reaction. Alter then responds to his perception of ego's reaction to him; and so forth. The result is that ego's opportunity structure is in some way modified, permitting either more or fewer legitimate or illegitimate opportunities.

When opportunities for a deviant career are expanding, the steady growing apart of the deviant and the control agents spawns open conflict. Some proportion of these encounters lead in the opposite direction, however, resulting in some kind of accommodation and a decrease in the opportunities for a deviant career (West, 1980).

This process of agent–deviant interaction is illustrated in the circumstances encountered by one of the respondents interviewed by Stebbins in a rare study of Canadian nonprofessional criminals:

> The respondent arrived in Toronto shortly after being released from prison in New Brunswick, only to be stopped while walking on a main street by two policemen in a prowl car. He was apparently immediately recognized and advised to return to his home province without further delay. But since he had just come from there, the respondent politely informed the police that he had important business in Toronto that would take a few days to accomplish, and after that he would consider leaving the city. This was not the sort of reaction the police were after, so they pressed their request again in a firmer manner. The respondent's reply was likewise more adamant, and the police left without success. That evening he was called from his rented room by his landlady only to be confronted by two different but "enormous" policemen who had just arrived in an ominous-looking police van. They again questioned him about his intentions to stay in Toronto, but the respondent, who could now see that he would probably remain in that city only in jail, replied that he had decided to return to New Brunswick after all. (Stebbins, 1976)

**continuance commitment**

Adherence to a criminal or other identity arising from the unattractiveness or unavailability of alternative lifestyles.

Another prominent contingency in secondary deviation is **continuance commitment**. Continuance commitment is "the awareness of the impossibility of choosing a different social identity . . . because of the imminence of penalties involved in making the switch" (Stebbins, 1976). Like value commitment mentioned earlier in this chapter, continuance commitment helps explain a person's involvement in a deviant identity. Unlike value commitment, which explains this involvement by stressing the rewards of the identity, continuance commitment explains it by describing the penalties gained from renouncing the deviant identity and trying to adopt a conventional identity.

As Ulmer (1994) notes, such penalties may be structural—flow from the social structure of the community—or personal—flow from the person's attitudes and sense of self. Stebbins's (1976) study of male, nonprofessional property offenders in Newfoundland revealed a number of commitment-related penalties of both types. As ex-offenders with prison records, the men in the study had difficulty finding jobs within their range of personally acceptable alternatives. The work they found was onerous, low in pay, and low in prestige.

Many of the men had amassed sizable debts before going to prison, which upon release, tended to discourage return to a conventional livelihood. Also penalizing were the questions from casual acquaintances about the nature of criminal life and the insulting remarks these people occasionally made about those who have been in jail. Even where their records were unknown, these nonprofessional offenders often heard people express unflattering opinions about men like them.

For these reasons and others, the man with a criminal record was often inclined to seek the company of those who understood him best—namely, other criminals—and to seek the way of life that afforded him at least some money and excitement—namely, crime. The police knew all this, and they would question local ex-offenders to determine whether they were possibly guilty of certain crimes. The ex-offenders, who were trying to "go straight," saw this as an additional penalty.

What is experienced as a string of penalties to the ex-offender is, from another perspective, a set of expressions of the societal reaction. In the everyday lives of ex-offenders, these expressions, when defined by the ex-offenders as penalizing, affect their deviant careers. Such expressions force many of them into the company of other deviants. Here they find greater understanding for their situation. Here, too, is at least the possibility of a better living than believed to exist in the conventional world.

What is the significance of the process of continuance of commitment for that of drift? Those teenagers and young adults who fail to drift out of crime into a more or less conventional way of life drift into a more or less solid commitment to crime. With a prison record and several years of secondary deviation, continuance commitment develops. Most deviants in this stage of their moral careers appear to be trapped in a self-degrading form of continuance commitment. The image they have of themselves is unflattering. It is one they wish they could abandon if only they could find a palatable way of leaving the world of crime (see also Schwendinger and Schwendinger, 1985).

But some criminals, including professional offenders, are quite attached to their deviant activities. Because the professionals find leaving crime for a conventional way of life no easier than it is for the nonprofessional offender, they are also committed to deviance. Nonetheless, theirs is self-enhancing commitment. For the professionals, continuance commitment is of minor consequence; they enjoy what they do and are disinclined to abandon it.

## Reactions to Commitment

Generally speaking, **self-enhancing commitment** presents no problem for deviants, even though they are more or less forced to retain their nonconformist role. There is little motivation to leave it for reasons of self-conception. Self-degrading commitment, however, presents a dramatically different situation. An individual committed to an identity in this manner has numerous alternatives.

Thus, people motivated by **self-degrading commitment** have the objective alternative of redefining the values and penalties associated with their committed identity, such that they become attached to them. Basically, this alters their perception of the balance of penalties. This psychological leap from

**self-enhancing commitment**

Commitment leading to a better opinion of oneself.

**self-degrading commitment**

Commitment leading to a poorer opinion of oneself.

self-degrading to self-enhancing commitment in the same deviant identity is exemplified by some of the repeat offenders in Shover's (1983) study. They wrestled with the frustrating gap between their legitimate aspirations and what they could actually achieve in life. Since conventional work offered little, they turned to living from day to day where crime was one of their more enjoyable activities.

Without really switching to a form of self-enhancing commitment, it is possible for some deviants to adjust, psychologically, to self-degrading commitment. This depends, of course, on how strong a motivating force the current state of self-degrading commitment actually is for them. Certain types of mildly rejected deviants seem to manage this form of adaptation. Lemert (1972) refers to them as "adjusted pathological deviants." The subsequent development of character disorders is another possibility under these circumstances (Griffiths and Verdun-Jones, 1994). Successful adjustment apparently depends, in part, on the availability of a role for them to play in the community.

Lemert also considers "self-defeating and self-perpetuating deviance." He cites alcoholism, drug addiction, and systematic cheque forgery as examples of this sort of vicious circle of cause and effect, characterized by an almost complete absence of durable pleasure for those involved. Finally, if the desire to escape self-degrading commitment is exceptionally strong, and none of the alternatives mentioned so far appeals to the committed individual, suicide becomes a prominent alternative.

Undoubtedly, there are many other alternatives to self-degrading commitment besides those discussed here. Much, it seems, depends on the nature of the identity to which the deviant is committed. There are different ways in which commitment can manifest itself. Extensive research is still needed to isolate the kinds and circumstances of commitment and the diverse reactions to it.

For many deviants, however, commitment is not a lasting contingency in their careers once aware of being trapped in that identity. In fact, this is one reason for stating the case for commitment in subjective terms. The deviant feels this way, which does not, however, always correspond to the objective state of affairs. Criminological theory and research support this observation. For instance, Matza (1990) holds that delinquents generally end their deviant careers at maturation, with few continuing on to adult crime (see Shannon, 1988). West (1980) and Wolfgang et al. (1987) found that many adult criminals also mature out of their antisocial ways. Thus, they take up a serious romantic relationship, find a legitimate job they like better than crime, or simply decide "to settle down" (see Chapter 14). Even deviants attached to their way of life often experience disillusionment and shifts of interest (Sommers, 2001), which is what "maturation" means in everyday terms in the world of crime (Jankowski, 1991). There is always the possibility of therapy for alcoholics, gamblers, and drug addicts. And, of course, some deviance requires youthful vigour, a quality lost with increasing years (Inciardi, 1974).

It is possible that self-enhancing commitment lasts longer than the self-degrading variety. Underlying this suggestion is the assumption that self-degrading commitment, while preferable to certain alternatives in the conventional world, is still undesirable in itself. A mortifying self-conception is a special penalty. It furnishes a significant part of the pressure to deal with an unpleasant state of affairs. Commitment to an identity or expectation leading to a negative self-image is a lesser-evil choice when initially compared with certain alternatives, and a greater-evil choice when subsequently compared with certain others. The strength of the individual's desire to abandon an unpleasant status is an important consideration in determining whether the transition will be made.

# Socialization into Crime

Most of the theories of criminality discussed elsewhere in this book help explain why people start a life of crime. By contrast, interactionism has been interested chiefly in what happens to criminals once their deviant activities commence. Still, two areas of interactionist theory, though not causal, can be properly seen as contributions to the study of socialization into crime. They are the processes of differential association and acquisition of a **criminal identity**.

## Differential Association

Sutherland first set out his theory of differential association in 1939 in *Principles of Criminology*. The statement there differs little from the most recent edition written by Sutherland and Cressey (1978). The theory consists of nine propositions describing the complicated pattern of interaction Sutherland called **differential association**:

1. people learn how to engage in crime;
2. this learning comes about through interaction with others who have already learned criminal ways;
3. the learning occurs in small, face-to-face groups;
4. what is learned is criminal technique (for example, how to open a safe), motives, attitudes, and rationalizations;
5. among criminals, one important learned attitude is disregard for the community's legal code;
6. one acquires this attitude by differentially associating with those who hold it and failing to associate with those who do not;
7. differential associations with criminals and non-criminals vary in frequency, duration, priority, and intensity;
8. learning criminal behaviour through differential association rests on the same principles as learning any other kind of behaviour; and,
9. criminal behaviour is a response to the same cultural needs and values as non-criminal behaviour. For instance, one individual steals to acquire money for a new suit of clothes, while another works as a carpenter to reach the same goal. Consequently, tying societal needs and values to crime fails to explain it.*

Based on what is known about the antecedents of crime, Sutherland's theory offers a valuable, albeit partial, explanation of theft, burglary, prostitution, and marijuana use. Also, differential association is often a major antecedent in the use of addictive drugs and dependence on alcohol. It may even play an explanatory role in some mental disorders.

**criminal identity**

This social category, imposed by the community, correctly or incorrectly defines an individual as a particular type of criminal. The identity pervasively shapes his or her social interactions with others. This concept is similar to master status.

**differential association**

Developed by Edwin Sutherland in the 1930s, this theory argues that crime, like any social behaviour, is learned in association with others. If individuals regularly associate with criminals in relative isolation from law-abiding citizens, they are more likely to engage in crime. They learn relevant skills for committing crime and ideas for justifying and normalizing it.

---

*Sutherland, Edwin H., and David R. Cressey. (1978). *Principles of Criminology (10th ed.)*. Philadelphia: Lippincott.

**FIGURE 13.2   Commitment**

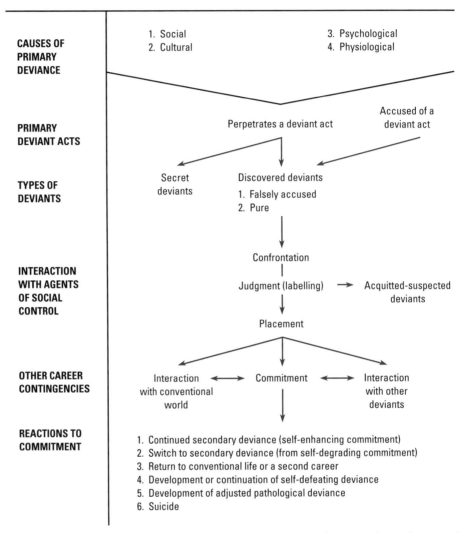

Source: Robert A. Stebbins. (1976). *Commitment to Deviance: The Nonprofessional Criminal in the Community*. Westport, Conn.: Greenwood Press. p. 66. Reproduced with permission of ABC-CLIO, LCC.

However, many other factors, which dilute the importance of differential associations, must be considered when explaining such behaviour. For example, two processes discussed earlier in this chapter—drift and primary deviance to secondary deviation—indicate that deviant motives and meanings are often gradually learned and tentatively applied and modified over time in interaction with both deviants and non-deviants (see Figure 13.2). The motives and meanings are not mere causal antecedents of criminal acts and memberships in criminal groups (Davis, 1980).

Birkbeck and LaFree (1993) reviewed another set of factors. Symbolic interactionism, they note, further aids our understanding of crime by directing attention to the motives and meanings operating in the situations in which crimes are committed. In this connection, Katz (1990) found that the expressive reasons behind many criminal acts (e.g., thrill, enjoyment) are as important as the instrumental reasons (e.g., money, status). Additionally, precisely how a crime is committed and even which crimes are committed depend, in part, on decisions made on the spot by the criminal. These decisions may relate to the possibility of being apprehended, serving a longer or shorter sentence, or enduring a hostile reaction from the community to the deviance being considered.

Although the theory of differential association has been widely tested, convincing support for it has always been blocked by the difficulty of operationalizing some of Sutherland's key concepts (for example, frequency, intensity, and duration of criminal and non-criminal associations). Nonetheless, in Matsueda's (2001) words,

> differential association theory represents one of the most important theoretical traditions in criminology. Historically, the theory brought a sociological perspective to the forefront of criminology and, with his path-breaking work on white-collar crime, established Edwin Sutherland as perhaps the most important criminologist of his generation. . . . Over 50 years later, differential association theory continues to stimulate revisions, extensions, and original research into the causes of crime.

The major contribution of differential association is highlighting the importance during the criminal career of ties to deviant peers. Daniel Wolf, an anthropologist who rode with the Rebels (an Edmonton biker gang) observed that the willingness of peers to stand up for one another can be crucial for maintaining power when faced with violent opposition from competitors:

> For an outlaw biker, the greatest fear is not of the police; rather, it is of a slight variation of his own mirror image: the patch holder of another club. Under slightly different circumstances those men would call each other "brother." But when turf is at stake, inter-club rivalry and warfare completely override any considerations of the common bonds of being a biker—and brother kills brother. None of the outlaws that I rode with enjoyed the prospect of having to break the bones of another biker. Nor did they look forward to having to live with the hate–fear syndrome that dominates a conflict in which there are no rules. I came to realize that the willingness of an outlaw to lay down his life in these conflicts goes beyond a belligerent masculinity that brooks no challenge. When a patch holder defends his colours, he defends his personal identity, his community, his lifestyle. When a war is on, loyalty to the club and one another arises out of the midst of danger, out of apprehension of possible injury, mutilation, or worse. (1991, 11)

There is a great deal of research evidence showing that having young offenders as friends is one of the strongest correlates of deviant behaviour. Several recent studies have also found that among at-risk youth, gang membership contributes to delinquency above and beyond the influence of associating with deviant peers. Sutherland's work helps us understand why this is true. Differential association theory also points to the need to learn the skills of committing certain crimes. These range from very simple techniques such as hitting a man over the head and stealing his watch, to taking an unlocked bicycle to sophisticated computer crimes. According to Sutherland, people learn necessary techniques and motives, drives, rationalizations, and attitudes of deviant behaviour from others with whom they associate.

Letkemann (1973), for example, described how a former penitentiary resident learned the now-obsolete art of safecracking:

> Prior to doing his first "can" [safe] [he] bugged an older safecracker in prison "until he finally divulged how to do it." This instruction, he added was "not like a teacher–student, it was just a matter of discussion during work."

When he left the prison he went back to his regular partner and described to him what he had learned about safes. His partner said this was ridiculous but [he] persuaded him to come along: "I followed the instructions to the letter. It opened—we were both overcome with it all—the ease of it all!"

This first job had been a punch job [breaking into a safe without explosives]—technically the simplest. Following this [he] and his partner "opened many doors by trial and error." . . . This went on for four years; they had not yet used explosives, nor had they ever been caught punching safes. They became increasingly eager to try explosives since they found so many safes that couldn't be opened any other way.

> During this time, [he] was associating with other safecrackers.... He eventually asked another safecracker whether he could borrow some grease [nitroglycerine]. "I wouldn't admit that I knew nothing about it." He obtained the grease and chose a small safe, but was unsuccessful. The next day, he discussed his problem with some more experienced safecrackers. He found he had used too long a fuse and was advised to use electric knockers [detonators]. This he did with success. (Letkemann, 1973, 136)

## Criminal Identities

A *criminal identity* is a social category into which deviants are placed by others in the community and into which, eventually, they may place themselves. That is, the process of identification of an individual as deviant has two sides. Based on a variety of criteria (for example, appearance, actions, associates, location), members of the community come to view someone as a particular kind of criminal. The woman wearing garish, suggestive clothing who frequents a street corner in the red-light district is identified as a prostitute. The man with long, unkempt hair, dirty jeans, and a black leather jacket who rides a Harley-Davidson motorcycle is identified, as we saw earlier, as a member of a gang bent on rape, violence, and drunkenness.

Moreover—and this is the second side—community identification of people tends to be very persuasive, even for deviants. That is, with officials, neighbours, relatives, and others asserting that these people are outlaws, it becomes increasingly difficult for them to deny the charge. At the very least, the alleged prostitute must accommodate her everyday life to such opinion, whether or not she is selling sex. The biker has the same problem.

Acquiring a community reputation, or identity, for unsavoury behaviour often helps further individual criminality. This is especially likely when the reputed criminal is forced into association with others of similar status and away from those who are "respectable." Once deviant ties are forged and non-deviant ties sufficiently weakened, the socializing potential of differential association begins to take effect.

# Limitations

Like all theories of crime and deviance, interactionist theory has its limitations, for it is not itself a complete explanation of crime. It falls well short of explaining all crime under all the conditions in which it is committed. Throughout this chapter, we have discussed the strengths of the theory (summarized in Table 13.1). We now examine its limitations, viewed according to three critiques: neo-Marxist, empiricist, and ethnomethodological (taken from Glassner, 1982). Each critique is also the nucleus of still another approach to the study of crime.

## The Neo-Marxist Critique

The principal neo-Marxist objection to interactionist theory is its failure to relate crime and other forms of deviance to the larger society. It fails to account for historical and contemporary political and economic interests. After all, deviant acts and careers do occur within such contexts.

It is further charged that in explaining deviance, labelling theorists overlook the division between the powerful and the powerless. Powerful members of society also violate laws and other norms even while, as moral entrepreneurs, establishing some of their own. Consider an internal investigation of the Toronto police force in 2004 which recommended that 218 criminal charges be laid against a dozen officers for offenses such as paying informants with drugs seized in other cases, stealing drugs and weapons from suspects and selling them, and extorting money from bar owners (CBC News Toronto, 2007). Charges were laid against six officers and the cases of five were still in the courts in December 2010.

**TABLE 13.1    Interactionist Theories**

| Theory | Theorists | Key Elements |
|---|---|---|
| Labelling | Lemert Becker | Primary deviance is infrequent deviance that involves little change in routine or lifestyle. Secondary deviance occurs when deviance becomes a way of life and a part of the deviant's self-image. |
| Differential Association | Sutherland | Crime and delinquency are primarily learned in interaction with others in small, face-to-face groups. This involves learning techniques of deviance and justifications for it. |

The concept of moral entrepreneur and the categories of secret and falsely accused deviants suggest, however, that interactionists have some understanding of the power differences in society. Perhaps the fairest criticism is that they have failed to go as far as they might in linking power to ideas like labelling, deviant career, and agent of social control. Still, the observation that labelling theory overlooks the larger social context of deviance is apt. The perspective is predominantly social-psychological.

## The Empiricist Critique

The empiricists find several research weaknesses in labelling theory and its empirical support. Glassner (1982) discusses three of these. First, interactionists are said by the empiricists to examine only, or chiefly, labelled deviants—those who have been officially identified as having deviated (charged and convicted, examined, and hospitalized). It is true that labelling theorists have frequently followed this narrow conception of the labelling process. Some deviants—for example, religious fanatics or occultists—are deviant and labelled by the community as such, even though they rarely if ever gain official recognition. This exposes interactionists to the criticism that community labelling makes no practical difference to the individual.

Second, the empiricists argue that labelling as a cause of deviance is inadequately conceptualized. This is a misunderstanding. As this chapter shows, interactionists see labels as interpretations, not causes. The label of deviant is a career contingency, an event, a process, or a situation interpreted by deviants as having a significant impact on their moral careers.

Third, the empiricists claim that labelling theory lacks testable propositions. Consequently, data in this area can be explained in many different ways. They hold that tests by quantitative statistical means are the only definitive way of confirming propositions. Interactionists defend their approach by pointing out that qualitative methods, particularly participant observation, are more appropriate for the study of interaction, labelling, career, and self-conception. These phenomena rest on definitions of the situation, images of self and others, negotiations of reality, and similar processes that are difficult to measure and, therefore, largely unquantifiable. Nevertheless, qualitative research often proceeds from the intense examination of individual groups and cases. Such studies are complicated and time-consuming, so there are relatively few of them. They tend to be exploratory rather than confirmatory.

## The Ethnomethodological Critique

**ethnomethodology**

A sociological theory developed by Harold Garfinkel. Roughly translated, the term means the study of people's practices or methods. The perspective does not see the social world as an objective reality, but as something people constantly build and rebuild through their thoughts and actions. Ethnomethodologists try to uncover the methods and practices people use to they create their taken-for-granted world.

The ethnomethodologists and conversational analysts are the modern-day inheritors of the phenomenology of Alfred Schutz. (In fact, Glassner refers to them as "phenomenologists" in his review). Phenomenology is the study of how we perceive and understand the objects and events of reality. Reality, the phenomenologists hold, is not independent of human perception, of human consciousness. The chief concern of the ethnomethodologists with labelling theory is its tendency to neglect this question: How do people make sense of their social world?

Leiter (1980) defines **ethnomethodology** as the study of common-sense knowledge. Three phenomena are encompassed by this definition:

(1) ethnomethodologists study the stock of knowledge people have of their social and physical world; (2) with this knowledge, they engage in common-sense reasoning about events, processes, things, and characteristics experienced in everyday life; and (3) when people reason together this way, their thoughts often coalesce into a supra-human reality—a social reality. This reality transcends the thoughts of the individuals involved. Ethnomethodologists do not seek to confirm the validity of common sense. Rather, they note that whether common sense is scientifically right or wrong, it is how "we experience the social world as a factual object" (Leiter, 1980).

However, the people of interest to the ethnomethodologist are not always deviant. Rather, ethnomethodologists study how agents of social control and ordinary citizens make sense of deviants and deviant acts. Interactionists are accused of ignoring the ways in which the conventional world identifies and classifies morally offensive individuals and their behaviour. The important data for ethnomethodologists are the clues people use to identify kinds of deviants and deviant acts. People use this knowledge to reach such conclusions as "guilty" or "innocent."

To some extent, interactionists are guilty as charged. Although there are occasional hints of ethnomethodological thinking in the interactionist literature on deviance, there has been until recently a tendency to rely heavily on official definitions, or labels, of what and who is deviant. But even official definitions and their applications are informed by common sense. They, too, warrant ethnomethodological analysis.

## Implications

The most profound implication of interactionist theory is that the theory offers a unique perspective on deviance, which enhances understanding of this phenomenon. For instance, observations on moral enterprise underscore the arbitrariness of criminal law and call attention to patterns of local and national power (though rarely to the extent neo-Marxists would like). Practically speaking, little that can be done to counteract most moral enterprise. But interactionist research, at least, exposes its existence.

On a more practical level, interactionist theory stresses the damaging effects of the deviant label. These effects are of at least two types. One, the label (to the extent that the wider community is aware of it) makes re-entry into that community problematic. Non-deviants are inclined to avoid known deviants. Why? Because their own reputations could be damaged from associating with deviants and, possibly, because they are revolted by the deviant's lifestyle and moral behaviour. Deviants are more than rule violators. They are also outcasts.

Two, labels colour the judgments many people make of those who are labelled. Labels are names for stereotyped images. Both the images and the labels help non-deviants, including practitioners, define situations involving deviants. These two effects of the deviant label have led Empey et al. (1999), among others, to argue that the juvenile courts should be used for only the most serious cases. Juvenile diversion and decriminalization programs, including

Canada's Youth Criminal Justice Act, are practical responses to this implication of interactionist theory.

Interactionist theory calls attention to the deviant career as a process that helps explain deviance beyond its initial causes. One practical implication of this career is that, over time, people often become committed to certain lifestyles. But, to the extent that they make substantial "side bets" (Becker, 1963) in one or more conventional identities, they are unlikely to deviate. Their possible deviance, if discovered and labelled, could ruin their reputations in the conventional world (for example, the politician exposed in the press for patronizing a prostitute).

One antidote to initial or continued deviance, then, is to give people every possible opportunity to build strong side bets in "respectable" pursuits. By this reasoning, juveniles and adult ex-offenders should be encouraged to drift toward conventional interests. The interactionist concept of career is also useful here, albeit the career in mind is one of serious leisure (Stebbins, 2007). This is the leisure of amateurs, hobbyists, and skilled and knowledgeable volunteers, where participants find a career in activities such as music, woodworking, or outdoor pastimes, leading to personal development realized through the acquisition of new skills, knowledge, and experience related to a leisure activity. Two outcomes of this process are positive change in sense of self-worth as well as production of a respectable social identity.

## SUMMARY

- Interactionist theory centres on the deviant interchanges among people and the meanings of these interchanges in the present, past, and future.

- A deviant career is the passage of an individual through the stages of one or more related deviant identities.

- Primary deviation occurs in the early stages of the deviant career. Here, deviance is enacted with little change in the person's everyday routine or lifestyle.

- The deviant drifts between two moral worlds. In youth offender subcultures, deviance is facilitated by certain moral rhetorics and by other aspects of the subterranean tradition.

- Agents of social control help check deviant behaviour. Moral entrepreneurs create and enforce rules, violation of which constitutes deviance. Thus, only some people get labelled deviant.

- When deviants see their lives as substantially modified by deviance, they have moved into secondary deviation. The rules are applied to some people and not others. Those publicly labelled deviant generally face some sort of societal reaction to their misdeeds. Labelled deviants may have to cope with stigma.

- Continuance commitment, or forcing a person to remain in an identity, sometimes results from these encounters. When self-degrading commitment sets in, those affected are inclined to redefine continuance penalties or otherwise adjust to this unsettling situation.

■ Although the theory of criminal socialization is not central in the interactionist perspective, interactionists have contributed to the theory in two major ways. First, people learn crime through differential association with others who are already criminal. Second, they are further socialized into it by being placed in and coming to accept (often grudgingly) a criminal identity.

■ Limitations to the interactionist theories have been noted by neo-Marxists, empiricists, and ethnomethodologists. At the moment, however, none of these approaches has progressed beyond finding weaknesses in the interactionist perspective such that it could become a distinct orientation itself.

■ Interactionist theory has certain theoretical and practical implications. One is that, wherever possible, continuance commitment to deviance among juveniles should be eschewed by avoiding the official label of criminal.

## QUESTIONS FOR CRITICAL THINKING

1. Identify and describe a recent change in existing criminal law or a recent passing of a new criminal law initiated by moral entrepreneurs.
2. Select a vulnerable category (e.g., lower-class male youths, Aboriginal peoples) and describe how they could be falsely accused of certain crimes. How does such an explanation relate to deviant identity?
3. Identify some factors contributing to secondary deviation among heroin users.
4. Identify some legitimate "side bets" people make that help them avoid criminal acts and criminals make that help them avoid further criminality.
5. Because of the influence of labelling theory, society has become more sensitive to the costs of deviant labels. List some measures taken in our youth and adult courts to reduce the number of people officially labelled by those institutions.

## NET WORK

Gun control is an issue that has seen groups of moral entrepreneurs with different viewpoints trying to influence lawmakers. Bill C-68, the Firearms Act, has been particularly controversial, with both sides working hard to have their views accepted. On one side of the issue is the National Firearms Association (NFA), which strongly objects to restricting ownership and use of firearms as set out in Bill C-68 (see **www.nfa.ca**).

On the other side is the Coalition for Gun Control. Arguments favouring gun control can be found at their website (**www.guncontrol.ca**).

1. What claims are these two sets of moral entrepreneurs making?
2. What reasons lie behind their conflicting views?
3. What strategies has the National Firearms Association used to fight implementation of Bill C-68? What arguments has the Coalition for Gun Control used in their successful fight to persuade the government to pass Bill C-68?

## KEY TERMS

career; pg. 409
career contingency; pg. 417
continuance commitment; pg. 418
criminal identity; pg. 421
deviant career; pg. 408
differential association; pg. 421
drift; pg. 410
empirical evidence; pg. 412
ethnic group; pg. 414
ethnomethodology; pg. 426
interactionist theories; pg. 408
labelling; pg. 409

master status; pg. 416
moral entrepreneur; pg. 412
moral rhetoric; pg. 411
primary deviation; pg. 410
secondary deviation; pg. 410
self-degrading commitment; pg. 419
self-enhancing commitment; pg. 419
stigma; pg. 411
symbolic interactionism; pg. 408

## BIBLIOGRAPHY

Becker, Howard S. (1963). *Outsiders: Studies in the Sociology of Deviance*. New York: Free Press.

Birkbeck, Christopher, and Gary LaFree. (1993). "The Situational Analysis of Crime and Deviance." In Judith Blake and John Hagan (eds.), *Annual Review of Sociology* 19. Palo Alto, CA: Annual Reviews, Inc.

Blumer, Herbert. (1986). *Symbolic Interactionism*. Berkeley: University of California Press.

CBC News Toronto. (2007). "Toronto Police Corruption Probe Laid a Fraction of Charges: Report." Available at http://www.cbc.ca/canada/toronto/story/2007/04/29/toronto-police-probe.html, accessed December, 2010.

Cohen, Albert K. (1965). "The Sociology of the Deviant Act." *American Sociological Review* 30:5–14.

Davis, Nanette J. (1980). *Sociological Constructions of Deviance*. (2nd ed.). Dubuque, IA: Wm. C. Brown.

Empey, Lamar T., Mark C. Stafford, and Carter H. Hay. (1999). *American Delinquency: Its Meaning and Construction*. (4th ed.). Belmont, CA: Wadsworth.

Glassner, Barry. (1982). "Labelling Theory." In M. Michael Rosenberg, Robert A. Stebbins, and Allan Turowetz (eds.), *The Sociology of Deviance*. New York: St. Martin's Press.

Goffman, Erving. (1986). *Stigma: Notes on the Management of Spoiled Identity*. Oneonta, NY: Touchstone.

Griffiths, Curt T., and Simon N. Verdun-Jones. (1994). *Canadian Criminal Justice*. (2nd ed.). Toronto: Harcourt Brace Canada.

Hewitt, John P., and Peter M. Hall. (1973). "Social Problems, Problematic Situations, and Quasi-Theories." *American Sociological Review* 38:367–74.

Hirschi, Travis. (2001). *Causes of Delinquency*. New Brunswick, NJ: Transaction.

Inciardi, James A. (1974). "Vocational Crime." In Daniel Glaser (ed.), *Handbook of Criminology*. Chicago: Rand McNally.

Jankowski, Martin S. (1991). *Islands in the Street: Gangs and American Urban Society.* Berkeley, CA: University of California Press.

Katz, Jack. (1990). *Seductions of Crime: Moral and Sensual Attractions in Doing Evil.* New York: Basic Books.

Leiter, Kenneth. (1980). *A Primer on Ethnomethodology.* New York: Oxford University Press.

Lemert, Edwin. (1951). *Social Pathology.* New York: McGraw-Hill.

———. (1972). *Human Deviance, Social Problems, and Social Control.* (2nd ed.). Englewood Cliffs, NJ: Prentice Hall.

Letkemann, Peter. (1973). *Crime as Work.* Englewood Cliffs, NJ: Prentice Hall.

Linden, Rick, and Cathy Fillmore. (1981). "A Comparative Study of Delinquency Involvement." *Canadian Review of Sociology and Anthropology* 18:343–61.

Link, Bruce G., and Jo C. Phelan. (2001). "Conceptualizing Stigma." In Karen S. Cook and John Hagan (eds.), *Annual Review of Sociology,* Vol. 27. Palo Alto, CA: Annual Reviews.

Matsueda, Ross L. (2001). "Differential Association Theory." In Patricia A. Adler, Peter Adler, and Jay Corzine (eds.), *Encyclopedia of Criminology and Deviant Behavior,* Vol. 1. Philadelphia: Brunner-Routledge.

Matza, David. (2010). *Becoming Deviant,* rev ed. New Brunswick, NJ: Transaction.

———. (1990). *Delinquency and Drift.* New Brunswick, NJ: Transaction.

Prus, Robert C., and C.R.D. Sharper. (1991). *Road Hustler: Grifting, Magic, and the Thief Subculture,* (expanded edition). New York: Kaufman and Greenberg.

Schwendinger, Herman, and Julia S. Schwendinger. (1985). *Adolescent Subcultures and Delinquency.* New York: Praeger.

Shannon, Lyle W. (1988). *Criminal Career Continuity.* New York: Human Sciences Press.

Short, James F. (1990). *Delinquency and Society.* Englewood Cliffs, NJ: Prentice Hall.

Shover, Neal. (1983). "The Later Stages of Ordinary Property Offender Careers." *Social Problems* 31:208–18.

Sommers, Ira B. (2001). "Criminal Careers." In David Luckenbill and Dennis Peck (eds.), *Encyclopedia of Criminology and Deviant Behavior,* Vol. 2. Philadelphia: Brunner-Routledge.

Spector, Malcom, and John I. Kitsuse. (2000). *Constructing Social Problems.* New Brunswick, NJ: Transaction.

Stebbins, Robert A. (1970). "On Misunderstanding the Concept of Commitment: A Theoretical Clarification." *Social Forces* 48:526–29.

———. (1976). *Commitment to Deviance: The Nonprofessional Criminal in the Community.* Westport, CT: Greenwood.

———. (1997). "Lifestyle as a Generic Concept in Ethnographic Research." *Quality and Quantity* 31:347–60.

———. (2007). *Serious Leisure: A Perspective for Our Time.* New Brunswick, NJ: Transaction.

Sutherland, Edwin H., and David R. Cressey. (1978). *Principles of Criminology.* (10th ed.). Philadelphia: Lippincott.

Ulmer, Jeffery T. (1994). "Revisiting Stebbins: Labeling and Commitment to Deviance." *The Sociological Quarterly* 35:135–57.

Watson, J. Mark. (1984). "Outlaw Motorcyclists: An Outgrowth of Lower Class Cultural Concerns." In Delos H. Kelly (ed.), *Deviant Behavior.* (2nd ed.). New York: St. Martin's Press.

West, W. Gordon. (1980). "The Short Term Careers of Serious Thieves." In Robert A. Silverman and James J. Teevan, Jr. (eds.), *Crime in Canadian Society.* (2nd ed.). Toronto: Butterworths.

Wolf, Daniel R. (1991). *The Rebels: A Brotherhood of Outlaw Bikers.* Toronto: University of Toronto Press.

Wolfgang, Marvin E., Terence P. Thornberry, and Robert M. Figlio. (1987). *From Boy to Man, from Delinquency to Crime.* Chicago: University of Chicago Press.

# Social Control Theory

**Rick Linden**

**UNIVERSITY OF MANITOBA**

We begin this chapter by examining some of the early social disorganization theories exploring the relationship between social structure and deviance. These theories were very important, because along with Merton's work (Chapter 10) they challenged the earlier view that the sources of crime lay within the individual. Instead, they proposed that the structure and culture of the American city was responsible for deviant behaviour. Social disorganization theorists felt that disorganized communities did not provide meaningful employment to residents and did not have strong families, schools, and churches. This lack of effective social controls led to high rates of crime and other types of deviance. While the early theorists looked at the relationship between community characteristics and crime, later theorists focused more on the way the social bonds of individuals help to constrain crime and delinquency. Final sections of this chapter deal with some of issues surrounding control theory and with the policy implications of the theory.

## Learning Objectives

After reading this chapter, you should be able to

- Understand the early social disorganization theories that sought to explain why crime rates were highest in neighbourhoods characterized by poverty, physical deterioration, and ethnic conflict.

- Know the importance of the social bonds of attachment, involvement, commitment, and belief in the causation of delinquency and crime.

- Explain the role of the family, the school, and the church in the causation of delinquency and crime.

- Describe the criticisms that have been made of social control theory and understand the validity of these criticisms.

- Understand the social policy implications of social control theory.

**Social control theory** assumes that human beings are neither good nor evil. However, we are born with the capacity to do wrong. Unlike most theories of criminality, control theory requires no special motivation to impel people to deviate. Since our natural propensity is to gratify ourselves with no concern for right and wrong, and since the "wrong" way may be the quickest and most efficient way of achieving these goals, it is conformity rather than deviance that must be explained. Other theorists ask "Why do they do it?" but the control theorist is concerned with the question "Why don't we *all* do it?" The answer given by control theory is "We all would, if only we dared, but many of us dare not because we have loved ones we fear to hurt and physical possessions and

**social control theory**
The theory proposes that people refrain from committing criminal acts because they do not want to jeopardize their bonds to conventional society.

social reputations we fear to lose" (Box, 1971, 140). All societies have developed ways of making people conform, and the control theorist is concerned with these processes that bind people to the social order.

# Theories of Social Disorganization— Durkheim, Thrasher, and Shaw and McKay

## Durkheim and Social Integration

The earliest social control theories explained how some types of social structure led to high rates of crime and deviance. Communities characterized by poverty, physical deterioration, and racial or ethnic conflict were too disorganized to exert effective control over the behaviour of residents. These early social disorganization theorists included Durkheim, Thrasher, and Shaw and McKay.

In his monograph *Suicide* (1951), Durkheim pointed out the importance of **social bonds** in the understanding of deviant behaviour. Egoistic suicide results from a situation in which a person's social ties are weakened to the extent that the person is freed from social constraints and acts only on the basis of private interests. Anomic suicide occurs when a lack of social integration, caused by factors such as rapid economic change, leaves a society without a clear system of moral beliefs and sentiments. In each case, social organization is weak and the individual lacks moral guidance. If the rules are strong and if there is consensus about their validity, there will be little deviance. If the rules are weak and if there is minimal agreement about their applicability, society will be unable to regulate morality effectively, and deviance will be common. Without socially regulated goals, deviance is more likely, as people pursue their aspirations without check.

We saw in Chapter 10 that in Merton's reformulation of anomie theory he shifted from Durkheim's emphasis on a society's failure to define appropriate goals to an emphasis on the failure to define the appropriate means of reaching common culture goals, and on the unequal distribution of legitimate means of reaching these goals. The social disorganization theorists—among them Thrasher, and Shaw and McKay—were more faithful to Durkheim's view of the effects of the social bond on deviance.

## Thrasher and *The Gang*

Thrasher and Shaw and McKay focused their attention on ecological studies of the city. Thrasher's classic study *The Gang* is still the most extensive study of juvenile gangs ever done. Thrasher located gangs both geographically and socially where there are breaks in the structure of social organization. They occur "in city slums characterized by physical deterioration, rapid succession of inhabitants, mobility, and disorganization; along economic and ecological boundaries; along political frontiers; …and during adolescence, an interstitial period between childhood and maturity" (Kornhauser, 1978, 51). Gangs arise spontaneously in areas where social controls are weak. Gangs are not necessarily delinquent, though delinquency will often be the natural result of the

**social bond**

The degree to which an individual has ties to his or her society. In Hirschi's theory, social bonds include attachment, commitment, involvement, and belief.

**National Gang Center (U.S.A.)**
www.nationalgangcenter.gov

activities of groups of adolescents in communities where social institutions are not able to control their behaviour (Thrasher, 1963). In a slum setting, delinquency was often the most exciting and interesting thing for these youths to do.

## Shaw and McKay—Ecological Analysis

In one of the earliest sociological explanations of crime and delinquency Shaw and McKay saw the origins of deviance not in the pathology of individuals, but in social disorganization. They concluded that the social structure of a community affected its rates of crime and delinquency.

Shaw and McKay found that some areas in Chicago had disproportionately high rates of officially recorded crime and delinquency. Rates were highest in slum areas near the city centre and generally declined as one moved outward. Areas with high crime and delinquency rates were characterized by "physical deterioration, decreasing population, high rates of dependency, [and a] high percentage of foreign-born and Negro population" (Thrasher, 1963, 361). In many of these neighbourhoods, crime rates remained high over a long period of time, even though the racial and ethnic characteristics of the residents changed as new waves of immigrants moved into the city. Shaw and McKay attributed these high rates of crime to the failure of neighbourhood institutions and organizations such as families, schools, and churches to provide adequate social controls. Like Thrasher, they also emphasized the importance of exposure to the criminal subculture that developed in these areas and which attracted young people to deviant behaviour.

Control theory was not fully developed in the work of Thrasher and Shaw and McKay, but from the 1930s to the 1960s subcultural and strain theories so dominated the field that there were very few additions to the social disorganization model (Kornhauser, 1978). Several reasons explain why control theory all but disappeared from the scene following this rather promising beginning. The most important reason was that the early research was methodologically flawed. The relationships among **independent variables** such as social class, mobility, and community diversity were consistent with social control theory, but they also were consistent with other perspectives such as strain theory, and Shaw and McKay never directly measured the degree of social control that existed in a particular community. They inferred, but did not demonstrate, that higher-income communities were better organized than were lower-class slums. The type of research done by Shaw and McKay was also subject to the problem of the **ecological fallacy**. For example, consider the finding that official crime rates are higher in lower-class than in middle-class areas. The conclusion usually drawn from this finding is that being a member of the lower class makes one more likely to become involved with crime. However, this inference is not necessarily true. Perhaps most crimes in lower-class areas are committed by middle-class residents of those census tracts. Perhaps the resident population is not responsible for crime at all. Engstad (1975) showed that some businesses in Edmonton such as licensed hotels, bars, and shopping centres attract people from other parts of the city and provide opportunities for crime. Chambliss (1973) found that middle-class adolescents migrated to other parts of the city to commit their delinquencies. Finally, the vague and often value-laden term "social disorganization" fell into disrepute among sociologists.

**independent variable**

A presumed cause of a dependent variable. If unemployment is thought to cause crime rates to increase, unemployment is the independent variable, and crime rates the dependent variable.

**ecological fallacy**

A research error made when data or information is gathered at a group level (the unemployment rate of various communities or neighbourhoods) and then conclusions are drawn about individuals (the unemployed person). Areas with high unemployment may have high crime rates, but this does not tell us that those crimes are necessarily committed by unemployed persons.

Despite these problems, Thrasher and Shaw and McKay did lay the foundations for a control theory of crime and delinquency. They found that delinquents come from communities that are poorly organized and whose institutions are not well integrated. Families are unable to adequately socialize their children, and their schools are poor. These elements all reappear in the work of later theorists. Unfortunately, most of the later work focused only on individuals rather than on neighbourhood variables. However, recent research from Statistics Canada has focused attention again on the correlation between neighbourhood conditions and crime in several Canadian cities. This research showed that crime was heavily concentrated in economically disadvantaged neighbourhoods (Savoie, 2008), just as it had been in Chicago during the time of Shaw and McKay.

# Early Social Control Theories—Reiss and Nye

## Albert Reiss

While the social disorganization theorists had been concerned with controls at the community and family level, Reiss (1951) was the first to distinguish between *social* controls, which include ties to primary groups such as the family and to the community and its institutions, and *personal* controls, which have been internalized by an individual. If these controls are absent, if they break down, if they are in conflict, or if they cannot be enforced, delinquency will result. Using information collected in the court files of a group of male juvenile probationers, Reiss found that success or failure on probation was associated with the absence of both social and personal controls.

## Ivan Nye

Theoretically, the work of Nye (1958) simply expanded on that of Reiss, but methodologically, it represented a great advance. While Reiss had relied on court records of youths who were officially defined as delinquent, Nye developed a technique for measuring self-reported delinquency and gathered his data from a random sample of high school students in three small American cities. His book represented one of the first attempts at unravelling the causes of delinquency using the self-report approach.

While Reiss did not elaborate on the theory underlying personal and social controls, Nye was quite explicit in stating his theoretical perspective: "control theory assumes delinquency is not *caused* in a positive sense (motivated by the gains to be derived from it) but *prevented* (determined by the relative costs of alternative benefits).... Weak controls free the person to commit delinquent acts by lowering their cost relative to available alternatives" (Kornhauser, 1978, 140–41, emphasis added). Individuals are motivated to achieve certain goals as quickly as possible but are prevented from doing so by the laws and customs that societies establish to protect their members.

Nye believed the family was the most significant group in the development of social controls. The extent to which the family enforced controls and the degree to which family members got along with one another determined the extent to which a child would develop internal controls. His research supported his hypotheses concerning the relationship between the family and delinquency. Children who came from close families in which there was agreement on basic values were unlikely to be delinquent.

The work of Reiss and Nye provided a promising beginning for contemporary control theory and subsequent research received much more empirical support than did the theories of Merton, Cohen, Cloward and Ohlin, Miller, and Sutherland, which dominated the field. However, it took a number of years before control theory became widely accepted by criminologists as one of the major theories explaining crime and delinquency.

# Travis Hirschi and the Social Bond

Control theory began to receive renewed attention in 1969 with the publication of Hirschi's *Causes of Delinquency*. Hirschi developed a clear and concise version of control theory and demonstrated empirically that it explained delinquency better than did competing theories. Like earlier control theorists, Hirschi postulates that individuals are more likely to turn to illegitimate means if their bond to society is weak or broken. For Hirschi, four interrelated aspects of the social bond constrain our behaviour: attachment, commitment, involvement, and belief.

# Attachment

**Attachment** refers to the degree to which the individual has affective ties to other persons, particularly those who belong to their primary groups. If an individual is sensitive to the feelings of others and close to those others, this attachment will constrain his or her behaviour because that individual will not want to hurt or embarrass the people he or she likes. Those lacking such ties will not have to consider the feelings of others and will be free to deviate. Thus, youth who do not get along with their parents will be more free to commit acts of delinquency than those who are close to their families.

**attachment**
The degree to which an individual has affective ties to other persons. One of the social bonds in Hirschi's theory.

## Commitment

The essence of **commitment** lies in the pursuit of conventional goals. "The idea, then, is that the person invests time, energy, himself, in a certain line of activity—say, getting an education, building up a business, acquiring a reputation for virtue" (Hirschi, 1969, 20). If a person decides to engage in deviance, that person will be putting his or her investment at risk. Thus the student who has worked hard in school and who aspires to become a professional may avoid the temptations of delinquency for fear of jeopardizing this future career. However, the youth who is failing in school and who has no career aspirations may not feel as constrained. For the second youth, the immediate rewards of delinquency might outweigh the potential long-term costs. Both

**commitment**
The degree to which an individual pursues conventional goals. One of the social bonds in Hirschi's theory.

commitments and attachments can change over time. For example, the phenomenon of maturational reform—as we get older, we behave better—can be explained by the fact that adults typically have a greater investment in conventional lines of activity than do adolescents so their deviance may have higher costs.

## Involvement

**involvement**

The degree to which an individual is active in conventional activities. One of the social bonds in Hirschi's theory.

Hirschi felt that people's level of **involvement** has an impact on delinquency. According to control theory, if people are busy with conventional activities, they will not have time to engage in deviant behaviour. For example, if a student is busy at school and is involved in extracurricular activities, that student will not have as much opportunity to commit delinquencies as will peers who are not as involved.

## Belief

**belief**

The degree to which an individual believes in conventional values, morality, and the legitimacy of law. One of the social bonds in Hirschi's theory.

Our **belief** in conventional values, morality, and the legitimacy of the law will constrain our behaviour. Unlike some conflict theorists (Chapter 11), who believe that deviants are tied to value systems different from those of the rest of the population, Hirschi claims that society does have a common value system. However, individuals vary in the degree to which they believe they should obey the rules. While conflict theorists tell us that acts that are deviant from the perspective of those who have the power to make and enforce the rules are *required* by the beliefs of members of certain subcultures, the control theorist says that deviant acts are made possible by the *absence* of beliefs forbidding them.

For the most part, research has supported Hirschi's theory, particularly for the variables of attachment and commitment. Belief in the law has also been found to be related to delinquency (Gomme, 1985). The evidence concerning involvement is mixed in that involvement in school activities is related to lower involvement in delinquency, while participation in sports, hobbies, and part-time jobs is not (Hirschi, 1969).

## Self-Control—The General Theory of Crime

Hirschi's early work focused on external sources of social control such as family, friends, and school. In 1990 Gottfredson and Hirschi published *A General Theory of Crime*, in which they proposed that individuals with low self-control have a greater propensity to commit crimes when they have the opportunity to do so. They will also be more likely to engage in other risky behaviour such as smoking, drinking, and dangerous driving. Gottfredson and Hirschi believe this theory applies to all types of crime.

Individuals who lack self-control are impulsive people who focus on the moment rather than planning for the future, who have unstable personal relationships, and who are less likely to feel shame or remorse when their actions hurt others. As Gottfredson and Hirschi have stated, when "desires conflict with long-term interests, those lacking self-control opt for the desires of the moment, whereas those with greater self-control are governed by the restraints imposed by the consequences of acts displeasing to family, friends, and the law" (1990, xvi).

Why do some people lack self-control? For Gottfredson and Hirschi, the answer lies in early childhood socialization. Children will have low self-control if they have poor relationships with their parents or if their parents do not have good parenting skills. Those who fail to develop self-control in childhood will be more likely to be involved in crime throughout their entire lives, so the impact of poor early socialization may persist for many years. Their behaviour will be constrained only by the lack of opportunities to commit crimes and other deviant acts.

Several Canadian researchers have studied the relationship between self-control and criminal behaviour. Using data collected during a night-time roadside survey of Ontario drivers, Keane et al. (1993) found that men and women who were lower in self-control had higher levels of blood alcohol than other drivers. Sorenson and Brownfield (1995) also found a correlation between self-control and drug use. However, they found that ties to delinquent friends were correlated more strongly with drug use than any of their self-control variables. Marc LeBlanc (1997) has suggested that low self-control is just one of several psychological traits that should be a part of a comprehensive social control theory of offending. LeBlanc found that Quebec youth with "egocentric personalities"—a construct similar in some respects to Gottfredson and Hirschi's notion of low self-control—have weaker social bonds and higher levels of delinquency than their peers (LeBlanc et al., 1988). In their study of Edmonton youth, LaGrange and Silverman (1999) found that self-control explained part of the difference in delinquency involvement between males and females.

While some research does support this theory, other evidence suggests that it will not replace more traditional versions of control theory. In the general theory of crime, Gottfredson and Hirschi turned away from Hirschi's earlier view that ongoing social bonds will make involvement in crime and delinquency less likely. Instead, they proposed that early childhood experiences can produce low levels of self-control that will result in higher levels of deviance throughout the entire life course. However, Sampson and Laub (1993) have cast doubt on this hypothesis. They followed boys from ages 17 to 25 and found that those who developed adult social bonds, including stable jobs and cohesive marriages, were less likely to be involved in criminality than peers who did not develop these ties. Thus, rather than remaining stable over the life course, the propensity to deviate appears to be variable and to depend on changes in one's social bonds. Childhood patterns of deviance are not necessarily carried into adulthood. Several other studies, including the work by LaGrange and Silverman (1999) and 21 studies reviewed by Pratt and Cullen (2000), suggest that self-control provides at best only a partial explanation of crime and delinquency and does not explain "all crime, at all times," as Gottfredson and Hirschi claim (117).

In the remainder of this chapter, we will look in detail at some of the research evidence bearing on control theory, discuss some issues with the theory, suggest ways in which the theory might be revised, and consider its social policy implications.

# FOCUS BOX 14.1

## CAN MARSHMALLOWS PREDICT BEHAVIOUR?

Walter Mischel has conducted a fascinating study of self-control. Mischel's daughters attended a nursery school on the campus of Stanford University where he taught psychology. Mischel set up a very simple study to examine why some people were able to delay gratification while others were not. He asked children to sit down at a small desk in a room at the nursery school. Each child was asked to choose a treat, such as a marshmallow, from a tray and then told that they could eat the treat immediately or, if they were willing to wait, they could have a second treat. The researcher then left the room and the children were filmed while they tried to avoid eating the treat until the researcher returned.

In the years following this research, Mischel's daughters occasionally discussed their friends and he noticed that the children who were able to delay eating the treat seemed to be doing better in school than those who could not wait. He formally followed up as many of the children as he could find and found that those who were able to delay gratification were doing better than the others in many dimensions of their lives (Shoda, Mischel, and Peake, 1990). They had fewer behavioural problems, better coping skills in adolescence, higher college entrance test scores, and less illicit drug use (Mischel et al., 2011). Other research has found that the ability to delay gratification is associated with lower levels of aggression, higher self-esteem, and less involvement in bullying (Mischel et al., 2011). As Mischel has stated: "If you can deal with hot emotions, then you can study ... instead of watching television ... and you can save money for retirement. It's not just about marshmallows" (Lehrer, 2009, 29).

Mischel and his colleagues have found evidence that there is a neurobiological component to the ability to delay gratification and have also found that this ability can be improved through training.

This work represents an interesting dimension of self-control theory and is potentially helpful because researchers in this area have suggested strategies for improving children's abilities to control their behaviour through measures such as reframing the situation to make the stimulus (in this case, the marshmallow) less immediately appealing.

For an amusing look at children confronted by a marshmallow, go to http://www.youtube.com/watch?v=6EjJsPylEOY.

# Family Relationships

Social control theory emphasizes family relationships since these provide children with the attachments that restrain their involvement in delinquency. Several aspects of family relationships are related to delinquency. Among these are strength of family ties, parental supervision and discipline, and the role model provided by parents.

## Strength of Family Ties

Strong family ties are important in the development of the social bond. If parents are close to their children and provide a congenial atmosphere in the home, family relationships should act as a deterrent to delinquency. Children

**"A Summary of Family Life, Delinquency, and Crime: A Policymaker's Guide"** Office of Prevention, Texas Youth Commission

www.tyc.state.tx.us/prevention/family_life.html

who care about what their parents think of them should be less likely to become involved in delinquency.

A number of studies confirm this view. Warm, affectionate family relationships are associated with low rates of delinquency, while mutual rejection and hostility are typical of the families of delinquents (Glueck and Glueck, 1950; Nye, 1958; Gove and Crutchfield, 1982). Some of this research has also found that conflict between the parents also characterizes the families of delinquents. A study of Edmonton youth discovered that boys who found their families attractive and who were concerned with pleasing their parents were less likely to be delinquent than boys who did not have close ties to their parents (Kupfer, 1966).

## Parental Supervision and Discipline

Children who are adequately supervised by their parents and whose parents discipline them in an appropriate fashion will have lower delinquency rates than will their peers who do not. Many studies have demonstrated the importance of parents' knowing what their children are doing and ensuring that they play with friends whom the parents consider suitable (Hirschi, 1969; West and Farrington, 1973; Wilson, 1980). Studies in Montreal and Edmonton have found that supervision was more strongly related to delinquency than any other family variable (Kupfer, 1966; Caplan, 1977; Biron and LeBlanc, n.d.).

Closely related to supervision is parental discipline. While critics of control theory have complained that the theory advocates the harsh treatment of children, control theorists do not view physical punishment as the best way to control behaviour. Rather, they believe "disapproval by people one cares about is the most powerful of sanctions. Effective punishment by the parent or major caretaker therefore usually entails nothing more than explicit disapproval of unwanted behaviour" (Gottfredson and Hirschi, 1990, 99–100). Studies have consistently found the disciplinary practices of delinquent families to be different from those of non-delinquent families. Families in which discipline was inconsistent or lax were much more likely to have delinquent children (Glueck and Glueck, 1950; West and Farrington, 1973). Children do not appear to learn from discipline unless it is administered in a clear, consistent manner.

There is also evidence of a relationship between higher rates of delinquency and very strict discipline, particularly if it is associated with harsh physical punishment (Fischer, 1980) and if parental warmth and supportiveness is lacking (Simons et al., 2000). Very strict discipline is seen as unfair and may lead to feelings of frustration and resentment on the part of the child. Harsh punishment may gain immediate compliance, but moderate discipline is more effective in encouraging children to internalize a set of values that will ensure long-term compliance (Aronson, 1984).

In his study of youths in a poor inner-city community, Anderson describes how what he calls "street-oriented" parents—those who do not try to emulate the "decent-family model"—discipline their children:

> In these circumstances, a woman—or a man, although men are less consistently present in children's lives—can be quite aggressive with children, yelling at them and striking at them for the least little infraction of the rules she has set down. Often little, if any, serious

explanation follows the verbal and physical punishment. This response teaches children a particular lesson. They learn that to solve any kind of interpersonal problem, one must quickly resort to hitting or other violent behaviour. (Anderson, 1994, 83)

The importance of parenting style is clearly shown in Canada's National Longitudinal Survey of Children and Youth (NLSCY), which is following the development of more than 23 000 children (Statistics Canada, 1998). The researchers asked the children's parents about their parenting styles, including punitiveness, hostility, consistency, and the amount of positive interaction. Parenting style had a strong correlation with relationship and behavioural problems in children. Children who were exposed to hostile or ineffective parenting were *nine* times more likely to have behavioural problems than were children who were not exposed to these parenting styles. Parenting style, particularly hostile parenting and parental harshness (Ho et al., 2008), was more strongly related to behavioural problems than other factors, including income and family structure. The most aggressive children at ages 10 and 11 were much more likely than their peers to report having negative relations with families and to feeling rejected by their parents (Sprott and Doob, 2000).

"National Longitudinal Survey of Children and Youth" Statistics Canada
http://www.statcan.gc.ca/daily-quotidien/981028/dq981028-eng.htm

## Parental Role Model

Hirschi argued that strong ties to parents will act as a deterrent to delinquency regardless of the criminality of the parents. However, there does appear to be a relationship between the criminality of the parent and that of the child. West and Farrington (1973) found that boys with at least one parent convicted of a criminal offence were more than twice as likely to become delinquent as those whose parents had no convictions. "Youthful crime often seems to be part of a family tradition" (West, 1982, 44). West does not feel that the parents deliberately transmit criminal values to their offspring because few of the children were involved in their parents' criminality, and the parents expressed disapproval of their children's involvement in delinquency. The relationship is at least partially explained by the fact that parents with criminal records were lax in applying rules and did not supervise their children effectively. Consider this comment from a high-risk auto theft offender in Winnipeg (interviewed for my own current research) who was required to wear an electronic monitoring bracelet that would notify officials if he left home after his curfew time:

> My friends would come over and we would party at my house, my mom didn't like that. We partied every day and she would get mad, trip out and bitch at me to turn the music down. When she was in my face I would feed her pieces [crack] until she left me alone.

In light of West's findings that criminal fathers were likely to be on social assistance and unemployment benefits and that this dependency was repeated among their sons, it would appear that families with criminal parents may have a variety of problems that are manifested in both parental criminality and poor family relationships. West and Farrington (1977) also suggest that part of the relationship may be due to labelling because an act of delinquency leading to arrest was more likely to result in a conviction if a boy came from a criminal family.

While direct modelling of parental behaviour does not appear to be a major cause of delinquency, it may be a factor in some types of offences. Rutter and Giller suggest that "criminal parents may provide a model of aggression and antisocial attitudes, if not of criminal activities as such" (1984, 183). The fact that a high proportion of abusive parents were themselves abused as children supports the view that family violence is learned in the home (Steinmetz and Straus, 1980). Abusive parents contribute to delinquency in another way. In a study of homeless youths in Toronto, Hagan and McCarthy (1997) found that some of their respondents were living on the streets in order to escape abuse at home. Once on the street, their need for food, shelter, and money led to delinquent behaviour.

# Schooling

Like the family, the school plays a primary role in socialization and is an important determinant of delinquency. The school is a pervasive influence in a young person's life. For most of the year, children spend all day in classes and return to school after hours for other activities such as sports and dances. More important, the school is an arena in which an adolescent's performance is constantly being judged. Those who are successful enjoy the prestige conferred by teachers and parents as well as by many of their classmates. Those who fail may feel that they have been rejected by the adult world as well as by their peers (Polk and Richmond, 1972). For those who are successful in school and who enjoy their educational experience, the school provides a stake in conformity. However, those who fail do not have this stake and hence are more likely to become involved in delinquency. The correlation between school failure and delinquency is relatively strong and has been replicated in Canada (Gomme, 1985), Britain (Hargreaves, 1967), and the United States (Polk and Schafer, 1972).

The school affects delinquency in two distinct but interrelated ways. First, the school is "one of the fundamental determinants of an individual's economic and social position" (Polk and Schafer, 1972, 10). The school has taken over many of the occupational socialization functions that in earlier times were performed by the family. Formal educational qualifications have become the basis for entry into most occupations. Thus a child's experiences in school will have a profound impact on that child's future life chances. Second, the school is related to delinquency through its effects on child's daily life. For some, the experience is interesting, pleasant, and enriching. For others, it is irrelevant, degrading, and humiliating.

Both types of impact have an effect on a student's stake in conformity. Those whose school experiences will clearly not qualify them for meaningful occupations may not have the same degree of commitment as their peers whose expectations are higher. The daily consequences of failure and the resulting lack of attachment to the school also affect the child. In fact, research suggests that the daily problems of coping with school failure may be more strongly related to delinquency than is concern about the future. Linden (1974) found that measures reflecting present school status (whether the child liked school, finished homework, skipped school, valued good grades, and got along with teachers) were more highly correlated with delinquency than were measures of educational aspirations and expectations. Arum and Beattie (1999) showed that students who had a school environment with small class sizes and course work that was relevant to their lives had lower rates of adult incarceration than those with less positive school experiences, even when their education did not provide any labour market benefit. Using data from Canada's National Longitudinal Study of Children and Youth, Sprott (2004) found that the classroom environment had an impact on later delinquency. Children who attended an emotionally supportive classroom between the ages of 10 and 13 had lower rates of violence two years later. Further, those with an academically supportive classroom environment had lower levels of property crime over the same period.

Some criminologists see a broader relationship between schools and delinquency. From a structural perspective, the school "cuts adolescents off from participating in the social and economic life of the community: it reduces their commitments and attachments" (West, 1984, 169). Even within the school, the educational process involves the student in only a passive way. Polk and Schafer (1972) illustrate the irrelevance of the student role by asking what happens when a student dies. The student disappears without leaving a social ripple aside from family bereavement. The student's role is not one that has to be filled by someone else. This marginality may contribute to delinquency by leaving the adolescent relatively free of the commitments that constrain deviance.

## Religion

Conventional wisdom has long held that people with strong religious commitment are not likely to become criminals. In the early penitentiaries that were the predecessors of our current prison system, Bible study was a major rehabilitative tool (Rothman, 1971). The first educational programs in prisons were intended to provide inmates with the basic literacy skills needed to read the Bible and other religious literature, which was expected to motivate the offender to mend his ways.

This view was supported by several early studies that showed a modest negative relationship between religious involvement and criminality. However, in 1969, Hirschi and Stark reported the results of a study that found that religious commitment was not related to delinquency. Neither church attendance, nor the belief in supernatural sanctions for rule breakers, nor the religiosity of parents was associated with delinquency. Because the work of Hirschi and Stark was methodologically superior to that of earlier researchers (and perhaps because of a secular bias among criminologists), the results of this study were commonly accepted as definitive. Most contemporary theories of the causes of crime do not consider religion to be an important factor.

However, subsequent studies found strong negative correlations between church attendance and delinquency (Higgins and Albrecht, 1977; Albrecht et al., 1977). How are we to reconcile these conflicting findings? One plausible answer has been given by Stark et al. (1982), who concluded that the key to resolving the contradiction was to look at differences in the communities studied. The studies that found there was no relationship between religiosity and delinquency were done in communities where religious participation was low, while the studies that found a relationship between religiosity and delinquency were done in communities that had high religious participation.

Stark et al. provided additional evidence to support this view. They compared samples of boys from Provo, Utah, where the church membership rate is very high, with boys from Seattle, where church membership rates are among the lowest in the United States. In Provo, the correlation (gamma) between church attendance and delinquency was –0.45, while in Seattle, it was only –0.13. This means that the relationship between attending church and not being involved in delinquency was much stronger in Provo than in Seattle. The relationship also holds for adult crime. In another paper (Stark et al., 1980), they found a negative relationship between church membership and crime rates for 193 U.S. cities. Stark et al. conclude that religiosity is related to reduced levels of involvement in crime and delinquency in communities where religion is important, but not in highly secularized communities.

Their explanation of this finding has broader implications for social control theory. Stark et al. believe that an **individualistic**, psychological view of the manner in which religion constrains behaviour has led researchers astray. Rather than looking at religion as affecting deviance through an individual's fear of religious sanctions, they suggest that "religion only serves to bind people to the moral order if religious influences permeate the culture and the social interactions of the individuals in question" (Stark et al., 1982). Religion will have its greatest impact where it binds its adherents into a moral community. In such a community, religious teachings will be salient and consistently reinforced. Under these circumstances, an individual is less likely to consider deviant behaviour. The costs to someone who decides to violate community norms may be high, and the likelihood of finding reference groups that support such a violation will be relatively low. Religion will have a greater impact if it is part of the community's institutional order than if it is a private matter.

**individualistic**
A theory that focuses on explaining the behaviour of individuals and using factors or features of the individual in explaining this behaviour.

It seems clear that religion constrains involvement in delinquent and criminal behaviour. However, this relationship is complex—it is greatest where there is a strong religious community; to some extent, it is mediated by one's relationships with family and friends (Elifson et al., 1983); and it has the most impact on behaviour (such as marijuana use) that may not be universally condemned by other segments of society (Linden and Currie, 1977).

## Issues with Social Control Theory

The evidence is generally supportive of control theory—in fact, many observers believe that empirical research provides more support for control theory than for its competitors. However, a number of issues have been raised about the theory that will be addressed in this section.

## How Does Control Theory Explain Upper-World Crime?

Control theory has focused on street crime and juvenile delinquency, not on occupational crime committed by high-status adults. In fact, upper-world crime would appear to contradict control theory's emphasis on the role of commitment in preventing crime because high-status people have a great stake in conformity. However, control theory can be used to understand such crime.

In his analysis of the Watergate cover-up in the United States, Hagan (1985, 171–73) provided a control theory of upper-world crime. The Watergate affair took place over a two-year period from 1972 to 1974. It involved the attempt by highly placed U.S. government officials to conceal their involvement in an unsuccessful plot to break into the offices of the Democratic National Committee. Ultimately, these events led to the resignation of President Richard Nixon and to the imprisonment of a number of his senior advisors.

From a control perspective, such illegal events could have been prevented by the belief that such acts were wrong. However, our society has not clearly defined upper-world morality. Politicians and business leaders rarely receive more than token punishments for illegal activities and are more likely to see their behaviour as only technically wrong than to see it as criminal. Transcripts of tapes made by Nixon reveal no concern with morality or ethics. In the absence of moral constraints, "the occurrence of such behaviors will depend largely on the risk and rewards ... associated with violating public and financial trust" (Hagan, 1985, 173). As you will see in Chapter 17, the rewards of upper-world crime are often very great. What, then, about the risks?

> The situational controls operative at the time of the initial Watergate offenses were inadequate. White House aides were able to manipulate funds and personnel for criminal political reasons with little expectation of detection. One reason why there was so little expectation of detection, of course, was that the criminals in this case were people who controlled the institutions of legal control (who could have been better positioned to deviate than those who controlled the FBI, the Justice Department, etc.?). Furthermore, once "caught," punishment became problematic in an atmosphere confused by promiscuous discussions of pardons. The uncertainties surrounding these events emphasize, then, the porous nature of the controls operative in one upper-world setting. (Hagan, 1985, 173)

In the next section of this chapter, you will learn that the theory has a message for those who wish to control deviance: monitor behaviour, recognize deviance, and punish deviant behaviour. While these principles are intended as advice for parents raising children, they are also applicable to upper-world crime. As Hagan tells us: "If there is a message to the policy-minded in the Watergate experience ... it is that checks and balances on power are crucial. Upperworld vocations, particularly politics and business, often carry with them a freedom to deviate unparalleled in the underworld. As control theory reminds us, unchecked freedom is a criminogenic condition" (1985, 173).

## Does Everyone Have the Same Motivation to Deviate?

**The Role of Delinquent Peers**  To the control theorist, we would *all* be criminal or delinquent but for the restraints provided by social controls so there is no need to account for the motivation to deviate. However, this appears to be only a partial explanation. Several factors may increase the likelihood of deviance among those who lack ties to the conventional order. We shall consider just one of these here—ties to deviant peers, which have been found to be strongly correlated to delinquency. For example, Sorenson and Brownfield (1995) found that ties to delinquent peers were a better predictor of drug use among Seattle youths than several measures of social control. Thornberry et al. (1993) studied a group of youths in Rochester, New York, and found that these youths were more likely to have committed delinquent acts while they were active members of juvenile gangs than they were either before or after their gang membership.

One way to deal with this is to integrate differential association (see Chapter 13) and control theories. These two theories present conflicting notions about the causation of crime and delinquency. For the differential association theorist, the crucial concept is ties to others; the pure control theorist claims that individuals with no ties to others—not even deviant others—are the most likely to become deviant.

Control theory conceives of an individual's social bond as having only a single dimension, weak to strong. When we incorporate differential association's emphasis on the importance of ties to deviant peers into the theory, however, we should see the social bond as multidimensional: conventional—weak to strong; unconventional—weak to strong. In bringing the two perspectives together, it is proposed that the first step is a weakness in the controls that bind an individual to the conventional system. An individual without these ties does not have to consider the consequences his or her actions will have on institutional and personal relationships. With the person "adrift" in this way (Matza, 1964), delinquency is a possible alternative. We are then faced with the problem of accounting for the motivation to commit acts of crime and delinquency (if we wish to go beyond the control theorists' reliance on natural motivation) and with explaining how one learns the techniques and rationalizations that facilitate deviance.

At least part of the answer to these questions can be found in differential association theory. We can postulate that the adolescent's lack of ties to the conventional order will increase the likelihood of association with deviant peers since the adolescent no longer has anything to lose by such affiliation. These ties will, in turn, increase the probability that the adolescent will be involved in deviance (see Figure 14.1).

This extension of control theory explains more of the variation in delinquency than either of its parent theories alone (Linden and Hackler, 1973; Linden and Fillmore, 1981). However, both of these studies used cross-sectional data rather than the longitudinal data that are more appropriate to the sequential theory we have proposed. Recently Maume et al. (2005) have used longitudinal data to study the relationship between marriage, delinquent peer attachment, and marijuana use, and their research also supports the integrated theory. They found that desistance from marijuana was influenced by marriage and, to a lesser extent, by a reduction in ties to deviant peers following a person's marriage.

The sequential model proposed here is more consistent with control theory than with Sutherland's differential association. The control–differential

**FIGURE 14.1**   **Control-Differential Association Theory**

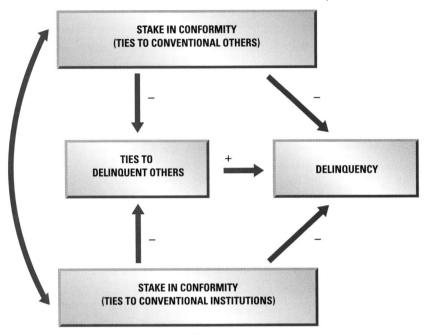

Source: Rick Linden and Cathy Fillmore. (1981). "A Comparative Study of Delinquency Involvement." *Canadian Review of Sociology and Anthropology* 18:343–61.

association model does not necessarily entail the strong element of normative approval required by Sutherland's cultural deviance perspective. Even if this normative approval is not a factor, delinquency may be fun and profitable and is not disapproved of by the delinquent's peer group. The internal dynamics of the group are such that it would be difficult for a reluctant member not to go along. Several researchers (Short and Strodtbeck, 1965; Velarde, 1978) have found that delinquent boys may try to look "bad" or "tough" in front of the group, even though they may express different views privately, because each believes the others are committed to such values. "An individual delinquent may wonder if or even think that his/her friends are not committed to delinquencies, but he/she can never confront the others to be sure of the degree of commitment they have" (Velarde, 1978). Several of the Winnipeg high-risk auto thieves who were on electronic monitoring said that they welcomed the bracelets because they allowed gave them an excuse to avoid going out with their friends to steal cars.

Other criminologists have also integrated control theory with competing perspectives. The most comprehensive extension of control theory has been carried out by Marc LeBlanc and several colleagues at the University of Montreal (Caplan and LeBlanc, 1985; Fréchette and LeBlanc, 1985; LeBlanc and Tremblay, 1985; LeBlanc, 1997). In addition to control and differential association variables, these researchers have also included the variables of external social control, personality traits, and the structural conditions of sex and social status. Most recently, Hardwick (2002) has shown that personality variables such as childhood temperament and self-control interact with social bonding variables and other social variables to produce delinquent and criminal behaviour. Because none of the theories you have studied in this text provides a complete explanation of crime and delinquency, it is likely that this integrative work will continue.

## Is Control Theory a Conservative Theory of Crime?

There is no simple explanation of crime, but different perspectives can help to explain it. In the absence of any consensus, some criminologists have taken an ideological approach in which theories are accepted or rejected on the basis of whether they are sufficiently conservative or radical. Robert Bohm has observed that "political and value preferences, ideology, empiricism, and positivism...stand in the way of any unity between traditional and radical criminologists" (1987, 327). For example, some conflict criminologists have been very critical of theories of crime, such as control theory, which do not focus on the political and economic structures that produce crime.

To some degree, this critique is a fair one. Control theorists have emphasized people's immediate environment, and from the time of Shaw and McKay until recently, have not considered the political and economic structures of their communities. However, these critics mistakenly reject the theory rather than recognize the fact that control variables can be incorporated within a structural perspective. For example, Shaw and McKay pointed out the importance of community variables in the development of social bonds. The ways in which control theory explains individual differences in criminal involvement are compatible with any number of structural theories, including conflict theories, and provide the link between society and individual that structural theories lack.

While control theory focuses on an individual's relationships with social institutions, structural factors condition these relationships. Although crime involves the behaviour of individuals, it has its origins in the social structure in which these individuals live. Lynch and Groves point out that "persons are more likely to conform when they stand to gain by doing so. But to make conformity attractive, society must do something for the individual; it must provide minimal satisfaction for both human and culturally defined needs. Social structures that provide for these needs are more likely to encourage conformity" (1989, 78).

If social institutions work together to encourage and to support conforming behaviour, rates of deviance should be low. However, if these institutions do not work together and if individuals and groups are alienated from their society's institutions, rates of deviance will be high. Consider the problems faced by Canada's Aboriginal people. They have far less power and fewer resources than other Canadians. They must cope with systems of education and religion imposed from outside which are not compatible with Aboriginal customs and traditions. Forced attendance at residential schools and forced adoption outside the community have destroyed family ties, and crippling rates of unemployment mean no job ties. School curricula that are irrelevant to Aboriginal students weaken children's attachment to their schools. Many Aboriginal Canadians face daily encounters with racism. They must submit to government policies that have not allowed Aboriginal communities to

**"Manitoba Aboriginal Justice Inquiry 1991 Summary"**
www.ajic.mb.ca/volume.html

achieve effective institutional integration. Under these conditions, strong social bonds are very difficult to develop, and the high rates of crime described in Chapter 5 can be expected. Recent work by Fitzgerald and Carrington (2008) has supported this view by showing the relationship between the structural characteristics of Winnipeg's disadvantaged neighbourhoods and Aboriginal involvement in crime.

Manitoba's Aboriginal Justice Inquiry concluded: "From our review of the information available to us, including the nature of the crimes committed by aboriginal people, and after hearing the hundreds of submissions presented to us in the course of our hearings, we believe that the relatively high rates of crime among aboriginal people are a result of the despair, dependency, anger, frustration, and sense of injustice prevalent in aboriginal communities, stemming from the cultural and community breakdown that has occurred over the past century" (Hamilton and Sinclair, 1991, 91). The impact of structural conditions on social bonds and on rates of crime and other deviance is illustrated in the discussion of life in Davis Inlet, Labrador, in Box 14.2. By incorporating control elements within a structural perspective, the example demonstrates the complementarity of the control and conflict approaches.

# FOCUS BOX 14.2

## THE MUSHUAU INNU OF DAVIS INLET

On several occasions over the past 20 years, Canadians were saddened by television images of young children sniffing gas in Davis Inlet in Labrador. The first incident was described by a team of researchers who studied the Mushuau Innu of Davis Inlet:

One day in February 1992, six children in the Innu community of Davis Inlet in Labrador burned to death in a house fire. Almost a year later, six of their friends, depressed at the approaching anniversary of the tragedy and convinced that the ghost of a young Innu was telling them that they should end their own lives, barricaded themselves in an unheated shack in temperatures of –40 and tried to kill themselves by sniffing petrol. The local Innu policeman reached them in time and, with great presence of mind, videotaped their responses as they were removed to safety. Then, to show the

world the horrors of life in Utshimassits (as the Innu call Davis Inlet), he passed the tape on to a television station.

Over the next few days, his graphic pictures of wild-eyed children hurling themselves against the wall and screaming "Leave me alone! I want to die!" shocked Canada and made Utshimassits, after years of official neglect, the focus of national and international media attention. Journalists and television crews suddenly converged on Davis Inlet from all over North American and Europe to try to discover how a supposedly "modern" and enlightened country like Canada could produce such a vision of desolation and despair. They were scandalized by what they found.

Utshimassits is a community living in almost unimaginable squalor and disarray. Rows of battered wooden shacks, looking more like a Third World refugee camp than

*(continued)*

a 'western' village, line unmade roads that for most of the year are no more than sheets of dirty ice. Virtually none of the houses—except for a handful belonging to non-Innu professionals like the priest, schoolteachers and nurses—have running water or mains drainage. Sewage is simply thrown onto the ground, where it is eaten by dogs or trampled by the gangs who roam the settlement.... These conditions are reflected in the appalling health and mortality statistics for Davis Inlet, where family breakdown, sexual abuse, drunkenness and alcohol-related disease, violence, accidents and self-harm have become endemic. (Samson et al., 1999, 6)

These problems did not exist prior to European colonization. Thus Samson and his colleagues conclude that the cultural and social disintegration of the Mushuau Innu has been caused by their past and current relationship with Canadian society. While many Aboriginal communities in Canada are healthy and thriving, particularly those that own valuable land and resources, many others share at least some of the problems of the Innu (see Shkilnyk, 1985).

How did colonialism cause the decline of a healthy people? The Mushuau Innu were successful nomadic hunters. However, colonial governments did not consider hunting to be an economically viable way of life and effectively forced the Innu to give up their centuries-old way of life and settle in sedentary communities:

After Newfoundland and Labrador joined Confederation in 1949, the federal government began to build new houses for the Innu. The houses were small (750 square feet), built close together and had few amenities. While equipped with tubs, toilets and sinks, the houses had no water or sewage services, few pieces of furniture and a single power outlet. Many families used hot plates or diesel fuel to start fires to warm their homes (Innu Nation, 1995). Gradually, the residents of Davis Inlet found themselves slipping out of touch with their traditional migratory way of life while having difficulty

fully embracing a "modern" sedentary life-style. (Burns, 2006, 68)

After their initial settlement, the entire community was moved three times. The first move, in 1948, was a forced migration from Davis Inlet to Nutak, which was over 300 kilometres away (Denov and Campbell, 2002). The Innu were moved without their consent to a location far away from their traditional hunting grounds, ostensibly to improve their economic prospects. The band did not accept the move and walked back to their former location. In 1967, they were moved to an island on Davis Inlet, again for economic reasons. However, as with the earlier move, there were no economic opportunities on the island and they were isolated during the spring thaw and fall freeze-up when the island was accessible only by air. Their new houses lacked running water and sewer systems and quickly degenerated to Third World standards (Denov and Campbell, 2002). While the move was intended to help the Innu become more economically self-sufficient, there were few jobs in the area. Finally, in 2002–03, they were moved back to the mainland to a new community at Natuashish. The latest move was done with the consent of the Innu, and for the first time they were consulted about the structure of their new community.

In addition to the shift from a nomadic to a sedentary life, the horrible living conditions, and the disruption caused by the moves of the community, other factors have contributed to the problems of the Innu. Missionaries tried to replace traditional spiritual practices with Christianity. Massive hydroelectric projects, mining, and logging have destroyed part of the natural environment of the Innu without their approval and without compensation. All these changes have disrupted the cultural continuity of the people of Davis Inlet by altering their relationship with their traditional lands:

...land is of central importance to aboriginal culture, identity and well-being. Aboriginal people have a unique relationship with the land that guides their daily life and provides them with great meaning....Isolating people

*(continued)*

from their traditional habitat, therefore, breaks the spiritual relationship with the land that exists within many aboriginal communities. (Denov and Campbell, 2002, 24)

The Innu have been cut off from their ties to the land and their knowledge of how to survive on the land is not relevant to their sedentary lifestyle: "Displacement among the Innu can thus be seen as part of a painful process of dispossession and alienation of their society from the land and from the cultural and spiritual roots it nurtures, ultimately leading to a sense of powerlessness" (Denov and Campbell, 2002, 24).

This discontinuity (what Durkheim would call anomie) is particularly acute among young people. The school system is a major source of their problems. Schooling interfered with learning traditional skills and yet did not prepare them for mainstream jobs. Because the schools did not use the Innu language, many young people could not communicate with their Innu-speaking elders. Several generations of Innu have been cast adrift between two cultures and prepared for what Samson has called "a way of life that does not exist....Many Innu have gradually become neither hunters nor 'modern' Canadians" (2003, 13) and as a result have strikingly high rates of suicide, gas sniffing, alcoholism, interpersonal violence, and vandalism. In the words of one young

Innu: "We were taught in school to be doctors, nurses, store managers, teachers, that's what we were taught in school, to be one of those people. I was never taught to be a hunter or to learn about my culture, I was never taught like that, it was always the white culture that was focused in the school.... I see a lot of kids that have failed in school...They feel so ashamed about not learning to speak English and then they will start drinking, they will drink and drink, and a lot of those people are still drinking because they are ashamed, they don't know how to write, how to speak the language" (Samson et al., 1999, 22).

In looking at the tragic story of the Mushuau Innu, we can see the complementarity of the control and conflict approaches. At one level, members of groups with high rates of crime and other deviance typically lack the social bonds that might tie them to the social order. However, if we ask why the strength of social bonds is less among those who, like many Aboriginal people, are forced to live on the margins of society, we must turn to the work of conflict theorists and their analyses of the political and economic forces that have created the poverty, powerlessness, and inequality that shape their lives.

Source: Samson, Colin, James Wilson, and Jonathan Mazower. (1999). *Canada's Tibet: The Killing of the Innu*. London: Survival.

# Policy Implications of Control Theory

Early control theorists were strongly aware of the policy implications of their work. For example, Shaw established and worked for many years with the Chicago Area Project, trying to strengthen community ties in a slum area. To illustrate some of the possible uses to which the findings of research done from a social control perspective might be put, we can consider the role of the family and the school in delinquency prevention.

## Policy Implications—The Family

Research has shown the importance of family relationships in the causation of delinquency. However, we are a long way from knowing what to do about this problem. How can we strengthen the family and make sure that parents love and care for their children? If anything, we are living in an era in which the family is becoming less stable as an institution.

While many of the problems in the family relationships of delinquents may require structural solutions, some small beginnings have been made in the task of trying to re-establish a bond between parent and child. One of the best examples of this is the work of Gerald Patterson and his colleagues at the Oregon Social Learning Center.

Based on his experiences treating several hundred families of antisocial children and on detailed observation of interaction patterns within these families, Patterson concluded that since "antisocial acts that are not punished tend to persist" (1980, 89), the key to changing the behaviour of these troublesome children was to punish their misdeeds. Hirschi observed that "this conclusion may come as no surprise to those millions of parents who have spent years talking firmly to their children, yelling and screaming at them, spanking them, grounding them, cutting off their allowances, and in general doing whatever they could think of to get the little bastards to behave; but it is exceedingly rare among social scientists, especially those who deal with crime and delinquency" (1983, 53).

While this approach might seem disturbingly authoritarian to some, Patterson is, in fact, merely advocating techniques used by families that are successful in avoiding delinquency. You will recall that parental supervision and disciplinary practices were strongly related to delinquent behaviour. Patterson has determined that the key aspects of this process involve several steps that have been summarized as "(1) monitor the child's behavior; (2) recognize deviant behavior when it occurs; and (3) punish such behavior" (in Hirschi, 1983, 55). In a properly functioning family, the parents understand this process, and the system is activated by the bonds of affection and caring between parent and child. The key is not just punishment—many parents of problem children were found to punish them more often and more harshly than did the parents of normal children. However, the parents of problem children did not know *how* to punish their children, and punishment actually made things worse. Discipline was used, but it was erratic and unpredictable and not directed specifically at the child's misbehaviour. "The failure of parents to use reasonable reinforcements contingent on steadily monitored behaviour places the child in a situation in which he comes to understand that he cannot control by his own actions what happens to him" (Wilson, 1983, 53). As a result, the children in effect train their parents (and others, such as teachers) to accept their misbehaviour.

Working with the families of pre-adolescent problem children, Patterson has taught parents how to shape their children's behaviour by using non-physical punishments (such as time-outs), by rewarding good conduct, and by interacting more positively as a family. This training process is often long and difficult. Many of the parents did not like their children, did not identify with the role of parent, and refused to recognize that their children were deviant (Patterson, 1980). Many were trying to cope with difficult economic and family situations as well as with the problems created by their antisocial children, and they resisted help.

Despite these problems, the results suggest that this program has potential. One evaluation showed that stealing was reduced from an average of 0.83 incidents per week to 0.07 incidents per week after the parent training program.

**Oregon Social Learning Center**
www.oslc.org/

The treatment effects persisted for six months, but within one year, stealing rates had gone back to pretreatment levels (Moore et al., 1979). This suggests that parental retraining may be necessary. Longer-term results were obtained with children diagnosed as aggressive, with whom program effects lasted longer than 12 months. The program also had a positive impact on siblings, indicating that the parenting skills of the parents had improved.

Richard Tremblay and his colleagues (1991) have evaluated a program similar to Patterson's in which preventive treatment was provided for disruptive kindergarten boys in a low-income community in Montreal. The treatment combined teaching social skills to the boys with training their parents to be consistent and constructive toward their children. Two years after the treatment, the treated boys reported less fighting and less theft than comparison groups of boys who did not receive the treatment. The classroom behaviour of the treated boys also showed improvement.

Programs like these may be too expensive to be implemented on a broad scale. However, given the high concentration of criminality in a relatively small proportion of families, they do have some potential for reducing crime rates. The demonstration that improved parenting can have an impact on

# FOCUS BOX 14.3

## PARENTING DELINQUENT YOUTHS

"When I met him, he was six and a half years of age. There was nothing about his appearance that identified him as the boy who had set the record."

These words are those of Gerald R. Patterson, a family therapist at the Oregon Social Learning Center in Eugene. The "record" to which he referred was the frequency—measured with painstaking care by the Learning Center's staff—with which Don, a small boy, displayed rotten behavior. Nearly four times a *minute* while in his home, Don would whine, yell, disobey, hit, or shove. When he was not at home, telephone calls from teachers and merchants would mark his progress through the neighborhood: "He left school two hours early, stole candy from a store, and appropriated a toy from a neighborhood child."

Don had "a sleazy look about him," Patterson wrote, "like a postcard carried too long in a hip pocket." His violent outbursts were frightening; any simple request or minor provocation would trigger obscene shouts, attacks on other children, or assaults on the furniture. His mother was tired, depressed, and nearly desperate as a result of coping unaided with this monster—no babysitter would take on the job of minding Don, whatever the pay. She nevertheless persevered, changing his wet sheets, bathing and dressing him, even feeding him, all the while talking to him in tones that vacillated between cajolery and scolding, murmurs and shouts. When her seemingly bottomless patience was at last at an end, she would threaten or hit him with a stick. That produced only temporary compliance. When the father was home, things were not much different. The shouting and fighting between Don and his younger brother continued, occasionally punctuated by the father slapping both children.

Children like Don are the youthful precursors not only of difficult teenagers, but sometimes of delinquents and adult criminals. The progression from violent, dishonest youngster to violent, dishonest teenager is not automatic, but it is common.

Source: James Q. Wilson. (1983). "Raising Kids," *The Atlantic* (October), p. 45.

misbehaviour should encourage those advocating structural changes (e.g., less unemployment) that are aimed at least in part at providing more family stability and programs (e.g., foster care) that provide substitute parents for children. The results also suggest that research should be done on other methods of increasing parenting skills, such as providing training in high schools and for the parents of newborn children.

One of the potential problems with this approach is that it can easily lead to blaming parents for their children's behaviour when the parents themselves have been victimized by their social and economic circumstances. For example, there is considerable documentation of the impact of the residential school system which forcibly removed Aboriginal children from their parents for most of the year and put them into school situations where many were physically and sexually abused and where attempts were made to destroy their cultures (Miller, 1996). Not surprisingly, many victims of the residential school system did not know how to raise their own children.

## The Schools and Social Policy

In their assessment of the role of the school in delinquency, Schafer and Polk suggest that the school fails in two ways: "The school not only fails to offset initial handicaps of lower-income and minority group children, but actively contributes to education failure and deterioration. If this is true, the school itself becomes an important active force in the generation of delinquency insofar as it is linked to failure" (1967, 236).

Research suggests that some schools and some teachers are better than others in helping children to function both academically and behaviourally. Rutter and Giller (1984) have suggested a number of factors differentiating good and bad schools. These include the standards and values set and maintained by the school, the degree to which students are allowed to participate in decision making, school and class size, staff turnover, and the degree of concentration of intellectually and socially disadvantaged pupils. Each of these factors has rather obvious policy implications.

A number of studies have looked at the impact of the teacher–student relationship on students' behaviour. British researchers (Hargreaves et al., 1975) have found that some teachers provoked deviance, while others were able to get students to cooperate. Failure to get along with teachers may weaken an adolescent's commitment to school. It may also affect grades by leading teachers to make negative judgments about a youth's abilities and character. Thus the classroom process may help to weaken an adolescent's attachment and commitment to the school.

Others have proposed changes in the type of curriculum and in the manner in which it is taught. Weis and Hawkins (1979) have recommended a greater use of programs such as performance-based education, which involves establishing learning goals for each student and developing individually paced programs with rewards for improvement. They also suggest the use of cross-age tutoring and other ways of involving students in the operation of the school to enhance their level of commitment.

Other research (Elliott, 1966; LeBlanc, 1983) suggests the importance of mechanisms for ensuring a transition from school to work, especially among those students who are not going on to university.

Schools must also ensure that their curriculum is relevant to the lives of their students. This was not achieved by the system of residential schools that has served Aboriginal youths in the Canadian North. A child who grows up in a small settlement on the Arctic coast will be flown south to Yellowknife or another southern point for high school. Besides being cut off from family and community, the student is educated into a way of life that is very different from that which exists in the home village. As a result, students may no longer fit into their home communities, but, at the same time, they are not completely acculturated into southern ways (Brody, 1975). Increasing rates of crime and other deviance among people who lack strong community ties can be consequences of this system.

It will not be easy to make changes in the schools to reduce the likelihood that students will get involved in delinquency and subsequent adult criminality. It is hard to make significant changes in large institutions that must satisfy a number of different interest groups. Even if we could make changes quickly, we could not be certain that they would have the desired effect. For example, programs that separate misbehaving students may have unintended consequences. Schafer and Polk (1967) discuss a program in which students with academic and behaviour problems were placed in special classes and provided with individual instruction by specially selected teachers. The outcome of the program was negative—placement in a class with other poorly motivated students compounded their problems and further alienated them from the mainstream of school life. The students may also have suffered from being labelled as troublemakers.

Despite these potential problems, there is merit in trying to work within the school system. The research that has been done represents a promising beginning, but what is needed is a program in which the lessons learned are systematically applied to the schools on an experimental basis. The types of reforms that would be most likely to succeed would be beneficial to all students and possibly reduce delinquency as well.

**TABLE 14.1    Social Control Theories**

| Theory | Theorists | Key Elements |
|---|---|---|
| Social disorganization theories | Durkheim, Thrasher, Shaw and McKay | Deviance will be highest in disorganized communities that lack social controls. |
| Early social control theories | Reiss, Nye | Stresses the importance of personal controls, particularly those provided by the family. |
| Social bond theory | Hirschi | The four elements of the social bond: attachment, commitment, involvement, and belief. |
| General theory of crime | Gottfredson Hirschi | Individuals with low self-control have a greater propensity to commit crimes when they have the opportunity to do so. |
| Control-differential association theory | Linden | Lack of ties to the conventional order will increase the likelihood of association with deviant peers. These ties will, in turn, increase the probability of delinquency involvement. |

# SUMMARY

- Rather than asking "Why do some people break the law?" social control theorists ask "Why don't we all do it?" The answer to this question lies in the processes that bind people to conventional society (see Box 14.1).

- Early theorists, including Thrasher and Shaw and McKay, looked at community-level controls. Disorganized communities that did not provide meaningful employment to residents and did not have strong families, schools, and churches could not provide adequate social controls and would have high rates of crime and other types of deviance.

- Later social control theories focused on the social bonds of individuals. Travis Hirschi described four interrelated aspects of the social bond that constrain our behaviour: attachment, commitment, involvement, and belief.

- Research on social control theory has pointed to the importance of the family and the school in restraining involvement in delinquency. While less research has been done with adults, it suggests that stable employment and a cohesive marriage are important factors.

- Among the criticisms of social control theory are these: it does not adequately explain white-collar crime; it does not account for the motivation to deviate; it is too individualistic; and it is too conservative.

- Recent theoretical work has returned to the social disorganization tradition and has once again linked societal and community factors to individual-level bonds.

## QUESTIONS FOR CRITICAL THINKING

1. How could you apply the principles of social control theory to reduce the amount of white-collar and corporate crime in Canada?
2. Discuss three of the criticisms that have been made of social control theory. How would you defend the theory against these criticisms?
3. Several of the theorists discussed in this chapter have looked at the relationship between the community and crime. Starting with the example of the tragic situation in Davis Inlet, discuss some of the government policies that have led to high rates of crime and other types of deviance among Canada's Aboriginal people.
4. Based on your knowledge of social control theory, what changes would you make to the public school system to help reduce delinquency?

## NET WORK

In 1998 the Canadian government established a $100-million fund to support the Aboriginal Head Start program. The program is intended to help reserve communities meet the educational, emotional, social, health, and nutritional needs of children under the age of six. Some early childhood education programs have proven very successful in reducing rates of crime and delinquency. This program is based on the U.S. Head Start program. You can find out more about Head Start at **http://www.acf.hhs.gov/programs/opre/hs/impact_study/index.html.**

Using some of the evaluations you will find on this link, do the following exercises:

1. What do you think would be the impact of Head Start programs on delinquency and crime? Do you think they are a cost-effective way of reducing crime?
2. The most effective early childhood education program is the Perry Preschool program, which you can read about at **http://www.highscope.org/Content.asp?ContentId=219.** What lessons can those running Head Start programs learn from the Perry Preschool program?
3. How important do you think it is to involve parents in Head Start programs? Does the research show that programs involving parents are more effective than those based only in the schools?

## KEY TERMS

attachment; pg. 437
belief; pg. 438
commitment; pg. 437
ecological fallacy; pg. 435
independent variable; pg. 435

individualistic; pg. 445
involvement; pg. 438
social bond; pg. 434
social control theory; pg. 433

## BIBLIOGRAPHY

Albrecht, Stan I., Bruce A. Chadwick, and David S. Alcorn. (1977). "Religiosity and Deviance: Application of an Attitude–Behavior Contingent Consistency Model." *Journal for the Scientific Study of Religion* 16: 263–74.

Anderson, Elijah. (1994). "The Code of the Streets." *The Atlantic Monthly* (May): 81–94.

Aronson, Elliot. (1984). *The Social Animal.* New York: W.H. Freeman.

Arum, Richard, and Irenee R. Beattie. (1999). "High School Experience and the Risk of Adult Incarceration." *Criminology* 37(3):515–36.

Biron, Louise, and Marc LeBlanc. "Family and Delinquency." Unpublished paper, Université de Montréal.

Bohm, Robert. (1987). "Comment on 'Traditional Contributions to Radical Criminology' by Groves and Sampson." *Journal of Research in Crime and Delinquency* 24 (November): 324–31.

Box, Steven. (1971). *Deviance, Reality and Society.* London: Holt, Rinehart and Winston.

———. (1981). *Deviance, Reality and Society* (2nd ed.). London: Holt, Rinehart and Winston.

Brody, Hugh. (1975). *The People's Land.* Markham, ON: Penguin Books.

Burns, Ausra. (2006). "Moving and Moving Forward: Mushuau Innu Relocation from Davis Inlet to Natuashish." *Acadiensis* 2 (Spring): 64–84.

Caplan, Aaron. (1977). "Attachment to Parents and Delinquency." Paper presented at the annual meeting of the Canadian Sociology and Anthropology Association, Fredericton, NB.

Caplan, Aaron, and Marc LeBlanc. (1985). "A Cross-Cultural Verification of a Social Control Theory." *International Journal of Comparative and Applied Criminal Justice* 9(2):123–38.

Chambliss, William. (1973). "The Saints and the Roughnecks." *Society* 11:24–31.

Denov, Myriam, and Kathryn Campbell. (2002). "Casualties of Aboriginal Displacement in Canada; Children at Risk among the Innu of Labrador." *Refuge* 20(2):21–33.

Durkheim, Émile. (1951). *Suicide*. Translated by John A. Spaulding and George Simpson. New York: Free Press.

Elifson, Kirk W., David M. Petersen, and C. Kirk Hadaway. (1983). "Religiosity and Delinquency: A Contextual Analysis." *Criminology* 21:505–27.

Elliott, Delbert S. (1966). "Delinquency, School Attendance and Dropout." *Social Problems* 13 (Winter): 307–14.

Engstad, Peter A. (1975). "Environmental Opportunities and the Ecology of Crime." In Robert A. Silverman and James J. Teevan (eds.), *Crime in Canadian Society* (pp. 193–211). Toronto: Butterworths.

Fischer, Donald G. (1980). *Family Relationship Variables and Programs Influencing Juvenile Delinquency*. Ottawa: Ministry of the Solicitor General.

Fitzgerald, Robin, and Peter Carrington. (2008). "The Neighbourhood Context of Urban Aboriginal Crime." *Canadian Journal of Criminology and Criminal Justice* 50:523–57.

Fréchette, M., and Marc LeBlanc. (1985). *Des délinquantes: émergence et développement*. Chicoutimi: Gaëtan Morin.

Glueck, Sheldon, and Eleanor Glueck. (1950). *Unraveling Juvenile Delinquency*. Cambridge, MA: Harvard University Press.

Gomme, Ian. (1985). "Predictors of Status and Criminal Offences Among Male and Female Delinquency in an Ontario Community." *Canadian Journal of Criminology* 26:313–23.

Gottfredson, Michael R., and Travis Hirschi. (1990). *A General Theory of Crime*. Stanford, CT: Stanford University Press.

Gove, Walter R., and Robert D. Crutchfield. (1982). "The Family and Juvenile Delinquency." *The Sociological Quarterly* 23:301–19.

Hagan, John. (1985). *Modern Criminology: Crime, Criminal Behavior and Its Control*. New York: McGraw-Hill.

Hagan, John, A.R. Gillis, and John Simpson. (1985). "The Class Structure of Gender and Delinquency: Toward a Power-Control Theory of Common Delinquent Behavior." *American Journal of Sociology* 90:1151–78.

Hagan, John, and Bill McCarthy. (1997). *Mean Streets: Youth Crime and Homelessness*. Cambridge: Cambridge University Press.

Hamilton, A.C., and C.M. Sinclair. (1991). *Report of the Aboriginal Justice Inquiry of Manitoba*, Vol. 1. Winnipeg: Queen's Printer.

Hardwick, Kelly. (2002). "Unravelling 'Crime in the Making': Re-examining the Role of Informal Social Control in the Genesis and Stability of Delinquency and Crime." Unpublished Ph.D. Thesis, University of Calgary.

Hargreaves, David H. (1967). *Social Relations in a Secondary School*. London: Routledge and Kegan Paul.

Hargreaves, David H., Stephen K. Hester, and Frank J. Mellor. (1975). *Deviance in Classrooms*. London: Routledge and Kegan Paul.

Higgins, Paul C., and Gary L. Albrecht. (1977). "Hellfire and Delinquency Revisited." *Social Forces* 55:952–58.

Hirschi, Travis. (1969). *Causes of Delinquency*. Berkeley: University of California Press.

———. (1983). "Crime and the Family." In James Q. Wilson (ed.), *Crime and Public Policy* (pp. 53–68). San Francisco: ICS Press.

Hirschi, Travis, and Rodney Stark. (1969). "Hellfire and Delinquency." *Social Problems* 17: 202–13.

Ho, Caroline, Deborah Bluestein, and Jennifer Jenkins. (2008). "Cultural Differences in the Relationship Between Parenting and Children's Behavior." *Developmental Psychology* 44:507–22.

Keane, Carl, Paul S. Maxim, and James J. Teevan. (1993). "Drinking and Driving, Self-control and Gender: Testing a General Theory of Crime." *Journal of Research in Crime and Delinquency* 30:30–46.

Kornhauser, Ruth Rosner. (1978). *Social Sources of Delinquency*. Chicago: University of Chicago Press.

Kupfer, George. (1966). "Middle Class Delinquency in a Canadian City." Unpublished Ph.D. dissertation, Department of Sociology, University of Washington.

LaGrange, Theresa, and Robert Silverman. (1999). "Low Self-Control and Opportunity: Testing the General Theory of Crime as an Explanation for Gender Differences in Delinquency." *Criminology* 37(1):41–72.

LeBlanc, Marc. (1983). "Delinquency as an Epiphenomenon of Adolescence." In Raymond R. Corrado, Marc LeBlanc, and Jean Trepanier (eds.), *Current Issues in Juvenile Justice* (pp. 31–48). Toronto: Butterworths.

———. (1997). "A Generic Control Theory of the Criminal Phenomenon." In Terence P. Thornberry (ed.), *Developmental Theories of Crime and Delinquency* (pp. 215–85). New Brunswick, NJ: Transaction Publishers.

LeBlanc, Marc, Marc Ouimet, and Richard Tremblay. (1988). "An Integrative Control Theory of Delinquent Behavior: A Validation 1976–1985." *Psychiatry* 51:164–76.

LeBlanc, Marc, and Richard Tremblay. (1985). "An Integrative Control Theory of Delinquent Behavior: A Validation 1976–1985." Paper presented at the annual meeting of the American Society of Criminology, San Diego.

Lehrer, Jonah. (2009). "Don't: The Secret of Self-Control." *The New Yorker*, May 18, pp.26–32.

Linden, Eric. (1974). "Interpersonal Ties and Delinquent Behavior." Unpublished Ph.D. dissertation, University of Washington.

Linden, Rick, and Raymond Currie. (1977). "Religiosity and Drug Use: A Test of Social Control Theory." *Canadian Journal of Criminology and Corrections* 19:346–55.

Linden, Rick, and Cathy Fillmore. (1981). "A Comparative Study of Delinquency Involvement." *Canadian Review of Sociology and Anthropology* 18:343–61.

Linden, Rick, and James C. Hackler. (1973). "Affective Ties and Delinquency." *Pacific Sociological Review* 16:27–46.

Lynch, Michael, and W. Byron Groves. (1989). *A Primer in Radical Criminology* (2nd ed.). Albany, NY: Harrow and Heston.

Matza, David. (1964). *Delinquency and Drift*. New York: Wiley.

Maume, Michael, Graham Ousey, and Kevin Beaver. (2005). "Cutting the Grass: A Re-examination of the Link between Marital Attachment, Delinquent Peers and Desistance from Marijuana Use." *Journal of Quantitative Criminology* 21 (March): 27–53.

Miller, James. (1996). *Shingwuak's Vision: A History of Native Residential Schools*. Toronto: University of Toronto Press.

Mischel, Walter, Ozlem Ayduk, Marc Berman, B.J. Casey, Ian Gotlib, John Jonides, Ethan Kross, Theresa Teslovich, Nicole Wilson, Vivian Zayas, and Yuichi Shoda. (2011).

"'Willpower' Over the Life span: Decomposing Self-Regulation." *Social Cognitive and Affective Neuroscience* 6:252–56.

Moore, D.R., B.P. Chamberlain, and L. Mukai. (1979). "Children at Risk for Delinquency: A Follow-up Comparison of Aggressive Children and Children Who Steal." *Journal of Abnormal Child Psychology* 7:345–55.

Naffine, Ngaire. (1987). *Female Crime: The Construction of Women in Criminology*. Sydney: Allen and Unwin.

Nye, F. Ivan. (1958). *Family Relationships and Delinquent Behavior*. New York: Wiley.

Patterson, G.R. (1980). "Children Who Steal." In Travis Hirschi and Michael Gottfredson (eds.), *Understanding Crime: Current Theory and Research*. Beverly Hills: Sage.

Polk, Kenneth, and F. Lynn Richmond. (1972). "Those Who Fail." In Kenneth Polk and Walter E. Schafer (eds.), *Schools and Delinquency* (pp. 55–69). Englewood Cliffs, NJ: Prentice Hall.

Polk, Kenneth, and Walter E. Schafer. (1972). *Schools and Delinquency*. Englewood Cliffs, NJ: Prentice Hall.

Pratt, Travis, and Francis T. Cullen. (2000). "The Empirical Status of Gottfredson and Hirschi's General Theory of Crime: A Meta-Analysis." *Criminology* 38 (3):501–34.

Reiss, Albert J., Jr. (1951). "Delinquency as the Failure of Personal and Social Controls." *American Sociological Review* 16:196–207.

Rothman, David J. (1971). The Discovery of the Asylum. Boston: Little, Brown and Company.

Rutter, Michael, and Henri Giller. (1984). *Juvenile Delinquency: Trends and Perspectives*. New York: The Guilford Press.

Sampson, Robert J., and John H. Laub. (1993). *Crime in the Making: Pathways and Turning Points Through Life*. Cambridge: Harvard University Press.

Samson, Colin. (2003). *A Way of Life That Does Not Exist: Canada and the Extinguishment of the Innu*. London: Verso.

Samson, Colin, James Wilson, and Jonathan Mazower. (1999). *Canada's Tibet: The Killing of the Innu*. London: Survival.

Savoie, Josee. (2008). "Neighbourhood Characteristics and the Distribution of Crime." Ottawa: Statistics Canada, available at http://www.statcan.gc.ca/pub/85-561-m/85-561-m2008010-eng.htm; accessed May 5, 2011.

Schafer, Walter E., and Kenneth Polk. (1967). "Delinquency and the Schools." In *The President's Commission on Law Enforcement and Administration of Justice, Task Force Report: Juvenile Delinquency and Crime* (pp. 222–77). Washington, DC: U.S. Government Printing Office.

Shoda, Yuichi, Walter Mischel, and Philip Peake. (1990). "Predicting Adolescent Cognitive and Self-Regulatory Competencies from Preschool Delay of Gratification Identifying Diagnostic Conditions." *Developmental Psychology* 26(6):978–86.

Simons, Ronald, L.Chyi-In Wu, Kuei-Hsui Lin, Leslie Gordon, and Rand D. Conger. (2000). "A Cross-Cultural Examination of the Link Between Corporal Punishment and Adolescent Antisocial Behavior." *Criminology* 38:47–80.

Shkilnyk, Anastasia M. (1985). *A Poison Stronger Than Love: The Destruction of an Ojibwa Community*. New Haven, CT: Yale University Press.

Short, James, Jr., and Fred Strodtbeck. (1965). *Group Process and Gang Delinquency*. Chicago: University of Chicago Press.

Sorenson, Ann Marie, and David Brownfield. (1995). "Adolescent Drug Use and a General Theory of Crime: An Analysis of a Theoretical Integration." *Canadian Journal of Criminology* 37:19–37.

Sprott, Jane. (2004). "The Development of Early Delinquency: Can Classroom and School Climates Make a Difference?" *Canadian Journal of Criminology and Criminal Justice* 46:553–72.

Sprott, Jane, and Anthony Doob. (2000). "Bad, Sad, and Rejected: The Lives of Aggressive Children." *Canadian Journal of Criminology* 42:123–33.

Stark, Rodney, Daniel P. Doyle, and Lori Kent. (1980). "Rediscovering Moral Communities: Church Membership and Crime." In Travis Hirschi and Michael Gottfredson (eds.), *Understanding Crime: Current Theory and Research* (pp. 43–52). Beverly Hills: Sage.

———. (1982). "Religion and Delinquency: The Ecology of a 'Lost' Relationship." *Journal of Research in Crime and Delinquency* 19:4–24.

Statistics Canada. (1998). "National Longitudinal Study of Children and Youth." *The Daily*, October 28.

Steinmetz, Suzanne K., and Murray A. Straus. (1980). "The Family as a Cradle of Violence." In Delos H. Kelly (ed.), *Criminal Behavior* (pp. 130–42). New York: St. Martin's Press.

Thornberry, Terence P., Marvin D. Krohn, Alan J. Lizotte, and Deborah Chard-Wierschem. (1993). "The Role of Juvenile Gangs in Facilitating Delinquent Behavior." *Journal of Research in Crime and Delinquency* 30:55–87.

Thrasher, Frederic M. (1963). *The Gang*. Chicago: University of Chicago Press.

Tremblay, Richard E., Joan McCord, Helene Boileau, Pierre Charlebois, Claude Gagnon, Marc LeBlanc, and Serge Larivee. (1991). "Can Disruptive Boys Be Helped to Become Competent?" *Psychiatry* 54:148–61.

Velarde, Albert J. (1978). "Do Delinquents Really Drift?" *British Journal of Criminology* 18 (1):23–39.

Weis, Joseph G., and J. David Hawkins. (1979). *Preventing Delinquency: The Social Development Approach*. Seattle: Center for Law and Justice, University of Washington.

West, D.J. (1982). *Delinquency: Its Roots, Careers, and Prospects*. London: Heinemann.

West, D.J., and D.P. Farrington. (1973). *Who Becomes Delinquent?* London: Heinemann.

———. (1977). *The Delinquent Way of Life*. London: Heinemann.

West, W. Gordon. (1984). *Young Offenders and the State: A Canadian Perspective on Delinquency*. Toronto: Butterworths.

Wilson, Harriet. (1980). "Parental Supervision: A Neglected Aspect of Delinquency." *British Journal of Criminology* 20:30–39.

Wilson, James Q. (1983). "Raising Kids." *The Atlantic Monthly*: 45–56.

# Deterrence, Routine Activity, and Rational Choice Theories

**Rick Linden**

UNIVERSITY OF MANITOBA

**Daniel J. Koenig**

FORMERLY OF UNIVERSITY OF VICTORIA

This chapter introduces you to several perspectives on crime that have their roots in the Classical theory of crime discussed in Chapter 8. Most sociological and psychological theories of crime seek to explain why people break the law and focus on the backgrounds, character, and motivation of offenders. In contrast, *deterrence theories* such as Beccaria's Classical theory focus on the factors influencing an individual's decision whether or not to commit an offence and assert that the legal system can be used to affect that decision.

The other theories discussed in this chapter—rational choice theory and routine activities theory—also examine the decision to commit specific criminal events so they also focus more on the crimes than on the background of those who commit these crimes. *Rational choice theory* assumes that people break the law because they believe this will provide them with some reward: a burglar steals money to pay living expenses, an addict smokes crack to get high and to avoid withdrawal, and a gang member shoots a rival to protect his drug distribution business. The criminal's decision may or may not appear rational to the rest of us, but it does meet a goal for the offender. *Routine activities theory* tells us that crime will not occur unless there is a motivated offender, a suitable target, and ineffective guardianship of that target. As you will learn later in this chapter, the routine activities approach has been particularly useful in helping develop ways of preventing crime because it moves beyond the simple consideration of penalties advocated by proponents of deterrence theory.

## Learning Objectives

After reading this chapter, you should be able to

- Understand the role of law as a deterrent to crime and recognize the limits of deterrence.
- Discuss how offenders make choices whether or not to commit offenses and understand the assumptions of rational choice theory.

- Discuss the routine activities approach to crime and understand the role of the motivated offender, suitable target, and ineffective guardianship in any criminal event.
- Know the rationale underlying situational crime prevention and be familiar with the research demonstrating its effectiveness.
- Understand the need for comprehensive crime prevention initiatives.

## Deterrence Theory

You will recall from Chapter 8 that Beccaria's Classical theory was based on rational choice—people will break the law if they think that doing so will advance their own interests. If it is to our advantage, and if we think we can get away with it, we will break the law. This implies that the best way to control crime is to set up a system of punishment that will ensure that people do not find lawbreaking to be in their best interest. Beccaria proposed that punishments should be severe enough to deter people from breaking the law but should also be proportionate to the nature of the crime. A person who might be tempted to break the law would consider the positive and negative consequences of this act and a well-crafted justice system would ensure that most people would choose good over evil. Beccaria believed that effective punishment should also be both swift and certain.

At the heart of Classical theory was the belief that humans were rational beings who carefully calculated the consequences of their behaviour. Crime would be prevented if the potential criminal realized that the costs of committing the crime would be greater than the rewards. Classical theorists had great faith in the ability of a well-designed criminal code to deter criminal behaviour.

How effective is the law as a deterrent? This is a critical question because our legal system is based in large part on its ability to deter. We know that at one level, deterrence is effective. Most people do not deliberately park where they know their car will be towed away and do not normally speed if they see a police car behind them. On the rare occasions when the police have gone on strike, crime has risen dramatically. In one notable police strike in Montreal in 1969, armed robberies began to occur within minutes of the strike and huge mobs of people ran through the shopping district, breaking windows and stealing whatever they could get their hands on. Many people were injured and a police officer was shot to death.

While the law clearly does deter, for policy makers the more important question concerns the limits of deterrence. Specifically, how can we change our current system to make it more effective as a deterrent? Many people, including 'law and order' politicians, believe that the best way to reduce crime is to increase the length of prison sentences and, since 2006, Canada's Parliament has passed several pieces of legislation designed to put more people in jail for longer periods of time. Prisons are expensive—the cost of keeping someone in a federal penitentiary is $102 000 per year (Correctional Service of Canada,

2010). This means it is very important to know whether sending more people to jail for longer periods has an impact on crime rates or whether other crime reduction strategies would keep Canadians safer.

Research on this issue suggests that *certainty* of punishment is more important than the *severity* of punishment, a finding that Classical theorists might have predicted. A simple example of the impact of increasing certainty is that obscene and harassing telephone calls declined dramatically after the introduction of caller ID services. Penalties did not increase, but the new technology made it much more certain the offending caller could be identified and charged. This proved much more effective than a new policy of increased penalties for the very rare offenders who ever got convicted.

Unfortunately, governments have found it easier to pass tougher sentencing laws than to find way of increasing the certainty of punishment. Tougher laws in the United States have led to a 500 percent increase in rates of imprisonment between 1972 and 2009 (Bureau of Justice Statistics, 2009) and they are now the highest in the world. Much of this increase was because of harsher penalties for drug offenders but there is no evidence that this mass incarceration has had any impact on the sale and use of illegal drugs.

## Does Imprisonment Deter Crime?

Steven Durlauf and Daniel Nagin (2011b) conducted a comprehensive review of the evidence on the deterrent effect of imprisonment. Most of the research they reviewed was done in the United States, much of it done in response to the massive increases in imprisonment in that country. Durlauf and Nagin conclude that long prison sentences "are difficult to justify on a deterrence-based, crime prevention basis" (2011, 38). Some of the research reviewed by Durlauf and Nagin suggests that imprisonment may actually *increase* an individual's likelihood of future criminal behaviour. Labelling theorists (see Chapter 13) would suggest that this is because punishment may stigmatize people and reduce their opportunities for a life in the non-criminal world. Offenders may also be able to adjust to prison life, so the threat of prison does not deter them; they may learn criminal values and skills in prison; or imprisonment may create feelings of resentment against society that may result in increased criminality when they are released.

The most conclusive studies reviewed by Durlauf and Nagin are the evaluations of mandatory minimum sentences, an issue which will be considered in the next section. However, one of the most interesting studies in their review examined whether young people reduced their offending when they reached age 18, when they began to be treated as adults in the court. Many people believe that youth courts coddle offenders and that the more serious penalties prescribed for adults will deter criminal behaviour. However, Florida research by Lee and McCrary cited by Durlauf and Nagin showed that there was only a slight reduction in offending when youth turned 18, so apparently the threat of adult penalties did not act as a deterrent.

# Do Mandatory Minimum Sentences Deter Crime?

The most informative work on the deterrent effect of imprisonment looks at the impact of mandatory minimum prison sentences for particular offenses or for offenders with significant prior records. These sentences have become widely used, but there has been much debate about their effectiveness.

What are mandatory minimum sentences? The Criminal Code provides a broad range of penalties for many offenses. For example, breaking into someone's home can result in penalties ranging from an absolute discharge to life imprisonment. This means that judges have a great deal of discretion, though appeal courts limit this discretion to some degree. When public complaints follow a particularly light sentence or when a paroled offender commits a serious crime, politicians may try to limit judicial discretion by legislating mandatory minimum penalties for certain offences. The most severe mandatory sentencing law in any western country is California's three strikes law. While the law is complicated, one of its components is a mandatory sentence of 25 years in prison for a third felony conviction following two earlier convictions for serious felonies (a category which includes residential burglary). This has resulted in some bizarre sentences, including cases where two men will spend the rest of their lives in prison, one for stealing a slice of pizza and the other for shoplifting a small package of meat. This punishment may seem to be far too harsh, at least for minor felonies like shoplifting and other forms of petty theft. However, in 2003 the U.S. Supreme Court ruled that it did not violate the Constitutional protection against cruel and unusual punishment. This decision covered two cases, one involving a defendant who received a sentence of 25 years without parole for stealing three golf clubs, and the second a defendant who was given two consecutive 25-year sentences (50 years in all) for stealing nine videotapes in two separate incidents (see Box 13.1).

The three strikes law has been very costly. According to the California State Auditor (2010), one-quarter of California's prison inmates were serving time under the three strikes law and estimated that the cost of serving these sentences was $20 billion more than if they had been sentenced for the actual crimes they committed rather than for the 'strikes' against them. Partly as a result of three strikes laws, California cannot afford its prison system and, in 2011, the U.S. Supreme Court ordered the state to release 32,000 inmates because of severe overcrowding. Mandatory minimum sentences also significantly increase court costs because individuals facing long mandatory penalties are more likely to insist on a trial rather than pleading guilty. The law is also very hard on the offenders and their families.

The high social and financial costs of mandatory minimum sentences might be worthwhile if they reduced crime rates. However, they do not. Michael Tonry has reviewed the research on the impact of mandatory minimum sentences and concluded: "Mandatory penalties are a bad idea. They often result in injustice to individual offenders. .... And the clear weight of the evidence is, and for nearly 40 years has been, that there is insufficient credible evidence to conclude that mandatory penalties have significant deterrent effects" (2009, 100).

Tonry bases this conclusion in part on a series of evaluations of California's three strikes laws. While California's crime rate has declined since the passage of three strikes in 1994 this decline was not a result of the three strikes laws. Only one of 15 studies reviewed by Tonry concluded that the legislation reduced crime rates. Several studies, including those by Marvell and Moody (2001) and Chen (2008), showed that crime rates in California did not decline faster than in other states even though the penalties in California were far more severe than in any other state. Kovandzic et al. (2004) arrived at similar findings using cities rather than states as the unit of analysis. Other studies compared the California counties that made the most use of three strikes with the counties that made the least use of the law and found no differences in reductions in total crime or in violent crime following the three strikes law (Legislative Analyst's Office, 2005). Several of these comparative studies also found that three strikes laws produced *increases* in homicide rates, possibly because offenders facing a third strike conviction wanted to eliminate people who could identify them.

Why don't severe penalties such as mandatory sentences deter crime? One reason is because offenders may not feel they are at risk of getting caught. Potential offenders are actually correct in believing that their next crime is unlikely to lead to punishment.

Crime statistics show that most criminal offenses are not reported, most reported offenses do not result in arrests, most arrests do not lead to convictions, and most convictions do not result in imprisonment. Nearly 2.2 million crimes were reported to Canadian police in 2009 (Dauvergne and Turner, 2010). Victimization surveys have shown that less than one-third of all crimes are reported to the police, so there are likely over seven million crimes each year in Canada. Despite this huge number of offenses, only about 5000 people were sentenced to federal penitentiaries (which includes all sentences of two years or more) and 80 000 to provincial custody (Public Safety Canada, 2011). Thus, the likelihood of being arrested, convicted, and punished for any offence is so low that tinkering with the level of punishment makes no difference. Governments promise to 'crack down' on crime, but this promise is kept so rarely that it is ignored by potential offenders who know from their own experience (and from that of their peers) that the odds of getting away with a crime are in their favour. This means that a harsh system like California's is really one of randomized severity in which some offenders received very harsh sentences while many others with similar patterns of offending remain on the streets.

Deterrence is also affected by the fact that many offenders have alcohol, drug, or mental health issues that may lead them to make bad decisions (see Box 15.1). Further, some offenders are unaware of the sentence they face if convicted. A study of serious firearms offenders came up with a very striking finding: "even felons who had been *prosecuted, sentenced, and were interviewed while incarcerated* dramatically underestimated the magnitude of their *current* sentence" (Kennedy, 2009, 26). An inmate, who was the first person sentenced under a new U.S. federal three strikes law, said that

> I ain't never heard anything about the law until they applied it on me. I never thought anything like this would happen to me, man. … It is going to make a few guys think, but some other guys don't even watch TV or care; they don't know nothing about the law. (Kennedy, 2009, 26)

One of the biggest failures of mandatory sentencing and other deterrence policies has been the war on drugs. Billions of dollars have been spent trying to reduce drug trafficking and consumption without reducing the problem. Over 30 000 people were killed in Mexico's drug wars between 2006 and 2010 (CNN, 2010). Even the risk to Mexican drug dealers of being murdered by other traffickers or of being killed by the police has not deterred new recruits to the drug business, which is so lucrative that when one distributor is killed or arrested, another will very quickly take his place.

Another possible reason harsh sentences have little impact is that prosecutors and judges can find ways of evading penalties such as mandatory minimum sentences that they feel are too severe. Cases may be plea-bargained to lesser charges or prosecutors may simply lay related charges that do not have a mandatory minimum penalty. A study of the use of Section 85 of Canada's Criminal Code, which imposed a mandatory minimum sentence for certain firearms offenses, found that many of the charges laid under this section were dealt with through plea bargaining and that about two-thirds of the charges were stayed, withdrawn, or dismissed (Roberts, 2005). If the Canadian government proceeds with its plan to pass legislation in 2011 requiring a mandatory sentence of at least six months in prison for growing as few as six marihuana plants if the grower is involved in marihuana trafficking, it is very likely that some prosecutors and judges would work around the law in cases where they don't feel a jail term is desirable. However, other similar offenders who face less sympathetic prosecutors and judges will go to jail.

Finally, it is likely that the existing level of punishment is severe enough for most of us. To give just one example, there is no evidence that capital punishment

# FOCUS BOX 15.1

## THE LIMITS OF DETERRENCE

Not all people can be deterred. Jacobs (2010) describes an incident in which

an offender stabbed a victim after a traffic dispute in a fully lit Taco Bell drive-thru window. The ...stabbing took place in view of at least ten potential eyewitnesses. The entire encounter was captured on surveillance video and (subsequently) broadcast worldwide on YouTube. The offender began the altercation with the victim *while the victim was on the phone with the police* (to report the traffic accident) *and under the reasonable presumption that the police were on their way.* The offender did not attempt to conceal or disguise his identity in any way. The offender attacked the victim despite the fact that he (the offender) had $6,000 worth of marihuana packaged for sale under the front seat of his car—a quantity that would trigger a charge of intent to distribute (as opposed to simple possession) if the police were to discover it (recall that the police were on their way). The offender attacked the victim despite the presence and direct intervention of two peacemakers (a cousin of the offender and an unrelated customer). Following the stabbing, the offender made no attempt to flee, despite the fact that he knew the police were coming. (2010, 428)

is any greater deterrent to crime than lengthy terms of imprisonment. In fact, one international study found that homicide rates actually went down after capital punishment was abolished (Archer et al., 1983).

# The Impact of Increasing the Certainty of Punishment

Increasing the *severity* of punishment beyond current levels does not seem to have a deterrent effect. Even the minority of studies which found that longer sentences help to reduce crime do not show a sufficient impact to justify the enormous costs of increasing prison populations. However, you will recall that Beccaria also discussed the need for *certainty* of punishment if the law was to be an effective deterrent. There is now a substantial body of research which shows that efforts to increase certainty can have a large deterrent effect (Durlauf and Nagin, 2011b). Two of these measures are **hot spots policing** and **individualized deterrence**.

## Hot Spots Policing

Most studies of the impact of increased certainty have focused on the police because their actions can increase or decrease the certainty of punishment. One promising strategy is 'hot spots' policing. This strategy is based on the fact that a small number of addresses produce a high percentage of calls to the police. For example, an early study of crime location found that half the calls to the Minneapolis police came from just three percent of the city's addresses (Sherman et al., 1989) and a more recent study found that half of the commercial robberies in Boston took place at one percent of the addresses (Braga et al., 2011). Several studies have shown that concentrating police resources in these high crime areas can significantly reduce crime by increasing the certainty of apprehension (Braga, 2008).

## Individualized Deterrence

The most dramatic results demonstrating the importance of certainty of punishment have come from the new strategy of **individualized deterrence**. This involves directly informing individuals about the consequences that will result from future misbehaviour and then ensuring that those promises are kept.

**Boston's Operation Ceasefire** The best-known example of the individualized deterrence strategy is the gang violence reduction program called Operation Ceasefire. The program was developed in response to high homicide rates among young, African-American males in Boston.

The project was a cooperative effort involving a significant number of agencies and groups. Police, probation workers, and gang outreach workers sought to deter gang violence by telling gang members that violence would not be tolerated and that gangs that continued to use violence would be targeted for intensive enforcement. Boston's Operation Ceasefire was not just a police effort

**hot spots policing**
Most crimes occur at a small number of addresses in any community. Hot spots policing concentrates police resources on these high-crime locations.

**individualized deterrence**
Offenders who are heavily involved in criminal activity are individually warned that their actions are being monitored and that future violations of the law will be dealt with immediately. Extra police and/or probation resources are added to ensure that the legal system does keep its promises.

but involved other law enforcement and criminal justice agencies as well as academics from Harvard University. The planning team also recruited social service agencies, local churches and community groups to work with youth in their communities. These community groups also made it clear to the gang members that their violent behaviour was not going to be tolerated by the community and used whatever formal and informal sanctions they could to enhance the certainty of deterrence. While suppression was a major component of the project, the project also offered gang members training, counselling, mentoring, and remedial education to help them get out of the gang lifestyle. Community organizations, including faith-based agencies, were involved in providing these services.

The impact of the project was dramatic. Operation Ceasefire was responsible for a 63 percent decline in youth homicide over a period of nearly three years (Kennedy et al., 2001). Many of the gang members said they actually welcomed the intervention because it gave them an excuse to avoid being pressured into violence by peers and because they felt safer themselves because rival gangs were also constrained. However, when the Boston Police Department dropped the program and several of the community groups also ended their involvement, rates of youth homicide returned to previous levels and continued to climb until at least 2006 (Pollack, 2006).

The U.S. government further tested the individualized deterrence model through the Strategic Approach to Community Safety Initiative, which sponsored programs in 10 cities (Roehl et al., 2006). The results were also very positive. For example, in Indianapolis there was a 32 percent reduction in homicide, in New Haven there was a 32 percent reduction in gun crime, and in Portland there was a 42 percent reduction in homicide and a 25 percent decrease in other violent crime. The model is now being promoted nationally in the United States through Project Safe Neighborhoods.

**Project HOPE**   Another project based on individualized deterrence is Hawaii's Project HOPE. This project was designed by Judge Steven Alm to reduce high rates of noncompliance with probation conditions requiring abstinence from drugs. He was concerned that probationers were allowed to commit many violations before any action was taken. When sanctions were imposed, they often involved revocation of probation which could result in lengthy periods of reincarceration. Judge Alm believed that short, certain penalties might work better than the uncertain threat of lengthy prison sentences.

In Project HOPE, probationers are first given a clear warning that if they fail to show up for drug testing, if they fail a drug test, or if they violate any other probation condition they will immediately be brought before a judge who will send them to jail for a brief period of time if they are found to have violated the terms of their probation. However, their probation is not revoked and after a few days in jail they are released and placed back on probation. Each probationer must call HOPE staff every morning and receive random drug testing at least once a week. Treatment is provided for some offenders, particularly those who have committed several probation violations. This program is much more intensive than normal probation supervision which consisted of monthly meetings with probation officers and no random drug testing.

An evaluation of the program (Hawken and Kleiman, 2009) showed a major improvement in drug-testing outcomes among the group assigned to HOPE. Over a six-month period, rates of positive drug tests among the HOPE participants dropped from 53 percent to only four percent, a decline of 93 percent. Over the same period, failure rates for the probationers in the comparison group who received normal probation declined by only 14 percent (from 22 percent to 19 percent). As a result, HOPE participants had a rate of probation revocation that was only one-third that of the comparison group. Despite the automatic use of custody for violators in the HOPE program, the overall number of days spent in prison was over 50 percent less for the HOPE probationers. This demonstrates that intensive community supervision can lead both to less crime and to lower prison costs.

In Canada, the Winnipeg Auto Theft Suppression Strategy is an award-winning crime reduction program that includes an individualized deterrence component. This program, which has reduced auto theft by over 80 percent, is discussed in detail at the end of this chapter.

The evidence demonstrates that the legal system can deter crime. Despite the fact that many politicians promise us that harsher sentences will reduce crime rates, there is compelling evidence that policies that increase certainty of punishment are both more effective and less costly than policies that increase the severity of punishment.

## Rational Choice Theory

Rational choice theory was developed by researchers at Britain's Home Office who were trying to develop better crime prevention programs. While similar in some respects to deterrence theory, rational choice theory incorporates an extensive body of research on how offenders actually make their choices about whether or not to commit crimes. Rather than simply assuming that potential offenders will be deterred by the threat of legal sanctions, rational choice theory took a much more empirically grounded view of offender decision-making. Offenders told researchers that they selected targets based on their perception of risks and rewards, they described characteristics of desirable and undesirable targets, and they gave detailed descriptions of their criminal actions. The research showed that while criminal behaviour was goal-oriented, there was little planning involved in most crimes and offenders did not carefully plan the benefits and costs of their criminal behaviour.

This work was the basis of **rational choice theory** (Cornish and Clarke, 1986) which postulated that crime was the result of deliberate choices made by offenders based on their calculation of the risks and rewards of these choices. The basic assumption of rational choice theory was that "crime is purposive behaviour designed to meet the offender's commonplace needs for such things as money, status, sex, and excitement, and that meeting these needs involves the making of (sometimes quite rudimentary) decisions and choices, constrained as these are by limits of time and ability and the availability of relevant information" (Clarke, 1995, 98).

**rational choice theory**

Rational choice theory claims that crime is the result of deliberate choices made by offenders based on their calculation of the risks and rewards of these choices.

Rational choice theory did not focus on the potential offender's background, but rather on the situational dynamics involved in the decision whether or not to commit a crime. Rational choice theorists do not believe that all crimes result from the same social processes. Thus the analysis of particular crime problems is the key to understanding the dynamics of the offense and to planning prevention programs. The factors involved in the decision to commit crime can vary even within the same crime category—the decision-making process is much different for professional thieves who steal cars to sell abroad than for a 14-year-old who sees a car running in front of a convenience store and takes it for a joyride before deliberately crashing it. One of the most important findings of this research was that offenders' behaviour was typically based more on short-term costs and benefits than on long-term considerations such as possible penalties (Felson and Clarke, 1998). The immediate rewards of a heroin injection are more important than a jail term or the long-term health risks, and the approval of peers for assaulting a member of a rival gang outweigh the possible costs of an assault conviction.

## Environmental Criminology

The work of Patricia and Paul Brantingham on *environmental criminology* is an extension of rational choice theory. Their work examines the target search process that precedes involvement in a crime. Like everyone else, criminals have activity patterns, and the environmental opportunities they encounter in the course of these activities influence their decisions to commit particular criminal acts (Beavon, Brantingham, and Brantingham, 1994). Criminals are more likely to commit their offenses along the paths they travel in the course of their daily activities; therefore, criminal opportunities are shaped by road networks and other factors that shape potential criminals' daily routines. Even if these actors are not actively seeking criminal opportunities, they may take advantage of vulnerabilities they encounter in the course of their daily affairs. Brantingham and Brantingham (1995) analyzed crime patterns in terms of nodes, paths, and edges. Nodes are important places to would-be offenders—the places where they live, work, and socialize—and they frequently commit crimes in the areas around these nodes. Paths are routes between nodes and these routes are vulnerable to crime. For example, a convenience store on the route from junior high school students' homes to their school is vulnerable to shoplifting, and homes that are on the route from a large bar to the area where patrons have parked their cars may be vulnerable to vandalism and other types of minor disorder as well as to burglary (Engstad, 1975). Edges are boundaries or barriers between different types land use. An example is a street that separates an industrial area from an adjoining residential neighbourhood. Crime rates are often high in these areas because neighbourhood social control may be weaker and because they may contain properties that attract or generate criminal activity. Beavon, Brantingham, and Brantingham (1994) studied the influence of street networks on patterns of property crime in Maple Ridge and Pitt Meadows, British Columbia. They found that property crimes are most likely to occur on street segments that are readily accessible, have high flows of traffic or people, and include attractive targets. Planners can use this knowledge to help prevent crime when designing roads and accessibility routes in new communities.

## Routine Activities Theory

Routine activities theory is closely linked to rational choice theory. Both theories focus on the circumstances of the criminal event. Routine activities theory was developed from research on patterns of crime, such as when and where it occurs, the immediate circumstances of crime, the relationship between victims and offenders, and the reasons why some people are more likely than others to be victimized by crime.

Hindelang et al. (1978) used this approach to develop the **lifestyle/exposure theory** to account for personal victimization. This theory states that the lifestyle and routine activities of people place them in social settings with higher or lower risks of being victimized. For example, people who spend a lot of time in public places at night have a higher risk of being robbed than people who spend their evenings at home. According to 2009 Canadian General Social Survey (GSS), those who reported engaging in 30 or more of these evening activities a month had violent victimization rates four times higher than those who engaged in 10 or fewer of these activities a month (Perreault and Brennan, 2010). Similarly, people whose lifestyles put them in frequent contact with people who commit crimes are more likely to be victimized than those whose time is spent with law-abiding companions. For example, members of organized crime gangs have higher rates of homicide victimization than most other Canadians. They have chosen a lifestyle in which violence is used as a means of settling disputes and in which factors like the competition for the exclusive right to sell drugs in particular areas ensure that there will be many disputes to settle. While much of gang violence has been between competing gangs, it is also used as a means of settling accounts within gangs. The homicide rate among sex workers is also very high. Robert Pickton was convicted of killing six sex workers in Vancouver (and is likely responsible for the deaths of at least 20 more) and investigations into similar serial killings are underway in several other Canadian cities. The working conditions of street prostitutes, as well as their association with the drug culture, place them at very high risk of victimization.

Additional confirmation of lifestyle/exposure theory comes from studies of repeat victimization. If victimization is more likely among people with risky lifestyles, then we would expect that people who have been victimized once should have a higher probability of being victimized a second time than people who have not been victimized. This is, in fact, the case. Repeated victimization of the same victim (or victim's household), by both the same type of crime and different crimes, has been observed frequently in surveys both in the United States (U.S. Dept. of Justice, 1974a, 1974b; Sparks, 1981) and in Canada (Koenig, 1977; Sacco and Johnson, 1990). In the 2004 Canadian GSS, of those who stated that they had been victimized by a crime during the preceding 12 months, 40 percent reported that they had been victimized more than once (Gannon and Mihorean, 2005).

**lifestyle/exposure theory**

A theory of crime victimization that acknowledges that not everyone has the same lifestyle and that some lifestyles expose people to more risks than others do.

**FIGURE 15.1**    **The Routine Activities Approach**

**routine activities approach**

An extension of the lifestyle/exposure theory, this approach assumes that crimes are the expected outcomes of routine activities and changing social patterns.

Cohen and Felson (1979) made the assumptions of lifestyle exposure theory more explicit when they formulated the **routine activities approach to crime** (Figure 15.1). This approach begins with the observation that three factors must be present at the same time and space for a crime to occur:

1.  A motivated offender. Unless someone wants to commit a crime, it will not take place. Most of the theories of criminal behaviour that you studied in earlier chapters try to explain why some people are motivated to commit crimes.
2.  A suitable target. A theft will not take place unless there is property to steal and an assault cannot happen unless there is someone to attack.
3.  A lack of guardianship of that target. If a target is well-guarded, it will be much less likely to be victimized.

Changes in any of these factors can lead to increases or decreases in crime. Thus even without additional motivated offenders, an increase in the number, the value, or the accessibility of suitable targets can result in increases in crime. For example, 30 years ago electronic equipment was bulky, heavy, and difficult to carry. Today, potential criminals have the opportunity to steal laptop computers, expensive phones and MP3 players, and other valuable electronics that weigh very little and that are easy to conceal. Cohen and Felson predicted that unless small, attractive items are carefully protected, theft rates will increase as these items become more common, and their data support this view. Less suitable targets are less frequently stolen. For example, Cohen and Felson observed that not many people steal refrigerators and washing machines because these are worth far less per pound than electronic equipment and because they are much harder to carry away.

An example of the importance of suitable targets was the discovery by young people in Winnipeg and Regina that some models of Chrysler vehicles built in the 1990s were very easy to steal. This discovery helped to fuel a boom in joyriding that saw rates of motor vehicle theft soar in both cities (Anderson and Linden, 2002). On the other hand, vehicles protected by electronic ignition immobilizers, which are almost impossible to start without a key, are very rarely stolen unless the owners leave their keys in the car. In another example, as the value of all types of metal rose dramatically in the middle of the last decade, thieves started stealing metal items such as manhole covers, aluminum billboards and road signs, and stainless steel tanker trailers. In Prince George, British Columbia thieves even tried to steal the head of a bronze statue of Terry Fox in order to recover the metal. Several people in Canada have died because they cut into live power lines in an attempt to steal the copper wire.

**Effective guardianship** refers to actions such as having neighbours who watch your home when you are on vacation, drawing a steel mesh curtain overnight across glass display windows of jewellery, and taking evening walks on busy, well-lit streets rather than walking alone in an isolated park or down a dark alley. Changes in guardianship affect crime rates. Cohen and Felson showed that as daytime occupancy of homes (guardianship) decreased because of factors such as the increased employment of women outside the home and increases in the length of vacations, there was a substantial increase in daytime residential burglaries while the proportion of commercial burglaries declined.

This perspective is consistent with the results of interviews with offenders. Bennett and Wright (1984a) concluded that risk factors were the major consideration in target selection or **target suitability**. Burglars would be deterred if they believed that someone was home or by the apparent visibility of possible entrances from nearby overlooking buildings or by passers-by and neighbours. When Wright and Decker asked their respondents to describe unsuitable targets, most said they would avoid targets in areas where it looked like neighbours would look out for each other. Older people were considered to be especially likely to report suspicious behaviour to the police:

> The thing is if you got a lot of elderly people on one block, that'll get you killed mostly.... I wanted to do [a burglary] over here by the bakery shop, but that's a retired area. Almost everybody that live on that block is retired and they constantly lookin' out windows and watchin' [out] for each other. Ain't nothin' you can do about that. (Wright and Decker, 1992, 87)

The routine activities perspective has been extended to incorporate two additional variables—*intimate handlers* and *crime facilitators*. Felson has described "the 'handled offender', the individual susceptible to informal social control by virtue of his or her bonds to society, and the 'intimate handler,' someone with sufficient knowledge of the potential offender to [control the offender]" (1986, 119). This variable incorporates into routine activities theory social bonds such as ties to parents and other community members that have been shown to reduce involvement in delinquency and crime (see Chapter 14). Clarke and Eck (2003) proposed that the decision whether or not to commit a crime can also depend on the presence of physical, social, or chemical crime facilitators. Physical facilitators are objects such as guns to be used in an armed robbery or scanning devices that enable restaurant employees to steal debit card numbers along with their associated PINs. Social facilitators can be peers who teach the individual the techniques of committing crime and who provide social support during the criminal event. Chemical facilitators include drugs and alcohol which reduce inhibitions and lead to acts that might not be committed if the individual was not under their influence. These substances can also make potential victims more vulnerable.

**effective guardianship**

An aspect of the routine activities approach to understanding crime victimization that argues that three key factors are required for crime to happen: a motivated offender, a suitable target, and ineffective guardianship of that target. Effective guardianship would include having locks on bikes, security lights in the backyard, or putting goods in the trunk of the car. Measures like this can reduce the risk of being victimized.

**target suitability**

Because of their vulnerability, some potential crime targets are more attractive than others. A home that is unlit, has shrubs blocking a view of the front door, and has no alarm system will be seen as a more suitable target than a well-protected home.

The importance of chemical facilitators is illustrated by the results of the 2009 GSS victimization survey. The survey found that alcohol consumption and illicit drug use increase one's likelihood of being a victim of crime. Those who reported consuming more than four alcoholic drinks in one sitting in the past month experienced about three times as many incidents of violent victimization during the preceding 12 months as did non-drinkers (Perreault and Brennan, 2010). Those who reported using illicit drugs every day had violent victimization rates that were eight times higher than those who did not use illicit substances. Regular drug users also had much higher rates of property victimization. The majority of victims of physical assault reported that the crime was due to the offender's alcohol or drug use. These findings are consistent with the fact that the western provinces, which have the highest rates of crime in Canada (see Chapter 5) also have the highest rates of alcohol and drug use problems (Veidhuizen et al., 2007).

## The Diverse Attractions of Crime

Critics of rational choice and routine activities theories suggest that they may account for financially-motivated crimes, but that they do not account for expressive crimes that involve strong emotions (Hayward, 2007). Proponents of rational choice and routine activities theories do take the view that "opportunity causes crime" (Felson and Clarke, 1998, 9). This notion is easy to understand when we think of situations like a person leaving an expensive bike unlocked and unattended in a high-crime neighbourhood or when managers of a convenience store near a junior high school do not take precautions against shoplifting. However, these theorists have also realized that the attractions of crime are very diverse and that motivations for criminal behaviour can be quite complex.

Consider the reasons armed robbers give for committing their offenses in the interviews quoted below. Most of us can understand the financial motives of the first robber, but the other three quotes show that robberies are not just committed for economic reasons. These might seem like bad decisions to most of us and few of the robberies had much advance planning. However, it is clear that for the offenders, robbery is the result of a rational choice that satisfies certain needs and desires:

> It's the fastest and most direct way to get money. There's no thrill in getting it. It's for the cash, the money that I do it. (Gabor et al., 1987, 63)
>
> When I have a gun in my hands, nothing can stop me. It makes me feel important and strong. With a revolver you're somebody. It's funny to see the expression of people when they have a .38 in their face. Sometimes when I went home at night I thought of it and laughed. I know that it's bad to say that. Maybe I was just fascinated. (Gabor et al., 1987, 63)
>
> I was mad and I had to do something to get it out of my system. I was mad at my cousins and my girlfriend. I was mad at my mom at the time. (Feeney, 1986, 58)
>
> Just to cause some trouble. Well, we just wanted to try that, you know. Goof around, you know, have some fun—jack up somebody … We thought we were really big and stuff like that. (Feeney, 1986, 58)

Some of the motivations for homicide are discussed in Box 15.2.

# FOCUS BOX 15.2

## THE DYNAMICS OF HOMICIDE

Researchers following the interactionist approach (see Chapter 13) have interviewed violent offenders and analyzed the accounts of homicides contained in police files to better understand the dynamics of homicide events. Luckenbill (1977) examined the typical roles played by offenders, victims, and bystanders in situations that resulted in homicide. He looked at the social context in which homicides occurred and concluded that many of them were confrontations that escalated into "character contests"; that is, violence became a means of saving face for the individuals. While their choice to use violence may not make sense to most of us, from their perspective it was a rational decision.

In most cases, the individuals involved were with family, friends, or acquaintances. Often the victim and the offender had previous histories of disputes that led them to anticipate or even to seek out confrontation with the others involved. In some cases, one of the parties insulted the other either intentionally or inadvertently; in others, there was a refusal to carry out some requested action. This was interpreted as being offensive and rather than ignoring the insult or leaving the scene, the offended individual responded aggressively in order to save face. In some cases, other people at the scene either encouraged a violent response or did nothing to try to defuse the situation. These points are illustrated in one of Luckenbill's examples:

> The offender, victim, and three friends were driving in the country drinking beer and wine. At one point the victim started laughing at the offender's car which he, the victim, scratched a week earlier. The offender asked the victim why he was laughing. The victim responded that the offender's car looked like junk. The offender stopped the car and all got out. The offender asked the victim to repeat his statement. When the victim reiterated his characterization of the car, the offender struck the victim, knocking him to the ground. (1977, 181)

What is striking about this incident is just how trivial it was. A joking remark made among friends ultimately led to the death of one young man and a long prison sentence for another. This case is not like most of those you see on television or in movies or read about in the headlines, but it is more representative of the "typical" homicide than are the cases of Paul Bernardo, Clifford Olson, or Robert Pickton, which get so much of the media's attention.

Can you think of some reasons why "respect" was so important to the young men involved in this case or in the following account of a Toronto murder trial:

> When prosecutor Laura Bird began speaking yesterday, it sounded for all the world as though she had borrowed her story line from a violent video game or, in another age, a Bugs Bunny and Road Runner cartoon.
>
> Hers was a tale of characters with childish nicknames who seethed with preening masculinity, nourished ridiculous grievances over months and whose ludicrous code of behaviour is redolent with more ritual gestures than a formal audience with royalty.
>
> It would have been comic, but Ms. Bird was describing the real lives of real people and the terrible and senseless death of one of them.
>
> Wayne Anthony Reid, a young black man, died in a hail of bullets on June 15 last year and, Ms. Bird said, he died because the friend he was with that night had, almost a full year earlier, either not nodded in respect, or not nodded vigorously enough, or not been seen to nod, in deference to a friend of the man now alleged to have killed him.

*(continued)*

The prosecutor was delivering her opening address, designed to give jurors an overview of her case, in the second-degree murder trial of Leon Patrick Boswell....

The victim, the alleged killer and their two friends either lived or grew up in the notorious housing complexes of the Jamestown area of northwest Toronto, a neighbourhood where territory is so clearly marked that, Ms. Bird said, "When you walked through the turf of someone else you were expected to acknowledge the other person in order to show your respect for them. Failure to nod, or otherwise hail them up, could be considered to be extremely disrespectful."

And, she said, "Disrespect was taken seriously and could be expected to result in violent retaliation" such that a code of silence envelops the whole community, "preventing citizens from coming forward to report crimes for fear that they may be next in line at the morgue."*

*Adapted from Christie Blatchford. (2002). "Doesn't Take a Lot to Get You Killed," in National Post, November 27. Reprinted with permission of National Post.

# Preventing Crime

Many of the criminologists who developed rational choice and routine activities theories were looking for ways to reduce crime. Their work led to situational crime prevention which has been very successful in reducing crime. In this section, we will focus mainly on situational prevention but will also discuss the social development approach to crime reduction which you learned about in Chapter 7. Finally, the chapter will conclude with a discussion of a highly successful auto theft reduction program that combines several different approaches to crime prevention into one comprehensive program.

## Situational Crime Prevention

Over three decades ago, robberies of city bus drivers declined dramatically when transit systems installed very sturdy fare boxes and implemented exact change systems so the drivers did not have to carry cash. (See Box 15.3 for a similar discussion about bank robberies.) Most models of new cars have very low theft rates because they have electronic immobilizers that make them virtually impossible to steal without using the keys or towing them. Researchers in England found that break-in victims were often victimized again within a few weeks of the initial crime. Based on this knowledge, they worked with the victims to improve physical home security measures (such as better locks) and they established "cocoon" Neighbourhood Watch programs that enlisted the help of the victims' immediate neighbours. Subsequent break and enter rates declined dramatically compared with similar areas that did not have this follow-up. These are all examples of **situational crime prevention**.

Situational crime prevention is premised on the belief that much crime is opportunistic and contextual rather than on the belief that offenders are driven

**situational crime prevention**
Premised on the belief that most crime is opportunistic rather than being the outcome of those driven to commit a crime no matter what the circumstances, this form of prevention attempts to reduce the opportunities for crime rather than just relying on the police after the crime has occurred.

# FOCUS BOX 15.3

## THE END OF BANK ROBBERIES?

Routine activities theory would predict that if targets become less attractive or if guardianship becomes more effective there should be less crime. This is exactly what has happened to bank robberies, which used to be a major problem in Canada. In fact, several decades ago, Montreal was the bank robbery capital of North America. Well-organized and well-armed gangs were responsible for as many as 900 bank robberies a year in that city and often took their skills on the road to rob banks and jewellery stores in Toronto and other cities. Often gangs of four men would carry out precisely coordinated bank robberies. One of the men would remain in the getaway car, another would stand guard at the door with a sawed-off shotgun and count out the time remaining to the other two men who were gathering up the money. The gang assumed that the alarm had been sent to the police as soon as they entered the door, so it was critical to finish the job and leave as quickly as possible. However, the number of bank robberies in Montreal has declined to about 100 per year and has also been declining in the rest of the country (Ha, 2002). The Montreal police department has abolished its specialized holdup squad, which had attracted some of the city's best police officers. By 2008, there were only 1240 robberies of financial institutions in Canada, a decline of 38 percent from 1999 (Dauvergne, 2010).

What has caused this dramatic decline in bank robberies? According to Tu Thanh Ha (2002), a number of factors were involved. First, banks have less cash on hand because of changes in banking patterns. Most people now have their paycheques deposited directly into their bank accounts so banks no longer have long lineups of people cashing their cheques at the end of the week. Also, many Canadians do their banking by using automatic teller machines, debit cards, or the Internet and do not depend on getting cash at the tellers' counter. Second, banks have developed more effective security methods, including time-release locks and closed-circuit camera systems. Finally, the police make arrests in 80 to 90 percent of bank robberies (McLean, 2000) so many potential bank robbers have decided crimes such as drug selling are easier ways of making money.

to commit a crime no matter what. You will recall that Cohen and Felson stated that three components—target suitability, ineffective guardianship, and a motivated offender—must converge in space and time for a crime to occur. Efforts to reduce crime can focus on any or all of these components. Clarke (2005) has identified five categories of situational crime prevention techniques and has provided examples of strategies that have been used for each category (see Table 15.1):

1. Increasing the *effort* required to commit a crime by target hardening or by controlling access to targets or the tools required to commit a crime.
2. Increasing the *risks* by increasing levels of formal or informal surveillance or guardianship.
3. Reducing the *rewards* by identifying property in order to facilitate recovery, by removing targets, or by denying the benefits of crime.
4. Reducing *provocations* by controlling for peer pressure or by reducing frustration or conflict.
5. Removing *excuses* by setting clear rules and limits.

**TABLE 15.1**    Ronald Clarke's Twenty Five Techniques of Situational Prevention

| *Increase the Effort* | *Increase the Risks* | *Reduce the Rewards* | *Reduce Provocations* | *Remove Excuses* |
|---|---|---|---|---|
| 1. Target harden<br>• Steering column locks and immobilizers<br>• Anti-robbery screens<br>• Tamper-proof packaging | 6. Extend guardianship<br>• Take routine precautions: go out in group at night, leave signs of occupancy, carry phone<br>• "Cocoon neighbourhood watch | 11. Conceal targets<br>• Off-street parking<br>• Gender-neutral phone directories<br>• Unmarked bullion trucks | 16. Reduce frustrations and stress<br>• Efficient queues and polite service<br>• Expanded seating<br>• Soothing music/muted lights | 21. Set rules<br>• Rental agreements<br>• Harassment codes<br>• Hotel registration |
| 2. Control access to facilities<br>• Entry phones<br>• Electronic card access<br>• Baggage screening | 7. Assist natural surveillance<br>• Improved street lighting<br>• Defensible space design<br>• Support whistle blowers | 12. Remove targets<br>• Removable car radio<br>• Women's refuges<br>• Pre-paid cards for pay phones | 17. Avoid disputes<br>• Separate enclosures for rival soccer fans<br>• Reduce crowding in pubs<br>• Fixed cab fares | 22. Post instructions<br>• "No Parking"<br>• "Private Property"<br>• "Extinguish camp fires" |
| 3. Screen exits<br>• Ticket needed for exit<br>• Export documents<br>• Electronic merchandise tags | 8. Reduce anonymity<br>• Taxi driver IDs<br>• "How's my driving?" Decals<br>• School uniforms | 13. Identify property<br>• Property marking<br>• Vehicle licensing and parts marking.<br>• Cattle branding | 18. Reduce emotional arousal<br>• Controls on violent pornography<br>• Enforce good behavior on soccer field<br>• Prohibit racial slurs | 23. Alert conscience<br>• Roadside speed display boards<br>• Signatures for customs declarations<br>• "Shoplifting is stealing" |
| 4. Deflect offenders<br>• Street closures<br>• Separate bathrooms for women<br>• Disperse pubs | 9. Utilize place managers<br>• CCTV for double-deck buses<br>• Two clerks for convenience stores<br>• Reward vigilance | 14. Disrupt markets<br>• Monitor pawn shops<br>• Controls on classified ads.<br>• License street vendors | 19. Neutralize peer pressure.<br>• "Idiots drink and drive"<br>• "It's OK to say NO"<br>• Disperse troublemakers at school | 24. Assist compliance<br>• Easy library checkout<br>• Public lavatories<br>• Litter bins |
| 5. Control tools/weapons<br>• "Smart" guns<br>• Disable stolen cell phones<br>• Restrict spray paint sales to juveniles | 10. Strengthen formal surveillance<br>• Red light cameras<br>• Burglar alarms<br>• Security guards | 15. Deny benefits<br>• Ink merchandise tags<br>• Graffiti cleaning<br>• Speed humps | 20. Discourage imitation<br>• Rapid repair of vandalism<br>• V-chips in TVs<br>• Censor details of modus operandi | 25. Control drugs and alcohol<br>• Breathalyzers in pubs<br>• Server intervention<br>• Alcohol-free events |

Source: "Twenty Five Techniques of Situational Prevention". POP Center. Available: http://www.popcenter.org/25techniques. Accessed 13 June 2011.

Hundreds of studies have shown the effectiveness of situational prevention programs. Some of the research cited by Clarke (2005) illustrates the potential of the approach:

- In the U.K. suicide rates declined when natural gas was detoxified, making it impossible for people to commit suicide by putting their heads in a gas oven.

- Graffiti was almost eliminated in the New York subway system when graffiti was removed immediately so the 'artists' could not see their work on display.

- U.S. cell phone companies were able to dramatically reduce fraudulent phone calls by developing 'anti-cloning' technology.

- Electronic tagging of library books has reduced theft from libraries.

- Better inventory control reduced employee thefts from an electronics retailer.

- Tighter procedures for mailing credit cards helped reduce rates of credit card fraud.

Table 15.1 shows the broad variety of situational techniques that can be used to reduce crime.

These and other situational techniques have been very effective in reducing crime. However, some critics have pointed out that it is also important to reduce the number of motivated offenders:

> The control of crime involves interventions on all levels: on the social causes of crime, on social control exercised by the community and the formal agencies, and on the situation of the victim. Furthermore, that social causation is given the highest priority, whereas formal agencies, such as the police, have a vital role, yet one which has in the conventional literature been greatly exaggerated. It is not the "Thin Blue Line", but the social bricks and mortar of civil society which are the major bulwark against crime. Good jobs with a discernable future, housing [projects] that tenants can be proud of, community facilities which enhance a sense of cohesion and belonging, a reduction in unfair income inequalities, all create a society which is more cohesive and less criminogenic. (Young, 1997, n.p.)

w(w)w

**Institute for the Prevention of Crime**
www.socialsciences.uottawa.ca/ipc/eng/

## Reducing Motivated Offenders

**Crime Prevention Through Social Development** The initiatives that Young describes are called **crime prevention through social development** programs. Stephen Schneider studied crime prevention in Vancouver's Downtown Eastside, one of Canada's most crime-ridden neighbourhoods. Schneider's experience in this community led him to a conclusion similar to Young's—that crime problems eventually must be addressed through "a comprehensive strategy that ultimately is based upon a reinvigoration of civil society, the centrality of the local community in social problem solving, and

**crime prevention through social development**
An approach to crime prevention that focuses on reducing the number of motivated offenders by changing the social environment.

the empowerment and participation of those who are in the most need. This means that a greater share of public resources and power be allocated to the local level and to the poorest communities in particular" (Schneider, 2007, 306). The work of Young and Schneider has led them to conclusions that are very different from those of politicians who promise us that a bit of tinkering with the justice system will quickly end most of our crime problems and their work helps to place the solutions suggested by routine activities theory into a broader perspective. Situational measures are an important way of reducing crime, but we must also consider other methods that will help to overcome the serious social problems that breed motivated offenders.

Social development programs are intended to reduce the pool of motivated offenders by altering the conditions that breed crime. These programs (several of which are described in Chapter 7) focus on factors such as family problems, peer issues, poverty, and a range of school and community factors. Some have tried to improve the parenting skills of high-risk parents, while others have provided job training and employment for young people who are cut off from the labour market because they live in poor communities. Social development strategies are often targeted at young people, who appear to be the most amenable to intervention and who make up the next generation of offenders.

One of the most promising areas is the provision of preschool programs for children from deprived backgrounds. One of the few social development programs that has undergone a long-term evaluation is a Michigan program called the Perry Preschool Project. The students were 123 black children from poor families. Children aged three and four attended a preschool with an active learning curriculum five mornings a week, and teachers visited the children's homes once a week. The program lasted 30 weeks each year. A control group did not receive these services. Like the earlier Head Start program, this project sought to remedy the impact of the children's impoverished backgrounds on their later school success.

The most recent follow-up of the Perry Preschool project looked at the participants at age 40 (Schweinhart et al., 2005). Far fewer of the program participants than controls had been arrested five or more times (36 percent versus 55 percent) and had less than half the arrest rate for drug offences (14 percent versus 34 percent). The program group had higher incomes, were more likely to own their own homes, and were less likely to have been on welfare. They had greater educational achievement and lower rates of illiteracy. Program group members were more likely to have had stable marriages and females had lower rates of out-of-wedlock births. The costs of the program were more than recovered because of gains in reduced welfare costs and increased earnings of the graduates. Schweinhart et al. estimate that the saving was over $17 for every dollar invested in the program. Those responsible for this program strongly suggest that the intervention must be made while the children are young and must be thorough enough to overcome the range of disadvantages faced by the participants. The Canadian government has responded to this research by establishing early childhood

Perry Preschool Program
www.highscope.org/Content.
asp?ContentId=219

education programs in a number of communities and by establishing a national Aboriginal Head Start program.

## The Need for Comprehensive Crime Reduction Initiatives

Some critics have expressed fears that situational techniques may lead to a fortress society or to a 'big brother' state where our actions are always subject to scrutiny through technology such as surveillance cameras. Other practitioners and academics have viewed social development as the only acceptable way of preventing crime. They have gone from the reasonable position that society needs to do something about the root causes of crime to the not so reasonable position that social development programs are the only ones that are acceptable.

In fact, developmental and situational approaches are complementary. We can distinguish between 'criminal involvement' and 'criminal events' (Clarke, 1995). Criminal involvement relates to criminal careers and is appropriately addressed by social development approaches. Criminal events are short-term acts that may be more appropriately addressed by situational prevention.

The most sensible strategy to pursue is one that recognizes that all crime prevention strategies have their strengths and weaknesses. A comprehensive strategy should include prevention programs that involve cooperation among different levels of government and other agencies and groups that can contribute to the solution (see Chapter 7), that are targeted to areas where they are most needed, that use a broad range of prevention approaches tailored to the specific needs of the communities, and that draw upon programs that have been shown to be effective in other places.

To illustrate the potential of this approach as a guide to preventing crime, consider a Winnipeg program that one of this chapter's authors help to develop and implement.

### The Winnipeg Auto Theft Suppression Strategy (WATSS) From 2003 to 2008 Winnipeg had North America's highest rate of auto theft. Nearly one in every five Criminal Code offenses in the city was an auto theft and the 2006 rate was 67 percent higher than the next highest Canadian city. In addition to the property loss involved in these thefts, there was also significant physical violence. In 2007, two people were killed by drivers of stolen vehicles and an early morning jogger was seriously injured after being deliberately run down by a youth driving a stolen car. In one 16-month period in 2007–2008, eight drivers deliberately tried to run down police officers with stolen vehicles. Vehicle thieves also frequently attempted to ram police cars. Some youth engaged in other dangerous behaviour such as jamming down vehicle accelerators and launching driverless vehicles down city streets and into parking garages.

Research done by the Manitoba Auto Theft Task Force found that auto theft rates were so high because auto theft had become an important part of youth culture in parts of the Winnipeg. Virtually all the stolen vehicles were used for joyriding or as temporary transportation and were eventually recovered, often with major damage. Interviews with young offenders found that they stole cars for excitement and to show off for their peers and that they were very committed to auto theft. For example, one of the respondents said he stole cars "for a joyride … for the rush!" and another reported that "[stealing cars] is addicting. When you find something you're good at, you want to keep doing it" (Anderson and Linden, 2002, 10).

This auto theft culture developed after a few young people learned how easy it was to steal some models of cars and realized that the probability of arrest was very low. These offenders told their friends and schoolmates about this new pastime and the number of people willing and able to steal cars grew quickly. Children in some neighbourhoods learned to steal cars at a very early age (a number of young people were able to steal dozens of cars before they were 12 years of age), and a peer culture developed that focused on car theft. Cars were often stolen by groups of friends, and over half the respondents reported that they had taken part in contests to see who could steal the most cars in a given period of time. This culture was reinforced by the mass media as well as by peer groups. Most of the interviewed youth played video games such as *Grand Theft Auto*, which glamorizes stealing cars and using them to create mayhem on the streets. Several also said that movies such as *Gone in 60 Seconds* had helped teach them some of the techniques of stealing cars.

For almost a decade, the favourite targets were Chrysler products manufactured in the early 1990s, which were particularly easy to steal. Although recent models are much more difficult to steal, older model Chrysler vehicles can be entered and started in a few seconds using only an ordinary screwdriver.

The solution to this problem focused on all three components of routine activities theory:

1. *Effective Guardianship.* Earlier in this chapter we discussed the notion of individualized deterrence. In the language of routine activities theory, increasing certainty is a way of making guardianship more effective. The most serious auto theft offenders were typically in the community under conditions of release such as curfews. The WATSS program provided intensive supervision to enforce these conditions. Youth were contacted in person every day by youth probation workers or the police Stolen Auto Unit and were contacted by phone every three hours. Youth who violated their conditions of release were immediately apprehended by the police so they did not have the opportunity to reoffend.

2. *Target Suitability.* The vulnerability of certain models of vehicles was a major reason why young people were able to learn to steal vehicles. Thus a major part of the prevention strategy was a mandatory program requiring electronic vehicle immobilizers for the 100,000 most at-risk vehicles in Winnipeg. These immobilizers were immediately effective: five years after the program began, none of the immobilizers approved by the program's sponsor, Manitoba Public Insurance, had yet been defeated by vehicle thieves.

3. *Motivated Offenders*. The third component of WATSS involved addressing the social causes of auto theft by working with young people and their families to try to reduce the number of young people who find auto theft an appealing form of recreation. Much of this work is done by youth probation staff. Support programs for high-risk offenders and their families are run with community partners including the Winnipeg School Division, Big Brothers and Big Sisters, and New Directions for Children, Youth, Adults and Families. The goals are to move current offenders away from auto theft and to end the flow of new recruits to this dangerous and costly pastime.

This program has been very effective in reducing crime. As shown in Figure 15.2, rates have declined dramatically since WATSS was fully implemented. Between 2006 and July 2011 auto thefts declined by 83 percent. There has not been displacement to other crimes; offenses such as break and enter, robbery, and theft from vehicles also declined over this period. Because of this reduction in vehicle thefts, Winnipeg drivers are paying about $40 million less each year in vehicle insurance premiums.

The success of WATSS and other programs based on rational choice and routine activities theories of crime demonstrate the need for governments to invest in evidence-based approaches to crime reduction rather than simply building more jails. The deterrent effects of increased certainty are demonstrably more likely to reduce crime than increasing severity by legislating longer sentences. Further, many situational prevention programs have been more successful than those that rely on the justice system to reduce crime, particularly when these programs are part of broad, comprehensive initiatives.

**FIGURE 15.2**    **Rates of Auto Theft**

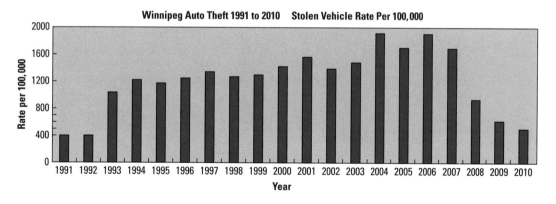

| Year: | 1991 | 1992 | 1993 | 1994 | 1995 | 1996 | 1997 | 1998 | 1999 | 2000 | 2001 | 2002 | 2003 | 2004 | 2005 | 2006 | 2007 | 2008 | 2009 |
|---|---|---|---|---|---|---|---|---|---|---|---|---|---|---|---|---|---|---|---|
| SVs: | 393 | 391 | 1034 | 1223 | 1183 | 1242 | 1352 | 1270 | 1308 | 1425 | 1581 | 1405 | 1493 | 1932 | 1712 | 1932 | 1714 | 956 | 629 |

Sources: 1991–1994: Winnipeg Police Service, Annual Report data; 1998–2010: Canadian Centre for Justice Statistics, Statistics Canada.

# Summary

- Deterrence theories focus on the factors influencing an individual's decision whether or not to commit an offence and assert that the legal system can be used to affect that decision. Research on the deterrent effects of imprisonment show that increasing the severity of our current laws is not likely to have an impact on crime rates. However, several studies show that increasing the certainty of punishment can reduce crime, particularly in programs targeted at frequent offenders.

- Rational choice theory assumes that people commit crimes because they believe this will provide them with some reward. A person's decision to commit a crime may or may not appear rational to the rest of us, but it does meet a goal for the offender.

- Routine activities theory is based on the observation that crime results from the simultaneous presence of a motivated offender, a suitable target, and ineffective guardianship of that target. This approach was used to develop lifestyle/exposure theory which is based on the idea that the lifestyle and activities of some people place them at higher risk for crime victimization

- The routine activities approach leads to a number of crime reduction strategies. These include situational measures, crime prevention through social development, and incapacitation of high-rate offenders.

- The most effective way to reduce crime is to implement comprehensive crime prevention programs that focus on reducing the number of motivated offenders, increasing guardianship, and reducing target suitability.

## QUESTIONS FOR CRITICAL THINKING

1. Understanding patterns of crime means that you can reduce your chances of becoming a victim of crime if you change certain aspects of your lifestyle. Some people argue that they should not have to change the way they dress, work, or play to avoid being victimized. What do you think?

2. As a student at a university or college, how do you assess your risk of victimization? What changes could you or others make that might reduce your chances of being a crime victim?

3. Many of our politicians suggest that the best way to deal with crime is to toughen up the Youth Criminal Justice Act and to increase the penalties for crime. After reading this chapter, do you think these politicians are correct?

4. The evidence presented in this chapter suggests that longer prison sentences are not an effective way of reducing crime. Despite this evidence, many Canadians strongly support these 'get tough' campaigns. Why do you think people support the 'get tough' approach?

## NET WORK

In this chapter, you have learned about the routine activities approach to crime. This approach has had an impact on the nature of crime prevention programs in North America and Europe by drawing attention to the role of the attractiveness of the target and the importance of effective guardianship. To see how these insights are used in crime prevention, go to the website of a major U.S. report on the effectiveness of crime prevention programs at **www.ncjrs.gov/works/**.

Read Chapter 7 of the report ("Preventing Crime at Places"). Find three projects that are intended to reduce the attractiveness of the target and three projects that increase effective guardianship. Have these projects been successful in reducing crime?

## KEY TERMS

crime prevention through social
   development; pg. 481
effective guardianship; pg. 475
hot spots policing; pg. 469
lifestyle/exposure theory; pg. 473
individualized deterrence; pg. 469

rational choice theory; pg. 471
routine activities approach; pg. 474
situational crime prevention;
   pg. 478
target suitability; pg. 475

## BIBLIOGRAPHY

Anderson, Jeff, and Rick Linden. (2002). "Pilot Study of Juvenile Auto Theft Offenders in Winnipeg." Unpublished manuscript, University of Manitoba.

Bennett, Trevor, and Richard Wright. (1984a). *Burglars on Burglary.* Brookfield, VT: Gower Publishing.

———. (1984b). "Constraints to Burglary: The Offender's Perspective." In Ronald Clarke and Tim Hope (eds.), *Coping with Burglary* (pp. 181–200). Boston: Kluwer-Nijhoff Publishing.

Blatchford, Christie. (2002). "Doesn't Take a Lot to Get You Killed." *National Post, November 27.*

Braga, Anthony. (2008). "Police Enforcement Strategies to Prevent Crime in Hot Spot Areas." *Crime Prevention Research Review* (No. 2) Washington, DC: Office of Community Oriented Policing, U.S. Department of Justice.

Braga, Anthony, David Hureau, Andrew Papachristo. (2011). "The Relevance of Micro Places to Citywide Robbery Trends: A Longitudinal Analysis of Robbery Incidents at Street Corners and Block Faces in Boston." *Journal of Research in Crime and Delinquency* 48(1): 7–32.

Bureau of Justice Statistics. (2009). *Sourcebook of Criminal Justice Statistics.* Available at http://www.albany.edu/sourcebook/tost_6.html#6_a, accessed June 6, 2011.

California State Auditor. (2010). "California Department of Corrections and Rehabilitation: Inmates Sentence Under the Three Strikes Law and a Small Number of Inmates Receiving Specialty Health Care Represent Significant Costs." *Report 2009-107.2,*

*May 2010.* Available at http://www.bsa.ca.gov/reports/summary/2009-107.2, accessed June 7, 2011.

Chen, Elsa. (2008). "Impacts of 'Three Strikes and You're Out' on Crime Trends in California and Throughout the United States." *Journal of Contemporary Criminal Justice* 24: 345–70.

Clarke, Ronald. (1995). "Situational Crime Prevention." In Michael Tonry and David Farrington (eds.), *Building a Safer Society: Strategic Approaches to Crime Prevention* (pp. 91–150). Chicago: University of Chicago Press.

Clarke, Ronald. (2005). "Seven Misconceptions of Situational Crime Prevention". In Nick Tilley (ed.), *Handbook of Crime Prevention and Public Safety* (pp. 39–70). Portland: Willan Publishing.

Clarke, Ronald V., and John Eck. (2003). *Becoming a Problem-solving Crime Analyst.* London: Jill Dando Institute of Crime Science.

CNN. (2010). "Mexican Drug War Deaths Surpass 30, 100." CNN, December 17; available at http://articles.cnn.com/2010-12-17/world/mexico.violence_1_drug-war-border-city-drug-related-violence?_s=PM:WORLD, accessed June 8, 2011.

Cohen, Lawrence E., and Marcus Felson. (1979). "Social Change and Crime Rate Trends." *American Sociological Review* 44: 588–607.

Correctional Service of Canada. (2010). *Statistics—Key Facts and Figures.* Ottawa: Correctional Service of Canada.

Dauvergne, Mia. (2010). "Police-Reported Robbery in Canada, 2008." *Juristat* 30(1).

Dauvergne, Mia, and John Turner. (2010). "Police-Reported Crime Statistics in Canada, 2009." *Juristat* 30(2).

Desroches, Frederic J. (1995). *Force and Fear: Robbery in Canada.* Toronto: Nelson.

Durlauf, Steven, and Daniel Nagin (2011a). "The Deterrent Effect of Imprisonment." Available at http://www.nber.org/chapters/c12078.pdf, accessed June 9, 2011.

———. (2011b). "Imprisonment and Crime: Can Both Be Reduced?" *Criminology and Public Policy* 10(1): 13–54.

Feeney, Floyd. (1986). "Robbers and Decision-Makers." In Derek Cornish and Ronald Clarke (eds.), *The Reasoning Criminal: Rational Choice Perspectives on Offending* (pp. 53–71). New York: Springer-Verlag.

Felson, Marcus, and Ronald Clarke. (1998). *Opportunity Makes the Thief: Practical Theory for Crime Prevention.* Police Research Series Paper 98. Home Office: London.

Gabor, Thomas, Micheline Baril, Maurice Cusson, Daniel Elie, Marc LeBlanc, and Andre Normandeau. (1987). *Armed Robbery: Cops, Robbers, and Victims.* Springfield: Charles C. Thomas.

Gannon, Maire, and Karen Mihorean. (2005). "Criminal Victimization in Canada, 2004." *Juristat* 25(7).

Ha, Tu Thanh. (2002). "The Demise of the Bank Heist." *The Globe and Mail*, November 11: A1, A7.

Hawken, Angela, and Mark Kleiman. (2009). *Managing Drug-involved Probationers with Swift and Certain Sanctions: Evaluating Hawaii's HOPE.* Washington, DC: U.S. Department of Justice.

Hayward, Keith. (2007). "Situational Crime Prevention and Its Discontents: Rational Choice Theory Versus the 'Culture of Now'." *Social Policy &Administration* 41(3): 232–50.

Hindelang, Michael J., Michael R. Gottfredson, and James Garofalo. (1978). *Victims of Personal Crime: An Empirical Foundation for a Theory of Personal Victimization.* Cambridge, MA: Ballinger Publishing.

Kennedy, David. (2009). *Deterrence and Crime Prevention: Reconsidering the Prospect of Sanction.* London: Routledge.

Kennedy, David, Anthony Braga, Anne Piehl, and Elin Waring. (2001). *Reducing Gun Violence: The Boston Gun Project's Operation Ceasefire.* Washington, DC: National Institute of Justice.

Koenig, Daniel J. (1977). "Correlates of Self-Reported Victimization and Perceptions of Neighbourhood Safety." In Lynn Hewitt and David Brusegard (eds.), *Selected Papers from the Social Indicators Conference, 1975* (pp. 77–90). Edmonton: Alberta Bureau of Statistics.

Kovandzic, Tomislav, John Sloan, and Lynne Vieraitis. (2004). "Striking Out as Crime Reduction Policy: The Impact of 'Three Strikes' on Crime Rates in U.S. Cities (1980–1999)." *Justice Quarterly* 21(2): 399–424.

Legislative Analyst's Office, California Legislature. (2005). *A Primer: Three Strikes: The Impact After More Than a Decade.* Sacramento: Legislative Analyst's Office.

Luckenbill, David. (1977). "Criminal Homicide as a Situated Transaction." *Social Problems* 25(2): 176–86.

Marvell, Thomas, and Calisle Moody. (2001). "The Lethal Effects of Three Strikes Laws." *Journal of Legal Studies* 30(1): 89–106.

McLean, Gene. (2000). "The New Age of Bank Security." *Canadian Banker* 107 (4).

Perreault, Samuel, and Shannon Brennan. (2010). "Criminal Victimization in Canada, 2009." *Juristat* 30(2).

Pollack, Stanley. (2006). "Bringing Peace to Boston's Streets." *The Boston Globe*, July 18.

Public Safety Canada. (2011). *Corrections and Conditional Release Statistical Overview—2010.* Ottawa: Public Safety Canada; available at http://www.publicsafety.gc.ca/res/cor/rep/2010-ccrso-eng.aspx#a7, accessed June 8, 2011.

Roberts, Julian. (2005). *Mandatory Sentences of Imprisonment in Common Law Jurisdictions: Some Representative Models.* Ottawa: Department of Justice.

Roehl, Jan, Dennis Rosenbaum, Sandra Costello, James Coldren, Amie Schuck, Laura Kunard, and David Forde. (2006). *Strategic Approaches to Community Safety Initiative (SACSI) in 10 U.S. Cities: The Building Blocks for Project Safe Neighborhoods.* Washington, DC: U.S. Department of Justice.

Sacco, Vincent F., and Holly Johnson. (1990). *Patterns of Criminal Victimization in Canada.* Ottawa: Statistics Canada (Housing, Family and Social Statistics Division), Minister of Supply and Services Canada.

Schneider, Stephen. (2007). *Refocusing Crime Prevention: Collective Action and the Quest for Community.* Toronto: University of Toronto Press.

Schweinhart, L.J., J. Montie, Z. Xiang, W.S. Barnett, C.R. Belfield, and M. Nores. (2005). *Lifetime Effects: The High/Scope Perry Preschool Study Through Age 40.* Ypsilanti: The High/Scope Press.

Sherman, Lawrence, Patrick Gartin, and Michael Buerger. (1989). "Hot Spots of Predatory Crime: Routine Activities and the Criminology of Place." *Criminology* 27: 27–55.

Sparks, Richard F. (1981). "Multiple Victimization: Evidence, Theory and Future Research." In *Victims of Crime: A Review of Research Issues and Methods.* Washington, DC: U.S. Dept. of Justice.

Tonry, Michael. (2009). "The Mostly Unintended Effects of Mandatory Minimum Penalties: Two Centuries of Consistent Findings." In Michael Tonry (ed.), *Crime and Justice: A Review of Research, Volume 38* (pp. 65–114). Chicago: University of Chicago Press.

U.S. Department of Justice. (1974a). *Crime in Eight American Cities. Advance Report.* Washington, DC: U.S. Dept. of Justice.

———. (1974b). *Crimes and Victims: A Report on the Dayton-San Jose Pilot Study of Victimization*. Washington, DC: U.S. Dept. of Justice.

Wasserman, Gail, Kate Keenan, Richard Tremblay, John Coie, Todd Herrenkohl, Rolf Loeber, and David Petechuk. (2003). *Risk and Protective Factors of Child Delinquency*. Washington, DC: Office of Juvenile Justice and Delinquency Prevention.

Wright, Richard T., and Scott H. Decker. (1992). *Burglars on the Job: Streetlife and Residential Break-Ins*. Evanston: Northeastern Books.

Young, Jock. (1997). "The Left and Crime Control." Available at http://www.malcolmread.co.uk/JockYoung/, accessed September 4, 2007.

# Patterns of Criminal Behaviour

Many different types of behaviour are illegal but they vary widely in serious-ness. Murder, for instance, is in a different category than not putting enough change in a parking meter. In Part III, we look at some of the kinds of miscon-duct that frequently occur in Canada.

When the average citizen thinks of crime, the images that most commonly come to mind are the so-called street crimes—robbery, assault, break and enter, and so on. These offences have been discussed throughout of most of this text because these crimes occupy most of the time and attention of the criminal justice system, they are the focus of the media, and they have been the concern of most criminologists.

This section of the text will look at two other types of crime. Chapter 16 looks at the "organized" criminals who are in the business of providing access to illegal goods and services. Chapter 17, the final chapter in the text, looks at crimes committed by "respectable" people: many of our leading citizens are white-collar criminals, and many of our largest businesses are corporate offenders. This chapter makes the important point that the power we give to those in positions of authority and ownership in modern corporations may encourage them to become involved in illegal activities that cause a great deal of social harm.

# Organized Crime

## Stephen Schneider

**SAINT MARY'S UNIVERSITY**

# 16

Organized crime can be distinguished by *how* crimes are carried out and by the ultimate *goal* of these crimes—financial profit. Criminal activity is "organized" if it is perpetrated by a group of people who conspire together on a continuing and secretive basis with the goal of obtaining a financial or other material benefit. Scale is also an important factor in determining the extent to which criminal activity is organized. The larger the scope of the criminal activities, the greater the need for a high level of organization and, often, for the involvement of people in several different jurisdictions.

## Learning Objectives

After reading this chapter you should be able to

- Define a criminal organization according to the *Criminal Code of Canada*.
- Understand the characteristics, complexity, and diversity of organized crime.
- Identify the dominant organized crime "genres" operating in Canada.
- Analyze the competing theories on the causes of organized crime and the social, economic, and political factors that give rise to organized crime in North America, and in Canada specifically.
- Compare competing theories on the structure of organized crime.
- Understand the role Canada plays in global organized crime.

## Defining Organized Crime

Different countries have different legal definitions of organized crime. Section 467.1 of the *Criminal Code of Canada* defines a criminal organization as "a group, however organized, that

(a) is composed of three or more persons in or outside Canada; and

(b) has as one of its main purposes or main activities the facilitation or commission of one or more serious offences that, if committed, would likely result in the direct or indirect receipt of a material benefit, including a financial benefit, by the group or by any of the persons who constitute the group."

The legislation goes on to state that a criminal organization "does not include a group of persons that forms randomly for the immediate commission of a single offence." While this caveat does provide some conceptual precision, the legal definition in Canada of a criminal organization remains exceptionally broad and provides little help in understanding the complexity of organized crime.

The Commission of the European Communities and EUROPOL define a criminal organization as "a structured association, established over a period of time, of more than two persons, acting in concert with a view to committing offences which are punishable by deprivation of liberty of a maximum of at least four years or a more serious penalty; whether such offences are an end in themselves or a means of obtaining material benefits and, where appropriate, of improperly influencing the operation of public authorities" (2001, 42). To complement and elucidate this definition, 11 fundamental traits of a criminal organization have been identified:

1. collaboration of more than two people
2. each with own appointed tasks
3. for a prolonged or indefinite period of time (refers to the stability and potential durability)
4. using some form of discipline and control
5. suspected of the commission of serious criminal offences
6. operating at an international level
7. using violence or other means suitable for intimidation
8. using commercial or businesslike structures
9. engaged in money laundering
10. exerting influence on politics, the media, public administration, judicial authorities, or the economy
11. determined by the pursuit of profit and/or power.*

European Law Enforcement Agency
http://www.europol.europa.eu/

This definition is useful because it recognizes that not every organized crime group encompasses all of these traits. To be deemed a criminal organization for law enforcement and prosecution purposes, an identified conspiracy need only exhibit six of the 11 traits. Yet, the European Union (EU) also recognizes the need to identify core characteristics (#1, 3, 5, and 11) that are present in all types of criminal organizations: the collaboration of more than two people, for a prolonged or indefinite period of time, who are engaged in the commission of serious criminal offences, for the pursuit of profit and/or power.

## Characteristics of Organized Crime

This section sets out the core characteristics of organized crime (summarized in Table 16.1) which can be divided into four categories: structural/organizational, institutional, commercial, and behavioural. Not all of these characteristics are present in every organized criminal conspiracy.

---

*Commission of the European Communities and EUROPOL. (2001). *Towards a European Strategy to Prevent Organised Crime*. Brussels: Commission of the European Communities. March.

**TABLE 16.1** A Comprehensive Classification of Organized Crime

| Structural/ Organizational | Institutional | Commercial | Behavioural |
|---|---|---|---|
| Two or more people involved | Continuing enterprise | Illegal activities committed for financial or other material benefit | Rationality |
| Conspire together to commit (serious) illegal acts | Sophistication | Consensual and predatory crimes | Contempt for civil society |
| A systematic pattern to the relationship of the offenders | Motivation | Legal commercial activities | Rules, regulations, and codes |
| Assigned tasks/ Specialization/ Division of labour | Career criminals | Goods and services | Discipline |
| Insulation against law enforcement and prosecution | Limited or exclusive membership | Tactics to support commercial activities: corruption, violence, money laundering | |
| Specialized channels and modes of communication | Recruitment | Multiple enterprises | |
| Multi-jurisdictional/ Transnational in scope | Secrecy | Constant demand for goods and services | |

## Structural/Organizational Characteristics

**Two or More People Involved** One of the core traits of organized crime is that it involves multiple individuals. The more offenders involved in a criminal conspiracy, the greater the chance it will constitute an organized criminal conspiracy.

**Conspire to Commit (Serious) Illegal Acts** A distinguishing characteristic of organized crime is that the individuals involved have come together with the express purpose of committing illegal acts and/or the resulting organization is wholly or overwhelmingly used as a vehicle to commit illegal acts for financial profit. This distinguishes criminal organizations from other organizations, such as corporations or governments, which are legitimately formed but may commit illegal acts in the course of otherwise legitimate business or governmental affairs. Further, the illegal acts should be "serious" in nature.

**A Systematic Pattern to the Relationship of the Offenders** To constitute an organized criminal conspiracy, there must not only be multiple offenders, there must be a *systematic pattern* to the relationship among these offenders. This systematic pattern separates organized crime from other forms of collective criminal action such as riotous mobs.

A major controversy in the study of organized crime concerns the nature of the relationships among the offenders and how organized criminal conspiracies are structured.  There is no single pattern to such relationships, just as there is no single type of organizational structure. The pattern of relationships may be based on kinship, friendship, or business ties, while the structure of a criminal organization or network may be hierarchical (based on power relations among the offenders involved) or more symmetrical (based on the specialized tasks of or resources available to the conspirators).

In his study of criminal networks in New York City, Ianni (1974) identified two basic forms of relationships among individuals involved in organized criminal conspiracies. The first are "associational networks" held together by close personal relationships among members. Examples of these personal relationships are kinship and shared ethnicity, as embodied by the Italian mafia "family." The second follows an "entrepreneurial model," where the bond among the offenders is less personal and more determined by business interests. The historical trend in organized crime has seen business relationships replacing associational networks as the principal binding force among offenders.

**Specialization/Division of Labour**   Many organized crime groups have a division of labour whereby the individuals involved are assigned certain functions (Abadinsky, 2007). In a hierarchical criminal organization, this division of labour often corresponds to the member's position in the power structure. In the more symmetrical network model, individuals have different roles based on their particular skills or resources.  For example, the Colombian cocaine cartels established an intricate division of labour in which each individual (or cell of individuals) specialized in one specific function, such as refining the raw coca into cocaine, transportation, bribing government officials, money laundering, wholesale distribution, security, and managing "stash" houses in destination countries (President's Commission on Organized Crime, 1986b; United States Senate Committee on Governmental Affairs, 1989).

**Insulation Against Enforcement and Prosecution**   A hierarchical organizational structure helps to insulate the upper echelons of a criminal group against law enforcement actions. This is done by ensuring that the hands-on execution of illegal activities is carried out by those at the lowest level of the organization or even outside the organization (the "prospects," "hangers-on," "associates," or "puppet club" members in the case of an outlaw motorcycle gang). The more buffers between those who physically carry out crimes and those in the upper echelons of the organization, the more the latter will be insulated from prosecution. The Cali Cartel from Colombia used an innovative network organizational structure that was explicitly designed to protect the organization and its members from law enforcement. This was accomplished by ensuring that the identities of offenders working within one 'cell' of the network were unknown to those working in other cells. If one should be compromised, the operations of the other cells (and the larger organization) would not be endangered (President's Commission on Organized Crime, 1984, 562; Constantine, 1994).

The insulation is also helped by a code of silence within criminal organizations. For example, central to the Italian Mafia is a code of *omerta*. At the most practical level, *omerta* is about secrecy; members are expected to keep the operations of the family secret from non-members and, ultimately, protect its leaders, and the organization itself from law enforcement (Edwards and Nicaso, 1993, 2–7).

**Specialized Modes and Channels of Communication** Because of the danger of electronic eavesdropping by police, those taking part in organized crime must often be very guarded about how they communicate and what they say to avoid providing law enforcement with evidence that can be used in court.

Communication can be protected in one of two ways. First, offenders can structure their communication so it cannot be interpreted by police; this is most often accomplished by talking in abstract codes. Second, criminal groups will undertake measures to ensure that their conversations are not intercepted by police, such as physically "patting down" people to guard against surreptitious recording, using electronic devices that can detect recording bugs, encrypting digital communication, and using multiple disposable cellular telephones.

**Transnational in Scope** One of the most significant recent trends in organized crime has been the internationalization of criminal groups and their illegal activities. Despite the historical prevalence of organized international smuggling, until the 1970s most criminal groups operated in specific local territories and usually did not attempt to operate outside their spheres of influence. Organized crime is now international. The unprecedented frequency with which criminal groups and activities cross national boundaries, combined with the global structure and reach of some crime groups, has led to the emerging spectre of what is referred to as "**transnational organized crime**" (TOC).

UN Transnational Organized Crime Threat Assessment
http://www.unodc.org/documents/data-and-analysis/tocta/TOCTA_Report_2010_low_res.pdf

**transnational organized crime**

Organized crime that is coordinated and conducted across national borders.

# FOCUS BOX 16.1

## STRUCTURAL AND ORGANIZATIONAL CHARACTERISTICS OF OUTLAW MOTORCYCLE GANGS (OMGS)

To outsiders a biker gang may represent the epitome of wild, unrestrained anarchism. However organizations like the Hells Angels are actually very structured, tightly-knit, and quite hierarchical. There is an organizational hierarchy to each chapter, complete with management positions; a division of labour; and skill-based advancement. There is general uniformity in style of dress, colours, and motorcycles (large modified Harley-Davidsons). Most clubs have a written constitution and bylaws, minutes of meetings are recorded, dues and other revenues are collected, and accounting records maintained.

The organizational structure of an OMG chapter is relatively consistent. Most have a president, vice president, secretary-treasurer, enforcer, sergeant-at-arms, road captain, rank-and-file members, and prospects. The Chapter president is often elected and has final say over all the business of the club. The Club presidents often receive all sorts of booty and tribute from members. The Secretary Treasurer is responsible for collecting dues on behalf of

*(continued)*

the chapter, acts as bookkeeper and secretary (such as keeping the minutes of a meeting), and keeps track of who owes what and to whom. The Sergeant-At-Arms maintains order at meetings and on the chapter's "biker runs." This position is usually filled by the toughest member of the chapter. He may also serve as an enforcer and has the power to discipline a club member. The Road Captain organizes the logistics and security for the time-honoured biker run.

Members of an OMG are those who are allowed to wear its official "colours." In general, a chapter will have no less than six and no more than 25 members. Each chapter has prospective members (called "strikers" or "prospects") who spend from one month to one year on probation. To become a member, one must first be sponsored by an existing member, who is responsible for his prospect. During this time, the prospect must prove himself worthy of membership by following orders and committing crimes. A vote is ultimately taken by chapter members to determine if the prospect can become a full, patch-wearing member.

The OMG and its leader are insulated from law enforcement through the chapter's organizational hierarchy and through a strict code, which ensures ultimate loyalty to the club. Strikers, prospects, hangers-on, puppet club members, and external associates will often take the fall for a particular crime that may involve an OMG member, especially one who occupies a management position in the chapter.

Many of the larger OMGs have developed specialized units to carry out important functions, such as enforcement, violence, and even murder. Hells Angels enforcers are adorned with Nazi storm trooper-like lightning bolts tattooed underneath the words "Filthy Few," the Outlaws have their "SS Death Squad," and the Pagans have the "Black T-Shirt Squad." The Hells Angels' former puppet gang in Quebec—the Rockers—had a special assassination squad called the "football team." The Rockers also operated a "baseball team, "which was made up of members and associates who were responsible for carrying out brutal beatings of rivals" (*Canadian Press*, 2002).

While OMG chapters exhibit a formal organizational structure, individual members often maintain a network of associates and connections through which he carries out his criminal rackets. For business purposes, each member is at the centre of a network that operates independently of the chapter. In other words, the formal structure of the OMG chapter is not necessarily the same as its revenue-generating commercial structure which is broader than the gang. But, "members can call upon the muscle of the club in the event of conflict, making them formidable entrepreneurs" Abadinsky (2000, 238). Lavigne (1996, 246) adds, "The Hells Angels are truthful when they say they are not a criminal organization. Rather, they are an organization of criminals." Indeed, "Belonging to the Hells Angels guarantees to each member the possibility of running an illicit activity" (Nicaso, 2001).

The structure of the OMG chapter was not originally designed as an infrastructure for a criminal organization. However, its reputation, pooled resources, connections with other chapters, criminal associates, and the strict rules and regulations, especially those demanding the utmost secrecy, are essential to carrying out the criminal operations of its members.

## Institutional Characteristics

**Continuity/Continuing Enterprise** Organized crime groups are designed to last beyond the life of the current membership (Abadinsky, 2007, 4). The interests of individuals are subordinate to those of the organization and personnel can be replaced as a matter of course. There is a line of succession to leadership and, as a rule, there are no indispensable members (Salerno, 1967, 7). The Hells Angels have officially existed since the 1950s, with roots stretching back to the immediate post-war period (see Box 16.1). Some of the five major New York mafia families, as well as the Montreal-based mafia, have survived for more than 75 years. Some Chinese triad societies date back hundreds of years. The *Criminal Code of Canada* recognizes organized crime as a continuing enterprise by emphasizing that a criminal organization "does not include a group of persons that forms randomly for the immediate commission of a single offence."

**Career Criminals**   One of the reasons organized crime groups and networks persist over time is that the offenders involved are usually career criminals. For official membership in some traditional crime groups, a criminal record is a prerequisite. Once initiated, many criminal groups require their members to undertake a wide range of illegal activities. Traditional crime groups, such as the Italian mafia or the Japanese Yakuza, require a lifetime membership; this means that offending can extend indefinitely. Members of criminal organizations often do not have legitimate jobs (although some will hide behind the pretence of artificially-created jobs or businesses) and even after accumulating considerable wealth or spending long periods of time in jail, many will continue with their illegal activities.

**Motivation**   Organized crime groups are not motivated by political ideologies, religious dogma, or a desire to change society. Their goal is the accumulation of financial and other material benefits. While influencing political and government officials may be a tactical objective of organized crime, the purpose of corruption is to gain government protection and/or immunity to continue their illegal operations. This non-ideological stance distinguishes criminal organizations from terrorist groups in which the illegal activities are driven by the goal of social and political change.

**Sophistication**   To maximize profits and to avoid incarceration some organized crime groups have become quite sophisticated. The level of sophistication with which both legal and illegal activities are carried out separates organized from unorganized crime, and the larger, transnational criminal groups from smaller localized gangs or networks. According to Criminal Intelligence Service Canada:

> Only a small number of organized crime groups are capable of operating elaborate criminal operations. These groups are engaged in diverse and complex activities. For the most part, they operate out of the largest urban areas but have secondary operations or criminal influence in other cities or rural areas. These groups are distinguished by sophisticated operations, often involving importation, manufacture or distribution of a wide range of illicit commodities as well as the ability to commit complex frauds, money laundering or financial schemes. In addition, many of these groups display the capability to target, coerce or employ individuals in legitimate business, professionals, such as lawyers and accountants, and other community members in order to facilitate their criminal activities. Many of these groups are difficult to target as they strategically insulate themselves from law enforcement.

Source: *2007 Annual Report on Organized Crime in Canada*, p. 14, Criminal Intelligence Service Canada, 2007. Reproduced with the permission of the Minister of Public Works and Government Services Canada, 2011.

Criminal Intelligence Service
Canada
www.cisc.gc.ca

**cybercrime**

The illegal acts in which a computer and a network are central to be committing a crime and the target of the crime.

Another indication of sophistication is the expanding use of technology by organized crime groups. Police have uncovered criminal conspiracies that have produced exact replicas of credit cards, passports, and currency. Some crime groups possess the computer technology to steal personal identification directly from bank cards or through the Internet. Computer hackers who are able to decode complex security systems and firewalls of corporations have been increasingly linked to organized criminals whose intentions are theft for financial gain (Brown, 2007; Verizon Business Risk Team, 2009). "**Cybercrime** groups" even develop and market "crimeware"—malicious software specifically designed to steal confidential personal and financial information (Criminal Intelligence Service Canada, 2010, 12). Some crime groups have engineered intricate encryption codes and software to communicate surreptitiously online while others possess the technology to conduct radar sweeps of drug surveillance planes to map out gaps in coverage. Submarines have even been used to smuggle contraband (Kaihla, 2002).

**Limited or Exclusive Membership** Traditionally, most organized crime groups place restrictions on membership. Group membership is based on factors such as ethnicity, race, nationality, kinship, or criminal record. Ethnicity and/or nationality has long been a major binding tie for members of organized crime groups, which explains why most of the dominant organized crime groups are referred to by ethnic backgrounds (the Sicilian mafia, Chinese triads, Japanese Yakuza, Colombian cartels, Jamaican posses, etc.).

Membership in some criminal groups is not merely symbolic. Once a member of a mafia family, the "made guy," "wise guy," or "good fellow" can now oversee his own crew and/or have jurisdiction over a neighbourhood to carry out his criminal activities. He also has greater access to criminal markets, government, private sector or union officials, and other resources that could not be used by most ordinary criminals. More importantly, criminal organizations such as the mafia or Hells Angels provide members with intimidating power, affluence, and credibility within the criminal underworld.

One of the most important changes in the world of organized crime has been the emergence of organized criminal networks that have abandoned any form of traditional restrictions on membership, such as ethnicity or nationality. Instead, the only criterion that qualifies an individual to become part of this criminal network is the ability to contribute to the accumulation of profits (see Figure 16.3).

**Recruitment** Organized crime groups need "an institutionalized process for inducting new members and inculcating them with the values and ways of behaving" (Cressey, 1969, 36). Recruitment is increasingly important to modern criminal organizations because of the need for specialized skills or resources. According to the Criminal Intelligence Service Canada (CISC), "Where critical skills necessary to facilitate criminal activities are absent within a criminal group, skilled outsiders are recruited or exploited to provide this service. The individual may be considered an outside contractor or part of the criminal network" (2009, 13).

**Secrecy** Organized crime groups protect the secrecy of their operations through violence, intimidation, insulation, rules, and codes of conduct.

The importance of maintaining the secrecy of an organized crime group is personified by the mafia's code of *omerta*, where a mafioso is defined in part by his ability to conceal the existence and operations of *the family* especially in the face of law enforcement interdiction.

## Commercial Characteristics

**Profit-oriented Criminal Activities** The business of organized crime is making money. This characteristic distinguishes organized crime from crimes of passion, vandalism, and terrorism. Organized crime groups generate money through a myriad of illegal (and legal) activities (see Table 16.2). Drug trafficking is the biggest money maker for most organized crime groups. The Criminal Intelligence Service Canada estimates that 80 percent of all identified criminal organizations in Canada are involved in the illegal drug trade (2007, 13; 2009, 9). However, many criminal groups have shown they will become involved in virtually any activity that will make them money.

**Consensual and Predatory Criminal Activities** Organized criminals are involved in both consensual and predatory crimes. A consensual crime is one

United Nations World Drug Report 2010
http://www.unodc.org/documents/wdr/WDR_2010/World_Drug_Report_2010_lo-res.pdf

**Table 16.2**  Common Organized Criminal Activities

| Consensual | Predatory/Consensual (includes both a victim and a consumer) | Predatory |
|---|---|---|
| Drug smuggling/trafficking | Automobile theft **Human trafficking** (indentured slavery and forced prostitution) | **Extortion** ("protection rackets") |
| Smuggling and marketing of legal consumer products (tobacco, liquor, fuel, digital products, clothing) | Environmental crimes (illegal dumping of waste) | Business and labour racketeering |
| Gambling | Counterfeiting and product piracy (bank cards, government documents, currency, consumer products) | Murder, grievous bodily injury |
| Migrant smuggling | Corruption (of government officials, labour racketeering) | Kidnapping |
| Loansharking | Illegal trade in wildlife | Consumer Fraud (Ponzi schemes, telemarketing) |
| Prostitution | Illegal trade in organs and tissue (human and animal) | Government fraud (tax, health care, employment insurance, social insurance and assistance) |
| Money laundering | Illegal trafficking in arms, ammunition and explosives | Corporate fraud (credit card, insurance, mortgage) |
| | Trafficking in nuclear and radioactive substances | Stock market manipulation |
| | Illegal trade in stolen artefacts, art, jewellery, precious gems | Theft (including robbery, burglary, hijacking) |
| | Trafficking in endangered plant species | Computer crime (computer hacking) |

where no 'victim' exists; that is, two or more individuals voluntarily engage in an illegal transaction. The business of organized crime has been described as providing goods and services that are in demand by the public but that have been made illegal or are tightly regulated by the state.

Predatory crimes are those in which a victim suffers a direct physical, emotional, or financial loss. Predatory crimes carried out by organized criminal groups include **extortion** (protection rackets), theft, **human trafficking**, currency counterfeiting, and various types of fraud.

A clear-cut delineation between consensual and predatory crimes is often difficult to make given that even consensual crimes can harm the individual consuming the good or service (e.g., a drug addict or compulsive gambler) as well as society at large. Table 16.2 summarizes the wide range of illegal activities associated with organized crime and categorizes each according to whether they are a consensual crime, a predatory crime, or both.

**Goods and Services** Organized illegal enterprises provide both goods and services. Popular illegal goods include drugs, legal contraband (such as cigarettes or liquor), stolen goods, weapons, counterfeit currency, pirated commercial products, and even human or animal organs. Common illegal consensual services include gambling, prostitution, **loansharking**, migrant smuggling, and illegal waste dumping (which is provided to legitimate businesses seeking to avoid the high costs of obeying environmental laws).

**Legal and Illegal** While most products supplied by organized crime groups are illegal, they supply goods and services that are legal but whose distribution is controlled by the state. For example, while cigarettes and liquor are legal products, they are also distributed through black markets. Most black markets for legal consumer products exist due to high government taxes. The United States has lower taxes on cigarettes and alcohol than Canada, so organized groups smuggle large quantities of these products across the border where they are sold to Canadians well below their retail price. Other legal products are stolen and then fenced through underground markets or through legal businesses such as bars or pawn shops. In addition to selling legal products illegally in underground markets, organized crime groups have also become involved in legitimate and legal businesses for purposes of generating revenue, to legitimize the offender, or to launder money.

**Constant Demand for Goods and Services** One of the most important factors that keeps organized crime groups in business is a loyal customer base that voluntarily consumes its products and services. Without drug users, gamblers, "johns," or people wanting to immigrate, organized crime would be much less profitable. Indeed, one of the reasons it is so difficult to eradicate organized crime is that its activities are supported by the 'law-abiding' public.

**Monopolistic Goals** Organized crime groups often seek a monopoly over the sale of a particular good or service in a particular geographic area. These monopolies are typically sought and maintained through violence, the threat of violence, or by corrupt relationships with government, businesses, or union

**extortion**
An offender unlawfully obtains money, property or services from an individual or entity through coercion and intimidation.

**human trafficking**
The illegal trade in people for the purposes of commercial sexual exploitation and other forms of forced labour.

**loansharking**
Lending money at very high interest rates, often enforced through physical force.

officials (Abadinsky, 2007). Competition for market share often leads to serious violence, as demonstrated by the biker war that erupted in Quebec in the 1990s. More than 160 people were killed when the Hells Angels tried to monopolize the lucrative cocaine trade in that province (Sher and Marsden, 2003).

**Tactics to Support Commercial Activities** While many organized crime activities directly generate revenue, others are carried out to facilitate the profit-making enterprises of the criminal organization. Like a legitimate corporation, criminal groups must undertake certain activities to support the production, distribution, and marketing of its products and services. One factor that separates organized crime from unorganized crime is the use of tactical illegal activities, such as corruption, violence/intimidation, and money laundering.

The corruption of public officials, labour unions, political parties, and the judiciary has historically formed an integral part of organized crime tactics, although this has not been as common in Canada as in other countries. However, in recent years, police in Canada have uncovered numerous conspiracies to corrupt officials working in marine ports and airports, to facilitate the international movement of drugs, contraband, and the cash proceeds of crime (Criminal Intelligence Service Canada, 2004, 10–14; Schneider, 2009, 366–367).

Gang violence may seem indiscriminate but it is often used rationally to ensure that certain individuals—usually competing gangsters, victims, witnesses or informants, and in some cases government officials—do not obstruct the criminal organization from reaching its objectives. Violence is also used to maintain internal discipline within crime groups and to enhance the reputation of the group.

One tactic used to protect the profits of organized crime is money laundering, which is the process of legitimizing illegally-earned revenue. Cash is the universally accepted mode of payment in the underground economy. Thus organized criminals—drug traffickers, in particular—accumulate large amounts of cash, often in small denominations. This can make them targets for law enforcement and taxation officials. To avoid this problem, organized criminals must devise creative methods for converting large amounts of cash into other assets while concealing the criminal source of the funds. A typical money laundering technique is to open a cash-based business, such as a restaurant or bar, and then deposit the cash proceeds of crime into a bank account under the guise of revenue from this legitimate business.

A final tactical imperative used by more sophisticated criminals is intelligence gathering and counter-surveillance, which includes the use of eavesdropping technology or placing gang associates inside enforcement agencies or other government agencies, to gather information.

## Behavioural Characteristics

**Rationality** Rational choice theory (see Chapter 15) contends that most offenders are self-maximizing decision-makers who calculate the advantages and disadvantages associated with specific criminal acts (Clarke and Cornish, 1985). Arguably, organized crime represents one of the most rational forms of criminality because it responds to the laws of supply and demand in the same way as legitimate business. This rationality is then reflected in the criminal organization itself. In this context, criminal groups "selling illicit goods and services must, if they are to capitalize on the great demand for their wares, expand by establishing a division of labour. ... The next rational move is consolidation and integration of separate divisions of labor into a cartel designed to minimize competition and maximize profits" (Cressey, 1969, 34–35). Even violence is used rationally by criminal groups because it is meant to support the goals of the group.

**Contempt for Civil Society** Members of traditional organized crime groups, such as the Italian mafia, Japanese Yakuza, the Russian **vory v zakone**, and outlaw motorcycle gangs, openly rebel against conventional social rules and values that govern civil society and organize their behaviour according to the norms of their criminal group. This attitude is exemplified by the term 'wiseguy,' which is used to refer to members of Italian-American mafia groups. A wiseguy believes that anybody who follows the commonly accepted rules and laws of civil society is a sucker and deserves to be victimized. Pileggi adroitly captures the wiseguy attitude toward society: "They lived in an environment awash in crime, and those who did not partake were simply viewed as prey. To live otherwise was foolish. Anyone who stood in line was beneath contempt" (1985, 36).

**vory v zakone**

A "thieve in law" is a high-ranking, well-respected organized crime figure in the old Soviet underworld and the new republic of Russia. Akin to the Italian Mafia, the code of the "Thieves World" emphasizes the rejection of the traditional norms of society, in particular a rejection of government authority. The origins of the "vor" pre-date the Czar, but many were inmates interned in soviet prison camps who organized themselves in an attempt to rule the criminal underworld.

**Rules, Regulations, and Codes** Like legitimate organizations, traditional organized crime groups have established rules and regulations that members are expected to follow (Abadinsky, 2007, 5). In some groups these rules are implicit, while in others they are explicit and may actually be written out. The most important rules focus on secrecy and loyalty because these values help to protect illegal organizations from the threats posed by law enforcement officials and by other organized crime groups.

**Discipline** In order to ensure that the rules and regulations are obeyed, most criminal groups have strict forms of discipline based on loyalty, a code of honour, and most importantly, the fear of reprisal (death).

## Dominant Organized Crime Genres and Groups

This section provides an overview of some of the dominant organized crime genres and groups in Canada, which can be categorized as: Italian, Chinese/Asian, Colombian/South American, outlaw motorcycle gangs, Russian/Eastern European, and Aboriginal. The specific criminal groups that fall within each of these genres embody many of the characteristics previously described in this chapter, and are highly sophisticated, powerful, and widespread:

> There are varying levels of criminal capabilities amongst organized crime groups across Canada. At present, those with higher levels of criminal capabilities are largely represented by a number of Asian criminal groups in the B.C. Lower Mainland and southern Ontario, some Italian crime groups in Ontario and Quebec, certain Hells Angels chapters in B.C., Ontario and Quebec, and several independent groups across the country. This relatively small number of criminal groups is distinguished by their large-scale, sophisticated operations involving

# FOCUS BOX 16.2

## RULES, RITES, AND RITUALS OF THE 'NDRANGHETA

In 1971, while Toronto police were searching the home of a suspected member of the Canadian cell of an Italian organized crime network, they found 27-page document, handwritten in an antiquated Italian script, in his kitchen cupboards.

Experts from Canada and Italy would later conclude that the papers outlined the rules, rites, rituals, and structure of the *Honorata Società* (known as the 'ndrangheta). It was the first time such an authentic document had fallen into the hands of police in North America. The heading on the first page was *Come Formare una Società* ("How to Form a Society") and the preamble partially read: "My stomach is a tomb, my mouth a bleated work of humility." Another section dictates the initiation rites of an inductee who symbolically vows to take "a bloody dagger in my hand and a serpent in my mouth" should he betray the Honoured Society.

A 1972 *Globe and Mail* article described the remainder of the document as a "a tangle of centuries old archaic Italian, the phrases laced with flowery, mystic imagery dealing with such matters as collecting opinions from society members,

punishing members who don't surrender their guns at meetings, catechism-like initiation rituals and the proper words to be used when separating a member from the group."

The papers also outlined the basic structure of a 'ndrangheta cell, which includes three levels or ranks. There were also references to the pledges and obligations of members, the most important being a vow of silence. The document uses the term *mastro di sgarru*, the obligation of members to exact vendettas against enemies of the Society. Another common term was *baciletta*, which can be defined as "extorted money" collected by Society members that should be "given to the ones who need it, the ones who have been arrested, for the defence lawyers, to help the people the police are looking for."

The discovery of this document was a significant breakthrough in efforts by police to prove the existence of a secret criminal society in North America with roots in Southern Italy.

Source: Based on *Globe and Mail*. (1972). "Metro Police Raid Turned Up Copy of Mafia Linked Society's Secret Rituals, Court is Told." *Globe and Mail*, June 2.

the importation, manufacture or distribution of a wide variety of contraband, as well as through financial crimes such as fraud and money laundering. However, these kinds of criminal groups have demonstrated an ability to shield themselves from disruption by law enforcement and rival criminal groups.

Source: *2006 Annual Report on Organized Crime in Canada*, p. 6, Criminal Intelligence Service Canada, 2006. Reproduced with the permission of the Minister of Public Works and Government Services Canada, 2011.

**Italian** Italian organized crime in Canada can be broken down into three categories: the Sicilian "mafia," the 'ndrangheta, and the Canadian arm of Italian-American crime families, often referred to as la cosa nostra (LCN) (Criminal Intelligence Service Canada, 2002, 16). Since the late 1940s, Italian-Canadian organized crime has been most influenced by the 'ndrangheta, which traces its roots to the Southern Italian province of Calabria (see Box 16.2). Most of the founders, leaders, and members of Italian-Canadian crime groups emigrated from Calabria or at least could trace their roots to this province. Despite this lineage, for many years Italian-Canadian criminal organizations operated as wings of Italian-American mafia families. The Montreal mafia was controlled by New York's Bonanno family, while many of the Italian-Canadian crime groups in Ontario were answerable to a family in Buffalo. Beginning in the 1960s, Italian-Canadian crime groups were established in Toronto that had strong ties to the 'ndrangheta in Southern Italy.

Today, Italian prosecutors allege there are seven dominant Calabrian mafia families in Toronto, involving both Italian and Canadian nationals, that are part of an international network of 'ndrangheta cells (*National Post*, 2010b; 2010c). Since the late 1970s, the Montreal-based mafia has been dominated by made members of Sicilian heritage. Under the command of the Rizzuto family, it is run independently of other crime groups in either Italy or the United States, and is involved in drug trafficking, illegal gambling (bookmaking), extortion (protection rackets), and has been accused of rigging bids related to commercial construction and public works contracts. Once considered the most powerful mafia group in this country, in recent years it has experienced a decline because of intensive law enforcement crackdowns, the jailing of its leader Vito Rizzuto in the United States on murder charges, competition from rival crime groups, and the 2010 murder of Vito's father and the family patriarch, 86-year-old Nicolo Rizzuto (Lamothe and Humphreys, 2006; Schneider, 2009, *Montreal Gazette*, 2011).

**Chinese/Asian** Contemporary Asian organized crime in Canada can be broken down into six categories: (1) localized street gangs made up of both youth and adults; (2) Chinese triads, which evolved from gangs in Toronto's Chinatown in the 1970s to sophisticated transnational criminal syndicates with links to Hong Kong, Taiwan, and Mainland China; (3) non-triad Chinese criminal networks that tend to specialize in one particular criminal activity, such as drug trafficking or migrant smuggling; (4) a loose network of criminals from Mainland China (originally referred to as the Big Circle Boys) who commit a wide variety of crimes; (5) Vietnamese crime groups, which include violent street gangs in Toronto and Vancouver and now include some of the biggest marijuana producers and traffickers in Canada; and (6) Indo-Canadian crime groups that are largely confined to British Columbia and are involved in cocaine, marijuana, and synthetic drug trafficking and smuggling.

The most dominant and historically entrenched of the Asian organized crime genre are Chinese criminal groups. During the first half of the twentieth century, Chinese merchants in Vancouver were behind some of the largest opium smuggling and trafficking rings in the country. Canada's first Chinatown in Victoria was home to illegal gambling halls, brothels, and opium dens, most of which were controlled by leading Chinese merchants. During the 1950s, the RCMP uncovered illegal Chinese immigrant smuggling operations from Hong Kong. Beginning in the 1970s, Southeast Asian heroin began to supplant the Turkish variety in North America and, before long, Chinese drug trafficking syndicates became some of the world's biggest heroin suppliers. By the mid-1970s, a rash of extortions within Toronto's Chinese community exposed the presence of Canada's first modern triad, the Kung Lok. Around the same time, Chinese street gangs emerged in Vancouver. A few years later, aggressive

Vietnamese gangs began to challenge the Chinese triads for supremacy in the Asian underworld in both cities. At the end of the 1980s the Big Circle Boys, originally a group of former soldiers from Mainland China, were being blamed for a series of violent robberies, home invasions, and other crime in Vancouver and Toronto. Within 10 years, this loose network would evolve into one of Canada's largest, most sophisticated criminal conspiracies, committing a wide range of highly profitable crimes, including drug trafficking (production, smuggling, and/or wholesale distribution of marijuana, heroin, cocaine, and synthetic drugs), bank card fraud, product piracy, people smuggling, human trafficking, contraband tobacco manufacturing and distribution, and currency counterfeiting (Schneider, 2009; Dubro, 1992; Criminal Intelligence Service Canada, 2004).

**Outlaw Motorcycle Gangs** Outlaw motorcycle gangs (OMGs) emerged in the United States following World War II and were originally formed for camaraderie and excitement. Biker gangs gradually moved into for-profit criminal pursuits, initially working as muscle-for-hire and as street-level drug distributors. The Hells Angels Motorcycle Club is the world's largest OMG, with almost 200 chapters located in numerous countries. While Canada once had many competing biker gangs, today the Hells Angels predominate. Its first chapter was founded in Montreal in 1976 and over the next 40 years, it became the first truly national criminal organization, with chapters, puppet clubs, and/or associates in every province. Indeed, Canada has become an international stronghold for the motorcycle club; there are more Hells Angels members per capita in Canada than any other country in the world. While drug trafficking remains a significant source of income for the Hells Angels, they are also involved in the illegal trafficking of firearms and explosives, protection rackets, automobile theft and export, fraud, and prostitution. To facilitate its international smuggling operations, the Hells Angels rely on corruption and internal conspiracies at international ports of entry and are believed to have successfully infiltrated shipping lines, port corporations, and longshoreman's unions in Canada and abroad (Sher and Marsden, 2004; Schneider, 2009).

**Colombian/South American** South American organized crime is overwhelmingly tied to the cocaine traffic and has traditionally been dominated by Colombian groups. While much of the world's coca leaf production occurs in Bolivia and Peru, most refined cocaine is manufactured in Colombia. Up until the mid 1990s, two Colombian "cartels"—Cali and Medellin—monopolized the wholesale cocaine market worldwide. During their ascendancy in the 1970s and 1980s, the two cartels were the largest and most sophisticated transnational crime groups in the world. Both established cells in Canada to wholesale cocaine. Cocaine smuggling into Canada in the early 1970s relied primarily on a large number of couriers who smuggled small quantities across the border. Eventually, the cartels flew cocaine into Canada on small planes with as much as 500 kilos on board, some of which was destined for the U.S. market. Colombian groups have been linked to the corruption of Canadian airport officials, including baggage handlers, ramp crews, and customs officials, to facilitate the importation of cocaine and the export of drug money (Schneider,

2009). The two cartels were eventually put out of business and their role has been filled by countless smaller operators from Columbia and Peru, although criminal groups from Mexico are now dominant in the international trafficking and marketing of cocaine, marijuana, and methamphetamine (United States Department of State, 2010).

**Russia/Eastern European** Organized crime factions from Russia, the Ukraine, and other former republics of the Soviet Union are active throughout the former communist bloc as well as Western Europe, North America, Israel, and Australia. Russian criminal organizations that trace their roots back for decades, like the *vory v zakone*, have been joined by younger career offenders, street criminals, former Soviet intelligence officers, government officials, and businessmen. Other eastern European crime groups originate in Yugoslavia, Albania, Croatia, and Serbia and most of these are involved in smuggling drugs, guns, and weapons in the Balkans and Europe. While Russian and Eastern European organized crime exploded in the chaotic atmosphere that followed the fall of the Soviet Union in the early 1990s, they had been operating on a small scale in North America since the 1970s. These loosely-networked groups operated mostly in New York, Los Angeles, and Toronto.

In Toronto, during the 1970s and 1980s, Eastern European criminals were involved in extortion, gambling, loansharking, and drug trafficking, much of it in conjunction with the Ontario arm of the American Costa Nostra (Lamothe and Nicaso, 1994, 45; Federal Bureau of Investigation, 1995; *Toronto Star*, 1996; Rawlinson, 1997). Russian and other Eastern European crime groups are most active in large cities in Ontario, Quebec, and British Columbia. They have varying degrees of organization and sophistication, and engage in a wide array of crime, from petty theft to sophisticated fraud schemes. Financial frauds, in particular **debit card fraud** schemes, are major activities for these groups. They are also involved in prostitution, contraband smuggling, illegal drug importation, as well as the theft and illegal export of vehicles to Eastern Europe (*Globe and Mail*, 1998; Criminal Intelligence Service Canada, 2002, 14–15; 2004, 7–9).

**debit card fraud**

Debit card fraud is a four step process: (1) create fake debit cards, (2) steal personal identification and banking information from legitimate cards, (3) emboss the stolen information on the fake cards, and (4) use the illegal debit cards.

**Aboriginal** Aboriginal organized crime in Canada can be divided into: (1) criminal groups and activities in Central Canada (Ontario and Quebec) that revolve around smuggling and contraband cigarette production, and (2) criminal gangs located in the prairie provinces. The former have played a central role in smuggling, due primarily to geo-political factors that facilitate the movement of contraband across the Canada–U.S. border. In 1994, RCMP Commissioner Norman Inkster said that as much as 70 percent of the contraband tobacco entering Canada was coming through the Akwesasne reserve. Populated by the Mohawk nation, the 14 000-acre reserve has the unique distinction of straddling the U.S.–Canada border, making it ideally suited for smuggling. The reserve's territory actually falls within five jurisdictions—Canada, the United States, Ontario, Quebec, and New York State—and agreements have been negotiated with federal, state, and provincial governments in both countries that uphold the right of the Mohawk people to freely cross the borders that cut through the reserve. These factors, combined with a well-honed smuggling infrastructure, have meant that a variety of contraband, drugs, and weapons cross through the reserve, with resident smugglers constantly shifting products based on demand and profitability. Aboriginal groups are active in the smuggling of alcohol, tobacco, drugs, firearms, explosives, jewellery, vehicles, electronic equipment, and people (*Montreal Gazette*, 1996; United States Congress, 2000; Schneider, 2009). Aboriginal crime groups in Central Canada are also involved in distribution of contraband goods at the wholesale and retail levels. In recent years, cigarette manufacturing plants and retail outlets have been established on several aboriginal reserves in Ontario and Quebec. These outlets, combined with cigarette smuggling from the United States, have been blamed for a flood of contraband cigarettes on the streets of Quebec, Ontario, and other parts of Canada (Royal Canadian Mounted Police, 2008; Canadian Convenience Store Association, 2009; *National Post*, 2010a).

Aboriginal criminal groups in the prairie provinces mostly operate as street gangs and, according to the CISC "are generally involved in opportunistic, spontaneous and disorganized street-level criminal activities, primarily low-level trafficking of marihuana, cocaine and crack cocaine and, to a lesser extent, methamphetamine. The gangs are also involved in prostitution, break-and-enters, robberies, assaults, intimidation, vehicle theft and illicit drug debt collection" (2004, 20–21). These Aboriginal gangs have connections to Asian and outlaw motorcycle criminal groups, from which they purchase drugs at a wholesale level.

While these organized crime genres include some of the largest and most sophisticated criminal groups and networks, they do not monopolize organized criminal activities. Today, organized crime is represented by a diverse number of "genres," that have emerged from numerous ethno-cultural and national backgrounds. Moreover, while a defining characteristic of these dominant organized crime genres has been a shared nationality, ethnicity, and/or language, in recent years it has become apparent that these factors are no longer the most important criteria in determining who participates in a particular organized criminal conspiracy. There are thousands of individual criminal entrepreneurs who work together, on an *ad hoc* or ongoing basis, in the pursuit of illegal revenues, regardless of ethnicity, nationality, or language. In this sense, modern organized crime can best be characterized as a fluid network of many autonomous buyers, brokers, financiers, middlemen, and distributors from different groups, ethnicities, nationalities, and countries that come together to make deals by capitalizing on each other's specialties and strengths. The proliferation and increasing diversity of criminal groups in Canada began in the early 1970s and gathered speed in subsequent decades. By 2009, the Criminal Intelligence Service estimated there were 750 criminal gangs in Canada (Criminal Intelligence Service Canada, 2009, 9).

## Theories of Organized Crime

Theories that help to explain organized crime can be divided into two categories: those that try to identify and analyze the causes of organized crime (etiological theories) and those that attempt to understand the structure of organized criminal conspiracies.

## Etiological Theories

Several theories have tried to explain the causes and existence of organized crime in North America. Some of the theories are specific to organized crime while others are based on selected theories of criminality you have read about in this text and have been adapted to organized crime. This chapter will focus on presenting theories specific to organized crime, which can be grouped into the following categories: (1) Alien Conspiracy Theory, (2) Ethnic Succession Theory, (3) Economic Theories, and (4) Public Policy Impetus.

**Alien Conspiracy Theory**  One of earliest theories of the origins and causes of organized crime in America is alien conspiracy theory. Originally developed to explain the origins and scope of Italian organized crime in the United States, it has also been applied to other ethnic-based organized crime genres, including Chinese Triads, Colombian cocaine cartels, Jamaican posses, Nigerian crime groups, and Russian/Eastern European crime groups.

Proponents of alien conspiracy theory believe that organized crime in America is the result of the importation of secret criminal societies that are rooted in foreign cultures. Thus organized crime does not emerge from American culture, but rather has been thrust upon the country by specific immigrant groups. When used to explain Italian-American crime groups, the theory also contends that a nation-wide criminal network exists—made up of about two dozen "families" of Italian lineage all of which were governed by a national commission—collectively known as the "mafia" or "**la cosa nostra**."

The theory was not developed by scholars but was most forcefully promoted in the early 1950s by a U.S. Senate committee, chaired by Senator Estes Kefauver (United States Congress, 1951). The committee's report alleged that a sinister secret organization originating in Sicily made its way to the United States during the period of massive Italian immigration in the late nineteenth and early twentieth centuries (Kelly, 1987, 13). This secret society grew into a monolithic nation-wide criminal conspiracy, under "centralized direction and control" which subverted and eroded the fundamental law-abiding values of American society (Smith, 1975, 138). Similar allegations were made by several later commissions including the President's Commission on Law Enforcement and Administration of Justice (1967). Criminologist Donald Cressey lent scholarly credence to this theory in his work as a consultant to the President's Commission and in a subsequent book *Theft of a Nation*, which over-estimated the scope and power of the Italian mafia in America while implying the subversion of American values and institutions by an invading alien force.

Like many conspiracy theories, alien conspiracy theory has some tenuous roots in reality. However, subsequent scholarly research, as well as evidence gathered by criminal justice agencies, has refuted the two main pillars of this theory as an almost fictional exaggeration of the roots and scope of ethnic Italian organized crime in North America.

First, the origins and perpetuation of La Cosa Nostra in America cannot simply be blamed on the importation of a secret society from Sicily. The American LCN can trace a part of its family tree to the Sicilian mafia, and the early secret societies in North America were made up of Italian immigrants, some of whom brought with them the traditions and criminal activities of the

**la cosa nostra**

This term is used to denote Italian-American organized crime. It was originally applied by the FBI in an attempt to make this criminal fraternity sound ominous and threatening. Members of the so-called LCN never used this label themselves, although they often referred to their secret society as "this thing of ours," which roughly translates into Italian as "la cosa nostra."

Sicilian mafia (or the Calabrian 'ndrangheta). However, the LCN, and indeed modern organized crime, is overwhelmingly an American (and to a lesser extent Canadian) creation. It is a product of North American culture, profitably fuelled by popular vices and the spirit of capitalism, and facilitated by corruption in the private and public sectors (Bell, 1953).

Second, there is little evidence to corroborate the existence of a nation-wide criminal conspiracy with centralized control. There were a number of Italian organized crime groups spread out across North America that were linked via ideology, ethnicity, methods, illegal networks, and criminal activities. Attempts were made by some influential Italian organized crime figures to create a "commission" that would coordinate and regulate competing interests of the various Italian crime groups. However, a *national* commission never fully materialized and most groups worked independently in their own cities with some sporadic cooperation (and conflict) between groups and across jurisdictions (Albini, 1971; Smith, 1975). The so-called "Commission" was largely confined to New York and had tenuous jurisdiction over the five mafia families in that city. Notwithstanding its limited jurisdiction, during the 1970s and 1980s, the Commission was respected and admired among certain mafia groups in Quebec and Ontario. The Commission (or its individual members) frequently dictated the activities of its Canadian mafia cells, was called in to help settle internal disputes, and had to be consulted if a made mafia member in Canada was to be killed as a result of an internal dispute.

In his 1975 book *The Mafia Mystique*, Dwight Smith argues that the alien conspiracy theory arose in the United States in part because self-serving governmental commissions, politicians, and law enforcement officials were fabricating fictional or exaggerated accounts to help secure greater enforcement and prosecutorial resources.

The notion of a national organized crime conspiracy generally did not resonate among Canadian scholars or government and law enforcement officials. In fact, up until the early 1960s police, politicians, and judicial inquiries typically denied the mafia existed in Canada (*Toronto Star*, 1948; *Toronto Telegram*, 1961; Roach, 1962). Thus, Canadian officials erred in the opposite direction of their American counterparts. While many of the early ethnic Italian criminal societies in this country were made up of immigrants who brought with them some basic ideologies and criminal methods from Sicily and Calabria, organized crime evolved and prospered in this country due to the same indigenous conditions that existed in America. While there was never any nation-wide confederation of Italian crime groups in Canada with a centralized command and control, law enforcement evidence and scholarly research has indicated that some ethnic Italian crime groups in Quebec and Ontario operated as cells of American mafia families and were also linked through international criminal conspiracies including drug trafficking, immigrant smuggling, and bookmaking. 'Ndrangheta cells operated in Toronto in years past and there is operating there today (*National Post*, 2010b, 2010c).

**Ethnic Succession Theory**   Other theories place greater emphasis on North American conditions that contribute to the origins and growth of modern organized crime on this continent. This perspective is epitomized by the adage: "societies get the crime they deserve." These theories situate the root causes of organized criminality in the broader social, political, cultural, and economic environment of North America. Several general theories of crime and criminality, detailed in previous chapters, have helped inform this approach.

In particular, strain theory (see Chapter 10) forms the basis of the ethnic succession theory of organized criminality, which contends that many immigrant ethnic groups are disproportionately involved in organized crime in the United States because of the barriers they encounter in their pursuit of the American dream (Bell, 1953; Ianni, 1974). Thus the ethnic basis of many organized crime groups in North America is not tied to the importation of foreign criminal cultures or secret societies, but results from minority groups struggling for prosperity. Each successive immigrant group experiences strains such as discrimination, unemployment, poverty, lack of political power, and social exclusion, and some members of these groups respond by becoming involved in criminal activities. As time passes and as legitimate and socially acceptable avenues of mobility open up to these ethnic groups, the strain subsides, members of the particular ethnic group rely less and less on crime to get ahead, and move more fully into mainstream society. Ethnic succession occurs when a subsequent immigrant groups fills this criminal void in their attempt to climb the ladder of success. According to this thesis, persons or entire ethnic groups that are implicated in organized crime are not committed to a deviant subculture, but are merely using available, albeit illegal, opportunities to achieve economic and social success (see Box 16.3). Thus, involvement in organized crime is a rational response to blocked opportunities (Abadinsky, 2003, 43).

# FOCUS BOX 16.3

## CAN ETHNIC SUCCESSION THEORY BE APPLIED TO CANADA?

The history of organized crime in Canada provides some evidence supporting ethnic succession theory. In the mid-to-late nineteenth century, Irish immigrants were disproportionately represented in violent criminal gangs in Upper and Lower Canada, in part because they were discriminated against by the English and Scots who held most positions of power.

During the first half of the twentieth century, Irish gangs were eclipsed by more sophisticated Jewish criminals who dominated such organized rackets as gambling and drug trafficking, particularly in Montreal, where anti-Semitism was rife.

Samuel Bronfman is an illustration of ethnic succession theory. Bronfman was born in Canada to immigrant Jewish parents, made his fortune supplying American bootleggers during Prohibition, and eventually headed Seagram's distilleries, one of Canada's largest corporate empires.

During the early twentieth century, Chinese merchants in British Columbia were involved in selling opium, gambling, and prostitution. Their clientele were Chinese immigrant labourers, who found refuge in such vices in the face of constant racial hatred, violence, and legislative disenfranchisement by the white population.

The Prohibition era in the 1920s witnessed the rise of the Italian racketeers, many of whom emerged from the poverty-stricken tenements of Southern Ontario and Montreal and were unable to find legitimate employment because of discrimination.

By the 1970s, Italian-Canadian crime groups were in decline, with the void being filled by other groups that had more recently immigrated to Canada, from China, Vietnam, Jamaica, and Russia (Carrigan, 1991; Schneider, 2009).

Critics of ethnic succession theory point to the fact that many people of Italian or Chinese heritage remained active in organized crime long after these groups were assimilated into mainstream society and many of their members had become successful through legitimate means. Potter (1994) concludes that members of immigrant ethnic and racial groups may turn to organized crime, but they do not necessarily replace existing ethnically and racially-based criminal groups. Moreover, this theory does not explain why those from the middle-class become involved in organized crime, nor does it account for the organized economic crimes committed by the wealthy and the powerful (Abadinsky, 2007). Finally, this theory fails to explain how criminal organizations that are made up primarily of White Anglo-Saxon Protestants—such as outlaw motorcycle gangs—emerge within North American society.

**Economic Theories** An economic analysis does not view organized crime as pathological, but as a rational system that operates according to the laws of supply and demand. In fact, basic economic concepts such as supply, demand, and price elasticity are quite applicable to underground markets. For example, research has shown that the price of illegal or contraband commodities is related to supply and demand (Caulkins and Reuter, 1998; Office of National Drug Control Policy, 2004; Royal Canadian Mounted Police, 2007). Thus, if the local cocaine supply is plentiful, the price will be low but if the local market has a limited supply the price will usually rise.

An economic approach focuses on how criminal organizations make money supplying goods and services that are in demand, but which have been declared illegal by the state. Underground markets also profit by providing the public with a cheaper supply of certain goods, primarily by evading taxes (e.g., contraband tobacco and liquor) or by supplying stolen or counterfeit goods. One significant implication of this economic analysis is that organized crime is not viewed as alien to the societies in which it operates, but a part of its commercial markets. Rather than viewing organized crime as an alien parasite that preys upon society and gives nothing back, an economic analysis recognizes that there is a symbiotic relationship between criminal organizations (as suppliers) and segments of society (as consumers) (Martens and Longfellow, 1982, 4; Dickie and Wilson, 1993, 216). In short, organized crime fulfils certain commercial functions for the societies in which it operates.

One critique of this economic perspective is that underground markets are highly distorted relative to legitimate markets. Naylor (2004, 21) declares that "the facile analogy between legal and illegal firms is at best a serious over-simplification, at worst simply wrong. In illegal markets that are highly segmented, decisions are personalized, information flows constricted, capital supplies short term and unreliable, objective price data lacking, and the time horizons (indeed the very existence) of enterprises coterminous with those of the entrepreneurs." Moreover, the application of traditional economic theory to organized crime only captures consensual crimes, while ignoring predatory criminal activities, such as theft, hijacking, kidnapping, extortion, and fraud.

**Public Policy Impetus** The government decides whether goods or services that people desire are to be made available in legal or illegal markets. A product or service only becomes illegal when the government passes laws prohibiting its use. For the most part, the products or services that have been criminalized by the state are deemed to constitute immoral vices that are personally and/or socially harmful, such as drugs, alcohol, gambling, or prostitution.

When a government outlaws a particular product or service that the public still wishes to use, it drives supply and demand to the "underground market," while creating the opportunity for the monopolization of a product or service by criminal entrepreneurs. In short, one of the fundamental reasons explaining why we have organized crime is because governments have criminalized certain vices. The best-known historical example of how government policies create illegal markets and fuel the rise of organized crime was the outlawing of liquor in the United States and Canada in the 1920s and early 1930s. Prohibition catapulted organized crime into a new level of profitability, power, and sophistication and set the stage for today's large, profitable criminal organizations.

Goods and services do not have to be criminalized to fuel organized crime. Taxation policies have been the impetus for the involvement of organized crime in trafficking legal goods such as alcohol, fuel, and tobacco. International and domestic smuggling of legal products is usually the result of a disparity in the level of taxes that have been applied to a product by different jurisdictions (see Box 16.4).

# FOCUS BOX 16.4

## GOVERNMENT CIGARETTE TAXATION POLICIES, SMUGGLING, AND ORGANIZED CRIME

Since the end of the American Revolution, legitimate consumer goods have been illegally smuggled into Canada from the United States due to much lower prices south of the border, which is largely because of import duties or high taxes imposed on similar products in Canada.

Historically, tobacco products have been the most popular contraband. In the 1890s, the Canadian government imposed an import duty to protect domestic cigarette manufacturers from foreign competition. This duty raised the cost of a small package of cigarettes imported into Canada to 10 cents while in the United States they could be purchased at half that price. The result, according to an 1895 Toronto Star article entitled "Smuggle the vile cigarette," was that tobacco smugglers were now "doing business on a tremendously large scale, bringing the goods both to Toronto and to Montreal."

Cigarette smuggling persisted for the next century but increased dramatically in the 1970s.

In 1991, the Canadian Government increased the excise tax on the domestic sale of cigarettes by almost 140 percent. However, no similar tax hikes were imposed on Canadian tobacco products destined for export. This resulted in a substantial difference between the price of exported Canadian cigarettes and those sold domestically. This price difference initiated a wave of smuggling that involved the lawful export of tax-exempt Canadian cigarettes to the United States and the smuggling of these cigarettes back into Canada. In less than two years following the tax hike, cigarette exports to the United States rose from 1.7 billion to 15.7 billion cigarettes (Canadian Tobacco Manufacturers Council, n.d.). This increase can almost exclusively be attributed to the burgeoning Canadian

*(continued)*

black market. According to a report on smuggling by the Canadian Association of Chiefs of Police (1994, 7), most of the contraband tobacco products in Canada during this period were supplied by well-organized smuggling groups and networks.

Today, legitimately-produced cigarettes are smuggled into Canada from the United States, counterfeit cigarettes are surreptitiously imported from China, while cigarette factories have sprung up on First Nations reserves in Ontario and Quebec. The RCMP estimate 175 criminal groups are involved in the illicit tobacco trade in Canada (Canadian Press, 2010; *National Post*, 2010a) including criminal gangs based in China, outlaw motorcycle gangs, Eastern European crime groups, as well as many more independent criminal groups and professionals.

## Theories of the Structure of Organized Criminal Conspiracies

As noted earlier, a defining characteristic of organized crime is a systematic pattern to the relationship among the offenders, which, in turn, helps define the organizational structure of a particular ongoing criminal conspiracy. In general, four theoretical models capture the different types of relationships and structures of ongoing organized criminal conspiracies: (1) the bureaucratic/hierarchical model, where there is a vertical power structure with at least three permanent ranks; (2) the kinship model, in which the Italian-American mafia family is portrayed as being structured around blood relationships; (3) the patron–client model, where influential professional criminals become "patrons" to others by providing contacts, resources, influence, and direction, and (4) the syndicate model, which is characterized by a fluid network of like-minded criminal offenders who are connected through symmetrical business partnerships based on complementary areas of specialization or resources.

**The Bureaucratic/Hierarchical Model** The bureaucratic/hierarchical model views criminal groups as highly structured, and tightly controlled hierarchical organizations. This model was first applied to Italian-American organized crime groups. Italian-American mafia families are viewed as structured hierarchically, with a deliberate and rational arrangement of positions and roles based on a well defined vertical power structure and division of labour (President's Commission on Law Enforcement and Administration of Justice, 1967; Cressey, 1969). In Canada, the ethnic Italian criminal organizations that predominated during the 1950s through to the early 1980s did appear to have a hierarchical structure, although it was somewhat less complex and flatter than that detailed by Cressey in his work for the 1967 President's Commission on Law Enforcement and Administration of Justice. For example, during the late 1960s and early 1970s, Montreal's Cotroni mafia group, which was a wing of New York City's Bonanno mafia family, was headed by Vic Cotroni. Underneath him at any one time were four or five senior lieutenants. Each lieutenant was in charge of a particular geographic region of Montreal and had his own crew made up of several "soldiers" who were in charge of, or had business ties with, a number of other people outside of the Cotroni group (Charbonneau, 1975; Quebec Police Commission, 1977; Edwards, 1990).

Many researchers have been critical of the application of this model to Italian organized crime. Ianni and Reuss-Ianni, state that the bureaucratic analogy arose as "honest attempts to explain syndicate organization in terms that are familiar to the public"(1972, 110). They argue there was "another, more suspect motivation," behind this model, which was its support of the government-promoted theory that the mafia was a national conspiracy, which "demands the existence of a national organization." For some critics, many aspects of a bureaucracy, such as lengthy chains of command, rigidity, and the centralization of power at the top, may not apply to Italian mafia families.

Despite the criticisms, this model may be applied to other criminal organizations such as the Colombian cocaine cartels. Many analysts have concluded that these cartels emulated the hierarchical, multinational corporation in their organizational structure. The Colombian cartels were structured to control each step required in processing, exporting and wholesaling cocaine. To facilitate this vertical integration, "each of the trafficking groups in Medellin, Bogota, and Cali contain various sections, each with a separate function, such as manufacturing, transportation, distribution, finance and security" (President's Commission on Organized Crime, 1984, 562). Although the exact structure of a Colombian cartel varied between groups and was quite fluid over time, Figure 16.1 provides one generic version of this structure.

**Kinship Model** Ianni and Reuss-Ianni (1972) suggest that the Italian-American mafia family has nothing to do with modern bureaucratic or corporate principles, but rather is primarily a social grouping shaped by culture, patterned by tradition, and structured around kinship relationships. Italian-American crime families are just that: structures that parallel families interconnected by blood or marriage (and in some cases, simply a shared ethnicity). There is no real vertical hierarchy; instead this social unit is built around a symbiotic relationship between a "patron" and a "client," a pattern of relationships that was first proposed by Joseph Albini (1971).

In their study of one Italian-American organized crime family, Ianni and Reuss-Ianni (1972) found that members of the Lupollo family (a pseudonym) were sustained in action by the force of kinship, rather than driven by fear or motivated by crime. Moreover, it was bonds of kinship, not criminal activities or a secret society, which bound this mafia family and tied it to other Italian-American mafia families. The Lupollo family operated as a "social unit with social organization and business functions merged," and all "leadership positions, down to 'middle management' level," were assigned on the basis of kinship (Ianni and Reuss-Ianni, 1972, 106).

Ianni and Reuss-Ianni (1972) outline some of the differences between mafia families and corporations. Formal organizations are composed of positions, not personalities. The duties and rights of a corporate executive, for instance, are clearly delineated so that the organization can swiftly replace an incumbent

**FIGURE 16.1** Generic Organizational Structure of the Cali Cartel

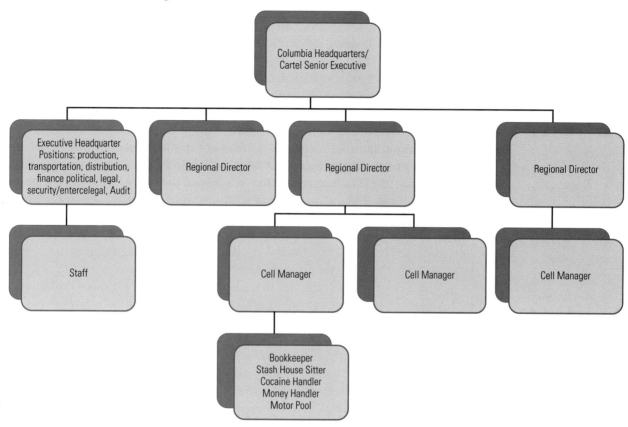

Sources: United States. Comptroller General. (1989). *Nontraditional Organized Crime: Law Enforcement Officials Perspectives on Five Criminal Groups.* Washington, DC: U.S. Government Printing Office; United States Drug Enforcement Administration. (n.d.). *Major Traffickers and Their Organizations.* Washington, DC: U.S. Drug Enforcement Administration; Thomas Constantine. (1994). "Statement before the U.S. Senate Drug Caucus." February 24. Washington, DC: United States Drug Enforcement Administration; Howard Abadinsky. (2000). *Organized Crime.* New York: Wadsworth Publishing, p. 149.

who dies or resigns. In some mafia families, however, particular members are indispensable because they possess special skills or have established highly personal contacts. The death of a member who acts as a "corrupter" may significantly disrupt the functioning of the family's criminal operations because no immediate substitute has the same level of political connections. Formal organizations are also supposed to be rationally organized with persons rising to leadership because of their demonstrated skill, intelligence, dedication, and expertise. Ianni and Reuss-Ianni (1972) argue that family standing and tradition are equally important—perhaps more important than the criteria of merit—in determining which family members will assume leadership roles. In the Lupollo mafia family, power accrued to an individual not because he was the best qualified but because kinship or tradition demanded it.

**Patron–Client Model** For Ianni and Reuss-Ianni (1972), the ongoing criminal operations of the Italian-American mafia family involve a loose system of power and "business" relationships and thus requires a middleman who becomes a patron to others by providing the right contacts, influence, and criminal opportunities. Over time, the patron comes to dominate a network of individuals in a geographic area (Ianni and Reuss-Ianni, 1983). At the centre of the patron–client model of the mafia is the Capo or Don. Unlike the head of a corporation, the role of the Capo is less a chief executive officer and more of a patron to his family and associates; he is at the centre of a network of family and business relationships. In this role he is a provider of services, especially for those who can't or won't turn to the government—from the peasantry in Sicily or Calabria where a government presence was sparse, to the Italian immigrant unfamiliar with or suspicious of the government in a new land, all the way to the thief or murderer who cannot go to the government for help. The Capo's role is to help ensure the welfare and security of his family, friends, and associates, such as putting up start-up capital to assist new enterprises, handing the flow of graft money to politicians and other government officials, regulating the use of violence, and resolving disputes among members (Albini, 1971; Hess, 1973; Gambetta, 1993). The role of the Capo is to serve as an intermediary, whether it is a commercial agent who brings legitimate businessmen or criminals together to make a deal, a political power broker who helps friends get elected to public office, or a mediator who arbitrates a conflict between two parties.

As seen in Figure 16.2, the Capo is at the centre of this patron–client structure, immediately surrounded by members of the crime family to whom he acts as a patron (and receives a monetary tribute or tax from each). In addition, each made member cultivates his own network of clients, which include external associates. These clients may represent a wide spectrum of society, including other criminals, politicians, law enforcement officials, judges, businessmen, and union leaders (Albini, 1971). The functional benefit of the patron–client structure is the potential to cultivate a wide range of money-making connections, both by the Capo and other made members of the mafia family. Missing from this graphic are the direct connects between the Capo and associates external to the family (other mafia family heads, politicians, businessmen, etc.).

While the patron–client model was developed primarily to describe Italian-American crime families, it also appears to have some relevancy to other organized crime groups. For example, individual official members of organizations such as the Hells Angels or Chinese triads are known to have an extensive network of associates (non-members), whose criminal activities revolve around that member.

**Network Model** The network model does not view organized crime as a monolithic, self-contained organization but as a loosely-knit, fluid network of like-minded independent criminal entrepreneurs, none of whom has any long-term authority over the others. A network model of organized crime views the patterns of relationships, not as hierarchical in nature, but as symmetrical business partnerships based on complementary areas of specialization that contribute to one particular deal or a series of ongoing criminal conspiracies. In a network, the structure of the relationship among the offenders is not defined by power, but by the particular function that the individual performs in the criminal conspiracy and/or by a financial investment made by a "business partner" in that venture.

**FIGURE 16.2**    The Patron–Client Organizational Model

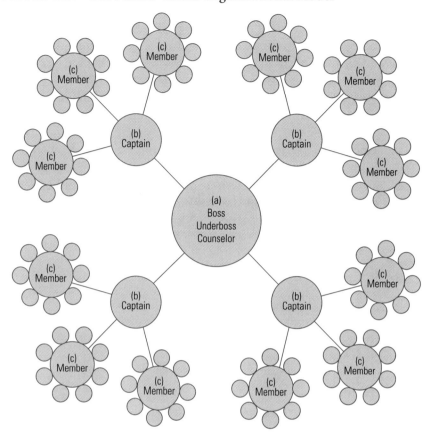

(a) At the centre of each organized crime family (famiglin: Family) is the boss (capo). He is assisted by an underboss (sottocapo) and a counselor (consigliere).

(b) Surrounding the boss are his clients, the captains (cepiregime).

(c) Orbiting around each captain are his clients, the lowest ranking members who have been formally initiated into the Family (soldati: "made guys").

(d) The members act as patrons to nomember clients.

(e) Each unit is tied to other Families throughout the country by the capo, whose soveriegnty is recognized by the other bosses.

Source: From ABADINSKY. *Organized Crime, 8E.* © 2007 Wadsworth, a part of Cengage Learning, Inc. Reproduced by permission. www.cengage.com/permissions

In her analysis of Chicago crime groups, Anderson (1979) concludes that the network model may be viewed as a combination of the bureaucratic/ hierarchical model and the kinship/patron–client model. She argues that well-defined criminal organizations do exist and some entail a hierarchical structure. She found that traditional organized crime groups do have layers of positions, such as boss, underboss, lieutenant, etc., but they also include various associates who were not true members themselves. These associates carry out many activities (both legal and illegal) necessary for the success of the group. These associates—who may include small time crooks, sophisticated criminal entrepreneurs, legitimate businessmen, politicians, or even other criminal organizations—all enter into patron–client type arrangements with the members of this criminal group. Figure 16.3 shows how Al Capone and his senior partners were linked in a network with different groups of associates.

In a Statistics Canada survey of police agencies, respondents indicated that 93 percent of the criminal organizations they investigated in had links with other crime groups. The purposes of these linkages were to combine expertise, to share personnel, facilities, or smuggling routes, to exchange goods

**FIGURE 16.3   Al Capone's Crime Network**

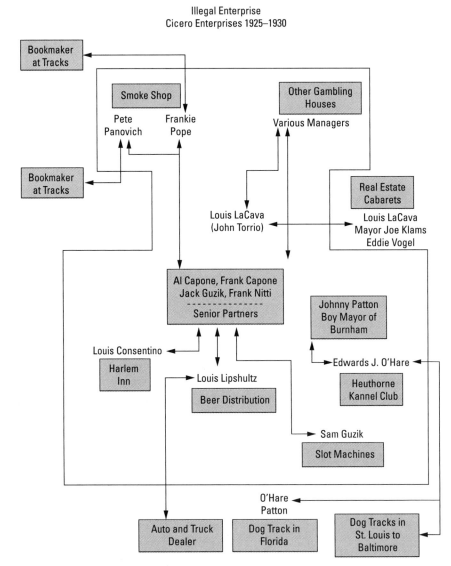

Source: Mark Haller (1990) "Illegal enterprises: A theoretical and historical interpretation", *Criminology*, 28 (2): 207

and services, or to expand into new markets (Sauvé, 1999). In its 2006 annual report, the CISC elaborated on these relationships:

> … law enforcement is identifying crime groups that are based on temporary alliances of individual criminals who merge their particular skills to better achieve success in specific criminal enterprises. Once a specific criminal venture is completed, these individuals may continue to collaborate on further criminal activities, or the group may dissolve. Although the individuals may go their separate ways, they sometimes reform into new groups based upon the skill requirements of new criminal opportunities. The nature and success of such networks are largely determined by individual characteristics and skills among those who act as their component parts.

Source: *2006 Annual Report on Organized Crime in Canada*, p. 6, Criminal Intelligence Service Canada, 2006. Reproduced with the permission of the Minister of Public Works and Government Services Canada, 2011.

In his research into organized crime in Canada, Morselli (2005, 2008, 2009), identifies a number of "networked" aspects of contemporary organized criminal conspiracies, including how such conspiracies arise via personal contacts and social networking among offenders, the "flexible order" of criminal conspiracies that make them resistant to law enforcement targeting and enforcement, and the important centralizing role of "brokers" within loosely structured criminal group ventures.

The network model is perhaps most applicable to large-scale drug importation and trafficking conspiracies, which rarely are carried out by single organized crime groups. Heroin finds its way on the streets of Toronto through the efforts of numerous individuals and groups, each of whom operate independently. These include farmers who grow the opium, chemists who refine the opium into heroin, transportation brokers who arrange for safe passage of the product, shippers who physically transport the product, wholesalers who arrange for the heroin to be cut and then distributed to street dealers who sell it at the 'retail' level. A good example of the network model for large-scale international drug trafficking was the legendary "French Connection" beginning in the 1940s which consisted of partnerships between Turkish farmers, who cultivated the opium; Instanbul-based brokers, who trafficked the morphine; French Corsican gangsters, who processed the morphine into heroin in France and then moved the final product across the Atlantic; American and Canadian mafia groups, who coordinated its importation and wholesale distribution in North America; and a diverse list of individuals and groups who sold the drugs at the retail level (Charbonneau, 1975; Naylor, 2004; Schneider, 2009).

In short, the traditional bureaucratic/hierarchical model of organized crime stresses hierarchy and centralized control, while the network model envisions greater decentralization, with separate enterprises that pool resources and provide local management. Such decentralization according to Haller (1990, 222), renders a business less vulnerable to law enforcement. By spreading the risks among separate partnerships, entrepreneurs minimize losses from bankruptcy or police raids of any single enterprise. Decentralization also makes sense for another important reason: "criminal entrepreneurs generally have had neither the skills nor the personalities for the detailed, bureaucratic oversight of large organizations. They are, instead, hustlers and dealers, for whom partnership arrangements are ideally suited. They enjoy the give and take of personal negotiations, risk-taking, and moving from deal to deal." (Haller, 1990, 222).

# Conclusion: Canadian Organized Crime

Organized crime in Canada spans more than 400 years: from pirates who pillaged ships and towns off the Atlantic coast during the seventeenth and eighteenth centuries; bank robbers, smugglers, horse thieves, cattle rustlers, and currency counterfeiters in the nineteenth century; opium traffickers, white slave traders, and professional gamblers of the early twentieth century; bootleggers during the era of Prohibition; to the Italian mafia, outlaw motorcycle gangs, Chinese triads, Colombian cocaine "cowboys," and today's other criminal groups.

In the last 40 years there has been a proliferation of criminal groups, networks, and organized conspiracies in Canada and worldwide. As the number of crime groups has multiplied, so has the scope, diversity, and profitability of organized criminal activities. In 2010 the head of the United Nations Office on Drugs and Crime reported that organized crime generates revenues of more than $120 billion globally every year, with drug smuggling by far the most lucrative activity (*Montreal Gazette*, 2010).

Canada continues to serve as a branch plant for transnational crime groups and as a transit point for the international movement of illegal drugs. According to the U.S. State Department (2002, V6) "heroin, cocaine, and MDMA (ecstasy) are trafficked through Canada, as international drug traffickers take advantage of Canada's proximity to the United States, less stringent criminal penalties as compared to the U.S., and the constant flow of goods across the U.S.-Canada border." Canada is also a conduit for undocumented immigrants, primarily from Asia, who illegally enter the U.S. Canada supplies an embarrassingly rich assortment of illegal and contraband goods, a tradition that began when British Columbia became a major producer of smokable opium in the early part of the twentieth century. This tradition continued through Prohibition, when Canada was America's main source of illegal liquor, and found new life in the 1970s, when the country surfaced as a major producer of synthetic drugs (Schneider, 2009). By the start of the new millennium, Canada had established itself as the continent's preeminent supplier of high-grade marijuana, methamphetamines, and ecstasy, "as various organized crime groups have taken great advantage of opportunities to diversify their criminal activities, enabling them to swiftly advance from domestic trafficking to global distribution" (Royal Canadian Mounted Police, 2007, 1). In recent years, police in British Columbia have discovered fields planted with opium poppies (*Globe and Mail*, 2010a; 2010b). Canada has also become a centre for telemarketing fraud and the counterfeiting of currency, bankcards, and digital entertainment products. All of these developments led the *Wall Street Journal* to assert that Canada has become "one of the most important bases for the globalization of organized crime" (*Wall Street Journal*, 1998).

Why does organized crime have such an active presence in Canada? Many of the answers can be found in the theories discussed earlier in this chapter. Indeed, the etiological theories included in this chapter may be as applicable to Canada as they are to the U.S.

Alien conspiracy theory explains some of Canada's organized crime problem. Many of the dominant organized crime genres active in this country—the Italian mafia and 'ndrangheta, Chinese triads, U.S.-based outlaw motorcycle gangs, Russian and Eastern European crime groups, Colombian cartels, Jamaican posses, etc.—find their origins in other countries. As an immigrant nation, the ethnic composition of organized crime in Canada is a reflection of the multicultural make-up of the country.

Ethnic succession theory may help shed some light on the historically-rooted institutionalized racism in Canada that has contributed to the "ethnic" basis of criminal gangs and organized crime groups in this country. Shut out of legitimate economic and political opportunities, members of certain minority groups have turned to the underground economy to eke out a living. Similar social factors and structural forces have produced a growing underclass of young men, often from minority groups, which has contributed to the recent proliferation of gangs and criminal organizations in Canada. The post-war political economy has helped forge the structural preconditions for spatial concentrations of crime in many larger urban centres by fuelling socio-economic disparities and the spatial amalgamation of poverty and other social problems within certain neighbourhoods and/or racial groups. The wealth of Canada and other Western nations is being held by a shrinking number of individual and corporate elites, the gap between the rich and the poor has been widening, urban centres have become segregated along socio-economic lines, and poverty has become more concentrated in certain neighbourhoods, communities, and racial groups. These trends and developments, according to critical criminologist Jock Young, are leading developed nations like Canada towards a "dystopia of exclusion," where "the poor are isolated in inner-city ghettos, in orbital estates, and in ghost towns" (Young, 2001, 20).

Another indigenous factor that contributes to organized crime in this country is the symbiotic relationship between crime groups and the Canadian public. There is a strong demand for illegal goods and services in this country creating a prosperous economic foundation for organized crime. Canada's public policies also contribute to the proliferation of organized crime by creating contraband markets through the criminalization of heroin, marijuana, and other substances in demand by the public. Government policies have also helped bolster the smuggling trade, underground markets, and organized crime (in particular the contraband cigarettes and liquor trade) through the application of high taxes.

Geo-political causes can also be identified. There is probably no country in the world that has as many factors conducive to a vibrant smuggling trade: an enormous land mass and airspace, three ocean coastlines that are impossible to adequately monitor and protect, the longest unguarded border in the world (with the U.S.,), and a relatively small tax base with which to police it. Most uniquely, perhaps, is the large concentration of Canadians living within a short

**Department of State International Narcotics Strategy Reports**
http://www.state.gov/p/inl/rls/nrcrpt/2010/index.htm

**RCMP Annual Drug Situation Reports**
http://www.rcmp-grc.gc.ca/drugs-drogues/index-eng.htm

distance of that border, which provides a convenient market for the contraband as well as a sympathetic and skilled labour pool from which to draw smugglers and distributors.

Globalization has also increased opportunities for criminal groups in Canada, which now export drugs and other contraband to the United States and overseas. The large-scale demand for premium Canadian illicit products, such as the highly coveted "B.C. Bud" marijuana, has played a role in fostering organized crime in this country. The influx of sophisticated and international criminal groups into Canada has also increased this country's position as a global hotbed of illegal drug production, currency and credit card counterfeiting, product piracy, and telemarketing fraud.

The historical and contemporary narrative of organized crime in Canada can help shed light on the character of the country and its people. In other words, while influenced by global forces, modernization, and the U.S., organized crime in Canada is also a reflection of our own society. (See Box 16.5 for a discussion of new legislative measures implemented in Canada to combat organized crime.)

# FOCUS BOX 16.5

## NEW LEGISLATIVE MEASURES TO COMBAT ORGANIZED CRIME

Historically, offenders involved in organized criminal conspiracies in Canada have been charged with individual illegal offences, most of laid them out in the Criminal Code or federal drug statutes. Relevant sections of the Criminal Code used to this effect include illegal gaming and betting (Sections 201 to 209), extortion (Section 346), criminal interest rate (Section 347), forgery (Sections 366 to 378), and fraud (Sections 380 to 396). There were no substantive criminal offences specifically related to organized crime.

This began to change in the mid 1990s. As Freedman notes, "Canada and a host of other countries have created new forms of individual criminal liability through targeted organized crime legislation. … These new laws specify culpability for individual conduct but place the act within the context of group activity, rationalizing more onerous individual punishment as deterrence of group-oriented criminality"(2006, 172). This new breed of organized crime legislation creates new offences and penalties for committing crimes in the context of an ongoing organized criminal conspiracy.

The U.S. was the first country to introduce such laws through the *Racketeer Influenced and*

*Corrupt Organizations* (RICO) statute of 1970, which makes it unlawful to acquire, operate, or receive income from an enterprise through a pattern of racketeering activity.

For decades Canada resisted legislation that created specific organized crime offences. It was not until 1997, when Bill C-95—officially called *An Act to amend the Criminal Code (criminal organizations) and to amend other Acts in consequence*—became law. Enacted in the wake of the violent events associated with the turf war between outlaw biker gangs in Quebec, for the first time the *Criminal Code* defined a "criminal organization," included a "criminal organization offence" and "participation in a criminal organization offence," and proscribed specific penalties for conviction under these sections.

Following further amendments that took effect in 2002, Section 476 of the Criminal Code now defines "criminal organization" and designates three criminal organization offences:

467.11: knowingly participating in or contributing to any activity of a criminal organization for the purpose of enhancing the

*(continued)*

ability of said organization to facilitate or commit an indictable offence under a federal statute (with a maximum penalty of five years in prison)

467.12: committing an indictable offence under a federal statute for the benefit of, at the direction of, or in association with, a criminal organization (with a maximum penalty of 14 years in prison)

467.13: being a member of a criminal organization, and instructing another person to commit an offence under a federal statute for the benefit of, at the direction of, or in association with, a criminal organization (with a maximum penalty of life in prison).

In July 2005, Madam Justice Michele Fuerst found two members of an Ontario chapter of the Hells Angels guilty of extortion and of committing that crime "in association" with a criminal organization. The ruling was viewed as a significant victory for the government, not only because it upheld Section 467.12, but because it ruled the Hells Angels to be a criminal organization. On January 23, 2002, the two men were both wearing their motorcycle club colours when they arrived at the home of a Barrie, Ontario, businessman who had allegedly sold them faulty equipment that was supposed to steal satellite television signals. By wearing their Hells Angels colours, the two men "presented themselves not as individuals, but as members of a group with a reputation for violence and intimidation," Justice Fuerst wrote in her decision. "They committed extortion with the intention to do so in association with a criminal organization, the HAMC (Hells Angels Motorcycle Club) to which they belonged" (*Toronto Star*, 2005).

## Summary

- Organized crime can be broadly defined by *how* crimes are carried out and by the ultimate *goal* of the criminal activity; it is perpetrated by a group of people who conspire together on a continuing and secretive basis with the goal of obtaining a financial or other material benefit.

- Dominant organized crime genres in Canada include: Italian, Chinese/Asian, Colombian/South American, outlaw motorcycle gangs, Russian/Eastern European, and Aboriginal.

- While a defining characteristic of these organized crime genres has been a shared nationality, ethnicity and/or language, in recent years these factors are no longer the most important criteria determining who participates in a particular organized criminal conspiracy. There are thousands of individual criminal entrepreneurs who work together, on an *ad hoc* or ongoing basis, in the pursuit of illegal revenues, regardless of the ethnicity, nationality, or language of the participants.

- Two competing and diametrically opposed theoretical camps on the origins of organized crime in North America are (1) alien conspiracy theory which holds that organized crime in North America is the result of the importation of secret criminal societies that are rooted in foreign cultures and (2) ethnic succession theory, which emphasizes how conditions indigenous to North America contribute to the growth of organized criminality on this continent.

■ In the last 40 years there has been a proliferation of criminal groups, networks, and organized criminal conspiracies in Canada and worldwide. Canada continues to serve as a branch plant for transnational crime groups and as a transit point for the international movement of illegal drugs. The country is also a major producer of illegal drugs, including marijuana, methamphetamines, and ecstasy. Canada has also become an international centre for telemarketing fraud and the counterfeiting of currency, bankcards, and digital entertainment products.

## QUESTIONS FOR CRITICAL THINKING

1. Compare and contrast the *Criminal Code of Canada* definition of a criminal organization with other definitions of organized crime. From an enforcement point of view, what are the strengths and weaknesses of this definition? Try to answer this question by examining the court decisions (case law) that have been made concerning this section of the Criminal Code.
2. Are the organized crime characteristics presented in this chapter complete? Can you think of any characteristics that may have been missed?
3. We often distinguish organized crime genres through nationality (Italian, Nigerian, Russian, etc.). Do you believe there is a distinctive "Canadian organized crime"? If so, how would you characterize it? How does Canadian history, norms, values, institutions and other characteristics contribute to the formation of Canadian organized crime?
4. How is organized crime distinguished from other types of criminal conspiracies carried out by groups of people and organizations, such as terrorism or corporate crime, or state crime? In particular, compare and contrast corporate crime with organized crime. Do you believe there are forms of corporate crime or state crime that should be classified and prosecuted as organized crime?
5. When thinking about organized crime, what are the parallels between the prohibition of alcohol, during the 1920s and the current prohibition of marijuana? Do you think it would be in the best interests of society to decriminalize or even legalize the personal use of marijuana? Why?
6. How does the information presented in this chapter compare with the depictions of organized crime in the popular entertainment media (television, movies, games, etc.)?

## NET WORK

Using resources available through the Internet, examine a particular organized crime genre (e.g., outlaw motorcycle gangs) and group (e.g., the Hells Angels) by applying what you have learned in this chapter. In particular, apply the following frameworks: (1) Characteristics of organized crime (2) Etiological theories of organized crime and (3) Theories of the Structure of Organized Criminal Conspiracies.

For many years, the Criminal Intelligence Service Canada had published an annual report examining organized crime in Canada. Recent reports can be found on their website at **http://www.cisc.gc.ca.** Based on an analysis of recent reports, describe the impact that organized crime has on Canada.

One can play various interactive games on the Internet (or through smart phone apps) that centre on organized crime. Join in on one of these games and assess the extent to which the game reflects the information presented in this chapter.

## KEY TERMS

cybercrime; pg. 500
debit card fraud; pg. 508
extortion; pg. 502
human trafficking; pg. 502
la cosa nostra; pg. 510

loansharking; pg. 502
transnational organized
   crime; pg. 497
vory v zakone; pg. 504

## BIBLIOGRAPHY

Abadinsky, Howard. (2000). *Organized Crime.* New York: Wadsworth Publishing.

———. (2003). *Organized Crime.* Belmont, CA: Thomson Wadsworth.

———. (2007). *Organized Crime.* Belmont, CA: Thomson Wadsworth.

Albini, Joseph L. (1971). *American Mafia: Genesis of a Legend.* New York, NY: Appleton-Century-Crofts.

Anderson, Annelise G. (1979). *The Business of Organized Crime: A Cosa Nostra Family.* Stanford, CA: Hoover Institution Press. Arlacchi, Pino. (1979). "The Mafioso: From Man of Honour to Entrepreneur [Social Basis of Mafioso Traditions]." *New Left Review* November/December: 53–72.

Bell, Daniel. (1953). "Crime as an American Way of Life." *The Antioch Review* June (13) 131–54.

Brown, Bob. (2007). "Cybercrime Update: Is Organized Crime Moving into Cybersphere? FBI says Malware Currently Purview of Loosely Organized Criminals." *NetworkWorld. com*, May 9; available at http://www.networkworld.com/news/2007/050907-fbi-organized-crime-cybercrime.html; accessed June 8, 2007.

Canadian Association of Chiefs of Police. (1994). *Organized Crime Committee Report, 1994: Smuggling Activities in Canada.* Ottawa: CACP.

Canadian Convenience Store Association [CCSA] (2009). *Contraband Tobacco in Canada: Time for Action: 2009 Status Report.* CCSA. Available at http://www.stopcontrabandtobacco.ca/en/Portals/0/media/gle-brochureen_acda.pdf; accessed 10 December 2009.

Canadian Press. (2002). "Montreal Trial told Hells Angels Videotaped Funeral of Cotroni Family Member." July 9.

———. (2010). "Border Agents Intercept 10 million Counterfeit Cigarettes in B.C." November 30.

Canadian Tobacco Manufacturers Council. [no date]. *Cigarette Export Statistics.* Ottawa, ON: Canadian Tobacco Manufacturers Council.

Carrigan, D. Owen. (1991). *Crime and Punishment in Canada: A History.* Toronto: McClelland & Stewart.

Caulkins, J. and P. Reuter. (1998). "What Price Data Tell Us About Drug Markets." *Journal of Drug Issues* 28(3): 593–612.

Charbonneau, Jean-Pierre [Translated into English by James Stewart]. 1975. *The Canadian Connection.* Ottawa, ON: Optimum Publishing.

Clarke, Ronald, and Derek Cornish. (1985). "Modeling Offender's Decisions: A Framework for Policy and Research." In M. Tonry and N. Morris (eds.), *Crime and Justice: An Annual Review of Research Volume 6* (pp. 147–185). Chicago: University of Chicago.

Commission of the European Communities and EUROPOL. (2001). *Towards a European Strategy to Prevent Organised Crime.* Brussels: Commission of the European Communities. March.

Constantine, Thomas. (1994). "Statement Before the U.S. Senate Drug Caucus." February 24. Washington, DC: United States Drug Enforcement Administration.

Cressey, Donald. (1969). *Theft of a Nation: The Structure and Operations of Organized Crime in America.* New York: Harper and Row.

Criminal Intelligence Service Canada. (2002). *Annual Report on Organized Crime in Canada, 2002.* Ottawa: CISC.

———. (2004). *Annual Report on Organized Crime in Canada, 2004.* Ottawa: CISC.

———. (2006). *Criminal Intelligence Service Canada Annual Report, 2006.* Ottawa: CISC.

———. (2007). *Criminal Intelligence Service Canada Annual Report, 2007.* Ottawa: CISC.

———. (2009). *Annual Report on Organized Crime in Canada, 2009.* Ottawa: CISC.

———. (2010). *Annual Report on Organized Crime in Canada, 2009.* Ottawa: CISC.

David Freedman. (2006). "The New Law of Criminal Organizations in Canada." *The Canadian Bar Review* 85(2): 172–219.

Dickie, Phil, and Paul Wilson. (1993). "Defining Organized Crime: An Operational Perspective." *Current Issues in Criminology* 4 (March 3): 215–24.

Dubro, James. (1986). *Mob Rule: Inside the Canadian Mafia.* Toronto: Totem Books.

———. (1992). *Dragons of Crime: Inside the Asian Underworld.* Toronto: McClelland & Stewart.

Edwards, Peter. (1990). *Blood Brothers: How Canada's Most Powerful Mafia Family Runs Its Business.* Toronto: McClelland-Bantam.

Edwards, Peter, and Antonio Nicaso. (1993). *Deadly Silence: Canadian Mafia Murders.* Toronto: Macmillan Canada.

Federal Bureau of Investigation. (1995). "Eurasian Criminal Enterprises." In *Overview of International Organized Crime* (pp. 13–37). Washington, DC: U.S. Department of Justice, Federal Bureau of Investigation.

Finckenauer, James. (2004). "The Russian 'Mafia.'" *Society* 41 (5): 61–64.

Gambetta, Diego. (1993). *The Sicilian Mafia: The Business of Private Protection.* Cambridge, MA: Harvard University Press.

*Globe and Mail.* (1972). "Metro Police Raid Turned Up Copy of Mafia Linked Society's Secret Rituals, Court is Told." *Globe and Mail*, June 2.

*Globe and Mail.* (1998). "Canada Braces for Eastern European Mafia Flood." November 30.

———. (2010a). "B.C. RCMP Seize 60,000 Poppy Plants in Record Haul." August 26.

———. (2010b). "Delta Police Seize Opium Poppy Pods Worth $760,000." September 15.

Haller, Mark. (1990). "Illegal Enterprise: A Theoretical and Historical Interpretation." *Criminology* 28(2): 207–234.

Hess, Henner. (1973). *Mafia and Mafiosi: The Structure of Power*. Lexington, MA: Heath Lexington Books.

Ianni, Francis. (1974). *Black Mafia: Ethnic Succession in Organized Crime*. New York, NY: Simon & Schuster.

Ianni, Francis, and Elizabeth Reuss-Ianni. (1972). *A Family Business: Kinship and Social Control in Organized Crime*. New York, NY: Russell Sage Foundation.

Ianni, Francis, and Elizabeth Reuss-Ianni. (1983). "Organized Crime." In Sanford Kadish (ed.), *Encyclopedia of Crime and Social Justice* (pp. 1094–1106). New York, NY: Free Press.

Kaihla, Paul. (2002). "The Technology Secrets of Cocaine Inc." www.business2.com.

Kelly, Robert. (1987). "The Nature of Organized Crime." In Herbert Edelhertz (ed.), *Major Issues in Organized Crime Control* (pp. 5–43). Washington, DC: National Institute of Justice.

Krukowska, Ewa, and Mathew Carr. (2011). "Organized Crime Blamed for Roiling $110 Billion Carbon Market." *Bloomberg.com*, January 31; available at http://www.bloomberg.com/news/2011-01-31/organized-crime-may-have-stolen-carbon-permits-amid-weak-security-eu-says.html; accessed 17 April 2011.

Lamothe, Lee, and Antonio Nicaso. (1994). *Global Mafia*. Toronto: MacMillan Canada.

Lamothe, Lee, and Adrian Humphreys. (2006*). The Sixth Family: The Collapse of the New York Mafia and the Rise of Vito Rizzuto*. Toronto: John Wiley & Sons

Lavigne, Yves. (1996). *Hells Angels: Into the Abyss*. New York: Harper Collins.

Lupsha, Peter. (1981). "Individual Choice, Material Culture and Organized Crime." *Criminology: An Interdisciplanary Journal* 19 (3): 3–24. Martens, Frederick, and Colleen Miller-Longfellow. (1982). "Shadows of Substance: Organized Crime Reconsidered." *Federal Probation* 46 (December): 3–9. *Montreal Gazette*. (1996). "Smuggling Illegal Immigrants Increasing, U.S. Cop Says." October 5.

——. (2010). "Organized Crime Generates $120 Billion Annually: UNOD." October 18.

——. (2011). "Cops Comb Woods Behind Rizzuto Home." January 10.

Morselli, Carlo. (2005). *Contacts, Opportunities and Criminal Enterprise*. Toronto: University of Toronto Press.

——. (2009). *Inside Criminal Networks*. New York: Springer.

Morselli, Carlo, and Julie Roy. (2008). "Brokerage Qualifications in Ringing Operations." *Criminology* 46 (1): 71–98.

*National Post*. (2010a). "'There's Nothing We've Done that's Illegal' Mohawk Leaders Deny that Organized Crime is Involved in the Industry." September 21.

——. (2010b). "A New Mafia: Crime Families Ruling Toronto, Italy Alleges." September 24.

——. (2010c). "Mafia 'Ndrangheta in Canada." September 25.

Naylor, Tom. (2002). *Wages of Crime. Black Markets, Illegal Finance, and the Underworld Economy*. Ithica: Cornell University Press.

Nicaso, Antonio. (2001). "Angels With Dirty Faces. Part 15—How the World's Richest and Most Ferocious Motorcycle Gang is Expanding Its Wings in Canada." *Tandem News*, June 24.

Office of National Drug Control Policy. (2004). *Technical Report for the Price and Purity of Illicit Drugs: 1981 Through the Second Quarter of 2003*. Washington DC: Executive Office of the President (Publication Number NCJ 207769).

Pileggi, Nicholas. (1985). *Wise Guy: Life in a Mafia Family*. New York, NY: Pocket Books.

Potter, Gary. (1994). *Criminal Organizations: Vice, Racketeering, and Politics in an American City*. Prospect Heights, IL: Waveland Press.

President's Commission on Law Enforcement and Administration of Justice. (1967). *Task Force Report: Organized Crime*. Washington, DC: United States Government Printing Office.

President's Commission on Organized Crime. (1984). *Organized Crime and Cocaine Trafficking. Record of Hearing IV, November 27–29, 1984*. Washington, DC: U.S. Government Printing Office.

———. (1986). *America's Habit. Drug Abuse, Drug Trafficking, & Organized Crime*. Washington, DC: United States Government Printing Office.

Quebec Police Commission. (1977). *The Fight Against Organized Crime in Quebec: Report of the Commission on Organized Crime and Recommendations*. Québec: Editeur officiel du Québec.

Rawlinson, Patricia. (1997). "Russian Organized Crime: A Brief History." In Phil Williams (ed.) *Russian Organized Crime: The New Threat?* (pp. 28–52). London: Frank Cass Publishing.Roach, Wilfrid. (1962). *Report of The Honourable Mr. Justice Wilfrid D. Roach as a Commissioner Appointed Under the Public Inquiries Act by Letters Patent Dated December 11, 1961*. Toronto: Commission of Inquiry.

Royal Canadian Mounted Police. (1945). *Report of the Royal Canadian Mounted Police for the Year Ended March 31, 1945*. Ottawa, ON: F.A. Acland.

———. (2007). *Drug Situation Report, 2007*. Ottawa: RCMP, Criminal Intelligence Directorate.

———. (2008). *2008 Contraband Tobacco Enforcement Strategy*. RCMP. http://www.rcmp-grc.gc.ca/pubs/tobac-tabac/tobacco-tabac-strat-2008-eng.pdf.

Salerno, Ralph. (1967). "Syndicate Personnel Structure." *Canadian Police Chief* 55(3).

Sauvé, Julie. (1999). *Organized Crime Activity in Canada, 1998: Results of a 'Pilot' Survey of 16 Police Services*. Ottawa, ON: Statistics Canada, Canadian Centre for Justice Statistics.

Schneider, Stephen. (2009). *Iced: The Story of Organized Crime in Canada*. Toronto: John Wiley & Sons.

Sher, Julian, and William Marsden. (2004). *The Road to Hell: How the Biker Gangs Conquered Canada*. Toronto: Knopf Canada.

Smith, Dwight. (1975). *Mafia Mystique*. New York: Basic Books.

*Toronto Star*. (1895). "Smuggle the Vile Cigarette." August 2.

———. (1948). "Windsor Grills Detroit's Chief on Race Data." February 27.

———. (1996). "Russian Crime Hits Metro Area." June 1.

———. (2005). "Being Hells Angel is Now a Crime: Court Case a Test of Anti-gang Law." July 1.

*Toronto Telegram*. (1961). "RCMP, FBI Suspect Mafia of Ruling Metro Gangland." April 14.

Tyler, Gus. (1962). *Organized Crime in America*. Ann Arbor: University of Michigan Press.

United States Congress. Senate. (1951). Special Committee to Investigate Organized Crime in Interstate Commerce. Final Report of the Special Committee to Investigate Organized Crime in Interstate Commerce. Pursuant to S. Res. 202 (81st Cong.) As amended by S. Res. 60 and S. Res. 129 (82d Cong.). Washington, DC: U.S. Government Printing Office.

United States Senate Committee on Governmental Affairs. Permanent subcommittee on Investigations. (1989). *Structure of International Drug Trafficking Organizations Hearings*. Washington, DC: United States Printing Office.

United States Congress. United States House of Representatives, Committee on the Judiciary, Subcommittee on Immigration and Claims. (2000). *Law Enforcement Problems at the Border Between the United States and Canada: Drug Smuggling, Illegal Immigration and Terrorism.* One Hundred Sixth Congress, First Session, April 14, 1999. Washington, DC: U.S. Government Printing Office, p. 158.

United States. Comptroller General. (1989). *Nontraditional Organized Crime: Law Enforcement Officials Perspectives on Five Criminal Groups.* Washington, DC: U.S. Government Printing Office.

United States Drug Enforcement Administration. (n.d.). *Major Traffickers and Their Organizations.* Washington, DC: U.S. Drug Enforcement Administration.

———. (2001). *Drug Trafficking in the United States.* September. Washington, DC: DEA.

United States Department of State. (2002). *International Narcotics Control Strategy Report, 2002.* Washington, DC: Department of State; Available at: www.state.gov/documents/organization/8696.pdf, accessed September 1, 2011.

———. (2010). International Narcotics Control Strategy Report, 2010. Volume 1: Drug and Chemical Control. Washington, DC: Department of State.

*Vancouver Sun.* (2005). "Ruling Hobbles Organized Crime Battle, Police Say." December 13.

———. (2010). "Police Fear More Drugs and Violence are Coming as Mexican Cartels Begin Operating in B.C." October 18.

Verizon Business Risk Team. (2009). *2009 Data Breach Investigation Report,* New York: Verizon Business; available at www.verizonbusiness.com/resources/security/reports/2009_databreach_rp.pdf.

*Victoria Times-Colonist.* (2005). "Police Net Can Be Cast Too Wide." December 14.

*Wall Street Journal.* (1998). "Organized Crime Begins using Canada as a Base for Operations Ranging from Drugs to Car Theft." July 6.

Wolf, Daniel. (1991). *The Rebels: A Brotherhood of Outlaw Bikers.* Toronto: University of Toronto Press.

Young, J. (2001). "Identity, Community and Social Exclusion." In M. Roger and J. Pitts (eds.), *Crime, Disorder, and Community Safety: A New Agenda*? (pp. 26–53). London: Routledge.

# 17

# Corporate and White-Collar Crime

**John Hagan**

NORTHWESTERN UNIVERSITY

**Rick Linden**

UNIVERSITY OF MANITOBA

We know far more about street crime and organized crime than we do about corporate and white-collar crime. While cases such as the multibillion-dollar Enron bankruptcy and the Conrad Black trial (Chapter 1) have raised the profile of these crimes, few Canadians are aware of the harm that is done by corporate and white-collar criminals. In fact, these crimes are much more costly in dollar terms than street crime. The $6 billion lost to investors in the Bre-X fraud discussed later in this chapter is far more than the money lost in all the robberies in Canadian history. Few bank robbers get away with more than a few thousand dollars, but Julius Melnitzer, an Ontario lawyer, defrauded banks and friends of $90 million to support his lavish lifestyle. Corporate and white-collar crimes are also dangerous; many occupational deaths and injuries are due to unsafe and illegal working conditions.

The term "white-collar crime," introduced by Sutherland (1940) more than a half-century ago, may be one of the most popularly used criminological concepts in everyday life. While there is a disagreement about the precise meaning of the term, the concept of white-collar crime has forced a reconsideration of some very basic criminological assumptions.

No longer is it possible to take for granted the way in which crime itself is defined. No longer can the official data collected on crime by agencies of crime control be accepted uncritically. No longer can it be assumed that the poor are necessarily more criminal than the rich. The criminological enterprise took on new form and substance when the topic of white-collar crime became a central part of the discipline. This chapter will consider issues of class, crime, and the corporations; the social organization of work; and legal sanctions. Each is part of the topic of white-collar crime.

## Learning Objectives

After reading this chapter, you should be able to

- Describe the concept of white-collar crime and explain the impact the notion of white-collar crime had on the discipline of criminology.
- Understand the occupational and organizational components of white-collar crime.

- Explain the physical and social harm caused by white-collar crime in Canada.
- Analyze how the structure of the modern corporation facilitates criminal activity.
- Understand the nature and extent of occupational crime.
- Understand the causes and consequences of our weak laws concerning corporate and white-collar crime.

# The Extent and Nature of Corporate and White-Collar Crime

## The Extent of Corporate and White-Collar Crime

The business section in your daily paper normally deals with stories involving company profits, mergers, and economic forecasts. However, in recent years criminal matters have become a routine part of business reporting. To give you some idea of the extent of corporate and white-collar crime, consider the following stories from the May 9, 2003, edition of the business section of the *Globe and Mail*:

- Two Ontario men were charged with theft and fraud because of activities that resulted in over $40 million in losses. Mark Eizenga and James Sylvester were accused of selling shares to support investments in Cuba and the Caribbean. Over 800 investors were misled by the pair, and most of the money disappeared. (Sylvester committed suicide just before his preliminary hearing in 2007. Eizinga was convicted and sentenced to eight years in prison.)

- Stock traders working for a unit of the Royal Bank were accused of placing stock orders late in the day in order to artificially inflate the closing price of a stock at the end of a reporting period. This helped to make the performance of a stock portfolio look more positive than it actually was.

- The Ontario Securities Commission accused a Peterborough man of collecting at least $25 million by falsely guaranteeing individuals a high rate of return on investments.

- There is a flaw in Microsoft's Internet Passport service that could make it possible for computer hackers to gain access to the accounts of customers visiting Internet shopping sites. The system also controls access to Microsoft's Hotmail system. The security flaw placed Microsoft in possible violation of a U.S. Federal Trade Commission order to ensure that personal consumer information was protected by the Passport system.

- Rupert Murdoch, owner of a global media empire that includes Fox TV, appeared before a U.S. Congressional committee seeking approval of a takeover of DirecTV, which is the largest provider of satellite television in the United States. Critics fear that the deal would violate competition laws by allowing Murdoch's company to use its huge size to force smaller competitors out of business.

■ The U.S. government is pursuing fraud charges against HealthSouth Corporation, the largest owner of physical therapy clinics and rehabilitation clinics in the United States. Many of the company's executives have pleaded guilty to making fraudulent reports that made the company appear to be more profitable than it actually was. This inflated the stock price. Many investors who bought the stock because of its apparent profitability lost most of their money when the fraud was revealed.

■ A New York stockbroker was accused of using his clients' money to pay off former employees who had threatened to reveal his illegal stock trading. He had been previously charged with "churning" investors' accounts. "Churning" is the practice of making unnecessary trades to generate higher commissions.

■ The Dutch company Ahold NV, one of the world's largest supermarket companies, lowered its earnings estimates by $880 million after these earnings had been artificially inflated by some of its American executives in order to make the company's performance look better than it really was.

■ The U.S. Securities and Exchange Commission is looking into potential accounting fraud charges against Qwest Communications, a large phone company. The company overstated its revenues by $2.2 billion over a three-year period ending in 2001.

■ Halliburton Company, once run by former U.S. Vice-President Dick Cheney, admitted paying $2.4 million in bribes to an official of the Nigerian government in order to get tax breaks for its operations in that country.

In addition to these stories involving violations and possible violations of criminal laws and securities regulations, several articles from the same issue of the newspaper dealt with ethical and regulatory issues. Among these were stories dealing with the need for better regulation of the stock market; the debate over the need to better regulate complex financial instruments known as derivatives; ethical questions about whether it was proper for Gerry Schwartz, the chief executive of the large Canadian company Onex, to appoint his wife to the board of directors of his company; the problems that were created for the Calgary-based oil company Talisman when it was accused of producing revenues that helped the Sudanese government to repress its own people in a civil war; a discussion of the reluctance of major pharmaceutical manufacturers to provide low-cost AIDS drugs for developing countries that cannot afford to pay for these treatments; and the ethics of Molson's sex-laden campaign for Bavaria beer.

More recently, the *Globe and Mail* published another significant list of occupational crimes, but this time it is in the sports section rather than in the business news. On July 25, 2007, several sports scandals made the headlines:

■ National Basketball Association referee Tim Donaghy resigned after being accused of betting on basketball games, including some that he had refereed.

He was also accused of providing inside information to gamblers. Donaghy subsequently pleaded guilty to two charges.

- Barry Bonds was nearing Hank Aaron's Major League Baseball home run record. While Bonds broke the record later that season, his accomplishment was tarnished by accusations that he used muscle-building steroids to help him develop his hitting power. Bonds was later charged with lying to a grand jury about his alleged steroid use. Many other Major League Baseball players including potential Hall of Famers such as Mark McGwire and Roger Clemens have also been accused of using drugs to help their performance.

- Top cyclist Alexandre Vinokourov was sent home after testing positive for performance-enhancing drugs while riding in the prestigious Tour de France. Later that week, race leader Michael Rasmussen was also sent home because of suspicion that he had used doping to improve his performance. The race has been dogged by doping allegations for years, and in 2006, race winner Floyd Landis was disqualified after a positive drug test.

- Officials of Formula One motor racing team McLaren-Mercedes were accused of illegally obtaining confidential technical documents from the rival Ferrari team. McLaren-Mercedes and its star drivers Fernando Alonso and Lewis Hamilton had been the leading racing team in 2007. Ultimately, McLaren-Mercedes were fined $100 million for their offence.

Sports scandals continue. In 2011, the same week that Roger Clemens faced trial on charges of perjury and obstruction of justice related to allegations of his use of performance-enhancing drugs, Toronto doctor Anthony Galea pleaded guilty in a Buffalo, New York, courtroom to unlawfully bringing drugs, including human growth hormone, into the United States. Galea had a very lucrative practice treating athletes including Tiger Woods and baseball star Alex Rodriquez (both of whom have denied receiving performance-enhancing drugs from Galea). Over 30 athletes were dropped from their national teams because of doping violations prior to the 2010 Vancouver Olympics. Obviously the pressure to win is sufficient to overcome any sense of ethics and fair play that some sports executives and athletes might possess.

The sheer volume of these stories clearly shows that corporate and white-collar crime is a major problem. Although most of these stories will remain on the business pages, many others that you will read about in this chapter have become front-page news. The public is finally becoming aware of the harm being done by corporate and white-collar criminals.

## The Nature of Corporate and White-Collar Crime

Corporate and white-collar offenders have many ways of making money. Figure 17.1 shows the range of offences committed by corporations and by individuals in the course of practising legitimate occupations. We will not discuss all these crimes, but in this chapter you will first learn about corporate crimes and then about crimes committed by individual practitioners.

**FIGURE 17.1    Types of Corporate and White-Collar Crime**

**Crimes against the Public**

*Corporate and Business Crime*

 Price-fixing (conspiring on contract bids or on prices for selling to the public)

 Manipulation of stocks and securities

 Commercial and political bribery and rebates

 Patent and trademark infringements

 Misrepresentation and false advertising

 Fraudulent grading, packaging, and labelling

 Tax fraud

 Adulteration of food and drugs

 Illegal pollution of the environment

*Crimes by Individual and Professional Practitioners*

 Obtaining fees, payments, or charges through fraud and deception

 Deceiving or defrauding patients, clients, customers

 Immoral practices in relations with clients

 Unprofessional conduct and malpractice

 Falsification of statements on vital documents

**Crimes within the Organization**

*Offences against the Organization*

 Theft of funds by employees

 Theft of inventory by employees

*Offences against Employees*

 Violation of workplace health and safety laws

 Violation of labour laws

 Discriminatory employment practices

 Harassment

Source: Adapted from Ronald Akers. (1973). *Deviant Behaviour: A Social Learning Approach.* Belmont, Wadsworth, p 180–181. Reprinted with permission of the author.

## Class, Crime, and the Corporations

### Occupation, Organization, and Crime

White-collar crimes are often committed through, and on behalf of, corporations. Corporate involvement in crime has been recognized at least since the early part of this century, when Ross (1907) wrote of a new type of criminal "who picks pockets with a 'rake-off' instead of a jimmy, cheats with a company prospectus instead of a deck of cards, or scuttles his town instead of his ship." Particular actions of corporations have been criminal offences in Canada since 1889 (Casey, 1985). However, it was not until after the Great Depression that Edwin Sutherland (1940) finally attached a lasting label to these offenders. Sutherland proposed that **white-collar crime** be defined "as a crime committed by a person of respectability and high social status in the course of his occupation."

  Since Sutherland came up with this term, there has been confusion about the role of *occupation* and *organization* in the study of white-collar crime. Wheeler and Rothman (1982) note that two influential works—Clinard's (1952) and Hartung's (1950) studies of black-market activities during World War II—defined

**white-collar crime**

An important concept but one with changing definitions. As used by Sutherland in 1940, the concept referred to corporate behaviour that caused social harm and for which there was a legal sanction. This sanction need not be criminal; it could be regulatory. Since that time, criminologists have also included the illegal actions of executives or employees who commit crimes against their employer or use organizational resources to gain personal benefit.

**Scams and Frauds RCMP Site**
www.rcmp-grc.gc.ca/scams/
index_e.htm

white-collar crime in two rather different ways. Clinard defined white-collar crime occupationally, as "illegal activities among business and professional men," while Hartung included an organizational component, defining such crimes as "a violation of law regulating business, which is committed for a firm by the firm or its agents in the conduct of its business." A distinction is still often drawn today (see, for example, Coleman, 1985, 8) between "**occupational crime**—that is, white collar crime committed by an individual or group of individuals exclusively for personal gain," and "**organizational crime**—white collar crimes committed with the support and encouragement of a formal organization and intended at least in part to advance the goals of that organization." Organizational crime is also known as corporate crime.

The problem is that the occupational and organizational components of many white-collar crimes cannot be easily separated. Clinard and Yeager (1980) make this point with the example of a Firestone tire official who aided his corporation in securing and administering illegal political contributions benefiting the corporation, but then embezzled much of the funds for himself. Many offenders benefit their companies and themselves. Nonetheless, it is important to note that locating white-collar offenders in their ownership and authority positions in occupational and organizational structures is a key part of the class analysis of white-collar crime (Geis, 1984; Hagan and Parker, 1985; Weisburd et al., 1990). Sutherland's emphasis on "respect" and "status" in defining white-collar crime opens up the issue of class position and the role it plays in any understanding of white-collar crime. A key element of social class is the power to commit major white-collar crimes that only ownership and authority positions in occupational and organizational structures can make possible.

Sutherland (1945) insisted that insofar as there exists a "legal description of acts as socially injurious and legal provision of a penalty for the act," criminologists should consider such acts as crimes. This is the case even though many such acts go undetected and unprosecuted. For example, many stock and securities frauds can be prosecuted under provincial securities legislation or under the Criminal Code of Canada. Securities laws are considered "quasi-criminal" statutes. Yet the behaviours prosecuted under either body of law may be identical. Prosecutorial discretion determines whether these behaviours are defined clearly and officially as crimes. Sutherland insisted that in either case, the behaviours were to be regarded as criminal. This can make a major difference in the relationship observed between class and crime.

Consider the issue of deaths and accidents that result from events in the workplace. Occupational deaths outnumber deaths resulting from murder (Sharpe and Hardt, 2006). While it cannot be assumed that most of these deaths result from the illegal actions of employers, there nonetheless is good reason to believe that many are not simply the result of employee carelessness.

One rather dated estimate (Reasons et al., 1981) holds that more than one-third of all on-the-job injuries are due to illegal working conditions, and that another quarter are due to legal but unsafe conditions. At most, one-third of all such accidents are attributed to unsafe acts on the part of employees. There are numerous well-documented examples of employers intentionally, knowingly, or negligently creating hazards. These include failing to follow administrative orders to alter dangerous situations and covering up the creation and existence of such

**occupational crime**

Refers to violations of the law in the course of practising a legitimate occupation.

**organizational or corporate crime**

White-collar crime committed with the support and encouragement of a formal organization and intended, at least in part, to advance the goals of that organization.

"Get Tough on Corporate Crime"
Aaron Freeman and Craig Forcese, Democracy Watch On-line
www.web.net/dwatch/camp/corpcr94.html

hazards. The penalties for these offences are very light. For example, a 2007 accident took the lives of three B.C. farm workers and injured 14 others. The workers
were packed into a 10-passenger van and were sitting on wooden benches without
seatbelts. While the RCMP recommended 33 criminal charges in this case, none
were laid. The driver was fined $2000 but the labour contracting company that
owned the van and employed the workers was not penalized (Sandborn, 2010).

The administrative decisions within the Johns-Manville Corporation that
failed to protect workers from asbestos poisoning is one of the best-known examples
of employer liability. Asbestos has been recognized as a serious health hazard since
the turn of the century but asbestos workers were not informed, and governments
and the medical community ignored the hazard. At the Johns-Manville plant in
Toronto, company doctors regularly diagnosed lung diseases among the asbestos
workers, but they never told the workers that their lung problems were related to
asbestos. Many of the workers subsequently died of asbestos-related illnesses. In
2005, asbestos-related deaths accounted for nearly one-third of workplace fatalities
in Canada (Sharpe and Hardt, 2006). While asbestos use is now tightly-controlled
in Canada, in 2011 Canada was the only country preventing the United Nations
from listing asbestos as a hazardous product in the Rotterdam Convention even
though less than 500 Canadian jobs depend upon mining and exporting asbestos.

The construction industry has high rates of death and injury because of
failure to implement workplace health and safety regulations. For example, one
Manitoba company was fined $75 000 because of the death of a bridge painter who
was working on a platform with no guard rails, and another was fined $27 500
for its role in the death of a young worker who was electrocuted when he
was allowed to work on a high-voltage light fixture while the wires were live
(McIntyre, 2001). Swartz (1978) concludes that these deaths should be recognized as a form of murder, or what is sometimes called "corporate homicide."
However, as with the Westray mine disaster (Box 17.1), corporate executives
are almost never held personally responsible for their negligence. At most, their
companies are ordered to pay small fines.

This chapter does not attempt to debate the fine points in the definition of
corporate homicide or to establish with any precision how many such homicides occur. It is enough to note that such deaths occur in considerable numbers. Of immediate interest here is the meaning of corporate homicide, and
crimes like it, for the relationship between class and crime.

## Social Class and Crime

There is increasing evidence that a relatively small number of offenders account
for a rather large proportion of serious street crimes (see Chapter 15). The same
may be true of many kinds of white-collar crime. For example, crimes such
as corporate homicide may occur much more frequently among particular
employers in particular kinds of industries. The mining, asbestos, and construction industries are examples that have already been noted. It may be difficult to pinpoint such employers in conventional research designs, and this may
obscure the relationship between class position and this type of criminality.

Implicit in the discussion of street crimes and corporate homicide is the high
likelihood that crime is not unidimensional. That is, these are different kinds of
crime that likely have different connections to the concept of class. Among adults,

class is negatively related to making the direct physical attacks involved in street crimes of violence, and class probably is positively related to causing harms less directly through criminal acts involving the use of corporate resources. Similarly, among juveniles, it may be that some common acts of delinquency (for example, forms of theft that include illegal copying of computer software and music and the unauthorized use of credit and bank cards) are related positively to class (Cullen et al., 1985; Hagan and Kay, 1990), while less frequent and more serious forms of delinquency are negatively related to class (see Chapter 5). The study of white-collar crime and delinquency provides increasing reason to believe that measures of class are connected to crime and delinquency in interesting, albeit complicated, ways.

Why do higher-status people get involved in criminal behaviour? Shover and Hochstetler (2006) suggest three cultural components of middle- and upper-class life that may shape their criminality: a competitive spirit, arrogance, and a sense of entitlement. The unethical acts of many of the sports figures described at the beginning of this chapter were carried out in order to help them win. Athletes are told that "winning is the only thing" and some respond to this pressure by cheating. According to Shover and Hochstetler, employees at Enron (discussed later in this chapter) were continuously evaluated and 15 percent were always rated unacceptable. This competitive pressure and the resulting insecurity of employees helped to foster a culture that encouraged misconduct. The fact that success in business is often measured by the size of one's salary can help to explain why executives who are already making huge salaries will break the rules so they can make even more money.

# FOCUS BOX 17.1

## WESTRAY—A DISASTER OF CRIMINAL PROPORTIONS

"In the early morning of 9 May 1992 a violent explosion rocked the tiny community of Plymouth, just east of Stellarton, in Pictou County, Nova Scotia. The explosion occurred in the depths of the Westray coal mine, instantly killing the 26 miners working there at the time" (Richard, 1997, vii). These words begin the report of a judicial inquiry into the Westray mine explosion that tells a shocking story of corporate and government misconduct that resulted in one of the largest occupational disasters in Canadian history.

Glasbeek and Tucker (1994) point out that the Westray explosion was not an accident, but like other occupational health and safety damage resulted from conscious decisions by those responsible for the miners' safety. This conclusion was reinforced by the title of Justice Richard's inquiry: *The Westray Story: A Predictable Path to Disaster*.

The explosion was not an accident but nobody intended to kill the miners. Rather, their deaths were the result of "a complex mosaic of actions, omissions, mistakes, incompetence, apathy, cynicism, stupidity, and neglect" (Richard, 1997, viii). The inquiry concluded that Westray managers "displayed a certain disdain for safety and appeared to regard safety-conscious workers as the wimps in the organization" (Richard, 1997, ix).

The mine was built in an area that was known to be treacherous because of geological faults and high levels of methane gas. However, only minimal safety precautions were taken. The mine owners and governments were more concerned about the economics of mining than about protecting the workers. The government

*(continued)*

relied on the company to meet safety standards and provided very limited compliance inspections. The company, Curragh Corporation, was having financial difficulties and put pressure on Westray to increase production levels in order to increase company revenues. Safety violations were common and some miners quit; others stayed because of the lack of alternative employment in the province. The safety of the mine was eloquently summed up by Justice Richard:

> I find that the source of ignition was sparks struck by the cutting bits of the continuous miner working in the Southwest 2 section of the mine. But it became apparent as the Inquiry proceeded that conditions at Westray were of greater significance to what happened than was the source of the ignition. Had there been adequate ventilation, had there been adequate treatment of coal dust, and had there been adequate training and an appreciation by management for a safety ethic, those sparks would have faded harmlessly. (1997, 3)

Despite clear evidence of these violations, the government did not exercise its responsibility under the Mineral Resources Act to shut down the mine until it was safe.

Five employees of the Nova Scotia Natural Resources Department and the Department of Labour were fired for their role in the explosion, but nobody from the mining company will ever be held legally responsible for the tragedy. Clifford Frame, president of Curragh Corporation, refused to testify at the inquiry and was never charged with any offence. Mine managers Gerald Philips and Roger Parry were charged with manslaughter and criminal negligence, but these charges were stayed by the Crown because a conviction was unlikely. This is but one of many cases that illustrate the inability of our laws to control corporate crime. The weakness of the current law was addressed by Justice Richard in recommendation 73 of his report:

> The government of Canada . . . should institute a study of the accountability of corporate executives and directors for the wrongful or negligent acts of the corporation and should introduce in the Parliament of Canada such amendments to legislation as are necessary to ensure that corporate executives and directors are held properly accountable for workplace safety. (1997, 57)

While there was a change in the law after the Inquiry, it has had little impact on worker safety.

Shover and Hochstetler proposed that people who are used to power and authority can develop an arrogance that convinces them that the rules that apply to the rest of us do not apply to them. Conrad Black explicitly contrasted his abilities and position with those of people who were not among the rich and powerful. You will recall from Chapter 1 that Black was expelled from Upper Canada College for several offences, including selling copies of final examinations. In his memoirs he justified his actions by describing his contempt for the school staff:

> All those who, by their docility or obsequiousness, legitimized the excesses of the school's penal system, the several sadists and few aggressively fondling homosexuals on the faculty, and the numerous swaggering boobies who had obviously failed in the real world and retreated to Lilliput where they could maintain their exalted status by contract threat of battery: all that gradually produced in me a profound revulsion. (Olive, 2007, 1)

At a rehearing in 2011 following his appeal, he continued to blame the U.S. justice system rather than his own behaviour for his time in prison:

I regret to have to write that I have also discovered in this mundane Odyssey that Canada, too, has its share of obtuse judges. But it does not actively encourage pre-trial media lynchings; requires a plausible test before charges are laid and not just the mockery of the American grand jury; has reasonably even and impartial procedural rules; the defence speaks last in trials; acquittals are not immediately reversible for sentencing purposes; few prosecutors revert to the private sector in Canada, and very few become politicians; and most judges are not, as they are in the United States, ex-prosecutors. (Black, 2011)

A sense of entitlement may also play a role in motivating white-collar criminals. Shover and Hochstetler cite research that showed that doctors who had been convicted of defrauding the U.S. medicare system felt they were entitled to the money they took illegally because of their status as doctors. Many corporate executives who have been accused of criminality have long histories of using their position for their own benefit in a manner that would not be allowed for any of their subordinates. Another quote from Conrad Black illustrates this sense of entitlement. In the 1980s Black was trying to take for himself funds that were in his employees' pension plan; he accused them of stealing from him and used this accusation to support his claim on the money (a battle Black later lost in court):

It's sometimes difficult to work myself into an absolute lachrymose [tearful] fit about a work force that steals on that scale. . . . We are not running a welfare agency for corrupt union leaders and a slovenly work force. (Olive, 2007, 1)

**2002 Fraud and Misconduct Survey KPMG**
www.kpmg.ca/en/services/advisory/forensic/fmdSurvey2002.html

## White-Collar Crime and the Social Organization of Work

Not all white-collar crimes are committed by high-status persons. For example, much embezzlement is committed by relatively low-status bank tellers (Daly, 1989) and blue collar workers also commit crimes in the course of practising their legal occupations. However, if it is true that white-collar crime is positively related to class position, it is also reasonable to ask why it should be so. The answer may lie in the power derived from ownership and authority positions in modern corporations. These positions of power carry with them a freedom from control that may be criminogenic. That is, to have power is to be free from the kinds of constraints that may normally inhibit crime. The modern corporation facilitates this kind of freedom.

## Crime and the Corporation: Executive Disengagement

The organization of the corporation is crucial to understanding most corporate crime (Reiss, 1980; Ermann and Lundman, 1982; Hagan, 1982). As Wheeler and Rothman (1982) noted, the corporation "is for white-collar criminals what the gun or knife is for the common criminal—a tool to obtain money from victims."

The corporation itself is a "legal fiction," with, as H. L. Mencken aptly observed, "no pants to kick or soul to damn." The law chooses to treat corporations as **juristic persons**, making them formally liable to the same laws as

**juristic person**

The legal concept that corporations are liable to the same laws as natural persons. Treating corporations as individuals raise practical difficulties for legal enforcement and punishment.

"natural persons." Some of the most obvious faults in this legal analogy become clear when the impossibility of imprisoning or executing corporations is considered. However, there are more subtle differences between corporate and individual actors with equally significant consequences:

> When individuals are placed in an organizational structure, some of the ordinary internalized restraints seem to lose their hold. And if we decide to look beyond the individual employees and find an organizational "mind" to work with, a "corporate conscience" distinct from the consciences of particular individuals, it is not readily apparent where we would begin—much less what we would be talking about. (Stone 1975)

Stone goes on to suggest some interesting ways in which the corporate conscience and corporate responsibility could be increased. However, these mechanisms, or others, have not been put in place. Corporate power in this sense remains unchecked, and it is in this sense criminogenic.

The problem is in part the absence of cultural beliefs that discourage corporate criminality (Geis, 1962). C. Wright Mills (1956) captured part of the problem in his observation that "it is better, so the image runs, to take one dime from each of ten million people at the point of a corporation than $100 000 from each of ten banks at the point of a gun." There is some evidence that cultural climates vary across time and regimes. For example, Simpson (1986) studied antitrust violations in the United States between 1927 and 1981 and found that such violations were more common during Republican than Democratic administrations. However, even when condemnatory beliefs about corporate crime have been strong, there have been too few controlling mechanisms in place to impose their controlling influence effectively.

Many modern global corporations are huge, with hundreds of thousands of employees and many layers of bureaucracy. It is very difficult for the boards of directors who are responsible for corporate governance to know many details concerning the daily operations of the corporation. Top officers and directors are liable to suit by the corporation itself (via a shareholders' action) if they allow a law violation to occur through negligence. However, the courts have not imposed a duty on directors to uncover corporate wrongdoing. This provides an incentive for senior managers and directors to remain uninformed about illegal activities.

**executive disengagement**
The custom by which lower-level employees assume that executives are best left uninformed of certain decisions and actions of employees, or the assumption that executives cannot be legally expected to have complete control over their individual staff.

The bankruptcy of Britain's Barings Bank provides an example of **executive disengagement**. Barings Bank, which had been controlled by the same family since 1762, was brought down by the actions of a 28-year-old trader. Nicholas Leeson lost almost $1 billion of the company's money on financial derivatives, which were essentially bets on the future performance of the Tokyo stock market. When the Tokyo market fell, Barings collapsed when it could not cover the losses. The size of this gamble was in violation of British banking laws. While bank officials were quick to blame Leeson, it is very likely that senior bank officials at least tacitly approved of Leeson's trading activities. Several financial experts have suggested that the profits Leeson had previously made for Barings led bank officials to allow him to risk their shareholders' money by making illegal trades (Drohan, 1995).

Canadian law in this area was tested in the case of YBM Magnex, a company that ostensibly sold a variety of products, including industrial magnets and bicycles, primarily to eastern European markets. Starting its Canadian life as a shell corporation on the Alberta Stock Exchange, YBM Magnex stock rose in value from 85 cents to $20 in less than three years. It was one of the stocks used in the Toronto Stock Exchange 300 index and had a total share value of about $1 billion. Several eminent Canadians served on its board of directors, including former Ontario premier David Peterson. However, despite these eminent directors, the company had a very shady background. The company was controlled by Semion Mogilevich, one of Russia's most powerful organized criminals (Howlett, 2002). YBM Magnex had been investigated in Britain for a variety of offences, including money laundering. The RCMP had been investigating the company since it was established in 1995 (Rubin, 1999). Stockholders' money disappeared in 1998 when the Ontario Securities Commission (OSC) stopped all trading in the company's shares. Auditors had refused to accept the company's financial statements, and the U.S. law enforcement officials had raided the company's Pennsylvania headquarters investigating charges of fraud and money laundering. Directors and auditors of the company were sued for $635 million and were charged by the OSC with withholding information from the public concerning the fact that the company was under investigation for its ties to organized crime. In 2003 the OSC banned five of the former directors of YBM Magnex from becoming directors or officers of any companies for periods ranging from five years to life. Other directors, including former premier Peterson, were not punished. Shareholders recovered some money through lawsuits against company executives. While these penalties were not nearly as harsh as those in similar U.S. cases, boards of directors are now taking their responsibilities more seriously and programs have been set up to train directors how to perform their supervisory roles more effectively.

## The Criminogenic Market Structure

Corporate crime research suggests not only a freedom at the top of organizations from the need to know and to accept responsibility for criminal activity below, but also a growing pressure from managers that is also criminogenic. Farberman (1975) has referred to such pressures in the automotive industry and in other highly concentrated corporate sectors as constituting a **criminogenic market structure**. The crime-generating feature of these markets is their domination by a relatively small number of manufacturers who insist that their dealers sell in high volume at a small per-unit profit. Dealerships that fail to perform risk the loss of their franchises. A result is high pressure to maximize sales and minimize service. Farberman suggests that car dealers may be induced by the small profit margins on new cars to compensate through fraudulent warranty work and repair rackets. The connection between these findings is that the executives of the automotive industry can distance themselves from the criminal consequences of the "forcing model" (high volume/low per-unit profit) they impose. The result is an absence of control over repair and warranty frauds at the dealership level.

**criminogenic market structure**

An economic market that is structured in such a way that it tends to produce criminal behaviour.

## The Large Scale of Corporations

Access to corporate resources makes it possible to commit very large-scale crimes. Wheeler and Rothman (1982) categorized white-collar offenders into three groups: individual offenders, occupational offenders, and those who committed offences in which both organization and occupation were ingredients (organizational offenders). The study demonstrated the enormous advantages accruing to those who use formal organizations in their crimes. For example, across a subset of four offences, the median "take" for individual offenders was $5279, for occupational offenders $17 106, and for organizational offenders $117 392. In a parallel Canadian study, Hagan and Parker (1985) reported that securities violators who make use of organizational resources commit crimes that involve larger numbers of victims and are broader in their geopolitical spread. Why the organizational edge? Wheeler and Rothman (1982) answer with an example:

> Represented by its president, a corporation entered into a factoring agreement with a leading . . . commercial bank, presenting it with $1.2 million in false billings over the course of seven months; the company's statements were either inflated to reflect much more business than actually was being done, or were simply made up. Would the bank have done this for an individual? Whether we conclude that organizations are trusted more than individuals, or that they simply operate on a much larger scale, it is clear that the havoc caused when organizations are used outside the law far exceeds anything produced by unaffiliated actors.

Just as the organizational form has facilitated economic and technological development on a scale far beyond that achieved by individuals, so too has this form allowed criminal gains of a magnitude that men and women acting alone would find hard to attain.

The structure of the modern corporation allows a power imbalance to prevail in which those individuals at the top experience a relative freedom, while those at the bottom often experience pressure applied from the top that encourages various kinds of white-collar crime. The corporate form itself can be used effectively to perpetrate "bigger and better crimes" than can be achieved by individuals acting alone. Access to these corporate resources is a unique advantage of class positions involving ownership and authority in business organizations. It is in this sense that it can be said that in the world of the modern corporation, the social organization of work itself is criminogenic.

## Corporate Accounting Scandals

While corporate crime has always been a major problem in North America, the new millennium saw scandals that shocked even the most avid supporters of free enterprise. Several of America's largest corporations, including energy company Enron and the telecommunications company WorldCom, went bankrupt, stock markets crashed, the economy declined. Just a few years later, corporate misconduct dealt the world economy another severe blow as a mortgage financing scandal in the United States and very risky lending policies in several other countries led to another major financial crisis. Why do we keep facing these crises caused by what one observer has called a "scandalous rot" (DeCloet, 2002)?

While these crises have many causes, an explanation can start with the way in which corporate executives are paid. Many companies provide their senior executives with stock options that allow the executive to purchase shares in his or her company at a later date for a price that is guaranteed at the time the options are issued. This means that if the stock goes up in the future, the executive can buy it at the guaranteed price and keep the difference between the issue price and the value of the stock at the time it is purchased. If the stock goes down, the executive will not use the option, so will not lose money. The intent of stock options is to provide executives with an incentive to work hard and raise the company's value. This will ensure that the company's shareholders benefit from the company's growth. Many companies also pay their senior employees very large bonuses if the company meets specified profit targets.

While some executives took a long-term perspective and worked to build up the value of their companies, other executives took a short-term approach that proved disastrous for their shareholders. They used a variety of short-term measures to raise both company profits and the stock price so they could make enormous profits on their stock options and bonuses very quickly. For example, "Chainsaw Al" Dunlap (named for his willingness to reduce costs by firing employees) was the chief executive officer (CEO) of the household appliance company Sunbeam. Dunlap's aggressive methods included artificially inflating sales figures so the company's profits appeared higher than they actually were. Sunbeam eventually went bankrupt and Dunlap was fired and fined $15 million, which was only a share of the illegal gains he made from Sunbeam stock.

During the late 1990s, the stock market rose dramatically and CEOs became corporate superstars. Many paid themselves enormous sums of money—many CEOs of large companies earned $50 to $100 million per year. Executives convinced themselves that they deserved these high levels of pay even when their companies were losing money. The greed of senior executives led directly to two of the largest bankruptcies in American history: Enron and WorldCom.

**The Collapse of Enron** How did senior managers of Enron cost their investors $63 billion? Enron was once a pipeline company that delivered natural gas. This business was very profitable, but to CEO Kenneth Lay and his senior executives it was a boring business that lacked the potential for quick profit growth. They developed a business model that involved trading futures contracts that are bets on the future prices of commodities such as natural gas, electricity, and pulp and paper. Initially, this new focus proved very profitable, and the value of the stock climbed quickly. Enron became the seventh most valuable company in the United States. However, the company took greater risks and the new business model broke down. To keep the company growing, Enron executives used illegal financial measures to make it appear as though profits were still increasing. Some of these complex measures involved the company selling its own assets to itself and showing the "profits" from this sale in its revenues. The company also tried to hide its debts by transferring them to outside "partnerships" that had actually been established by Enron.

Enron developed a culture of greed. Many senior Enron employees acted like children in a candy store and took massive personal profits from the financial schemes organized by the company. Several finance department employees invested $125 000 of their own funds in one of Enron's illegal financial transactions and made $30 million in a few months (Butler, 2002). As the illegal schemes began to unravel and the company began to slide into bankruptcy, Enron paid bonuses of $681 million to 140 top executives, including $67 million to CEO Kenneth Lay, who continued to encourage employees and members of the public to buy Enron stock even as he and his executives stripped the company of its remaining value (Kranhold and Pacelle, 2002). Ultimately, creditors, stockholders, and other Enron employees suffered huge losses when the financial arrangements fell apart.

Enron executives must take most of the blame for the company's demise and several have received very lengthy jail terms. However, they also had help from the managers of other large corporations. The Arthur Andersen accounting firm, one of the world's largest, allowed Enron's many lapses of legal and ethical standards to slip by its auditors in order to help it obtain lucrative consulting contracts with Enron. Many of Wall Street's largest banks and brokerage firms collaborated with Enron in order to profit from stock commissions, consulting contracts, and interest from loans. One of Canada's largest banks, CIBC, was accused of helping Enron with its fraudulent financial dealings and while not admitting any wrongdoing, in 2005 CIBC paid $2.4 billion to settle a lawsuit over its dealings with Enron.

**WorldCom** The Enron debacle was quickly followed by an even larger bankruptcy. The failure of WorldCom, the largest long-distance telephone service provider in the United States, cost investors a massive $175 billion as its share value dropped from $64.50 a share to only 83 cents (Kadlec, 2002). WorldCom, led by CEO Bernard Ebbers, a former Edmonton milkman, admitted it overstated earnings by $3.8 billion over a period of 15 months. That is, the company reported earning $3.8 billion more than it actually made. While the Enron fraud was very complex, WorldCom used a simple method of inflating its non-existent profits. It simply treated its everyday expenses (mainly payments to local phone companies for using their services to complete calls) as capital investments that could be written off over a period of several years. This made its profits look higher than they really were because it did not have to deduct these expenses from the money it took in from its customers. This would be like you pretend that you are paying your current tuition over a period of four years instead of in the current academic year. This pretence would make your accounts look better than they really are, but eventually you are going to have to account for the missing money. These revelations led to a collapse in the company's stock. Ebbers, the company's CEO, is now serving a 25-year prison sentence and has lost most of the fortune he made from his company.

Arthur Andersen, the global company that was responsible for auditing Enron, WorldCom, and several other companies accused of misleading accounting, was found guilty of a felony count of obstructing the Securities and Exchange Commission's investigation into Enron. Andersen employees had shredded documents and tried to persuade others to cover up the scandal. Following the verdict, the company announced that it was going out of business. It was victim of a corporate culture in which generating revenue for the company became a greater concern than protecting the public by doing its job competently.

**Canada's Nortel** In 2000, Nortel, a Canadian-based telecommunications company was the most valuable company in Canada. Its shares were valued at $124 each, but unfortunately for investors its financial statements greatly overstated the company's revenues. At a time when the market for technology stocks was collapsing, revelations that Nortel was not as profitable as it had claimed to be, along with a realization that the company had greatly overpaid for smaller companies that it had purchased, drove its shares below $1. While some shareholders lost 99 percent of their investments, John Roth, Nortel's CEO, retired after cashing in most of his shares at the top of the market. Executives who followed Roth were given bonuses if they could return Nortel to profitability. Nortel did report a profit in 2003 and the executives were given nearly $300 millions in bonus payments. However, in 2004 the company revealed that most of the profits were due to faulty accounting and company shareholders again suffered a devastating loss. In 2008 the RCMP charged three Nortel officials, including former CEO Frank Dunn, with several fraud-related charges over these false reports. In 2009 the company filed for bankruptcy protection and Canada lost one of the world's pre-eminent technology companies.

**The Financial Collapse of 2008** The collapse of Enron and WorldCom and an earlier wave of crimes involving U.S. savings and loan institutions both led to economic crises involving major stock market crashes and increased unemployment. You might think that governments would respond to these financial disasters by increasing regulation and making financial institutions more accountable for their activities. However, this was not the case, at least in part because financial institutions strongly resisted increased regulation, claiming that free market forces would ensure that businesses operate properly. Thus U.S. financial institutions were allowed to engage in extremely risky investments. The collapse of these institutions in 2008 caused a financial catastrophe that cost trillions of dollars, led to the loss of hundreds of thousands of jobs in North American and Europe, and bankrupted several countries.

This massive financial collapse was very complex, but the major cause was the fact that major financial institutions in the United States and several other countries took on excessive risk and engaged in reckless lending practices. One example is the NINJA mortgages issued by some mortgage companies. The term NINJA means No Income, No Job or Assets. Normally people in those circumstances would not be issued mortgages because they would be likely to default and the bank would lose its money. However, in the United States, those issuing these mortgages would repackage them and sell them to other financial institutions and to individual investors. Many banks and mortgage companies were involved and few have been punished. One exception was Wells Fargo bank which was recently fined $85 million for falsifying loan documents and for pushing homeowners into more costly types of mortgages during the housing boom (Rugaber and Kravitz, 2011). This fine represents an insignificant amount for a company which is one of the largest mortgage lenders in the United States.

The greed of many of the people responsible for the U.S. banking system led to a major financial catastrophe. Even those whose behaviour was at least technically legal failed to do their jobs in assessing risk, so purchasers of these toxic mortgages were not aware of what they were buying. Journalist Matt Taibbi describes how Goldman Sachs, the largest investment bank in the United States, sold these mortgages:

> Goldman.... bundled hundreds of different mortgages into instruments they called Collateralized Debt Obligations [CDO]. Then they sold investors on the idea that, because a bunch of those mortgages would turn out to be O.K., there was no reason to worry so much about the shitty ones: The CDO, as a whole, was sound......
>
> [However, they were not sound] "Take one $494 million issue.... Many of the mortgages belonged to second-mortgage borrowers and the average equity they had in their homes was *0.71 percent.* Moreover, 58 percent of the loans included little or no documentation—no names of the borrowers, no addresses of the homes... Yet, both of the major ratings agencies, Moody's and Standard & Poor's, rated 93 percent of the issue as investment grade. Moody's projected that less than 10 percent of the loans would default. In reality, 18 percent of the mortgages were in default *within 18 months.* (Taibbi, 2010, n.p.)

When mortgage holders defaulted in large numbers, the impact spread quickly through the financial system. However, Goldman Sachs even profited from the defaults because in separate transactions, the company made market bets against the mortgages it was selling to others. This is only part of the reason why Taibbi described Goldman Sachs as "a great vampire squid wrapped around the face of humanity, relentlessly jamming its blood funnel into anything that smells like money." (Taibbi, 2010, n.p.)

Several senior officials of Enron and WorldCom were charged and sentenced for their misconduct, as were some of the people responsible for the earlier savings and loan scandal. However, while hundreds of charges have been laid against minor players in the mortgage industry, no high-ranking officials from the companies involved in precipitating the latest financial crisis have been prosecuted (Morgenson and Story, 2011). Instead, the U.S. taxpayers were forced to pay to bail out many of these companies because of the economic danger of their failure. An illuminating footnote to this story is that Canadian financial institutions were relatively unaffected by the crisis, and our mortgage market is very stable. This is because Canadian politicians and regulators did a much better job of ensuring that financial institutions did not become reckless in their search for profits. In this, and in many other types of corporate and white-collar crime, aggressive regulation and enforcement can do a great deal to reduce misconduct. Unfortunately this is often lacking.

## Consumer Safety Issues

Beginning in the 1960s the consumer movement began to hold manufacturers accountable for the safety of their products. Ralph Nader's book *Unsafe at Any Speed,* which described the deaths and injuries caused by the faulty design of the General Motors Corvair automobile, helped to focus the public's attention on consumer safety. Widely publicized cases like the calculation by Ford executives that it would be cheaper to pay for lawsuits brought by the families of Ford Pinto drivers who had been burned to death in accidents than to fix the fuel tank design flaw that caused the fires, and the production of Firestone tires that came apart at high speed, led to tougher safety regulations and convinced companies that it was good business to manufacture safe products. Over the next 40 years, governments became more active in regulating consumer goods and products became much safer.

In 2007, people who took product safety for granted were surprised to learn of several incidents in which unsafe products manufactured in China were being sold in the North American market. The first was the melamine-contaminated pet food that you read about in Chapter 11 of this text. The second was the sale of counterfeit Colgate toothpaste in discount stores throughout Canada. The toothpaste contained potentially harmful chemicals. The third scandal involved children's toys, including Elmo, Big Bird, and Dora, that were recalled by manufacturers because of safety concerns. A few months later Mattel, the maker of Fisher-Price toys, was forced to issue three recalls involving millions of toys. Some of the toys had lead paint, which can be poisonous, while others had design flaws, including loose magnets that children could swallow.

The toy recall provides an example of a criminogenic market structure that has resulted from globalization. Mattel manufactures most of its toys in China because of low wage levels and an absence of environmental and workplace health and safety regulations mean that it is much cheaper to manufacture toys in China. However, in China the toy companies contract out their production to local companies where quality control is difficult to maintain. The president of Mattel blamed Chinese manufacturers for the safety problems, but in fact the responsibility must be shared more broadly.

Some of the blame does fall on China where regulation is lax, corruption and bribery are common, and the government tacitly approves of a wide range of illegal practices. However, Mattel is also at fault. It is no secret that quality control is not nearly as effective in China as it is in North American factories. Thus the toy companies are ultimately responsible for doing sufficient testing of their Chinese-made products to ensure that they are safe. And what about Canadian and American governments? There are toy safety regulations, but we know that unless regulations are actively enforced some businesses will ignore them. Neither country does routine testing of toys, leaving that task to the toy companies. Unfortunately, even if safety violations are found, neither country is likely to impose any sanctions against the violators. Ultimately, it is the consumer who will enforce safety regulations. If Mattel and other companies have to keep issuing safety-related recalls, customers will stop putting their children at risk by buying these companies' products and will turn to more reliable suppliers.

# White-Collar Crime and Legal Sanctions

Given the distribution of freedom and pressure that has been identified within the structure of the modern corporation and the power this gives to those who run it, the question that recurs is this: What does the law do to remedy the potential for abuse?

"We have arranged things," writes Christopher Stone (1975), "so that the people who call the shots do not have to bear the full risks." This is the consequence of the limited liabilities borne by modern corporate actors:

> Take, for example, a small corporation involved in shipping dynamite. The shareholders of such a company, who are typically also the managers, do not *want* their dynamite-laden truck to blow up. But if it does, they know that those injured cannot, except in rare cases, sue them as individuals to recover their full damages if the amount left in the corporations' bank account is inadequate to make full compensation. . . . What this means is that in deciding how much money to spend on safety devices, and whether or not to allow trucks to drive through major cities, the calculations are skewed toward higher risks than suggested by the "rational economic corporation/free market" model that is dreamily put forth in textbooks. If no accident results, the shareholders will reap the profits of skimping on safety measures. If a truck blows up, the underlying human interests will be shielded from fully bearing the harm that they have caused. And then, there is nothing to prevent the same men from setting up a new dynamite shipping corporation the next day; all it takes is the imagination to think up a new name, and some $50 in filing fees. (Stone, 1975, 462–63)

Large corporations are not quite as free as the small corporation in the example to dissolve and reconstitute their operations. However, the separation of shareholder and management interests gives rise to a related problem of liability. Damage judgments against corporations are taken from the companies' revenues and rarely affect the salaries of the managers who made the decisions leading to the penalties. Thus the shareholders suffer for the misdeeds of corporate managers while the managers are shielded by the corporate structure.

The broader issue is how and why the law is used to control white-collar crime. It has already been seen that civil remedies are not very effective. We turn now to criminal sanctions. How does the state decide what kinds of upperworld indiscretions will be called criminal? The most interesting work that has been done on this issue in Canada involves the development of anticombines legislation. Given the powerful economic interests involved in forming the **monopolistic enterprises** this legislation presumably seeks to prevent, one might wonder how an **anticombines law** was ever passed in the first place. Goff and Reasons (1978) indicate that the initiative for the original legislation in 1899 "came not from the general populace but from small businessmen, who felt their firms were at the mercy of big business interests." However, more recently

**monopolistic enterprise**
Any corporation that controls all, or the majority, of the market for a particular product or service.

**anticombines law**
In order to protect the principle of competition, valued by all liberal, capitalistic societies, laws have been created to prevent and punish corporations that work together to reduce competition.

Smandych (1985) has noted that a Royal Commission on Labour and Capital, created for the purpose of investigating industrial conditions in Canada, interviewed and recorded testimony from numerous trade-union representatives and workers. This testimony, cited in the Commission's 1899 report, specifically sought legislation against monopolistic practices, and Smandych argues that "the possibility that worker demands for the elimination of combines went unnoticed by the government of the day is extremely doubtful."

Smandych concludes that "the first flourishing of Canadian anti-combines legislation was the product of an essential confrontation between labour and capital, and of the state's effort to find an acceptable solution." This is not to say that this legislation was strong or effective because it was not (Snider, 1979). Efforts over the years to strengthen the legislation with "proconsumer and pro-competition" amendments were unsuccessful because of business opposition. The legislation has done much less than it promised to reduce monopolistic practices and to punish those who promote them. Prosecutions are rarely successful, and when they are, the fines are so low that they do not act as an effective deterrent to anticompetitive behaviour.

What of the few white-collar offenders who are held criminally liable and processed through the criminal justice system? Notions of "equality before the law" are perhaps nowhere more subjective in meaning than in their application to the sentencing of white-collar offenders (Hagan and Albonetti, 1982). This is reflected in at least two kinds of comments made by judges about the sentences they impose for white-collar crimes. It is reflected first in the suggestion that white-collar offenders experience sanctions in a different way from other kinds of offenders, and second in the assertion that different kinds of sanctions are appropriate in white-collar cases.

The view, common among judges, that white-collar offenders experience sanctions differently is summarized in Mann et al.'s (1980) study of a sample of judges who have tried such cases: "Most judges have a widespread belief that the suffering experienced by a white-collar person as a result of apprehension, public indictment and conviction, and the collateral disabilities incident to conviction—loss of job, professional licenses, and status in the community—completely satisfies the need to punish the individual." This belief persists in the face of Benson's (1989, 474) findings that "although they commit the most serious offences, employers and managers are least likely to lose their jobs after conviction for a white-collar crime." Judges feel that the defendant, having suffered enough from the acts of prosecution and conviction, does not require a severe sentence. However, the sentence must still provide a deterrent. Mann et al. (1980) concluded that most judges seek a compromise in resolving this dilemma so they use weekend sentences and short jail sentences which they feel might deter others.

The role of fines in sentencing white-collar offenders is controversial. Some judges feel that fines are the only penalties that should be given to white-collar offenders. Posner (1980) argues that if fines are suitably large, they are an equally effective deterrent and cheaper to administer, and therefore socially preferable to imprisonment and other punishments. It has already been noted that corporate entities are liable to little else than fines. However, Mann et al. (1980) find judges to be skeptical of the effectiveness of fines. The sense that emerges from this research is that judges are acutely aware of the issues of deterrence, disparity, and discrimination in the sentencing of white-collar offenders, and that they attempt to respond to these issues by fashioning sentences that combine sanctions in a compromise fashion. Consistent with this view, Hagan and Nagel (1982) found in a sentencing study covering the period from 1963 to 1976 in the Southern District of New York that judges attempted to compensate for the shorter prison terms given to white-collar offenders by adding probation or fines to their sentences. Similarly, fines were most frequently used in conjunction with prison and probation sentences. In any case, all these findings suggest that white-collar offenders are advantaged by the specific types and combination of legal sanctions that are imposed on them.

In both Canada and the United States, there is some evidence that the mid-1970s brought a new and somewhat harsher attitude toward white-collar crime. Katz (1980) speaks of a "social movement against white-collar crime" that began in the United States in the late 1960s, and the evolution of public opinion documents an increasing concern with the occurrence of such crimes (Cullen et al., 1982). This new concern seems at least in part to have been a response to incidents such as the American experience with Watergate and a major Canadian scandal involving dredging contracts. It was illustrated by the proactive prosecutorial policies of several U.S. attorneys (Hagan and Nagel, 1982) and in the increased prosecution of large-scale securities violations in Ontario (Hagan and Parker, 1985). In 1987 the Canadian government passed new environmental legislation that provides for fines of up to $1 million per day and jail terms of up to five years for guilty executives. Further, the government of Ontario has increased the fine for insider trading of securities from $25 000 to $1 million, and it has increased the possible jail term from one to two years.

So there *appears* to be a move toward tougher legal sanctions for white-collar offences. Of course, charges must be laid before sanctions can be imposed, and the power of corporations and of persons in high social-class positions makes the decision to prosecute problematic (see Benson et al., 1988). Hagan and Palloni (1983) reported an increased use of imprisonment with white-collar offenders after Watergate, but they also indicate that the length of these prison sentences was unusually short. The Canadian study of the enforcement of securities laws in Ontario (Hagan and Parker, 1985) reveals a similar pattern of trade-offs in the severity with which white-collar offenders are treated. Overall, treatment of white-collar offenders seems to have been lenient in the past, and despite some examples of harsher sentences, there is no unambiguous evidence that this situation has changed markedly. Even where white-collar offenders have received prison sentences, they typically obtain parole very early in their terms.

In recent years the massive losses due to the failures of companies such as Enron and WorldCom have led to harsher treatment of corporate criminals in the United States. These crimes led to a serious loss of confidence in the stock market—why would someone want to invest money in companies whose earnings reports could not be trusted? The scandals were so pervasive that it became obvious that major changes were needed in regulation and corporate governance. While corporate lobbying has limited regulatory changes, governments in the United States have made their laws tougher and have put more resources into investigating and prosecuting corporate crime. Many senior executives have been publicly arrested and taken into custody in front of the media in the so-called "perp walks," designed to show the public that politicians have acted. The jail sentences received by high-profile offenders in cases such as Enron and WorldCom have been very harsh—two executives received sentences of over 20 years—so there is at least anecdotal evidence that the new guidelines are having an impact.

However, there is no evidence that Canadian courts have become more punitive toward corporate criminals and the police and securities regulators have not made much effort to clean up the business world. The fact that Conrad Black was prosecuted in the United States rather than in Canada is indicative of the fact that the U.S. justice system is now much tougher on corporate malfeasance cases than is the Canadian system. Even Jim Flaherty, the federal Minister of Finance, has said that Canada's securities regulations are ineffective.

Why does the justice system not deal with white-collar crimes more effectively? The complexity of corporate crime makes it costly to investigate and to prosecute. The public is usually more concerned about violent crime and neighbourhood safety issues, so police chiefs are under pressure to invest their resources in these offences. Thus local police typically do little white-collar crime enforcement and federal and provincial governments have not invested sufficient resources to these investigations. Investigations are extremely lengthy and expensive.  The investigation of the alleged Nortel frauds took four years and required 50 people to go through 20 million documents (*Toronto Star*, June 20, 2008). The amount of information collected in these complex cases results in lengthy delays in going to trial. It is difficult to keep good investigators because they are attracted away by much higher salaries in private industry. Many of these offences also involve multiple jurisdictions which can further complicate investigations. Even if prosecution is successful, white-collar offenders are seen as good parole risks and are often back in the community very quickly.

In response to these problems, in 2003 the federal government established the Integrated Market Enforcement Team (IMET) to deal with stock market frauds and in 2004 passed new legislation to make it easier to prosecute some fraud-related offences. The IMET team has members from several different federal agencies including the RCMP and the Department of Justice. The IMET program was criticized for a lack of successful prosecutions (Le Pan, 2007) and some measures were taken to improve IMET's performance. From 2003 to 2010 there were 24 major IMET investigations. Charges were laid in 9 of these, 5 were discontinued, and 10 were still ongoing. The average length of time between referral to IMET and the laying of charges is nearly three years (Public Safety Canada, 2010).

## Occupational Crime

In the rest of this chapter you will learn about crimes that are committed by individuals who violate the law in the course of practising a legitimate occupation. As with corporate crime, at the heart of much occupational crime is a violation of positions of trust (Shapiro, 1990).

## Unprofessional Conduct and Malpractice

Historically we have known little about unprofessional conduct and malpractice among groups such as lawyers and doctors because most of it has been dealt with privately by the governing bodies of professional associations. However, in recent years society has become less tolerant of professional deviance. Complainants have become more vocal and more violations have come to the attention of the public. Governments have also been more willing to prosecute in cases that involve violations of the criminal law.

Every occupation includes people who violate legal or ethical codes for their own benefit. However, the problem is made worse when those responsible for regulating the conduct of individual practitioners fail to do their job. The examples of sexual abuse by members of the clergy and malpractice by doctors illustrate how the failure by church and medical authorities to respond to complaints against members of their professions has led to greater harm being done.

Perhaps the most widely publicized cases of unprofessional conduct over the past decade have involved sexual abuse by members of the clergy. In Canada, the Anglican Church has been named as a co-defendant in over 1200 complaints from former students of Indian residential schools, and several Catholic priests have been convicted of sexual assault charges in which the victims were former residential school students. Aboriginal children who attended residential schools have not been the only victims of abuse. The first major case to come to the attention of the Canadian public involved the Mount Cashel Orphanage in St. John's, Newfoundland, which was run by members of the Christian Brothers order. Abuse at the orphanage was hidden for many years. In 1975 a police investigation heard testimony which included this statement from a former resident:

> I am 11 years old .... I have been at Mount Cashel Orphanage for about five years. I am happy at the orphanage except for Brother Burke, Brother Ralph and Brother English. I don't like Brother Burke because he beats me across my bare backside with a stick about three days ago Brother Burke took me into a closet and made me pull down my pants he hit me five or six times across my backside with a stick. He beat me because I threw a after shave tin into the garbage and it made a noise and Brother Burke was watching T.V. Both Brother Ralph and Brother English on seven or eight times have caught a hold of me and have felt my legs and felt my bird. Sometimes this has happened when I have been in bed. Brother Ralph would sit down on the bed and feel my bird inside my pyjama pants. Most times Brother English would feel my bird when I was in the dining Hall he would do it sometimes when I was in bed. (Law Commission of Canada, 2000, 28)

When the investigating officers recommended laying charges against members of the Christian Brothers, the chief of the Royal Newfoundland Constabulary refused to allow charges. No further action was taken until a Royal Commission was established in 1989 following a series of public complaints from former residents of the orphanage. The commission found that

w w w

Survivors Network of Those
Abused by Priests
www.survivorsnetwork.org

senior Catholic Church officials covered up accusations of sexual and physical abuse as did the police chief and a provincial deputy minister. As a result, 15 members of the Christian Brothers were charged and both the Newfoundland government and the Christian Brothers order were forced to make multimillion-dollar payments to abused victims.

This failure of church officials to deal with abusive clergy is by no means unique. Former Boston cardinal Bernard Law resigned his post in 2002 after facing criticism that he had failed to act in many cases of sexual misconduct by priests. Not only did he fail to take action, but he covered up many instances of misconduct and reassigned several priests who had been accused of abusing children to positions where they would continue to work with children. A number of these priests reoffended, including Father John Geoghan, who has been accused of fondling or raping 150 children. Geoghan received a sentence of 9 to 10 years for one case, and by 2002 the Catholic Church had paid out over $10 million in settlements with 86 of his victims. Geoghan had been moved to a number of parishes in the Boston area in response to complaints, but the Church otherwise took no action until after the case had received wide publicity.

The scandal has not been limited to North America. In 2011, following the release of a government report on child abuse by Catholic priests, Irish Prime Minister Enda Kenny expressed his anger at the failure of the church hierarchy to protect Irish children:

> The Cloyne report excavates the dysfunction, disconnection, elitism, the narcissism that dominate the culture of the Vatican to this day… The rape and torture of children were downplayed or "managed" to uphold instead, the primacy of the institution, its power, standing and "reputation". Far from listening to evidence of humiliation and betrayal with St Benedict's "ear of the heart"… the Vatican's reaction was to parse and analyse it with the gimlet eye of a canon lawyer…. The [Prime Minister] was moving an all-party motion that "deplores the Vatican's intervention which contributed to the undermining of the child protection frameworks and guidelines of the Irish state and the Irish bishops." (Fitzgerald, 2011)

Medical doctors have been accused of many types of violations, ranging from false billing to ethical lapses in the treatment of patients and sexual misconduct with patients. Perhaps the most serious violations by doctors involve malpractice. Most doctors are competent professionals, but accusations of malpractice are not uncommon. For example, in 2009 patients began 891 legal actions against physicians, although typically only about one-third of these actions are successful (Canadian Medical Protective Association, 2010). Examples of cases that have resulted in action against doctors include one Manitoba doctor who was sanctioned for sewing beads into the stitches of an Aboriginal woman, and an American doctor who was convicted of assault for carving his initials into a patient (Henderson, 2000). In one rather bizarre case, a South Carolina doctor was fined and reprimanded for using an amputated foot as bait in his crab trap (*Vancouver Sun*, 2000).

One tragic case of malpractice involved a Winnipeg surgeon who specialized in pediatric cardiac surgery. In 1994, 12 young children died while undergoing surgery at the Health Sciences Centre. A judicial inquiry found that at least five of the deaths were likely preventable (Sinclair, 2000). The inquiry determined that the surgeon was at fault, but also blamed the hospital, which failed to ensure that the surgeon was qualified, and his supervisors, who failed to take action even when there were complaints about his performance. There was a culture of secrecy surrounding the work of the doctor, and nurses who complained about the program were ignored by hospital officials.

The failure by professional licensing and regulatory bodies to hold their members accountable has seriously harmed clients and patients. For example, Dr. Richard Neale lost his surgical privileges in British Columbia after a series of complaints. He was allowed to retrain for six months and then to return to his surgical duties. In 1981, an Ontario patient died as a result of Dr. Neale's incompetence, but he continued to operate and to injure patients until he was finally banned from practice in 1985 as a result of the 1981 case. Leaving Canada, he continued to practise in England, where he had a complication rate five times higher than that of his colleagues (Wente, 2000). Even though British authorities had been warned about Neale, they did not remove him from practice until 2000.

In 2007, Toronto real estate agent Krista Stryland died of complications following liposuction surgery at the Toronto Cosmetic Clinic. Her condition deteriorated after surgery that removed more than the standard amount of fat and liquids from her body and the doctor who treated her did not respond appropriately to her complications.

The surgery was carried out by Dr. Behnaz Yazdanfar, a family physician who was not a qualified plastic surgeon. However, Dr. Yazdanfar was permitted to perform cosmetic surgery in Ontario without formal surgical training. The year before Ms. Stryland's death, another doctor had complained about Dr. Yazdanfar's lack of qualifications and about her advertising but the College of Physicians and Surgeons of Ontario determined that she was qualified to conduct cosmetic surgery procedures and allowed her to continue doing liposuction and breast augmentations.

In 2009 the College of Physicians and Surgeons conducted hearings into a number of complaints against Dr. Yazdanfar including the Stryland case. The Discipline Committee determined that Dr. Yazdanfar committed professional misconduct by failing to meet the standard of practice, that she violated advertising regulations, and that she acted in a manner that was "disgraceful, dishonourable or unprofessional" (College of Physicians and Surgeons of Ontario, 2009, 1). Finally, the Discipline Committee concluded that Dr. Yazdanfar is incompetent and has prohibited her from performing further surgery.

College of Physicians and Surgeons Judgment in Yazdanfar case:

http://www.cpso.on.ca/docsearch/details.aspx?view=4&id=%20 67947

## Investment and Securities Fraud

Many people rely on financial advisors to help them prepare for their retirement. In most cases, this is a good idea, but unfortunately not all advisors can be trusted. For example, Earl Jones, a Montreal investment advisor, defrauded clients of over $50 million in order to support his lavish lifestyle. Many investors trusted Jones with their life savings and were financially devastated by his actions (Sutherland, 2009). While disastrous for his victims, Jones' crimes pale by comparison with those of Bernie Madoff who victimized thousands of people and lost close to $20 billion. Both Jones and Madoff used **Ponzi schemes** to defraud their clients. In a Ponzi or pyramid scheme (Evola and O'Grady, 2009), investors are solicited through the promise of high returns on investments. Investors are initially paid dividends on their investments; however, the funds paid out are not generated from actual investments. Indeed, the money is generally not invested. Instead, payouts to clients come from the contributions of new investors. That is why the "returns" to investors are often quite high, in order to attract more investors to generate investment funding that can be spent by the organizers and/or paid out to investors. Eventually the new money runs out and the scheme collapses.

**Ponzi scheme**

A fraud in which old investors are paid with the funds invested by new investors. When the scheme runs out of new investors, the scheme collapses.

Madoff, once a highly-respected Wall Street financier, is now serving a prison term of 150 years in the United States. Jones was sentenced to 11 years in prison, but will likely be released after serving only a few years of this term.

Another type of securities fraud is insider trading which occurs when someone, usually an owner or employee of the company, receives information about the company that is not available to the general public. It is unlawful to buy or sell stock using this information because this would give the insider an advantage over other investors. In 2000, Glen Harvey, former president of Alberta-based Golden Rule Resources, was sentenced to one year in jail and fined $3.95 million for trading $4 million worth of company stock while withholding assay results showing that the company had almost no gold on one of its properties. When the news was finally released, the company shares dropped by over half. Harper was only the second person to be sentenced to jail in Canada for insider trading (Canadian Press, 2000) and successful prosecutions for this offence are rare.

A third type of investment fraud is the "pump and dump." In this scam, stock promoters take a worthless company, invent a story about the company, then tell that story in order to get people to buy the stock. If they are successful, the stock price will rise and the promoters will sell their shares for a profit and other investors will be left only with worthless shares. The story of Bre-X, the most expensive stock fraud in Canadian history, is described in Box 17.2.

# FOCUS BOX 17.2

## BRE-X: THE ANATOMY OF A STOCK FRAUD

The speculative segment of the Canadian stock market has had a very bad reputation. *Forbes* magazine once called Vancouver the "scam capital of the world" because of the fraudulent stocks that were sold on the Vancouver Stock Exchange. Until recently, governments failed to regulate the activities of some of the more aggressive stock promoters. Perhaps, then, it is fitting that Canada was the home of one of the world's largest stock swindles.

*(continued)*

According to the autopsy report that marked the end of one of history's largest frauds: "Testimonies of witnesses and existing evidence indicate that victim Michael Antonius [*sic*] de Guzman did not fall by accident but that he deliberately ended his life by dropping himself from the helicopter" (Wells, 1998, 29). Michael de Guzman was the chief geologist of Bre-X, a Canadian gold mining company that claimed to have discovered one of the world's largest gold mines. Shortly after de Guzman's death, assay reports revealed that there was no gold and that the Bre-X property in Indonesia was worthless. Investors lost $6 billion when Bre-X stock collapsed.

Mines have been "salted" for hundreds of years. Owners of a worthless property could attract investors by scattering gold at the mine site or by adding it to rock samples after they had been collected. Despite this long history of fraud and deception, investors around the world fell for the story of Bre-X. Many of these investors lost their life savings, and at least one killed himself after Bre-X stock collapsed.

Bre-X was built on a flimsy structure of lies. However, greed led many to ignore the risks and warning signs and to believe the story spun by the Bre-X principals and by their supporters in the financial world. Jennifer Wells describes the press release by company president David Walsh, a man whose stock promoting career had been, up until Bre-X, a disaster:

> The Walsh press release described the prospect as a "deposit," which it was not, the presumed gold resource as "reserves," which they were not, and said that drilling on the property by the previous tenant had yielded numerous intersections of more than two grams of gold per tonne, which was a lie. (1998, 122)

To raise exploration money, Walsh was essentially announcing that he had a producing gold mine, even though the company had not even begun to explore the property.

After initial samples showed no signs of gold, somebody—most likely de Guzman—began salting the samples. Not surprisingly, tests of these samples were more successful, and Bre-X officials used the results to regularly increase their estimates of the amount of gold. As the mythical gold reserves increased, the stock began to soar. Shares that once sold for six cents per share were soon worth hundreds of dollars.

In addition to the problems with the mine, Bre-X also had to contend with the corrupt Indonesian government, which eventually took nearly half of the project. When this happened company officials simply doubled their estimates of the amount of gold. Investors were comfortable even though over half their investment had been assigned to the Indonesians and to a large mining company selected by the Indonesian government (Wells, 1998).

The involvement of this company, Freeport McMoRan, spelled the beginning of the end for Bre-X and its investors. When Freeport carried out its own testing program, assay results showed there was no gold on the Bre-X property. The last nail was hammered into the Bre-X coffin by Graham Farquharson, an independent analyst whose report concluded:

> The magnitude of the tampering with core samples that we believe has occurred and resulting falsification of assay values at Busang, is of a scale and over a period of time and with a precision that, to our knowledge, is without precedent in the history of mining anywhere in the world. (Wells, 1998, 368)

Nobody will ever be punished for the Bre-X fiasco. De Guzman committed suicide and David Walsh died of natural causes in 1998. John Felderhof, the company's chief geologist, was acquitted of fraud charges in 2007. The company is bankrupt and nobody associated with Bre-X has the resources to replace the billions of dollars lost by investors.

## Internet Fraud

White-collar criminals have been quick to adopt new technologies. As the Internet becomes more prevalent and as more people use it to conduct economic transactions, Internet crime is becoming more common. Some individuals have found it profitable to advertise on Internet auction sites such as eBay, to collect cheques from purchasers, and then fail to deliver the promised article. Others have used spam e-mail to get people to order products such as Norton Anti-Virus. Some of these spam advertisers deliver a pirated copy of the software that cannot be registered or updated; others simply use the customer's credit card number to order other goods. Other online criminals swindle funds through phony investment schemes or sell phony products.

Another type of Internet fraud victimized Cryptologic, a Canadian firm that develops software for Internet gambling. In 2001, a computer hacker broke into the company's servers and altered Cryptologic's programs for online slot machines and craps games at two web casinos to ensure that players would always win. As a result, several online gamblers made a total of $1.9 million.

## The Justice System: Wrongful Convictions

Even people who work in the justice system sometimes break the rules or exhibit incompetence. As Box 17.3 shows, one of the consequences of this can be the imprisonment of innocent people. In addition to the cases involving Dr. Smith, Canada has had several other high-profile cases of wrongful conviction including those of Guy Paul Morin, Thomas Sophonow, David Milgaard, and Donald Marshall. One factor these cases have in common is that justice system personnel had "tunnel vision" focused on only one suspect and so failed to properly investigate the cases or to adequately assess evidence that might have cleared the suspects during the investigation or at trial. In some of these cases police and prosecutors deliberately withheld evidence from that defence that might have resulted in an acquittal of the accused.

## Tax Fraud

No current estimates are available, but many billions of dollars are lost to tax fraud. The Auditor General estimated loss in 1997 was $12 billion (Auditor General of Canada, 1999), a sum greater than the budget of the Department of National Defence. The income tax system in Canada is one that requires all taxpayers to report their incomes honestly. However, they clearly do not do so, and there is evidence that in some occupations, the rate of non-compliance is as high as 90 percent (Gabor, 1994).

How do so many people avoid taxes? People who are working at jobs where all their income is paid by an employer have little opportunity to avoid tax because the employer deducts the tax and reports salary information to the government. However, a large segment of the working population has jobs that enable them to hide income. Many of you have likely worked as servers in the restaurant industry or have friends who work in this field. Since much of

# FOCUS BOX 17.3

## DR. CHARLES SMITH: WRONGFUL CONVICTIONS

Dr. Smith was a forensic child pathologist who gave crucial testimony in many child fatality cases. He worked at Toronto's Hospital for Sick Children and was widely-recognized as an authority in his field despite a lack of training in forensic pathology. He was heavily involved testifying in court from 1990 to 2005 when criticism finally led to a review of his work. This review concluded that Smith had made serious errors in almost half the 45 child autopsies reviewed, and that there was serious doubt about 13 cases which had resulted in convictions. Among those convicted and later released after Smith's evidence was refuted by other experts were: Louise Reynolds, who served 22 months for fatally stabbing her daughter who had actually been mauled by dogs; William Mullins-Johnson who served 12 years after being convicted of raping and murdering his niece; and Tammy Marquardt who was freed in 2011 after serving 14 years for murdering her son. As with many others responsible for wrongful convictions, Dr. Smith was overly zealous in trying to secure convictions. He did not perform as an independent expert, whose proper role was to provide objective evidence to the court rather than to support the Crown's case. Instead, Smith began his investigations with the idea that a child had died as the result of a crime instead of an accident or misfortune. He saw his job as helping the Crown prosecutor prove that an accused was guilty. Along with sloppy techniques, a lack of knowledge of forensic pathology, and a lack of professionalism, this approach to his job led to many miscarriages of justice (Goudge, 2008).

According to a judicial inquiry, Dr. Smith's competence should have been questioned much earlier, but his supervisors ignored complaints about the accuracy of his work. His supervisors and justice officials including prosecutors and judges all failed to ensure that his work was competent and fair:

> As this review demonstrates, for over a decade, while the danger signals about Dr. Smith kept coming, those in charge at the [Office of the Chief Coroner for Ontario] who ultimately might have done something about the mounting problem did far too little. It is a graphic demonstration of how the oversight of pediatric forensic pathology could and did fail, almost completely. In large measure, responsibility for this failure lies in three areas: the grave weaknesses that existed in the oversight and accountability mechanisms, the inadequate quality control measures, and the flawed institutional arrangements of pediatric forensic pathology in particular, and forensic pathology as a whole. (Goudge, 2007, 31)

As in so many other instances of corporate and white-collar wrongdoing, much of the harm done by Dr. Smith could have been avoided if governments had provided adequate regulatory frameworks and if those responsible for supervision had actually done their jobs competently.

the income of servers comes from tips, the employer usually does not keep a record of this income and, as a result, many servers do not pay tax on this portion of their earnings. Restaurants and other businesses have purchased electronic sales suppression software for their cash registers that allows them to hide some of their sales so the owners do not have to pay tax (Canada Revenue Agency, 2008). Unscrupulous contractors will offer customers a reduced price if the customer will pay in cash so they will not have records of income that could be uncovered through an audit. These workers are part of what is called the "underground economy," whose size in 2008 was estimated at $36 billion (Statistics Canada, 2011).

People often justify tax fraud because they feel that taxes are too high and governments are taking money that rightfully belongs to the taxpayer. Many Canadians were particularly upset when the GST was implemented, and there is some evidence that people in businesses such as contracting turned to the underground economy as a way of avoiding the GST.

Other types of tax fraud have involved exaggerating income tax deductions. Over 100 000 Canadians have had their claims for charitable deductions rejected by the Canada Revenue Agency because they were grossly inflated. People who donated funds to phony charities would receive tax receipts for many times the value of their donation. About $1.4 billion in tax revenue was lost because of this scam (Donovan, 2007) and it was highly unlikely that any of the donated money actually reached people in need. Large numbers of Canadians also circumvent the tax system by purchasing smuggled cigarettes, alcohol, and other forms of contraband.

## Political Corruption

While Canadian politicians have been more honest than their counterparts in many other countries, we have had our share of political scandals. In 1873, just six years after Confederation, the government of John A. Macdonald was forced to resign over allegations of bribery in the selection of a contractor to build and operate the Canadian Pacific Railway. Perhaps the most corrupt political regime in Canada was that of Maurice Duplessis, the premier of Quebec for most of the period between 1936 and 1959. He created a powerful political machine that routinely violated election rules and violated many of Quebeckers' basic rights, such as the right to freedom of political expression. In addition, his supporters used inside information to make money on the stock market and accepted financial kickbacks from people who wanted to do business with the Quebec government (Corrado, 1996).

Corrado (1996) has documented many of the corrupt activities engaged in by members of Brian Mulroney's Conservative government between 1984 and 1993. Mulroney's use of patronage was widespread, as political supporters were given government jobs and contracts, often without competitions. Although this practice is not illegal, it set the tone for other misconduct. Several cabinet ministers and MPs were forced to resign after being charged with bribery and influence peddling and many other Conservative Party officials were prosecuted for similar offences in connection with party fundraising activities. There were also allegations that the government interfered with the judicial process in an attempt to cover up some of these illegal activities. Dissatisfaction with the ethical standards of Prime Minister Mulroney and his colleagues was one reason that the federal Conservative Party was almost wiped out in the 1993 election.

Many years later, a judicial inquiry investigated the links between Prime Minister Mulroney and German-Canadian businessman Karlheinz Schreiber. Shortly after Mr. Mulroney left the prime minister's office (but while he was still sitting as a Member of Parliament), he received the first of three cash-stuffed envelopes from Mr. Schreiber. This cash was not documented in any business documents, no receipts were issued, and Mr. Mulroney did not declare the money on his tax forms. He also did not mention the money when he was questioned about his relationship with Mr. Schreiber during a lawsuit Mr. Mulroney filed against the Canadian government. Even the amount of money involved is in doubt as Mr. Mulroney claims he received $225 000 while Mr. Schreiber testified that he gave $300 000 (Oliphant, 2010).

While no charges were ever laid in this matter, Justice Oliphant, who headed the Inquiry, could find no evidence that Mr. Mulroney performed any services for the money and concluded that: "the business and financial dealings between Mr. Schreiber and Mr. Mulroney were inappropriate. I also found that Mr. Mulroney's failure to disclose those business and financial dealings was inappropriate" (2010, 51).

The most recent major scandal involved the Liberal government of Prime Minister Jean Chrétien. In 2002 a newspaper ran a story about a Montreal advertising company that had received over half a million dollars for a report that was never completed. The auditor general investigated and concluded there had been massive misspending in a government program that provided federal funding for the sponsorship of events, most of which were in the province of Quebec. In many cases, money was given to companies that did not actually do any work for the government. The auditor general concluded: "I think this is such a blatant abuse of public funds that it is shocking. I am actually appalled by what we've found" (Canadian Broadcasting Corporation, 2004, n.p.).

Following this report, an inquiry headed by Justice John Gomery was established to further investigate what had become known as the Sponsorship Scandal. Justice Gomery's report was released in 2005 and concluded that over $150 million of taxpayers' money was given by the Liberal government to five advertising and communications companies in Quebec with ties to the federal Liberal Party, and in many cases nothing was done by these companies to earn the money. Several of the executives who received this money subsequently made large donations to the Liberal Party and paid the salaries of Liberal party workers. Justice Gomery concluded that "whether legal or illicit, there was at least an implicit link between the contributions [to the Liberal party] and the expectation that the government contracts would be awarded" (2005, 79). Thus government money appears to have been returned to the party to use for its own purposes.

The report laid some of the blame for the scandal on Prime Minister Chrétien, his chief of staff Jean Pelletier, and Public Works Minister Alfonso Gagliano, all of whom failed to ensure that government funds were spent properly. While no elected officials were charged, one government official and several of the marketing executives have been convicted and sentenced to jail for their roles in this affair. Justice Gomery stated that his report "chronicles a depressing story of multiple failures to plan a government program appropriately and to control waste—a story of greed, venality and misconduct both in government and advertising and communications agencies, all of which contributed to the loss and misuse of huge amounts of money at the expense of Canadian taxpayers. They are outraged and have valid reasons for their anger" (Gomery, 2005, xix).

Corruption is only one type of government malfeasance. Many countries are governed by politicians who abuse their citizens by repressing dissent and denying people their basic human rights. These problems are most prevalent in dictatorial regimes such as Zimbabwe and China, but even democratic societies are not immune. During the U.S. president George Bush's "War on Terror" following the attacks on New York's World Trade Center on September 11, 2001, the government imposed a series of restrictions on civil liberties. Legislation such as the Patriot Act and the Protect America Act allowed the government to open people's mail and to carry out wiretaps and other types of electronic surveillance without the judicial supervision required by the Constitution. Suspected terrorists were held in a U.S. military base in Guantanamo Bay, Cuba, rather than in the United States so that American laws would not apply, and prisoners were tortured and humiliated by the U.S. soldiers at the Abu Ghraib prison in Iraq.

## Blue-Collar Crime

The concept of white-collar crime also fits many people who wear blue collars. Because of this, some have suggested that the term *occupational crime* may be a better one to use. Many trades people defraud the government by doing work "off the books" to avoid provincial sales tax and the GST. Some blue-collar businesses have very bad records of consumer fraud. For example, Robert Sikorsky (1990) documented an appalling degree of misconduct in the automobile repair business. Travelling across Canada, he visited 152 repair shops. Before each visit, he disconnected the idle air control in his car, triggering a warning light on the instrument panel. The repair was obvious and very simple—reinsert the connector. Over half the shops Sikorsky visited performed unnecessary work, overcharged him for work that was done, or lied about the work that had been done. In one case he was presented with an estimate of $570. A similar study was conducted by Menzies (2000). In this case a mechanic disabled one of the sparkplugs on a car that was otherwise in good working order. In each case Menzies requested and paid for an engine diagnosis that ranged in price from $69 to $103, so there was ample information available to do the repair that should have cost about $20. Menzies visited only four Toronto repair shops, but his study reinforced Sikorsky's findings. Only one shop, a Honda dealership, repaired the problem without recommending any further work. Of the other three, Goodyear estimated the repair would cost $234, Speedy Auto Service estimated $300, and Canadian Tire estimated $648 would be required to return the car to working order.

## Employee Fraud

Corporations are also often the victims of crime. A 2001 survey sponsored by the accounting company Ernst & Young found that about 25 percent of the Canadian workforce reported either having committed fraud against their employer or witnessing someone committing fraud during the previous year. Given these numbers, it is not surprising that an earlier survey of employers found that 80 percent reported having been victimized by employee fraud (Canadian Broadcasting Corporation, 2001). Examples of frauds reported to Ernst & Young include taking kickbacks from suppliers in exchange for contracts, creating phony invoices and collecting the money, stealing company property, and stealing cash from the company. Canadian retailers estimate that in 2001 they lost $1 billion to employee theft, almost as much as their losses from shoplifting and other types of customer theft. To put this figure in perspective, the Retail Council of Canada reported that in 2002, losses due to robberies were $5.6 million and losses from credit card fraud were $204 million (2002). Corporations of all sizes are victimized, but often the toll has been greatest on small companies. For example, many small restaurants have been forced out of business because of theft of money and food by staff. Lisa Leduc interviewed Ottawa restaurant employees about ways of "scamming" their employers. One of the interviewees described some of these methods:

> A manager would bring in his friends, a table of, let's say, eight, and [they would have] wings and beer, and he would go into the cooler where the beer was and grab it when the bartender wouldn't even notice, and [there would be] free dinner and beer for this person's friends.... Also, people weren't punching in drinks and [were] pocketing the money. Cooks [were] taking food home, all staff [were] taking dishes and cutlery. (Quoted in Gabor, 1994, 78–79)

In recent years technology and changes in financial practices have made larger corporations more vulnerable to the actions of individual employees. Earlier in this chapter you read about the illegal trades by Nicholas Leeson that drove Barings Bank into bankruptcy. Since the Leeson case, there have been several others where an individual trader has done significant harm to his company. Toronto's Stephen Duthie lost $182 million through unauthorized trading that was essentially gambling with his company's money. Duthie would have received a huge bonus if his gamble had succeeded in making large profits for his company. However, the trades lost money, and Duthie's employer, Phoenix Trading and Research, was forced to close. These cases have become so common that the term *rogue trader* has been invented to describe the actions of people like Leeson and Duthie.

## Summary

- The study of white-collar crime has altered our view of some of the major issues in criminology. It has demonstrated that the relationship between class and crime is more complicated than early criminologists had believed. Our theories of crime must account for the crimes of the privileged as well as for the crimes of the poor.
- Even when they come to the attention of the authorities, white-collar crimes are often not reported in official crime statistics because they are dealt with under quasi-criminal statutes.
- Corporations are instruments that enable people to commit crimes that are vast in scope. The financial and physical costs of corporate crimes are very high.

- The structure of the modern corporation provides managers with a great deal of freedom from control. This has the unintended consequence of encouraging crime. In some industries, high-level managers demand such unreasonably high levels of profit that their subordinates feel pressured to break the law.

- While corporations are subject to legal regulation, the laws that govern them are weak. Even when punishment is administered, it is often so light that it does not act as a deterrent but is an accepted cost of doing business.

- There is some evidence that penalties for white-collar offenders are increasing in the United States, but this does not appear to be the case in Canada.

- One of the major contributors to many types of occupational crime is the failure of professional organizations to adequately control the behaviour of their members. Another is the fact that many people do not strongly condemn crimes such as tax fraud.

## QUESTIONS FOR CRITICAL THINKING

1. The argument is made in this chapter that the structure of the corporation facilitates crime. What changes could be made in the organization and operation of corporations that would increase corporate responsibility?
2. Why do you think the government has refused to implement laws that would hold corporate officials more responsible for their actions?
3. In previous chapters of this text, you have studied a number of theories of criminal behaviour. Select one of these theories and assess how well it explains white-collar and corporate crime.
4. Some judges give light sentences to white-collar offenders because they feel that these offenders have already suffered from the publicity surrounding their conviction and because their employment prospects have suffered. Do you feel that these are appropriate sentencing criteria?
5. Can you think of three different actions that might be taken by governments and/or corporations to reduce the amount of white-collar and corporate crime in Canada?

## NET WORK

There are several websites dealing with fraud. Two of the best are **www.scambusters.com** and **www.fraud.org.**

1. Go to these websites and briefly describe three different types of fraud. How can each of these frauds best be prevented?
2. How have the white-collar criminals who carry out these frauds adapted to new communications technology?

# KEY TERMS

anticombines law; pg. 550

criminogenic market structure; pg. 543

executive disengagement; pg. 542

juristic person; pg. 541

monopolistic enterprise; pg. 550

occupational crime; pg. 537

organizational or corporate crime; pg. 537

white-collar crime; pg. 536

# BIBLIOGRAPHY

Akers, Ronald. (1973). *Deviant Behavior: A Social Learning Approach*. Belmont: Wadsworth.

Auditor General of Canada. (1999). "The Underground Economy Initiative." *Report of the Auditor General of Canada*. Ottawa: Office of the Auditor General of Canada.

Baumhart, Raymond. (1961). "How Ethical Are Businessmen?" *Harvard Business Review* 39:5–176.

Benson, M. L. (1989). "The Influence of Class Position on the Formal and Informal Sanctioning of White-Collar Offenders." *Sociological Quarterly* 30:465–79.

Benson, M. L., W. J. Maakestad, F. T. Cullen, and G. Geis. (1988). "District Attorneys and Corporate Crime: Surveying the Prosecutorial Gatekeepers." *Criminology* 26:505–18.

Black, Conrad. 2011. "Our Mighty Treasure House." *National Post*, July 2. Available at http://www.nationalpost.com/news/MIGHTY+treasure+house/5038319/story.html, accessed July 5, 2011.

Butler, Steve. (2002). "Colossal Enron Collapse a Good Thing for the Rest of Us." *Winnipeg Free Press*, February 22:A15.

Canada Revenue Agency. (2008). "Businesses Warned Against Using Tax Cheating Software." *Tax Alert*. Ottawa: Canada Revenue Agency.

Canadian Broadcasting Corporation. (2001). "Study Shows Employee Fraud Prevalent in Workplace." Available at http://cbc.ca/cgi-bin/templates/print.cgi?/news/2001/01/08/workplace_ fraud010108, accessed January 9, 2001.

———. (2004). "Auditor-General's Report 2004." Available at http://www.cbc.ca/news/background/auditorgeneral/report2004.html, accessed September 10, 2007.

Canadian Medical Protective Association. (2010). *2009 Annual Report*. Ottawa: Canadian Medical Protective Association.

Canadian Press. (2000). "CEO Jailed for Insider Trading." *Winnipeg Free Press*, September 19:B8.

Casey, John. (1985). "Corporate Crime and the State: Canada in the 1980s." In Thomas Fleming (ed.), *The New Criminologies in Canada* (pp. 100–101). Toronto: Oxford University Press.

Clinard, Marshall. (1952). *The Black Market: A Study of White Collar Crime*. New York: Holt, Rinehart and Winston.

Clinard, Marshall, and Peter Yeager. (1980). *Corporate Crime*. New York: Free Press.

Coleman, James. (1974). *Power and the Structure of Society*. New York: W. W. Norton.

———. (1985). *The Criminal Elite*. New York: St. Martin's Press.

College of Physicians and Surgeons of Ontario. (2011). *Yazdanfar, Behnaz CPSO #: 67947*. Available at http://www.cpso.on.ca/docsearch/details.aspx?view=4&id=%2067947, accessed July 7, 2011.

Corrado, Raymond. (1996). "Political Crime in Canada." In Rick Linden (ed.), *Criminology: A Canadian Perspective*. (3rd ed.) (pp. 459–93). Toronto: Harcourt Brace.

Cullen, Francis, Martha Larson, and Richard Mathers. (1985). "Having Money and Delinquency Involvement: The Neglect of Power in Delinquency Theory." *Criminal Justice and Behavior* 12(2):171–92.

Cullen, Francis, Bruce Link, and Craig Polanzi. (1982). "The Seriousness of Crime Revisited: Have Attitudes toward White Collar Crime Changed?" *Criminology* 20:83–102.

Daly, Kathleen. (1989). "Gender and Varieties of White-Collar Crime." *Criminology* 27: 769–93.

DeCloet, Derek. (2002). "Deceit Began This Scandalous Rot." *National Post*, July 11.

Donovan, Kevin. (2007). "$1.4B Tax Scams Nail Donors." *TheStar.com*, September 29.

Drohan, Madelaine. (1995). "Barings Was Warned of Risk." *The Globe and Mail*, March 6:A1.

Ermann, M. David, and Richard Lundman. (1982). *Corporate Deviance*. New York: Holt, Rinehart and Winston.

Evola, K., and N. O'Grady. (2009). "As Fraud Schemes Proliferate—Are You the Next Investor to Crash and Burn?" *Journal of Investment Compliance* 10:14–17.

Farberman, Harvey. (1975). "A Criminogenic Market Structure: The Automobile Industry." *Sociological Quarterly* 16:438–57.

Fitzgerald, Rory. (2011). "Enda Kenny's Attack on the Vatican Reflects Ferocious Public Anger." *Catholic Herald*, July 21. Available at http://www.catholicherald.co.uk/commentandblogs/2011/07/21/enda-kenny%E2%80%99s-attack-on-the-vatican-reflects-ferocious-public-anger/, accessed August 24, 2011.

Gabor, Thomas. (1994). *Everybody Does It*. Toronto: University of Toronto Press.

Geis, Gilbert. (1962). "Toward a Delineation of White-Collar Offenses." *Sociological Inquiry* 32:160–71.

———. (1984). "White Collar Crime and Corporate Crime." In Robert F. Meier (ed.), *Major Forms of Crime*. Beverly Hills: Sage.

Glasbeek, Harry, and Eric Tucker. (1994). "Corporate Crime and the Westray Tragedy." *Canadian Dimension* (January–February):11–14.

Goff, Colin, and Charles Reasons. (1978). *Corporate Crime in Canada*. Scarborough: Prentice Hall.

Gomery, Mr. Justice John. (2005). *Who Is Responsible? Fact Finding Report*. Montreal: Commission of Inquiry into the Sponsorship Program and Advertising Activities.

Goudge, Mr. Justice Stephen. (2008). *Inquiry in Pediatric Forensic Pathology in Ontario. Volume 1: Executive Summary*. Available at http://www.attorneygeneral.jus.gov.on.ca/inquiries/goudge/report/v1_en.html, accessed July 10, 2011.

Hagan, John. (1982). "The Corporate Advantage: The Involvement of Individual and Organizational Victims in the Criminal Justice Process." *Social Forces* 60(4): 993–1022.

Hagan, John, and Celesta Albonetti. (1982). "Race, Class and the Perception of Criminal Injustice in America." *American Journal of Sociology* 88:329–55.

Hagan, John, and Fiona Kay. (1990). "Gender and Delinquency in White-Collar Families: A Power-Control Perspective." *Crime and Delinquency* 36(3):391–407.

Hagan, John, and Ilene Nagel. (1982). "White Collar Crime, White Collar Time: The Sentencing of White Collar Criminals in the Southern District of New York." *American Criminal Law Review* 20(2):259–301.

Hagan, John, and Alberto Palloni. (1983). "The Sentencing of White Collar Offenders Before and After Watergate." Paper presented at the American Sociological Association Meetings, Detroit.

Hagan, John, and Patricia Parker. (1985). "White Collar Crime and Punishment: The Class Structure and Legal Sanctioning of Securities Violations." *American Sociological Review* 50(3):302–16.

Hartung, Frank E. (1950). "White Collar Offenses in the Wholesale Meat Industry in Detroit." *American Journal of Sociology* 56:25–34.

Henderson, Tanya. (2000). "Delivered and Signed." Available at http://abcnews.go.com/onair/2020/2020_000428_zorro_feature.html, accessed May 12, 2003.

Howlett, Karen. (2002). "The Two Faces of YBM Magnex." *The Globe and Mail*, December 29:B13.

Kadlec, Daniel. (2002). "WorldCon." *Time* (July 8):15–20.

Katz, Jack. (1980). "The Movement against White-Collar Crime." In Egon Bittner and Sheldon Messinger (eds.), *Criminology Review Yearbook*, Vol. 2. Beverly Hills: Sage.

Kranhold, Kathryn, and Mitchell Pacelle. (2002). "Enron Paid Top Managers $681 Million, Even as Stock Slid." *The Wall Street Journal*, June 17:B1, B4.

Law Commission of Canada. (2000). *Restoring Dignity: Responding to Child Abuse in Canadian Institutions*. Ottawa: Law Commission of Canada.

Le Pan, Nick. 2007. *Enhancing Integrated Market Enforcement Teams, Achieving Results in Fighting Capital Markets Crime*. Report submitted to the Commissioner of the RCMP.

Mann, Kenneth, Stanton Wheeler, and Austin Sarat. (1980). "Sentencing the White Collar Offender." *American Criminal Law Review* 17(4):479.

McIntyre, Mike. (2001). "Deaths Cost Firms Dearly." *Winnipeg Free Press*, March 3:A1, A4.

Menzies, David. (2000). "Looking for Mr. Goodwrench." *National Post*, September 23.

Mills, C. Wright. (1956). *The Power Elite*. New York: Oxford University Press.

Morgenson, Gretchen, and Louise Story. (2011). "In Financial Crisis, No Prosecutions of Top Figures." *The New York Times*, April 14.

Oliphant, Jeffrey. (2010). *Commission of Inquiry into Certain Allegations Respecting Business and Financial Dealings between Karlheinz Schreiber and the Right Honourable Brian Mulroney*. Ottawa: Minister of Public Works and Government Services Canada.

Olive, David. (2007). "An Anthology of Black Quotes." *Toronto Star*, March 11. Available at http://www.thestar.com/News/article/190677, accessed September 16, 2007.

Posner, Richard A. (1980). "Optimal Sentences for White Collar Criminals." *American Criminal Law Review*:409–18.

Public Safety Canada. (2010). *Final Report: 2009–2010 Evaluation of the Integrated Market Team Initiative*. Evaluation Directorate, Public Safety Canada.

Reasons, C., L. Ross, and C. Paterson. (1981). *Assault on the Worker: Occupational Health and Safety in Canada*. Toronto: Butterworths.

Reiss, Albert. (1980). *Data Sources on White Collar Law Breaking*. Washington: National Institute of Justice.

Retail Council of Canada. (2002). *2001 Canadian Retail Security Report*. Toronto: Retail Council of Canada.

Richard, Justice K. Peter. (1997). *The Westray Story: A Predictable Path to Disaster, Executive Summary.* Halifax: Government of Nova Scotia.

Ross, E. A. (1907). *Sin and Society.* Boston: Houghton Mifflin.

Rubin, Sandra. (1999). "RCMP Investigated YBM in Early 1995." *The Financial Post,* January 9.

Rugaber, Christopher, and Derek Kravitz. (2011). "Wells Fargo Fined in Mortgage Case." *The Globe and Mail,* July 21:B7.

Sandborn, Tom. (2010). "Hard Thanksgiving for Injured Farm Workers." *The Tyee,* October 11. Available at http://thetyee.ca/News/2010/10/11/InjuredFarmWorkers, accessed July 7, 2011.

Shapiro, Susan P. (1990). "Collaring the Crime, Not the Criminal: Reconsidering the Concept of White-Collar Crime." *American Sociological Review* 55:346–65.

Sharpe, Andrew, and Jill Hardt. (2006). "Five Deaths a Day: Workplace Fatalities in Canada, 1993-2005." *CSLS Research Paper 2006-04.* Ottawa: Centre for the Study of Living Standards.

Shover, Neal, and Andy Hochstetler. (2006). *Choosing White-Collar Crime.* New York: Cambridge University Press.

Sikorsky, Robert. (1990). "Highway Robbery: Canada's Auto Repair Scandal." *Reader's Digest* (February):55–63.

Simpson, Sally. (1986). "The Depression of Antitrust: Testing a Multilevel, Longitudinal Model of Profit-Squeeze." *American Sociological Review* 51:859–75.

Sinclair, Judge Murray. (2000). *The Report of the Manitoba Pediatric Surgery Inquest.* Winnipeg: Provincial Court of Manitoba. Available at http://www.pediatriccardiacinquest.mb.ca, accessed May 12, 2003.

Smandych, Russell. (1985). "Marxism and the Creation of Law: Re-Examining the Origins of Canadian Anti-Combines Legislation, 1890–1910." In Thomas Fleming (ed.), *The New Criminologies* (pp. 87–99). Toronto: Oxford University Press.

Snider, Laureen. (1979). "Revising the Combines Investigation Act: A Study in Corporate Power." In Paul J. Brantingham and Jack M. Kress (eds.), *Structure, Law and Power: Essays in the Sociology of Law* (pp. 105–19). Beverly Hills: Sage.

———. (1988). "Commercial Crime." In Vincent F. Sacco (ed.), *Conformity and Control in Canadian Society* (pp. 231–83). Scarborough: Prentice Hall.

Statistics Canada. (2011). "Study: The Underground Economy in Canada." *The Daily,* June 27. Ottawa: Statistics Canada.

Stone, Christopher. (1975). *Where the Law Ends: The Social Control of Corporate Behavior.* New York: Harper and Row.

Sutherland, Anne. (2009). "Montreal Man's $50M Disappearance 'Shatters' Friends. *Montreal Gazette,* July 13. Available at http://www.canada.com/news/Montreal+disappearance +shatters+friends/1787353/story.html, accessed August 16, 2009.

Sutherland, Edwin. (1940). "White Collar Criminality." *American Sociological Review* 5: 1–12.

———. (1945). "Is 'White Collar Crime' Crime?" *American Sociological Review* 10:132–39.

Swartz, Joel. (1978). "Silent Killers at Work." In M. David Ermann and Richard Lundman (eds.), *Corporate and Governmental Deviance* (pp. 114–28). New York: Oxford University Press.

Taibbi, Matt. (2009). "The Great American Bubble Machine." *Rolling Stone,* July 9–23. Available at http://www.rollingstone.com/politics/news/the-great-american-bubble-machine-20100405, accessed July 10, 2010.

*Vancouver Sun.* (2000). "Doctor Baited Crab Trap with Human Foot." August 9:A3.

Weisburd, David, Elin Waring, and Stanton Wheeler. (1990). "Class, Status and the Punishment of White-Collar Criminals." *Law and Social Inquiry* 15(2):223–46.

Wells, Jennifer. (1998). *Fever: The Dark Mystery of the Bre-X Gold Rush.* Toronto: Viking.

Wente, Margaret. (2000). "Dr. Bloody and Mr. Whizzo." *The Globe and Mail*, July 25:A17.

Wheeler, Stanton, and Michael Rothman. (1982). "The Organization as Weapon in White Collar Crime." *Michigan Law Review* 80(7):1403–26.

Wheeler, Stanton, David Weisburd, and Nancy Bode. (1982). "Sentencing the White Collar Offender: Rhetoric and Reality." *American Sociological Review* 47:641–59.

# Glossary

**absolute deprivation**
The inability to sustain oneself physically and materially. *p. 334*

**actuarial**
Refers to statistical calculations of risk across time and groups. *p. 387*

***actus reus***
All the elements contained in the definition of a criminal offence—other than the mental elements (***mens rea***). *p. 74*

**administrative record**
A collection of information about individual cases. An administrative record contains information that can be the basis of statistics, provided that clear procedures are developed for handling the data and generating statistical descriptions. *p. 105*

**anomie**
A concept developed by Émile Durkheim (1858–1917) to describe an absence of clear societal norms and values. Robert Merton (1910–2003) used the term more narrowly to refer to a situation in which people would adopt deviant means to achieve goals beyond their means. *p. 324*

**anticombines law**
In order to protect the principle of competition, valued by all liberal, capitalistic societies, laws have been created to prevent and punish corporations that work together to reduce competition. *p. 550*

**Antisocial Personality Disorder**
A personality disorder that involves disregard for the rights of others, as well as impulsive, irresponsible, and aggressive behaviour. *p. 298*

**assumption of discriminating traits**
The view that offenders are distinguished from non-offenders by, for example, their high levels of impulsiveness and aggression. *p. 285*

**assumption of offender deficit**
The view that offenders who break the law have some psychological deficit that distinguishes them from normal law-abiding citizens. *p. 285*

**atavism**
Cesare Lombroso (1836–1909) believed that some criminals were born criminals; they were atavistic. This suggested that they were throwbacks to an earlier stage of human evolution and that this limited evolutionary development meant that they were morally inferior. This inferiority could be identified through a series of physical **stigmata**. *p. 270*

**attachment**
The degree to which an individual has affective ties to other persons. One of the social bonds in Hirschi's theory. *p. 437*

**attentive gaze**
A methodological requirement that researchers immerse themselves where crime occurs in the everyday world in order to better understand the ways in which crime is experienced and interpreted by individuals. *p. 391*

**autonomic reactivity**
A measurement of the extent to which an individual's physical organism reacts to external stimuli. *p. 295*

**belief**
The degree to which an individual believes in conventional values, morality, and the legitimacy of law. One of the social bonds in Hirschi's theory. *p. 438*

**bourgeois class**
The term *bourgeois class*, or *bourgeoisie*, was used by Marx to refer to the capitalist or ruling class in modern societies. *p. 45*

**broken windows policing**
Just as houses with broken windows indicate that nobody cares about the neighbourhood, proponents of this policing style feel that tolerating minor misbehaviour will mean that residents will be afraid to use their streets. They feel that police should quickly deal with minor incivilities such as panhandling, vandalism, and other behaviours that contribute to fear of crime. Critics feel this policing style potentially discriminates against the poor. *p. 400*

**Canadian Centre for Justice Statistics**
A division of Statistics Canada, formed in 1981, with a mandate to collect national data on crime and justice. *p. 107*

**capital**
Each person enters a field of activity already possessed of certain powerful qualities or "capital." For example, a student who has a large vocabulary and is able to use this vocabulary competently will likely have an advantage in achieving a "feel for the game" within the academic field. *p. 392*

**career**
In common use, this refers to the sequence of stages through which people in a particular occupational sector move during the course of their employment. It has also been applied to the various stages of personal involvement with criminal activity. *p. 409*

**career contingency**
An unintended event, process, or situation that occurs by chance, beyond the control of the person pursuing the career. *p. 417*

***Charter—Charter of Rights and Freedoms***
The *Canadian Charter of Rights and Freedoms*, enacted by the *Canada Act 1982 (UK)* c. 11. The Charter provides protection for a wide range of individual rights typical of liberal democracies that until this time were protected by common law rather than constitutional guarantee. As a part of the Constitution of Canada, the Charter cannot be changed without the consent of both Parliament and provincial legislatures. The Charter includes provisions to protect freedoms of speech, conscience, and religion; protection against unreasonable search and seizure; rights to due legal process; and mobility and minority language rights. *p. 73*

**class conflict theory**
Laws are passed by members of the ruling class in order to maintain their privileged position by keeping the common people under control. *p. 20*

**classical conditioning**
A basic form of learning whereby a neutral stimulus is paired with another stimulus that naturally elicits a certain response; the neutral stimulus comes to elicit the same response as the stimulus that automatically elicits the response. *p. 292*

**Classical School**
Considered to be the first formal school of criminology, Classical criminology is associated with 18th and early 19th century reforms to the administration of justice and the prison system. Associated with authors such as Cesare Beccaria (1738–1794), Jeremy Bentham (1748–1832), Samuel Romilly (1757–1818), and others, this school brought the emerging philosophy of liberalism and utilitarianism to the justice system, advocating principles of rights, fairness, and due process in place of retribution, arbitrariness, and brutality. *p. 262*

**collective solidarity**
A state of social bonding or interdependency that rests on similarity of beliefs and values, shared activities, and ties of kinship and cooperation among members of a community. *p. 34*

**commitment**
The degree to which an individual pursues conventional goals. One of the social bonds in Hirschi's theory. *p. 437*

**common law**
The common law tradition found in English Canada derives from feudal England, where it had become the practice for the king to resolve disputes in accordance with local custom. Customs that were recognized throughout the country were called common custom, and decisions made by the king and by subsequent courts set up to settle disputes became known as common law; the body of judge-made law that has evolved in areas not covered by legislation. *p. 45, 73*

**community psychology**
A perspective that analyzes social problems, including crime, as largely a product of organizational and institutional characteristics of society. It is closely related to sociology. *p. 286*

**compensation from the state**
Victims of crimes that suffered physical or other injuries may apply to a provincial agency to receive lump sum or monthly payments according to provincial legislation. *p. 222*

**conduct norms**
Specification of rules or norms of appropriate behaviour generally agreed upon by members of the social group to whom the behavioural norms apply. *p. 348*

**conflict perspective**
The focus on the inherent divisions of societies based on social inequality and the way these social divisions give rise to different and competing interests, with the central assumption that social structures and cultural ideas tend to reflect the interests of only some members of society rather than society as a whole. *p. 323*

**consensus perspective**
Also known as *functionalism*, this perspective assumes that societies have an inherent tendency to maintain themselves in a state of relative equilibrium through mutually adjustive and supportive interaction of their principal institutions. It also assumes that effective maintenance of society is in the common interest of all its members. *p. 323*

**consensus theory**
Laws represent the agreement of most of the people in society that certain acts should be prohibited by the criminal law. *p. 19*

**conservative approach**
An approach that understands "difference" between men and women as biologically based sex differences. Women are viewed as "naturally" inferior or unequal to men. *p. 180*

**conspiracy**
An agreement by two or more persons to commit a criminal offence. *p. 86*

**continuance commitment**
Adherence to a criminal or other identity arising from the unattractiveness or unavailability of alternative lifestyles. *p. 418*

**correlate**
Any variable that is related to another variable. Age and sex are the two strongest correlates of crime. *p. 133*

**correlation**
A relationship that exists when two or more variables, such as age and crime, are associated or related to one another. *p. 133*

**counselling**
Procuring, soliciting, or inciting another person to commit a crime. *p. 84*

**counting procedure**
A consensus on how to count units and data elements. For example, if an offender goes on a break-and-enter spree and steals from a half dozen houses, is this to be counted as one incident or six? *p. 105*

**crime**
Conduct that is prohibited by law and that is subject to a penal sanction (such as imprisonment or a fine). *p. 68*

**crime prevention through social development**
An approach to crime prevention that focuses on reducing the number of motivated offenders by changing the social environment. *p. 481*

**crime rate**
Criminologists calculate crime rates (or rates of incarceration, conviction, or recidivism) by dividing the amount of crime by the population size and multiplying by 100 000. This produces the standard rate per 100 000; occasionally it is useful to calculate a rate per million or some other figure when looking at less frequently occurring offences. *p. 102*

**criminal attempt**
A criminal attempt occurs when an individual does—or omits to do—anything for the purpose of carrying out a previously formed intention to commit a crime. The conduct in question must constitute a substantial step toward the completion of the crime that is intended. *p. 85*

**criminal identity**
This social category, imposed by the community, correctly or incorrectly defines an individual as a particular type of criminal. The identity pervasively shapes his or her social interactions with others. This concept is similar to **master status**. *p. 421*

**criminal law**

A body of jurisprudence that includes the definition of various crimes, the specification of various penalties, a set of general principles concerning criminal responsibility, and a series of defences to a criminal charge. *p. 70*

**criminal procedure**

A body of legislation that specifies the procedures to be followed in the prosecution of a criminal case and defines the nature and scope of the powers of criminal justice officials. *p. 71*

**criminogenic market structure**

An economic market that is structured in such a way that it tends to produce criminal behaviour. *p. 543*

**criminology**

The body of knowledge regarding crime as a social phenomenon. It includes the processes of making laws, breaking laws, and reacting to the breaking of laws. Its objective is the development of a body of general and verified principles and of other types of knowledge regarding this process of law, crime, and treatment. *p. 9*

**cultural conflict**

A theory that attempts to explain certain types of criminal behaviour as resulting from a conflict between the conduct norms of divergent cultural groups. *p. 348*

**cultural construction**

A perspective on a subject that is shaped by cultural assumptions rather than having a natural or objective basis. For example, concepts of masculine and feminine suggest how men and women should behave, but very few of these gender differences are determined by biological sex. *p. 192*

**cultural explanation**

An explanation for crime that is phrased in terms of the values and beliefs of a society or its component subgroups. *p. 151*

**culturally prescribed aspiration**

A rejection of the notion that aspirations are entirely self-created; rather, they are defined by culture and transmitted by other members of the society. *p. 325*

**cybercrime**

The illegal acts in which a computer and a network are central to be committing a crime and the target of the crime. *p. 500*

**dangerous knowledge**

A form of knowledge that leaves no concept, notion, or idea un-touched by criticism. To achieve this relentlessly critical stance, cultural criminologists will often turn to diverse sources of information (e.g., novels and street-level observation) as means to reveal alternative perspectives that might shake the foundations of our taken-for-granted assumptions about crime. *p. 391*

**dark figure of crime**

The amount of crime that is unreported or unknown. The total amount of crime in a community consists of crimes that are known or recorded and the dark figure of crime. Criminologists have used differing methods (such as victimization surveys) to try to decrease the amount of unknown or unrecorded crime. *p. 109*

**data element**

Specification about what, exactly is to be collected. Operational issues may require more detail than the statistical system does. Also, statistical needs may require that operational agencies collect data that they do not need (or do not think that they need) for operational purposes. In any statistical system, there must be detailed agreements on exactly what is to be collected. *p. 105*

**debit card fraud**

Debit card fraud is a four step process: (1) create fake debit cards, (2) steal personal identification and banking information from legitimate cards, (3) emboss the stolen information on the fake cards, and (4) use the illegal debit cards. *p. 508*

**deconstruction**

An opening up of seemingly closed "things." It intends to encounter the hidden and excluded elements of language, meaning, and experience. *p. 398*

**deterrence**

As used in criminal justice, it refers to crime prevention achieved through the fear of punishment. *p. 266*

**differential association**

Developed by Edwin Sutherland in the 1930s, this theory argues that crime, like any social behaviour, is learned in association with others. If individuals regularly associate with criminals in relative isolation from law-abiding citizens, they are more likely to engage in crime. They learn relevant skills for committing crime and ideas for justifying and normalizing it. *p. 421*

**diffuseness of roles**

A characteristic of relatively simple societies in which people encounter one another in a variety of overlapping roles—there is little occupational specialization and no clear separation of private and public spheres of life. People are continuously reminded of their extensive bonds with others. *p. 34*

**discipline**

A meticulous manner or method of training. It intends to ensure constant subjection and obedience. It involves hierarchal observation, normalizing judgment, and examinations. *p. 384*

**drift**

A psychological state of weak normative attachment to either deviant or conventional ways. *p. 410*

**duress**

Duress may be a defence to a criminal charge when the accused was forced to commit a crime as a consequence of threats of death or serious bodily harm made by another person. *p. 92*

**ecological fallacy**

A research error made when data or information is gathered at a group level (the unemployment rate of various communities or neighbourhoods) and then conclusions are drawn about individuals (the unemployed person). Areas with high unemployment may have high crime rates, but this does not tell us that those crimes are necessarily committed by unemployed persons. *p. 435*

**effective guardianship**

An aspect of the **routine activities approach** to understanding crime victimization that argues that three key factors are required for crime to happen: a motivated offender, a suitable target, and ineffective guardianship of that target. Effective guardianship would include having locks on bikes, security lights in the backyard, or putting goods in the trunk of the car. Measures like this can reduce the risk of being victimized. *p. 475*

**ego**
A psychoanalytical term that denotes the rational part of the personality. It mediates between the *id* and the *superego* and is responsible for dealing with reality and making decisions. *p. 287*

**empirical evidence**
Evidence as observed through the senses; it can be seen, touched, heard, smelled, tasted, and, to some extent, measured. This is the only form of scientifically acceptable evidence. *p. 412*

**ethnic group**
A group of individuals having a common, distinctive subculture. Ethnic group differ from races by implying that values, norms, behaviour, and language, not necessarily physical appearance, are important distinguishing characteristics. *p. 414*

**ethnomethodology**
A sociological theory developed by Harold Garfinkel. Roughly translated, the term means the study of people's practices or methods. The perspective does not see the social world as an objective reality, but as something people constantly build and rebuild through their thoughts and actions. Ethnomethodologists try to uncover the methods and practices people use to they create their taken-for-granted world. *p. 426*

**executive disengagement**
The custom by which lower-level employees assume that executives are best left uninformed of certain decisions and actions of employees, or the assumption that executives cannot be legally expected to have complete control over their individual staff. *p. 542*

**extortion**
An offender unlawfully obtains money, property or services from an individual or entity through coercion and intimidation. *p. 502*

**extraversion**
A personality characteristic associated with sociability, impulsiveness, and aggression. *p. 293*

**feminist approach**
Understands "difference" between men and women as structurally produced by inequalities of class, race, and gender that condition and constrain women's lives. *p. 188*

**feudalism**
A system of economic and social organization found historically in several areas of the world. In western Europe, feudalism was at its height between about 1000 and 1500. The economic foundation of the system was the feudal manor that included a central farm owned by a landlord and small land holdings for a class of bonded farm labourers (serfs). The serfs were required to work the central manorial farm and to provide the lord with produce and money payments in return for their right to use the land. The system gradually declined as cities and towns grew and power became centralized in nation-states under monarchies. *p. 44*

**field**
A basic unit of social activity. The social world is divided into many fields (e.g., the "artistic" field, the "academic" field, or the "economic" field). Each field of activity is defined by its own market through which certain practices or dispositions are valued more than others. *p. 392*

**free trade zone**
A specially designated geographical area within a nation that is exempt from the regulations and taxation normally imposed on business. These zones are intended to facilitate cross-border production and trade. Examples of these zones are found along the United States–Mexico border, where they are referred to as *maquilladora*. *p. 55*

**gender-ratio problem**
Poses the question of why are there sex differences in rates of arrest and types of criminal activity between men and women. *p. 186*

**generalizability problem**
Raises the issue of whether mainstream theories of crime—which have largely been developed with men in mind—can be made to "fit" women. *p. 186*

**governmentality**
The art of governing. It transcends and is considerably broader than the traditional understanding of government as a state-directed activity. Government, then, encompasses a wide array of techniques, within and outside of the state, intended to (re) shape and (re)direct human actions. *p. 384*

**gross counts of crime**
A count of the total amount of crime in a given community, making no distinction between crime categories. *p. 112*

**group conflict theory**
A theory that attempts to explain certain types of criminal behaviour as resulting from a conflict between the interests of divergent groups. *p. 348*

**habitus**
A set of durable dispositions acquired through experience that allow one to achieve a "feel for the game" within a specific field of activity. These are internalized practices that serve as a "second nature" responsive to the immediate demands of everyday life. *p. 392*

**harm to victims**
The direct impact of crime on victims includes harm, such as loss, injury, pain, and emotional trauma. These can be exacerbated by the experience with the police, courts, corrections, and others. *p. 220*

**hegemonic masculinity**
A particular idealized form of masculinity that is culturally glorified, honoured, and exalted. For example, associating 'the masculine' with physical strength, aggression, independence, ambition, lack of emotion, and heterosexuality. *p. 208*

**hot spots policing**
Research has shown that most crimes occur at a small number of addresses in any community. Hot spots policing concentrates police resources on these high-crime locations. *p. 469*

**human capital**
The talents and capabilities that individuals contribute to the process of production. Companies, governments, and individuals can invest in human capital, just as they can invest in technology and buildings or in finances. *p. 336*

**human rights**
The minimum conditions required for a person to live a dignified life. Among the rights set out by the Universal Declaration of Human Rights are the right to life, liberty, and security of the person; the right to be free of torture and other forms of cruel and degrading punishment; the right to equality before the law; and the right to the basic necessities of life. *p. 15*

**human trafficking**
The illegal trade in people for the purposes of commercial sexual exploitation and other forms of forced labour. *p. 502*

**id**
A psychoanalytical term that denotes the most inaccessible and primitive part of the mind. It is a reservoir of biological urges that strive continually for gratification. The **ego** mediates between the *id* and the **superego**. *p. 287*

**ideal type**
An ideal type is a theoretical construct which is abstracted from experience and brings together observed characteristics of real social relationships. Observed empirical instances are combined to create a social form that has a conceptual coherence which is never entirely observed in any actual community but can be used as a standard against which to compare any real community. *p. 34*

**ideology**
A linked set of ideas and beliefs that act to uphold and justify an existing or desired situation in society. Ideologies offer explanations and justifications of features of society such as the distribution of wealth, status, and power. *p. 104*

**inchoate crime**
A criminal offence that is committed when the accused person seeks to bring about the commission of a particular crime but is not successful in doing so. The three inchoate offences in the *Criminal Code* are attempt, conspiracy, and counselling. *p. 83*

**independent variable**
A presumed cause of a dependent variable. If unemployment is thought to cause crime rates to increase, unemployment is the independent variable, and crime rates the dependent variable. *p. 435*

**individualistic**
A theory that focuses on explaining the behaviour of individuals and using factors or features of the individual in explaining this behaviour. *p. 445*

**individualized deterrence**
Offenders who are heavily involved in criminal activity are individually warned that their actions are being monitored and that future violations of the law will be dealt with immediately. Extra police and/or probation resources are added to ensure that the legal system does keep its promises. *p. 469*

**instrumental Marxism**
The state is viewed as the direct instrument of the ruling or capitalist class. Instrumentalism is based on the notion that the processes of the superstructure are determined by the economic base. *p. 355*

**intoxication**
Intoxication caused by alcohol and/or other drugs may be a defence if it prevents the accused from forming the intent required for a specific intent offence, such as murder or robbery. *p. 91*

**involvement**
The degree to which an individual is active in conventional activities. One of the social bonds in Hirschi's theory. *p. 438*

**juristic person**
The legal concept that corporations are liable to the same laws as natural persons. Treating corporations as individuals raises practical difficulties for legal enforcement and punishment. *p. 541*

**justice**
For Derrida, since it is perpetually deferred, justice cannot be defined adequately. It is not contained in or constrained by law. It is infinite. It is "to come." *p. 400*

**la Cosa Nostra**
This term is used to denote Italian-American organized crime. It was originally applied by the FBI in an attempt to make this criminal fraternity sound ominous and threatening. Members of the so-called LCN never used this label themselves, although they often referred to their secret society as "this thing of ours," which roughly translates into Italian as "la cosa nostra." *p. 510*

**labelling**
According to labelling theory, deviance is not a quality of the act but of the label that others attach to it. This raises the question of who applies the label and who is labelled. The application of a label and the response of others to the label may result in a person becoming committed to a deviant identity. *p. 409*

**legal definition of crime**
Crime is an act that violates the criminal law and is punishable with jail terms, fines, and other sanctions. *p. 15*

**levels of aggregation**
This refers to how data are to be combined. Do we want city-level, provincial, or national data? *p. 105*

**liberal approach**
Distinguishes sex (biological) from gender (cultural) and sees differences between men and women as resulting from gender roles and socialization patterns. *p. 182*

**lifestyle/exposure theory**
A theory of crime victimization that acknowledges that not everyone has the same lifestyle and that some lifestyles expose people to more risks than others do. *p. 473*

**loansharking**
Lending money at very high interest rates, often enforced through physical force. *p. 502*

**master status**
A status overriding all others in perceived importance. Whatever other personal or social qualities individuals possess, they are judged primarily by this one attribute. *Criminal* exemplifies a master status that influences the community's identification of an individual. *p. 416*

**maturational reform**
The observation that involvement in crime tends to decrease as people age. *p. 138*

***mens rea***
Criminal intent. The mental elements (other than voluntariness) contained in the definition of a criminal offence. *p. 76*

**methodology**
Refers to the study or critique of methods. There are many philosophical issues about the use of a particular method or about positivism or measurement itself. *p. 102*

**micro-powers**
Small and mundane relations of governance, with an appreciable effect on human behaviour. For example, the arrangement of a traditional classroom, with the professor or instructor at the front and all students facing her/him, is infused with power relations that rarely gain our attention. *p. 384*

**mistake of fact**
Mistake of fact may be a defence where the accused person acts under the influence of an honest mistake in relation to any of the elements of the **actus reus** of the offence charged. *p. 89*

**mode of production**
The dominant form of social and technical organization of economic production in a society. Historically, a variety of modes of production can be distinguished based on both technology and the structure of social relationships. *p. 33*

**modelling**
A form of learning that occurs as a result of watching and imitating others. *p. 294*

**monopolistic enterprise**
Any corporation that controls all, or the majority, of the market for a particular product or service. *p. 550*

**moral development theory**
Refers generally to theories of individual psychology that investigate how moral reasoning emerges in the individual and develops as the individual matures. *p. 292*

**moral entrepreneur**
Someone who defines new rules and laws or who advocates stricter enforcement of existing laws. Often such entrepreneurs have a financial or organizational interest in particular definitions or applications of law. *p. 412*

**moral rhetoric**
In the study of crime, this is the set of claims and assertions deviants make to justify their deviant behaviour. The moral rhetoric of a group is an important component of socialization into a deviant identity. *p. 411*

**naked life**
For Agamben, naked life is akin to Homo Sacer—an individual who is excluded from possessing human rights and can be killed by anyone but cannot be sacrificed during a religious ceremony. *p. 395*

**NCRMD**
The special verdict of "not criminally responsible on account of mental disorder." In order to be found NCRMD, it must be proved on the balance of probabilities that,

because of mental disorder, the accused lacked the capacity to appreciate the nature and quality of the act or omission in question or of knowing that it would be considered morally wrong by the average Canadian. *p. 87*

**necessity**
Necessity may be a defence to a criminal charge when the accused person commits the lesser evil of a crime in order to avoid the occurrence of a greater evil. *p. 92*

**negative *social* capital**
The way in which one's network of formal social resources (e.g., organizations designed to provide social services) can be used to more effectively regulate and control rather than empower an individual. *p. 393*

**negative *symbolic* capital**
The way in which stigma cast upon a neighbourhood might be symbolically transferred to the neighbourhood's residents, placing them in a deficit with respect to their ability to improve their social standing. *p. 393*

**norms**
Established rules of behaviour or standards of conduct. *p. 14*

**objective *mens rea***
The *mens rea* elements of a criminal offence are considered to be objective if they are based on a determination of whether a reasonable person, in the same circumstances and with the same knowledge as the accused, would have appreciated the risk involved in the accused's conduct and would have taken steps to avoid the commission of the **actus reus** elements of the crime in question. *p. 77*

**occupational crime**
Refers to violations of the law in the course of practising a legitimate occupation. *p. 537*

**operant conditioning**
The basic process by which an individual's behaviour is shaped by reinforcement or by punishment. *p. 296*

**opportunity structure**
Opportunity is shaped by the way the society or an institution is organized or structured. *p. 334*

**organizational or corporate crime**
White-collar crime committed with the support and encouragement of a formal organization and intended, at least in part, to advance the goals of that organization. *p. 537*

**over-representation**
A group that has a number of its members in some condition in greater numbers than their population would suggest. If a group makes up 20 percent of the population, then a researcher might predict, other things being equal, that they would represent 20 percent of offenders. *p. 147*

**paramount chieftainship**
A political system similar to a kingdom that brings together a number of partly autonomous villages or communities under the hierarchical rule of a grand chief. *p. 43*

**party to a crime**
The *Criminal Code* specifies that one is a party to—and liable to conviction of—a criminal offence if one actually commits it, aids and/or abets it, becomes a party to it by virtue of having formed a common intention with others to commit a crime, or counsels the commission of an offence that is actually committed by another person. *p. 82*

**patriarchy**
A system of male domination that includes both a structure and an ideology that privileges men over women. *p. 191*

**Ponzi scheme**
A fraud in which old investors are paid with the funds invested by new investors. When the scheme runs out of new investors, the scheme collapses. *p. 557*

**population**
The term population refers to all members of a given class or set. For example, adult Canadians, teenagers, Canadian inmates, or criminal offenders can each be thought of as populations. *p. 103*

**Positive School**
The first scientific school, it consisted of the Italian criminologists Cesare Lombroso (1836–1909), Raffaelo Garofalo (1852–1934), and Enrico Ferri (1856–1929).

They supported the assumptions of positivism and argued that criminality is determined—the effect in a cause–effect sequence—and that the mandate of criminology should be to search for these causes. It was believed that with the exception of those deemed to be born criminals, the discovery of the causes of crime would allow for effective treatment. *p. 268*

**power**
Power, for Foucault, extends beyond the state. It is not a quantity to hold or possess. It is, rather, relational, such that power is only ever evident in its exercise. *p. 384*

**primary deviation**
Occurs when an individual commits deviant acts but fails adopt a primary self-identity as a deviant. *p. 410*

**provocation**
Provocation may be a partial defence to a charge of murder (if successful, it reduces the offence from murder to manslaughter). The required elements of provocation are (i) that the accused responded to a wrongful act or insult that was of such a nature that an ordinary person would have been likely to lose the power of self-control and (ii) that the accused acted "on the sudden and before there was time for his (or her) passion to cool." *p. 93*

**radical feminism**
A perspective that views the problem of gender inequality and of women's subordination in society as rooted in the institution of patriarchy. *p. 365*

**rational choice theory**
Rational choice theory claims that crime is the result of deliberate choices made by offenders based on their calculation of the risks and rewards of these choices. *p. 471*

**regulatory offences**
Regulatory offences arise under legislation (either federal, provincial, or territorial) that regulates inherently legitimate activities connected with trade, commerce, and industry or with everyday living (driving, fishing, etc.). These offences are not considered to be serious in nature and usually carry only a relatively minor penalty upon conviction. *p. 72*

**relative autonomy**
A term used in the structural Marxist perspective to indicate that the state has a certain amount of independence from the capitalist class and is therefore able to enact laws that are not in the immediate interests of the capitalist class. *p. 357*

**relative deprivation**
Deprivation in relation to others around you, rather than judged against an absolute standard of sustainability. Relative deprivation and **absolute deprivation** are often contrasted. Absolute deprivation refers to the inability to sustain oneself physically and materially. However, in relative terms, deprivation is not judged against some absolute standard of sustainability but against deprivation in relation to others around you. You may have sufficient money to meet your needs and even meet them adequately, but you may feel relatively deprived because others around you have more. *p. 334*

**reliability**
Identifies one of the standards (another being **validity**) against which the tools used to measure concepts are judged. Reliability refers to consistency of results over time. If a bathroom scale is used to measure the concept of weight, one must ask: Is this tool (the bathroom scale) reliable? Does it provide consistent results? Notice that the bathroom scale or any other measure may be reliable and yet be inaccurate. *p. 102*

**repeat victimization**
The phenomenon of a person being a victim of a crime more than once. *p. 220*

**restitution from the offender**
Victims of any type of crime may request that the offender pay the victim money as reparation for financial or other losses caused by the crime. *p. 222*

**rights of crime victims**
Legislators in different countries and intergovernmental agencies such as UN have recognized various fundamental principles of justice and rights for victims of crime, such as the right to be informed, to receive restitution, or to be present in court. *p. 221*

**risk**
The calculated probability of an eventuality. *p. 387*

**risk society**
An emerging societal form characterized by the production and increased awareness of human-made "risks," such as nuclear destruction and environmental devastation. More importantly, the risk society is organized around the management of such risks. *p. 388*

**role convergence**
Explanation for the rising crime rate among women has been that their roles have become similar to (converged with) those of men. *p. 144*

**routine activities approach**
An extension of the **lifestyle/exposure theory**, this approach assumes that crimes are the expected outcomes of routine activities and changing social patterns. For example, those with more property can expect to be the victims of property crime more often than those with less property. Young people who like to hang out in the evenings are more likely to be victims than are those who go to organized activities or remain at home to study. *p. 474*

**sample**
A group of elements (people, offenders, inmates) selected in a systematic manner from the population of interest. *p. 117*

**secondary deviation**
Occurs when an individual accepts the label of deviant. The result is adoption of a deviant self-identity that confirms and stabilizes the deviant lifestyle. *p. 410*

**self-defence**
The *Criminal Code* permits the use of force in self-defence in certain circumstances where the individual concerned becomes the object of an unlawful assault. Where the individual acted in self-defence without intending to inflict death or grievous bodily harm on the assailant, it must be shown that no more force was used than was necessary in the circumstances. Where the individual concerned inflicted death or grievous bodily harm, then it must be shown that he or she acted under a reasonable

apprehension of death or grievous bodily harm and under a reasonable belief that he or she had no alternative but to employ lethal force. *p. 94*

**self-degrading commitment**
Commitment leading to a poorer opinion of oneself. *p. 419*

**self-enhancing commitment**
Commitment leading to a better opinion of oneself. *p. 419*

**self-report study**
A method for measuring crime involving the distribution of a detailed questionnaire to a sample of people, asking them whether they have committed a crime in a particular period of time. This has been a good method for criminologists to determine the social characteristics of offenders. *p. 125*

**seriousness rule**
If there are several crimes committed in one incident, only the most serious crime is counted. UCR1.0 uses the seriousness rule. *p. 110*

**sexism**
Attributing to women socially undesirable characteristics that are assumed to be intrinsic characteristics of that sex. *p. 180*

**situational crime prevention**
Premised on the belief that most crime is opportunistic rather than being the outcome of those driven to commit a crime no matter what the circumstances, this form of prevention attempts to reduce the opportunities for crime rather than just relying on the police after the crime has occurred. An example is the exact fare system used on buses, which removes the opportunity to rob the driver. *p. 478*

**social bond**
The degree to which an individual has ties to his or her society. In Hirschi's theory, social bonds include **attachment**, **commitment**, **involvement**, and **belief**. *p. 434*

**social control theory**
The theory proposes that people do not become criminal because they do not want to jeopardize their bonds to conventional society. *p. 433*

**social structure**
The patterned and relatively stable arrangement of roles and statuses found within societies and social institutions. The idea of social structure points out the way in which societies, and institutions within them, exhibit predictable patterns of organization, activity, and social interaction. *p. 324*

**socialist feminism**
A perspective that views women's exploitation under capitalism and oppression under patriarchy as interconnected. Neither the class structure of capitalism nor patriarchal gender relations are given priority in socialist feminism, rather gender and class relations are viewed as mutually dependent. *p. 366*

**socialization**
The interactive process whereby individuals come to learn and internalize the culture of their society or group. *p. 288*

**sovereign**
One who holds supreme power in a territory or space. Agamben, following Carl Schmitt, claims the sovereign is the one who is empowered to declare a state of exception. *p. 395*

**state**
As defined by Max Weber (1864–1920), the state is an institution that claims the exclusive right to the legitimate exercise of force in a given territory through the use of police to enforce laws or the army to maintain civil stability. While there have been stateless societies, most complex societies have state systems of formal government and administrative bureaucracies. *p. 33*

**state of exception**
A period of time where the sovereign declares civil liberties suspended: typically in a time of national crisis. *p. 395*

**Statistical School**
Associated with early social scientists such as Adolphe Quetelet (1795–1874) and André-Michel Guerry (1802–1866), who began to explore the structure of emerging European societies with the assistance of statistical methods. While their early use of statistics is important, they also developed a **structural explanation** of crime and other social problems. *p. 267*

**stigma**
As used by Erving Goffman (1922–1982), a personal characteristic that is negatively evaluated by others and thus distorts and discredits the public identity of the individual. For example, a prison record may become a stigmatized attribute. The stigma may lead to the adoption of a self-identity that incorporates the negative social evaluation. *p. 411*

**stigmata**
Physical signs of some special moral position. Cesare Lombroso (1836–1909) used the term to refer to physical signs of the state of **atavism** (a morally and evolutionary inferior person). *p. 270*

**strain theory**
The proposition that people feel strain when they are exposed to cultural goals they are unable to reach because they do not have access to culturally approved means of achieving those goals. *p. 323*

**structural explanation**
An explanation for crime that focuses on **social structure** (usually this refers to inequality, poverty, or power differentials). For example, the patriarchal structure of the family might help explain the abuse of women and children within the family. *p. 151*

**structural Marxism**
The state is viewed as acting in the long-term interests of capitalism as a whole, rather than in the short-term interests of the capitalist class. *p. 356*

**subculture**
A group of people who share a distinctive set of cultural beliefs and behaviours that differs in some significant way from that of the larger society. *p. 334*

**subjective *mens rea***
The ***mens rea*** elements of a criminal offence are considered to be subjective if they are based on a determination of "what actually went on in the accused person's mind." The forms of subjective *mens rea* are intention and knowledge; recklessness; and wilful blindness. *p. 77*

**superego**
A psychoanalytical term that denotes the ethical and moral dimensions of personality;

an individual's conscience. The **ego** mediates between the *superego* and the *id*. *p. 287*

### surplus

The excess of production over the human and material resources used up in the process of production. In simple societies, there was often little if any surplus since the production from hunting and gathering was entirely used up in subsistence. With the development of animal herding and settled agriculture, production exceeded immediate subsistence needs, and social inequality and class division became possible when particular individuals or groups were able to take control of this surplus. *p. 36*

### surveillance

The direct or indirect observation of conduct toward producing a desired outcome (i.e., conformity). *p. 384*

### symbolic interactionism

A sociological perspective that focuses on the dynamics of how people interpret social situations and negotiate the meaning of these situations with others. It differs from more structurally focused perspectives in seeing individuals as actively creating the social world rather than just acting within the constraints of culture and social structure. *p. 408*

### target suitability

Because of their vulnerability, some potential crime targets are more attractive than others. A home that is unlit, has shrubs blocking a view of the front door, and has no alarm system will be seen as a more suitable target than a well-protected home. *p. 475*

### terrorism

The illegitimate use of force to achieve a political objective by targeting innocent people. *p. 24*

### theory

A theory consists of a set of concepts and their nominal definition or assertions about the relationships between these concepts, assumptions, and knowledge claims. All sciences use theory as a tool to explain. It is useful to think of theory as a conceptual model of some aspect of life. We may have a theory of mate selection, of the emergence of capitalist societies, of criminal behaviour, or of the content of dreams. In each case, the theory consists of a set of concepts and their nominal definition or assertions about the relationships between these concepts, assumptions, and knowledge claims. *p. 104*

### token economy

A behaviour therapy procedure based on operant learning principles. Individuals are rewarded (reinforced) for positive or appropriate behaviour and are disciplined (punished) for negative or in appropriate behaviour. *p. 297*

### trace

The mark of absence in words that is the necessary condition of thought and experience (Derrida, 1976). *p. 399*

### transnational corporation

A corporation that has sales and production in many different nations. As a result of their multinational reach, these corporations are often thought to be beyond the political control of any individual nation-states. *p. 51*

### transnational organized crime

Organized crime that is coordinated and conducted across national borders. *p. 497*

### tribalism

Where social bonds are based primarily on people's real or assumed common descent from an ancestor or group of ancestors, and this shared identification distinguishes the group from outsiders. In such societies, all social relationships tend to be direct and quasi-familial. *p. 39*

### "true crime"

A "true crime" occurs when an individual engages in conduct that is not only prohibited but also constitutes a serious breach of community values; as such, it is perceived by Canadians as being inherently wrong and deserving of punishment. Only the Parliament of Canada, using its criminal law power under the *Constitution Act, 1867*, may enact a "true crime." *p. 72*

### Tudor

Refers to the period of English history from 1485 to 1603, when the nation's monarchs were descended from Owen Tudor and Catherine (1401–1437), widow of Henry V. *p. 58*

### Uniform Crime Reports (UCR)

Since 1962, Statistics Canada has published the Uniform Crime Reports based on a standardized set of procedures for collecting and reporting crime information. *p. 110*

### validity

The extent to which a tool or instrument (questionnaire, experiment) actually measures the concept the researcher claims to be interested in and not something else. For example, measuring people's feet to learn about the concept of intelligence, on the surface at least, does not seem valid. *p. 102*

### value

A collective idea about what is right or wrong, good or bad, and desirable or undesirable in a particular culture. *p. 19*

### victim fine surcharge

A monetary penalty similar to a fine, which can be assessed at sentence or added to a fine such as in a traffic violation, but can only be used by the government to fund services for victims. *p. 226*

### victimization surveys

A survey of a random **sample** of the population in which people are asked to recall and describe their own experience of being a victim of crime; surveys of the general public to identify who has been a victim of crime, whether they reported the crime to police, and other related aspects of victimization. *p. 117, 219*

### white-collar crime

Crime that is committed by middle- and upper-class people in the course of their legitimate business activities. An important concept but one with changing definitions. As used by Sutherland in 1940, the concept referred to corporate behaviour that caused social harm and for which there was a legal sanction. This sanction need not be criminal; it could be regulatory. Since that time, criminologists have also included the illegal actions of executives or employees who commit crimes against their employer or use organizational resources to gain personal benefit. *p. 15*

# Index